HEALTH POLICY

Crisis and Reform in the
U.S. Health Care Delivery System

HEALTH POLICY

Crisis and Reform in the U.S. Health Care Delivery System

Fifth Edition

Edited by

Charlene Harrington, PhD, RN
Professor of Sociology and Nursing

Carroll L. Estes, PhD
Professor of Sociology

Department of Social and Behavioral Sciences School of Nursing
University of California, San Francisco

With assistance from

BROOKE HOLLISTER
Health Policy

JONES AND BARTLETT PUBLISHERS
Sudbury, Massachusetts
BOSTON   TORONTO   LONDON   SINGAPORE

World Headquarters

Jones and Bartlett Publishers
40 Tall Pine Drive
Sudbury, MA 01776
978-443-5000
info@jbpub.com
www.jbpub.com

Jones and Bartlett Publishers
Canada
6339 Ormindale Way
Mississauga, Ontario L5V 1J2
Canada

Jones and Bartlett Publishers
International
Barb House, Barb Mews
London W6 7PA
United Kingdom

Jones and Bartlett's books and products are available through most bookstores and online booksellers. To contact Jones and Bartlett Publishers directly, call 800-832-0034, fax 978-443-8000, or visit our website www.jbpub.com.

Substantial discounts on bulk quantities of Jones and Bartlett's publications are available to corporations, professional associations, and other qualified organizations. For details and specific discount information, contact the special sales department at Jones and Bartlett via the above contact information or send an email to specialsales@jbpub.com.

The authors, editor, and publisher have made every effort to provide accurate information. However, they are not responsible for errors, omissions, or for any outcomes related to the use of the contents of this book and take no responsibility for the use of the products and procedures described. Treatments and side effects described in this book may not be applicable to all people; likewise, some people may require a dose or experience a side effect that is not described herein. Drugs and medical devices are discussed that may have limited availability controlled by the Food and Drug Administration (FDA) for use only in a research study or clinical trial. Research, clinical practice, and government regulations often change the accepted standard in this field. When consideration is being given to use of any drug in the clinical setting, the health care provider or reader is responsible for determining FDA status of the drug, reading the package insert, and reviewing prescribing information for the most up-to-date recommendations on dose, precautions, and contraindications, and determining the appropriate usage for the product. This is especially important in the case of drugs that are new or seldom used.

Library of Congress Cataloging-in-Publication Data
Health policy : crisis and reform in the U.S. health care delivery system / [edited by] Charlene Harrington, Carroll L. Estes. — 5th ed.
    p. ; cm.
  Includes bibliographical references and index.
  ISBN-13: 978-0-7637-4657-5 (alk. paper)
  ISBN-10: 0-7637-4657-6 (alk. paper)
  1. Medical policy—United States. 2. Health care reform—United States. 3. Medical care—United States—Finance. I. Harrington, Charlene. II. Estes, Carroll L.
  [DNLM: 1. Delivery of Health Care—economics—United States. 2. Delivery of Health Care—trends—United States. 3. Health Care Reform—United States. 4. Health Policy—United States. 5. Health Services Accessibility—United States. W 84 AA1 H43478 2008]
  RA395.A3H42554 2008
  362.1'0973—dc22
                                                                                                2006102359

6048

Production Credits
Executive Editor: Kevin Sullivan
Production Director: Amy Rose
Acquisitions Editor: Emily Ekle
Associate Editor: Amy Sibley
Editorial Assistant: Patricia Donnelly
Production Assistant: Amanda Clerkin
Senior Marketing Manager: Katrina Gosek
Composition: Auburn Associates, Inc.
Manufacturing Buyer: Therese Connell
Cover Design: Kate Ternullo
Cover Image: © VisualField/ShutterStock, Inc.
Printing and Binding: Malloy, Inc.
Cover Printing: Malloy, Inc.

Printed in the United States of America
11 10 09 08 07 10 9 8 7 6 5 4 3 2

CONTENTS

v

FOREWORD

The issues discussed in this fifth edition of *Health Policy* are truly the issues of the millennium, though many of them have remained the same over the years since the first edition of this book was published. That they seem so intractable should not surprise us, because reaching consensus on issues such as universality of health care, the poor, access to care, and organization of care is difficult for all of the countries in the world, whether industrialized or developing. However, Americans' idiosyncratic views about money and justice, among other things, lead to ambivalence and changeability with regard to political solutions on both the local and national levels in the United States. There appears to be little question that the public has great concern about the current state of health care, and the flaws in current approaches. In fact, as this edition is being published, polls place concerns about health care at the top of Americans' priorities and various political approaches are anticipated to quell these concerns. It is unfortunate that some of these approaches seem beneficial to much of the public but have potentially negative implications for costs of pharmaceuticals and for the continuing power of the private for-profit sector in dominating health care delivery.

In the United States, there has not been a strong national coalition behind the development of a public movement for a universal health care system. As a result of the inability to mobilize the political force of the nation, a number of states have made efforts to get the question of universal care on their own agendas. Ultimately, the value placed on quality of care and access to care by the American public has to be revealed in the voting booth. If that value is high, change is inevitable; if the American public is fearful of the consequences of an inclusive health care policy, decades will pass with millions of people unserved, underserved, and receiving care of questionable quality.

The fifth edition of *Health Policy* retains a few articles from the previous edition. These articles are classic in that they provide a frame of reference and backdrop for understanding the problems in the U.S. health care system and the basic health policy issues. Most articles in this volume are new, however, and permit us to keep up with the constantly changing issues in health policy at the leading edge of current discussions.

Part I begins with a review of what health policy is and how the political system operates. Focusing on issues of health status of the population and vulnerable groups, Part II details issues of race, gender, and income disparities as well as discrimination. Some of the issues at the core of access are the growing uninsured population, social inequality, mental health, aging, long-term care, and end-of-life care policies.

In discussing health care delivery system issues, the articles in Part III deal with organizational change, labor issues, and quality of care. Mergers and restructuring, primary care, staffing issues in hospitals and nursing homes, shortages in the workforce, errors in health care, and public reporting of quality indicators are invaluable for health professionals both on first reading and as references for repeated readings and use.

Part IV discusses the economics of health care with articles on public and private financing and insurance and managed care. Part V deals with reform of the health care system in the United States. Along the way, the outstanding analysts of health care systems discuss trends and systems in Canada, the United Kingdom, and other industrialized countries. In addition, definitions of health policy, failures in policy, crises in nursing caused by misapplied policy and public inaction, and potential solutions through health reform are presented.

The fifth edition of *Health Policy* is designed for all health professionals and anyone interested in or involved in the health care field. The authors are all experts in their subject matter. In their thoughtful articles, the most challenging issues facing the United States are explicated. The content provides information that will enrich the reader's understanding of the specifics and generalities of the problems Americans face in health care, both in the present and in the future. It also provides the impetus for individual and collective action.

Claire M. Fagin, PhD, FAAN

INTRODUCTION

This edited volume is designed for health professionals and for students of health policy and economics. Health policy and economics are constantly changing, and the literature in the area is expanding at an alarming pace. This growth makes it difficult for those learning about the area to identify the most important topics for study and the changing issues and trends. This volume highlights the key issues and trends that we cover in our policy courses in the Department of Social and Behavioral Sciences at the University of California, San Francisco. We have selected our favorite articles about health status and access, delivery systems, costs and economics, politics, and health reform.

Health policy is a new arena for many health professionals, and many realize that they must become knowledgeable in this area to improve health care both for their own patients and for the public at large. Health professionals working in organizations, public health, primary and specialty care, private practice, and management positions are all directly affected by the organization and financing of the health care system, including those policies and politics that shape the system. Health policy does not come naturally to many health professionals who may have undergone long and arduous clinical training focusing on caring for individuals and families. The organizational, systemic, and political issues sometimes seem too overwhelming to comprehend. Nevertheless, health professionals must move beyond their basic training to become more politically aware and active in shaping policy and advocating for their own interests and the interests of their patients. They also must move beyond clinical research into policy-relevant research, addressing the larger issues affecting their patients and the health professions as a whole. Indeed, a research and policy focus on organizations, financing, and systems of care can have more impact than any single clinical study.

This book is designed to focus on the "big picture" issues and to present the viewpoints of sociologists, economists, political scientists, and health experts. The language these experts use is different and sometimes difficult, but understanding it is essential to be able to communicate with public policy makers and health services and policy researchers.

Health professionals come to the policy arena with many strengths and liabilities. Their greatest strength is that they are viewed positively by the public and the policy makers as caring providers with a real commitment to patients and the health of the public. Consequently, the public and the policy makers are willing to listen to their perspectives on health issues. They are knowledgeable about the day-to-day problems of their patients and families and are able to present these problems in a way that the public and policy makers can understand. Moreover, health professional organizations can use their size and energy to have a major influence on policy making.

In the past, health professionals have had relatively little political impact and power because they have not exercised their potential influence. Many health professionals have had little education about policy and system issues. In addition to having a wide range of political views (from liberal to conservative), and affiliations (from Republican to Democrat to Independent), health professionals are divided into many specialty groups and organizations, with only a small percentage participating in their national organizations. These individuals are frequently reluctant to pay membership dues and to volunteer their time and energy to perform organizational work. This hesitancy is understandable because health professionals are often managing jobs, families, caring for sick parents and children, and going to school, among many other day-to-day responsibilities, leaving little time for political action. As the overall competition in the job market intensifies, professional work pressures and stress may further reduce health professionals' participation in professional and political organizations.

This book is designed to persuade health professionals that they need to add political work to their lives. The strength to influence health policy can come only when health professionals are better informed about policy, economics, and politics and unite behind some common goals. To be effective, political and professional actions should be undertaken through organizations rather than as individual health professionals. Enthusiasm for their own specialty organizations should not divert health professionals from participation in the local, state, and national organizations that address the broader issues related to the health profession.

This book focuses on the important policy issues of our times. It attempts to arm health professionals with facts about the system and the names of key policy shapers. Because health care statistics are updated frequently, it is important not to memorize facts but rather to learn the most important sources for information so that current information can be retrieved when needed. The book also highlights trends that tend to move forward until public policy changes or private system changes alter their progress.

Public policies are actions that are taken by policy makers at the federal, state, and local levels. These actions can include budgetary changes, legislative changes, regulatory changes, and often judicial rulings. Before health professionals can advocate for public policy changes, they need a clear understanding of the current federal policies that affect the health system and its operation, including the financial incentives that influence health providers and organizations.

Part I of this book begins with an understanding of health policy and the political process. The vested interests in and politics of the failure of President Bill Clinton's health plan are examined, as well as the potential role of health professionals in changing the health system. Part II examines the health status of the U.S. population, examining health disparities and discrimination among different population groups, including issues of access to care, aging, disability, and long-term care. The overall poor health status of the U.S. population is, in part, the result of limited access to services, especially for the poor, uninsured, and vulnerable populations. Part III discusses dramatic changes occurring in the health care delivery system and in organizations, including labor issues and quality of care.

Part IV focuses on how economics drives the entire health system in the United States and affects the day-to-day operations of health care organizations and professionals. Trends in financing health care services and the health industry are described, including the growth in public financing of Medicare and Medicaid and private financing. Private insurance and managed care are emphasized because of the rapid shift to managed care.

Part V, the final section of the book, is dedicated to health care reform. Articles examine health systems in other countries—particularly Canada—as potential models for the United States. Finally, a vision for the future of health care reform is presented.

This book is not designed to represent a broad spectrum of political ideas but rather to provide the perspectives of expert health services researchers as well as policy leaders who are both consumer-oriented and advocates for health reform. Most articles are critical of the existing health care system and hold the underlying assumption that changes in the system are needed. The status quo of millions of individuals in the United States continuing without access to health insurance, and millions of women and children with unacceptably poor health status, must be corrected.

Although reform is clearly needed, as yet a consensus has not emerged among health professionals and the public about how such reform should be accomplished. In this book, we show the urgent need for reform and urge health professionals to become politically active, using their political power and influence to improve the current system. Although the political problems of our health care system may seem overwhelming, the system *can* be changed if we develop an understanding of the underlying problems and unite behind reform strategies. The failed efforts of health reform in the early 1990s can be corrected in the coming decade.

ACKNOWLEDGMENTS

We would like to thank Brooke Hollister, doctoral student in sociology at the University of California, San Francisco, for her extensive work in identifying and collecting the articles, editing the articles, and obtaining the permissions for this edition. We would also like to thank Kevin Sullivan, Amy Sibley, and Amanda Clerkin for their editorial assistance.

PHOTO CREDITS

PART I

HEALTH POLICY

Health policy can be a confusing concept and field of study. As an orientation to the field, Block describes the array of definitions and the dynamic and complex policy-making process. Health policy is designed to address problems or changes that need to be made, but the key to success is initially identifying and understanding the problem and then following a model to direct or intervene in the public policy-making process.

As health professionals have begun to better appreciate the importance of policy and politics in their practices, they are increasingly becoming involved in politics and political actions. Because participating in the political process effectively is an art, health professionals need to know the basic rules of politics. The article by Dodd, an experienced nurse who previously held a high-level presidential administrative appointment and served as a top staff person to Congresswoman Nancy Pelosi, Democratic Majority Leader in the U.S. House of Representatives, gives practical guidelines for understanding and participating in politics.

The political scene in the United States is not a pretty picture, with large corporate health insurers, health care organizations, and the pharmaceutical industry wielding sometimes intimidating influence through massive political contributions. An example of the political control of corporations is the historical failure of national health insurance legislation over the years and the failure of President Bill Clinton's health reform legislation in 1994. Even the most conservative economists have noted the power that the health industry has had to stop any significant government reform. Interest-group politics are involved, and the health industry seeks to protect its economic position.

Corporations have not wanted government-guaranteed benefits that give workers more power and freedom to move between companies, and in and out of the workforce, without penalty. Even the Clinton health plan, which was designed to appeal to large corporate interests, was not able to win their support. The media and academia are also heavily influenced by corporate ideology in America, such that the public views of health reform they have presented in the past were aligned with those of the corporate world in opposition to the changes. The complexities of health reform are limited by the U.S. constitutional framework, making any change difficult, and the enormous influence of corporate and wealthy interests over the political and electoral processes.

1

Steinmo and Watts address why the United States does not have a comprehensive national health insurance program, showing that American political institutions are biased against reform. The U.S. political system places power in the hands of special-interest groups, and the political structure is decentralized, making it relatively easy to block legislation. Because of this political structure, it is difficult for any legislation to be passed. Thus, if Americans want Congress to act on a reform agenda, they need to focus on reforming political institutions and minimizing the influence of special-interest groups to make it easier for a democratic majority to get ground-breaking legislation enacted.

CHAPTER 1

Health Politics and Political Action

Teacher talking with students

Health Policy: What It Is and How It Works

Lester E. Block, DDS, MPH

INTRODUCTION

The usage and popularity of the word *policy* in regard to health has significantly increased over the past four decades. During the decade between 1992 and 2002, 2,132 books were published with the words *health* and *policy* in their titles as compared to 75 during the decade between 1959 and 1969 (WorldCat, 2003).

For the past 20 years, articles have been published about the emergence of health policy as an increasing concern to health professionals and the need for them to develop an adequate foundation of knowledge of health policy to be able to better analyze and influence the formulation of policies to support their professional objectives (Bodenheimer, 2001; Longest, 1997; Reeves, Bergwall, and Woodside, 1984; Rodgers, 1989; Roemer, 1980). Rodgers indicated that this was being hindered by the lack of a clear concept and definition of what policy is and that meager and inadequate attempts to define it give the assumption that its definition is too often assumed to be self-evident (Rodgers, 1989).

Almost 10 years before Rodgers' article was published, Falcone had written that deriving a useful definition and concept of health policy is complicated by the lack of a viable definition of the word *policy*, "not because of a scarcity of meanings with some currency but the lack of commonly accepted conceptions" (Falcone, 1981, p. 5). Ten years after the Rodgers article was published, Milstead (1999) commented that there still is not a clear definition of policy, and she, too, called for health professionals to be knowledgeable in their role as makers of public policy.

Although numerous attempts have been made in the past 20 years to clarify the meaning of *policy*, much of the ambiguity Rodgers referred to in 1989 remains. Ambiguity in regard to health care terms is not restricted, however, to the word *policy*. Many other health care–related terms, such as quality, reform, rationing, freedom of choice, managed care, spirituality, alternative care, and comprehensive care, are equally ambiguous. Even the simple word *is* has been questioned in regard to what *is* is (Ferguson, 2000).

The goal of this article is to provide a framework enabling the reader to examine the public policy issues discussed in this book. It is hoped that this framework can be used to better comprehend the policy-making process, to determine whether the policies in question appropriately address the public interest, and to view policy making as a process to solve problems. It should be noted that the major purpose of health policy is to enhance

Lester E. Block, DDS. (1997). Health policy: What it is and how it works. Dr. Block is Professor Emeritus at the School of Public Health at the University of Minnesota, School of Public Health. This article was prepared for the third edition of this book.

health or facilitate its pursuit by the public and the defining purpose of the governmental health policy is to support the public in its quest for health (Longest, 1998).

WHAT IS HEALTH POLICY?

One of the reasons for the ambiguous usage as to the meaning of the word *policy* is that it has two quite different Greek roots, one meaning "demonstration or proof" and the other meaning "citizenship" (Chrichton, 1981). Definitions of policy based on the root meaning "demonstration or proof" include (a) a certificate of insurance more commonly known as an insurance policy and (b) a method of gambling in which bets are made on numbers to be drawn from a lottery (*Oxford English Dictionary*, 1989).

Definitions of policy derived from the root meaning *citizenship* include the following:

a. "Principles that govern action toward given ends" (Leavitt and Mason, 1998). "A guiding principle considered expedient, prudent, or advantageous in reference to conduct or action. For example, honesty is the best policy, or it was a good policy to consent" (*Webster's Dictionary*, 1986).
b. "A way and means of doing things; a modus operandi" (Raymond, 1992, p. 380).
c. "Statements that express the wisdom, philosophy, experiences, and beliefs of an organization's senior management for future guidance toward attainment of goals and objectives" (Timmreck, 1997, p. 559). An example of the usage of policy in the context of this definition is management guru Peter Drucker's comment on change: "The first policy and the foundation for all others—is to abandon yesterday" (Drucker, 1999, p. 74).
d. "Any stated position on matters at issue, such as an organization's policy statement on universal health care" (Subcommittee on Health and Environment, 1976, p. 124).
e. "A plan or course of action of a government or business intended to influence and determine decisions, actions, and other matters. Examples include American foreign policy or a company's personnel policy" (*Webster's Dictionary*, 1986).
f. "A course of action adopted and pursued by a government, party, statesman, or other individual or organization" (Subcommittee on Health and Environment, 1976, p. 124).
g. "Measures that government (that is, the public sector) adopt or can adopt to achieve given ends or goals" (Brown, 1988).
h. "Authoritative decisions and guidelines that direct human behavior toward specific goals either in the private or the public sector" (Hanley, 1998, p. 125).
i. "Authoritative decisions made in the legislative, executive, or judicial branches of government that are intended to direct or influence the actions, behaviors, or decisions of others" (Longest, 1998, p. 243).

Definitions a–d, although commonly used, do not reflect the meaning of policy as used in the context of the public policy-making process; definitions e–i do. The most applicable and appropriate definition for policy as applied to the public sector is definition i.

In addition to these divergent definitions of policy, another confounding factor is that policy is considered as a field, an entity, as well as a process. As a field it is considered in a manner similar to that of the field of sports, nursing, or teaching. As an entity it is often used to refer to goals, programs, and proposals as well as the "standing decisions" or formal documented directives of an organization (Milstead, 1999). As a process it is used to represent the public policy-making process (Iatridis, 1995). Charles O. Jones confirms the importance of defining policy more precisely although he thinks the task is not an easy one since the word *policy* is often used interchangeably with goals, programs, decisions, laws, standards, proposals, and grand designs. He suggests that when a reference is made to policy, the following question should be asked: Is the person referring to national goals, current statutes, or recent decisions, or "characterizing certain behavioral consistencies by decision makers"? His reason for asking these questions is not to "enforce one particular definition of the term *policy* but rather to clarify meanings and thereby improve understanding" (Jones, 1984, p. 6).

Jones, as well as Eulau and Prewitt, suggests that while the word *policy* is often used as an adjective, as in policy goals, policy programs, policy decisions or choices, and policy effects, using the word interchangeably as in the above terms can be confusing (Jones, 1984; Eulau and Prewitt, 1973).

A common misuse of the word *policy* appears in the following statement: "It is our policy to reduce national spending on medical care" (Laster, 1996, p. 864). Reducing national spending is certainly a most admirable goal, but it is not a policy. To achieve that goal, however, would require the formulation and implementation of public policies. Health policies include:

- Health-related decisions made by legislators that are codified in the statutory language enacted in legislatures—laws.
- Rules/regulations designed to implement legislation or to operate government and its various health-related programs.
- Judicial decisions related to health (Longest, 1998).

The question has been raised as to whether programs such as Medicare and Medicaid should be referred to as policies as well as programs. Brown (1992, p. 21) indicates that "laws when they are more or less freestanding legislative enactments aimed to achieve specific objectives" should more appropriately be referred to as programs, not policies. Based on Brown's thinking, Medicare and Medicaid created by "freestanding legislative enactments aimed to achieve specific objectives" as well as rules and judicial decisions should rightly be thought of as programs *comprising* a collection of laws, rules, and judicial decisions—that is, policies.

GLOSSARY OF PUBLIC POLICY-RELATED TERMS

In an attempt to address the aforesaid inconsistencies and definitional confusion, the following glossary suggests the most appropriate meanings of policy-related terms, as applied to the public policy process.

A Policy—"Authoritative decision that is made in the legislative, executive, or judicial branches of government. It is intended to direct or influence the actions, behaviors, or decisions of others." As Longest so perceptively points out, the word *authoritative* is the crucial element of this definition (Longest, 1998, p. 4).

Policies/Policy–"Authoritative decisions made in the legislative, executive, or judicial branches of government that are intended to direct or influence the actions, behaviors, or decisions of others" (Longest, 1998, p. 243). While all policies are solutions, not all solutions are policies.

Solutions–Ideally, the "definitive answers that solve problems or make them disappear" (Nadler and Hibino, 1998, p. 306). It is often the case that improvement rather than total resolution is a more realistic expectation.

Private Policy–Policy made by nongovernmental agencies and organizations that includes directives and guidelines governing such issues as conditions of employment, product lines, pricing, marketing strategies, and other related service provisions (Leavitt and Mason, 1998; Longest, 1998).

Public Policy–Policy made at the legislative, executive, and judicial branches of federal, state, and local levels of government that affects individual and institutional behaviors under the respective government's jurisdiction. Public policy includes all policies that come from government at all levels (Magill, 1984). It can be considered as the response of government to address society's problems (Weissberg, 1986) or as government's attempt to seek solutions in response to society's problems (Jones, 1984). Examples include legislation passed by Congress and signed by the president, regulations written to address that legislation, and judicial decisions made by the courts (Leavitt and Mason, 1998).

The three major public policy categories are defense, domestic, and foreign. Included under the rubric of domestic policy are employment and labor, transportation, tax, economic, and social policy. Social policy includes health and welfare policy (Dunn, 1994). Examples of health policies are the 1965 federal public law (P.L. 89–97) that established Medicare and Medicaid and a state's procedures for the regulation of health care professionals (Longest, 1998).

There are two main types of public policy: regulatory and allocative. Regulatory policies such as the regulation of health care professions by the states are designed to influence the actions, behaviors, and decisions of others. "Allocative policies provide net benefits to some distinct group or class at the expense of others in order to ensure that public objectives are met" (Longest, 1998, p. 9). Although it is true that a rich and complex blend of public and private sector policies and actions shape American health policy and America's pursuit of health, given that this book primarily addresses policy at governmental levels, the word *policy* will be used interchangeably with *public policy.*

Health Policy–"The collection of authoritative decisions made within government that pertain to health and to the pursuit of health" (Longest, 1998, p. xxi). "It is at any given time, the entire set of health-related policies/authoritative decisions made at any level of government that can be said to constitute that level's health policy" (Longest, 1998, p. 5). It should be noted that the term *health policy* is considered by some to include policies in the private sector as well (Hanley, 1998).

Health Policies–Policies that pertain to health or influence the pursuit of health. Additional examples of health policies include a city government's banning smoking in public buildings, the requirement of nonsmoking sections in restaurants within the jurisdiction of that city, or the U.S. Supreme Court's rulings on the legality of abortion (Longest, 1998).

Social Policy–Public policies and directives that promote the welfare of the public (Leavitt and Mason, 1998). Along with education, crime and correction, and economic security, a nation's health policy is part of its overall social policy (Barker, 1995).

Intentions–"The true purpose of an action" (Jones, 1984, p. 27).

Goals–"The stated ends to be achieved" (Jones, 1984, p. 27).

Plans or Proposals–"Specified means for achieving goals" (Jones, 1984, p. 27).

Programs–"Authorized means for achieving goals" (Jones, 1984, p. 27).

Decisions or Choices–"Specific actions taken to set goals, develop plans, implement and evaluate programs" (Jones, 1984, p. 27).

Effects–"The measurable impacts of programs or policies which can be intended or unintended" (Jones, 1984, p. 27).

Unintended Consequences (also known as *blowback*)–Unanticipated or unintended effects arising from actions of people and especially of government, both of a positive and negative nature. They are, however, usually considered as "perverse unanticipated effects of governmental policy" (Norton, 2003, p. 1).

Policy Analysis–A term used to describe both the overall policy-making process as well as a specific component of that process, with the latter being the preferred meaning (Dunn, 1994; Hanley, 1998). The dual definition creates confusion. The primary role of policy analysis in the public policy-making process is to provide the knowledge and information required for making public policy utilizing various evaluation and measurement processes by which broad questions of need, scope, allocation, utilization, capacity, resources, and goals are critically assessed (Dunn, 1994).

Policy analysis is carried out by people from various disciplinary and professional backgrounds. The policy analysis field falls under the umbrella of general social sciences as well as within the disciplines of economics, political science, and sociology (Einbinder, 1995). Policy analysts investigate the causes, consequences, and performance of public policies and programs (Dunn, 1994) and assist in the public policy-making process by providing input into the structuring of the problems, forecasting, making recommendations, monitoring, and evaluating (Barker, 1992).

Thus, policy analysis as contrasted with policy making is concerned primarily with explanations rather than with prescriptions. It involves the careful investigation into the causes and consequences of policies and not the making of proposals. It is a set of techniques that seeks to determine what the probable effects of a proposed policy will be and what were the effects subsequent to policy implementation (Dunn, 1994).

THE PUBLIC POLICY-MAKING PROCESS

The public policy-making process in the United States is complex, dynamic, confusing, and at times mysterious. It is complex because the making of public policy involves an interaction among various government institutions whose players have differing political and social perspectives, interests, and political party affiliations. In addition, the process includes the participation of self-interest groups, private and nonprofit organizations, and the public at large. To varying degrees and depending on the policy issue at play, all of these players are operating in the policy-making process, doing their best to influence the adoption of their policies and to sabotage opposing ones. While the process is ostensibly an open one, the reality is that much of the process is not visible to the public, making it seem all the more confusing and mysterious. Given that the three main arenas of living in a society—government, the economy, and private life—are interrelated, complicated, multi-layered, and dynamic, it is not surprising that the process of making policies that mediate these relationships is also complicated, multilayered, and dynamic (Einbinder, 1995). The public policy formation process has been dominated by three major players: interest groups concerned about and affected by a particular policy area; the agency of the executive branch of government that has administrative responsibility over the related policy area; and the committees and subcommittees in Congress with responsibility for legislative authority in those areas. These three players have been termed the *Iron Triangle* in deference to their lock on policy development (Kronenfeld, Whicker, and Lynn, 1984).

A variety of public policy-making models has been suggested by policy scholars (Chrichton, 1981; Dunn, 1994; Hanley, 1998; Jones, 1984; Kingdon, 1995; Leavitt and Mason, 1998; Longest, 1998; Magill, 1984; Milstead, 1999; Paul-Shaheen, 1990). While these models have commonalities, there are differences among them. The problem-centered model proposed in this article is based primarily on the work of Dunn (1994), Kingdon (1995), Longest (1998), and Paul-Shaheen (1990). It relies on the premise that policies emanate from problems, whether they are real, perceived as real, or claimed to be real. Given the significance of problem conceptualization in the policy-making process, a discussion of "problems" will precede the presentation of the model.

Meaning and Definition of Problems

Just as there is ambiguity in regard to the meaning of *policy*, there is ambiguity regarding the meaning of *problem*. The definition of a problem ranges from a medical condition or a mathematics or physics proposition to definitions that contain the concept of a problem as something that is a perplexing situation of concern. The following two definitions of *problem* specifically apply to the policy-making process:

   a. "an unsettled matter demanding a solution or decision and requiring considerable thought or skill for its proper solution or decision" (*Webster's Dictionary*, 1986).
   b. "a difficult or puzzling question proposed for a solution" (*Oxford English Dictionary*, 1989).

Thus, the two requisites of a problem are (1) a perplexing or vexing situation and (2) an invitation for a solution.

Dornblaser has provided a useful conceptualization of a problem in the context of the making of public policy. He considers a problem as a discrepancy between "the way the world is and the way it should be," and he defines a problem as the "gap between what is and what ought to be" (Dornblaser, 1995, p. 3). More specifically, a problem is an unachieved goal—"it is a condition or a set of circumstances that a person or group *thinks* should be changed" (Nadler and Hibino, 1998, p. 39). Dornblaser has suggested for purposes of policy making that the problem should be stated in the form of a question that begs for a solution/policy (Dornblaser, 1995).

There is a difference between a problem and a condition or a situation. People put up with many conditions and situations every day. Situations and conditions become problems when it is believed that something should be or needs to be done about them. Kingdon suggests, for example, that losing a finger is not a problem but a situation (Kingdon, 1995). It can become a problem if the person missing the finger is a concert pianist.

Both Dornblaser and Dunn have emphasized the importance of asking the right questions when examining a problem statement because problems that initially may appear to be insoluble may be reformulated so that previously undetected solutions emerge. "A problem well formulated," Dunn wrote, "is a problem half solved" (Dunn, 1994, p. 2; Dornblaser, 1995). Ackoff (1974, p. 8) perceptively suggests that "successful problem solving requires finding the right solution to the right problem. We fail more often because we solve the wrong problem than because we get the wrong solution to the right problem." Raiffa (1968, p. 263) also emphasized the importance of identifying the correct problem and warned against making "an error of a third kind: solving the wrong problem." He also proposed an "error of the fourth kind: solving the right problem too late." Another warning worth noting is the importance of not developing a policy in search of a problem.

Defining or structuring a problem is essentially a process of separating causes from symptoms and repeatedly asking "why is that a problem" until the point is reached at which the essential problem has been defined. The appropriate parallel in science is the popular aphorism that "If in the course of performing an experiment, you pose the question in the wrong way, you are doomed to arrive at the wrong answer" (Hall, 2000, p. 17).

Proposed Model for the Making of Public Policy

The public policy-making process in real life is a complex, dynamic, nonlinear, cyclical, evolutionary, and iterative process. In the two-dimensional proposed model shown in Figure 1.1.1, an attempt has been made to reflect this reality. Given the premise that policies emanate from problems and that the policy-making process is problem centered, "problems" has been placed in the center of the model. Another premise of the model is that problem recognition is a necessary condition for the formulation of a policy but it is not a sufficient condition for policy formulation; that is, all policies result from problems, but problems do not necessarily lead to policies. (See the following definition of Window of Opportunity/Policy Window.)

Although problems can be generated by any of the players directly or indirectly connected to the public policy-making process, the major players are legislators, members of the executive branch of government, and various interest groups (Dunn, 1994; Longest, 1998).

As mentioned previously, policy making and policy analysis are considered as two separate entities, with policy analysis providing the needed analytical information for the decision makers. Policy made in the legislative and executive branches of government usually follows this format. It is also the case, however, that policy making and policy analysis are often concurrently engaged in by individuals or groups of policy makers.

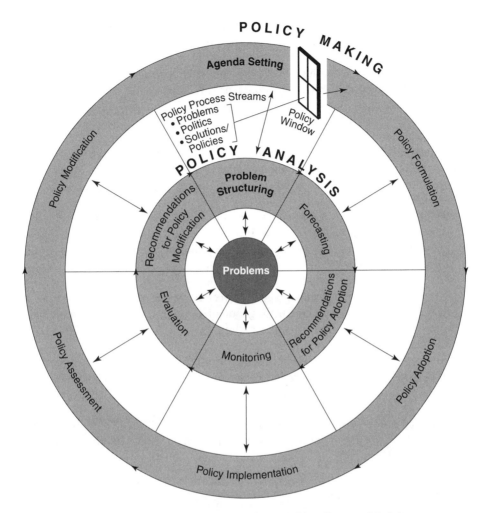

FIGURE 1.1.1   A Problem-Centered Public Policy-Making Process Model

Source: This model is derived from the writings of Dunn, Kingdon, Paul-Shaheen, and Longest.

In the proposed model, six phases of the policy-making process are identified. In a rationally evolving process, the order in which these components are listed should be the order in which they occur once the problem is identified and defined. Before examining the model, it would be helpful to review the following definitions of the model's components.

Phases of Policy Making

1. *Agenda Setting*—Agenda setting is the initial and crucial phase in the policy-making process. During that phase a multiplicity of problems compete for sufficient

recognition to warrant their passage through the window of opportunity/policy window to the policy formulation phase of the process. What determines whether a particular problem passes through this window is dependent on (1) the overall appeal of the problem (problems), (2) the political support it has generated (politics), and (3) the view of perceived viability of the proposed alternative solution (solutions). These three factors–problems, politics, and solutions–have been termed the three policy streams (Kingdon, 1995; Longest, 1998; Paul-Shaheen, 1990). For the policy window to open and allow the problem to pass through, the three policy streams must coalesce into a single policy stream (Kingdon, 1995).

   Window of Opportunity/Policy Window–The policy window is essentially a filter through which problems entrapped in the agenda-setting phase must pass to reach the policy-formulation stage to become serious contenders (Kingdon, 1995; Longest, 1998). The policy window is comparable to the gatekeepers at the entrance to an exclusive club or at an HMO.

2. *Policy Formulation*–The development or devising of alternative policies to address a problem (Longest, 1998).
3. *Policy Adoption*–The adoption of a policy alternative with the support of the legislative majority, consensus among agency directors, or a court decision (Longest, 1998).
4. *Policy Implementation*–The carrying out of an adopted policy by administrative units that mobilize human and financial resources to comply with the policy (Longest, 1998).
5. *Policy Assessment*–The determination of whether the implemented policy is in compliance with its statutory requirements and achieving its objectives in regard to the problem (Dunn, 1994).
6. *Policy Modification*–Depending on the results of the policy assessment and the political climate, the policy could be maintained, modified, or eliminated (Dunn, 1994). An example of the latter is the repeal of PL 100-360, the Medicare Catastrophic Coverage Act of 1988, in 1989 (Longest, 1998).

Phases of Policy Analysis

In the proposed model, the related components of policy analysis have been placed between problems and policy making for the reasons indicated previously.

1. *Problem Structuring*–The aspect of policy analysis that yields information about the conditions giving rise to a problem (Dunn, 1994).
2. *Forecasting*–Providing information about the future consequences of acting on policy alternatives, including taking no action (Dunn, 1994).
3. *Recommendations for Policy Adoption*–Providing information on the probable effects of adopting a policy and the "value or worth of the above mentioned consequences in solving or alleviating the problem" (Dunn, 1994, p. 14).
4. *Monitoring*–"Measuring and recording of the ongoing operation of a policy's implementation" (Longest, 1998, p. 234).
5. *Evaluation*–Providing information about the value or worth of the policy in solving or alleviating the problem.

6. *Recommendations for Policy Modification*—Providing information needed for determining the future status of the implemented policy.

SUMMARY

It is important to remember that the public policy-making process and its results are influenced by confounding factors that are often external to the process itself. Longest includes among those factors the preferences of individuals, organizations, interest groups, and a host of biological, cultural, demographic, ecological, economic, ethical, legal, psychological, social, technical, and political factors (Longest, 1998).

When reading articles about the wide variety of health policy-related issues, it would be instructive to first identify the primary problem and whether it has been appropriately defined and stated; second to determine what, if any, policies have resulted in response to the problem and whether those policies have helped alleviate the problem; and third to identify the outcomes of the policies in regard to unintended consequences. When confronted with a health-related issue or problem, common sense will often indicate whether a proposed policy is viable. In the early 1800s, Supreme Court Justice Oliver Wendell Holmes was well aware of the value of common sense when he said, "Science is a first rate piece of furniture for a man's upper chamber, if he has common sense on the ground floor" (Bartlett, 1992).

REFERENCES

Ackoff, R. L. (1974). *Redesigning the future: A systems approach to societal problems.* New York: Wiley.

Barker, R. L. (1995). *The social work dictionary.* Washington, DC: NASW Press.

Bartlett, J. (1992). *Familiar quotations.* Boston: Little, Brown.

Bodenheimer, T. S. (2001). *Understanding health policy: A clinical approach.* Stanford, CT: Appleton and Lange.

Brown, L. D. (1988). *Health policy in the United States: Issues and options.* New York: Ford Foundation.

Brown, L. D. (1992). Political evolution of federal health care regulations. *Health Affairs,* 11 (Winter), 17–37.

Chrichton, A. (1981). *Health policy making: Fundamental issues in the United States, Canada, Great Britain, Australia.* Ann Arbor, MI: Health Administration Press.

Dornblaser, P. (1995). Problem solving and decision making theory and technique. Unpublished monograph, Minneapolis: University of Minnesota, Department of Health Care Management.

Drucker, P. (1999). *Management challenges for the 21st century.* New York: HarperBusiness.

Dunn, W. N. (1994). *Public policy analysis: An introduction.* Englewood Cliffs, NJ: Prentice Hall.

Einbinder, S. D. (1995). Policy analysis. In: *Encyclopedia of social work* (19th ed., pp. 1849–1855). Washington, DC: NASW Press.

Eulau, H., & Prewitt, K. (1973). *Labyrinths of democracy.* Indianapolis, IN: Bobbs-Merrill.

Falcone, D. (1981). Health policy analysis: Some reflections on the state of the art. In: R. A. Straetz, M. Lieberman, & A. Sardell, eds. *Critical issues in health policy* (pp. 3–13). Lexington, MA: Lexington Books.

Ferguson, A. (2000, June 5). A license to revisit the word *is. Time,* 155(23), 47.

Hall, S. S. (2000, May 7). Split personality. *New York Times,* 105(19), 17.

Hanley, B. E. (1998). Policy development and analysis. In: J. K. Leavitt and D. J. Mason, eds., *Policy and politics in nursing and health care* (3rd ed.). Philadelphia: WB Saunders.

Iatridis, D. S. (1995). Policy practice. In: *Encyclopedia of social work* (p. 1855). Washington, DC: NASW Press.

Jones, C. O. (1984). *An introduction to the study of public policy* (3rd ed.). Fort Worth, TX: Harcourt Brace.

Kingdon, J. W. (1995). *Agendas, alternatives and public policies* (2nd ed.). New York: Addison Wesley Longman.

Kronenfeld, J., Whicker, J., & Lynn, M. (1984). *U.S. national health policy: An analysis of the federal role.* New York: Praeger.

Laster, L. (1996). Making sausage and making national health policy. *Journal of Health Politics, Policy and Law,* 24(1), 863–868.

Leavitt, J. K., & Mason, D. J. (1998). *Policy and politics in nursing and health care* (3rd ed.). Philadelphia: WB Saunders.

Longest, B. B. (1997). *Seeking strategic advantage through health policy analysis.* Chicago: Health Administration Press.

Longest, B. B. (1998). *Health policy making in the United States* (2nd ed.). Chicago: Health Administration Press.

Magill, R. S. (1984). *Social policy in American society.* Hingham, MA: Kluwer Academic Publishers.

Milstead, J. A. (1999). *Health policy and politics: A nurses' guide.* Gaithersburg, MD: Aspen.

Nadler, G., & Hibino, S. (1998). *Break through thinking—The seven principles of creative problem solving* (2nd ed.). Roseville, CA: Prima.

Norton, R. (2003). Unintended consequences. In: *The concise encyclopedia of economics.* Retrieved June 9, 2003, from http://www.econlib.org, p. 1.

The Oxford English dictionary (2nd ed.). (1989). Vol. XII. Oxford, UK: Oxford University Press.

Paul-Shaheen, P. A. (1990). Overlooked connections: Policy development and implementation in state–local relations. *Journal of Health Politics, Policy and Law,* 15(4), 833–856.

Raiffa, H. (1968). *Decision analysis: Introductiory lectures on choices under uncertainty.* Reading, MA: Addison-Wesley.

Raymond, W. J. (1992). *Dictionary of politics.* Lawrenceville, VA: Brunswick.

Reeves, P. N., Bergwall, D. F., & Woodside, N. B. (1984). *Introduction to health planning* (3rd ed.). Arlington, VA: Information Resources Press.

Rodgers, B. L. (1989). Exploring health policy as a concept. *Western Journal of Nursing Research,* 11(6), 694–702.

Roemer, R. (1980). Law and health policy. In: R. Roemer and G. McKray, eds. *Legal aspects of health policy issues and trends.* Westport, CT: Greenwood Press.

Subcommittee on Health and Environment of the Committee on Interstate Commerce, U.S. House of Representatives. (1976). *A discursive dictionary of health care.* #59-892-0. Washington, DC: U.S. Government Printing Office.

Timmreck, T. C. (1997). *Health services cyclopedic dictionary* (3rd ed.). Sudbury, MA: Jones and Bartlett.

Webster's third new international dictionary, unabridged. (1986). Springfield, MA: Merriam-Webster.

Weissberg, R. (1986). *Understanding American government* (2nd ed.). New York: Random House.

WorldCat. Retrieved June 4, 2003, from http://newfirstsearch.oclc.org/.

Play to Win: Know the Rules

Catherine J. Dodd, RN, MS

The result of Otto von Bismark's famous quote, "Laws are like sausages—it is better not to see them be made" (Brainy Quote.com, 2006), is that politics is often left to those with iron stomachs. Because legislation, according to health economist Paul Feldstein, "redistributes wealth" (1996, p. 17), it is essential that pragmatic idealists—both the self-appointed guardians of the public good and elected officials—participate in the political process. Only their cooperation can ensure that health policy is not designed by and implemented by the well-financed interest groups motivated only by profit.

Politics has been defined as "the art and science of government," and political affairs as "competition between competing interest groups of individuals for power and leadership" (Morris, 1962, p. 1015). The division of scarce resources is almost without exception political, being characterized by competition between interest groups, some more powerful than others. It is rarely fair. Political decisions are not made during the hearings in the hallowed halls of the Capitol. Rather, political decisions are made long before the day of the vote and are based on external influences that may or may not include expert knowledge.

Political decisions influence many aspects of our daily lives. Politics determines the outcomes of proposals in governing bodies, in the workplace, in the neighborhood, and at the dinner table. Parents may decide which child gets the largest piece of pie based on who has been the most helpful around the house or who has completed their homework. Similarly, a state legislator may vote to fund a new health center because many voters from that neighborhood support her, even though that decision may jeopardize another clinic in another legislative district. Those who fail to participate in the political process are allowing the decisions to be made by people who may seek to control resources for their own personal or political gain (Dodd, 2004).

Political expertise is essential for success in organizations, institutions, and local, state, and national governments. Developing and maintaining political power requires establishing and maintaining relationships. It also takes time and practice.

Catherine J. Dodd, RN, MS, FAAN. (2006). Play to win: Know the rules. Catherine Dodd has served as the District Director for Democratic Leader, Congresswoman Nancy Pelosi. Prior to that, she was an appointee of President Bill Clinton, serving as the Regional Director for the U.S. Department of Health and Human Services, Region IX, under Cabinet Secretary Donna Shalala. This article was revised from the fourth edition of this book.

TEN UNIVERSAL COMMANDMENTS
OF POLITICS AND REASONS TO OBEY THEM

1. The personal is political. Each of us is just one personal or social injustice away from being involved in politics.
2 In politics, friends come and go but enemies accumulate.
3. Politics is the art of the possible. The majority rules.
4. Be polite, be persistent, be persuasive, and be polite.
5. Ignore your mother's instructions. Talk to strangers.
6. Money is the mother's milk of politics.
7. Negotiate visibility. Take credit, and take control.
8. Politics has a "chit economy," so keep track.
9. Reputations are permanent.
10. Don't let 'em get to you.

1. The personal is political. Each of us is just one personal or social injustice away from being involved in politics. Every vote counts.

Injustices and tragedies, whether individual or collective, often ignite social movements that result in advocacy and collective action. Elected officials are inspired to introduce legislation because of their own personal experience or the experience of someone they know, or because of collective demands of constituents.

Representative Caroline McCarthy, LPN, ran for Congress and was elected after her husband and child were shot on the New York subway. She promised the voters that she would fight for stricter gun laws. She challenged the National Rifle Association (NRA) enthusiasts, who believe their personal freedom will be impinged upon by limiting access to automatic weapons, and who frequently initiate very successful letter writing and e-mail campaigns in key congressional districts to protect their "constitutional rights." NRA activists also raise money for *key* candidates from members all over the country.

MADD (Mothers Against Drunk Driving) was founded in 1980 by Cindy Lightner, whose 13-year-old daughter was killed by a drunk driver. Today, MADD is the largest crime-fighting organization in the country, with chapters in every state. Its members include relatives and friends of victims of drunk drivers as well as health professionals and supportive members of the public. MADD has been extremely effective in achieving its objectives at the local level, lobbying for speed bumps and the installation of stoplights; at the state level, increasing penalties for drunk driving, and at the national level, placing restrictions on alcohol advertising (Mothers Against Drunk Driving, 2006).

Many health advocacy organizations, such as Families USA (www.familiesusa.org), emerged from the movement to support access to health care. The recent proposals to privatize Social Security and Medicare helped increase the national membership of the National Committee to Preserve Social Security and Medicare (www.ncpssm.org). Environmental health (www.breastcancerfund.org) and social justice organizations have emerged to address the unfair burden of exposure to toxic chemicals borne by communities of color located in polluted neighborhoods (www.ejfoundation.org).

The more voices that participate in our democracy, the more likely that the weakest voices will be heard. Individuals who choose not to vote or not to be involved in politics, in essence, relinquish their power to those who do vote. Long ago, Plato advised that "One of the penalties for refusing to participate in politics is that you end up being governed by your inferiors" (en.thinkexist.com, 2006).

Every person can make a difference, especially when one considers how the outcome of an election may affect the lives of those who do not believe that their voices count. Many recent elections at all levels of government have been decided by one or fewer votes per precinct.

2. In politics, friends come and go but enemies accumulate.

This old adage can be applied to many relationships. Its application includes two important concepts: Never surprise your friends, and politics makes strange bedfellows. It is imperative to not jeopardize working relationships, with public officials or other advocates, by publicly opposing someone, by not inviting them to a meeting, or by voting against them without talking to them before taking action. Maintaining relationships does not require disclosing strategy; it means simply showing respect for the right of others to have a different perspective. Trust and respect are commodities in politics that once lost, are rarely regained. While you may disagree on one issue, there may exist agreement on another issue, and a relationship sustained by respect allows for discussion, compromise, and progress. Handling conflicts respectfully will allow for future collaboration. Maintaining working relationships allows for "strange bedfellows." Managing conflicts respectfully allows for future collaboration with partners who may agree with your position on other issues.

For example, advocates for women's and children's health frequently testify to protect women's reproductive freedom and argue against the testimony of advocates from conservative religious organizations. On issues affecting children's health, however, the two organizations come together as strange bedfellows and make powerful allies. Representative Henry Hyde and Senator Ted Kennedy disagree on most issues, but they worked together to create the State Children's Health Insurance Plan during President Clinton's administration.

3. Politics is the art of the possible. Count votes in advance. The majority rules.

The policies that are adopted and the legislation that is signed into law reflect compromise and rarely resemble what was initially introduced. Successful politicians strive for what is possible. In diverse political cultures where there are many different opinions and philosophies, the most successful legislators are those with an ability to find compromises acceptable to the majority that do not destroy the intent of the original legislation. Votes are not won during dramatic debate on the floor of the House or Senate. Instead, they are won one by one, by talking to individual legislators, seeking their support, and finding out what compromises would be required to gain their support. Sometimes asking others for assistance in lining up additional votes is necessary. Once commitments are made they are rarely changed, because trust is the basis of future relationships. If legislation is controversial, legislators may not commit to a position until the actual vote because no one wants to be the "deciding vote." Legislators do not willingly vote for legislation that is opposed by powerful lobbies if they believe the legislation is going to fail anyway (because friends come and go but enemies accumulate, and no one wants to alienate powerful lobbies if the bill will fail anyway).

For example, strange bedfellows came together to oppose the passage of the 2003 Medicare Modernization Act, which represented the first major change to Medicare in more than 25 years. The act added some coverage for prescription drugs for seniors. Conservative Republicans opposed the law because it would cost too much; almost all Democrats opposed it because it was not comprehensive and did not impose cost controls on the pharmaceutical industry. Some of the conservative Republicans finally agreed to support the legislation when a section was added to begin to privatize Medicare in 2010. This part of the act was not debated: The party in the majority makes the rules, and the Republicans ruled that no debate was needed, despite opposition to this move from Democrats. This amendment has far-reaching implications for the future of Medicare because it changes Medicare from a guaranteed benefit package to an insurance program that will compete in the market. On the day of the vote on the Medicare Modernization Act, pharmaceutical company lobbyists, who are known for their large campaign contributions, made calls to legislators who were uncommitted and who had competitive elections, as did President George W. Bush. The vote was ultimately "held open" into the middle of the night, longer than the rules allowed for, until enough votes had been changed to pass the bill.

If the margin for passage of a law is close, how a legislator votes usually depends on whether the voters in his or her district care about the issue and on whether major campaign contributors support or oppose the issue. Advocates need to be certain of those votes they can count on and then ensure that the supporting legislators, board members, and so forth will be in attendance the day the vote is scheduled, especially if it is expected to be close.

Many people wonder why so few pieces of legislation are passed and signed into law. Two factors explain this phenomenon.

Since the 1994 elections, Congress and state legislatures have become more partisan, and the voters have become disillusioned with "incumbents—career politicians." In 1993, Congress spent an entire year debating President Clinton's health care reform proposal. Special interests (against reform) targeted candidates in swing districts who supported reform, spending $400 million to ensure their defeat. For the first time in 40 years, the Republican Party gained a majority in both houses of Congress (the Senate and the House of Representatives; see Tables 1.2.1 and 1.2.2 for a summary of their organization). The 1994 elections produced a class of "freshmen" (new senators and representatives) dominated by business people/owners who lacked experience in negotiating with other people who hold entirely different philosophies or agendas. These new legislators simply refused to negotiate with their Democratic colleagues, leading to legislative gridlock. In the corporate world, of course, business owners who cannot agree on terms merely find other contractors.

The Republicans elected to the 104th Congress were also very conservative, and their majority created a more conservative Congress. This same trend was echoed throughout the country at the state and local levels as conservative (religious anti-women's reproductive freedom) campaign strategists successfully ran candidates in primaries who were then

TABLE 1.2.1   Congress at a Glance

Senate	*House of Representatives*
Upper House	Lower House
100 members, two from each state	435 members, apportioned every 10 years based on population changes
6-year terms	2-year terms
One third are up for election each 2 years	Up for election every 2 years

elected in general elections, defeating Democratic career-politician incumbents. All votes cast in the subsequent 104th Congress were significantly more conservative on health, education, human services, and environmental issues than those produced by previous Congresses. Democrats representing swing districts voted more conservatively than they might have previously in an attempt to appeal to moderate Republicans in their districts during an election year. Elected officials do not ordinarily have this option, because they are elected by and work for the voters rather than for themselves. However, the Republicans' control of the Congress gave them more power to determine what would be negotiated and what would not even be discussed.

After President Bush's election in 2000, the Republicans had total, one-party control of the federal legislative agenda. The majority of states also had Republican governors. Following the 2000 census, not surprisingly state legislatures redrew district lines to enhance the election of Republicans in many states. These new lines served to solidify the Republican majority in Congress for the rest of the decade.

For legislation to pass, a majority of members of the legislature need to vote in for it. The *majority* rules in more ways than one. All parties have their own philosophies and agendas. The *majority* party determines which issues will be debated and whether the

TABLE 1.2.2   Congressional Leadership

Senate	*House of Representatives*
• Vice President of the United States	• Speaker of the House (majority party)
• President Pro Tempore	
• Temporary Presiding Officer	
• Majority Leader	• Majority Leader
• Majority Whip	• Majority Whip
• Minority Leader	• Minority Leader
• Minority Whip	• Minority Whip

Note: State legislative leadership often has similar terminology.

The "majority" is the party with the most votes. The "leader" is tasked with setting the agenda for the party in Congress. The "whip" is tasked with ensuring that the party votes along party lines on issues agreed on by the party.

To gain a better understanding of party priorities, search the websites of the majority and minority "leaders" in each party.

debate will allow for alternatives or compromise. Many pieces of legislation are introduced and never put on the agenda for consideration if the party in the *majority* does not want the issue considered.

Partisan ideology has taken the place of pragmatic bipartisan compromise and problem solving. The Republican ideology emphasizes competition in the "market" to reduce budgets. In contrast, the Democratic ideology favors greater public protection through government regulation. The increased partisanship in halls of government across the United States has produced very few compromises. Leadership in both parties is necessary for legislators to work together and, one by one, meet, talk, and identify acceptable compromises.

4. Be polite, be persistent, be persuasive, and be polite.
Send thank-you notes, write, write, write, ghost write, and write.

In this era of instant messaging, it is difficult to determine the preferred method of communication for individual elected officials. Elected officials listen to those who elect them and/or support them financially in their campaigns. Perennial voters (those who vote in every election, rain or shine) tend to be more highly educated and are more likely to write a letter or craft an e-mail message. For that reason, an individually written letter (mailed, faxed, or e-mailed—but not a chain message) is the most effective lobbying tool. Preprinted letters or postcards and "linked" e-mails off advocacy Internet sites are effective only in specific mass strategy campaigns. In general, phone calls urging a vote are used in last-minute attempts and are considered an effective lobbying tool only if they are from constituents who leave their addresses and ask for a written response explaining how the elected official plans to vote (or has already voted).

Letters from voters who live in the elected official's or legislator's district do make a difference. Some elected officials, however, believe their constituency goes beyond their legislative district. For example, an RN legislator may consider and respond to the opinions of RNs regardless of where they live, or a gay legislator may consider and respond to letters from people in the lesbian/gay/bisexual/transgender community regardless of where they live.

If your legislator is not a member of the committee that will hear the bill in which you are interested, find out the staff person who is assigned to the committee, address your letter to the Chair of the Committee "care of" the staff person *at the committee's address*, and then send a copy of your letter to your legislator with a brief note.

It is best to gather information about the legislator's position in advance by communicating with the staff person responsible for the issue. Call the capitol office and ask to speak to the staff person responsible for the issue; if he or she is unavailable, ask for an e-mail address. Thousands of constituents are making similar requests, so keep your communication clear and concise. Thank the staff person for his or her assistance, and if your legislator agrees with your position, write your letter or message so that it acknowledges the lawmaker's position and states that you are pleased with it. Communication with legislators should establish the sender's credibility as a constituent (e.g., a nurse, a mother, student, expert) and should be polite, persuasive, and succinct. Communications should state the sender's position early in the communication, offer support for the position with research or personal experience or belief, and ask for a response prior to the vote. This message is not a term paper, so it need not be perfect grammatically, only persuasive. It is likely to be read only by staff (unless the sender has a personal relationship with the elected official).

Multiplying the effectiveness of your effort by demonstrating broad support or opposition can be accomplished by assisting, collecting, and mailing similar letters from friends, family, and colleagues. When 1 letter arrives in a legislator's office, it is recorded; when 10 arrive, it becomes an issue of constituent concern; when 20 individually written communications arrive, staff alert the elected official. To be effective, letters must arrive before the vote is scheduled, so send them early. If the bill fails and is introduced in subsequent years, you must write again, and again, and again, if necessary. Many bills are amended during the process, so it is important that you continue to communicate with your legislator if you no longer support or oppose the bill along the way.

Always be polite: In talking to legislators, staff, or the press, never say or put in writing anything you do not want printed on the front page of the newspaper. Reputations are permanent (Commandment 9). Many a career has ended because of an angry quote (Commandment 2: Friends come and go but enemies accumulate).

The two most effective kinds of communication are thank-you notes and letters to the editor. If the legislator, organizational board member, or coworker takes the desired action, follow your mother's advice: Write a thank-you note! Everyone enjoys being recognized and thanked. Those colorful envelopes in the mail are the first to be opened by each of us, and elected officials are no exception. This kind of communication also shows you are monitoring their vote. Politicians, like relatives and friends, remember people who send thank-you notes.

Letters to the editor and op-ed columns in local newspapers are extremely effective lobbying tools. The editorial section of the newspaper is the first section read by political staff each day because the opinions expressed are those of voters. Politicians give extra credence to letters to the editor for two reasons. First, the people who write these missives subscribe to the paper and are more likely to be perennial voters. Second, letters are not printed unless the paper has received more than one on the subject. Letters written by women are more likely to be printed because editors try to balance the page with equal numbers of letters from men and women. Agreeing with or lauding the paper for its coverage of an issue also increases the likelihood of publication. Letters from suburbs often have a better chance of being printed because they demonstrate a wide readership for the paper.

Health professionals have very high credibility, so a letter to the editor published in a local paper will have significant public influence that is recognized by politicians. Use your credentials.

Letters should be well written (they will be read by thousands of people) but should not exceed 250 words. (Many papers have publication policies that can be acquired from the paper's website or a call to the paper.) Letters can be e-mailed, faxed, or mailed and must include the address (and often the phone number) of the sender. Editors often contact the sender to verify or clarify the content of the letter. The same letter, with a different sender, can be submitted to a paper in another geographic area of the state or country.

Op-ed pieces should not exceed 750 words and usually require a four- to six-week lead time. Communicating first with the editor of the opinion page will increase the likelihood that an op-ed piece will be printed. Op-ed pieces are published on topics of broad interest. Generating letters to the editor to demonstrate interest in the subject or position prior to submitting an op-ed piece or following the publication of an op-ed piece is a more sophisticated and very effective strategy for influencing pubic opinion and hence the opinion of elected officials. The best way to plan an editorial page lobbying effort is to become acquainted with the editorial pages of the newspaper. If you want to be a future source as an expert, call the reporter and compliment him or her. If you are sending a positive letter to the editor, send a copy to the reporter because reporters do not see all the responses to their work.

Whether it is voting for a piece of legislation when it comes before the legislature or voting for a candidate in an election, health professionals are very persuasive. After all, if you can convince people to change their health behaviors, you can surely convince them to vote. Health professionals are very effective in campaigns. When health professionals walk door to door for candidates or work on phone banks, voters listen. The public especially loves nurses and health professionals. Just about everyone has a relative who is a nurse, or a relative who was just cared for by a nurse. Nurses poll higher in public trust measurements than members of any other profession.

In 2002, a political action committee (PAC) was formed called Physicians for a Democratic Majority (www.demdocs.org). Many types of health professionals and students support this organization with both their time and money. In every general election, they pay the expenses of students, nurses, and physicians who are willing to go work in elections where the race is very close. They wear lab coats and name tags, and they talk to voters about why their votes are important. Another benefit of working on campaigns in this way is that legislative staff frequently take time off to work on campaigns, so you may meet the very people you will be contacting regarding legislation in the future.

5. Ignore your mother's instructions. Talk to strangers, or network. Carry business cards. Build your network. Flaunt your professional credential proudly.

Talking to strangers comes naturally to health professionals. Every new patient/client is first a stranger. If you go to an event and know very few people, act like a host. Introduce yourself. Practice your introduction, emphasizing what you want people to remember about you. Shake hands firmly, and make eye contact. Repeat the person's name when you are ending your conversation (this both endears you to the person—people like hearing their names—and helps you remember the person's name). Exchange business cards—and include your credential on your card. Don't let the cards you collect just pile up. Immediately after the event, write the date and event on the card and something about the person. Then, enter your contacts into your database with a "note" section so you will remember them and/or can search for them.

Strangers cease to be strangers when their business cards become part of a phone list or database to be used for political action or fundraising. Follow up with an e-mail or "nice to meet you" card that endears you to your new network member. It really becomes a small world when strangers talk to strangers and they become friends and create networks.

In garnering support or opposition for issues or candidates, no one is a stranger to health professionals. If you are an RN, print "RN" on your checks after your name so candidates will know they've received hard-earned "nursing money."

6. "Money is the mother's milk of politics." Give it early; if you don't have it, raise it.

The invention of television, which allowed candidates to speak directly but not personally to voters, has diminished the importance of political parties as the mechanism for establishing party philosophy and disseminating political messages to voters. Television has not changed who has the right to run for office (any citizen can run, and only the president must be a native-born citizen of the United States), but it has changed who wins. Candidates who cannot afford television time invest targeted direct mail to bring their messages directly to your mailbox in well-planned, nonsubstantive glossy brochures. Targeted direct mail lists are purchased from campaign consultants who obtain voter information from the local Registrar of Voters and sort the data by any number and combination of fields depending on the target audience, such as who voted in the last three elections (called likely or perennial voters), political party, sex, age, votes by mail, owns or rents home, and neighborhood. The strategy in direct mail campaigning focuses on projecting how many votes are needed from the target audiences and then tailoring the message to that audience. The narrower the target, the higher the cost of the segmented campaign literature. Likewise, the more TV spots purchased during prime time, the higher the cost of the air time. Getting messages to voters is expensive.

Campaigns require money and more money, hence the saying, "Money is the mother's milk of politics" (Jesse Unruh, former State Treasurer of California). The amount of money candidates raise early in their campaigns determines each candidate's viability later in the race. The American Nurses Association (ANA) PAC is an example of a political organization that supports candidates who support nursing's positions on issues. It has raised (from members in contributions averaging $40) and contributed more than $1 million in each congressional election since 1994. In evaluating candidates before primaries (when there are often several candidates in the field) for possible early endorsement, the PAC staff members compile information on how much money each candidate has raised and how much is projected to be spent. How much money has been raised gives an idea of the candidate's viability. PACs do not support candidates who cannot raise enough money to win their election. If some candidates have not raised much money but others have, the field of possible endorsements is narrowed to those who are serious about winning.

EMILY's List (www.emilyslist.org) is an example of a national fundraising effort for pro-choice Democratic women candidates. EMILY stands for "Early Money Is Like Yeast": The organization believes that contributing to women candidates early helps them establish their viability as credible candidates and therefore to raise other funds. Republican women have a similar organization called the Wish List (www.thewishlist.org).

People and organizations that provide early financial support are always remembered once politicians get elected, because the winners know they would not have been elected without these early supporters. Relationships made early in campaigns may have exponential returns because many elected officials run for higher office—and those relationships are forever.

Many people are not affluent and cannot afford to make large contributions. Remember the networking principle (Commandment 5), and call friends, relatives, and colleagues to collect $10 to $50 from each contact. Collecting eight $25 contributions raises $200. Volunteering to help make fundraising calls is a key campaign activity. The worst that can happen is the person will say "no."

Most people can afford a contribution of $45 per year (less than $5 per month) to a PAC that stands for their beliefs or to a political party. Raising and contributing money to friends of health care is important both for the candidate and for your profession. Some candidates are "shoe-ins" or in safe seats (where the voter registration favors their party) and are likely to be elected or re-elected. Nevertheless, they need to raise money so they can assist candidates in other parts of the state or country. Gaining leadership positions in elected bodies and recruiting allies for legislation require the support of colleagues, and one way to garner that support is to help raise money for colleagues who are in tight races who are seeking leadership positions. This is especially true when the number of terms an elected official may serve is limited by statutory term limits; this constraint requires them to climb to a leadership position much faster.

7. Negotiate visibility. Take credit, and take control.

Throughout history, different professions have had varying degrees of influence in legislative bodies. Today, the American Medical Association, the HMO industry, the pharmaceutical industry, and the nursing home industry (to name only a few) have significant power in the legislature. Not surprising, all of these entities contribute generous sums to candidates from both parties. The profession of nursing, while held in high regard by the public, has not been given (or taken) credit for the essential role that nurses play within health care systems. Traditionally, nurses, social workers, and public health advocates have had little control over the systematic decisions being made by health corporations and the business people and physicians who often control them.

Taking control requires taking credit, whether in the health care system or in politics. When a "Nurses for Nancy Pelosi for Congress" group raises $1,000 and produces 10 volunteers every Saturday, its members must negotiate visibility for nursing or for a few key nurses in the campaign. Credit may take the form of listing nurses on every piece of campaign literature, or getting 10 seats at a large fundraising dinner instead of only 5, or being included in the candidate's policy "kitchen cabinet." Visibility is never offered; it must be asked for and negotiated. First-time candidates and candidates in swing or highly competitive races never forget individuals and constituencies who were visible in difficult races. The Physicians for a Democratic Majority ("DemDocs") PAC, for example, has been included on several citizen advisory committees organized by members of Congress because members' visibility was so effective in getting out the vote (GOTV) in key races.

8. Politics has a "chit economy," so keep track. Seniority counts.

Commandment 3 requires an ability to communicate, in some instances to ask for help, and then to count votes. Most people like to help—but this help comes at a price. The exchange of votes, lining up votes, raising money, and mobilizing volunteers to walk precincts are all activities that accrue chits. For elected officials, chits are exchanged for appointments to key committees and for leadership positions. At the federal level, the longer the tenure of the legislator, the higher his or her rank, regardless of the person's status as a member of the majority or minority party. Seniority is given consideration in committee assignments, so it is to a district's or state's advantage to re-elect incumbent legislators who have good voting records. For individuals, chits mean access, support on key issues, and appointments to board and commissions.

9. Reputations are permanent.

In politics, as in life, there is no asset more important to success than a positive reputation. No one assigns reputations; they are earned and remembered. A key ingredient in developing a positive reputation is dependability. Deliver promptly what has been promised, whether it is an article, names and addresses of possible supporters, campaign funds, or volunteers. Answer questions honestly and directly, and offer to research unknown information. Return calls and respond to requests for assistance. These are routine practices of dependable people. If you identify yourself as an RN or as a member of an organization, the impression you leave is a reflection of the profession and the organization you say you represent, so make them proud to have you represent them.

In a congressional election for an open seat (no incumbent running), an RN activist promised to provide the American Nurses Association's position statements on issues to assist with the candidate's platform development after the candidate had been endorsed by the ANA PAC. Within two days, the RN activist had been asked to draft the candidate's statements on health care, and she later became a staff member to that member of Congress. If the RN activist had failed to follow through on the promise of assistance, her credibility and nursing's reputation would have been tarnished.

10. Don't let 'em get to you.

Remember the words of childhood: "Sticks and stones may break my bones, but words can never hurt me." Use this mantra: "I'm glad I'm here, I'm glad you're here, I know what I know, and I care about you." Or just picture those who mock you or challenge your positions sitting on a bedside commode in a hospital patient gown (nobody is attractive in a patient gown)!

Eleanor Roosevelt once said, "No one can make you feel inferior without your permission." Unfortunately, a sense of inadequacy and inferiority has often been part of the socialization of women. To overcome this ingrained subliminal sense, when addressing hostile audiences (or any audiences, for that matter) the mantra mentioned previously does two things. First, it causes you to smile because it sounds so corny. Second, that smile warms the audience and makes them more friendly. This is as true of two-year-olds as it is of adults.

Regrettably, we live in a world that thrives on crises and negativity. Negative campaigns cast doubts on the character and abilities of candidates. Doubt translates into not voting for a particular candidate, or not voting at all. Recognize that negative comments are going to be made and reported. Rebuttals are not always possible and are often wasted on hysterical, angry responses. The best defense is a good offense: Accept that comments will be misinterpreted and reported, and measure your response just as you did on the playground in grade school. Correct the misinterpretation, refute the allegation, and repeat over and over to yourself: "Sticks and stones may break my bones, but words can never hurt me."

SUMMARY

Health care professionals have a unique and broad perspective on the health care delivery needs of individuals and populations. They also have excellent communication skills and organizational skills. Few other professions are so well suited to be activists, lobbyists, leaders, and legislators. Failure to apply these skills and unique expertise in politics is to fail the patients who rely on us. As Margaret Sanger, a graduate public health nurse who founded Planned Parenthood, once said, "If one is to truly live, one must put one's convictions into action." So get involved!

REFERENCES

BrainyQuote.com. Retrieved August 2006 from www.brainyquote.com.

Dodd, C. J. (2004). Making the political process work. In: C. Harrington and C. L. Estes, *Health policy: Crisis and reform in the U.S. Health Care Delivery System*. Sudbury, MA: Jones and Bartlett.

En.thinkexist.com. Retrieved August 29, 2006, from www.en.thinkexist.com.

Feldstein, P. J. (1996). *The politics of health legislation*. Chicago: Health Administration Press.

Morris, W. (1969). *The American heritage dictionary of the English language*. Atlanta: Houghton Mifflin.

Mothers Against Drunk Driving. Retrieved August 2006 from www.MADD.org.

Primer on Policy:
The Legislative Process at the Federal Level

Sara Hart and Nadine Jackson

INTRODUCTION OF A BILL

The legislative process formally begins when a member of Congress introduces a bill. It is then assigned a number with the designation of H.R. for a House of Representatives bill and *S* for a Senate bill. House or Senate leadership then assigns the bill to the subcommittee or committee that has jurisdiction over the particular issue that is addressed by the bill. This starts the legislative process rolling. The committee or subcommittee may choose to hold hearings, which allow supporters and opponents the opportunity to present their concerns. These same committees may also decide not to hold hearings or not to move the legislation forward in the process. Many bills die from neglect in committees or subcommittees. If the political climate is ripe and the issue is high on the congressional policy agenda, committee members may decide to move the bill out of committee. They accomplish this by calling for a mark-up, adding any amendments or deleting problem areas. The clean bill, once voted on, is reported out to either the full committee (if a subcommittee held the mark-up) or to the full chamber in which the bill originated if the full committee marked up the bill.

Aside from House and Senate Appropriations Committees, there are a number of committees in each chamber that have jurisdiction over health legislation. In the House they are the Commerce Committee, Subcommittee on Health and Environment; and the House Ways and Means Committee, Subcommittee on Health. On the Senate side, the Health, Education, Labor and Pensions Committee, Subcommittee on Public Health; and the Senate Finance Committee, Subcommittee on Health Care consider the majority of health-related legislation.

FLOOR ACTION AND CONFERENCE COMMITTEE

In the House, the legislation then goes to the powerful Rules Committee, which determines the terms and length of any floor debate and if amendments can be introduced from the floor. The Senate has no Rules Committee, but senators can filibuster (delay a floor vote) or add amendments to the existing legislation once the bill comes to the full Senate for a vote. The Speaker of the House or the Majority Leader in the Senate sets the legislative

Sara Hart and Nadine Jackson, 2000. Primer on Policy: The Legislative Process at the Federal Level. *Politics and Nursing Practice* 1:31–33.

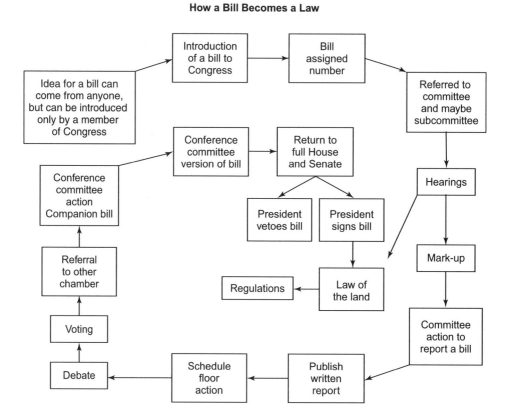

FIGURE 1.3.1   How a Bill Becomes a Law

calendar, which determines when and if a bill will actually reach the floor for debate. Once these processes are completed, representatives and senators are ready to cast their yea or nay vote. It may be a recorded roll call vote or a voice vote if leadership decides that this is more appropriate for the legislative issue under consideration. If the legislation is successful, it is referred to the other chamber to repeat the process. A bill must pass both chambers of Congress before it is sent to the president for his signature.

Often companion bills are introduced into the House and Senate. This means that the legislative process occurs simultaneously in both Houses. Companion bills speed up the lengthy legislative process. Because each bill may differ slightly from the other, once it passes its respective chamber it is sent to a conference committee to reconcile any differences.

The leadership in both chambers creates a conference committee, and committee chairpersons and prominent sponsors of the original bills are appointed to serve. When the conference committee reaches an agreement, a report is prepared that describes the recommended changes. The conference version of the bill must then be returned to the full House and Senate for a final vote.

EXECUTIVE ACTION

The legislation is now ready to be sent to the chief executive. He may sign the legislation or take no action for 10 days when the Congress is in session. Either way, the legislation becomes law. If the president vetoes the bill, a two-thirds majority vote of Congress is necessary to override the veto. If Congress sends the bill to the president and goes out of session, the president may use a pocket veto to kill the legislation. The president's options may be influenced by political pressures and party politics. Once the legislation is signed into law, it is referred to the appropriate regulatory agency for rulemaking. It is the regulatory process that puts the meat on the bones and enables a statute to become transformed into a fully functioning government program (see Figure 1.3.1).

CONCLUSION

Knowledge of the inner workings of the federal legislative process is an invaluable tool for nurses wishing to improve access and quality in health care. Effectively influencing the policy making process requires close monitoring of issues that are under consideration by policy makers. Establishing ongoing relationships with public officials creates an important line of communication that allows one to share his or her nursing expertise.

It's the Institutions, Stupid!
Why Comprehensive National
Health Insurance Always Fails in America

Sven Steinmo
University of Colorado

Jan Watts
Yale University

By the time this essay is published, both pundits and scholars will have analyzed and reanalyzed the failure of the Clinton health care plan. The most obvious explanations have already been offered. They blame President Clinton, his plan, his advisors, his wife, the Democrats, the Republicans, the medical industry, and the American voters. They will argue that if Clinton had only been smarter, tougher, or more savvy, or if his plan somehow had been more "in tune" with America, the Democrats would have retained their control of Congress. Clearly, they will argue, Americans want comprehensive health care reform as much as the American economy needs it. If Clinton had not missed this golden opportunity, surely Congress would have finally passed what every other democratic legislature in the world passed long ago. Bill Clinton's burden must be heavy.

We argue that this line of analysis is wrong; instead we believe that America did not pass comprehensive national care reform in 1994 for the same reason it could not pass it in 1948, 1965, 1974, and 1978. The United States is the only democratic country that does not have a comprehensive national health insurance system (NHI) because American political institutions are structurally biased against this kind of comprehensive reform.

This institutional bias begins with a political structure forged by America's founding fathers that was explicitly designed to pit faction against faction to protect minority factions from majority factions. Progressive reforms have exacerbated this bias by undermining strong political parties. Subsequently, several generations of congressional reforms unwittingly turned national politicians into independent political entrepreneurs. This institutional context explains (and could be used to predict) the failure of national health care reform in America—not flaws in the plan, the planners, or political strategy.

We offer a brief overview of the history of NHI politics through an institutionalist lens. It does not make sense to blame the Clinton administration for its inability to pass NHI yet forget the failures of the Roosevelt, Truman, Kennedy, Johnson, Nixon, Ford, and Carter administrations. With this history we show how the structure of American political institutions shaped the political strategies of both proponents and opponents of reform and thereby explain the unique and often curious health care reform policies that have passed in America. Finally, we suggest that the policies actually passed have confirmed the anti-statist "public understanding" (Jacobs 1993a) that is part of the American political culture.

SOME ARGUMENTS FOR REFORM'S FAILURE

Culture

The most common explanation for the absence of NHI is that the United States is exceptional because of its unique political culture (Anderson 1972; Jacobs 1993; Rimlinger 1971). America has developed unique individualistic and anti-statist political values that have biased the polity against the welfare state.

As intuitively appealing as this argument at first appears, flaws in both the logic and evidence that have been marshaled in its favor undermine its utility. First, and most obviously, public opinion polls have consistently shown that most Americans have favored some kind of comprehensive NHI system for most of the post-war era (see Table 1.4.1).

Second, even to the extent that Americans are highly individualistic, whether this general cultural predisposition translates into specific attitudes toward specific governmental programs is not clear. Political cultures, after all, contain various (and sometimes competing)

TABLE 1.4.1   Public Support for Greater Government Role in the Health Care Industry

Year	Percentage Expressing Support for Increasing Government Role in Health Care Delivery[a]
1937	80
1942	74
1961	67
1965	63
1976	66.7
1978	61.3
1992	75

[a]Data were taken from different polls that asked similar, but not identical, questions. See sources for exact questions.

Sources: Free and Cantril 1967: 10; Gallup 1961, 1965; *Fortune:* July 1942: 8–10, 12, 14, 18; *American Medical News* 1976, 1992: 27; What the Polls Show 1978: 20.

political values (Page and Shapiro 1992). Thus, although Americans do hold highly individualistic values, they are also profoundly egalitarian—especially with respect to the value of equal opportunity.

Third, a critical lacuna in the culturalist argument is the paucity of comparative historical evidence. The argument implies that Americans did not pass NHI but Europeans did because this program was demanded in Europe, whereas it was not in the United States. In truth, however, little evidence shows that NHI was the product of widespread public demand in other industrial democracies. Instead, the various comprehensive public health programs initiated throughout the world were, in fact, the product of governing elites' attempts to address pressing policy problems (Immergut 1992; Heclo 1974).

Finally, culturalist analyses tend to ignore or at least underemphasize the dynamic interactions between public preferences and public policy. Clearly what governments do (or do not do) affect attitudes toward government. But the emphasis on the permanence of cultural preferences belies this point.

In the end, culturalists offer quite static explanations. What we need is a better understanding of the relationship between what people think about government and what government does (or does not do). Politics is an iterative process, not a one-off game. Thus if government does well, it builds support. If it fails to act in response to public pressure, or if it acts poorly, we should not be surprised that citizens lose faith in public institutions.

Interests

Many of the best political histories of the politics of health care reform in the United States either explicitly or implicitly advance what we all an "interest" explanation (Poen 1979; Alford 1975; Navarro 1976). Although often explicitly sensitive to the peculiar cultural context of American politics, these analyses essentially argue that the United States has not developed an NHI scheme because of the determined opposition of powerful interest groups.

The evidence used to support this thesis in many ways is overwhelming. Any history of the politics of health care reform in the United States shows clearly that reformers in this country have faced an exceptionally well-organized and well-financed opposition, whereas the proponents of reform have been demonstrably less well organized and less well financed.

Still, as empirically satisfying as the interest explanation can be, we believe it has important analytic flaws. If the key explanation for the absence of NHI in the United States is that powerful interest group fought the reform, then proponents of this argument should be able to show that countries that did pass NHI legislation did not have powerful interest groups opposing their reforms. However, studies of the politics of health care reform in other democratic polities clearly show that physicians, hospitals, insurance companies, business interests, and conservative political forces generally bitterly opposed NHI in every country in which national health care policies eventually emerged. The important question is why the forces of opposition could stop some form of NHI in the United States but not in other democracies.

A second problem with the traditional interest explanation is that it cannot adequately explain why some policy reforms have been successful in the United States while others have not. The for-profit medical industry was opposed to the creation of Medicare and Medicaid in the early 1960s, just as they had opposed NHI in the 1940s and 1950s. They used many of the same tactics against this reform that they used successfully to prevent passage of earlier reforms. Why, if powerful interest groups can veto policies they oppose, did the Medicare/Medicaid legislation pass despite this opposition?

NATIONAL HEALTH REFORM FINALLY COMES OF AGE?

With the election of Bill Clinton, almost all observers believed that comprehensive NHI would finally become a reality in America. There were many reasons to predict the success, and they are all familiar to our readers. Health care costs had clearly spun out of control. Now even traditionally powerful anti-state interests such as the corporate sector indicated their readiness to accept fundamental reform—even if that meant greater government involvement in the health care sector (Martin 1993). More than thirty million Americans without health insurance and tens of millions more were seriously worried about losing their insurance, and thus even the middle class saw a clear need for reform. Poll after poll indicated that 70 to 82 percent of the American public favored NHI (Roper Center for Public Opinion Research 1994b, 1994c). Bill Clinton also made NHI the keystone of his electoral campaign. Finally, as the previous quote indicates, even the provider community appeared to concede that health care reform was not only politically inevitable but also morally and economically necessary.

So what happened? Why were almost all predictions wrong? Why, given the fact that all of the cards appeared to be stacked in the direction of health care reform, did nothing pass? The answer, of course, is that reformers such as Bill Clinton are not playing on a level table. The game of politics in America is institutionally rigged against those who would use government—for good or evil. James Madison's system of checks and balances, the very size and diversity of the nation, the Progressive reforms that undermined strong and programmatic political parties, and the many generations of congressional reforms have all worked to fragment political power in America.

This fragmentation of political power—which has become more severe in the past twenty years—offered the opponents of reform many opportunities to attack Clinton's plan. This institutional bias, and not flaws in the plan or the political strategy pursued by the administration, once again killed plans for comprehensive NHI in America. A very brief overview of some of the new cards that are stacked against health reform is instructive. First, as both Peterson and Morone have suggested, American political institutions are not the same as they were twenty, thirty, or forty years ago. With the reforms of the 1970s "[t]he oligarchy had been changed into a remarkably decentralized institution. . . . Congress as a whole generally became a more permeable and less manageable institution than ever before" (Peterson 1993b: 418). Whereas policy making could at one time be characterized as "iron triangles," now it appeared to be dominated by "issue networks" (Heclo 1974). But whereas Peterson and Morone appear to believe that these changes make reform more likely than before, we believe that the increased decentralization of institutional power makes meaningful reform less likely to pass today.

Second, the 1990s is marked by "an entirely new type of policy community." According to Peterson, it "has lost its cohesiveness and its capacity to dominate health care politics and the course of policy change" (Peterson 1993b: 408, 411). Now that health care is one-seventh of the U.S. economy, even more interests have something to lose if meaningful comprehensive health care reform were to pass. The fact that there are so many more interests (factions) that now have a stake in the extant system (a system that is enormously profitable) does not suggest to us that reform is more likely in the 1990s. Quite the contrary: Reformers now have to battle a medical/industrial/insurance complex that has more than $800 billion a year at stake.

Third, we must remember that the Clintons' bill needed support from *more than* 50 percent of the members of the House and 50 percent of the members of the Senate. Congressional rules (that is, institutions) in force in 1994 allowed a minority to block legislation as long as they could control just forty of one hundred votes in the Senate. No other democratic system in the world requires support of 60 percent of legislators to pass government policy. This institutional fact appears even more absurd when we remember that the Senate was so radically malapportioned.

Fourth, despite the fact that the 1990s was marked by the highest level of public support for government intervention in health care financing (Peterson 1993b: 406–7), the incredible $4,500,000,000,000+ debt facing American taxpayers (most of which has been accumulated in the past fifteen years) make government financing of health care reform exceptionally unlikely indeed.

Fifth, changes in the technology of electioneering have worked hand in hand with the increasing fragmentation of power in Congress to the point that members of Congress have become independent policy entrepreneurs. This means money. Between 1 January 1993 and 31 July 1994, candidates for the House and Senate received $38 million in campaign contributions from the health and insurance industries. The AMA had the most generous political action committee in the country, contributing more than $1,933,000 in 1993 and 1994 alone. These figures do not include small donations made by local constituents, nor do they include donations from small business, another bitter foe of Clinton's health reform plans. "By the end of the year we expect that the health and insurance industries will have spent over $100 million to crush health care reform," reported the public interest research organization, Citizen Action. "They will have spent over $40 million in campaign contributions and another $60 million in advertising, public relations, organizing and lobbying. In addition, previous reports have identified over $13 million in campaign contributions from other opponents of comprehensive [health] reform" (*Citizen Action* 1994: 2).

Sixth, the world around our political institutions has not remained static either. Undoubtedly, the most important change in modern politics is the role of an importance of the media. The techniques available for marketing research and media delivery are radically more sophisticated today than they were only fifteen or twenty years ago. This point was not lost on the opponents of health care reform. The insurance industry, for example, spent more than $14 million on the famous "Harry and Louise" advertisement alone. Moreover, as Hamburger and colleagues note, the American media increasingly falls into a ratings game, thereby eschewing serious discussion and presentation of policy issues in favor of misleading headlines and horse race reportage (Hamburger et al. 1994).

Finally, the repeated failure of American political institutions to address the polity's problems—even when there has been clear public will for action—has worked to undermine dramatically the public's faith in their governmental institutions.

EPILOGUE: WHITHER REFORM?

We opened this essay predicting that, after the failure of Clinton's health care reform plan, pundits and scholars alike would blame the president, his administration's policy team and their political strategy, the plan itself, interest groups' dirty campaign in the media, and/or the American political culture for the failure of NHI in America. Once again, we think these analyses miss the point. The failure of the president's health care reform plan is neither a failure of this president nor a failure of his specific plan. Rather it is a failure of American political institutions with which he has been forced to work and through which the plan had to be passed.

This suggests to us that reformers who want real reform rather than a continuation of the pattern of buying off interests and avoiding making tough choices should focus their efforts on reforming American political institutions rather than designing ever more sophisticated reform strategies that might be able to squeak or "slouch" through the American political system. Our history tells us that even if these more politically palatable piecemeal solutions do pass in some future Congress, they are likely to throw fat on the inflationary fire—while at the same time deepen the alienation between the American people and their government.

REFERENCES

Alford, Robert R. 1975. *Health Care Politics: Ideological and Interest Group Barriers to Reform*. Chicago: University of Chicago Press, 1975.

American Medical Association. Managing Health Care Costs: An American Association Research Report. *AMA Briefings and Surveys*. Chicago: AMA Membership Publications.

Citizen Action. 1994. Press Release: The Health and Insurance Industries Give $38 Million to Congressional Candidates. Washington, DC: Citizens Action. 3 November: 2.

Fortune. 1942. July: 18.

Free, Lloyd, and Hadley Cantril. 1967. *The Political Beliefs of Americans*. New Brunswick, NJ: Rutgers University Press.

Hamburger, Tom, Theodore Marmor, and Jon Meacham. 1994. What the Death of Health Reform Teaches Us about the Press. *The Washington Monthly* November: 35–41.

Heclo, Hugh. 1974. *Modern Social Politics in Britain and Sweden*. New Haven: Yale University Press.

Immergut, Ellen M. 1992. *Health Politics: Interests and Institutions in Western Europe*. New York: Cambridge University Press.

Jacobs, Lawrence. 1993a. *The Health of Nations; Public Opinion and Making of American and British Health Policy*. Ithaca: Cornell University Press.

———. 1993b. Health Reform Impasse: The Politics of American Ambivalence toward Government. *Journal of Health Politics, Policy and Law* 18:629–55.

Martin, Cathie Jo. 1993. Together Again: Business, Government, and the Quest for Cost Control. *Journal of Health Politics, Policy and Law* 18:359–93.

Navarro, Vincente. 1976. *Medicine under Capitalism*. New York: Prodist.

Page, Benjamin, and Robert Shapiro. 1992. *The Rational Public*. Chicago: University of Chicago Press.

———. 1993b. Political Influence in the 1990s: From Iron Triangles to Policy Networks. *Journal of Health Politics, Policy and Law* 18:396–438.

Poen, Monte M. 1979. *Harry S. Truman Versus the Medical Lobby: The Genesis of Medicare*. Missouri: University of Missouri Press.

Public Papers of the Presidents of the United States. 1961–1966. Washington, DC: Government Printing Office.

Rimlinger, Gaston. 1971. *Welfare Policy and Industrialization in Europe, America and Russia.* New York: Wiley.

The Roper Center for Public Opinion Research.

———. 1994b. A Polling Review of a Great Debate: The Public Decides on Health Care Reform. *The Public Perspective* 5(6).

———. 1994c. Survey for the University of Connecticut. *Public Opinion Online.*

Steinmo, Sven. 1993. *Taxation and Democracy: Swedish, British and American Approaches to Financing the Modern State.* New Haven: Yale University Press.

What the Polls Show. 1978. *U.S. News and World Report* 8 May.

PART II

HEALTH STATUS AND ACCESS TO CARE

Part II of this book examines the health status of the population in the United States. Many have challenged whether the United States really has the best health care in the world. The relatively poor health care indicators that the United States has compared with other countries in terms of low-birth-weight babies, mortality, life expectancy, and other factors suggest the U.S. has serious problems. The Commonwealth Fund score card shows the performance of the U.S. on multiple indicators. The major causes of the poor performance of the United States are complex, but certainly the lack of a national health care system is one factor, along with the failure to address smoking, drinking, and violence in society. The problems of income inequality in society are a major contributing factor to poor health.

The underlying factors that influence health behaviors, however, are not simply lifestyle problems, but rather are social problems created by the practices of organizations and industries that create environmental pollution and occupational hazards. Many large organizations and industries represent powerful special-interest groups, such as tobacco companies, alcohol industries, firearms manufacturers, automobile manufacturers, and large corporate polluters. Public policies have recently begun to shift toward limiting access to tobacco products (through higher taxes and restricting access to minors) and firearms. Regulation plays an important role in addressing these problems—for example, by penalizing corporate polluters and requiring safer automobiles. In addition, legal actions and large judgments against tobacco companies and pending legal actions against firearms makers are beginning to have a direct impact on corporate behavior.

The problems that create poor health status are not evenly distributed throughout U.S. society. Poverty and lower social status are associated with poor health, poor nutrition, poor housing, low incomes, and poor sanitation. These problems are detrimental to vulnerable populations, including infants, children, adolescents, older people, members of minority groups, and the disabled. Fiscella and Williams show that socioeconomic inequalities result in serious disparities in health status between individuals with resources and the poor. Persons with low incomes, education, or occupational status have worse health and die at younger ages than those who are well off. The effects of institutional, individual, and internalized racism also add to the poorer health of African Americans. Social factors are the primary reasons for health disparities.

Racial and ethnic diversity in society is increasing, while racial and ethnic discrimination persists both in the broader society and within the health system. Such discrimination has been documented in many studies of basic health care, including delivery of mental and physical health care, and prevents access to care and the appropriate treatment of health conditions. Kunitz and Pesis-Katz show that the mortality rates for African Americans are higher than the rates for whites, but especially so in the United States, which has inadequate health and welfare programs compared with Canada, which has a comprehensive health and welfare system for its citizens. Mortality rates for whites in the United States have not improved as much as the rates for white Canadians, in part because of the lack of access to health care for many in the United States.

Poverty is closely associated with gender and ethnicity, especially for female heads of households. Sarto highlights the challenges for women's health, which are compounded by gender differences in health status and disease. For example, women are more likely to have comorbidities related to myocardial infarction, and less likely to have diagnostic procedures and to be given interventions. As women age, they are more likely than men to have multiple health problems and to be poor and less likely to have income security. Moreover, child poverty is a serious problem in rich countries such as the United States (UNICEF report). The proportion of children living in poverty has risen in a majority of the world's developed counties over the past decade, and this increase has resulted in poor health and higher morality rates among these populations.

To remedy the problems of poor health status that are directly related to disadvantage and inequality, a number of social policies need to be addressed. Education achievement, access to health services, and income support for those who are poor are all important ways to improve the health of the population.

ACCESS TO HEALTH INSURANCE AND TO HEALTH CARE

The lack of health insurance and access to appropriate care in the United States is a serious and growing problem for the poor as well as for the growing millions of low-income workers in the United States. The uninsured rates are especially high among young adults, children, African Americans, Hispanics, the poor, and middle-income families in this country. The latest information from the U.S. Census Bureau shows that poverty is increasing and the number of Americans without health insurance is increasing. The uninsured come from many different occupational groups, and include many nursing assistants, dietary workers, and housekeeping employees working in the health care sector.

The lack of access to care is directly reflected in a failure to diagnose problems and delays in needed treatments. Those without access are vulnerable to poor health, injury, and death. Health care services in the United States are rationed to those who can pay, but those who cannot pay are excluded altogether. In addition, most Americans are underinsured for preventive services and long-term care. Many researchers have documented the serious negative consequences of a lack of access to health insurance on general health as well as on specific conditions, including primary prevention and screening services, cancer care, chronic disease care, and hospital care. Health status and mortality also correlate with access to health care.

Many individuals and small businesses cannot afford to purchase health insurance. This is especially a problem for service-sector and non-unionized employees. Some large businesses are also limiting health benefits to their employees or requiring employees to pay for insurance for themselves and their dependents. In 1996, Congress passed legislation that prohibited private health insurance companies from denying private insurance to individuals with preexisting medical conditions in an effort to prevent abuses in the insurance sector. This legislation did not prohibit the insurance industry from raising premiums beyond the reach of individuals needing insurance, however. Unregulated private health insurance premiums continue to escalate beyond the financial reach of a large portion of Americans.

Congressional legislation that expanded Medicaid in the early 1990s made a dramatic difference for millions of poor and uninsured women. In spite of these gains, Medicaid still fails to cover a majority of these women and children. In particular, Medicaid does not cover a large percentage of the poor for whom it was designed because of state underfunding of the program. As health care costs escalate, Medicaid underfunding tends to worsen, and federal and state governments are not responding to the growing need for coverage for the poor, including prenatal care (a need unique to women and their unborn children). These gaps became worse after the 1996 welfare reform act caused many women and children to lose access to Medicaid services. Although Congress enacted the State Children's Health Insurance Program (SCHIP) for low-income children in 1997, large numbers of children still lack access to health services.

Despite the limitations in the Medicaid program and the variations in benefits found across states, Medicaid and health insurance in general are critical factors in reducing the racial and ethnic disparities in health care in the United States. A sizable share of health disparities could be reduced for Hispanics and African Americans if they were insured at levels comparable to whites.

Access to mental health services is a serious public policy issue because mental illness is so prevalent in the United States, and many people with serious mental illnesses have not received treatment. Unfortunately, many individuals with mental health problems are not fully covered by most private health insurance. In 1996, Congress passed legislation requiring that mental health care insurance would be equal to that for physical health care, but in subsequent sessions Congress did not continue the parity legislation. Since that time, many states have passed state parity laws on the use of mental health services. Harris, Carpenter, and Bao show that these state parity laws have improved access to mental health care for patients with relatively mild mental health problems, but have not resolved the problems of inadequate mental health care for individuals with more serious mental health problems. The public debate needs a new infusion of energy from health professionals and others advocating for appropriate mental health insurance coverage, housing, and humane care for the mentally ill.

AGING, DISABILITY, AND LONG-TERM CARE

The aging of the population is another challenge to the U.S. health care system. The older population has the greatest incidence of disability and chronic illness and needs substantially more health care services than younger populations. The aging of the population and the social and economic challenges in providing long-term care must be faced by society. Additionally, a growing proportion of the U.S. population has disabilities or limitations in activities because of disabling conditions (Estes and Wallace). The percentage of the population affected increases dramatically with age. Few realize, however, that many people with disabilities are younger than 65 years of age. The disabled also constitute a large group that is underserved by the current U.S. health system.

LaPlante and colleagues estimate the amount of unmet need for personal assistance services related to activities of daily living. The shortfall is greatest for those who live alone. The adverse consequences of this unmet need may include discomfort, weight loss, dehydration, falls, burns, and dissatisfaction. The costs of expanding services range from $1.2 billion to $2.7 billion, which should be politically feasible considering the benefits of providing services.

Estes and Wallace point out that care of the aged and disabled is shockingly inadequate in the United States. Society views the aged and disabled as problems, a view socially constructed through negative perceptions, myths, and messages. These societal views are then translated into social policies that adversely affect the aged and disabled. Moreover, the U.S. health system treats aging as a disease, medically and economically exploiting the aged and disabled who have a need for assistance. Social and health care policies for the aged and disabled should be redesigned to remove discriminatory practices and to meet real needs.

Home and community-based services in the United States are underdeveloped, and there is a need to focus on developing appropriate care delivery systems as alternatives to institutional care (Lynch, Estes, and Hernandez). Medicare, as the primary health program for the aged and disabled, has been focused on hospital and physician care, but paid little attention to long-term care and chronic disease management. Lynch et al. recommend a number of policies that might improve care for Medicare beneficiaries, including risk assessment, case management, information systems, physician training, evidenced-based protocols, and disease management programs.

Recent policy trends in Medicaid and Medicare programs have threatened access to care for low-income individuals who are aged and disabled. O'Brien points out that Medicare's high premium costs and cost-sharing requirements create a heavy burden for individuals with low incomes. The federal subsidies to Medicare managed care plans have not improved access for individuals with low incomes because the premiums are increasing along with out-of-pocket charges and the benefits are declining. The proposed reductions in federal Medicaid programs for low-income individuals threaten to reduce access to aged and disabled patients who depend on long-term care paid for by the Medicaid program. Moreover, many state Medicaid programs are forcing individuals into managed care programs and waiver programs where the benefits can be limited and cost sharing can be increased. Overall, the federal policy efforts to control the costs of public programs present a major threat to access to services for the most vulnerable low-income groups.

Social security is a critical factor for successful aging and good health. Estes shows that older women—especially women of color—are more dependent on the U.S. Social Security program than men. Current proposals to privatize Social Security could have serious negative consequences for older women and for other individuals who depend heavily on this resource for their primary source of income. The proposals to privatize Social Security are led by parties with ideological positions that want to limit the role of government and expand Social Security to the private financial markets.

CHAPTER 2

Health Status of the Population
Why Not the Best?

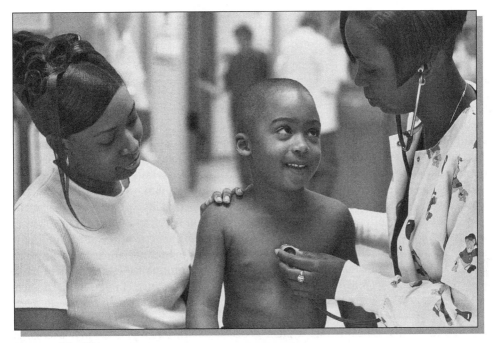

Nurses with child

Why Not the Best?
Results from a National Scorecard
on U.S. Health System Performance

The Commonwealth Fund Commission on
a High Performance Health System
September 2006

EXECUTIVE SUMMARY

Once upon a time, it was taken as an article of faith among most Americans that the U.S. health care system was simply the best in the world. Yet growing evidence indicates the system falls short given the high level of resources committed to health care. Although national health spending is significantly higher than the average rate of other industrialized countries, the U.S. is the only industrialized country that fails to guarantee universal health insurance and coverage is deteriorating, leaving millions without affordable access to preventive and essential health care. Quality of care is highly variable and delivered by a system that is too often poorly coordinated, driving up costs, and putting patients at risk. With rising costs straining family, business, and public budgets, access deteriorating and variable quality, improving health care performance is a matter of national urgency.

The Commonwealth Fund Commission on a High Performance Health System has developed a National Scorecard on U.S. Health System Performance (Table 2.1.1). The Scorecard assesses how well the U.S. health system is performing as a whole *relative to what is achievable*. It provides benchmarks for the nation and a mechanism for monitoring change over time across core health care system goals of health outcomes, quality, access, efficiency, and equity.

Scores come from ratios that compare the U.S. national average performance to benchmarks, which represent top performance. If performance in the U.S. was uniform for each of the health system goals, and if, in those instances in which U.S. performance can be compared with other countries, we were consistently at the top, the average score for the U.S. would be 100. But, the U.S. as a whole scores an average of 66. Several different measures or indicators were examined for each of the goal areas and dimensions of health system performance. There are wide gaps between national average rates and benchmarks in each of the dimensions of the Scorecard, with U.S. average scores ranging from 51 to 71.

Adapted from: The Commonwealth Fund Commission on a High Performance Health System. (2006). *Why Not the Best? Results from a National Scorecard on U.S. Health System Performance.* New York: The Commonwealth Fund.

By showing the gaps between national performance and benchmarks that have been achieved, the Scorecard offers performance targets for improvement. And it provides a foundation for the development of public and private policy action, and a yardstick against which to measure the success of new policies.

SCORECARD HIGHLIGHTS AND LEADING INDICATORS

Long, Healthy, and Productive Lives: Total Average Score 69

- The U.S. is one-third worse than the best country on mortality from conditions "amenable to health care"—that is, deaths that could have been prevented with timely and effective care. Its infant mortality rate is 7.0 deaths per 1,000 live births, compared with 2.7 in the top three countries. The U.S. average adult disability rate is one-fourth worse than the best five U.S. states, as is the rate of children missing 11 or more days of school because of illness or injury.

Quality: Total Average Score 71

- Despite documented benefits to timely preventive care, barely half of adults (49%) received preventive and screening tests according to guidelines for their age and sex.
- The current gap between national average rates of diabetes and blood pressure control and rates achieved by the top 10 percent of health plans translates into an estimated 20,000 to 40,000 preventable deaths and $1 billion to $2 billion in avoidable medical costs.
- Only half of patients with congestive heart failure receive written discharge instructions regarding care following their hospitalization.
- Nursing home hospital admission and readmission rates in the bottom 10 percent of states are two times higher than in the top 10 percent of states.

ACCESS: TOTAL AVERAGE SCORE 67

- In 2003, one-third (35%) of adults under 65 (61 million) were either underinsured or were uninsured at some time during the year.
- One-third (34%) of all adults under 65 have problems paying their medical bills or have medical debt they are paying off over time. And premiums are increasingly stretching median household incomes.

EFFICIENCY: TOTAL AVERAGE SCORE 51

- National preventable hospital admissions for patients with diabetes, congestive heart failure, and asthma (ambulatory care sensitive conditions) were twice the level achieved by the top states.

- Hospital 30-day readmission rates for Medicare patients ranged from 14 percent to 22 percent across regions. Bringing readmission rates down to the levels achieved by the top performing regions would save Medicare $1.9 billion annually.
- Annual Medicare costs of care average $32,000 for patients with congestive heart failure, diabetes, and chronic lung disease, with twofold spread in costs across geographic regions.
- As a share of total health expenditures, U.S. insurance administrative costs were more than three times the rates of countries with the most integrated insurance systems.
- The United States lags well behind other nations in use of electronic medical records: 17 percent of United States doctors compared with 80 percent in the top three countries.

EQUITY: TOTAL AVERAGE SCORE 71

- On multiple indicators across quality of care and access to care, there is a wide gap between low-income or uninsured populations and those with higher incomes and insurance. On average, low-income and uninsured rates would need to improve by one-third to close the gap.
- On average, it would require a 20 percent decrease in Hispanic risk rates to reach benchmark white rates on key indicators of quality, access, and efficiency. Hispanics are at particularly high risk of being uninsured, lacking a regular source of primary care, and not receiving essential preventive care.
- Overall, it would require a 24 percent or greater improvement in African American mortality, quality, access, and efficiency indicators to approach benchmark white rates. Blacks are much more likely to die at birth or from chronic conditions such as heart disease and diabetes. Blacks also have significantly lower rates of cancer survival.

SYSTEM CAPACITY TO INNOVATE AND IMPROVE: NOT SCORED

Innovations in the ways care is delivered—from more integrated decision-making and information sharing to better workforce retention and team-oriented care—are necessary to make strides in all dimensions of care.

Investment in research to assess effectiveness, develop evidence-based guidelines, or support innovations in care delivery is low. The current federal investment in health services research, estimated at $1.5 billion, amounts to less than $1 out of every $1,000 in national health care spending. Ideally a national Scorecard would include indicators of the system's capacity to innovate and improve, but good indicators in this area are not currently available—itself a problem.

SUMMARY AND IMPLICATIONS

The Case for a Systems Approach to Change

The Scorecard results make a compelling case for change. Simply put, we fall far short of what is achievable on all major dimensions of health system performance. The overwhelming picture that emerges is one of missed opportunities—at every level of the system—to make American health care truly the best that money can buy.

And let there be no doubt, these results are not just numbers. Each statistic—each gap in actual versus achievable performance—represents illness that can be avoided, deaths that can be prevented, and money that can be saved or reinvested. In fact, if we closed just those gaps that are described in the Scorecard—we could save at least $50 billion to $100 billion per year in health care spending and prevent 100,000 to 150,000 deaths. Moreover, the nation would gain from improved productivity. The Institute of Medicine, for example, estimates national economic gains of up to $130 billion per year from insuring the uninsured.

The central messages from the Scorecard are clear:

- Universal coverage and participation are essential to improve quality and efficiency, as well as access to needed care.
- Quality and efficiency can be improved together; we must look for improvements that yield both results. Preventive and primary care quality deficiencies undermine outcomes for patients and contribute to inefficiencies that raise the cost of care.
- Failures to coordinate care for patients over the course of treatment put patients at risk and raise the cost of care. Policies that facilitate and promote linking providers and information about care will be essential for productivity, safety, and quality gains.
- Financial incentives posed by the fee-for-service system of payment as currently designed undermine efforts to improve preventive and primary care, manage chronic conditions, and coordinate care. We need to devise payment incentives to reward more effective and efficient care, with a focus on value.
- Research and investment in data systems are important keys to progress. Investment in, and implementation of, electronic medical records and modern health information technology in physician offices and hospitals is low—leaving physicians and other providers without useful tools to ensure reliable high quality care.
- Savings can be generated from more efficient use of expensive resources including more effective care in the community to control chronic disease and assure patients timely access to primary care. The challenge is finding ways to re-channel these savings into investments in improved coverage and system capacity to improve performance in the future.
- Setting national goals for improvement based on best achieved rates is likely to be an effective method to motivate change and move the overall distribution to higher levels.

Our health system needs to focus on improving health outcomes for people over the course of their lives, as they move from place to place and from one site of care to another. This requires a degree of organization and coordination that we currently lack. Whether through more integrated health care delivery organizations, more accountable physician groups, or more integrated health information systems (in truth, likely all of these), we need to link patients, care teams, and information together. At the same time, we need to deliver safer and more reliable care.

Furthermore, the extremely high costs of treating patients with multiple chronic diseases, as detailed in this report, serve as a reminder that a minority of very sick patients in the U.S. account for a high proportion of national health care expenditures. Payment policies that support integrated, team-based approaches to managing patients with multiple, complex conditions—along with efforts to engage patients in care self-management—will be of paramount importance as the population continues to age.

By assessing the nation's health care against achievable benchmarks, the Scorecard, in a sense, tracks the vital signs of our health system. With rising costs and deteriorating coverage, leadership to transform the health system is urgently needed to secure a healthy nation.

TABLE 2.1.1   National Scorecard on U.S. Health System Performance

Indicator	U.S. National Rate	Benchmark	Benchmark Rate	Score: Ratio of U.S. to Benchmark
1. Mortality amenable to health care, Deaths per 100,000 population	115	Top 3 of 19 countries	80	70
2. Infant mortality, Deaths per 1,000 live births	7.0	Top 3 of 23 countries	2.7	39
3. Healthy life expectancy at age 60, Years	16.6	Top 3 of 23 countries	19.1	87
4. Adults under 65 limited in any activities because of physical, mental, or emotional problems, %	14.9	Top 10% states	11.5	77
5. Children missed 11 or more school days due to illness or injury, %	5.2	Top 10% states	3.8	73
6. Adults received recommended screening and preventive care, %	49	Target	80 Various	61
7. Children received recommended immunizations and preventive care*	Various	Various	Various	85
8. Needed mental health care and received treatment*	Various	Various	Various	66
9. Chronic disease under control*	Various	Various		61
10. Hospitalized patients received recommended care for AMI, CHF, and pneumonia (composite), %	84	Top hospitals	100	84
11. Adults under 65 with accessible primary care provider, %	66	65+ yrs, High income	84	79
12. Children with a medical home, %	46	Top 10% states	60	77
13. Care coordination at hospital discharge*	Various	Various	Various	70
14. Nursing homes: hospital admissions and readmissions among residents*	Various	Various	Various	64

(continues)

TABLE 2.1.1   continued

Indicator	U.S. National Rate	Benchmark	Benchmark Rate	Score: Ratio of U.S. to Benchmark
15. Home health: hospital admissions, %	28	Top 25% agencies	17	62
16. Patients reported medical, medication, or lab test error, %	34	Best of 6 countries	22	65
17. Unsafe drug use*	Various	Various	Various	60
18. Nursing home residents with pressure scores*	Various	Various	Various	67
19. Hospital-standardized mortality ratios, Actual to expected deaths	101	Top 10% hospitals	85	84
20. Ability to see doctor on same/ next day when sick or needed medical attention, %	47	Best of 6 countries	81	58
21. Very/somewhat easy to get care after hours without going to the emergency room, %	38	Best of 6 countries	72	53
22. Doctor-patient communication: always listened, explained, showed respect, spent enough time, %	54	90th percentile Medicare plans	74	74
23. Adults with chronic conditions given self-management plan, %	58	Best of 6 countries	65	89
24. Patient-centered hospital care*	Various	Various	Various	87
25. Adults under 65 insured all year, not underinsured, %	65	Target	100	65
26. Adults with no access problem due to costs, %	60	Best of 5 countries	91	66
27. Families spending <10% of income or <5% of income, if low-income, on out-of-pocket medical costs and premiums, %	83	Target	100	83
28. Population under 65 living in states where premiums for employer-sponsored health coverage are <15% of under-65 median household income, %	58	Target	100	58
29. Adults under 65 with no medical bill problems or medical debt, %	66	Target	100	66
30. Potential overuse or waste*	Various	Various	Various	48

TABLE 2.1.1   continued

Indicator	U.S. National Rate	Benchmark	Benchmark Rate	*Score: Ratio of U.S. to Benchmark*
31. Went to emergency room for condition that could have been treated by regular doctor, %	26	Best of 6 countries	6	*23*
32. Hospital admissions for ambulatory care sensitive conditions*	Various	Various	Various	*57*
33. Medicare hospital 30-day readmission rates, %	18	10th percentile regions	14	*75*
34. Medicare annual costs of care and mortality for AMI, hip fracture, and colon cancer (annual Medicare outlays; deaths per 100 beneficiaries)	$26,829; 30	10th percentile regions	$23,314; 27	*88*
35. Medicare annual costs of care for chronic diseases: diabetes, CHF, COPD*	Various	Various	Various	*68*
36. National health expenditures spent on health administration and insurance, %	73	Top 3 of 11 countries	2.0	*28*
37. Physicians using electronic medical records, %	17	Top 3 of 19 countries	80	*21*
OVERALL SCORE				*66*

*Various denotes indicators that comprise two or more related measures. Scores average the individual ratios for each component. For detailed information on the national and benchmark rates for individual components, please refer to C. Schoen et al, "U.S. Health System Performance: A National Scorecard," *Health Affairs* Web Exclusive, Sept. 20, 2006.

AMI = acute myocardial infarction; CHF = congestive heart failure; COPD = chronic obstructive pulmonary disease

Commonwealth Fund National Scorecard on U.S. Health System Performance, 2006.

Special Theme Article

Health Disparities Based on Socioeconomic Inequities: Implications for Urban Health Care

Kevin Fiscella, MD, MPH, and David R. Williams, PhD, MPH

Differences in socioeconomic status, whether measured by income, educational achievement, or occupation, are associated with large disparities in health status.[1] This association persists across the life cycle[2] and across measures of health, including health status,[3] morbidity,[4] and mortality.[5] Although effects are largest for those living in poverty, gradients of disparity are seen across the socioeconomic spectrum.[6]

This article discusses health disparities based on socioeconomic status in the context of urban health care. We begin by discussing the relationships among race, socioeconomic status, and health. We trace disparities in health based on socioeconomic status throughout the course of an individual's life and review potential explanations for this relationship. We conclude by discussing the implications of these disparities for the provision of health care to urban, low-income, and minority patients. Studies for this review were identified through selected Medline searches, bibliographic searches of key articles, and the authors' knowledge of the literature. The size of the literature on health disparities precluded a complete, systematic literature search.

THE INTERRELATION OF RACE, SOCIOECONOMIC STATUS, AND HEALTH

Race, socioeconomic status, and health have historically been inextricably intertwined in the United States. Unlike most countries, however, the United States collects national health data primarily by race and not by socioeconomic status.[7] African Americans have experienced varying levels of social, economic, and political exclusion that have resulted in poorer health since their arrival on this continent as slaves several hundred years ago.[8] Historically, slavery in the United States was rationalized on the basis of racism—an ideology of oppression based on a belief in the inherent racial biological inferiority of one race and the superiority of another.[9] The construct of race, however, is socially derived with limited biological basis.[10]

To this day, as a legacy of this oppression, African Americans experience dramatically worse health across the age spectrum, including higher adult and infant mortality.[11] They

Adapted from: Kevin Fiscella and David Williams. (2004). Health disparities based on socioeconomic inequalities: Implications for urban health care. *Academic Medicine* 79(12), 1139–1147.

have significantly higher mortality rates from cardiovascular and cerebrovascular disease, most cancers, diabetes, HIV, unintentional injuries, pregnancy, sudden infant death syndrome, and homicide than do whites.[12] These health disparities have been rationalized on the basis of genetic "differences" despite evidence that genetics does not contribute significantly to these disparities.[13] Racial differences in socioeconomic status, not genetics, are the most important cause of these health disparities.[5]

Racism perpetuates these health disparities by operating at three distinct levels: institutionalized policies and practices that maintain racial disadvantage, individual racial discrimination and biased treatment, and internalized cognitive processes.[14] Each reinforces the others. Institutionalized racism, manifested through long-standing racial inequities in employment, housing, education, health care, income, wealth, and criminal justice, is reinforced through racist beliefs.[15] Individual racism, including unconscious bias, is manifested through discrimination in housing, banking and employment, racial profiling by police, harsher sentencing for minority defendants, lower educational expectations for minority students, and unequal medical treatment.[16] Racial stereotypes contribute to voting patterns and public policies that, in turn, reinforce institutionalized racism. Internalized racism refers to introjection of racial stereotypes by the minority group members. Internalized racism may contribute to self doubts, lower school performance, depressive symptoms, substance abuse, dropouts, and other risk behaviors.[17]

Residential segregation, a product of long-standing institutional and individual racism,[18] represents a fundamental cause of racial disparities in health because it perpetuates racial disparities in poverty, education, and economic opportunity that, in turn, drive disparities in health.[19] The social and spatial marginalization associated with segregation reinforces substandard housing, underfunded public schools, employment disadvantages, exposure to crime, environmental hazards, and loss of hope, thus powerfully concentrating disadvantage.[20]

HEALTH DISPARITIES ACROSS THE LIFE CYCLE

Fetal and Neonatal Health

Health disparities resulting from socioeconomic status begin early in life, but have potential for lasting effects.[21] Disparities in health potentially begin in utero because the health of the fetus is so closely linked to the health of the mother. A mother's low socioeconomic status is associated with multiple risk factors for adverse birth outcomes, including unplanned and unwanted pregnancy,[22] single and/or adolescent motherhood,[22] smoking,[23] urogenital tract infections,[24] chronic illness in the mother, and inadequate prenatal care.[25] Not surprisingly, a mother's low socioeconomic status, and to some extent the low socioeconomic status of the father, are associated with low birth weight[26] and infant mortality.[27]

Child Health

Socioeconomic disparities continue into childhood.[28] Children of low socioeconomic status have greater risks of death from infectious disease,[29] sudden infant death,[30] accidents,[31] and child abuse.[32] They have higher rates of exposure to lead poisoning[33] and household smoke.[34] They have higher rates of asthma,[35] developmental delay and learning disabilities,[36] conduct disturbances,[37] and avoidable hospitalizations.[38] They more often reside in families with marital conflict[39] and are more often exposed to intimate-partner[40] and community violence.[40] Low socioeconomic status and overcrowding are associated with infectious disease including tuberculosis[29] and *Helicobacter pylori* infection.[41] By their preteen years, children of low socioeconomic status report lower health status and more risk behaviors.[2]

Adolescent Health

Low socioeconomic status affects adolescents as well. Low socioeconomic adolescents report worse health; they have higher rates of pregnancy,[42] sexually transmitted disease,[43] depression, obesity,[44] and suicide.[45] They are more likely to be sexually abused,[46] drop out of high school,[47] or be killed.[48] Satisfaction with health, better family involvement, better problem solving, more physical activity, better home safety, having higher school achievement, and being in the best health profiles are all positively related to parental socioeconomic status during adolescence.[49]

Adult Health

By adulthood, health disparities related to socioeconomic status are striking. Compared with persons who have a college education, those with less than a high school education have life expectancies that are six years shorter.[5] People with low socioeconomic status experience higher rates of death across the spectrum of causes.[50] They experience premature chronic morbidity and disability including the onset of hypertension at an earlier age,[51] diabetes,[52] cardiovascular disease,[53] obesity,[54] osteoarthritis,[55] depression,[56] oral pathology,[57] many cancers,[58] and cardiovascular disease.[59]

Elderly Health

Health disparities among the elderly that are related to socioeconomic status begin to narrow slightly, perhaps due to healthy survivor effects.[60] Nonetheless, elderly people of lower socioeconomic status experience greater disability,[61] more limitations in activities in daily living,[62] and more frequent and rapid cognitive decline.[63] Having achieved higher educational levels tends to be associated with the prevention of functional limitations, while a higher income level is associated with both prevention and delayed progression of functional decline.[64]

EXPLANATIONS

The relationship between socioeconomic status and health is complex. Socioeconomic status has been defined as potential or realized access to resources in three major domains:

material, human, and social capital.[65] Thus, it is not surprising that a relationship between socioeconomic status and health has persisted across time, place, and changes in epidemiology. Socioeconomic status represents a fundamental cause of health.[66]

Reverse Causality

Undoubtedly, poor health can result in low socioeconomic status. Persons with disabilities, whether physical or psychiatric, often achieve lower educational, occupational, and income outcomes than do persons without such disabilities. Similarly, persons who experience serious illness or disability often face unemployment or downward mobility. While health status can affect socioeconomic status, there is compelling evidence that socioeconomic status strongly affects health.

Genetic Confounding

Genetic factors may partly confound the relationship between health and socioeconomic status, but socioeconomic status clearly affects health independently of genetic factors. Cognitive ability[67] and personality[68] are partly genetically determined; childhood IQ[69] predicts adult survival; and personality is associated with educational attainment.[70] However, socioeconomic status in childhood has been shown to predict adult health independent of childhood IQ,[71] and quantitative genetic studies show that the effects of the level of educational attainment are independent of genetic confounding.[72] Twin studies[73] and natural experiments[37] show that neighborhood environment and the socioeconomic status of parents affect children's health outcomes.

Social Causation

The available evidence suggests that socioeconomic status affects health through myriad pathways. As illustrated earlier, disparities in health begin early in life. There is growing evidence to support the Barker hypothesis that fetal growth restriction is associated with higher rates of obesity, hypertension, diabetes, and cardiovascular disease.[74]

The level of socioeconomic status during childhood independently predicts educational attainment and adult mortality.[75] The pathways through which socioeconomic status of children affects adult health include cognitive stimulation,[76] family conflict,[39] childhood abuse,[77] exposure to environmental toxins,[78] family structure,[79] divorce[80] and autonomy support.[75] These risks appear to be additive, if not multiplicative.[81]

Inadequate cognitive stimulation, child abuse, and neglect can have lasting effects on emotional development, psychiatric health, and risk-taking behavior.[82] Thus, early childhood effects may affect mental functioning of adults, which in turn can affect their physical health.[83]

Lack of resources—whether financial hardship, low literacy, limited access to health care, or social marginalization—is associated with chronic stress. Exposure to chronic stress is detrimental to health because it results in continued "wear and tear," termed "allostastic load."[84] Available evidence suggests that the stress associated with low socioeconomic status has cumulative physiological effects,[85] including adverse metabolic, autonomic, and brain effects such as hippocampal atrophy.[86] Conversely, high socioeconomic status is associated with improved psychological coping, including self-efficacy and perceived control, which in turn is associated with improved health and reduced mortality.[87]

Notably, low socioeconomic status is consistently related to reduced access to quality health care.[88] Low income is associated with higher rates of reduced access to health care, higher rates of uninsurance, and absence of a regular source of care.[89] Low income and type of insurance are associated with less preventative care for children or adults[90] lower-intensity hospital care,[91] including fewer cardiac or vascular procedures; and worse outcomes following these procedures.[92] Low-income persons receive lower quality ambulatory[93] and hospital care,[94] including fewer prescriptions for aspirin and/or provision of thrombolysis for myocardial infarction.[95] Absence of insurance has been consistently related to a range of adverse outcomes, including higher mortality.[96]

THE CONCENTRATION OF RISK

The effects of socioeconomic status on health are amplified because risk factors associated with low socioeconomic status tend to cluster within individuals, families, and communities. Risk factors are further concentrated by racial and socioeconomic residential segregation.[97] Moreover, each of the three domains of socioeconomic status (material, human, and social capital) are correlated with each other. Consequently, a person with little education is at risk for being low income and jobless. People of low socioeconomic status likely share a household with others of the same status and reside in a low-socioeconomic-status community. Although there are more poor white than black persons in the United States, one reason for the greater adverse impact of poverty on African Americans is that poor blacks are markedly more likely than are their white peers to reside in high-poverty residential areas.[20] Even if the health of a person of low socioeconomic status has not yet been affected, there is greater risk for ill health among his or her family members. Furthermore, living in a community of low socioeconomic status is associated with higher cardiovascular mortality independent of the socioeconomic characteristics of the individual.[98] Low-income children, particularly those living in racially segregated communities, typically attend schools where risk factors are further concentrated. Given these contextual effects, persons with low socioeconomic status are more likely to be exposed to crime, violence, and drug trafficking, and they are less likely to be exposed to successful role models[99] or social networks that facilitate upward mobility.[100] The cumulative toll from these concentrated risk factors can be devastating to individual, families, and communities.

IMPLICATIONS FOR URBAN MEDICINE

Most health care provided to the urban poor is delivered by safety-net providers,[101] including hospital outpatient clinics, community health centers, and other not-for-profit organizations.

However, this safety net of providers is endangered.[102] Half of all community health centers have endured financial crises,[103] and many struggle to retain physicians.[104]

Unique Challenges

Providers serving urban, low-socioeconomic-status, minority patients will be confronted with clinical, logistical, paperwork, and administrative challenges. Their work is more clinically challenging not simply because patients suffer greater levels of biomedical morbidity, but also because this morbidity is embedded within a complex web of psychosocial morbidity. Physicians are likely to confront problems in communication and shared understanding that are related to differences in language, culture, and health literacy.[105] Unlike suburban practices where patients often present with single problems, patients in low-income, urban practices often present with a complex array of problems.[106] Working with the urban poor means working with patients who not only have greater biopsychosocial morbidity and risk factors but also have far fewer resources at their disposal to cope with these problems.[107]

The number of patients presenting with complex biopsychosocial problems can be overwhelming to urban health care providers. Patients with low levels of health literacy require more time, not less, to explain treatment.[108] Specialty services are often not easily available for the uninsured.[109] Caring for a handful of such patients is challenging. Caring for multiple patients with complex needs can be overwhelming in the absence of adequate systems of care. Preventive care services may be neglected in the face of multiple and competing providers' demands.[110] Access to specialist, diagnostic, and behavioral health services may be limited.[111]

Providing medical care to urban low-income populations also poses administrative challenges. Appointment-time scheduling can be problematic. Missed appointments are significantly higher at practices with patients from low socioeconomic status.[112] Practices frequently compensate for missed appointments by overbooking patients, which results in long wait times for patients.

Paperwork demands are considerable. These include certification of employability for welfare, assessment of temporary or long-term disability, workers' compensation, disabled parking permits, case management, job training, childcare certification, school enrollment, Medicaid preauthorization for medications, transportation services, increase in Medicaid visit or medication thresholds, and medication refills. Although completing paperwork has become routine in primary care, the volume is magnified in practices with patients of low socioeconomic status who often lack adequate ancillary support.

Despite the greater amount of time and expense required to work with low-income patients, reimbursement is significantly lower. Medicaid reimburses physicians at significantly lower rates than does other insurance.[113] Moreover, most persons living at or below federal poverty are not eligible for Medicaid[114]; many have no health insurance or have health care coverage that fails to cover needed prescriptions, and high prescription costs deter adherence.[115] Even among patients with private insurance, reimbursement may be lower. Existing billing codes do not adequately capture complexity, time, and expense involved in caring for patients in low-socioeconomic-status urban areas. Given these challenges, it is hardly surprising that many physicians eschew working with poor[116] or uninsured patients.[117]

Health Care Quality

Despite these challenges, providing quality health care in urban practices is feasible.[118] Community health centers in particular have been shown to provide care comparable to that provided to more advantaged populations.[119] Providing quality care requires not only sound clinical skills, but also the ability to effectively integrate biomedical, psychological, and social factors; cultural competency; and patient-centered care.[120] It also requires the presence of systems designed to promote quality.[121] Reminder systems for busy health care providers can mitigate the effects of competing demands, tracking systems help ensure follow-up on abnormal results, chronic disease registries can be used to promote adherence to treatment guidelines, and outreach can be extended to hard-to-reach patients.[122] Electronic technology systems can facilitate these tasks.[123] Same-day appointment scheduling can improve access and reduce no-show rates.[124] On-side interpretation services are critical.[125]

Implementation of these measures should reduce disparities in health care quality based on patients' racial, ethnic, or socioeconomic status and facilitate progress toward the Healthy People 2010 goal of eliminating disparities in health. However, achieving this goal will likely require more than the elimination of disparities in health care; it will require a sustained national commitment to addressing the fundamental causes of disparities in health.

REFERENCES

1. Anderson RT, Sorlie P, Backlund E, Johnson N, Kaplan GA. Mortality effects of community socioeconomic status. *Epidemiology.* 1997;8:42–7.

2. Starfield B, Robertson J, Riley AW. Social class gradients and health in childhood. *Ambul Pediatr.* 2002;2:238–46.

3. Fiscella K. Is lower income associated with greater biopsyhosocial morbidity? Implications for physicians working with underserved patients. *J Fam Pract.* 1999;48:372–7.

4. Marmot M, Shipley M, Brunner E, Hemingway H. Relative contribution of early life and adult socioeconomic factors to adult morbidity in the Whitehall II study. *J Epidemiol Community Health.* 2001;55:301–7.

5. Wong MD, Shapiro MF, Boscardin WJ, Ettner SL. Contribution of major diseases to disparities in mortality. *N Engl J Med.* 2002;347:1585–92.

6. Marmot MG, Smith GD, Stansfield S, et al. Health inequalities among British civil servants: the Whitehall II study. *Lancet.* 1991;337:1387–93.

7. Williams DR. Race/ethnicity and socioeconomic status: measurement and methodological issues. *Int J Health Serv.* 1996;26:483–505.

8. Byrd WM, Clayton LA. An American health dilemma: a history of blacks in the health system. *J Nat Med Assoc.* 1992;84:189–200.

9. Zuberi Z. *Thicker than Blood: How Racial Statistics Lie.* Minneapolis: University of Minnesota Press; 2001.

10. American Anthropological Association. Statement on race. *Am Anthropol.* 1998;100:712–3.

11. Sorlie P, Rogot E, Anderson R, Johnson NJ, Backlund E. Black-white mortality differences by family income. *Lancet.* 1992;340:346–50.

12. Eberhardt MS, Ingram DD, Makuc DM. *Urban and Rural Health Chartbook, Health, United States, 2001.* Hyattsville, Md: National Center for Health Statistics, 2001.

13. Pearce N, Foliaki S, Sporle A, Cunningham C. Genetics, race, ethnicity, and health. *BMJ.* 2004;328:1070–2.

14. Jones CP. Levels of racism: a theoretic framework and a gardener's tale. *Am J Public Health.* 2000;90:1212–5.

15. Hilfiker D. *Urban Injustice: How Ghettos Happen.* New York: Seven Stories Press, 2002.

16. Institute of Medicine. *Unequal Treatment: Confronting Racial and Ethnic Disparities in Health Care.* Washington, DC: National Academy Press; 2002.

17. Patterson O. *Rituals of Blood: Consequences of Slavery in Two American Centuries.* New York: Basic Books; 1999.

18. Massey DS, Denton NA. Hypersegregation in U.S. metropolitan areas: black and Hispanic segregation along five dimensions. *Demographics.* 1989;26:373–91.

19. Williams DR, Collins C. Racial residential segregation: a fundamental cause of racial disparities in health. *Public Health Rep.* 2001;116:404–16.

20. Wilson WJ. *The Truly Disadvantaged: The Inner City, the Underclass, and Public Policy.* Chicago: University of Chicago Press; 1987.

21. Lundberg O. The impact of childhood living conditions on illness and mortality in adulthood. *Soc Sci Med.* 1993;36:1047–52.

22. Cubbin C, Braveman PA, Marchi KS, Chavez GF, Santelli JS, Gilbert BJ. Socioeconomic and racial/ethnic disparities in unintended pregnancy among postpartum women in California. *Maternal Child Health J.* 2002;6:237–46.

23. Gazmariarian JA, Adams MM, Pamuk ER. Associations between measures of socioeconomic status and maternal health behavior. *Am J Prev Med.* 1996;12:108–15.

24. Krieger N, Waterman PD, Chen JT, Soobader MJ, Subramanian SV. Monitoring socioeconomic inequalities in sexually transmitted infections, tuberculosis, and violence: geocoding and choice of area-based socioeconomic measures—the Public Health Disparities Geocoding Project (US). *Public Health Rep.* 2003;118:240–60.

25. Abel MH. Maternal characteristics and inadequate prenatal care. *Psychol Rep.* 1996;79:903–12.

26. Hessol NA, Fuentes-Afflick E, Bacchetti P. Risk of low birth weight infants among black and white parents. *Obstet Gynecol.* 1998;92:814–22.

27. Wise PH, Kotelchuck M, Wilson ML, Mills M. Racial and socioeconomic disparities in childhood mortality in Boston. *N Engl J Med.* 1985;313:360–6.

28. Chen E, Matthews KA, Boyce WT. Socioeconomic differences in children's health: how and why do these relationships change with age? *Psychol Bull.* 2002;128:295–329.

29. Drucker E, Alcabes P, Bosworth W, Sckell B. Childhood tuberculosis in the Bronx, New York. *Lancet.* 1994;343:1482–5.

30. Nam CB, Eberstein JW, Deeb LC. Sudden infant death syndrome as a socially determined cause of death. *Soc Biol.* 1989;36:1–8.

31. Marcin JP, Schembri MS, He J, Romano PS. A population-based analysis of socioeconomic status and insurance status and their relationship with pediatric trauma hospitalization and mortality rates. *Am J Public Health.* 2003;93:461–6.

32. Wolfner GD, Gelles RJ. A profile of violence toward children: a national study. *Child Abuse Negl.* 1993;17:197–212.

33. Bernard SM, McGeehin MA. Prevalence of blood lead levels > or = 5 micro g/dL among US children 1 to 5 years of age and socioeconomic and demographic factors associated with blood of lead levels 5 to 10 micro g/dL, Third National Health and Nutrition Examination Survey, 1988–1994. *Pediatrics.* 2003;112:1–13.

34. Mannino DM, Caraballo R, Benowitz N, Repace J. Predictors of cotinine levels in US children: data from the Third National Health and Nutrition Examination Survey. *Chest.* 2001;120:718–24.

35. Smith LA, Hatcher JL, Wertheimer R. The association of childhood asthma with parental employment and welfare receipt. *J Am Med Womens Assoc.* 2002;57:11–15.

36. To T, Cadarette SM, Liu Y. Biological, social, and environmental correlates of preschool development. *Child.* 2001;27:187–200.

37. Costello EJ, Compton SN, Keeler G, Angold A. Relationships between poverty and psychopathology: a natural experiment. *JAMA.* 2003;290:2023–9.

38. Hakim RB, Bye BV. Effectiveness of compliance with pediatric preventive care guidelines among Medicaid beneficiaries. *Pediatrics.* 2001;108:90–7.

39. Conger RD, Ge X, Elder GH Jr, Lorenz PO, Simons RL. Economic stress, coercive family process, and developmental problems of adolescents. *Child Develop.* 1994;65:541–61.

40. Sheehan K, DiCara JA, LeBailly S, Christoffel KK. Children's exposure to violence in an urban setting. *Arch Pediatr Adolesc Med.* 1997;151:502–4.

41. Malaty HM, Graham DY. Importance of childhood socioeconomic status on the current prevalence of *Helicobacter pylori* infection. *Gut.* 1994;35:742–5.

42. Gold R, Kennedy B, Connell F, Kawachi J. Teen births, income inequality, and social capital: developing an understanding of the causal pathway. *Health Place.* 2002;8:77–83.

43. Rice RJ, Roberts PL, Handsfield HH, Holmes KK. Sociodemographic distribution of gonorrhea incidence: implications for prevention and behavioral research. *Am J Public Health.* 1991;81:1252–8.

44. Goodman E, Slap GB, Huang B. The public health impact of socioeconomic status on adolescent depression and obesity. *Am J Public Health.* 2003;93:1844–50.

45. McCall PL. Adolescent and elderly white male suicide trends: evidence of changing well-being? *J Gerontol.* 1991;46:S43–51.

46. Moore KA, Nord CW, Peterson JL. Nonvoluntary sexual activity among adolescents. *Fam Plann Perspect.* 1989;21:110–4.

47. Vartanian TP, Gleason PM. Do neighborhood conditions affect high school dropout and college graduation rates? *J Socioecon.* 1999;28:21–41.

48. Dahlberg LL. Youth violence in the United States: major trends, risk factors, and prevention approaches. *Am J Prev Med.* 1998;14:259–72.

49. Starfield B, Riley AW, Witt WP, Robertson J. Social class gradients in health during adolescence. *J Epidemiol Community Health.* 2002;56:345–61.

50. Howard G, Anderson RT, Russell G, Howard VJ, Burke GL. Race, socioeconomic status, and cause-specific mortality. *Ann Epidemiol.* 2000;10:214–23.

51. Vargas CM, Ingram DD, Gillum RF. Incidence of hypertension and educational attainment: the NHANES I epidemiologic follow-up study. First National Health and Nutrition Examination Survey. *Am J Epidemiol.* 2000;1542:272–8.

52. Robbins JM, Vaccarino V, Zhang H, Kasl SV. Socioeconomic status and type 2 diabetes in African American and non-Hispanic white women and men: evidence from the Third National Health and Nutrition Examination Survey. *Am J Public Health.* 2001;91:76–83.

53. He J, Ogden LG, Bazzano LA, Vupputuri S, Loria C, Whelton PK. Risk factors for congestive heart failure in US men and women: NHANES I epidemiologic follow-up study. *Arch Intern Med.* 2001;161:996–1002.

54. Lantz PM, House JS, Lepkowski JM, Williams DR, Mero RP, Chen J. Socioeconomic factors, health behaviors, and mortality: results from a nationally representative prospective study of US adults. *JAMA.* 1998;279:1703–8.

55. Hannan MT, Anderson JJ, Pincus T, Felson DT. Educational attainment and osteoarthritis: differential associations with radiographic changes and symptom reporting. *J Clin Epidemiol.* 1992;45:139–47.

56. Lorant V, Deliege D, Eaton W, Robert A, Philippot P, Ansseau M. Socioeconomic inequalities in depression: a meta-analysis. *Am J Epidemiol.* 2003;157:98–112.

57. Chavers LS, Gilbert GH, Shelton BJ. Racial and socioeconomic disparities in oral disadvantage, a measure of oral health-related quality of life: 24-month incidence. *J Public Health Dent.* 2002;62:140–7.

58. Gorey KM, Vena JE. The association of near poverty status with cancer incidence among black and white adults. *J Community Health.* 1995;20:359–66.

59. Everson SA, Maty SC, Lynch JW, Kaplan GA. Epidemiologic evidence for the relation between socioeconomic status and depression, obesity, and diabetes. *J Psychosom Res.* 2002;53:891–5.

60. Von Dem KO, Luschen G, Cockerham WC, Siegrist J. Socioeconomic status and health among the aged in the United States and Germany: a comparative cross-sectional study. *Soc Sci Med.* 2003;57:1643–52.

61. Melzer D, Izmirlian G, Leveille SG, Guralnik JM. Educational differences in the prevalence of mobility disability in old age: the dynamics of incidence, mortality, and recovery. J *Gerontol B Psychol Sci Soc Sci.* 2001;56:S294–301.

62. Kington RS, Smith JP. Socioeconomic status and racial and ethnic differences in functional status associated with chronic diseases. *Am J Public Health.* 1997;87:805–10.

63. Farmer ME, Kittner SJ, Rae DS, Bartko JJ, Regier DA. Education and change in cognitive function. The Epidemiologic Catchment Area Study. *Ann Epidemiol.* 1995;5:1–7.

64. Zimmer Z, House JS. Education, income, and functional limitation transitions among American adults: contrasting onset and progression. *Int J Epidemiol.* 2003;32:1089–97.

65. Oakes J, Rossi P. The measurement of SES in health research: current practice and steps toward a new approach. *Soc Sci Med.* 2003;56: 769–84.

66. Link BG, Phelan J. Social conditions as fundamental causes of disease. *J Health Soc Behav.* 1995;Spec No:80–94.

67. Stoolmiller M. Implications of the restricted range of family environments for estimates of heritability and nonshared environment in behavior-genetic adoption studies. *Psychol Bull.* 1999;125:392–409.

68. McCrae RR, Jang KL, Livesley WJ, Riemann R, Angleitner A. Sources of structure: genetic, environmental, and artifactual influences on the covariation of personality traits. *J Personality.* 2001;69:511–35.

69. Whalley LJ, Deary IJ. Longitudinal cohort study of childhood IQ and survival up to age 76. *BMJ.* 2001;322:819.

70. Goodwin R, Engstrom G. Personality and the perception of health in the general population. *Psychol Med.* 2002;32:325–32.

71. Hart CL, Taylor MD, Davey SG, et al. Childhood IQ, social class, deprivation, and their relationships with mortality and morbidity risk in later life: prospective observational study linking the Scottish Mental Survey 1932 and the Midspan studies. *Psychosom Med.* 2003;65:877–83.

72. Lichtenstein P, Harris JR, Pedersen NL, McClearn GE. Socioeconomic status and physical health, how are they related? An empirical study based on twins reared apart and twins reared together. *Soc Sci Med.* 1993;36:441–50.

73. Caspi A, Taylor A, Moffitt TE, Plomin R. Neighborhood deprivation affects children's mental health: environmental risks identified in a genetic design. *Psychol Sci.* 2000;11:338–42.

74. Barker DJ. The fetal and infant origins of adult disease. *BMJ.* 1990;301:1111.

75. Bosma H, Mheen HD, Mackenbach JP. Social class in childhood and general health in adulthood: questionnaire study in contribution of psychological attributes. *BMJ.* 1999;318:18–22.

76. Hertzman C, Wiens M. Child development and long-term outcomes: a population health perspective and summary of successful interventions. *Soc Sci Med.* 1996;43:1083–95.

77. Rohner RP, Rohner EC. Antecedents and consequences of parental rejection: a theory of emotional abuse. *Child Abuse Negl.* 1980;4:189–98.

78. Lanphear BP, Hornung R, Ho M, et al. Environmental lead exposure during early childhood. *J Pediatr.* 2002;140:40–7.

79. McLanahan SS. Parent absence or poverty: which matters more? In: Duncan GJ, Brooks-Gunn J, eds. *Consequences of Growing up Poor.* New York: Russell Sage Foundation; 1997.

80. Friedman HS. Long-term relations of personality and health: dynamisms, mechanisms, tropisms. *J Personal.* 2000;68:1089–107.

81. Evans GW. The environment of childhood poverty. *Am Psychol.* 2004;59:77–92.

82. Dube SR, Felitti VJ, Dong M, Giles WH, Anda RF. The impact of adverse childhood experiences on health problems: evidence from four birth cohorts dating back to 1900. *Prev Med.* 2003;37:268–77.

83. Rutter M. Childhood experiences and adult psychosocial functioning. *Ciba Found Sympos.* 1991;156: 189–200.

84. McEwen BS. Stress, adaptation, and disease. Allostasis and allostatic load. *Ann N Y Acad Sci.* 1998;8740: 33–44.

85. Lynch JW, Kaplan GA, Shema SJ. Cumulative impact of sustained economic hardship on physical, cognitive, psychological, and social functioning. *N Engl J Med.* 1997;337:1889–95.

86. Seeman TE, Crimmins E, Huang MH, et al. Cumulative biological risk and socio-economic differences in mortality: MacArthur studies of successful aging. *Soc Sci Med.* 2004;58:1985–97.

87. Marmot MG, Bosma H, Hemingway H, Brunner E, Stansfeld S. Contribution of job control and other risk factors to social variations in coronary heart disease incidence. *Lancet.* 1997;350:235–9.

88. Fiscella K, Franks P, Gold MR, Clancy CM. Inequality in quality: addressing socioeconomic, racial, and ethnic disparities in health care. *JAMA.* 2000;283:2579–84.

89. Shi L. The convergence of vulnerable characteristics and health insurance in the US. *Soc Sci Med.* 2001;53:519–29.

90. Hahn RA, Teutsch SM, Franks AL, Chang MH, Lloyd EE. The prevalence of risk factors among women in the United States by race and age, 1992-1994: opportunities for primary and secondary prevention. *J Am Med Womens Assoc.* 1998;53:96–104, 107.

91. Yergan J, Flood AB, Diehr P, LoGerfo JP. Relationship between patient source of payment and the intensity of hospital servies. *Med Care.* 1988;26:1111–4.

92. Boxer LK, Dimick JB, Wainess RM, et al. Payer status is related to differences in access and outcomes of abdominal aortic aneurysm repair in the United States. *Surgery.* 2003;134:142–5.

93. Brook RH, Kamberg CJ, Lohr KN, Goldberg GA, Keeler EB, Newhouse JP. Quality of ambulatory care. Epidemiology and comparison by insurance status and income. *Med Care.* 1990;28:392–433.

94. Kahn EL, Pearson ML, Harrison ER, et al. Health care for black and poor hospitalized Medicare patients. *JAMA.* 1994;271:1169–74.

95. Rathore SS, Berger AK, Weinfurt KP, et al. Race, sex, poverty, and the medical treatment of acute myocardial infarction in the elderly. *Circulation.* 2000;102:642–8.

96. Institute of Medicine. *Care Without Coverage: Too Little, Too Late.* Washington, DC: National Academy Press; 2002.

97. Massey DS, Denton NA. *American Apartheid: The Making of the Underclass.* Cambridge, Ma: Harvard University Press; 1993.

98. Diuez Roux AV, Merkin SS, Arnett D, et al. Neighborhood of residence and incidence of coronary heart disease. *N Engl J Med.* 2001;345:99–106.

99. Elliot DS, Wilson WJ, Huizinga D, Sampson RJ. The effects of neighborhood disadvantage on adolescent development. *J Res Crime Delinq.* 1996;33:389–426.

100. Wegener B. Job mobility and social ties: social resources, prior job, and status attainment. *Am Soc Rev.* 1960;56:60–71.

101. Prinz TS, Soffel D. The primary care delivery system in New York's low-income communities: private physicians and institutional providers in nine neighborhoods. *J Urban Health.* 2003;80:635–49.

102. Institute of Medicine. *America's Health Care Safety Net: Intact but Endangered.* Washington, DC: National Academy Press; 2000.

103. McAlearney JS. The financial performance of community health centers, 1996-1999. Clear evidence that many CHCs are on the brink of financial insolvency. *Health Affairs.* 2002;21:219–25.

104. Singer JD, Davidson SM, Graham S, Davidson HS. Physician retention in community and migrant health centers: who stays and for how long? *Med Care.* 1998;36:1198–213.

105. Carrillo JE, Green AR, Betancourt JR. Cross-cultural primary care: a patient-based approach. *Ann Intern Med.* 1999;130:829–34.

106. Blankfield RP, Goodwin M, Jaen CR, Stange KC. Addressing the unique challenges of inner-city practice: a direct observation study of inner-city, rural, and suburban family practices. *J Urban Health*. 2002;79:173-85.

107. Weiner S. "I can't afford that!": dilemmas in the care of the uninsured and underinsured. *J Gen Intern Med*. 2001;16:412-8.

108. Schillinger D, Piette J, Grumbach K, et al. Closing the loop: physician communication with diabetic patients who have low health literacy. *Arch Internal Med*. 2003;163:83-90.

109. Weissman JS, Moy E, Campbell EG, et al. Limits to the safety net: teaching hospital faculty report on their patients' access to care. *Health Affairs*. 2003;22:156-66.

110. Jaen CR, Stange KC, Tumiel LM, Nutting P. Missed opportunities for prevention: smoking cessation counseling and the competing demands of practice. *J Fam Pract*. 1997;45:348-54.

111. Gusmano MK, Fairbrother G, Park H. Exploring the limits of the safety net: community health centers and care for the uninsured. *Health Affairs*. 2002;21:188-94.

112. Weingarten N, Meyer DL, Schneid JA. Failed appointments in residency practices: who misses them and what providers are most affected? *J Am Board Fam Pract*. 1997;10:407-11.

113. Perloff JD, Kletke P, Fossett JW. Which physicians limit their Medicaid participation, and why. *Health Serv Res*. 1995;30:7-26.

114. Guyer J, Broaddus M, Dude A. Millions of mothers lack health insurance coverage in the United States. Most uninsured mothers lack access both to employer-based covered and to publicly subsidized health insurance. *Int J Health Serv*. 2002;32:89-106.

115. Mojtabai R, Olfson M. Medication costs, adherence, and health outcomes among Medicare beneficiaries. *Health Affairs*. 2003;22:220-9.

116. Komaromy M, Lurie N, Bindman AB. California physicians' willingness to care for the poor. *West J Med*. 1995;162:127-32.

117. Reed MC, Cunningham PJ, Stoddard JJ. *Physicians pulling back from charity care*. Issue Brief Cent Stud Health Syst Change. 2001;1-4.

118. Bayer WH, Fiscella K. Patients and community together: a family medicine COPC project in an urban private practice. *Arch Fam Med*. 1999;8:546-9.

119. Starfield B, Powe NR, Weiner JR, et al. Costs vs quality in different types of primary care settings. *JAMA*. 1998;272:1903-8.

120. Fiscella K. Reducing health care disparities through collaborative care. *Fam Systems Health*. 2002;20:365-74.

121. Grumbach K, Bodenheimer T. A primary care home for Americans: putting the house in order. *JAMA*. 2002;288:889-93.

122. Bodenheimer T, Wagner EH, Grumbach K. Improving primary care for patients with chronic illness. *JAMA* 2002;288:1775-9.

123. Bodenheimer T, Grumbach K. Electronic technology: a spark to revitalize primary care? *JAMA*. 2003;290:259-64.

124. Kennedy JG, Hsu JT. Implementation of an open access scheduling system in a residency training program. *Family Med*. 2003;35:666-70.

125. Jacobs EA, Lauderdale DS, Meltzer D, et al. Impact of interpreter services on delivery of health care to limited-English-proficient patients. *J Gen Intern Med*. 2001;16:468-74.

Mortality of White Americans, African Americans, and Canadians: The Causes and Consequences for Health of Welfare State Institutions and Policies

Stephen J. Kunitz, with Irena Pesis-Katz

It has been widely recognized that both in the past and at present, white and African-American citizens have had very different mortality experiences. Perhaps somewhat less well known is the fact that the populations of the United States and Canada have also had, and continue to have, very different mortality rates. For most of the 20th century Canada had a small but significant advantage with regard to life expectancy. Figure 2.3.1 provides more detail and shows that white American life expectancy was the same as, or better than, that of all Canadians for most of the period from 1850 to 1950 (Haines and Steckel 2000, 696–7). Only in the 1970s did the Canadian figure rise above that of white Americans. For the entire 20th century, however, the life expectancy of African Americans was substantially below that of both white Americans and Canadians, which accounts for most of the Canadian advantage until 1970. After that time, the life expectancy of both white and black Americans has been lower than that of Canadians.

DISPARITIES DUE TO CONDITIONS AMENABLE TO INTERVENTION BY THE HEALTH CARE SYSTEM

It has been known for some time that proportionately more African Americans than whites die of causes amenable to interventions by the health care system (Carr et al. 1989; Rene et al. 1995; Schwartz et al. 1990; Woolhandler et al. 1985). Among the causes accounting for the greatest disparity in life expectancy of African Americans and whites are cerebrovascular and cardiovascular diseases and hypertension (Wong et al. 2002). Although there has been a decline in both causes of death among African Americans, which began in the 1950s but was generally more rapid for whites (Farley and Allen 1987, 42–3), there still is a very large difference in the rates for the two populations. Some of the difference is due to lower rates of vascular surgery among African Americans than among whites (Gittelsohn, Halpern, and Sanchez 1991; Wenneker and Epstein 1989).

Adapted from: Stephen J. Kunitz and Irena Pesis-Katz. (2005). Mortality of white Americans, African Americans, and Canadians: The causes and consequences for health of welfare state institutions and policies. *Milbank Quarterly* 83(1), 5–39.

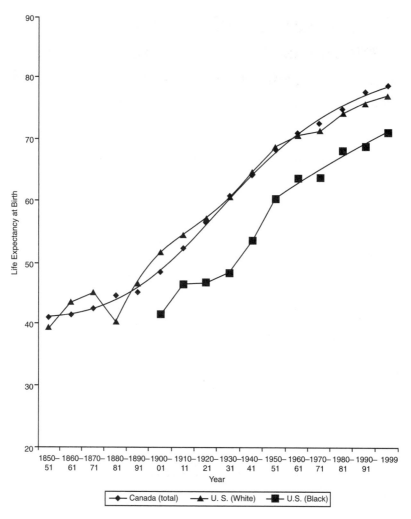

FIGURE 2.3.1   Life Expectancy in Canada and the United States, 1850–2000

The two populations show similarly large differences in the other causes of death amenable to interventions by the health care system. A few have had very dramatic declines (Hodgkin's disease, cervical cancer, peptic ulcer, and tuberculosis). Indeed, the number of cases of tuberculosis began falling in each group early in the 20th century even before effective therapy was available (Ewbank 1994, 123; Farley and Allen 1987, 42–3). Other causes have shown little or no change (breast cancer, appendectomy, cholecystectomy and hernia, and maternal mortality). Of these, breast cancer has been of particular concern. There is reasonably persuasive evidence that mammography has lowered the death rate from breast cancer (Tabar et al. 2003). But African-American women have benefited less than white women because they tend to be screened less frequently, to have lower rates of repeat mammography, and to have fewer follow-up examinations for abnormal findings

(Jones, Patterson, and Calvocoressi 2003). Factors such as breast density and obesity, which are more common among African-American than white women, may also reduce the efficacy of mammography when it is used. Thus the story is complicated, but the evidence suggests that programs specially targeted to African-American women do increase the use of mammography and may well be beneficial (Jones, Patterson, and Calvocoressi 2003).

Unlike the preceding conditions, there has been a noticeable increase in asthma mortality among both African Americans and whites, although greater in the former than the latter. Hospital admissions for acute asthmatic attacks are much more common for African-American than for white youngsters and are much more common from inner-city than from other urban or suburban neighborhoods. It has been suggested that both adverse environmental conditions and lower-quality primary care are responsible for the differences (McConnochie et al. 1999).

HIV/AIDS and diabetes, two of the causes of death that account for much of the difference between white and African-American life expectancy, were not mentioned by the European Community Consensus Conference (Wong et al. 2002). Nonetheless, there is reason to believe that the health care system has much to offer in each case with regard to advice about prevention and treatment. Since 1980, the increase in both HIV/AIDS and diabetes has been more dramatic for African Americans than for whites. In the case of HIV/AIDS, however, there has been a sharp decline in mortality since the 1990s, the result of both preventive and therapeutic interventions (Wong et al. 2002). This decline parallels the accelerating drop in the death rate from tuberculosis in the same period, suggesting that the two are associated. In the case of diabetes, there has been no such decline. Indeed, the number of deaths from diabetes has been much higher for African Americans than for whites, and the evidence suggests that blacks are admitted to hospital with advanced disease requiring amputation more frequently than whites are (Gittelsohn, Halpern, and Sanchez 1991).

It is difficult to say definitively how much of the disparity in death rates from conditions amenable to health care interventions is the result of unequal access to the full range of health services and how much is due to circumstances beyond the reasonable reach of health care systems. Insurance (or its lack) has an important impact on access to care but does not explain all the racial differences in access that have been reported (Zuvekas and Taliaferro 2003). Nonetheless, such consistent differences lead to the conclusion that a great deal is indeed due to unequal access, much of which is built into patterns of segregation in both urban and rural America.

In addition, there is evidence that (1) the quality of primary care physicians who treat most African Americans may not be as good as that of other physicians (Bach et al. 2004) and that (2) even when whites and African Americans have similar types of health care coverage—for example, Medicare—and are admitted to hospitals, the care they receive differs. Notwithstanding the importance of Medicare as an integrative force in health care (Marmor 2000b), studies of Medicare fee-for-service and managed care programs still reveal "differences in care patterns . . . for cancer treatment, treatment after acute myocardial infarction, use of surgical procedures, hospice use, and preventive care" (Virnig et al. 2002, 224).

These differences may result from the providers' racism, the patients' lack of information, and differences in Medigap coverage, as well as other causes. Whatever the reason, as David Barton Smith (1998) showed, many of these differences in quality of hospital care can be attributed to the lax enforcement of requirements for equal treatment in facilities receiving federal funds. After a brief burst of enthusiasm for civil rights following the passage of Medicare in 1965, the federal enforcement of equal treatment in hospitals weakened. Smith cited several reasons why this occurred, among which were the executive branch's diminished commitment to civil rights enforcement, the growing preoccupation with cutting costs and shrinking the federal bureaucracy, and organizational changes within the U.S. Department of Health and Human Services. This contributed to continuing disparities in the treatment of African Americans and whites, Thus even when mechanisms exist for enforcing equal treatment, the federal government has failed to make adequate use of them.

COMPULSORY HEALTH INSURANCE IN CANADA AND THE UNITED STATES

If the health disparities between African Americans and whites were caused by the institutional and policy legacy of slavery and racism, how that legacy was expressed was determined by political institutions. These same institutions also contribute much to the differences between the United States and Canada. An important feature of the American presidential system is that "individual members of the legislature owed their primary loyalty to their constituencies" (Huntington 1966, 390–1), powers are divided among the branches of the government, and party discipline is weak. According to Huntington (1966), this system, inherited from the Tudor model of government, was made obsolete by the parliamentary revolution in England just as it was being adopted in the United States.

Canada adopted the parliamentary system, and institutionalists argue that the difference in the U.S. and Canadian political systems helps explain the creation of national health insurance in Canada and its failure in the United States (Hacker 1998; Maioni 1998). But as the American example should have made clear, the larger political culture and economy have also had a profound effect. The absence of a social democratic party in the United States is an important reason why there is no compulsory health insurance, and the fact that the United States does not have a parliamentary system may partly explain why it does not have a social democratic third party (Gutman 1976; Lipset and Marks 2000; Sombart 1906). It does not explain, however, either why one of the two major American parties is not social democratic (Lipset and Marks 2000, 79–81) or why the most important third party in Canada is.

Just as American attitudes toward race, as expressed through political institutions, contribute much to the differences in health between African Americans and whites, so have the differences between the American and Canadian political cultures and institutions greatly affected the differences in health care and mortality in the two countries.

MORTALITY OF CANADIANS AND WHITE AMERICANS

The life expectancy of Canadians and white Americans diverged in the 1970s and the difference has increased subsequently in each decade since then. Significantly, the differences between social insurance coverage in the two countries became apparent in the 1950s, when Canada instituted broader protection than the United States offered. By then, both countries had industrial accident, pension, and unemployment insurance, but in 1944 Canada also offered a system of family allowances. The gap in social insurance opened much wider after Canada implemented a universal health insurance program in 1972 (Kuderle and Marmor 1982, 83–5), in contrast to the far from universal programs, Medicare and Medicaid, created in the United States in 1965.

In addition, Canada's social insurance programs are more redistributive than America's, and the result has been much greater income equality in the former than the latter country. Although between 1974 and 1985, income inequality worsened in both Canada and the United States, the trend in Canada reversed in the following decade, whereas it continued in the United States. Between 1985 and 1997, Canadian patterns of income taxation and transfer payments were far more redistributive than those in the United States (Wolfson 2000; Wolfson and Murphy 2000).

After universal health insurance was implemented in Canada, several studies were made of the consequences for health care utilization. The results were mixed. Some showed that the inequalities among income groups in utilization and health status have persisted (Dunlop, Coyte, and McIsaac 2000; Dunn and Hayes 2000; Wilkins, Berthelot, and Ng 2002; Wood et al. 1999), but for the most part, utilization has increased, especially among the poor (McDonald et al. 1974; Munan, Vobecky, and Kelly 1974; Siemiatycki, Richardson, and Pless 1980). Although waiting times for elective and semiurgent procedures have lengthened since the 1970s, the degree to which the increase has reduced life expectancy, as contrasted with quality of life, is not significant (Naylor 1999). Moreover, (1) the differences among socioeconomic groups with respect to avoidable hospitalizations are far greater in American than in Canadian cities (Billings, Anderson, and Newman 1996); (2) the risk of inadequate prenatal care is greater for poor American women than for poor Canadian women (Katz, Armstrong, and LoGerfo 1994); (3) survival from some heavily technology-dependent conditions, for example, end-stage renal disease, is better in Canada than in the United States (Hornberger, Garver, and Jeffery 1997), perhaps the result of the high prevalence of for-profit dialysis centers in the United States; and (4) among hospitalized victims of myocardial infarction, Americans have more technologically intense interventions than Canadians but the same one-year survival (Anderson, Newhouse, and Roos 1989; Tu et al. 1997). In contrast, survival from hip fractures is worse in Manitoba than in New England (Roos et al. 1990), although comparisons with adjacent U.S. states might have been more appropriate. In general, however, most causes of death as well as mortality differences among income groups in Canada have declined since the 1970s (Wilkins, Berthelot, and Ng 2002). Furthermore, the use of U.S. services by Canadians is too small to have had a measurable impact on cause-specific mortality or life expectancy (Katz et al. 2002).

The Canadian system of comprehensive care, free of charge at the point of service, and with a greater emphasis than in the United States on primary care, may be generally more effective than the American system for the total population. In light of the great inequalities between whites and African Americans, however, the question is whether the differences between the two countries can be explained by the high rates of death among African Americans or whether these differences affect white Americans as well. Both the lower life expectancy of white Americans than Canadians since the 1970s and the results of the analyses of cancer survival suggest that there should be differences in most of the causes of death amenable to intervention by the health care system. This is important, because if the U.S.-Canadian differences can be explained only by the high rates of preventable deaths among African Americans, then equality between the United States and Canada could be addressed by equalizing the care received by African Americans and leaving the rest of the system untouched. But if the U.S.-Canadian differences are also attributable to differences between white Americans and Canadians, then equalization would require more than simply addressing the problems affecting African Americans, important though that is as an end in itself.

In virtually every case, Canadians have lower rates than white Americans. The exceptions are breast cancer, all respiratory diseases in children, and peptic ulcer, for which the rates are very similar or the same. Moreover, in those conditions for which the rates are falling, they tend to be falling more rapidly among Canadians. These conditions are hypertension and cerebrovascular disease, Hodgkin's disease, appendectomy, cholecystectomy and hernia, cervical cancer, and chronic rheumatic heart disease. Ischemic heart disease has fallen at about the same rate in each population. HIV/AIDS mortality increased more rapidly and to higher levels among white Americans than Canadians, and in the 1990s it fell more rapidly. Nonetheless, the rates still are higher in the United States. Diabetes mortality is increasing in both populations as well, but far more rapidly among white Americans than among Canadians.

These comparisons strongly suggest that the Canadian health care system, though not without serious problems (Blumenthal et al. 2004), serves the interests of Canadians better than the U.S. health care system serves the interests of white Americans, not to mention African Americans. Even the use of American-made pharmaceuticals does not seem to have led to higher death rates in Canada, which should allay the fears of those concerned about reimporting drugs to the United States from Canada. Moreover, the lower death rates of Canadians have been achieved at about half the cost of what Americans pay for health care (Reinhardt, Hussey, and Anderson 2004). In 1999, in current U.S. dollars, the per capita health expenditures in Canada were $1,939, compared with $4,271 in the United States (World Bank 2003).

CONCLUSION

The reported differences between white Americans and all Canadians in causes of death that a well-functioning health system ought to be expected to address are consistent, which raises questions about the impact of health services that cannot simply be dismissed. Beginning in the last third of the 19th century, public health interventions have had a major impact on mortality (e.g., Cain and Rotella 2001; Condran 1987; Condran and Cheney 1982; Condran and Crimmins-Gardner 1978; Crimmins and Condran 1983; Fulton 1980; Wells 1995), and evidence strongly supports the effect of health services on population mortality in the late 20th century (McKee 1999; Nolte and McKee 2004).

Clearly, much more than unequal access to health services, no matter how broadly construed, accounts for the disparities I have reported between whites and African Americans, but health services cannot simply be deemed insignificant. In contrast, more of the disparity between white Americans and Canadians seems to be attributable to access to health services, largely because the timing of the divergence coincides so closely with the creation of universal coverage in Canada, and because the difference is so much smaller. Other factors must also be important. Among the most frequently cited is income inequality. I noted earlier that income inequality is greater in the United States than in Canada, the result of the same differences in political culture and institutions that led to such different health care systems. It is thus difficult to disentangle the effects of income inequality and health services. But the evidence cited here regarding patterns of survival of cancer patients with similar incomes in the two countries, as well as differences in prenatal care among poor women in the two countries, suggests that the impact of health care is significant apart from the fact of income inequality.

Although the past has shaped the present, the future is not immutable. Unfortunately, the Canadian system of health care is more likely to become like the American system than the American system is to become like the Canadian, because parliamentary systems are better able to change direction than the American system is. A cohesive and tightly disciplined party structure, the very feature of the Canadian system that made dramatic change possible in the first place, may make a change of direction more likely. Nonetheless, in comparison with the system in the United States, the Canadian system is likely to be able to be changed more quickly and more radically, both to expand and to contract benefits. Indeed, the American system was designed to make radical changes in policy difficult. Regardless of the permanence or impermanence of the Canadian system of health care, however, the inability to create a similar universal health care system in the United States has had a measurable impact on the health of all Americans over the past 30 years.

REFERENCES

Anderson, G.M., J.P. Newhouse, and L.L. Roos. 1989. Hospital Care for Elderly Patients with Diseases of the Circulatory System: A Comparison of Hospital Use in the United States and Canada. *New England Journal of Medicine* 321:1443–8.

Bach, P.B., H.M. Pham, D. Schrag, R.C. Tate, and J.L. Hargraves. 2004. Primary Care Physicians Who Treat Blacks and Whites. *New England Journal of Medicine* 351:575–84.

Billings, J., G.M. Anderson, and L.S. Newman. 1996. Recent Findings on Preventable Hospitalizations. *Health Affairs* 15:239–50.

Blendon, R.J., L.H. Aiken, H.E. Freeman, and C.R. Corey. 1989. Access to Medical Care for Black and White Americans: A Matter of Continuing Concern. *Journal of the American Medical Association* 261:278–81.

Blumenthal, D., C. Vogeli, L. Alexander, and M. Pittman. 2004. *A Five-Nation Hospital Survey: Commonalities, Differences, and Discontinuities.* New York: Commonwealth Fund.

Cain, L.P., and E.J. Rotella. 2001. Death and Spending: Urban Mortality and Municipal Expenditure on Sanitation. *Annales de demographie historique* 1:139–54.

Carr, W., N. Szapiro, T. Heisler, and M.I. Krasner. 1989. Sentinel Health Events as Indicators of Unmet Needs. *Social Science and Medicine* 29:705–14.

Condran, G.A. 1987. Declining Mortality in the United States in the Late Nineteenth and Early Twentieth Centuries. *Annales de demographie historique* 1:119–41.

Condran, G.A., and R.A. Cheney. 1982. Mortality Trends in Philadelphia: Age- and Cause-Specific Death Rates 1870–1930. *Demography* 19:97–123.

Condran, G.A., and E. Crimmins-Gardner. 1978. Public Health Measures and Mortality in U.S. Cities in the Late 19th Century. *Human Ecology* 6:27–54.

Crimmins, E.M., and G.A. Condran. 1983. Mortality Variation in U.S. Cities in 1900. *Social Science History* 7:31–59.

Dunlop, S., P.C. Coyte, and W. McIsaac. 2000. Socio-Economic Status and the Utilization of Physicians' Services: Results from the Canadian National Population Health Survey. *Social Science and Medicine* 51:123–33.

Dunn, J.R., and M.V. Hayes. 2000. Social Inequality, Population Health, and Housing: A Study of Two Vancouver Neighborhoods. *Social Science and Medicine* 51:563–87.

Ewbank, D.C. 1994. History of Black Mortality and Health before 1940. In *Health Policies and Black Americans*, edited by D.P. Willis, 100–28. New Brunswick, N.J.: Transaction.

Farley, R., and W.R. Allen. 1987. *The Color Line and the Quality of Life in America.* New York: Russell Sage Foundation.

Fulton, J.P. 1980. Socioeconomic Forces as Determinants of Childhood Mortality Decline in Rhode Island, 1860–1970: Comparison with England and Wales. *Comparative Social Research* 3:287–308.

Gittelsohn, A.M., J. Halpern, and R.L. Sanchez. 1991. Income, Race, and Surgery in Maryland. *American Journal of Public Health* 81:1435–41.

Gutman, H.G. 1976. *Work, Culture, and Society in Industrializing America.* New York: Knopf.

Hacker, J.S. 1998. The Historical Logic of National Health Insurance: Structure and Sequence in the Development of British, Canadian and U.S. Medical Policy. *Studies in American Political Development* 12:57–130.

Haines, M.R., and R.H. Steckel, eds. 2000. *A Population History of North America.* Cambridge, England: Cambridge University Press.

Hornberger, J.C., A.M. Garver, and J.R. Jeffery. 1997. Mortality, Hospital Admissions, and Medical Costs of End-Stage Renal Disease in the United States and Manitoba, Canada. *Medical Care* 35:686–700.

Huntington, S.P. 1966. Political Modernization; America vs. Europe. *World Politics* 18:378–414.

Jones, B.A., E.A. Patterson, and L. Calvocoressi. 2003. Mammography Screening in African American Women: Evaluating the Research. *Cancer* 97 (suppl.):258–72.

Katz, S.J., W. Armstrong, and J.P. LoGerfo. 1994. The Adequacy of Prenatal Care and Incidence of Low Birthweight among the Poor in Washington State and British Columbia. *American Journal of Public Health* 84:986–91.

Kuderle, R.T., and T.R. Marmor. 1982. The Development of Welfare States in North America. In *The Development of Welfare States in Europe and America*, edited by P. Flora and A.J. Heidenheimer, 81–121. New Brunswick, N.J.: Transaction.

Lipset, S.M., and G. Marks. 2000. *It Didn't Happen Here: Why Socialism Failed in the United States.* New York: Norton.

Maioni, A. 1998. *Parting at the Crossroads.* Princeton, N.J.: Princeton University Press.

Marmor, T.R. 2000. Review of *Atlantic Crossings* and *Shifting the Color Line. Public Opinion Quarterly* 64:110–3.

McConnochie, K.M., M.J. Russo, J. McBride, P. Szilagy, A.M. Brooks, and K.J. Roghmann. 1999. Socioeconomic Variations in Asthma Hospitalization: Excess Utilization or Greater Need? *Pediatrics* 103:e75.

McDonald, A.D., J.C. McDonald, V. Salter, and P.E. Enterline. 1974. Effects of Quebec Medicare on Physician Consultation for Selected Symptoms. *New England Journal of Medicine* 291:649–52.

McKee, M. 1999. Does Health Care Save Lives? *Croatian Medical Journal* 40:123–8.

Munan, L., J. Vobecky, and A. Kelly. 1974. Population Health Care Practices: An Epidemiologic Study of the Immediate Effects of a Universal Health Insurance Plan. *International Journal of Health Services* 2:285–95.

Naylor, C.D. 1999. Health Care in Canada: Incrementalism under Fiscal Duress. *Health Affairs* 18:9–26.

Nolte, E., and M. McKee. 2004. *Does Healthcare Save Lives? Avoidable Mortality Revisited.* London: Nuffield Trust.

Reinhardt, U.E., P.S. Hussey, and G.F. Anderson. 2004. U.S. Health Care Spending in an International Context: Why Is U.S. Spending So High, and Can We Afford It? *Health Affairs* 23:10–25.

Rene, A.A., D.E. Daniels, W. Jones, Jr., and R. Jiles. 1995. Mortality Preventable by Medical Interventions: Ethnic and Regional Differences in Texas. *Journal of the National Medical Association* 87:820–5.

Roos, L.L., E.S. Fisher, S.M. Sharp, J.P. Newhouse, G. Anderson, and T.A. Bubolz. 1990. Postsurgical Mortality in Manitoba and New England. *Journal of the American Medical Association* 263:2453–8.

Schwartz, E., V.Y. Kofie, M. Rivo, and R.V. Tuckson. 1990. Black/White Comparisons of Deaths Preventable by Medical Intervention: United States and the District of Columbia 1980–1986. *International Journal of Epidemiology* 19:591–8.

Siemiatycki, J., L. Richardson, and I.B. Pless. 1980. Equality in Medical Care under National Health Insurance in Montreal. *New England Journal of Medicine* 303;10–5.

Smith, D.B. 1998. Addressing Racial Inequality in Health: Civil Rights Monitoring and Report Cards. *Journal of Health Politics, Policy and Law* 23:75–105.

Sombart, W. 1906. *Why Is There No Socialism in the United States?* London: Macmillan.

Tabar, L., M.-F. Yen, B. Vitak, H.-H.T. Chen, R.A. Smith, and S.W. Duffy. 2003. Mammography Service Screening and Mortality in Breast Cancer Patients: 20-Year Follow-up before and after Introduction of Screening. *Lancet* 361:1405–10.

Tu, J.V., C.L. Pashos, C.D. Naylor, E. Chen, S.-L. Normand, J.P. Newhouse, and B.J. McNeil. 1997. Use of Cardiac Procedures and Outcomes in Elderly Patients with Myocardial Infarction in the United States and Canada. *New England Journal of Medicine* 336:1500–5.

Virnig, B.A., N. Lurie, Z. Huang, D. Musgrave, A.M. McBean, and B. Dowd. 2002. Racial Variations in Quality of Care among Medicare+Choice Enrollees. *Health Affairs* 21:224–30.

Wells, R.V. 1995. The Mortality Transition in Schenectady, New York, 1880–1930. *Social Science History* 19:399–423.

Wenneker, M.B., and A.M. Epstein. 1989. Racial Inequalities in the Use of Procedures for Patients with Ischemic Heart Disease in Massachusetts. *Journal of the American Medical Association* 261:253–7.

Wilkins, R., J.-M. Berthelot, and E. Ng. 2002. *Trends in Mortality by Neighbourhood Income in Urban Canada from 1971 to 1996.* Suppl. to *Health Reports,* vol. 13. Ottawa: Statistics Canada.

Wolfson, M. 2000. Income Inequality in Canada and the United States. *The Daily,* Statistics Canada. Available at http://www.statcan.ca/Daily/English/000728/d000728a.htm (accessed July 28, 2004).

Wolfson, M., and B. Murphy. 2000. Income Inequality in North America; Does the 49th Parallel Still Matter? *Canadian Economic Observer,* August, 1–24.

Wong, M.D., M.P. Shapiro, W.J. Boscardin, and S.L. Etmer. 2002. Contribution of Major Diseases to Disparities in Mortality. *New England Journal of Medicine* 347:1585–92.

Wood, E., A.M. Sallar, M.T. Schechter, and R.S. Hogg. 1999. Social Inequalities in Male Mortality Amenable to Medical Intervention in British Columbia. *Social Science and Medicine* 48:1751–8.

Woolhandler, S., D.U. Himmelstein, R. Silber, M. Bader, M. Harnly, and A.A. Jones. 1985. Medical Care and Mortality: Racial Differences in Preventable Deaths. *International Journal of Health Services* 15:1–22.

World Bank. 2003. *World Development Indicators 2002,* CD-ROM. Washington, D.C.

Zuvekas, S.H., and G.S. Taliaferro. 2003. Pathways to Access: Health Insurance, the Health Care Delivery System, and Racial/Ethnic Disparities, 1996–1999. *Health Affairs* 22:139–53.

The Gender Gap:
New Challenges in Women's Health

Gloria E. Sarto, MD, PhD

At the turn of the 20th century, life expectancy for women was 47 years. Women commonly died in childbirth from blood loss and infection. The only treatment for pelvic inflammatory disease was bed rest and warm douches. Medical research was a laissez-faire proposition. Drug companies sold products with outrageous claims for efficacy, but with no guarantee of safety. Worthless, impure, and dangerous patent medicines and foods were on the market.

Today, overall life expectancy is 76 years. Many factors brought about this improved outcome, but women's health research, education, and health policy played major roles. In the early 1900s, women organized to support the original Food and Drug Act, enacted in 1906, creating the first government regulatory agency. This act provided for monitoring drugs for strength and purity, but with no requirements for safety testing. It wasn't until 1938, when a revised federal Food, Drug, and Cosmetic Act was passed, that the industry was required to prove drug safety before market release. Further amendments in 1962 put into place a process that required testing in animals before testing in humans, and manufacturers had to demonstrate not only safety but efficacy. The 1962 Food, Drug, and Cosmetic Act required the Food and Drug Administration (FDA) to collect reports of adverse reactions, to require drug advertising to include risks as well as benefits, and to inform participants if a drug was investigational and obtain their consent.

Research and the availability of antibiotics—initially, sulfa in the 1930s, and then penicillin in the 1940s—played a major role in improving the health of women. Blood transfusions and immunizations were instrumental in reducing maternal and infant mortality. Medical and scientific research in the 1940s and 1950s brought new understanding to disease processes and new therapies. Over the ensuing years, the focus of the research was primarily pregnancy and contraception, and as a result, great strides were made in making pregnancy safe. But "women's health" became narrowly defined as reproductive health.

In 1977, after the tragedies caused by the use of thalidomide and DES in pregnant women, the FDA issued new guidelines, which recommended against including women of childbearing potential in the early phases of drug testing, except in life-threatening illnesses. Although the intent was to protect women, an unintended consequence was that women were excluded from research and, thus, from its substantial benefits. At this same time, women were seeking more knowledge about their bodies and greater involvement in their own health care. The Boston Women's Health Collective's *Our Bodies, Ourselves* was published, and women's studies courses were developed at universities. With their changing role in society, women became increasingly critical of their health care and health care providers. By 1985 the Assistant Secretary for Health established a Public Health Task Force on Women's Health Issues.

In 1986, the Task Force released a report stating that "the historical lack of research focus on women's health concerns has compromised the quality of health information available to women, as well as the health care they receive." It went on to urge, "biomedical and behavioral research be expanded to ensure emphasis on conditions and diseases unique to, or more prevalent in, women in all age groups." Guidelines were issued by the National Institutes of Health (NIH) that urged applicants for research funding to include women in clinical research.

In 1991, the NIH Office of Research on Women's Health called for investigation of cardiovascular disorders, osteoporosis, domestic violence, and the psychosocial biological aspects of women's health, in addition to such traditional areas as reproductive health, sexually transmitted diseases, and endometriosis.

The Women's Health Initiative, one of the largest U.S. prevention studies, which focuses on the major causes of death, disability, and frailty in postmenopausal women, was one result. Another study, by the Agency for Health Care Research and Quality, examined hysterectomy and its contingent morbidity and studied alternatives to hysterectomy for treatment of certain disorders. The National Institute on Aging initiated the Study of Woman Across the Nation (SWAN), to characterize menopause—hormonally and behaviorally—in diverse populations of women.

The FDA issued guidelines in 1993 calling for the study of both women and men in the evaluation of medicines. These guidelines allowed the restriction of women of childbearing potential to be lifted and for women to be included in early phase clinical trials to allow detection of clinically significant gender/sex differences.

GENDER DIFFERENCES IN HEALTH

Research has shown that gender differences in health and disease are significant. Coronary heart disease presents in women 10 to 15 years later than it does in men. Men are more likely to present with myocardial infarction as a manifestation of the disease, but women are more likely to die within 1 year of having an initial recognized myocardial infarction. Women are more likely to have co-morbidities such as congestive heart failure, hypertension, and diabetes. Women have fewer diagnostic procedures than men and are less likely to be given effective interventions such as aspirin, [beta]-blockers, and thrombolytic agents (Table 2.4.1).

Blood pressure is higher in men than in women of comparable ages until menopause. Then blood pressure in women increases to levels higher than those in men. Women live significantly longer after colon cancer resection than men with comparable disease. Women smokers are more likely to develop lung cancer than men, taking into account baseline exposure, body weight, and body mass index. Women are 2.7 times more likely to develop autoimmune diseases, including multiple sclerosis, rheumatoid arthritis, and lupus.

TABLE 2.4.1   Women's Health: New Challenges

Key Issues

- Differences in health and disease exist between males and females that cannot be attributed to hormones.
- Understanding the basic biology for these differences will improve diagnosis and treatment of those disorders that affect women differently than men.
- Disparities in health status and health outcomes exist among diverse populations of women with poorer health among minority women, with few exceptions, across a range of illnesses.
- Recent research indicates that along with level of education, individual behavior, access to care, environmental. factors, income and possession of insurance, differences in the quality of health care is a contributing factor in disparities in health status and health outcomes.
- Women are living longer but often with decreased function.
- Factors such as gender, education, economic status, race, and ethnicity all are predictors of health status, but quality of life, as one grows older, is more than absence of disease, and aging successfully requires more than being healthy.

Men and women respond differently to medications. Women are at higher risk for adverse reactions to drugs as diverse as antihistamines and antibiotics. Antiarrhythmic drugs can induce a potentially lethal cardiac rhythm, torsades de pointe. Hypokalemia, hypomagnesemia, bradycardia, and QT interval prolongation that may be affected by the menstrual cycle increase susceptibility to this event.

Women generally perform articulatory tasks and fine motor tasks more quickly than males. Men demonstrate an advantage in visual–spatial ability. Certain classes of opioid analgesics are more effective in women than men.

The US Institute of Medicine (IOM) issued a report, *Exploring the Biological Contributions to Human Health: Does Sex Matter?* The committee concluded that sex does matter. It found that differences in the basic biochemistries of males and females on a cellular level can affect health, and that these exist across the life span. It also reported that differences in metabolism and susceptibility to pharmacologic agents exist. Additionally, there are behavioral and cognitive differences between males and females.

CLOSING THE GAPS

In 1999, of the nearly 140 million women living in the United States, women of racial and ethnic minorities comprised 39.6 million (28.3%) including African-American (12.5%); Hispanic (11.2%); Asian American/Pacific Islander (3.8%); and American Indian/Alaskan Native (0.7%). Disparities in health status and health outcomes, with poorer health among minority populations (with few exceptions), exist across a range of illnesses.

Cardiovascular disease is the leading cause of death for African-American, Hispanic, American Indian/Alaskan Native, and white women and is the second leading cause for Asian

American women. African-American women have the highest mortality rate from heart disease (147.6 per 100,000). In contrast, the mortality rate from heart disease for white, non-Hispanic women is 90.4 per 100,000; for Hispanic women, 64.7; for American Indian/Alaskan Native women, 92.8; and for Asian American/Pacific Islander, 49.3. Black women are less likely than other women to receive life-saving therapies for heart attacks. They are least likely to receive reperfusion therapy (44%), followed by black men (50%), white women (56%), and white men (59%). Black women are less likely than others to be referred for cardiac catheterization.

Cancer is the second leading cause of death for women of color, except for Asian American/Pacific Islander women, for whom it is the leading cause of death. Lung cancer, the leading cause of cancer deaths for women, is on the rise. For women of color, the rate is highest among American Indian/Alaskan Native women, 58 deaths per 100,000, and the lowest among Asian American/Pacific Islander women, 11.5 and 8.9, respectively. African-American women have the highest rate of death from breast cancer, 31 per 100,000, even though the incidence of breast cancer among African-American women is lower than that of white women.

Diabetes is more common among women of color than among Caucasian women. In 1997, diabetes was the fourth leading cause of death for African-American, American Indian/Alaskan Native, and Hispanic women. It is most common among American Indian/Alaskan Native women; 41% of older women in this population have diabetes. Among some subgroups of this population, the incidence is even higher. Additionally, the adverse outcomes associated with diabetes among some minorities are far worse than that of others. When compared with white women with diabetes (15%), African-American women with diabetes (25%) are more likely to develop end-stage renal disease, be blinded, have limbs amputated, and die of their disease.

Maternal mortality and infant mortality are added examples of marked disparities in health outcomes. Maternal mortality and infant mortality among African-American women are 4 and 2.5 times greater, respectively, than the national average. African-American women have the highest rate of low birthweight (2,500 g) births than any other racial or ethnic group.

The death rate due to cerebrovascular disease—primarily strokes—among black women is nearly twice that of all other women. HIV/AIDS, other sexually transmitted diseases, and co-morbidities likewise disproportionately affect women of color.

The IOM's report *Unequal Treatment: Confronting Racial and Ethnic Disparities in Health Care* concluded that "racial and ethnic minorities tend to receive a lower quality and intensity of health care than non-minorities, even when access-related factors, such as patients' insurance status and income is controlled." The committee recommended legal, regulatory, and policy changes; health systems interventions; programs to enhance patient education and empowerment; integration of cross-cultural studies into the education of health care professionals; and improved data collation.

AN AGING POPULATION

In the early 1900s, roughly one of every 25 persons was over age 65. By 1980, the ratio was one in eight. In the early 2000s, it will be one in every five. Today, 34 million Americans are 65 or older. Three out of five are women. By age 85, women outnumber men two to one.

Fifty percent of female Medicare beneficiaries have incomes of less than $10,000. Forty-two percent have less than 12 years of education. Some 24% report fair or poor health; 29% have three or more chronic conditions.

Of the 34.5 million Medicare beneficiaries over age 65, 19.4 million (56%) are women, and among those 85 and older, roughly 70% are women. The mean annual income for women 65 years and older in 1999 was $15,615; for men it was $29,171. The proportion of female Medicare beneficiaries, aged 65–84 years, with incomes below $10,000 was 26%, and over age 85, it was 44%, while in men, the numbers were 14% and 26%, respectively. Twenty-seven percent of women on Medicare have no prescription drug coverage and women on Medicare spend a greater portion of their incomes on health care than men (22% vs 17%, respectively). Women without drug coverage fill seven fewer prescriptions, on average, than do women with coverage, placing them at increased risk for complications of their health problems.

Given their longer lifespan, women are more likely than men to have multiple health problems. Although women live, on average, 7 more years than men, they live more of those years while functionally disabled. Major contributors are stroke, depression, hip fracture, osteoarthritis, and heart disease. Of the 10.6 million Medicare beneficiaries with long-term care needs (defined as one or more limitations in activities of daily living), 61% are women. Of the 1.5 million nursing home residents aged 65 and older, 75% are women, and, of the 2.4 million home healthcare users, 67% are women.

Poor health is not a foregone consequence of aging, yet, despite recognition of the importance of preventive care and healthy habits in improving quality of life in later years, women and their physicians miss opportunities to promote good health. Preventive health-care rates have changed very little over the past 10 years. Additionally, disparities exist in screening rates across income and education levels. Uninsured women are less likely to visit a physician on a regular basis and are less likely to have preventive care screening procedures.

The majority of women do not receive counseling from their physicians on a number of health issues. Although heart disease is the leading cause of death for women, only 34% of women report that their physicians discuss heart health with them. Fewer than 50% report that their doctors discuss the importance of exercise, diet and weight, and calcium intake. Less than a third reported discussions about smoking and drugs and alcohol. Only 8% report conversations about safety or violence in their homes. Although colon cancer is the third leading cause of cancer deaths for women, of women 50 years and older, only about half reported ever receiving sigmoidoscopy. Overweight and obesity elevate the risks of illness from heart disease, diabetes, hypertension, osteoarthritis, and other musculoskeletal problems. Regular exercise lessens these risks. In 2000, 39% of women reported no non-work-related physical activity. Among the elderly, musculoskeletal strength and exercise are important in preventing falls, yet, among non-institutionalized women over 75, 50% report no physical activity during leisure time.

Factors such as gender, education, economic status, race, and ethnicity all are predictors of health status, but quality of life as one grows older is more than the absence of disease, and aging successfully requires more than being healthy. Research is showing that possessing self-respect, having more control over one's life, enjoying quality connections with others, having purpose in life, and possessing a certain degree of resilience are key ingredients to aging successfully. Some of these are not acquired solely by one's own accord, nor can they be applied universally, but there is evidence that they are important ingredients for successful aging. Supportive family and friends, a life without violence, recognizable achievements, and appreciation for who one is and what one does are important ingredients.

An individual has to have financial security to have autonomy. Without this, one is dependent on family members. Purpose in life, a critical feature of wellness, requires a realization of one's potential and the ability to see life as meaningful. Possessing a certain amount of resilience gives one the ability to spring back from adversity, which occurs so commonly among older individuals, and transforms adversity into an opportunity to learn. Although not entirely clear, research suggests there may be a link between social well-being, happiness, and better function, and reduced mortality. Understanding what constitutes successful aging and how it is achieved is a new area for research.

CONCLUSION

Much of the improvement in women's health during the 1900s can be attributed to research, education, and policy changes in reproductive health. While there is a need for continued research and improvement in this area, new challenges must be addressed. These include the widespread disorders that affect women differently from men; the relatively poor health of minority women; and the specific needs of a growing population of elderly women.

Research and education, and where warranted, policy changes, must be directed toward existing, as well as newly emerging, health concerns, if there is to be continued improvement in the health of women.

SUGGESTED READINGS

Department of Health and Human Services, Centers for Disease Control and Prevention. National Center for Health Statistics. *Chartbook on Trends in the Health of Americans: Health, United States, 2002.*

Collins KS, Schoen C, Joseph S, Duchon L, Simantov E, Yellowitz M. *Health Concerns Across a Woman's Lifespan: The Commonwealth Fund 1998 Survey of Women's Health.* The Commonwealth Fund, May 1999.

Guralnik JM, Fried LP, Simonsick EM, Kasper JD, Lafferty ME (eds): *The Women's Health and Aging Study: Health and Social Characteristics of Older Women with Disability.* Bethesda, MD, National Institutes on Aging, 1995, 95-4009.

Misra D (ed): *Women's Health Data Book: A Profile of Women's Health in the United States.* 3rd edition. Washington, DC, Jacobs Institute of Women's Health and the Henry J. Kaiser Family Foundation, 2001.

Smedley BD, Stith AY, Nelson AR (eds): *Unequal Treatment: Confronting Racial and Ethnic Disparities in Health Care.* Washington DC, Institute of Medicine, National Academy Press, 2002.

Wizeman TM, Pardue ML (eds): *Exploring the Biological Contributions to Human Health: Does Sex Matter?* Washington DC, Institute of Medicine, National Academy Press, 2001.

Child Poverty in Rich Countries, 2005

United Nations International Children's Emergency Fund

INTRODUCTION

This 2005 review of child poverty in rich countries, from the UNICEF *Innocenti Research Centre*, finds that the proportion of children living in poverty in the developed world has risen in 17 out of the 24 OECD nations for which data are available. No matter which of the commonly-used poverty measures is applied, the situation of children is seen to have deteriorated over the last decade.

UNICEF believes that reversing this trend is a priority for the OECD countries. Allowing the kind of poverty that denies a child the opportunities that most children consider normal is a breach of the United Nations *Convention on the Rights of the Child* to which almost all OECD countries are committed. Reducing child poverty is also a measure of progress towards social cohesion, equality of opportunity, and investment in both today's children and tomorrow's world.

LEAGUE TABLE

At the top of the new child poverty league (Figure 2.5.1) are Denmark and Finland where the proportion of children in poverty is now less than 3 percent At the bottom are the United States and Mexico where child poverty rates are higher than 20 percent.

Such variation in itself demonstrates a central point of this report: there is nothing inevitable or immutable about child poverty levels; they reflect different national policies interacting with social changes and market forces. Significant variation therefore equals significant scope for improvement.

It is apparent from Figure 2.5.1 that most progress has been made in the Nordic countries, all four of which have child poverty rates below 5 percent. There follows a broad band of middle-ranking nations with rates between 5 and 15 percent, including all of the most populous European countries except Italy (which has the highest child poverty rate in Europe).

Below this group are to be found five countries—the United Kingdom, Portugal, Ireland, New Zealand, and Italy—all with exceptionally high rates of child poverty (15 percent to 17 percent).

Two other striking features of the rankings are that all six non-European nations—Australia, Canada, Japan, Mexico, New Zealand, and the United States—are to be found in the bottom half of the table. It may also be significant that the five countries with the lowest

Adapted from: United Nations International Children's Emergency Fund. (2005). *UNICEF Child Poverty in Rich Countries, 2005*. Florence, Italy: Innocenti Research Centre.

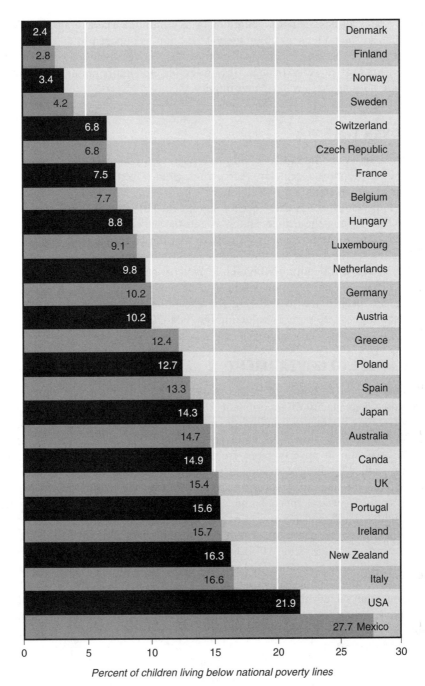

Percent of children living below national poverty lines

FIGURE 2.5.1   The Child Poverty League. The bars show the percentage of children living in 'relative' poverty, defined as households with income below 50 percent of the national median income.

child poverty rates all have small populations (4 to 9 million). The average population size for the top half of the table is approximately 16 million as opposed to 60 million for those in the lower half of the table. That small nations may have advantages in solidarity and cohesiveness, or that poverty may be less tolerable and more manageable in smaller economies, are notions that await further inquiry.

CHANGE OVER TIME

Although it is widely assumed that child poverty in rich countries is on a steady downward track. Over the most recent ten-year period, child poverty has risen in 17 of the 24 OECD countries for which data are available.

In only four countries has there been a significant fall. Three of those four—Australia, the United Kingdom and the United States—began the period with child poverty rates that offered much scope for improvement. In only one of the countries with low child poverty at the beginning of the period has the rate been further reduced: Norway therefore takes the accolade as the OECD nation where child poverty can be described as 'very low and continuing to fall'. Special mention might also be made of the United Kingdom where a commitment has been made to reducing the exceptionally high child poverty rate and where the first target—a 25 percent reduction by 2004–2005—is likely to have been met.

THE CHALLENGE TO GOVERNMENT

While acknowledging the power of labour market conditions and social changes, this report emphasises the capacity of governments to bring downward pressure on child poverty rates. It shows, for example, that higher government spending on family and social benefits is clearly associated with lower child poverty rates (Figure 2.5.2). But it also shows considerable variation in poverty rates—from 3 percent to 15 percent—even in countries with broadly similar levels of government spending. This suggests that poverty rates depend not only on the level of government support but on the manner of its dispensation; many OECD countries would appear to have the potential to reduce child poverty below 10 percent without a significant increase in overall spending.

Poverty levels are the result of a complex and sometimes difficult-to-predict interplay between government policy, family efforts, labour market conditions, and the wider forces of social change. It is therefore essential to have an up-to-date and evidence-based awareness of how government policy plays out in the real world. This is mostly a matter of detailed national analysis, but this report explores one means of making more visible the real impact of government tax and transfer policies on children in low-income families, and warns that in some countries the net result of current policies may be to support early retirement over investing in children.

Most fundamentally, the report urges all OECD governments to establish credible targets and timetables for the progressive reduction of child poverty. For most of those countries, a realistic target would be to bring child poverty rates below 10 percent. For the six nations that have already achieved this, the next aim might be to emulate the Nordic countries in bringing child poverty below 5 percent.

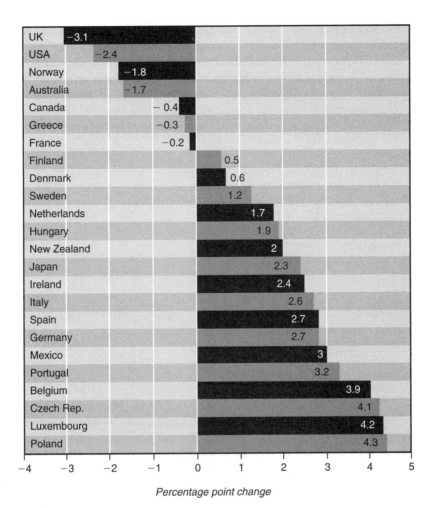

FIGURE 2.5.2   Changes in child poverty rates during the 1990s. The bars show the rise or fall in child poverty rates in each country during the 1990s.

THE DETERMINANTS OF POVERTY

This report concludes that a majority of OECD nations appear to be losing ground against child poverty, both in relation to annually-updated median incomes and in relation to the median incomes prevailing in the early 1990s.

What is driving child poverty rates upwards in so many of the world's wealthiest nations? And why are some OECD nations doing a much better job than others in protecting children at risk of poverty?

Each country can offer a different context for changes in its child poverty rate. But in all countries poverty levels are determined by some combination of the same three forces—social trends, labour market conditions, and government policies. These are the shifting tectonic plates that support the material well-being of children, and it is to their interplay that we must look for answers.

Social and family changes, first of all, are influencing poverty rates in all countries. The average age of parents is slowly rising, as in the average educational level. Meanwhile the average number of children per family is tending to fall. All of these forces tend to increase the economic resources available to children. On the other hand the incidence of single parenthood has risen in many countries—increasing the risk of child poverty.

CHAPTER 3

Access to Care

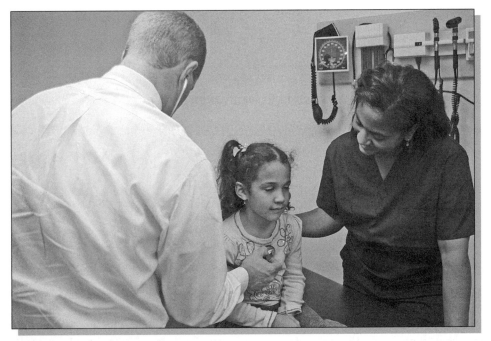

Doctor and nurse with child patient

Income, Earnings, and Poverty Data from the 2005 American Community Survey

U.S. Department of Commerce
Carlos M. Gutierrez,
Secretary

David A. Sampson,
Deputy Secretary

Economics and Statistics Administration
Vacant,
Under Secretary for Economic Affairs

U.S. CENSUS BUREAU
Charles Louis Kincannon,
Director

INTRODUCTION

This report looks at data on income, earnings, and poverty based on the 2005 American Community Survey (ACS), which provides a measure of the country's economic well-being. This report uses the unique ability of the ACS to produce estimates of detailed socioeconomic characteristics for the United States, states, and lower levels of geography.

The U.S. Census Bureau also reports income and poverty data based on the Annual Social and Economic Supplement (ASEC) to the Current Population Survey (CPS).

This report has three main sections: household income, earnings of men and women, and poverty. The income and poverty estimates in this report are based solely on money income received (exclusive of certain money receipts such as capital gains) before payments are made for items such as personal income taxes, social security, union dues, and Medicare deductions. Money income does not include the value of noncash benefits such as food stamps; health benefits; subsidized housing; payments by employers for retirement programs, medical, and educational expenses; and goods produced and consumed on the farm.

Adapted from: U.S. Census Bureau. 2006. *Income, Earnings, and Poverty Data from the 2005 American Community Survey,* ACS-02. Washington, DC: U.S. Government Printing Office.

MEDIAN HOUSEHOLD INCOME FOR THE UNITED STATES AND STATES

The ACS measured the median household income in the United States in 2005 at $46,242. Household income estimates varied from state to state, ranging from a median of $61,672 for New Jersey to $32,938 for Mississippi. New Jersey, Maryland, Connecticut, Hawaii, Massachusetts, and New Hampshire had median incomes above $55,000, while Mississippi, West Virginia, Arkansas, Louisiana, and Alabama had median incomes below $37,500.

Figure 3.1.1 displays the relationship of state median household incomes to the median for the United States. Median incomes in 19 states were above the U.S. median, while in 28 states the median incomes were below it.

The states in the Northeast tended to have median income above the U.S. median. Six of the nine Northeast states—Connecticut, Massachusetts, New Hampshire, New Jersey, New York, and Rhode Island—had median household incomes above the U.S. median, while Maine and Pennsylvania fell below the U.S. median.

Similarly, states in the West were likely to be above the U.S. median, with 7 of the 13 having household incomes above the median. They were Alaska, California, Colorado,

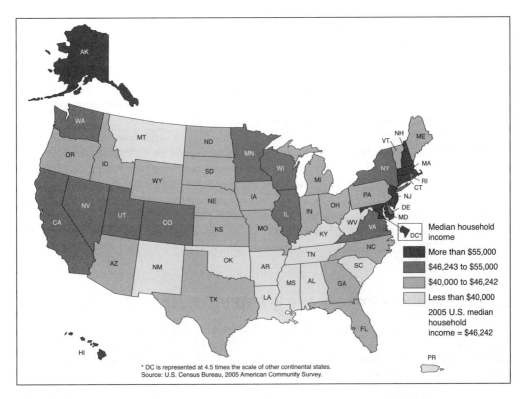

FIGURE 3.1.1   Median Household Income in the Past 12 Months by State: 2005 (In 2005 inflation-adjusted dollars)

Source: U.S. Census Bureau, 2005 American Community Survey

Hawaii, Nevada, Utah, and Washington. Those below the U.S. median in the West region were Arizona, Idaho, Montana, New Mexico, and Oregon.

The majority of states in the Midwest (8 out of 12) and the South (13 out of 17) had median incomes that were below the U.S. median. Illinois, Minnesota, and Wisconsin in the Midwest, and Delaware, Maryland, and Virginia in the South had incomes above the national median.

Incomes were generally higher on the East and the West Coasts than they were in the rest of the country. Of the five states bordering the Pacific Ocean—Alaska, California, Hawaii, Oregon, and Washington—only Oregon had a median income that was lower than the U.S. median. Of the 14 states bordering the Atlantic Ocean, 9 had medians above the U.S. median.

MEN'S AND WOMEN'S EARNINGS BY STATE

Some of the states that had high median household incomes, such as New Jersey, Connecticut, Massachusetts, and Maryland, also had median earnings for men that were above $50,000. No state had median earnings for women above $50,000, but in the District of Columbia, Maryland, and Connecticut, median earnings for women were significantly above $40,000.

For comparison to state and lower-level geographies, the ACS measured the median earnings of men in the United States in 2005 at $41,965, while women had median earnings of $32,168, or 76.7 percent of men's earnings. In each of the 50 states and the District of Columbia, women's median earnings were less than men's median earnings. The District of Columbia was the area with the highest ratio between men's and women's earnings (91.4 percent). One possible explanation for this high ratio is that the pay of federal workers is closer by gender, and the District of Columbia has a large federal workforce.

The South and the West regions have states in which women's earnings as a percentage of men's earnings were relatively high, as well as states in which the percentage was relatively low. In the South, three states and the District of Columbia had ratios significantly higher than the national ratio, as did two states in the West. There were no states in the Midwest and only one state in the Northeast with ratios significantly higher than the national ratio. As a result, women's earnings were closer to men's in more states in the South and the West than in the Northeast and the Midwest.

MEDIAN EARNINGS BY RACE AND HISPANIC ORIGIN

Asian men had the highest median earnings ($48,693) in 2005 of any single-race group. Non-Hispanic White men were the second highest ($46,807), followed by Native Hawaiian and Other Pacific Islander men ($35,426), Black men ($34,433), and American Indian and Alaska Native men ($33,520). Each of these race groups had higher median earnings than Hispanic men ($27,380). The lowest median earnings for men among the race groups were for those reported as Some Other Race ($27,041).

The pattern observed for women by race was similar to that of the men. Asian women ($37,792) had the highest median earnings, followed by non-Hispanic White women

($34,190). Next were Native Hawaiian and Other Pacific Islander women ($30,041) and Black women ($29,588). They were followed by American Indian and Alaska Native women ($27,977). Hispanic women ($24,451) earned less than the previous race groups, and women of Some Other Race ($23,678) had the lowest median earnings of any race group.

For the race and Hispanic groups, men had higher earnings than women. The race group with the lowest female-to-male ratio was non-Hispanic Whites, where women's earnings were 73.0 percent of men's earnings. The median earnings of women were larger than 85 percent of men's for the Some Other Race group and Hispanics.

MEDIAN EARNINGS BY INDUSTRY AND OCCUPATION

In each of the 20 industry sectors, men earned more than women. The sectors where the ratios between women's and men's earnings were the lowest were finance and insurance, where women earned 55.4 percent of men; management of companies and enterprises (55.9 percent); and professional, scientific, and technical services (61.6 percent).

When women and men were in the same occupational group, men had higher median earnings than women. Community and social services occupations was the only group where women's earnings as a percentage of men's earnings were higher than 90 percent. In contrast, women's earnings as a percentage of men's earnings were 70 percent or less for legal occupations, sales and related occupations, health care practitioner and technical occupations, and production occupations. Legal occupations had the lowest percentage of women's earnings when compared to that of men's earnings (49.5 percent).

Men earned the most in the legal occupations ($102,272) and the least in the food preparation and serving related occupations ($21,350). Women who worked in computer and mathematical occupations had the highest median earnings among women ($58,906). The occupational groups with the lowest median earnings for women were farming, fishing, and forestry occupations ($16,739) and food preparation and serving related occupations ($17,075).

MEDIAN EARNINGS BY EDUCATIONAL ATTAINMENT

A person's level of education is considered to be a predictor of earnings—the more education, the greater the potential earnings. The median earnings of men who were not high school graduates were $22,138. This increased to $31,683 for male high school graduates and to $39,601 for men with some college or an associate's degree. Men who completed college and received a bachelor's degree earned a median of $53,693. The highest median earnings, $71,918, were for men with a graduate or a professional degree.

Women who did not complete high school earned $13,076 in 2005, while graduating from high school increased women's earnings to $20,179. Attending but not completing college or receiving an associate's degree resulted in median earnings of $25,736, while women who completed a bachelor's degree had median earnings of $36,250. As with men, women who received a graduate or professional degree earned the most ($47,319).

While both men and women showed increased earnings with increased levels of education, at each level of education, men earned more than women. The ratio of female-to-male earnings was lowest for those with less than a high school education, where women earned 59.1 percent of men. The ratio increased as educational level increased, up to the completion of college. For men and women with a high school education, women earned 63.7 percent of what men earned, while they earned 65.0 percent when both had some college or an associate's degree. The ratio increased further when both men and women completed college. At that educational level, women earned 67.5 percent of what men earned. Additional education beyond a bachelor's degree decreased the earnings ratio. Women earned 65.8 percent of men's earnings when both had a graduate or a professional degree.

POVERTY

Poverty Status for the United States and States

According to the 2005 ACS data, about 38.2 million people, or 13.3 percent of the U.S. population, had income below the poverty threshold in the last 12 months (Figure 3.1.2).

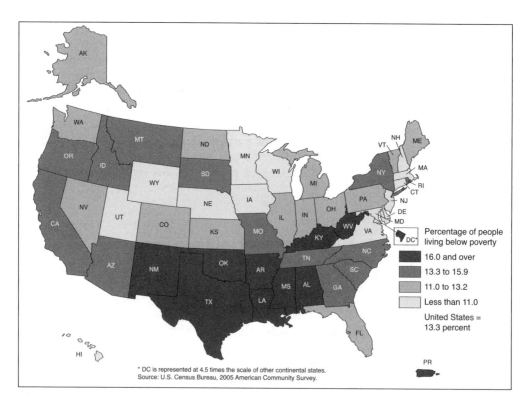

FIGURE 3.1.2   Percentage of People in Poverty in the Past 12 Months by State: 2005

Source: U.S. Census Bureau, 2005 American Community Survey

The data show differences in the level of poverty among states, counties, and places. Comparing poverty rates among the 50 states and the District of Columbia revealed variations ranging from a low of 7.5 percent in New Hampshire to a high of 21.3 percent in Mississippi. The estimated poverty rate for New Hampshire is not statistically different from that of Maryland, at 8.2 percent. The poverty rate for the District of Columbia was among the highest, at 19.0 percent, which is not statistically different from the rates of Louisiana, New Mexico, West Virginia, and Texas.

Poverty Status for Counties and Places

This section discusses poverty rates for counties and places with populations of 65,000 or more. This report categorizes these counties and places into two groups based on their population size—smaller areas are those with populations of 65,000 to less than 250,000, and larger areas are those with populations of 250,000 or more.

Among the counties with a population of 250,000 or more, Cameron County and Hidalgo County in Texas had the highest proportion of people with income below the poverty level in the past 12 months, at about 41 percent. Many of the counties with low poverty rates were not statistically different from each other. For example, Loudoun County, VA; Morris and Somerset Counties, NJ; Howard County, MD; and Waukesha County, WI, had poverty rates less than 5 percent. Maryland and Missouri both had counties or county equivalents on the high and low lists. The poverty rate for the large counties in Maryland ranged from a low of 3.4 percent in Howard County to a high of 22.6 percent in Baltimore city, while in Missouri, the poverty rate ranged from a low of 4.4 percent in St. Charles County to a high of 25.4 percent in St. Louis city.

The places with the highest proportions of people in poverty were Cleveland city, OH (32.4 percent), and Detroit city, MI (31.4), while the places with the lowest percentage in poverty were Plano city, TX (6.3 percent), and Virginia Beach city, VA (7.4 percent). The poverty rate for large cities in Texas ranged from 6.3 percent in Plano city to 27.2 percent in El Paso city.

As measured in the ACS, about 17.7 percent of the U.S. population had income below 125 percent of the poverty threshold. This proportion comprises about 5.7 percent of people with income below 50 percent of the poverty threshold, about 7.6 percent of people with income at or above 50 percent and less than 100 percent, and about 4.4 percent with income at or above the threshold but lower than 125 percent of the threshold.

Comparing the proportions of people with an income-to-poverty ratio under 50 percent among the states, New Hampshire (3.3 percent) had the lowest proportion, while the District of Columbia (10.8 percent) had the highest proportion.

About 50 million people, or 1 in 6, had an income-to-poverty ratio less than 125 percent, placing them in or near poverty. New Hampshire (10.0 percent) and Connecticut (10.9 percent) had the lowest proportions, while Mississippi (27.6 percent) had the highest proportion of people living at or near poverty. In addition, ten other states and the District of Columbia had over 20 percent of people with incomes that placed them at or near poverty.

Medicaid and the Uninsured
Who Are the Uninsured?
A Consistent Profile Across National Surveys

Kaiser Commission on Medicaid and the Uninsured

The growing number of uninsured Americans is one of the biggest and most debated problems we face in our health care system. The actual count of the number of uninsured gets considerable policy use and media interest—enough attention that when national estimates of the uninsured differ, it raises doubts about our ability to design solutions or gauge their impact.

This issue brief begins with a comparison of the total number of uninsured from three major national surveys, demonstrating that these estimates are actually more consistent than what is often perceived. In addition, and perhaps even more important to the public debate, the analysis shows that the surveys' profiles of the uninsured are also consistent. In other words, who the uninsured are does not vary much across national surveys.

Across all three surveys, more than half of the uninsured are in low-income families and about half are ethnic or racial minorities. The majority of uninsured adults are working, but their lack of education makes it more difficult for them to get jobs that offer employer-sponsored coverage.

ESTIMATES OF THE UNINSURED

Several surveys are able to provide national health insurance coverage estimates, including how many are uninsured. Since 1980 the Census Bureau's Current Population Survey (CPS) has produced annual estimates of Americans' health coverage, as part of its purpose to broadly monitor socioeconomic trends. In addition, both the Medical Expenditure Panel Survey (MEPS—conducted by the Agency for Healthcare Research and Quality) and the National Health Interview Survey (NHIS—from the National Center for Health Statistics) also provide regular and timely estimates of health insurance coverage. Different estimates of the number of uninsured released each year are not exactly the same and that has at times created questions about how large the problem really is.

Health insurance estimates from national surveys vary depending on how the questions are phrased and how long a period people are asked to recall their experiences. For example,

Adapted from: Kaiser Commission on Medicaid & the Uninsured. 2006. Who Are the Uninsured? Washington, DC: The Henry J. Kaiser Family Foundation.

respondents may be asked what their insurance coverage is in the month they are being interviewed or if they have been without coverage anytime in the past year or two years.

For this comparison, we contrast

- the 2003 NHIS published estimate (a point-in-time estimate),
- a 2003 MEPS single month estimate (July, 2003) and
- the 2004 March CPS, assuming that respondents generally answered questions relative to their health coverage at some point-in-time in 2003, rather than for the entire 2003 calendar year.

HOW MANY ARE UNINSURED?

Depending on the reference period respondents are asked to recall, national survey estimates of the uninsured have ranged as widely as 20 to 80 million. At one end, different surveys report 20 and 35 million being uninsured over the course of a full year, while as many as 80 to 85 million have been uninsured for at least part of a two year period. However, when comparisons are drawn using the same reference period in the NHIS, MEPS, and CPS (assuming it is a point-in-time estimate), the differences in the number of the uninsured are relatively small. For example, in 2003 the total number of nonelderly uninsured at any "point-in-time" in the year ranged from 41.1 million to 46.0 million, depending on which of these three surveys is used. The percentage of all the nonelderly who were uninsured ranged from 16.3% to 18.3%.

WHO ARE THE UNINSURED?

All three surveys show that about 80% of the uninsured are adults. Adults are more likely to be uninsured than children because most low-income children qualify for either Medicaid or S-CHIP, while low-income adults under age 65 qualify for Medicaid only if they are disabled, pregnant, or have dependent children. Because many eligible children are not enrolled in these public programs—often because their parents do not know they qualify—children make up 17% to 19% of all the uninsured. Adults are disproportionately represented among the uninsured and constitute the large majority, with those 18 to 44 years old making up roughly 60% of the uninsured.

Across all three surveys, more than half of the nonelderly uninsured come from low-income families, ranging from 52% to 59% of the uninsured across the surveys. Those with low incomes (less than 200% of the poverty level; or $37,620 for a family of four in 2003) are less likely to have jobs that offer employer-sponsored coverage and are also less likely to be able to afford their share of the premium. Roughly a third of the nonelderly population comes from low-income families, but they are disproportionately represented among the uninsured because their chances of being uninsured are over three times greater than those with higher incomes.

Looking just at working-age adults, the three surveys similarly estimate that at least two thirds of nonelderly uninsured adults are employed (Figure 3.2.1). Employers are the

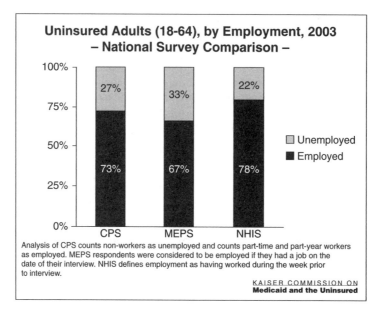

FIGURE 3.2.1   Uninsured Adults (18–64), by Employment, 2003–National Survey Comparison

Source: KCMU analysis.

most common source of health coverage for nonelderly Americans, but many uninsured workers either work for employers who do not offer coverage or cannot afford the coverage that they are offered. The share of the uninsured from working families is likely to grow if the percent of firms offering health benefits continues to decline and employee cost-sharing increases. In 2005, only 60% of employers offered health insurance to their workers, compared to 69% in 2000.

About two-thirds of uninsured adults in all three surveys have no college education and more than one-quarter of the uninsured did not graduate from high school. These groups tend to be less able to get high-skill jobs that come with health benefits. Those with less education are also more likely to be uninsured for longer periods.

The three surveys consistently show that about half of the uninsured are white (non-Hispanic) and half are racial and ethnic minorities. Minorities are more likely to have lower family incomes, which raises the risk of being uninsured. However, income disparities do not account for all of the racial and ethnic differences in health coverage. Minorities at both lower and higher income levels are more likely to be uninsured than their white counterparts. Uninsured rates are the highest among low-income Hispanics. Overall, Hispanics make up about 16% of the nonelderly population, but about 30% of the uninsured.

Besides painting a very similar economic and demographic profile, the NHIS, MEPS, and CPS also present a consistent picture of the health of the uninsured population. Each of these surveys estimates that about 10% of the uninsured report their health status as being fair or poor. Were it not for Medicaid, the insurance safety net for low-income persons with chronic and severely disabling conditions, more of the uninsured would not be in good health. Medicaid covers almost 60% of children who are in fair or poor health and over a third of adults who also are not in good health.

CONCLUSION

Three large national surveys—the CPS Annual Social and Economic Supplement, the MEPS, and the NHIS—produce timely estimates of health insurance coverage in the U.S. All of them are useful to policymakers and produce a fairly consistent picture of who the uninsured are. National estimates of the number of uninsured are also not substantially different when comparisons are made using a common reference period.

Because a basic goal of health insurance reform is to achieve better access to insurance—as the key to improving access to care—policymakers need a clear understanding of not only how many are uninsured, but who they are. The comparisons presented in this brief demonstrate that when the number of uninsured is measured consistently, the profile of these Americans varies little across surveys.

All of the major surveys point to the need to base policies on a realistic, data-based picture of who the uninsured really are and what they can actually afford. While more than two-thirds of uninsured adults are working, they are disproportionately low-income and less educated. Adults and racial and ethnic minorities also comprise a disproportionate share of the uninsured. Policies intended to expand coverage and improve access to care can be informed by these consistencies in our largest national surveys and with this knowledge can focus on those with the greatest need.

REFERENCE

1. The Kaiser Family Foundation and Health Research and Educational Trust. The 2005 Kaiser/HRET Annual Employer Health Benefits Survey, 2005. Available at http://www.kff.org/insurance/7315.

Access to Care and Utilization Among Children: Estimating the Effects of Public and Private Coverage

Thomas M. Selden, PhD, and Julie L. Hudson, PhD

The past quarter century has witnessed large changes in children's insurance coverage. The percentage of children younger than age 18 with private coverage steadily declined, falling from 73.6% in 1977 to 67.6% in 1987, 63.0% in 1996, and 60.6% in 2003.[1,2] This decline initially led to a sharp increase in uninsurance rates from 12.7% in 1977 to 17.8% in 1987. Since the late 1980s, however, declines in private coverage have been more than offset by expansions in public coverage, first through Medicaid and then through the State Children's Health Insurance Program (SCHIP). By 2003, 27.5% of children held public coverage, up from 13.6% in 1977 and 14.6% in 1987. As a result, the percentage of children who were uninsured in 2003 fell to 11.9%, the first time in 2 and a half decades that the rate of uninsurance had been less than its 1977 level.

These dramatic trends in coverage highlight the importance of understanding the relationship between children's insurance coverage and their access to and utilization of medical care. Numerous studies have shown that coverage is associated with increased access and utilization,[3,4] with private coverage often having larger effects than public coverage.

In this report, we use pooled data from the 1996–2002 Medical Expenditure Panel Survey (MEPS) to examine the relationship between children's insurance coverage and having a usual source of care, lacking a usual source of care for financial/insurance reasons, and medical care utilization of care by type of service.

RESULTS

On average during the period 1996-2002, 10.4% of all children age 18 and younger lacked a usual source of care (USC). Children with coverage were substantially less likely to lack a USC than those without coverage, with the lowest frequency being among children with private coverage.

Adapted from: Thomas M. Selden and Julie L. Hudson. 2006. Access to Care and Utilization Among Children: Estimating the Effects of Public and Private Coverage. *Medical Care.* 44(5): 119–126.

Nearly every access and utilization measure exhibits this same pattern, whereby access and use is greatest among children with private coverage, followed by those on public coverage, and then the uninsured. On average, children had only 63% of the recommended number of well-child visits. Among uninsured children, this average compliance rate was only 35.2%. The only 2 types of service that publicly insured children use at greater rates than privately insured children are emergency room visits and inpatient hospital stays.

These access and use differences can be misleading insofar as privately insured, publicly insured, and uninsured children vary on many potentially confounding dimensions. In particular, family income among children with private coverage averaged 426% of the federal poverty line (adjusted for family composition), versus only 109% for publicly insured children and 218% for uninsured children. Also, only 1.6% of privately insured children have "fair" or "poor" self-reported health status versus 5.4% of publicly insured children and 2.9% of uninsured children.

MULTIVARIATE ANALYSIS

Absent controls, public and private coverage reduce the probability of lacking a USC by 16.1% and 21.3% relative to being uninsured. With controls, the difference between public and private coverage essentially disappears. Lacking a USC due to financial reasons exhibits a similar pattern, although the univariate difference between public and private coverage is itself small.

Turning to our measures of use, our univariate results suggest that children with public coverage have a 5.0% lower visit frequency than children with private coverage when we do not include any controls. Adding controls gives us a difference of 4.5% points in the opposite direction. Multivariate analysis also has a large effect on our coverage effect estimates for well-child visits and dental visits. Absent controls, compliance with well-child visit guidelines appears to be similar for publicly insured and privately insured children. When we add controls, the private coverage effect becomes nearly 10% points smaller than that of public coverage. With respect to dental coverage, the univariate result is that children with private coverage have a dental visit rate nearly 20% points higher than children with public coverage. This difference by coverage type essentially disappears when we add controls. Controlling for covariates has relatively little effect in our models for having an inpatient hospital stay or an emergency room visit.

CONCLUSION

This report focuses on differences in access and use associated with public and private insurance for children. When we control for other factors such as poverty and health status, we generally find the access and use effects of public coverage to be as large or larger than those of private insurance. Relative to uninsured children, children with either type of coverage are far less likely to lack a usual source of care, and they are less likely to lack a usual source of care for financial reasons. They also have higher utilization rates for ambulatory care, well-child preventive care, and dental care.

We conclude that although insurance coverage is already well-known to improve children's access and utilization, the magnitude of estimated coverage effects may indeed depend upon the estimation method used. In the absence of data from random-assignment experiments, no one estimation method is likely to be definitive. Perhaps the best strategy is to explore alternative estimation methods, noting the strengths and weaknesses of each. Our efforts to apply instrumental variables to the estimation of the relationship between insurance and access and use suggest that coverage effects, particularly for public coverage, may well be larger than previously believed.

REFERENCES

1. Cunningham PJ, Monheit AC. Insuring the children: a decade of change. *Health Affairs.* 1990;9:76–90.

2. Rhoades JA, Cohen JW. *Health Insurance Status of Children in America, 1996–2003: Estimates for the U.S. Population under Age 18. Medical Expenditure Panel Survey Statistical Brief #44.* Rockville, MD: Agency for Healthcare Research and Quality; 2004.

3. O'Brien E, Mann C. *Maintaining the Gains: The Importance of Preserving Coverage in Medicaid and SCHIP.* Columbia, SC: Covering Kids & Families; 2003.

4. Buchmueller TC, Grumbach K, Kronick R, et al. The effect of health insurance on medical care utilization and implications for insurance expansion: a review of the literature. *Med Care Res Rev.* 2005;62:3–30.

The Effects of State Parity Laws on the Use of Mental Health Care

Katherine M. Harris, PhD,
Christopher Carpenter, PhD, and Yuhua Bao, PhD

Historically, health insurance plans have offered less generous coverage for mental health care services compared with that for general medical services. In an effort to "level the playing field," the federal government enacted legislation in 1996 requiring health insurers to eliminate yearly and lifetime dollar limits for mental health benefits. At the same time, however, the 1996 law did not prohibit other benefit restrictions or require purchasers to offer mental health benefits.[1] By the end of 2002, more than 30 states had enacted stricter and more comprehensive parity mandates than the federal government, affecting the roughly 70% of workers employed by nonself-insured firms subject to state benefit mandates.

The implementation of state parity laws during the late 1990s paralleled the trend toward managed behavioral health benefits. Case studies from this time period suggest that the effect of managed care in reducing inpatient and specialty care use "overwhelmed" the positive effects on use resulting from benefit expansions.[2-4] The overall result was stable or reduced total benefit costs on the order of 10% to 40%.

Three studies have looked at the effects of parity laws using nationally representative data from the Health Care for Communities (HCC) surveys, which were conducted in 2 cross-sectional rounds over the years 1997–1998 and 2000–2001.[5-7] Each study considered a different aspect of the data and used a distinct analytic strategy. These studies suggest that state parity laws have had small positive effects on mental health service use and consumers' perceptions of access to care.

The overall finding that parity resulted in increased use without corresponding increases in expenditures begs questions about the level of need among individuals who used more mental health care under parity and whether stable expenditures were achieved through offsetting reductions in use among other subgroups. To begin to address these questions, we used the National Survey on Drug Use and Health (NSDUH), a large, nationally representative survey, to study the effect of state parity laws on mental health care use among adults with private health insurance. We measured the effect of parity using a quasiexperimental design that compares changes over time in mental health care use in "experimental" states that implemented parity laws with changes over time in "control" states that did not implement parity laws during the same time period. Like with other studies,

Adapted from: Katherine M. Harris, Christopher Carpenter, and Yuhua Bao. 2006. The Effects of State Parity Laws on the Use of Mental Health Care. *Medical Care.* 44(6): 499–505.

we were not able to distinguish the effects of parity from the effect of changes in the management of mental health benefits.

Our study is the first to use population-based data to examine the effect of state parity laws on psychotropic medication use. This area has received considerably less attention in the parity literature despite the prominence of medications in the treatment of mental health problems.[8] Although state parity laws do not directly impact prescription drug benefits, state parity laws may have indirectly affected patterns of psychotropic medication use through a number of different mechanisms. For example, parity may decrease medication use by increasing the use of nonphysician providers. Alternatively, parity may increase use of medications to reduce the use of specialists and to shift costs onto general medical insurers traditionally at risk for medication costs. The only study to date on this topic found that the implementation of expanded first-dollar coverage and managed care was associated with slowing growth in psychotropic medication costs.[9]

RESULTS

Descriptive Results

As expected, the probability of using mental health care in the past year increases with the level of psychologic distress. With several exceptions, including the use of outpatient care among those in the upper group, active parity status was generally associated with higher rates of mental health service use. However, none of these differences were statistically significant except when all adults were considered.

Multivariate Results

Depending on the definition of active parity status, parity laws resulted in as much as a 1.2 percentage point increase in the probability of using any mental health care in the past year for those in the lower distress group, as much as a 1.8 percentage point increase in use for the middle group, and no statistically significant changes in the probability of use for those in the upper group. Although small changes in absolute terms, estimated effects were large in proportional terms when compared with baseline preparity service use rates.

Discussion

This study used a large, nationally representative dataset to measure the effect of state parity laws on the use of mental health care. To our knowledge, this study is the first to examine parity effects by the severity of mental health problems, to examine medication use in the context of parity, and to estimate models with a full set of unrestricted state-fixed effects. Overall, our results suggest that parity increased use of both prescription medications and outpatient care among the roughly two-thirds of adults with relatively low levels of mental and emotional distress.

Although estimates of increased use were small in level terms, they represent large proportional changes. An increase in service use from 6% to 8% among the roughly one-third of adults in the middle distress group represents tens of thousands of new users in a state with 1,000,000 adults covered by private insurance. Effects of this magnitude are consistent with studies showing substantial changes in mental health service use associated with changes in the organization and delivery of medical and mental health services and the implementation of managed behavioral health care.[3,8]

The results suggested that parity affected prescription medication and outpatient use differentially. However, no clear patterns of parity's effect on service mix emerged across the different definitions of active parity status, suggesting that changes in service mix occurred differentially across states and time periods.

We did not find evidence that parity affected the use of mental health care for those in the upper distress group. This group was substantially more likely to use mental health care in the period before widespread parity adoption and may have used care regardless of the changes in benefit design brought about by parity laws. Although this finding is consistent with the idea that price elasticity declines as the severity of mental health problems increases, the service use measures in the NSDUH are likely too crude to detect changes in the organization and delivery of care (e.g., the granting or denial of subspecialty referrals, visit limits) experienced by established users as a result of parity. Furthermore, the cross-sectional nature of the NSDUH also limits our ability to examine the indirect effects of parity on employment and insurance status that, if they exist, would disproportionately affect people with the most serious mental health problems.

Nonetheless, the lack of evidence in favor of increased use among those with higher distress remains somewhat puzzling. It is reasonable to expect that expanded first-dollar coverage would have generated increased service use given that the overwhelming majority of those in the upper distress group did not use any care in the past year and that financial considerations are mentioned more frequently than any other reason for not receiving needed mental health treatment.[9] The lack of an effect may indicate a lack of active outreach to this relatively needy subgroup.

REFERENCES

1. Frank RG, Goldman HH, McGuire TG. Will parity in coverage result in better mental health care? *N Engl J Med.* 2001;345:1701–1704.

2. Sturm R, Goldman W, McCulloch J. Mental health and substance abuse parity: a case study of Ohio's state employee program. *J Ment Health Policy Econ.* 1998;1:129–134.

3. Zuvekas SH, Regier DA, Rae DS, et al. The impacts of mental health parity and managed care in one large employer group. *Health Aff (Millwood).* 2002;21:148–159.

4. Rosenbach M, Lake T, Young C, et al. *Effects of the Vermont Mental Health and Substance Abuse Parity Law.* DHHS Publ No (SMA) 03-3822. Rockville, MD: Center for Mental Health Services. Substance Abuse and Mental Health Services Administration; 2003.

5. Pacula RL, Sturm R. Mental health parity legislation: much ado about nothing? *Health Serv Res.* 2000;35:263–275.

6. Sturm R. State parity legislation and changes in health insurance and perceived access to care among individuals with mental illness: 1996–1998. *J Ment Health Policy Econ.* 2000;3:209–213.

7. Bao Y, Sturm R. The effects of state mental health parity legislation on perceived quality of insurance coverage, perceived access to care, and use of mental health specialty care. *Health Serv Res.* 2004;39: 1361–1377.

8. Bao Y. Predicting the use of outpatient mental health services: do modeling approaches make a difference? *Inquiry.* 2002;39:168–183.

9. Office of Applied Studies. *Results from the 2001 National Household Survey on Drug Abuse: Volume I. Summary of National Findings.* DHHS Publication No SMA 02-3758, NHSDA Series H-17. Rockville, MD: Substance Abuse and Mental Health Services Administration; 2002.

CHAPTER 4

Aging and Long-Term Care

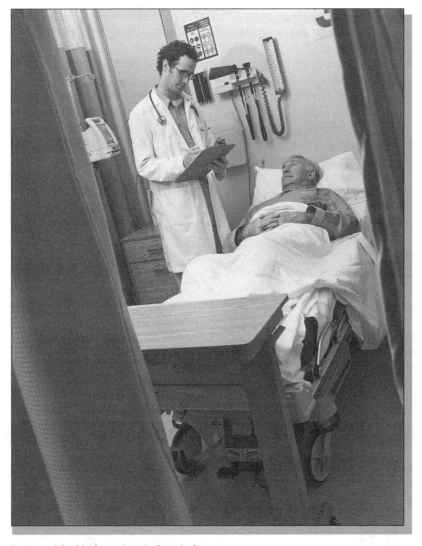

Doctor with elderly patient in hospital room

Older People

Carroll L. Estes and Steven P. Wallace

INTRODUCTION

Despite the growing academic and political interest in health equity and in social justice in health care, little attention has been paid to these issues as they relate to older people.

In the United States, *Healthy People 2010* has two central goals—one focusing on equity, to eliminate health disparities, and the other linked to aging, to increase the quality and years of healthy life. Although many of the *Healthy People 2010* targets focus on issues of concern to older persons, disparities among age groups are not included. This omission occurred while the United Nations was declaring 1999 the International Year of Older Persons and developing a program on "Building a Society for all Ages"[1] that links the status of older people to that of others in society. There is a burgeoning literature on disparities within the older population,[2,3] but there has been a decline during the past 30 years in attention given to ageism and inequities based on age. The growing popularity of trends such as "antiaging" medicine and the continuing efforts to blame the elderly for projected deficits in Medicare and Social Security suggest that older people are likely to face less equitable treatment because of their age in the future unless social policies and political ideologies change. Thus, it is important to consider both the inequities within the older population and between the older and younger populations.

Eliminating inequities in the determinants of health care and health status for older people is an ethical imperative. However, it is also in society's social and material interest to promote conditions in which older people can be healthy. Many older people continue to contribute to their families and communities through very old age,[4] and as the "baby-boom" generation ages, an even larger pool of older people with valuable skills and experiences will become important resources. If older people are not healthy, their ability to contribute to their communities declines, and the costs of their debilitating illnesses are borne by society.

THE IMPACT OF SOCIAL INJUSTICE ON THE HEALTH OF OLDER PEOPLE

Injustice among the elderly is well documented. Health status varies by race, ethnicity, income, and gender among older persons. Older African-Americans have worse health than do older whites across all measures of health status, including disease, disability, and self-

Adapted from: Carroll L. Estes and Steven P. Wallace. (2006). Older people. In: B.S. Levy and V.W. Sidel (Eds.), *Social injustice and public health* (pp. 113–129). Oxford, UK: Oxford University Press.

assessed health.[5] Older Latinos have lower rates than do non-Latino whites of some diseases, most notably heart disease and stroke, but higher rates of diabetes and of disability.[2] Poverty is strongly associated with all measures of poor health in old age. And women have more chronic conditions and disability than do men, despite their greater life expectancy.

Self-assessed health status, a good predictor of death and disability as well as current health status,[6] follows social categories of inequality. Older people with the lowest income are more than twice as likely as older people with high incomes to report reduced health status (Table 4.1.1). Both Latinos and non-Latino African-Americans are about 50 percent more likely to report reduced health status as are non-Latino whites. Women are somewhat more likely to report reduced health status than are men.

With the substantial reduction in deaths from acute infectious diseases during the past century, mortality is increasingly due to chronic conditions that are most common in old age. With aging, the disease profile shifts from predominantly infectious diseases to predominantly chronic and degenerative noncommunicable diseases, such as arthritis, hypertension, coronary artery disease, cerebrovascular disease, and cancer. This "epidemiological transition" has occurred in developed countries and is occurring in developing countries.[7] Many chronic diseases could be prevented or delayed through health promotion and disease prevention strategies. Older African-Americans have more chronic conditions than do older whites, and older women have more than do older men (Table 4.1.2).

Elderly people in the United States, where disability rates have declined in recent years, are projected to have healthier lifestyles and better health than comparably aged people in the past.[8] The global generalizability of this trend, however, remains to be established; instead,

TABLE 4.1.1   Percentage of Self-Assessed Health Status of Persons Aged 65 and Over by Income, Race/Ethnicity, and Gender, United States, 1999

	Fair/Poor Self-Assessed Health
Income	
Below poverty level	36.0
Low: 100–199% poverty level	31.9
Middle: 200–399% poverty level	22.4
High: ≥400% poverty level	16.4
Race/Ethnicity	
Non-Latino African-American	37.7
Non-Latino white	23.0
Latino	34.0
Gender	
Women	25.1
Men	23.7

Modified from Agency for Healthcare Research and Quality, Household Component Analytical Tool (MEPSnet/HC). Rockville, Md.: AHRQ, 2003.

TABLE 4.1.2　Percentage of Older People (Aged 65 or Older) with Chronic Conditions, by Race, Ethnicity, and Gender, United States, 2000

	Stroke	Diabetes	Mobility Limitation	Incontinence	Two or More Chronic Conditions*
Non-Latino whites	11.3	16.0	47.3	27.6	71.6
African-Americans	13.3	28.3	56.6	24.0	76.9
Latinos	9.9	23.3	47.6	21.4	67.9
Women	11.1	16.9	53.7	34.6	76.1
Men	11.7	18.8	40.1	15.9	65.6

*Hypertension, diabetes, arthritis, osteoporosis/broken hip, pulmonary disease, stroke, Alzheimer's disease, Parkinson's disease, skin cancer, other cancer.

From Center for Medicare and Medicaid Services (CMS). The characteristics and perceptions of the Medicare population: data from the 2000 Medicare Current Beneficiary Survey. Baltimore, Md.: CMS, 2003.

there may be increasing "population frailty,"[9] longer life but worsening health, and increased morbidity as people live longer, placing greater demands on the health care system.[10]

Inequities also exist in the access to health services by different population groups of older persons. The same social and economic characteristics that are associated with worse health outcomes account for documented differences in the level of use of health services. Unmet medical needs are more common among older African-Americans, those with incomes below the poverty line, and older women (Table 4.1.3). Although most older people have a regular site for health care, older African-Americans and those with incomes below the poverty line are less like to have a private physician as their regular source of care; they are more likely to seek care at clinics with reduced continuity of care and limited services.

In addition to differences in receiving any health care, there are disparities among older people in the quality of care they receive. The Institute of Medicine has determined

TABLE 4.1.3　Percentage Reporting Access to Health Care Problems, Persons Aged 65 and Over, by Race, Poverty, and Gender, United States, 1993

	Unmet Medical Needs	No Regular Source of Care	Regular Source of Care Not a Private Physician
Whites	9.9	6.1	7.2
African-Americans	18.4	6.6	22.1
Income at or above poverty level	8.8	5.6	7.8
Income below poverty level	27.2	8.2	15.5
Older men	8.7	6.7	10.9
Older women	12.0	5.7	7.0

From Cohen RA, et al. Access to health care, part 3: older adults (series 10, volume 198). Hyattsville, Md.: Vital Health Statistics, National Center for Health Statistics, 1997.

that racial and ethnic disparities in health care are independent of economic status, health insurance, and other factors.[11] Some of the differences in quality of care among older people are reflected in measures of satisfaction with care. Older African-Americans have the lowest satisfaction rates; Latinos, intermediate rates; and whites, the highest rates.

In sum, inequities exist in health status, access to health care, and the quality of care received among different groups of older people based on their social characteristics.

In addition to the inequities that exist within the older population, there is a continuing bias against older people as a group in several health-related dimensions. For example, there is much devaluing of older people by health professionals[12,13] and social-policymakers. Treatment decisions for older people are often influenced by the person's age, rather than a consideration of the costs and benefits of treatment. Older people, for example, are less likely to receive recommendations for cancer treatments that could extend their lives than younger people, even when there is no medical reason to avoid those treatments. The pattern of undertreatment is exacerbated by the underrepresentation of older people in most clinical trials.[14] Some even suggest that older people, such as those over age 80, should receive no curative treatments, regardless of their prognosis, because they have lived out their "natural" lives.[15]

Older people are often devalued in discussions of the costs of health and social programs that they use.[16] Some policymakers blame the rising costs of Medicare on older people, even though much medical treatment is driven by physician referral, not patient demand. In addition, the rapidly rising costs of prescription medications appear to be largely a function of manufacturer-induced demand (especially by direct advertising to consumers) for high-cost drugs, rather than use of new drugs that improve treatment of disease.[17]

Furthermore, our technology-intensive medical care system is increasingly inappropriate for the chronic disease challenges of older people, including hearing problems, falls, incontinence, and social isolation, as well as polypharmacy and the need for end-of-life care.[18-20] These challenges do not usually require expensive tests, surgical interventions, or state-of-the-art technology. An example is the current treatment pattern of older people with incontinence—a socially embarrassing condition that contributes to social isolation and increases the risk for deconditioning, falls, and institutionalization. It is often erroneously seen as a "normal" part of growing old.[21] Although behavioral therapy, including pelvic exercises, is the most effective treatment of urinary incontinence[22] drug therapy, surgery, and the use of adult diapers continue to be the most common forms of treatments. An estimated 8 percent of women aged 60 and older have ever had surgery for incontinence.[23] Among men and women over age 50 with incontinence, 20 percent use pads or other absorbent supplies.[24] Adult diapers and drugs produce significant profits for their manufacturers, creating incentives to promote those products; in contrast, behavioral therapy is time-consuming and not very profitable. As a result, many older people with incontinence do not receive adequate treatment for this condition.

WHAT NEEDS TO BE DONE

Given the cumulative lifetime disadvantage underlying much of the social injustice that affects the health of older people, measures need to be taken to improve the distribution of health and health services among both the current generation of older people and people who are now young and represent future generations of older people. Today's older people cannot easily change their lifetime history of employment earnings, living conditions, or other resources. Addressing social injustice among older people requires intervention with social policies that reduce inequities—by race, ethnicity, income, and gender—in retirement income, quality of medical care, and community integration.

To promote policy change, it is necessary to raise political awareness.[25] Because older people of color, older poor people, and older women tend to be disenfranchised from the political process,[26] it is important to increase understanding about the health status, process of care, and financial burdens of these groups of older people. Organizations that focus on race and ethnicity, poverty, and women's health need to join those that focus on aging to support this work.

Health policies that focus on structural factors, such as the organization and financing of medical care and the social environment where older people live, affect the entire population. Population-based interventions that potentially affect all older people, such as ensuring access to health care, have the potential political advantage of drawing support from others, including middleclass and politically influential people. Improving the health of older people in the United States therefore requires changing the health care system so that all older people receive appropriate care.

Public policy can influence other important changes in the health care system, including changes in the composition of the health care workforce and the financial incentives within the system. Because patients' satisfaction with physicians is higher when they can choose physicians of the same ethnicity,[27] equity in medical care depends, in part, on the racial and ethnic composition of the physician workforce. Members of racial and ethnic minority groups need to be provided the tools and incentives to pursue careers in health care.

There are also important community level changes that do not involve the medical care system that promote health. Building large supermarkets in inner cities, for example, can increase the consumption of fruits and vegetables by low-income older people.[28] Policies that encourage such construction—usually thought of as economic-development or zoning policies—are also important health policies that may help reduce disparities in nutrition and health. In general, providing older people with financial resources to obtain adequate housing, nutrition, and medical care would contribute to reducing many of the financing, process-of-care, and health-status inequities that they experience.

All of these types of policy changes will require broad coalitions of advocates. Policies that substantially improve the distribution of resources to older people, such as Social Security and Medicare, have been adopted when there has been a broad coalition of advocates, including organized labor, citizen's groups, and health professionals.[29]

FIGHTING BACK: RECLAIMING PUBLIC HEALTH AND THE STATE

Older people, women, minorities, and the poor have been largely absent from influential debates of the World Bank—against public pensions—and the World Trade Organization (WTO)—for the commercialization of care services. The major participants in these debates have been governments from rich countries, wishing to deregulate government provision of services, and corporations, wanting to expand into lucrative areas of work world-wide.[30-32] Major players in the international trade of health services include health insurance companies, drug companies, and medical equipment suppliers.

Opponents of globalization have been mobilized in areas of human rights, ecology, women's rights, race and ethnic justice, and worker rights. Elder rights advocates are invisible, except for the largely uncritical formal positions articulated in United Nations and WHO documents that offer little guidance or evidence of commitment to the goals of universal, collective, and social obligations enacted through government programs. Although not "wrong" in their entirety, current United Nations and WHO efforts are no match for the active efforts of the WTO, the International Monetary Fund, and the World Bank to privatize government provision of social care and support for the aged. The privatization of those services is now commonly inserted as a condition of development loans and debt relief to developing countries, known as structural adjustment.

Organizations representing older people need to link with larger organizations and forums working on a global justice agenda. The recent upsurge of political activity among pensioners in a number of countries[33] offers a potentially important platform upon which to build age-integrated social movement for social change. The joining of the movements of opposition to the worst abuses of globalization is essential and the role of older-people's organizations is pivotal because older people have much to lose should there be widespread privatization of public health and retirement programs.

An example of positive networking is in the actions of eastern European and Third-World women networking in struggles that define women's rights as human rights as a key principle of citizenship. These efforts have occurred through collaborations, such as Women's EDGE, the Association for Women in Development, the Center for Economic Justice, InterAction/Commission on the Advancement of Women (2000), and the Open Society Institute's Network Women's Program (2002). Declining female political participation and relegation to traditional women's work inspired the first independent Women's Forum in the former Soviet Union in 1991 that adopted the platform that "democracy without women is no democracy." Forms of resistance and collective action are also emerging in submerged networks (those without defined organizational structures), such as the Internet, and everyday forms of resistance, such as boycotts of certain products and business entities.[34] Globalization does not inexorably lead to minimal levels of social protection.[35,36] The road map for the work ahead consists of actions and activities that install pro-welfare, social-protection, and full-employment policies.[37]

CONCLUSION

Rights for older people must be defined as basic human rights: Social justice for older people must begin with the assertion of the human right to health, as established in the Universal Declaration of Human Rights and other international agreements. This includes the human rights of older people as a group, as well as subgroups of older people who have suffered lifelong injustice. Working to reduce the socioeconomic-health gradient at all ages promotes justice for both current and future cohorts of older people. Promoting public health approaches to aging will reduce the biomedicalization of old age. And activists must denounce macroeconomic adjustment policies and militarization of relationships among nations for their devastating effects on people's health and quality of life; they must demand ethical principles in politics and economics that work to satisfy people's needs.[38]

REFERENCES

1. United Nations. *Second World Assembly on Ageing adopts Madrid Plan of Action and Political Declaration.* Madrid, Spain: Second World Assembly on Ageing, 2002.

2. Wallace SP, Villa VM. Equitable health systems: cultural and structural issues for Latino elders. *Am J Law Med* 2003;29:247–67.

3. Dunlop DD, Manheim LM, Song J, Chang RW. Gender and ethnic/racial disparities in health care utilization among older adults. *J Gerontol Soc Sci* 2002;57B:S221–33.

4. Wallace SP. Community formation as an activity of daily living: the case of Nicaraguan immigrant elderly. *J Aging Stud* 1992;6:365–84.

5. Clark DO, Gibson RC. Race, age, chronic disease, and disability. In: Markides KS, Miranda MR, eds. *Minorities, aging and health.* Newbury Park, Calif.: Sage, 1997, pp 107–26.

6. Idler EL, Kasl SV. Self-ratings of health: do they also predict change in functional ability? *J Gerontol Ser B Psychol Sci Soc Sci* 1995;50:S344–53.

7. Kinsella K, Velkoff VA. *An aging world: 2001.* Series P95/01-1. Washington, D.C.: U.S. Government Printing Office, 2001.

8. Manton K, Corder L, Stallard E. Chronic disability trends in elderly in the US. *Proc Natl Acad Sci USA* 1997;94:2593–8.

9. Verbrugge LM. The dynamics of population aging and health. In: Lewis SJ, ed. *Aging and health: linking research and public policy.* Chelsea, Mich.: Lewis, 1989, pp 23–40.

10. Olshansky SJ, Rudberg MA, Carnes BA, et al. Trading off longer life for worsening health: the expansion of morbidity hypothesis. *J Aging Health* 1991;3:194–216.

11. Smedley BD, Stith AY, Nelson AR, eds. *Unequal treatment: confronting racial and ethnic disparities in health care.* Washington, D.C.: Institute of Medicine, National Academy Press, 2003.

12. Reuben DB, Fullerton JT, Tschann JM, Croughan-Minihane M. Attitudes of beginning medical students toward older persons: a five-campus study. *J Am Geriatr Soc* 1995;43:1430–6.

13. Kane RL. The future history of geriatrics: geriatrics at the crossroads. *J Gerontol A Biol Sci Med Sci* 2002;57:M803–5.

14. Muss HB. Older age—not a barrier to cancer treatment. *N Engl J Med* 2001;345:1128–9.

15. Callahan D. Aged based rationing of medical care. In: Williamson JB, Watts-Roy DM, Kingson ER, eds. *The intergenerational equity debate.* New York, N.Y.: Columbia University Press, 1999.

16. Binstock RH. Scapegoating the old: intergenerational equity and age-based health care rationing. In: Williamson JB, Watts-Roy DM, Kingson ER, eds. *The generational equity debate.* New York, N.Y.: Columbia University Press, 1999, pp 157–84.

17. Mintzes B, Barer ML, Kravitz RL, et al. How does direct-to-consumer advertising (DTCA) affect prescribing? A survey in primary care environments with and without legal DTCA. *CMAJ* 2003;169:405–12.

18. Tinetti ME, Inouye SK, Gill TM, Doucette JT. Shared risk factors for falls, incontinence, and functional dependence. Unifying the approach to geriatric syndromes. *JAMA* 1995;273:1348–53.

19. Hanlon JT, Schmader KE, Ruby CM, Weinberger M. Suboptimal prescribing in older inpatients and outpatients. *J Am Geriatr Soc* 2001;49:200–9.

20. Miller SC, Mor V, Wu N, et al. Does receipt of hospice care in nursing homes improve the management of pain at the end of life? *J Am Geriatr Soc* 2002;50:507–15.

21. Mitteness LS, Barker JC. Stigmatizing a "normal" condition: urinary incontinence in late life. *Med Anthropol Q* 1995;9:188–210.

22. Burgio KL, Locher JL, Goode TS, et al. Behavioral vs drug treatment for urge urinary incontinence in older women: a randomized controlled trial. *JAMA* 1998;280:1995–2000.

23. Diokno AC, Burgio K, Fultz H, et al. Prevalence and outcomes of continence surgery in community dwelling women. *J Urol* 2003;170:507–11.

24. Schulman C, Claes H, Matthijs J. Urinary incontinence in Belgium: a population-based epidemiological survey. *Eur Urol* 1997;32:315–20.

25. Weissert CS, Weissert WG. *Governing health: the politics of health policy.* 2nd ed. Baltimore, Md.: Johns Hopkins University Press, 2002.

26. Wallace SP, Villa V. Caught in hostile cross-fire: public policy and minority elderly in the United States. In: Minkler M, Estes CL, eds. *Critical gerontology: perspectives from political and moral economy.* Farmingdale, N.Y.: Baywood, 1998.

27. Laveist TA, Nuru-Jeter A. Is doctor-patient race concordance associated with greater satisfaction with care? *J Health Soc Behav* 2002;43:296–306.

28. Wrigley N, Warm D, Margetts B, Whelan A. Assessing the impact of improved retail access on diet in a "food desert": a preliminary report. *Urban Studies* 2002;39:2061–82.

29. Wallace SP, Williamson JB. The senior movement in historical perspective. In: *The senior movement: references and resources.* New York, N.Y.: G. K. Hall, 1992, pp vii–xxxvi.

30. Estes CL, Biggs S, Phillipson C. *Globalization and ageing: social theory, social policy and ageing.* London, England: Open University Press, 2003.

31. Vincent J. *Politics, power, and old age.* Buckingham, England: Open University Press, 1999.

32. Vincent J, Patterson G, Wale K. *Politics and old age.* Aldershot, Hampshire, England: Ashgate Books, 2002.

33. Walker A, Maltby A. *Ageing Europe.* Buckinghamshire, England: Open University Press, 1997.

34. Mittelman JH, Tambe A. Global poverty and gender. In: Mittelman JH, ed. *The globalization syndrome.* Princeton, N.J.: Princeton University Press, 2000.

35. Navarro V. Health and equity in the world in the era of globalization. *Int J Health Serv* 1999;29:215–26.

36. Navarro V. Are pro-welfare state and full employment policies possible in the era of globalization? *Int J Health Serv* 2000;30:231–51.

37. Kagarlitsky B. The challenge for the left: reclaiming the state. In: Pantich L, Leys C, eds. *Global capitalism versus democracy.* Woodbridge, Suffolk, England/New York, N.Y.: Merlin Press/Monthly Review Press, 1999, pp 294–313.

38. International Forum for the Defense of the Health of the People. Health as an essential human need, a right of citizenship, and public good: health is possible and necessary. *Int J Health Serv* 2002;32:601–6.

Medicare and Chronic Care at the Beginning of the 21st Century: Improving But a Long Way to Go

Marty Lynch, Carroll L. Estes, and Mauro Hernandez

INTRODUCTION

Given the growing number of elderly and disabled Americans who receive health care services through the Medicare program and the costs associated with their use of needed services, it is critical that we learn the best way to treat chronic conditions faced by many of these beneficiaries. Recent data (Thorpe and Howard, 2006) suggests that almost all of the increase in Medicare spending over the last 15 years is due to patients with multiple chronic diseases. This article discusses a series of recommendations that would improve the Medicare program's response to the growth of chronic disease problems. The recommendations provided here are based on findings from three major types of programs.

The first category includes innovative federal and state programs, which attempt to integrate medical, home, and community-based services for the people with chronic conditions. Some of the best-known programs of this type are the Program of All-inclusive Care for Elderly (PACE); the Social Health Maintenance Organization (SHMO), first and second generations (seen by some to have been a failure; Wolff and Boult, 2005); and state-sponsored initiatives for Medicare and Medicaid eligibles such as Minnesota Senior Health Options (MSHO) and Wisconsin Family Care.

A second major category includes disease management programs, which attempt to improve chronic disease medical management for populations suffering from these conditions (CBO, 2004; Center on an Aging Society, 2004). Examples of these programs include the Breakthrough Series Best Practice Collaborative approach to chronic disease care being conducted in a number of health care systems, including community health centers (Ellrodt, Cook, Lee, Cho, Hunt, and Weingarten, 1997; Katon et al., 1995; McCulloch, Price, Hindmarsh, and Wagner, 1998; Watner et al., 2001). Another example related to chronic medical management is the group clinic approach for patients suffering from chronic diseases practiced in some regions by Kaiser Permanente as well as by some other providers (Sadur et al., 1999; Scott et al., 2004). A third is the emphasis on teaching self-care included in many of the disease management approaches (Lorig, Sobel, Ritter, Laurent, and Hobbs, 2001; Norris, Engelgau, and Narayan, 2001).

Marty Lynch, Carroll L. Estes, and Mauro Hernandez. (2006). *Medicare and chronic care at the beginning of the 21st century: Improving but a long way to go.* San Francisco, CA: Institute for Health and Aging, University of California, San Francisco. This article was prepared for the book.

A third major category is the high-risk care management approach developed by a number of managed care organizations and medical groups, which seeks to identify high-risk members and provide special care management in an effort to improve care in general and to control high utilization rates and expenditures (Boult, Boult, Morishita, Dowd, Kane, and Urdangarin, 2001; Boult, Pualwan, Fox, and Pacala, 1998; Quinn, Prybylo, and Pannone, 1999). This approach is currently being tested by CMS as part of a Medicare fee-for-service plan in a "Case Management for High-Cost Beneficiaries" demonstration authorized by the Medicare Modernization Act (CMS, 2005b). Improvements in functional status and reductions in hospitalization costs have also been reported by nursing homes and managed care organizations that employ geriatric nurse practitioners who work collaboratively with primary care physicians of these more impaired long-term care residents (Buchanan, Bell, Arnold, Witsberger, Kane, and Garrard, 1990; Burl, Bonner, Rao, and Khan, 1998).

All of these approaches rely on the ability to track information about patients, their diagnoses, and their utilization rates. Ideally, such information can allow physicians and other providers to better follow patients with chronic conditions and link actual care delivery to evidence-based protocols (Baker, Lafata, Ward, Whitehouse, and Divine, 2001).

Findings from current and proposed CMS-backed demonstrations will ultimately help inform an approach to chronic illness (Wolff and Boult, 2005). However, successes of these various programs to date, insofar as we have data indicating success already available, lead us to make a number of recommendations for improving the Medicare program.

KEY ISSUES

At least some evidence indicates that the initiatives noted previously have had some success, whether it be the ability of the specialized plans like PACE, SHMO, and the dual-eligible programs to stay in business while managing a very complex set of patient needs, or the improvement of clinical outcomes and processes as measured in chronic disease collaboratives, or improvements in patient and provider satisfaction. Given the successes achieved to date, we might ask how these models could be extended to additional Medicare beneficiaries. Certainly, many of the disease management interventions can be delivered under existing regulations by Medicare Advantage programs. It is much more difficult for fee-for-service Medicare providers to deliver care management, group visits, self-care management training, and other potentially helpful services under existing regulations, although current demonstrations and initiatives are examining this question (CMS, 2004, 2005b, 2006).

Integrating the Different Types of Chronic Care Initiatives

Existing chronic care initiatives focus on linking acute medical care to home and community services or to expanding medical services to include education, self-care management, case management, and population-based clinical improvements. Approaches aimed at chronic long-term care services, care management with high-cost users, and specific disease management programs do not necessarily intersect. For example, PACE program might choose to implement disease management protocols side-by-side with its multidisciplinary approach to integrated care. Disease management programs might try to link patients to community services related to their functional needs. There is little evidence that this cross-initiative type of planning has been put in place to date, and it is probably safe to assume that few Medicare beneficiaries receive state-of-the-art care across a range of functional and disease management needs despite efforts to improve the disease management aspect of this care. Current CMS demonstrations do not appear to go beyond disease management and high-risk case management to integrate functional chronic care with clinical care.

This limited scope may be acceptable for those beneficiaries who have chronic disease management needs but no functional needs. On the flip side, however, we would expect that almost all participants in PACE, participants in dual-eligible programs, and SHMO members receiving chronic care benefits have multiple chronic diseases and could benefit from implementation—or at least modified implementation—of disease management techniques. Given the heavy burden of multiple chronic conditions faced by those who are nursing home eligible or at risk for nursing home placement, these patients may require a hybrid approach that would require implementation of a range of evidence-based clinical protocols and social interventions responding to their most critical functional problems. Requiring these specialized plans to implement disease management protocols or to participate in collaborative training in key chronic disease areas may be one solution, even as we acknowledge that they are already managing a wide range of services and may have limited resources to implement new programs without commensurate rate increases. Recent findings on cost increases driven by those with multiple chronic conditions (Thorpe and Howard, 2006) should spur additional exploration in this area.

Reaching Individual and Small Group Providers

Another challenging question is posed by the paucity of initiatives that reach private providers or small physician groups providing care under the traditional fee-for-service Medicare program. Chronic condition collaborative participants and demonstration participants, with few exceptions, have been medical centers, health plans, hospitals, safety net providers, community health centers, and others with some level of infrastructure—but not small private providers. This is also true for most programs that integrate medical, home, and community-based services. Most initiative approaches of both types require substantial organizational support and resources (Luft, 2001), including somewhat sophisticated information systems. The group and staff model plans that have birthed a number of these initiatives are more likely to be able to influence their physicians and to provide the necessary structural supports than plans that shift risk to IPA structures.

The outcomes of current Medicare demonstrations aimed at fee-for-service Medicare beneficiaries will be important in understanding the applicability of these models outside managed care structures. The CMS demonstrations in smaller practices are still relatively narrow in scope, and it will be several years before findings from their evaluations will become available. Incentives related to the ability to experience cost savings from reduced utilization of hospital days may also be important in systems implementing these initiatives and have been undertaken in health plans, hospitals, and medical centers. CMS is also attempting to structure risk sharing for chronic disease management providers in its fee-for-service demonstrations by allowing for sharing of savings and requiring cost reduction targets for participating groups (Super, 2004).

Medicare HMOs and Chronic Care

Given that the majority of initiatives discussed here have taken place in managed care settings, and that organizational structure, information systems, and financial incentives are better aligned to support disease management in health plans, can we not presume that supporting the growth of managed care in Medicare might also create a favorable climate for chronic disease management? At the same time, the Medicare Advantage program is volatile at this point in time, with plans pulling out of the business or out of specific geographic areas or, conversely, entering markets based on the rate structure. In 2001, 934,000 Medicare HMO members (13.6%) were displaced from their plans (Stuber, Dallek, and Biles, 2001). Since then, the Medicare Modernization Act has responded to plans' complaints and raised payment rates significantly, leading to increased plan interest and member growth. Enrollment growth in the long run will depend on whether rate increases are sustained and regulatory barriers moderated.

Plans have also not yet shown an interest in adding functionally oriented chronic and long-term care services to their products. Except for one SHMO II plan in Nevada, and pilot programs at other HMOs such as Kaiser Permanente, there has been little activity within Medicare Advantage plans to link medical and functional chronic care services. Growth of Medicare Advantage will provide a favorable environment for disease management programs given the presence of the necessary infrastructure and incentives to control overall costs.

There are, however, questions about whether health plans that rely on IPA subcontracts will be able to implement these initiatives as effectively as group or staff model HMOs. There are also at least some quality questions to be considered. Most comparisons of HMO and fee-for-service care have shown comparable quality between the two (Miller and Luft, 2001). However, even special demonstration programs such as the SHMO have had difficulty integrating services for disabled members (Harrington, Lynch, and Newcomer, 1993). It may be more difficult for non-demonstration projects to achieve integration of acute and functionally oriented chronic care.

Unfortunately, little research to date has considered how the disabled, in general, fare in HMOs. Earlier studies suggested that Medicare HMOs provide only half as much home care as traditional Medicare and have poorer health outcomes related to home care (Shaughnessy, Schlenker, and Hittle, 1994). Elderly arthritic HMO patients with persistent joint pain also showed less improvement in symptoms than Medicare fee-for-service patients (Schlesinger and Mechanic, 1993). When SHMOs provided chronic disability care, the specific plan to which a beneficiary belonged and the geographic area where it was located were at least as important as individual needs in determining the amount and type of care received (Lynch, Harrington, and Newcomer, 1999). Plan behavior and geographic location may also be critical factors in determining the availability of disease management programs, suggesting that regulatory requirements and uniform program expectations throughout Medicare will be critical in assuring that beneficiaries have equitable access to proven chronic care initiatives.

RECOMMENDATIONS

A number of factors may make it difficult to translate the successes enjoyed by existing smaller initiatives into traditional Medicare used by millions of older and disabled Americans. Nonetheless, there have already been a number of positive results from the chronic care programs mentioned earlier. Indeed, Medicare has already begun to make the transition to paying for additional preventive and educational services (immunizations, mammograms, and diabetes education, to name a few) and has undertaken demonstrations to look at disease management and care management activities. Following are a number of recommendations for continued improvements to the Medicare program, which would allow improved chronic care management.

Short-Term Methods to Bring Initiative Benefits to the Medicare Fee-for-Service Population

Risk Assessment for Medicare FFA

A number of care management programs (Quinn et al., 1999; Rich, Beckham, Wittenberg, Leven, Freedland, and Carney, 1995) have used risk assessment to identify members so as to target special chronic care services. CMS requires Medicare Advantage plans to conduct an assessment within 90 days of enrollment. CMS should identify high-risk Medicare beneficiaries in fee-for-service plans or provide incentives for primary care physicians to do the same, using standard screening instruments now used by health plans or through physician referral.

Case Management for All High-Risk Medicare Beneficiaries

Once high-risk patients are identified, make beneficiaries with serious chronic diseases eligible for case management services paid for by the Medicare program either on a per-member, per-month case management fee or on a fee-for-service basis. Medicare could either contract through physician providers for nurse or social work case management or with independent agencies certified to provide these services. These could be Area Agencies on Aging, case management programs, home health agencies, community health centers, or other vendors. Primary care physicians have great difficulty coordinating medical care with community-based services (Fox, 2001). Part of the charge for case managers would be for linking high-risk Medicare patients to existing community services. They would also be expected to teach the patient self-care skills. This benefit would extend the learning from disease management programs into the fee-for-service Medicare program. CMS is testing aspects of this approach in the Care Management for High Cost Beneficiaries Demonstration (CMS, 2005b).

Medicare-Provided Information Systems for Small Providers

Information system infrastructure may present a problem for non-health plan providers. Health plans, medical centers, hospitals, and community health centers that have participated in chronic disease collaboratives all have some capability to use their information systems to build disease registries. CMS is currently testing provision of a simplified Veterans Administration electronic health record software to physicians (CMS, 2005a). If successful, basic PC software for private providers and small medical groups, in essence, would allow them to build chronic disease registries for their practices (Watner, 2001). The program could include protocols for population-based approaches to chronic care, including tracking and reminder systems for both patients and doctors for critical testing and monitoring processes. Initiatives like the VA system demonstration should be continued and expanded to provide information system technology to all providers.

Pay to Train FFS Physicians in Best Practices

Given the scarcity of chronic disease initiatives in fee-for-service Medicare, offer reimbursement to independent primary care providers or small groups of providers to participate in collaborative training models focusing on chronic disease care. These could be established on a regional basis or could use teleconferencing capabilities or Internet-based distance learning tools to avoid the cost and time of travel.

Program Expectations to Use Evidence-Based Protocols

Given the positive outcomes associated with a number of chronic disease interventions (Knox and Mischke, 1999; Rich, 1999; Rossiter et al., 2000; Rubin, Dietrich, and Hawk, 1998), build Medicare program expectations for all providers to use evidence-based chronic disease interventions. Use Medicare professional review organizations to help publicize these guidelines, monitor providers, and build support systems for providers in implementing guidelines.

Encourage Use of Group Visits

Make the Medicare fee-for-service payment methodology flexible enough to encourage group visit models for chronic disease care. Encourage providers to use these visits as part of their chronic disease program, including reimbursement for the nursing and nutritionist services provided in these programs.

Improve Education of Primary Care Physicians

Medical School Education in Case Management and Teamwork

Our review of the literature suggests that there is inadequate training of physicians in chronic care management, self-management training, and working in multidisciplinary teams. Therefore, we suggest incentives for graduate medical education programs to train physicians in evidence-based chronic disease management protocols, teaching self-care tools, and working with case managers in interdisciplinary settings as a part of their graduate medical education programs (Eichner and Blumenthal, 2003). This training should also include orientation toward the Area Agency on Aging network and links to community-based social services (Fox, 2001).

Make it Easier for States to Improve Chronic Care and Integrate with Medicare

Help States Link Medicare and Medicaid

A major problem in integrating acute and chronic care is the split between Medicare and Medicaid coverage and incentives for state and federal government to shift costs from one payer to the other (Wiener and Stevenson, 1998). Yet obtaining waivers to link these two reimbursement streams has proved extremely difficult and often taken many years. We recommend that states be encouraged by CMS to offer voluntary enrollment in health plans that link both Medicaid and Medicare dollars for acute care integrated with home and community services for dual eligibles with chronic conditions—without requiring waivers or placing difficult regulatory barriers on cooperating plans, such as separate health plan certification processes for both Medicare and Medicaid.

Medicare Advantage

Make Disease Management an Expectation for Health Plans

Some Medicare Advantage programs have implemented disease management programs that have realized a number of positive outcomes, as mentioned earlier. We suggest that CMS make evidence-based chronic disease management a program expectation for Medicare Advantage contractors and consider payment incentives for those plans that show improved chronic disease process and outcome measures.

Educate Medicare Beneficiaries

Educate Beneficiaries in Self-Care Directly

Growing numbers of consumers have indicated a preference to have some control over the services they receive. Self-care education has also been an important part of disease management approaches. We recommend that CMS initiate a beneficiary education program using major elder and disabled advocacy organizations, insurance counseling programs, and foundation-sponsored programs such as the Center for Medicare Education to develop user-friendly materials about chronic disease self-care, necessary clinical testing, and advice for interacting with their physician or health plan. Beneficiaries should also be educated about consumer rights and Medicare appeals processes.

Link the Part D Benefit to Chronic Disease Management

Give Providers Part D Data

Pharmacy management and education are important aspects of chronic disease management. The Medicare Part D benefit could allow for tracking of pharmacy utilization, with a link to allow primary care physician to use these data in their chronic disease management efforts.

Long Term: Medicare Advantage

Assure That Risk-Adjusted Rates Support Chronic Care
Health plans have expressed concerns that special chronic care programs might encourage sicker beneficiaries to enroll. CMS should continue to develop its risk-adjustment models, which would, in essence, pay health plans to enroll members with chronic diseases while avoiding problems of adverse selection (Newcomer, 2001).

Integrate Chronic and Acute Care in Medicare

Medicare Needs to Recognize and Cover the Functional Needs of Chronic Care Patients
In the long run, CMS should work toward integrating home and community-based care services responding to the functional needs of beneficiaries with chronic conditions into the Medicare program. This move would avoid cost shifting between the Medicare and Medicaid programs and improve the quality and accessibility of care for consumers with chronic problems.

SUMMARY

Innovations in disease management and care coordination hold promise for improving chronic care in the Medicare program. Current Medicare demonstrations are beginning to test these programs more thoroughly. Medicare has not, however, made significant process in linking clinical chronic care with functionally oriented care for patients who suffer from disabilities. Bridging this chasm will be critical for consumers and their families, who must face both the medical and disability problems related to chronic care.

REFERENCES

Baker, A. M., Lafata, J. E., Ward, R. E., Whitehouse, F., and Divine, G. (2001). A Web-based diabetes care management support system. *Joint Commission Journal on Quality Improvement* 27(4), 179–190.

Boult, C., Boult, L. B., Morishita, L., Dowd, B., Kane, R. L., & Urdangarin, C. F. (2001). A randomized clinical trial of outpatient geriatric evaluation and management. *Journal of the American Geriatric Society* 49(4), 351–359.

Boult, C., Pualwan, T. F., Fox, P. D., & Pacala, J. T. (1998). Identification and assessment of high-risk seniors. HMO Workgroup on Care Management. *American Journal of Managed Care* 4(8), 1137–1146.

Buchanan, J. L., Bell, R. M., Arnold, S. B., Witsberger, C., Kane, R. L., & Garrard, J. (1990). Assessing cost effects of nursing-home-based geriatric nurse practitioners. *Health Care Finance Review* 11(3), 67–78.

Burl, J. B., Bonner, A., Rao, M., & Khan, A. M. (1998). Geriatric nurse practitioners in long-term care: Demonstration of effectiveness in managed care. *Journal of the American Geriatric Society* 46(4), 506–510.

CBO. (2004). *An analysis of the literature of disease management programs.* Washington, DC: Congressional Budget Office (CBO), U.S. Congress.

Center on an Aging Society. (2004). *Disease management programs: Improving health while reducing costs?* (Issue Brief 4). Washington, DC: Center on an Aging Society, Georgetown University.

CMS. (2004). Medicare awards for programs to improve care of beneficiaries with chronic illness. Centers for Medicare & Medicaid Services. Retrieved January 30, 2005, from www3.cms.hhs.gov/apps/media/press/release.asp?Counter=1274

CMS. (2005a). HHS announces grant to help implement electronic health records in family practice medicine. Centers for Medicare & Medicaid Services. Retrieved August 30, 2006, from www.cms.hhs.gov/apps/media/press/release.asp?Counter=1075

CMS. (2005b). Medicare to award contracts for demonstration projects to improve care for beneficiaries with high medical costs. Centers for Medicare & Medicaid Services. Retrieved August 30, 2006, from www.cms.hhs.gov/DemoProjectsEvalRpts/downloads/CMHCB_Press_Release.pdf

CMS. (2006). Medicare demonstration and evaluation reports. Centers for Medicare & Medicaid Services. Retrieved August 30, 2006, from www.cms.hhs.gov/DemoProjectsEvalRpts/MD/list.asp

Eichner, J., & Blumenthal, D. (Eds.). (2003). *Medicare in the 21st century: Building a better chronic care system.* Washington, DC: National Academy of Social Insurance.

Ellrodt, G., Cook, D. J., Lee, J., Cho, M., Hunt, D., & Weingarten, S. (1997). Evidence-based disease management. *Journal of the American Medical Association* 278(20), 1687–1692.

Fox, P. D. (2001). Personal communication with Peter Fox, President, PDF, Inc. Chevy Chase, MD.

Harrington, C., Lynch, M., & Newcomer, R. J. (1993). Medical services in social health maintenance organizations. *Gerontologist* 33(6), 790–800.

Katon, W., Von Korff, M., Lin, E., Walker, E., Simon, G. E., Bush, T., Robinson, P., & Russo, J. (1995). Collaborative management to achieve treatment guidelines. Impact on depression in primary care. *Journal of the American Medical Association* 273(13), 1026–1031.

Knox, D., & Mischke, L. (1999). Implementing a congestive heart failure disease management program to decrease length of stay and cost. *Journal of Cardiovascular Nurses* 14(1), 55–74.

Lorig, K. R., Sobel, D. S., Ritter, P. L., Laurent, D., & Hobbs, M. (2001). Effect of a self-management program on patients with chronic disease. *Effective Clinical Practice* 4(6), 256–262.

Luft, H. S. (2001). Personal communication with Hal Luft, Professor and Director, Institute for Health Policy Studies, University of California, San Francisco.

Lynch, M., Harrington, C., & Newcomer, R. (1999). Chronic care: Predictors of chronic services by impaired members in the Social Health Maintenance Organization demonstration. *Journal of Applied Gerontology* 19(3), 283–304.

McCulloch, D. K., Price, M. J., Hindmarsh, M., & Wagner, E. H. (1998). A population-based approach to diabetes management in a primary care setting: Early results and lessons learned. *Effective Clinical Practice* 1(1), 12–22.

Miller, R. H., & Luft, H. S. (2001). *HMO plan performance update: An analysis of recently published literature (1997–2000).* Prepared for the Council on the Economic Impact of Health System Change: 8th Princeton Conference: The Future of Managed Care.

Newcomer, R. (2001). Personal communication with Robert Newcomer, Professor and Chair, Department of Social and Behavioral Sciences, University of California, San Francisco.

Norris, S. L., Engelgau, M. M., & Narayan, K. M. (2001). Effectiveness of self-management training in type 2 diabetes: A systematic review of randomized controlled trials. *Diabetes Care* 24(3), 561-587.

Quinn, J. L., Prybylo, M., & Pannone, P. (1999). Community care management across the continuum: Study results from a Medicare health maintenance plan. *Care Management Journal* 1(4), 223–231.

Rich, M. W. (1999). Heart failure disease management: A critical review. *Journal of Cardiac Failure* 5(1), 64–75.

Rich, M. W., Beckham, V., Wittenberg, C., Leven, C. L., Freedland, K. E., & Carney, R. M. (1995). A multidisciplinary intervention to prevent the readmission of elderly patients with congestive heart failure. *New England Journal of Medicine* 333(18), 1190–1195.

Rossiter, L. F., Whitehurst-Cook, M. Y., Small, R. E., Shasky, C., Bovbjerg, V. E., Penberthy, L., et al. (2000). The impact of disease management on outcomes and cost of care: A study of low-income asthma patients. *Inquiry* 37(2), 188–202.

Rubin, R. J., Dietrich, K. A., & Hawk, A. D. (1998). Clinical and economic impact of implementing a comprehensive diabetes management program in managed care. *Journal of Clinical Endocrinology and Metabolism* 83(8), 2635–2642.

Sadur, C. N., Moline, N., Costa, M., Michalik, D., Mendlowitz, D., Roller, S., et al. (1999). Diabetes management in a health maintenance organization: Efficacy of care management using cluster visits. *Diabetes Care* 22(12), 2011–2017.

Schlesinger, M., & Mechanic, D. (1993). Challenges for managed competition from chronic illness. *Health Affairs (Millwood)*, 12(suppl), 123–137.

Scott, J. C., Conner, D. A., Venohr, I., Gade, G., McKenzie, M., Kramer, A. M., et al. (2004). Effectiveness of a group outpatient visit model for chronically ill older health maintenance organization members: A 2-year randomized trial of the cooperative health care clinic. *Journal of the American Geriatrics Society* 52(9), 1463–1470.

Shaughnessy, P. W., Schlenker, R. E., & Hittle, D. F. (1994). Home health care outcomes under capitated and fee-for-service payment. *Health Care Financing Review* 16(1), 187–222.

Stuber, J., Dallek, G., & Biles, B. (2001). *National and local factors driving health plan withdrawals from Medicare + Choice: Analyses of seven Medicare + Choice markets*. Washington, DC: Commonwealth Fund.

Super, N. (2004). *Medicare's chronic care improvement pilot program: What is its potential?* (Issue Brief 797). Washington, DC: National Health Policy Forum, Georgetown University.

Thorpe, K. E., & Howard, D. H. (2006). The rise in spending among Medicare beneficiaries: The role of chronic disease prevalence and changes in treatment intensity. *Health Affairs Web Exclusive.*

Wagner, E. H. (2001). Personal communication with Edward Wagner, Program Director, W. A. MacColl Institute for Health Care Innovation. Seattle, WA.

Wagner, E. H., Glasgow, R. E., Davis, C., Bonomi, A. E., Provost, L., McCulloch, D., et al. (2001). Quality improvement in chronic illness care: A collaborative approach. *Joint Commission Journal on Quality Improvement* 27(2), 63–80.

Wiener, J. M., & Stevenson, D. G. (1998). State policy on long-term care for the elderly. *Health Affairs* 17(3), 81–100.

Wolff, J. L., & Boult, C. (2005). Moving beyond round pegs and square holes: Restructuring Medicare to improve chronic care. *Annals of Internal Medicine* 143(6), 439–445.

Unmet Need for Personal Assistance Services: Estimating the Shortfall in Hours of Help and Adverse Consequences

*Mitchell P. LaPlante, Stephen H. Kaye,
Taewoon Kang, and Charlene Harrington*

Community-residing adults of all ages with needs for personal assistance services (PAS) in daily activities are at risk of all or some of their needs being unmet, which can reduce their quality of life, compromise safety, and increase risks of a number of adverse consequences (Allen & Mor, 1997; Desai, Lentzner, & Weeks, 2001; Lima & Allen, 2001). These include injuries from falls, burns, weight loss, dehydration, discomfort, and other problems that can further worsen health and disability and increase risks of institutionalization and death. Minimizing unmet need is the primary goal underlying long-term care policy.

PAS refers to human help provided to individuals in specific activities that are generally obligatory for bodily maintenance and for living in the community, comprising the activities of daily living (ADLs; bathing, dressing, transferring from a bed or chair, toileting, and eating) and the instrumental activities of daily living (IADLs; such as taking medications and shopping for groceries). PAS include all help, whether hands-on, standby, or supervisory, whether paid or unpaid. Unmet need occurs when assistance from others is needed but not provided or inadequate.

There are many causes of unmet need. Over 85% of all of the hours of assistance people receive with ADLs and IADLs are provided by family and friends (LaPlante, Harrington, & Kang, 2002). Informal helpers, who may have to balance other responsibilities, including work and child care, are often limited in the amount of help they can provide. People with low informal resources, such as those who live alone, are especially likely to have unmet needs and depend largely on formal assistance, if affordable and available. Public PAS remain biased toward institutional rather than community living (Harrington et al., 2000), and people who live in states that do not provide enough home- and community-based services may be at greater risk of unmet need (LeBlanc, Tonner, & Harrington, 2000, 2001; Muramatsu & Campbell, 2002).

To advance the understanding of unmet need beyond mere prevalence, it is useful to know how much help is lacking and what the cost might be to address it. Quantifying unmet need for PAS in terms of the shortfall in hours of help is an important step in that

Adapted from: Mitchell P. LaPlante, Stephen H. Kaye, Taewoon Kang, and Charlene Harrington. (2004). Unmet need for personal assistance services: Estimating the shortfall in hours of help and adverse consequences. *Journal of Gerontology: Social Sciences.* 59B (2): S98–S108. Copyright © The Gerontological Society of America. Reproduced by permission of the publisher.

direction. This analysis builds on a prior national study estimating hours of PAS received among adults of all ages (LaPlante et al., 2002) to examine the relationship of hours with unmet need. We define unmet need as the gap between felt need and expressed need.

METHODS

Data are from supplements to the National Health Interview Survey (NHIS), a large nationally representative survey of households in the United States conducted annually by the Census Bureau for the U.S. National Center for Health Statistics (U.S. NCHS). Respondents to the 1994 and 1995 NHIS (94% core response rate) were given a supplemental screening questionnaire, known as Phase I of the National Health Interview Survey on Disability (NHIS-D; U.S. NCHS, 1998a, 1998b).

Data from Phase II of the NHIS-D are used to estimate met and unmet need for assistance with ADLs/IADLs and to estimate hours of paid and unpaid help received. Individuals were asked if they were helped in any of 5 ADL and 10 IADL activities, including hands-on help, supervision, or stand-by help, and whether they needed help or more help (activities a person does not do for reasons other than health are excluded). Individuals who lacked help or needed more help in one or more ADL/IADL activities are defined as having unmet need.

We hypothesized that the percentage of people experiencing adverse consequences would be greater on every measure for those with unmet versus met need, which we tested using a one-tailed *t* test.

RESULTS

About 15.1 million community-residing adults need help in ≥1 of the 15 IADLs and ADLs, 21.4% of whom have unmet need. The percentage with unmet need is lowest for those who need help only in IADLs (18.3%) and generally increases with higher numbers of ADLs, from 23.6% with one ADL need to 34.6% at four ADLs; but declines to 25.9% at five ADLs. Most people with unmet need get some help but do not get all the help they need. We find that only 545,000 adults of the 3.2 million with unmet need receive no help at all, a population with a low level of disability, mostly needing help in IADLs only, and in particular the single activity of heavy housework. For most people with unmet need, the issue is not *whether* they get help, but *how much* help they get.

Relationship of Unmet Need to Hours of Help

We expect that people with unmet need would have fewer hours of help than those whose needs are met. We find only a small difference in the mean hours of help received between those with unmet versus met need among people who need help with just IADLs or only one ADL (<2 hours per week) but large and highly significant differences for those needing help in two or more ADLs. This group amounts to 949,000 people—almost a million—

with perceived unmet need, who average 16.1 fewer hours per week than those whose needs are met. Persons with unmet needs have fewer hours for each number of ADLs above one that they need help with, and the differences in mean hours are statistically significant for those needings help in two, three, or five ADLs.

Overall, people needing help in two or more ADLs and reporting unmet need receive 56.2 hours of help and are estimated to need an additional 16.6 hours of help per week. Those living alone receive 24.1 hours of help and need an additional 18.7 hours, a relative shortfall of 43.7% of their total needed hours. Those who live with others receive substantially more help (66.1 hours) but need an additional 16.0 hours; their relative shortfall is a more modest 19.5%. People with fewer than two ADLs with unmet need are omitted owing to their relatively small shortfall (4 hours) and lesser policy import.

Cost of Eliminating Unmet Need

We made a simple estimate of the cost of eliminating the shortfall in hours among people with low income (below 300% of the SSI eligibility level) who live alone and have perceived unmet need. The calculation is based on what it would cost to supply enough paid hours annually to eliminate the gap in weekly hours associated with unmet need. We assumed paid helpers would receive an hourly rate of $10. This comes to about $1.9 billion annually for the 195,000 people with incomes below 300% of the SSI level who live alone, and the 95% confidence interval is from $1.2 to $2.7 billion. The cost of eliminating the shortfall in hours associated with unmet need among the half-million people with low income who live with others comes to about $4.7 billion; the 95% confidence interval is from $2.2 to $7.1 billion.

Negative Consequences of Unmet Need and Dissatisfaction

Even people whose needs are usually met can experience adverse consequences owing to lack of help, if a helper is not available at the right time and place, or if the quality of help is inadequate. But we would generally expect people with perceived unmet needs to have a higher frequency of adverse experiences. For all comparisons where a significant difference is observed, people with unmet needs have a higher rate of adverse consequences. Of individuals who need help with two or more ADLs, those with unmet needs have significantly greater probability of adverse consequences than those whose needs are met on 29 of 34 measures tested. These measures include discomfort, distress, mobility restriction, doing activities oneself that the person needs help with, and more serious concerns such as going hungry, running out of food, getting burned, unintentional weight loss, and dehydration. Many of these measures specifically attribute lack of help as the cause of the events, such as going hungry because no help was available to eat.

People with unmet needs also experience a variety of secondary conditions at rates significantly higher than those whose needs are met, including falls and injuries due to falls, bedsores, and contractures. Of those with unmet needs, 51% attributed their falls to lack of help in getting around or inability of their helper to prevent their falling compared with 32% of those whose needs are met. People with unmet need are much less satisfied with their primary helper's availability and the amount of assistance they give as well as other aspects of their helping abilities, and they are more likely to be left alone and to lack backup helpers.

DISCUSSION

Unmet need is prevalent among adults of all ages who have substantial needs for PAS. About 29% of adults needing help in two or more of the five basic ADLs need more help than they receive. In a society where 85% of hours of help come from family and friends (LaPlante et al., 2002), the problem of unmet need for PAS is magnified among people who live alone, 45% of whom have unmet need, compared with 26% of those who live with others. This study demonstrates that an association exists between perceived unmet need and reduced hours of help, independent of level of disability, race, age, and income level. People who live alone and have unmet need (almost a quarter-million people) are estimated to lack 18.7 hours of help per week or 44% of the hours they need. Those with unmet needs who live with others lack 16.0 hours per week or 20% of the hours they need.

Unmet need is not a measure of individuals' insatiable demands for more help. The data confirm that unmet need is associated with higher rates of adverse consequences on 48 of 53 measures tested, including discomfort, going hungry, losing weight, dehydration, falls, injuries due to falls, burns, and dissatisfaction, at much higher rates than those whose needs are met, particularly for people who live alone. These are serious problems that compromise the safety, comfort, and hygiene of individuals with unmet needs, reducing their ability to live independently and increasing their risk of institutionalization and possibly death. Many of these events are specifically attributed by the respondent as resulting from lack of help. Inferring causality on other measures lacking such attributions, like contractures and bedsores occurring in the last 3 months, is hazardous because of the cross-sectional design of the survey. The occurrence of such events may have precipitated a need for more than the available level of help. Nevertheless, the weight of the evidence clearly suggests that unmet need is associated with and attributed to much greater adversity.

Access to paid help is critical for people who live alone because they are much more likely to receive paid help than are people who live with others (62% versus 24%). Of people who live alone, those whose needs are met are more likely than those whose needs are unmet to get paid help (70.2% versus 50.3%). More than half of that paid help is reported to be paid by Medicare or Medicaid. Among people living with others, the difference in getting paid help by unmet need is much smaller (25.7% versus 19.4%). Thus, expanding access to paid PAS appears crucial in reducing unmet need among those who live alone. A limitation of the data is that family helpers were not asked if they were paid, which may accentuate differences between paid and unpaid help by living arrangement.

If the estimated shortfall in hours were to be provided through public funds, the cost of eliminating unmet need among people who live alone with low incomes ranges from $1.2 to $2.7 billion, a relatively small amount However, the cost for people who live with others is more than twice as large, from $2.2 to $7.1 billion.

Legal precedents such as the Supreme Court's Olmstead decision (U.S. Government Accounting Office, 2001) and legislative initiatives such as the Medicaid Community Attendant Services and Supports Act (MiCASSA; Harkin & Spector, 2001) would enable individuals to live in the least restrictive setting they desire. However, such efforts to reduce society's reliance on institutions cannot work if individuals' needs are not well met in the community.

Previous research, by looking only at the prevalence of unmet need for PAS, creates a false impression that unmet need is a large and costly problem to resolve. In fact, only 6.6% of all needed hours of help are unmet among adults needing help in two or more ADLs. The reduction, if not the elimination, of unmet need for PAS is a financially achievable goal for the nation and one that long-term care policy should focus on.

REFERENCES

Allen, S. M., & Mor, V. (1997). The prevalence and consequences of unmet need: Contrasts between older and younger adults with disability. *Medical Care, 35,* 1132–1148.

Desai, M. M., Lentzner, H. R., & Weeks, J. D. (2001). Unmet need for personal assistance with activities of daily living among older adults. *The Gerontologist, 41,* 82–88.

Harkin, T., & Spector, A. (2001). Medicaid Community Attendant Services and Supports Act of 2001 (MiCASSA) S. 1298. Washington, DC: U.S. Congress.

Harrington, C., LaPlante, M. P., Newcomer, R. J., Bedney, B., Shostak, S., Summers, P., et al. (2000). *A review of federal statutes and regulations for personal care and home and community based services: A final report.* San Francisco: University of California.

LaPlante, M. P., Harrington, C., & Kang, T. (2002). Estimating paid and unpaid hours of personal assistance services in activities of daily living provided to adults living at home. *Health Services Research, 37,* 397–415.

LeBlanc, A. J., Tonner, M. C., & Harrington, C. (2000). Medicaid 1915(c) home and community based services waivers across the states. *Health Care Financing Review, 22*(2), 159–174.

LeBlanc, A. J., Tonner, M. C., & Harrington, C. (2001). State Medicaid programs offering personal care services. *Health Care Financing Review, 22*(4), 155–173.

Lima, J. C., & Allen, S. M. (2001). Targeting risk for unmet need: Not enough help versus no help at all. *Journal of Gerontology: Social Sciences, 56B,* S302–S310.

Muramatsu, N., & Campbell, R. T. (2002). State expenditures on home and community based services and use of formal and informal personal assistance: A multilevel analysis. *Journal of Health and Social Behavior, 43,* 107–124.

U.S. General Accounting Office. (2001). *Long-term care: Implications for Supreme Court's Olmstead decision are still unfolding* (GAO-01-1167T). Washington, DC: Author.

U.S. National Center for Health Statistics. (1998a). *1994 National Health Interview Survey on Disability, Phase I and II* (Machine readable data file and documentation; CD-ROM Series 10, No. 8A). Hyattsville, MD: Author.

U.S. National Center for Health Statistics. (1998b). *1995 National Health Interview Survey on Disability, Phase I and II* (Machine readable data file and documentation; CD-ROM Series 10, No. 10A). Hyattsville, MD: Author.

The Economic and Health Security of Today's Young Women

Brooke Hollister, BA, and Carroll L. Estes, PhD

INTRODUCTION

Whether through the gender wage gap, savings, pensions, earnings sacrificed due to care-giving, or health insurance and access to health care, females today continue to face disproportionate disadvantages compared to their male counterparts. Public policy, including Social Security and Medicare reform; patterns of health care insurance coverage and provision; and multiple other dynamic aspects of societal change will affect the ability of today's young women to attain and maintain economic and health security. Just as economic and political projections are made regarding the future of social insurance programs such as Social Security and Medicare, so parallel projections need to be made of women's economic and health security as they age and retire in the decades ahead. Such parallel projections underscore not only the many prevailing disadvantages faced by women in U.S. society, but also women's disproportionate stake in preserving and improving the nation's social insurance programs to meet the needs of tomorrow's women as they age.

WOMEN'S POVERTY

Women are disproportionately at risk of poverty throughout their lifetime, especially in old age (Smeeding, 1999). Several factors contribute to this disadvantage, including the prevailing gender wage gap, low personal savings, the increasingly limited availability of private pensions, women's role as informal caregivers, and the changing structure of the American family (Estes, 2004). For future generations, it is projected that older women's poverty will persist while older men's poverty is expected to decline (Hartmann, in press).

While historically the gender wage gap has narrowed, women's median annual earnings fell from 2003 to 2004 by 1%, to 76.6% of men's earnings (U.S. Census Bureau, 2006a). The typical 25-year-old woman with a college degree will make about $523,000 less in wages over her lifetime compared to a 25-year-old man with a comparable education (IWPR/AFL-CIO, 1999). Older women today have roughly 58% of the retirement incomes of older men (U.S. Census Bureau, 2002). The gender wage gap is even greater for

Brooke Hollister and Carroll L. Estes. (2006). Women's health security. Brooke Hollister is a doctoral student at the University of California, San Francisco and the project director of the non-profits Students for Social Security and Concerned Scientists in Aging. Carroll Estes, PhD, is a professor at the Institute for Health and Aging, University of California, San Francisco. This article was prepared for the fifth edition of this book.

women of color and ethnic minorities (U.S. Census Bureau, 2006a). It is projected that the gender income gap will persist for younger women into old age as measured by virtually every category of income (private pensions, Social Security earnings, assets, and other sources). Not surprisingly, this gender wage gap contributes importantly to the lifelong and cumulative disadvantages faced by women.

Americans today are saving less than one penny of each after-tax dollar of income, with savings rates having dropped by 10% since 1984 (U.S. Bureau of Economic Analysis, 2005). This trend is likely to continue as the economic inequality between the rich and the poor worsens, leaving more working Americans too poor to save for retirement. The National Women's Retirement Survey reported that women usually have little or no money left to save for retirement after paying their bills (Heinz Foundation and Sun America, 1998). In addition, half of all minority women say that they have no money saved for retirement (WISER, 2005). Younger women are particularly disadvantaged regarding saving. Women aged 21 to 34 carry significantly more credit card debt than do their male counterparts (47% and 35%, respectively), and more single young women (53%) are living paycheck by paycheck than are single young men (42%) (U.S. Census Bureau, 2006a).

Pension coverage is both uneven and increasingly uncertain, in terms of the availability of coverage, employer's contribution, and risk to the individual worker. In 1979, nearly two in five (37%) private-sector workers were covered under a pension at work. Today, that number has dropped to just one in five (21%) (AFL-CIO, 2006). While the gap in pension coverage between men and women has decreased over the past decade, there is still cause for concern. Even when women qualify for private pensions, they receive about half the median benefits received by men. In 2000, the median annual income from these pensions for women was only $3,816 compared to $8,148 for men (SSA, 2004). In 2002, compared to 18% of older white women, only 13% of older black and 7% of older Hispanic women received a pension income (SSA, 2004).

Defined-contribution retirement savings plans such as 401(k)'s are much more widely available than defined-benefit pension plans as workers' only retirement plan option on the job. In 2002, participation of working women in a pension or savings plan was only 43%, compared to men's contribution rate of 49% (Purcell, 2003). Of today's workers, 38% of African American women, 26% of Hispanic women, and 38% of Asian/Pacific Islander women are covered by pension plans at work (Department of Labor, 2000). The shift to defined-contribution plans is important given findings of gender differences in investment experience and outcomes; women are generally more conservative, steering clear of riskier investments (Hinz, McCarthy, and Turner, 1997). In addition, women are more likely to receive and spend their retirement lump-sum benefits, using this money for everything from everyday expenses, to health care costs, to their children's educations (Conley and Ryvicker, in press). As more pensions switch from defined contributions to defined benefits, the economic security of tomorrow's elders is likely to diminish (Hartmann, in press).

Women's work as informal caregivers continues to be the primary U.S. long-term care (LTC) policy. Informal caregivers provide 75% or more of the nation's LTC, and women provide 70% or more of the LTC of the non-institutionalized elderly (Gregory, Pandya, AARP, and Public Policy Institute, 2002). Women (12%) are more likely than men (8%) to care for sick or aging family members, and some face economic tradeoffs as a result (Salganicoff, Neuman, Cubanski, Ranji, and Voris, 2006). Costs of informal care likely exceed the conservative estimates of $257 billion annually. According to the National Family Caregivers Association, the values of family caregiver services are more than two times the combined amount spent on nursing home and home care services (Becwith, 2005). One study shows that "over 40% of adult offspring . . . report that the time spent on caregiving tasks was equivalent to the time required by a full time job" (Feldblum, 1985, p. 220). Women lose as much as $550,000 in earnings, missed promotions, raises, and benefits over their lifetimes and $2,100 per year in Social Security payments (Metlife Mature Market Institute, 1999). Policies surrounding the LTC and pensions systems that reward those who engage in paid labor at the expense of those who fill unpaid caregiving roles are a direct attack against women (Estes, Biggs, and Phillipson, 2004).

Social Security and Poverty

Currently, 20% of older Americans rely on Social Security for 100% of their income in retirement, and two-thirds rely on Social Security for the majority of their retirement income (SSA, 2003). Older women are more likely to depend on Social Security as their only source of income in retirement (Older Women's League, 2002; WISER, 2002). In 2002, 90% of women were collecting Social Security benefits, with the average benefit for retired women ($774) being about 20% less than the average benefit for men ($1,006) (SSA, 2004). Social Security keeps many older women out of poverty. Without Social Security, 52% of older white females, 65% of older African American females, and 61% of older Latina females would be forced into poverty (IWPR, 2005). As more pensions are shifted from defined benefits to defined contributions, many of today's younger workers will depend on Social Security as their only guarantee in retirement. Furthermore, Social Security provides today's young working adults with life and disability insurance policies that few would be able to afford otherwise (estimated at $400,000 and $350,000, respectively) (NCPSSM, 2006). Without Social Security, the National Committee to Preserve Social Security and Medicare (NCPSSM) estimates that the almost 18 million beneficiaries of Social Security disability and survivor beneficiaries would be left destitute and dependent on a failing Medicare system (NCPSSM, 2006).

Social insurance programs help alleviate some of the prevailing inequalities experienced in society by women as well as people of color and people with disabilities. Attempts to privatize Social Security and changes presented in the 2003 Medicare Modernization Act (MMA), therefore, threaten the needed security of social insurance coverage for all Americans.

Social Security and Pension Reform

Gender differences in late-life financial security are highly correlated with marital status, with many social insurance programs exacerbating this inequality through the linking of benefits to marital status (Estes, 2004). Women are more likely than men to be widowed, divorced, or never married, leaving them particularly vulnerable in old age (Society of Actuaries, 2006). Marriage and divorce rates, smaller families, informal caregiving, and living alone all threaten the future economic security of today's youth, and particularly the fate of younger women. As a consequence, the guaranteed benefit of Social Security income for retired workers is vital for women. However, improvements are needed to address the shifts in family structure that are most perilous for women, particularly those who are low income, are less educated, are members of a minority, or have children (Estes, 2004).

Suggestions for improving women's financial status in old age include the following:

- Provide credits for "Caring Years," ensuring more gender equity in Social Security.
- Establish a Social Security minimum benefit at or above the poverty level, thereby lifting more older women out of poverty.
- Improve benefits for divorced, widowed, and other nonmarried women, protecting them in light of changing family structure and dynamics.
- Increase education and information on saving and investing for retirement.
- Eradicate the gender wage gap and promote higher education for women and further advancement of women into better jobs with benefits and child day care services.
- Improve and expand Medicaid family planning.
- Allow for paid pregnancy leave and more flexible work schedules for families and single mothers.

WOMEN'S HEALTH

Much of recent health policy has supported the development of a huge medical industrial complex that has enriched the pharmaceutical, health insurance, and hospital industries, thanks to major costs being passed on to consumers and the government. The increasing cost of health care and rising number of uninsured appear to be enduring aspects of the U.S. medical care system that threaten the health security of women of all ages.

Today Americans are living longer than ever, with women living longer than men, and whites living longer than people of color, with the limited exception of the Latino paradox (Anderson, 1998). Given this increasing longevity, it is expected that Americans will live with chronic disease longer, and that the prevalence of illness in society at any given time will be higher (Olshansky, Rudberg, Carnes, Cassel, and Brody, 1991). Of more immediate relevance for today's youth, almost 3 in 10 of today's 20-year-olds will become disabled before reaching age 67 (SSA, 2006a). These trends toward higher prevalence and more extended duration of chronic illnesses will require significant increases in financial and medical resources from individuals, families, and the government.

Related to longer life expectancy is the growing proportion of older women living alone. Almost 60% of older women are single, compared to just 26% of men (WISER, 2002). Women have less help around the house, less assistance when in need of caregiving, lower incomes, and a higher risk of institutionalization (Estes, 2004; WISER, 2002; SSA, 2006b; Glasse, Estes, and Smeeding, 1999; U.S. Census Bureau, 1996, 2004; Yntema, 1997). This trend is exacerbated by a decline in marriage and an increase in divorce (Steurle, 1999). Marital status is a strong predictor of income (Burkhauser and Smeeding, 1994) and health security as measured by health insurance coverage (Harrington Meyer, Wolf, and Himes, 2006).

Deleterious health, mental health, and economic consequences often accompany women's informal caregiving (Schulz and Beach, 1999). Women are likely to encounter a great deal of stress through caregiving and fulfilling other multiple and competing roles, and it is common for women to put the physical and mental health needs of those they care for ahead of their own. Family caregivers are more likely to experience depression associated with the stress and emotional work of their caregiving (Covinsky et al., 2003). Strained elderly spouse caregivers have been found to be at 63% higher risk of mortality than non-caregivers (Schulz and Beach, 1999). In 1990, the potential caregiver-to-elder ratio was 11:1; in 2050, this ratio is projected to shrink to 4:1, due in part to lower reproductive rates (Washington State DSHS, 2005). Clearly, several aspects of today's changing family structure (divorce, later childbearing, smaller families, more women living alone, and longer life expectancy) will influence the availability and affordability of informal care in the future.

Rising medical costs present one of the strongest indictments against the nation's private for-profit medical insurance system. Spillman and Lubitz (2000) found that the total health care expenditures (in 1996 dollars) from the age of 65 years until death increases substantially with longevity, rising from $31,181 for persons who die at the age of 65 years to more than $200,000 for those who die at the age of 90, in part because of steep increases in nursing home expenditures for very old persons. Currently, a 65-year-old faces $44,000 of uncovered LTC costs in his or her lifetime (Knickman and Snell, 2002). In addition, the Congressional Budget Office (CBO, 1999) estimates that LTC expenditures will increase at a rate of 2.6% per year above the inflation rate for the next 30 years. By 2040, there will be nearly three times as many people in nursing homes as there were in 1990 (U.S. Census Bureau, 1996). The ratio of men to women in nursing homes is 3:1, explaining the higher LTC costs for women and their increased dependence on Medicare and Medicaid (Sahyoun, Pratt, Lentzner, Dey, and Robinson, 2001).

More than 50% of bankruptcies occur due to catastrophic health care costs (Himmelstein, Warren, Thorne, and Woolhandler, 2005). Health care spending for women is consistently higher than that for men, even after adjustment for women's increased longevity (Spillman and Lubitz, 2000). The present value of out-of-pocket prescription drug costs for older persons averages $12,000, uncovered medical care comes to $16,000, and uncovered insurance premiums total $18,000 (Knickman and Snell, 2002). While many countries cover these expenses publicly, most Americans bear all of the burden of these health care costs. Public policies made to support the ideology of individual responsibility are failing the majority of the public in light of skyrocketing health care costs and the increasing tendency to shift these costs from employers and insurers to the individual. Furthermore, there is little evidence that health care costs will decrease in the future (Collins, Estes, and Bradsher, 2001).

For the most part, America's system of private insurers, Medicare, and Medicaid is responding to increasing costs by shifting expenses back to the individual in the form of premiums, co-payments, and increasing restrictions on medical tests, procedures, and prescription drugs. *Cost control* is a term defined in very different ways depending on who defines it. Patients and ordinary citizens might hope that cost control would mean eliminating administrative waste, sales commissions, and marketing excesses. To health industry executives, however, cost control may mean reducing the wages of health care workers, laying them off, speeding up the remaining staff, breaking unions, or watering down the quality of medical services to patients (Andrews, 1995). Medicare's acute care emphasis, deductibles, and high out-of-pocket costs and co-payments are disproportionately difficult for older women (Liu, Perozek, and Manton, 1993). Median out-of-pocket costs are almost twice as much for older women (19%) as for older men (11%) who have no supplemental insurance (Salganicoff et al., 2006). The rising instability in employment and marital status across the life course means that a secure health insurance system will not be employment or family based.

The rising cost of health care, limits to public health programs, and gaps in employer coverage have left 46.6 million Americans uninsured (Kaiser Commission on Medicaid and the Uninsured, 2003, 2006). Four out of five uninsured persons are in working families, with low-wage workers (laborers, service workers, and those employed in small business) at the greatest risk of being uninsured (Kaiser Commission on Medicaid and the Uninsured, 2003; U.S.Census Bureau, 2006b). Young adults between the ages of 18 and 24 have the highest rate of being uninsured (U.S. Census Bureau, 2006b). Today, there are 13.7 million young adults who lack health insurance in the United States, an increase of 2.5 million since 2000 (Collins, Schoen, Kriss, Doty, and Mahato, 2006). Unmarried women are two to three times as likely to be uninsured or to rely on public programs such as Medicaid (Leigh and Jimenez, 2002). Additional disparities in access to health insurance coverage and health care have been found among women of color (Harrington Meyer, 1996) and women with low incomes (Lyons, Salganicoff, and Rowland, 1996). About half of the non-elderly uninsured are racial and ethnic minorities, with uninsured rates being the highest among Hispanics. Hispanics make up about 16% of the non-elderly population and about 30% of the uninsured population ((Kaiser Commission on Medicaid and the Uninsured, 2006).

The importance of having insurance to realizing access to health care is well documented (Kaiser Commission on Medicaid and the Uninsured, 2003; IOM, 2001, 2002; Lenhard-Reisinger, 1996). Uninsured adults are less likely to receive preventive care, more likely than those with insurance to be hospitalized for conditions that could have been avoided, and more likely to have serious conditions identified at a later stage than the insured (e.g., cancer) (Kaiser Commission on Medicaid and the Uninsured, 2003. In addition to negative health effects, 44% of the uninsured had a serious problem paying medical bills in 2002 (KFF, 2005). Lack of medical insurance—whether at a young age, in old age, or throughout the life course—has significant effects on health, financial stability, and retirement security, highlighting the importance of Medicare and Social Security.

With the growth of the medical industrial complex, longer life expectancy, more women living alone, the shrinking pool of caregivers, and the increasing cost of health care; many people will undoubtedly exhaust their income and retirement savings on chronic or catastrophic health care costs. Like Social Security, Medicare may be the only form of health care available to the elderly and disabled in the future.

Women and Medicare

Although Medicare has almost eliminated the number of uninsured elderly, the average older person spends 20% of his or her income on out-of-pocket health care costs, with this figure rising to 34% of income for the poor elderly (Rowland, 1999).

The CBO (1999) has documented that the public sector (Medicare and Medicaid) covered 59% of the $120 billion spent on LTC. Although most of us would hope to be able to rely on personal resources and the financial stability of children or spouses should we require LTC, several factors related to the changing face of the American family are likely to significantly limit the availability of informal care in the future.

Exclusions of LTC under Medicare forces individuals to "spend down" their savings and other assets to qualify for Medicaid LTC coverage. Women's reliance on Medicaid is critical in women's health, health care access, and outcomes. Of Medicaid beneficiaries older than age 14, 7 in 10 are women, with women "more likely to qualify for Medicaid than men because they tend to be poorer and tend to meet the program's strict eligibility criteria" (KFF, 2005, p. 1). Medicaid provides valuable family planning resources to women, with 1 in 10 women of reproductive age relying on Medicaid for her health and reproductive care (KFF, 2005).

Without Medicaid's services or the eventual development of a universal health care system, women's health problems, barriers to health care, and poor outcomes would be dramatically exacerbated. Despite the growing need for Medicaid coverage among women, the poor, the disabled, and the elderly, the federal government has responded to the growing health care costs of these populations by cutting funding, decreasing reimbursement rates, restricting eligibility criteria, and rationing the availability of certain health treatments.

The 2003 Medicare Modernization Act represents a threat to the traditional universal public Medicare program because it subsidizes the largely for-profit Medicare Advantage (HMO-type) plans. The introduction of higher payments for Medicare Advantage plans than for traditional Medicare is the product of the special interests that formulated this legislation (the insurance industry, private health plans, the pharmaceutical industry, and the government) and the ideology of "choice" within health care.

Medicare and Health Care Reform

Raphael and Bryant (2003) write that "women's health and well-being are particularly sensitive to decisions made in relation to the spending priorities of governments, the extent to which services are provided, and the degree to which women are supported in moves toward equity" (p. 63). Their research finds that in countries with a social welfare orientation, women's health and quality of life exceed those of their counterparts who live in countries with a market approach to policy. Their warnings about the growing market-oriented approaches in Canada support the call to stop the privatization of services and expand U.S. social welfare programs.

Suggestions for reforms to address women's health security include the following:

- Join all other developed countries in developing a national health care system with LTC to ensure access to quality care for all citizens.

In the absence of a national health care system, other suggestions include these measures:

- Ensure universal health care coverage through state and/or local government.
- Improve and expand Medicaid services and eligibility (increase asset limits).

- Extend COBRA provisions to five years.
- Create LTC coverage under Medicare to alleviate the burden of cost on and exploitation of informal caregivers.
- Dedicate research and advocacy to improving health care access for all disadvantaged populations, including women, racial and ethnic minorities, and people with disabilities.

SUMMARY

Today's youth face insecurity and risk in their future, guaranteeing an increase in reliance on social insurance programs. Today's youth will be left with less savings, less wealth, less pensions, and more barriers to health care than were available to previous generations. The intergenerational stakes, as represented by social insurance programs, are higher for women, especially minority women. The importance of preserving these programs continues to grow as today's young women face increasing challenges to a financially secure and healthy retirement.

REFERENCES

American Federation of Labor–Congress of Industrial Organizations (AFL-CIO). (2006). Defined benefit pensions. Retrieved October 15, 2006, from www.aflcio.org/issues/retirementsecurity/definedbenefitpensions/index.cfm

Anderson, R. (1998). *United States abridged life tables, 1996.* Hyattsville, MD: National Center for Health Statistics.

Andrews, C. (1995). *Profit fever: The drive to corporatize health care and how to stop it.* Monroe, ME: Common Courage Press.

Becwith, B. (2005). Critical perspectives on public policy and family caregiving issues. *Health Care and Aging. Newsletter of the Healthcare and Aging Network, American Society on Aging,* 12(3), 1, 6.

Burkhauser, R. V., & Smeeding, T. M. (1994). *Social Security reform: A budget neutral approach to reducing older women's disproportionate risk of poverty* (Policy Brief No. 2). Syracuse, NY: Maxwell School Center for Policy Research.

Collins, C. A., Estes, C. L., & Bradsher, J. E. (2001). Inequality and aging: The creation of dependency. In: C. L. Estes & Associates (Eds.), *Social policy and aging* (pp. 137–163). Thousand Oaks, CA: Sage.

Collins, S. R., Schoen, C., Kriss, J. L., Doty, M. M., & Mahato, B. (2006). *Rite of passage? Why young adults become uninsured and how new policies can help.* New York, NY: Commonwealth Fund.

Congressional Budget Office. (1999). CBO memorandum: Projections of expenditures for long term care services for the elderly. Retrieved October 15, 2006, from http://www.cbo.gov/showdoc.cfm?index=1123&sequence=0

Conley, D., & Ryvicker, M. (In press). The price of female headship: The effect of gender and family structure on savings, inheritance and wealth accumulation in the United States. *Journal of Income Distributions,* 13(3–4), 41–56.

Covinsky, K. E., Newcomer, R., Fox, P., Wood, J., Sands, L., Dane, K., & Yaffe, K. (2003). Patient and caregiver characteristics associated with depression in caregivers of patients with dementia. *Journal of General Internal Medicine,* 18, 1006–1014.

Department of Labor. (2000). U.S. Department of Labor, Pensions, and Welfare Benefits Administration. Private pension, health and welfare plan highlights. Pension coverage. Washington, D.C. Spring 2000.

Estes, C. L. (2004). Social Security privatization and older women: A feminist political economy perspective. *Journal of Aging Studies,* 18(1), 9.

Estes, C. L., Biggs, S., & Phillipson, C. (2004). *Social theory, social policy and ageing: A critical introduction.* Milton Keynes, UK: Open University Press.

Feldblum, C. (1985). Home health care for the elderly: Programs, problems and potentials. *Harvard Journal on Legislation,* 22, 193–254.

Glasse, L., Estes, C., & Smeeding, T. (1999). *Social Security reform and older women: How to help the most vulnerable.* Statement for the House Subcommittee on Social Security, Committee on Ways and Means. Washington, DC: Gerontological Society of America.

Gregory, S. R., Pandya, S. M., AARP, & Public Policy Institute. (2002). Women and long term care. Retrieved June 1, 2005, from http://assets.aarp.org/rgcenter/health/fs77r_women_2002.pdf

Harrington Meyer, M. (1996). Making claims as workers or wives: The distribution of Social Security benefits. *American Sociological Review,* 61(3), 449–465.

Harrington Meyer, M., Wolf, D. A., & Himes, C. L. (2006). Declining eligibility for Social Security spouse and widow benefits in the United States? *Research on Aging,* 28(2), 240–260.

Hartmann, H. (In press). *Women and retirement security.* New York: Russell Sage.

Heinz Foundation & Sun America. (1998). The national women's retirement survey.

Himmelstein, D. U., Warren, E., Thorne, D., & Woolhandler, S. (2005). Marketwatch: Illness and injury as contributors to bankruptcy. *Health Affairs,* Suppl Web Exclusives: W5–63.

Hinz, R. P., McCarthy, D. O., & Turner, J. A. (1997). *Are women conservative investors? Gender differences in participant-directed pension investments.* Philadelphia: University of Pennsylvania Press.

Institute of Medicine (IOM). (2001). *Coverage matters: Insurance and health care.* Washington, DC: National Academy Press.

Institute of Medicine (IOM). (2002). *Care without coverage: Too little, too late.* Washington, DC: National Academy Press.

Institute for Women's Policy Research (IWPR). (2005). Memo to John Roberts: The gender wage gap is real. www.iwpr.org

Institute for Women's Policy Research (IWPR)/American Federation of Labor–Congress of Industrial Organizations (AFL-CIO). (1999). *Equal pay for working families: National and state data on the pay gap and its costs.* Washington, DC: IWPR and the AFL-CIO Working Women's Department.

Kaiser Commission on Medicaid and the Uninsured. (2003). The uninsured and their access to health care. Retrieved October 15, 2006, from www.kff.org/uninsured/upload/The-Uninsured-and-their-access-to-health-care-Oct-pdf. Washington, DC: The Henry J. Kaiser Family Foundation.

Kaiser Commission on Medicaid and the Uninsured. (2006). Who are the uninsured? A consistent profile across national surveys. Retrieved October 15, 2006, from www.kff.org/uninsured/upload/7553.pdf. Washington, DC: The Henry J. Kaiser Family Foundation.

Kaiser Family Foundation (KFF). (2005). Medicaid: A critical source of support for family planning in the United States. Retrieved October 15, 2006, from www.kff.org/womenshealth/upload/Medicaid-A-Critical-Source-of-Support-for-Family-Planning-in-the-United-States-Issue-Brief-UPDATE.pdf

Knickman, J. R., & Snell, E. K. (2002). The 2030 problem: Caring for aging baby boomers. *Health Services Research,* 37(4), 849–884.

Leigh, W. A., & Jimenez, M. A. (2002). Women of color health data book. Retrieved October 15, 2006, from http://orwh.od.nih.gov/pubs/WomenofColor2006.pdf

Lenhard-Reisinger, A. (1996). Health insurance and women's access to health care. In: M. Falik & K. Scott Collins (Eds.), *Women's health: The Commonwealth Fund survey* (pp. 324–344). Baltimore, MD: Johns Hopkins University Press.

Liu, K., Perozek, M., & Manton, K. (1993). Catastrophic acute and long term care costs: Risks faced by disabled elderly persons. *Gerontologist,* 33, 299–307.

Lyons, B., Salganicoff, A., & Rowland, D. (1996). Poverty, access to health care, and Medicaid's critical role for women. In: M. Falik & K. Scott Collins (Eds.), *Women's health: The Commonwealth Fund survey* (pp. 273–295). Baltimore, MD: Johns Hopkins University Press.

MetLife Mature Market Institute. (1999). *The MetLife juggling act study: Balancing caregiving with work and the costs involved.* Westport, CT: MetLife Mature Market Institute.

National Committee to Preserve Social Security and Medicare (NCPSSM). (2006). Social Security primer. Retrieved October 15, 2006, from www.ncpssm.org/news/archive.ssprimer/

Older Women's League. (2002). *Social Security privatization: A false promise for women.* Washington, DC: Older Women's League. Retrieved October 15, 2006, from www.owl-national.org/owlreports/MothersDay2002.pdf

Olshansky, S. J., Rudberg, M. A., Carnes, B. A., Cassel, C. K., & Brody, J. A. (1991). Trading off longer life for worsening health: The expansion of morbidity hypothesis. *Journal of Aging and Health,* 3(2), 194–216.

Purcell, P. (2003). *Pension and retirement savings plans: Sponsorship and participation.* Washington, DC: Congressional Research Service.

Raphael, D., & Bryant, T. (2003). The welfare state as a determinant of women's health: Support for women's quality of life in Canada and comparison nations. *Health Policy,* 68, 63–79.

Rowland, D. (1999). The challenge of meeting the diverse needs of Medicare's beneficiaries. Paper presented at the Hearing on Medicare Reform, Committee on Finance, U.S. Senate.

Sahyoun, N. R., Pratt, L. A., Lentzner, H., Dey, A., & Robinson, K. N. (2001). The changing profile of nursing home residents: 1985–1997. *Aging Trends,* 4, 1–8.

Salganicoff, A., Neuman, T., Cubanski, C., Ranji, U., Voris, M. (2006). Health coverage and expenses: Impact on retired women's economic well being. In: Heidi Hartmann (Ed.), *Women and retirement security.* New York: Russell Sage Foundation.

Schulz, R., & Beach, S. R. (1999). Caregiving as a risk factor for mortality: The caregiver health effects study. *Journal of the American Medical Association,* 282(23), 2215–2219.

Smeeding, T. (1999). *Social Security reform and older women: Improving the system.* Syracuse, NY: Syracuse University Press.

Social Security Administration (SSA). (2003). Most retirees rely on Social Security for their incomes: Fast facts & figures about Social Security. Retrieved October 15, 2006, from www.aflcio.org/issues/retirementsecurity/socialsecurity/upload/chart4.pdf

Social Security Administration (SSA). (2004). Income of the population 55 or older; 2002. Retrieved October 15, 2006, from www.ssa.gov/policy/docs/statcomps/income_pop55/2002/

Social Security Administration (SSA). (2006a). Fact sheet: Social Security. Retrieved October 15, 2006, from www.ssa.gov/pressoffice/basicfact.htm

Social Security Administration (SSA). (2006b). Social Security is important to women. Retrieved October 15, 2006, from www.ssa.gov/pressoffice/factsheets/women.htm

Society of Actuaries. (2006). Key findings and issues: The impact of retirement risk on women. 2005 risks and process of retirement survey report. Retrieved October 15, 2006, from www.soa.org

Spillman, B. C., & Lubitz, J. (2000). The effect of longevity on spending for acute and long-term care. *New England Journal of Medicine,* 342(19), 1409–1415.

Steuerle, E. (1999). *The treatment of the family and divorce in the Social Security program.* Washington, DC: U.S. Senate Special Committee on Aging.

U.S. Bureau of Economic Analysis. (2005). Personal income and outlays. Retrieved June 1, 2005, from http://bea.gov/bea/newsrel/pinewsrelease.htm

U.S. Census Bureau. (1996). *Current population reports, special studies, P23-190, 65+ in the United States.* Washington, DC: U.S. Government Printing Office. Retrieved October 15, 2006, from www.census.gov/prod/1/pop/p23-190/p23-190.pdf

U.S. Census Bureau. (2002). *Money income in the United States.* Washington, DC: U.S. Government Printing Office. Retrieved October 15, 2006, from www.census.gov/hhes/www/income/income02.html

U.S. Census Bureau. (2004). We the people: Aging in the United States. Washington, DC: U.S. Government Printing Office. Retrieved October 15, 2006, from www.census.gov/prod/2004pubs/censr-19.pdf

U.S. Census Bureau. (2006a). *Income, earning, and poverty data from the 2005 American community survey.* Washington, DC: U.S. Government Printing Office. Retrieved October 15, 2006, from www.census.gov/prod/2006pubs/acs-02.pdf

U.S. Census Bureau. (2006b). *Income, poverty, and health insurance coverage in the United States: 2005.* Washington, DC: U.S. Government Printing Office. Retrieved October 15, 2006, from www.census.gov/prod/2006pubs/p60-231.pdf

Washington State DSHS. (2005). Informal/family caregivers. Retrieved October 15, 2006, from www.adsa.dshs.wa.gov/professional/factsheets/informal%20%20family%20caregivers%20fact%20sheet%2012-05.pdf

Women's Institute for Secure Retirement (WISER). (2002). *Minority women and retirement income: Your future paycheck.* Washington, DC: WISER.

Women's Institute for Secure Retirement (WISER). (2005). *Minority women and retirement income: Your future paycheck.* Washington, DC: WISER.

Yntema, S. (1997). *Americans 55 and older: A changing market.* Ithaca, NY: New Strategist Publications.

Social Security Privatization and Older Women: A Feminist Political Economy Perspective

Carroll L. Estes

INTRODUCTION

In social gerontology during the 1990s, increasing attention in policy circles was given to talk of issues of intergenerational relations and a hypothesized antagonism between the generations. Interestingly, in spite of bountiful rhetoric to the contrary, this "intergenerational conflict" has never been empirically demonstrated to be true either by public opinion polls or by other research (Cook, 2003). Attacks on Social Security have occurred almost in direct proportion to the strength of the politically motivated crisis constructions of Social Security, the population aging, the baby boom, the stepped-up attacks on women as welfare mothers and their reproductive choice and rights, and the political rise of the Christian Coalition and its moralistic stance regarding men as divinely chosen heads of the patriarchal family. Beginning with the Reagan Revolution and continuing throughout President Reagan's two terms, new popularized versions of a Social Security "crisis" have been continuously manufactured and reified in the political rhetoric of Congress, Wall Street power brokers, and conservative thinkers (Estes, 1996, 2001a). The power struggles surrounding attempts to privatize entitlements such as Social Security (as well as Medicare) signify the challenged and changing role of the state in the context of a rise in financial global capital and the dynamic struggles engendered by it. Periodic yet sustained attacks on the legitimacy of the state (Estes, 1991) emanating from former President Carter's campaign onward (as state governors ran against Washington, DC, politicians and bureaucrats) have only contributed more threats to Social Security.

WOMEN'S DEPENDENCY ON THE STATE

Social policy contributes to older women's dependency. The economic hardship and dependence of older women on the state are socially and structurally produced due largely to women's historic role and treatment in and by the family, the market, and the state (Dickinson & Russell, 1986; Orloff, 1993). These gendered institutions (Acker, 1988) and their gender regimes (Connell, 1987) reflect masculine domination (Bourdieu, 2001). The result is (a) gendered policy in the public and private sectors (b) wage inequality, sex discrimination, and unequal opportunity to work (which disadvantages women) and (c) reproductive labor (e.g., caregiving) that is neither financially remunerated nor accounted for under U.S. Social Security

Adapted from: Carroll L. Estes. (2004). Social Security privatization and older women: A feminist political economy perspective. *Journal of Aging Studies* 18, 9–26.

retirement policy (Estes, 1998; Harrington Meyer, 1996). Stated bluntly social policy reflects the dominant ideologies and state policies that enforce, bolster, and extend the market and the structure of white male advantage in the larger economic, political, and social order (Estes, 2001b).

The problem of Social Security is particularly important because women are more dependent on the state than men across the life course (Estes, 2001b). Further, older women's dependency on the state and its safety net programs increases with aging, widowhood, divorce, and associated spend-downs (decumulation) in their economic resources, just as women's health status becomes more problematic with age. By the time a woman is age 65, she is almost twice as likely as her male counterpart to be poor or near poor (Estes & Michel, 1999; Older Women's League (OWL), 1999). Marital status is definitly related to poverty (Harrington Meyer; 1996). Older women are thrice more likely to be widowed than older men (SSA, 1998). Almost 60% of older women are single compared with 26% of older men (Women's Institute for Secure Retirement (WISER), 2002, p. 12). Divorce rates have jumped more than threefold for midlife women (aged 45–49) in the United States (from 5.3% to 17.7% between 1970 to 1997) (Steuerle, 1999). Future projections are for the continued acceleration of these trends, with reductions in the percentage of married women in midlife as well as old age (Estes & Michel, 1999; OWL, 1999; Steuerle, 1999).

These trends in marital status are expected to substantially increase the poverty rates for older women who are never married, divorced, or separated (Smeeding, Estes, & Glasse, 1999). Declining rates for women who are married in old age are a major reason that older women's economic hardships are now projected to decline for baby boom and future generations of older women, while older men's poverty rate is projected to decline or disappear in the next several decades (Commonwealth Fund, 1988; Smeeding, 1999; Smeeding et al., 1999). Privatization, as is argued throughout this article, would be expected to significantly exacerbate the already difficult economic problems of older women.

Interestingly, in cross-national comparisons, U.S. older women who are single have the lowest income relative to married couples of the eight nations studied (Disney & Johnson, 2001; Disney & Whitehouse, 2002). With the nations in rank order, single older women's incomes fare from best to worst as follows: the Netherlands (the best), Italy, Canada, Australia, France, Germany, the UK, and the United States (the worst and dead last). In another study of 18 nations, Smeeding and Williamson (2001; Disney & Whitehouse, 2002) found that the United States was the second worst of all countries (surpassed only by Australia) in its "pensioner income poverty rate"–the percent of pensioners with incomes below one-half of the population median income. More than 20% of U.S. pensioners report incomes below one-half the median threshold. Finally, in studies of pensioner income inequalities in 16 countries, the United States ranks near the bottom, second only to Greece in the ratio of 90th percentile of pensioner income to the 10th percentile (Forster & Lellizzari, 2000; Disney & Whitehouse, 2002).

SOCIAL INSURANCE

In 1935, Social Security was designed to be the nation's bedrock of social insurance to address the universals of the uncertainty of retirement, illness, disability, and death. Social insurance is meant to meet both the defined needs of individuals and their family's and society's needs. The U.S. social insurance system is built around the provision of defined benefits derived on onset of principles. U.S. citizens know what they are entitled to in retirement income, with predictability and certainty. This is vastly different than what would occur under the alternative private proposal—a system of defined contributions that does not guarantee a certain level of benefits at the time of retirement, e.g., benefit adequacy: (discussed further below).

Robert Ball, former U.S. Commissioner of Social Insurance for three Presidents, describes the basic principles of social insurance: "The best form of self-protection is mutual aid on a universal scale. When everyone contributes, everyone can be protected" (Ball & Bethell, 1989, p. 3). The unique characteristics of social insurance that Ball identifies include coverage, earned benefit, equality, dedicated financing, and administration and responsibility (Ball & Bethell, 1989, pp. 71–79), as outlined below:

1. Coverage
   There is equitable protection for the entire population.
   No one is forced into poverty in retirement.
2. Earned benefit
   All beneficiaries or their families contribute to the program.
   There is an earned right to benefits, unlike stigmatized welfare.
3. Equality
   Everyone is in the same boat.
   There is broad support for the program.
   There are uniform defined benefits.
4. Dedicated financing
   A dedicated source of financing exists through the payroll tax.
   Low-income workers can be covered at an affordable cost.
   There is inflation protection.
   Cost containment and administrative efficiencies are realized.
5. Responsibility for program purpose and content
   There is a clear designation of congressional and federal administrative responsibility.
   There is program visibility (transparency) and public accountability.

The proposed privatization of Social Security is predicated on a repudiation of virtually all five of these principles of social insurance. Instead, individual responsibility, performance of workers in the market (but without recognition of women's contributed reproductive labor), and earned property rights (rather than citizenship rights) are the key principles that are philosophically enshrined and instantiated under privatization schemes. A central question is how these principles of privatization (or their repudiation) will affect women and other groups in society that are already disadvantaged by race/ethnicity, and lower socioeconomic status (social class) long before old age, disability, or widowhood are imposed on them.

TWO AGENDAS: PRIVATIZATION VERSUS SOCIAL INSURANCE

The proponents of Social Security privatization are seeking to advance the front battle lines of the conservative agenda. The proponents of the current social insurance system of Social

Security (who also oppose privatization) seek to advance a program that has historically achieved a delicate balance of equity and adequacy concerns. It is one on which social justice claimants, including feminists, could address anyone (or some combination) of the significant cumulative disadvantages of race, class, and gender. The agenda of the privatization versus social insurance/antiprivatization forces may be outlined as follows.

Privatization Adherents: The Conservative Agenda seeks to:

- Replace social insurance principles with market principles.
- Treat beneficiaries as citizens with property.
- Reinstate the traditional role of women in family and the reward structure for productive and reproductive labor; use policy to reward paid labor market behavior only.
- Change Social Security from a system of defined benefits to one of defined contributions, shifting responsibility from the public government to individual private responsibility.
- Shrink the welfare state by
    Reducing state costs/commitment to secure retirement.
    Reducing business costs/commitment (reduced payroll taxes).
- Give massive state subsidy to financial capital via Social Security privatization.
- Abolish all redistributive elements of the current Social Security system (i.e., remove all provisions designed to address gender, race, and class justice, such as those reflecting the "adequacy" principle in Social Security).

Social Insurance (Antiprivatization) Adherents: A Feminist and Progressive Agenda seeks to:

- Preserve principles of social insurance and universal entitlement.
- Treat beneficiaries as citizens with rights.
- Maintain and improve Social Security as a defined benefit.
- Increase public responsibility and fairness.
- Redress gender, race, and class justice through state policy.
- Recognize reproductive labor as contributions under Social Security.

WHY PRIVATIZATION IS BAD FOR WOMEN

Analyses of the women's issues that are raised by the proposed privatization of Social Security have been developed by a number of organizations and scholars. The brief analysis by the National Women's Law Center is reproduced here in toto because of the clarity and consistency of the analysis with the perspective of critical feminist political economy (Table 4.5.1).

CONCLUSION: A FEMINIST POLITICAL ECONOMY AND SOCIAL SECURITY

The Big Picture is twofold. First, Social Security privatization represents a major effort to shift responsibility from the state to the individual, with large and predictably negative

TABLE 4.5.1   Why Social Security Is a Better Deal Than Privatization for Women and Their Families

Social Security	Private Accounts
Retirement benefits for as long as you live This guarantee of lifetime income for retired workers and their survivors is especially important for women who tend to live longer, spend more years alone, and have less assets than men.	*Risk of outliving your account balance* Lifetime savings can be drained by a long life, health costs, bad luck, or misjudgment. Converting an account to an annuity consumes 15–20% of its value (women may pay more) and lifetime income will depend on how the market is doing when the annuity is purchased.
Guaranteed, predictable retirement benefits Social Security's defined benefit does not fluctuate with the stock market and provides the foundation of women's retirement security. This will be even more important in the future as employers move away from traditional pensions to 401(k)s.	*Risk that returns may go up or down* Everyone should try to save for retirement. However, investing has risks; some market downturns last for years. Investment fees cut deeply into returns: a fee of 1%/year would consume 20% of an account over 40 years. Small accounts are often charged higher fees than larger accounts.
Annual cost-of-living adjustments Social Security protections against inflation are especially important to women because they live longer than men.	*Inflation erodes purchasing power* Almost no private annuities offer COLAs. Inflation of 2.5%/year would cut the value of a 65-year-old's annuity payment by 40% by the time she is 85.
Progressive benefit formula Social Security provides a higher percentage of preretirement income for women who have worked for low wages and taken time out for caregiving.	*Those who have less, get less* Private accounts depend on how much an individual can put in and returns, minus costs. The system would not compensate for women's lower lifetime earnings.
Disability and survivors benefits for families Equivalent to a $300,000 life and $200,000 disability policy for an average wage earner and family, these benefits are especially important to minorities because of their higher rates of disability and death.	*No assurances of family insurance benefits* No plan to privatize has yet specified how these benefits would be maintained; workers would not have enough in an account to protect themselves and their families if their careers were cut short and many of those who need it most could not afford to buy comparable private insurance.
Automatic benefits for spouses/ surviving spouses Spousal benefits are available to both sexes, but 99% of those who depend on	*All spousal protections up in the air* Would workers be able to spend all of their account or leave whatever was left to

(continues)

TABLE 4.5.1   continued

Social Security	Private Accounts
them are women. Divorced spouses and divorced widows married 10 years receive benefits automatically, without reducing benefits for the worker or next spouse.	someone other than the spouse? At divorce, spouses would have to struggle over the division of limited account assets; women's experience with the division of other pension assets suggests that many will not receive an equitable share.

National Women's Law Center, estimated 2005.

effects on women, minorities, and lower-income men, while also transferring massive amounts of cash (up to $15 trillion in Social Security funds) from the state to private capital markets via Wall Street. Second, the power struggles surrounding Social Security privatization signal both (a) a major transfer of power and control *from* the state *to* private corporate capital and (b) a veiled effort to "discipline" the American citizen in the form of two bodies—the woman and her family and the wage worker. The discipline is in the message that, with privatization, those who are not highly educated and socioeconomically advantaged must accept the hardship of exploitative labor conditions over a long lifetime of work to have any chance of escaping deep economic deprivation in old age.

The present Social Security system is clearly more woman friendly than Social Security privatization designs that will vitiate or negate the principles of social insurance. Because the present design of Social Security is predicated on the more inclusive principle of social insurance, it institutionalizes a citizen-based rather than a market- and property-based social contract. It is the universally granted, state-guaranteed, and citizen-based contract envisioned in the initial framing of Social Security and one that offers vital assurances of some minimal income adequacy for all U.S. beneficiaries and their families in contrast to the higher risks and uncertainties attendant to privatized schemes. Under Social Security privatization, the distributional outcomes will be decidedly worse for women, minorities, and low-income workers compared with the present system of social insurance.

A significant limitation on old age policy is that the dominant power group, white men, does not share equally with women the benefits of the longevity revolution. I believe that this may well significantly account for policies that reflect and reward traditional intact family structures, male patterns of aging and health (e.g., Medicare for acute care and no universal public provision for long-term care that comprises women's unpaid work), and social positioning and privileging of whites and males.

A major goal of a critical feminist political economy of Social Security and the privatization debate is understanding how the state and Social Security policy work in tandem with capital and the sex and gender system in ways that render older women vulnerable and dependent throughout their life course (Estes, 1982, 1991, 2001b). An important consideration is how state policies that define, individualize, and comodify the problems of aging (i.e., as individual problems and personal private responsibility to be solved by the provision of services to individuals and sold at a profit) (see Estes, 1979; Estes, Gerard, Zones, & Swan, 1984; Estes, Harrington, & Pellow, 2001) are ideologically and practically consistent with state roles that advance the interests of capital accumulation and the legitimization of capitalist social relations (Estes, 1979; O'Connor, 1973). Although it is a widely shared feminist view that state policy has not succeeded in recompensing for the lifelong accumulation of social and material disadvantages of women and oppressed minorities, the present social insurance system offers greater protection and a basic set of principles that provides the scaffolding on which policies may be designed to further enhance social justice goals and reduce social inequities. Principles of market-based citizenship offer no such possibility.

REFERENCES

Acker, J. (1988). Class, gender and the relations of distribution. *Signs, 13,* 473–493.

Ball, R., & Bethell, T. (1989) *Because we're all in this together.* Washington, DC: Families USA Foundation.

Bourdieu, P. (2001). *Masculine domination.* Stanford, CA: Stanford University Press.

Commonwealth Fund. (1988). *Aging alone: Profiles and projections.* New York: Commonwealth Fund.

Connell, R W. (1987). *Gender and power: Society, the person, and sexual politics.* Stanford. CA: Stanford University Press.

Cook, F. L. (2003). *Public opinion and Social Security.* National Council on the Aging-American Society on Aging. Chicago, IL.

Dickinson, J., & Russell, R. (1986). *Family, economy and state: The social reproduction process under capitalism.* New York: St. Martin's Press.

Disney, R., & Johnson, P. G. (2001). *Pension systems and retirement incomes across DECD countries.* Aldershot, England: Edward Elgar.

Disney, R., & Whitehouse, E. (2002). The economic well-being of older people in international perspective: A critical review. In S. Crystal & D. G. Shea (Eds.), *Annual Review of Gerontology and Geriatrics. vol. 22* (pp. 59–94). New York: Springer.

Estes, C. L. (1979). *The aging enterprise.* San Francisco, CA: Jossey-Bass.

Estes, C. L. (1982). Austerity and aging in the United States: 1980 and beyond. *International Journal of Health Services,* 12(4):573–584.

Estes, C. L. (1991). The Reagan legacy: Privatization, the welfare state, and aging in the 1990's. In J. Myles & J. S. Quadagno (Eds.), *States, labor markets, and the future of old age policy* (pp. 59–83). Philadelphia, PA: Temple University Press.

Estes, C. L. (1996). *Crisis, the welfare state and aging* (Presidential Address). Paper presented to the Annual Meeting of the Gerontological Society of America, Washington, DC.

Estes, C. L. (1998). *Social Security and the older woman.* Organized by the Older Women's League for the Economic Security Task Force, National Council of Women's Organizations, Washington, DC.

Estes, C. L. (2001a). Crisis, the welfare state, and aging: Ideology and agency in the social security privatization debate. In C. L. Estes et al. (Eds.), *Social policy and aging: A critical perspective* (pp. 95–117). Thousand Oaks, CA: Sage.

Estes, C. L. (2001b). Sex and gender in the political economy of aging. In C. L. Estes et al. (Eds.), *Social policy and aging: A critical perspective* (pp. 119–135). Thousand Oaks, CA: Sage.

Estes, C. L., Gerard, L., Zones, J. S., & Swan, J. (1984). *The political economy, health, and aging.* Boston, MA: Little, Brown.

Estes, C. L., Harrington, C., & Pellow, D. N. (2001). The medical industrial complex and the aging enterprise. In C. L. Estes et al. (Eds.), *Social policy and aging: A critical perspective* (pp. 165–185). Thousand Oaks, CA: Sage.

Estes, C. L., & Michel, M. (1999). Social Security and women. In *Social Security in the 21st century. The taskforce on Women* (pp. 1–7). Washington, DC: Gerontological Society of America.

Forster, M. F., & Lellizzari, M. (2000). *Trends and driving factors in income distribution and poverty in the OECD area*. Labour Market and Social Policy Occasional Paper no. 42. Paris: OECD.

Gokhale, J., & Kotlikoff, L. J. (1999). Generational justice and generational accounting. In J. B. Williamson, D. M. Watts-Roy, & E. Kingson (Eds.), *The generational equity debate* (pp. 75–86). New York: Columbia University Press.

Harrington Meyer, M. (1996). Making claims as workers or wives: The distribution of social security benefits. *American Sociological Review, 61*, 449–465.

National Women's Law Center. *Why Social Security is a better deal than privatization for women and their families*. Washington, DC: National Women's Law Center.

O'Connor, J. (1973). *The fiscal crisis of the state*. New York: St. Martin's Press.

Older Women's League (OWL). (1999). *Privatization and older women: Mothers Day report*. Washington, DC: OWL.

Orloff, A. S. (1993). Gender and the social rights of citizenship: The comparative analysis of gender relations and welfare states. *American Sociological Review, 58*, 303–329.

Peterson, P. (1999). How will America pay for the retirement of the baby boom generation? In J. B. Williamson, D. M. Watts-Roy, & E. Kingson (Eds.), *The generational equity debate* (pp. 41–57). New York: Columbia University Press.

Smeeding, T. (1999). *Social Security reform and older women: Improving the system*. Syracuse, NY: Syracuse University Press.

Smeeding, T., Estes, C. L., & Glasse, L. (1999). *Social Security reform and older women: Improving the system*. Washington, DC: Gerontological Society of America.

Smeeding, T., & Williamson, J. (2001). *Income maintenance in old age: What can be learned from cross-national comparisons?* Working Paper No. 263, Luxembourg Income Study. Luxembourg: CEPS/INSTEAD.

SSA. (1998). *Fast facts and figures about Social Security*. Washington, DC: Office of Research, Evaluation and Statistics; Social Security Administration.

Steuerle, E. (1999). *The treatment of the family and divorce in the Social Security program*. Washington, DC: U.S. Senate Special Committee on Aging.

Thurow, L. C. (1999). Generational equity and the birth of a revolutionary class. In J. B. Williamson, D. M. Watts-Roy, & E. Kingson (Eds.), *The generational equity debate* (pp. 58–74). New York: Columbia University Press.

Williamson, J. B., Watts-Roy, D. M., & Kingson, E. (1999). *The generational equity debate*. New York: Columbia University Press.

Women's Institute for Secure Retirement (WISER). (2002). *Minority women and retirement income: Your future paycheck*. Washington, DC: WISER.

Informalization of Long-Term Caregiving: A Gender Lens

Carroll L. Estes and Donna M. Zulman

INTRODUCTION

As the baby boomers begin to age and the proportion of Americans older than 65 years increases rapidly, a growing number of elderly are turning to friends and family for care each year. As many as 70% of severely impaired elderly people rely solely on informal care from family and friends (Commonwealth Fund, 1989). According to the 1997 NAC/AARP National Family Caregiver Survey, this care is provided by nearly one in four (22.4 million) households in the United States. The 1997 survey reports that the typical caregiver is a married woman in her mid-forties with an annual household income of approximately $35,000, who works full-time and provides an average of 18 hours of caregiving each week (National Alliance for Caregiving and the American Association of Retired Persons, 1997).

As early as 1986, Estes identified a major trend in long-term care as the informalization of care, referring to the substantial and increasing care provided to the elderly by unpaid family and friends (Estes, 1986, 1988). The burden of unpaid caregiving for the elderly has always been substantial (Abel, 1991), but it was increased significantly when a change in Medicare reimbursement policy in 1983 gave hospitals major economic incentives (payment by diagnosis-related grouping, or DRG) to discharge the elderly from hospital care "sicker and quicker" (Estes et al., 1993). During the first year after DRGs, more than 37 million days of care were transferred from the hospital to the home and community. The rise of medical cost containment in the early days of the Reagan Administration and the promotion of for-profit medical care, which set off the first wave of major health care competition and restructuring commencing in the 1980s, were to be significant in contributing to the workload of informal caregivers and, therefore, to the workload of women in the provision of long-term care in the United States.

The acceleration of the informalization of caregiving for the elderly has reflected a shift of health care service delivery from formal delivery systems such as hospitals and other formal providers to the home and community. As a process, this kind of informalization represents the transfer of care delivery from the formal system of paid professional providers to unpaid providers such as friends and family (Binney, Estes, and Humphers, 1993).

Carroll L. Estes and Donna M. Zulman. (2004). *Informalization of long-term caregiving: A gender lens*. San Francisco, CA: Institute for Health and Aging University of California, San Francisco. This article was prepared for the fourth edition of this book.

This informalization process is continuing to grow as a result of the increasing influence of managed care, multiple forms of capitation, and health maintenance organizations (HMOs). Suzanne Gordon reports that "HMOs are cutting costs and saving money by having patients and their families perform duties formerly done by nurses," which raises the question about "Who is going to take care of the sick at home?" and the observation that "The mounting costs—emotional, physical, and financial—that families or patients have to bear are never part of the industry's cost-benefit analyses" (Gordon, 1998). Medical care industry competition and profit making pressures contribute to relentless efforts to cut costs and an important mechanism to do that is the reduction in lengths of stay in hospitals for coronary artery bypass graft surgery, hip replacements, and multiple other medical procedures. Technological advances including pharmaceutical developments further propel such trends.

Women have traditionally been expected to take on the responsibility of caregiving as a duty of the home. As women enter the workplace in increasing numbers, however, there is a growing need for policy, both at a national level and in the workplace, to accommodate the changing worlds of women and of informal caregivers. This article explores the informalization of caregiving, the experience of employed caregivers, the difficult circumstances of female caregivers, and the economic value produced by the informal care system. The outline of a theoretical framework is introduced and some of the most important policy issues are examined.

THE INFORMALIZATION OF CAREGIVING

The long-term care sector relies on informal care provision for a number of reasons. Most prominent is the economic value of close to $200 billion that is saved due to the work of millions of unpaid caregivers (Arno, Levine, and Memmott, 1999), which some scholars believe may be a serious underestimate of the cost of labor contributed. The magnitude of the value of unpaid work illustrates the importance of unpaid health work in sustaining the system of care outside of expensive formal care institutions. Another argument is that there may be a political advantage to obscuring the conditions under which care is provided from the public view (Close, Estes, and Linkins, 2001).

Informalization not only reflects the transfer of care to unpaid providers, but also produces the transfer of the physical, intellectual, emotional, and economic responsibility for that care (Binney et al., 1993). Women are disproportionately affected, as empirical studies irrefutably demonstrate that they are the most likely to take on these responsibilities. There are workforce disruptions associated with women's fulfillment of the societal expectations that they will be responsible for providing the bulk of long-term care (Estes and Close, 1994). This is in addition to the effects of informalization on the occupational disruptions of the careers of individual women, a topic that is yet to be well researched.

The Impact of Informalization on Caregivers in the Workforce

Recently, studies have begun to address the unique circumstances of individuals who juggle caregiving and outside employment.

The U.S. Department of Labor estimates that 30% of the workforce provides some level of care for an elderly relative (Workplace Task Force of the Last Acts Campaign, 1999). There has been an increase in the number of caregivers who are employed, from 55% in 1987 to 64% in 1997 (52% full-time and 12% part-time) (National Alliance for Caregiving and the American Association of Retired Persons, 1997; Wagner, 1997).

Tennstedt argues that rather than decreasing time or level of care, caregivers who are employed tend to make accommodations in their work schedules or make arrangements to meet their caregiving responsibilities (Tennstedt, 1999). The NAC/AARP findings support this, concluding that employment has no effect on the amount of care provided by caregivers. Of the employed caregivers in this study, half reported taking time off, coming in later, or working fewer hours. Only 6% and 3.6% (respectively) gave up work entirely or took early retirement due to caregiving (National Alliance for Caregiving and the American Association of Retired Persons, 1997).

The U.S. Department of Labor reports that 54% of Americans will likely be responsible for an elderly parent or relative in the next 10 years (Workplace Task Force of the Last Acts Campaign, 1999) and Wagner (1997) predicts that between 11 million and 15.6 million of these caregivers will also be participating in the workforce. Currently, however, only 23% of companies with 100 or more employees have programs in place to support caregivers (Galinsky and Bond, 1998). Given the projections for the future, it will be essential that the workplace adapt to provide an extensive support network that accommodates the needs and schedules of employed caregivers (Wagner, 1997).

The Experience of Female Caregivers: Balancing Work and Care Provision

Caregivers are predominantly female (Collins, Schoen, Joseph, Duchon, Simantov, and Yellowitz, 1999; U.S. Department of Labor: Women's Bureau, 1998), with women making up approximately three-fourths (73%) of caregivers (National Alliance for Caregiving and the American Association of Retired Persons, 1997). Studies have shown that employment does not preclude women from assuming caregiving roles (Moen, Robison, and Fields, 1994; Pavalko and Artis, 1997), and employed women are almost twice as likely as employed men to miss work to take care of sick relatives (Collins et al., 1999). Compared to men, women are less likely to have the job autonomy that enables them to provide care for someone without a reduction in income or other serious consequences. According to a Commonwealth Fund 1998 Survey of Women's Health that included interviews with 2,850 women, caregiving responsibilities appear to fall on women uniformly, regardless of income, race, or marital status, although family resources and income may influence the extent of these caregivers' responsibilities. Forty-three percent of female caregivers provide 20 hours or more of care per week (Collins et al., 1999).

Social Class, Gender, and Caregiving

While the Commonwealth Fund Survey reports that the percentage of female caregivers with incomes above or below the national median of $35,000 are almost identical (9% and

11%, respectively), their experiences appear to differ based on the resources and income available. For example, women from lower income levels are more likely to be living in the same community as relatives and parents, and are more likely than women from higher income levels to care continuously for their elderly parents (Glazer, 1993). They are also nearly twice as likely as wealthier women to live with the relative for whom they are providing care (62% compared to 36%) (Collins et al., 1999).

The economic, physical, and emotional toll of caregiving can also be significantly greater for lower-income women. Women in working-class jobs may not have the time or the job flexibility to make telephone calls. In addition, they may not have the resources to hire substitutes (Glazer, 1993). The Commonwealth Fund Survey found that lower-income women are more likely to be providing care for 20 hours or more per week (52% of women with incomes below $35,000 compared to 29% of women with incomes above $35,000).

Demographic trends suggest that the caregiving load for women will not lighten in the years to come. The labor force rate is projected to increase in the coming years, especially for women aged 55 to 64. In addition, as baby boomers age, life expectancy increases, family size shrinks, and as women delay childbearing, more women will be in the classic "sandwich generation" juggling both childrearing and elder care responsibilities. The U.S. Department of Labor (1998) estimates that 41% of caregivers are sandwiched between the generations. This may result in a decrease in the number of hours caregivers can provide to elder parents (Stone, 2000).

The Economic Value and Costs of Caregiving

Researchers have utilized a number of methods to estimate the value of uncompensated care provided by family members each year. For example, one study measured the wages and benefits lost by caregivers due to their caregiving responsibilities. Based on this method, the estimated value of care is $18 billion a year (Mellor, 2000). However, this approach does not account for caregiving provided by retired persons (Arno et al., 1999).

A third approach, utilized by Arno et al., applies a market wage rate to caregiving activity. Using this approach, Arno et al. (1999) estimate that the national economic value of informal caregiving for 1997 was $196 billion. When incorporating the possible range in numbers of caregivers, researchers determined that the estimated economic value could range from $115 billion to $288 billion. $196 billion is approximately 18% of total national health care expenditures, and dwarfs national spending for formal home health care ($32 billion) and nursing home care ($83 billion).

Health Costs to Caregivers in Morbidity and Mortality

In addition to the economic costs of caregiving, caregivers often report a toll on their health and well-being. Compared to non-caregiving women, female caregivers are 8% more likely to rate themselves in poor or fair health, and 13% more likely to suffer from a chronic health condition. Female caregivers also report higher rates of mental health concerns; 51% report high depressive symptoms, compared to 38% of non-caregiving women. Finally, 25%

of caregivers report difficulty obtaining needed health care (compared with 16% of other women), and female caregivers are twice as likely to not receive proper health care for themselves and to not fill a prescription because of cost (Collins et al., 1999).

Examining the additional "costs" outside of the economic sacrifices that informal caregivers make, it has been found that as many as 70% of caregivers report decreased physical health status due to their caregiving responsibilities (Snyder and Keefe, 1985). Documented increases in morbidity include increased rates of diabetes, arthritis, ulcers, and anemia, as well as increased rates of high blood pressure and cardiac problems in women (Prucho and Potasnik, 1989). Most frequently noted is the association between caregiving and depression. In a study of participants of the Nurses' Health Study, new caregivers for disabled spouses or parents demonstrated a decline in mental health and an increase in depressive symptoms. In addition, women who provided more than 36 hours of care per week were six times more likely than non-caregivers to exhibit depressive symptoms (Cannuscio, Rimm, Jones, Kawachi, Colditz, and Berkman, 2000).

While increased morbidity, especially emotional and mental strain, has been documented extensively among caregivers, researchers have only recently begun to address the possible mortality risks of providing informal care. A 1999 prospective population-based cohort study of elderly caregiving spouses (funded by the National Institutes of Health, National Institute on Aging) found that there was a 63% higher mortality risk among participants who were providing care and experiencing caregiver strain compared with non-caregiving controls. Participants who were providing care but not experiencing strain and those with a disabled spouse who were not providing care did not have elevated adjusted mortality rates. This research suggests that being a caregiver who is experiencing mental or emotional strain is an independent risk factor for mortality among elderly spousal caregivers (Schulz and Beach, 1999).

The magnitude of the problem of increasing demand for informal caregivers is a serious dilemma. The U.S. Census Bureau has even begun to report statistics on the "two-generation elderly support ratio," which is the ratio for "two elderly generations," or the number of persons aged 85 years and older per 100 persons aged 65 to 69 years (Siegel and Tauber, 1986). In 1990, the overall ratio was 30, but by 2050 that ratio will reach 100, indicating that the number of individuals aged 65 to 69 will equal the number of individuals aged 85 and older. As Collins, Estes, and Bradsher observe,

> Simply stated, this means that many more older persons, particularly women in their late 60s, will have the added burden of caring for relatives, parents, and spouses in their mid-80s or older. (Collins et al., 2001, pp. 144–145)

A Theoretical Framework for Understanding the Informalization of Care and Women's Unpaid Labor

The framework for the present analysis is predicated upon five major assumptions. The first premise is that caregiving is socially constructed (Estes, 1979); thus, what caregiving "is," its status in society and the marketplace, who does it, the conditions under which there is (or is not) remuneration, and public policy about it are all social products. Insofar as they are socially produced or constructed, they may be deconstructed or changed—albeit not without significant conflict and power struggles.

The second premise is that the problem of caregiving must be understood as structurally conditioned rather than merely as an individual activity or "choice." Considering the problem of caregiving as an individual experience without examining social structural factors obfuscates the influence of three major social institutions of the family, the labor market, and the state (public policy) in shaping the expectations and division of labor regarding the work of caregiving in the society (Estes, 2001).

The third premise is that the activity and experience of caregiving necessitates consideration from a life course perspective. Given that women provide caregiving for an estimated 18 years for their young and an equivalent number of years for adults and the elderly (estimated at 19 years) (Porter, 1995), the continuous and pervasive character of this activity is noteworthy. This also underscores that the labor of caregiving and its associated outcomes are very much products of intergenerational life experience and that caregivers of the old who are old themselves are especially vulnerable.

A fourth premise concerns the powerful influence of race, class, and gender as forces that shape the daily lives of those who perform paid and unpaid caregiving work of the society. Individual-level analysis does not account sufficiently for the structural influences of race, gender, class, and age (Estes and Binney, 1988) that help explain disparities in the work and costs of informal caregiving. In particular, the "life chances" of those who do the labor of unpaid caregiving in our society are seriously affected, as the data on the economic and health condition of care providers amply demonstrate.

The fifth premise is that any consideration of unpaid, informal caregiving, by definition, highlights the fact that, in U.S. society, it is women who do most of this work. Further, it is acknowledged that this work carries with it significant costs as well as rewards. The disadvantage to women is cumulative and enormous, and it is credited as the basis of the feminization of poverty including the feminization of old-age poverty (Harrington Meyer, 2001; Harrington, 2000; Estes, 2001).

Policy Options

Several policy options are available to address aspects of the problem of caregiving consistent with the approach of this article. Two levels of change are relevant:

1. On the more general societal level, institutional sexism in thought and practice is reflected through the sex/gender system (Rubin, 1975) that imposes norms and role expectations of women as the primary caregivers for their families. Under the current sex/gender system, the work of child care as well as elder care is seen as the private responsibility of the women in the family. This patriarchal concept of women is reflected in the lack of any formal national policy or provisions to provide or support child care and only minimal assistance for elder caregiving (e.g., means-tested nursing home placement) when needed. Thus both child and elder care continue to be treated essentially as private matters to be provided (contributed) by family (women) outside the paid labor market or (for those who have

economic resources) in the private-pay market. There is only minimal (and grudging) support from the state for these functions and only miserly assistance for welfare cases.

2. On the level of existing public policy, the economy and health security affect caregivers. Two policy arenas are targets for change—Social Security and long-term care. In the case of Social Security, policy changes are needed to redress the gender bias in not presently counting the unpaid caregiver years the same as paid labor. Other improvements needed are in the benefit structure that currently provides below-poverty-level benefits for many workers, particularly those who are in and out of the labor force due to caregiving, those who are divorced and single (widowed and non-married), and those who are low-income workers. Policy proposals include altering the special minimum benefit requirements and allowing lower-earning and caregiving spouses a number of "dropout years" that would not be counted against Social Security benefits (Hartmann, 1999; Smeeding, Estes, and Glasse, 1999).

In the area of long-term care (LTC), major reform could substantially lift some of the burden of responsibility currently assigned to informal caregivers and compensate (financially and in terms of Social Security credits) for some of the economic contributions made (and sacrifices endured) by informal caregivers. There is an inextricable link between the lack of support for informal long-term care work and the quality of life for the recipients of care as well. As Harrington Meyer et al. observe,

> Bureaucratization and stinting on resources deprive recipients of good care—jeopardizing the ability of our most vulnerable constituents to receive even the most basic of social rights. Moreover, inadequate recognition of, and compensation for, care work bars providers from participating as full citizens with full opportunities in political, social and economic institutions. (Harrington Meyer, Herd, and Michel, 2001, p. 4)

LTC needs to be provided and publicly financed for all Americans regardless of age or income. Such a policy could be modeled after the German LTC plan, which is financed by a small payroll tax (about 1.5%); is mandatory, with eligibility based on functional assessment; has no means testing; permits some opting out for private insurance; reverses the institutional bias of LTC with home care; and provides a service voucher benefit or cash option (Schunk and Estes, 2001). Virtually all types of services are provided by the German state: home care, day or night care facilities, respite care, and institutional care. Harrington et al. (1991) have proposed a plan of entitlement to social insurance for LTC, in which LTC is a right available to all (with universal access), with a continuum of social and medical support for informal care.

These policy suggestions argue against current proposals for the privatization of Social Security and the buildup of commercial private long-term care insurance, which are the major policy "solutions" proposed by the current Bush administration. The Bush initiatives are both considerably negative for women, given their longer life expectancy and more vulnerable economic state, having less income to invest either in the stock market (Smeeding et al., 1999) or for purchasing private LTC insurance (Estes and Bodenheimer, 1994). In contrast, what is essential are policy changes to provide solutions for both caregivers and care recipients that will address the serious health and economic security issues confronting unpaid informal care workers, as well as the inequities in the gendered division of labor. The suggested policy options would be only a modest step toward achieving the gender justice (England, Keigher, Miller, and Linsk, 1987; Kirp, Yudof, and Franks, 1986) in community care. Gender justice occurs "when men and women are given the opportunity and the capacity to choose" (Kirp et al., 1986). The U.S. national long-term care policy, bluntly described, is that women will do the work; they will do it without pay, and at great sacrifice. The result is that the nation is, to borrow the economist's term, "free riding" on the backs of women for the provision of long-term care. As England and her colleagues (1987) eloquently argue, there needs to be a shift toward policies to maximize gender justice by conceptualizing care-dependent individuals as a responsibility shared by family and government, with community care seen as a social utility—available according to a broad definition of need and with public provision as a foundation for care. It is consistent with the view of family care as a "social good," and the view that women are entitled to realize their economic potential (England et al., 1987; Harrington, 2000).

Even more far-reaching societal and institutional changes would be required to address the gender inequities in terms of the large and growing burden of unpaid caregiving that falls primarily upon the shoulders of women—and, as this article demonstrates, at great economic, health, and psychological cost. Achieving these changes will not be easy, inasmuch as they necessitate a shift in societal expectations and division of labor, implicating changes in the major power relations of gender, class, race/ethnicity, and generation.

REFERENCES

Abel, E. K. (1991). *Who cares for the elderly?* Philadelphia: Temple University Press.

Arno, P. S., Levine, C., & Memmott, M. M. (1999). The economic value of informal caregiving. *Health Affairs,* 18(2), 182–188.

Binney, E. A., Estes, C. L., & Humphers, S. E. (1993). Informalization and community care. In: C. L. Estes, H. J. Swan, & Associates (Eds.), *The long-term care crisis: Elders trapped in the no-care zone* (pp. 155–170). Newbury Park, CA: Sage.

Cannuscio, C. C., Rimm, E. B., Jones, C. P., Kawachi, I., Colditz, G. A., & Berkman, L. F. (November 13, 2000). *A longitudinal analysis of informal care provision and women's mental health status: Analysis in the Nurses' Health Study.* Paper presented at the 128th Annual Meeting of the American Public Health Association, Boston, MA.

Close, L., Estes, C. L., & Linkins, K. W. (2001). The political economy of health work. In: C. L. Estes & Associates (Eds.), *Social policy and aging: A critical perspective* (pp. 217–230). Thousand Oaks, CA: Sage.

Collins, C. A., Estes, C. L., & Bradsher, J. E. (2001). Inequality and aging: The creation of dependency. In: C. L. Estes & Associates (Eds.), *Social policy and aging.* Thousand Oaks, CA: Sage.

Collins, K. S., Schoen, C., Joseph, S., Duchon, L., Simantov, E., & Yellowitz, M. (1999). *Health concerns across a woman's lifespan: The Commonwealth Fund 1998 survey of women's health.* New York: The Commonwealth Fund.

Commonwealth Fund. (1989). *Help at Home: Long-Term Care Assistance for Impaired Elderly People* (Report of the Commonwealth Fund Commission on Elderly People Living At Home). New York: Commonwealth Fund.

Eisner, R. (1989). *The Total Incomes System of Accounts.* Chicago: University of Chicago Press.

England, S. E., Keigher, S. M., Miller, B., & Linsk, N. L. (1987). Community care policies and gender justice. *International Journal of Health Services,* 17(2), 217–232.

Estes, C. L. (1986). The politics of ageing in America. *Ageing and Society,* 6, 121–134.

Estes, C. L. (2001). From gender to the political economy of aging. In: C. L. Estes & Associates (Eds.), *Social policy and aging* (pp. 119–135). Thousand Oaks, CA: Sage.

Estes, C. L., et al. (Eds.). (2001). *Social policy and aging.* Thousand Oaks, CA: Sage.

Estes, C. L., & Bodenheimer, T. (1994). Paying for long-term-care. *Western Journal of Medicine,* 160(1), 64–69.

Estes, C. L., & Close, L. (1994). Public policy and long-term care. In: R. P. Abeles, H. C. Gift, & M. G. Ory (Eds.), *Aging and quality of life* (pp. 310–335). New York: Springer.

Estes, C. L., Swan, H. J., & Associates. (1993). *The long-term care crisis: Elders trapped in the no-care zone.* Newbury Park, CA: Sage.

Family Caregiver Alliance. (2000). *Family Caregiver Alliance update.* San Francisco, CA: Family Caregiver Alliance.

Family Caregiver Alliance. (2001a). *Family Caregiver Alliance update.* San Francisco, CA: Family Caregiver Alliance.

Family Caregiver Alliance. (2001b). *Family Caregiver Alliance update: Federal tax credit for caregivers reintroduced in Congress.* San Francisco, CA: Family Caregiver Alliance.

Folbre, N., & Nelson, J. A. (2000). For love or money—or both? *Journal of Economic Perspectives,* 14(4), 123–140.

Fox, P., Kohatsu, N., Max, W., & Arnsberger, P. (2001). Estimating the costs of caring for people with Alzheimer's disease in California: 2000–2040. *Journal of Public Health Policy,* 22(1), 88–97.

Galinsky, E., & Bond, T. (1998). *The 1998 business work-life study.* New York: Families and Work Institute.

Glazer, N. Y. (1993). *Women's paid and unpaid labor: The work transfer in health care and retailing.* Philadelphia: Temple University Press.

Gordon, S. (July 20, 1998). Not something for do-it-yourselfers. HMOs are cutting costs and saving money by having patients and their families perform duties formerly done by nurses. *Los Angeles Times* (OpEd).

Harrington, C., Cassel, C., Estes, C. L., Woolhandler, S., & Himmelstein, D. U. (1991). A national long-term care program for the United States. A caring vision. The Working Group on Long-Term Care Program Design, Physicians for a National Health Program. *JAMA,* 226(21), 3023–3029.

Harrington, M. (2000). *Care and equality: Inventing a new family politics.* New York: Routledge.

Harrington Meyer, M. (Ed.). (2001). *Care work: Gender, labor, and the welfare state.* New York: Routledge.

Harrington Meyer, M., Herd, P., & Michel, S. (2001). Introduction: The right to—or not to—care. In: M. Harrington Meyer (Ed.), Care work: *Gender, labor, and the welfare state* (pp. 1–4). New York: Routledge.

Hartmann, H. (September 13, 1999). *Keep the heart in Social Security.* Paper presented at the Testimony before the Forum on Social Security and Elderly Women, The Senate Democratic Task Force on Social Security.

Heymann, J. (2000). *The widening gap: Why America's working families are in jeopardy and what can be done about it.* New York: Basic Books.

Kempler, P. (1992). The use of formal and informal home care by the disabled elderly. *Health Services Research,* 27, 421–451.

Kirp, D. L., Yudof, M. G., & Franks, M. S. (1986). *Gender justice.* Chicago: University of Chicago Press.

Mellor, J. M. (2000). Filling in the Gaps in Long Term Care Insurance: Policy Implications for Informal Care Workers. In: M. H. Meyer (Ed.), *Care work: Gender, labor and the welfare State* (pp. 202–216). New York: Routledge.

Moen, P., Robison, J., & Fields, V. (1994). Women's work and caregiving roles: A life course approach. *Journal of Gerontology: Social Sciences,* 49(4), S176–S186.

National Alliance for Caregiving, and the American Association of Retired Persons. (1997). *Family caregiving in the U.S.: Findings from a national survey.* Bethesda, MD, and Washington, DC: American Association for Retired Persons.

Pavalko, E. K., & Artis, J. E. (1997). Women's caregiving and paid work: Causal relationships in late midlife. *Journal of Gerontology: Social Sciences,* 52B(4), S170–S179.

Porter, A. I. (1995). *The path to poverty: An analysis of women's retirement income* (Mother's Day Report). Washington, DC: Older Women's League.

Prucho, R. A., & Potasnik, S. L. (1989). Caregiving spouses: Physical and mental health in perspective. *Journal of the American Geriatric Society, 37*, 697–705.

Rubin, G. (1976). The traffic in women: Notes on the "political economy" of sex. In: R. R. Reiter (Ed.), *Toward an anthropology of women* (pp. 157–177). New York: Monthly Review Press.

Schulz, R., & Beach, S. R. (1999). Caregiving as a risk factor for mortality: The caregiver health effects study. *Journal of the American Medical Association, 282*(23), 2215–2219.

Schunk, M. V., & Estes, C. L. (2001). Is German long-term care insurance a model for the United States? *International Journal of Health Services, 31*(3), 617–634.

Smeeding, T., Estes, C. L., & Glasse, L. (1999). *Social Security reform and older women: Improving the system* (Report for the Task Force on Women). Washington, DC: Gerontological Society of America.

Snyder, B., & Keefe, K. (1985). The unmet needs of family caregivers for frail and disabled adults. *Social Work in Health Care, 10*, 1–14.

Stone, R. I. (2000). *Long-term care for the disabled elderly: Current policy, emerging trends and implications for the 21st century.* New York: Milbank Memorial Fund.

Tennstedt, S. (March 29, 1999). *Family caregiving in an aging society.* Paper presented at the U.S. Administration on Aging Symposium: Longevity in the New American Century, Baltimore, MD.

U.S. Department of Labor: Women's Bureau. (1998). *Work and elder care: Facts for caregivers and their employers* (98-1). Washington, DC: U.S. Department of Labor.

Wagner, D. L. (1997). *Comparative analysis of caregiver data for caregivers to the elderly 1987 and 1997.* Bethesda, MD: National Alliance for Caregiving.

Workplace Task Force of the Last Acts Campaign. (1999). *Synthesis of findings from studies with companies and caregivers.* Report of research studies directed by the National Health Council, the National Alliance for Caregiving, and the Last Acts Campaign.

PART III

HEALTH CARE DELIVERY SYSTEM ISSUES

ORGANIZATIONAL CHANGE

The health care industry has changed dramatically since President Clinton's national health care reform policy was debated in Washington in 1994. The $2 trillion health industry (or medical industrial complex) includes private profit-making insurance companies, health maintenance organizations, hospitals, physician groups, pharmaceutical companies, medical supply companies, and other health-related businesses, all of which have a vested interest in maintaining the current social structure and health system.

Mergers and acquisitions in the health care delivery system have resulted in larger companies within the industry. As discussed by Kitchener, these mergers have also consolidated the industry into a series of more horizontal organizations, in which many like organizations are joined together (such as many hospitals spread across the country), and vertical organizations, in which companies acquire different types of health care organizations (such as hospitals that own nursing facilities, physician groups, home health agencies, and other services). As a growing number of health corporations that are publicly traded on the stock exchange are consolidated, these companies are benefiting by gaining access to new financial capital for expansion. Their shareholders benefit when the prices of their stocks increase. Large corporate employers, employees, and even members of the public respond positively to "portable" benefits that enable members to obtain care through their plan or network of providers when they travel across the country or move to new locations.

The primary losers in mergers and consolidations are the nurses and health care workers, whose jobs may be eliminated through downsizing. Consumers of health care and local communities also lose power as the health industry consolidates into ever larger corporations. As billions of dollars are drained from clinical care, revenues are shifted to the investors and shareholders of large companies and to management; they are not reinvested in providing health services.

At the same time that large segments of the population lack health insurance and access to care, the waste in the health care system in the United States is growing. The proportion of total health care dollars going to overhead and profits is staggering. Estimates are that 25% of total U.S. dollars are spent on administration—a percentage far higher than

153

that in any other country. The greed associated with the corporatization of health care, where the major emphasis is on reaping profits for stockholders, is growing.

Moreover, there is a shift toward greater competition. Hospitals' competitive strategies raise the question about a new medical "arms race," even as there are indications of shortages of hospital beds, especially emergency room services (as Bazzoli and colleagues discuss). Hospitals and physicians are developing for-profit specialty services that may be provided either within or outside of traditional hospitals. These efforts by specialty physicians, which are designed to compete with community hospitals, may eventually threaten the financial health of hospitals, increase the overall costs of care, and decrease the quality of care. As these changes occur, health care organizations are shifting the delivery of care away from hospitals to ambulatory and community-based settings.

Conflicts of interest between physicians and other health care providers and the health industry have been identified for many years as a growing concern. When health providers refer patients to services or organizations where they have a financial interest, an obvious problem arises. More recently, the conflict of interest between health providers and researchers who test and market drugs and have a financial stake in the outcomes of selected drugs has been identified as a serious problem. Brennan and colleagues describe health industry practices that lead to conflicts of interests and suggest ways to avoid these ethical issues. These measures include stringent regulations that prohibit providers from accepting small gifts, pharmaceutical samples, continuing education, funds for provider travel, speakers bureaus, ghostwriting, and consulting and research contracts.

The proprietary health industry has experienced dramatic growth since the early 1980s, while nonprofit health care organizations have come under increasing strain. A number of studies have addressed the differences in nonprofit and for-profit health care organizations on quality and costs. Studies show for-profit nursing homes have lower costs and greater efficiencies than their nonprofit counterparts. For-profit organizations more aggressively mark up prices over costs; nonprofits are more trustworthy in delivering services, have more innovation, and offer better quality. Ownership does matter, and efforts should be made to preserve nonprofit health care.

Kitchener and Harrington examine the long-term care field, which has been historically dominated by nursing homes. After a century of efforts to build legitimacy and support for home and community-based services, the organizational field now supports both approaches. Kitchener and Harrington show that while for-profit nursing home chains still dominate long-term care, home and community-based alternatives are growing, especially in the private for-profit sector.

Shi and colleagues examine the current primary care delivery system and find serious problems with it. Namely, these authors reveal that access to primary care can reduce health disparities and mortality rates in the United States. Adopting new public policies and practices for a patient-centered primary care system would address the diverse needs and expectations of the population.

LABOR ISSUES

In 1995, the Pew Commission projected an excess supply of health professionals in the labor force, primarily because of the rapid growth in managed care. More recently, shortages of nursing personnel have been reported as the U.S. economy has experienced low unemployment and unprecedented economic growth. The cycles of excesses followed by shortages of personnel have a long history in the health field.

Physician workforce policy has relied primarily on the free-market approach. This policy is irrational and results in an endless cycle of labor shortages, such as the current shortage of primary care physicians. A planned approach would require government to be involved in regulating the entry into graduate medical education for specialties and that would reduce the reliance on international medical graduates.

Some argue that physicians are losing autonomy and power because of the growth of managed care and the consolidation of health organizations into large health care systems. Kitchener, Caronna, and Shortell show that physicians who work within large health care systems are adapting to these environments whose structures vary widely across the industry. Overall, they argue, physicians have been able to maintain their autonomy and power in most new health care systems.

For nursing, the health market continues to be competitive. Indeed, organizations are seeking to expand the supply of nurses. In another trend, health care employers are limiting wages and benefits and increasing employee responsibility. Unruh and Fottler predict that the future for the registered nursing workforce holds a large shortage of workers, a challenge magnified by stagnant wages and low levels of job satisfaction for nurses. The number of individuals entering nursing is expected to decrease, even as the percentage of RNs leaving nursing increases, and the percentage of RNs working in nursing and working in patient care declines. This trend will create problems in attracting students into the profession and for health care organizations that need to retain a skilled workforce. Policy solutions can focus on enhancing working conditions, improving staffing levels and wages and benefits, allowing more flexible hours of work, and increasing the nursing supply through legislative and regulatory approaches.

Health care employment has been of the greatest importance to women, African Americans, and other minorities, who have found many opportunities as the health labor force has grown rapidly over the past 25 years. An important case can be made that diversity in the health care workforce offers a way to address the growing health disparities for minorities. A culturally competent workforce should improve access to high-quality care for the medically underserved. Despite recent gains in diversity, however, minority representation in medicine, nursing, and other health professions lags behind minority representation in the overall population. Health policy approaches can address this huge challenge while improving care in the United States.

At a time when there are shortages in the health workforce, many problems within the work environment may potentially lead to dissatisfaction and high workforce turnover. Waehrer, Leigh, and Miller show that the cost of occupational injury and illness of health workers is a serious problem that can exacerbate workforce problems. The hospital industry is the third most expensive of 313 U.S. industries for worker's compensation costs, and the costs of occupation injury and illness in health care are varied across occupations.

The long-term care industry is also experiencing serious labor shortages, and its workforce remains adequate to address the growth expected with aging of the U.S. population. Unlike pediatrics, geriatrics has not been embraced as a specialty. There is a critical shortage of professionals in geriatrics. One way to address this growing problem is to require every health care worker to have some education in geriatrics and access to geriatric care experts. This situation will merely continue to exacerbate quality problems in long-term care unless new policies are developed.

One of the most rapidly growing areas in the health care labor market is unskilled workers to provide home care and personal assistance services. This segment of the labor market has grown as state Medicaid programs have begun to shift long-term care resources toward home and community-based services and away from institutional care, while the number of workers in nursing homes has remained at the same level. Proposed cuts in the state Medicaid programs could have a negative impact on these workers who provide services to the elderly and disabled. Low wages and benefits, however, pose a major threat to the stability of the unskilled health labor market.

QUALITY OF CARE

Given that they are spending large amounts per capita, members of the public rightly expect a high level of quality of care. Health research, however, suggests that poor quality of care is a serious hidden problem within the U.S. system. In 1999, the Institute of Medicine (IOM) released *To Error Is Human,* which estimated that 44,000 to 98,000 deaths occur each year as a result of medical errors in U.S. hospitals, and that these errors cost $17 billion to $29 billion per year. These estimates are viewed as only the tip of the iceberg with regard to medical errors across all types of health care settings.

Physicians and nurses have historically viewed this problem as one of individual mistakes, yet research shows that quality is more of an organizational and systemic problem. The best approach to preventing accidents, injuries, and deaths from health care services is to redesign the organizational systems and mechanisms for providing care. Nearly seven years after the publication of the IOM report, quality continues to be one of the United States' most serious problems. While hospitals are reporting improvements, it is clear that the effort to improve quality needs further work. Stronger regulations, better use of information technology, and improvements in workforce organization and training have shown some benefits, but error-reporting systems have made little impact to date and accountability has not improved.

One approach to addressing the poor quality of care found in many of the nation's hospitals is to improve the nurse staffing levels. Rothberg and his colleagues show that having a higher proportion of hours of care per day provided by RNs is a cost-effective intervention. Better staffing is associated with shorter lengths of stay and lower rates of urinary tract infections and gastrointestinal bleeding. Higher rates of RN hours were also associated with lower rates of pneumonia, shock, cardiac arrest, and failure to rescue patients from death due to complications. As a result of such research findings and the active involvement of nursing organizations, California implemented the first and strongest nurse staffing requirements for hospitals in the country, and other states are considering similar legislation.

When Kelley and colleagues examined 140 quality measures and 100 measures of access to care, they found wide variations in quality and pervasive health disparities throughout the U.S. health care system. The quality problems and disparities are especially notable in preventive care.

Harrington and colleagues have shown that serious quality problems with the nursing home industry in the United States persist despite 25 years of efforts to improve these conditions. This primarily profit-driven industry provides largely unprofessional health and social services for the most frail elderly in society. Research shows that the enforcement of federal standards for nursing homes is weak, and very few poorly managed homes are punished for failure to meet standards. In addition, enforcement of regulations varies widely across states. The many barriers to improved enforcement include a lack of political will to ensure that nursing homes meet standards. Although Congress passed strong enforcement legislation, it has consistently failed to implement the legislation, giving the public appearance of concern while not interfering with industry practices.

Schnelle and colleagues show that staffing levels in nursing homes are the best indicator of quality of care. Nursing homes with high staffing levels reported better processes of care on 13 of 16 care process measures. There is a threshold for staffing of about 4.1 hours per resident-day, such that facilities with staffing at lower levels tend to show poorer processes of care. Staffing levels on average are well below safe levels, and levels at some facilities are dangerously low. The dilemma is that the president and Congress are reluctant to increase the regulatory requirements for staffing because of the high cost to government, which pays about 60% of the total nursing home costs in the United States. Nursing homes have a high political profile, but reform has been difficult to achieve at the federal level. Greater success appears feasible at the state level, as some states have adopted tough new staffing standards.

Schlenker, Powell, and Goodrich examine home health care quality using new measures that home care agencies are required to report on Medicare patients. In 2000, the Centers for Medicare and Medicaid Services adopted a Medicare prospective payment system that pays a set rate for each episode of illness. Schlenker et al.'s findings show there were fewer patient visits and lower hospitalization and emergent care rates, but the quality of care was lower for wound care, incontinence care, and behavioral outcomes after the new payment system was adopted.

Both consumers and the government are demanding more detailed information about the quality provided by health care organizations. The state of the art for measuring health outcomes is improving but is far from a science. Some studies have shown that publicizing hospital performance indicators does have a positive impact by improving quality of care. Other studies have confirmed the positive effects of report cards. Unfortunately, the quality reports on private health plans and managed care have had little impact because many of the poorest-performing organizations refuse to make their data public. If voluntary compliance is not feasible, policy makers may need to mandate public reporting for health plans and other health care providers. Schneider, Zaslavsky, and Epstein reveal that outcome measures in for-profit health plans are lower than those in nonprofit health plans on four measures. They conclude that when standardized performance measures are used to compare performance, for-profit plans provide lower quality of care.

CHAPTER 5

Organizational Change

Overview of large hospital

Exploding the Merger Myth in U.S. Health Care

Martin Kitchener, PhD

INTRODUCTION

Many trends in the organization and policy of the U.S. health care market are driven by the effort to replace an element of the hitherto dominant professional logic (set of ideas and beliefs) that prescribes the appropriate structures and practices of provider organizations (Kitchener, 2002). For most of the last century, the strength of the professional logic ensured that certain organizational arrangements (e.g., quality assurance through peer review) attained two qualities of "rationalized myths" (Meyer and Rowan, 1991). First, they were taken for granted to the extent that they persisted without—or despite negative— evaluations of their effectiveness. Second, non-adoption of prescribed practices such as peer review threatened the legitimacy of an organization and its executives among their peers, patients, and purchasers (e.g., government and employers).

Primarily in response to purchasers' frustration with the cost of the organizational arrangements prescribed by professional logic, a loose alliance of reformers has vigorously promoted an alternative managerial logic for health care providers (Scott et al., 2000). Among other things, this effort seeks to definitively establish the efficacy of commercial practices such as mergers. While remnants of professional logic remain strong in the U.S. health care market, reformers continue with their attempts to replace the myths of that logic with alternatives that are rooted in managerial logic.

This article combines organizational concepts with research evidence to argue that mergers have become a powerful myth that is neither rational (value and interest-neutral) nor benign in terms of outcomes. The first section uses the concept of rationalized myth (Meyer and Rowan, 1991) to offer an explanation as to why there have been so many health care mergers despite the disappointing outcomes and costs of mergers generally, and the well-known implementation barriers in professional provider organizations. The second section considers the winners and losers under the health care merger myth (Fuchs, 1997).

MERGER AS MYTH

Variations on the theme of merging two or more organizations within a more centralized administrative structure developed in fields such as manufacturing, where managerial logic prescribes appropriate organizational arrangements. Despite these origins, research into

---

Martin Kitchener. (2003). *Exploding the merger myth in U.S. health care.* San Francisco: Department of Social and Behavioral Sciences, University of California, San Francisco.

mergers demonstrates two consistent outcomes. First, costs rise beyond initial estimates and nine-figure totals are increasingly common (Davis et al., 1995). Second, more than 75% of mergers fail to achieve the three most commonly stated goals of cost savings, improved market share/power, and enhanced service coordination (Marks and Mirvis, 2001).

During the 1980s, many variants of two main strains of "merger mania" spread across the U.S. health market: (1) "horizontal integration" between similar organizations (e.g., hospitals), and (2) "vertical integration" between various combinations of hospitals, HMOs, and physician groups (Fuchs, 1997). Between 1989 and 1996, the number of horizontal hospital mergers rose to 190 compared with 74 between 1983 and 1988 (Bogue et al., 1995). In 1996 alone, the 483 mergers among health providers and 33 mergers involving HMOs were valued at $27 billion and $13.3 billion, respectively (Hayes, 1998). Just as the three most commonly stated goals for these mergers mimicked the justifications used in commercial fields, the outcomes were similar: (1) economic outcomes evaluated as "moderate at best" (Snail and Robinson, 2001); (2) few mergers achieving their stated organizational aims (Weil, 2000; Commonwealth Fund Task Force on Academic Health Centers, 2000; Blumenthal and Edwards, 2000; Andreopoulos, 1997); and (3) little mention of the costs involved (Sirower, 1997; Dranove and Shanley, 1995; Gardside, 1999).

By the late 1990s, despite the evidence from commercial and health care fields, the efficacy of health care mergers became taken for granted. The myth then spread to the field academic health centers (AHCs), which have been described as one of the last bastions of professional logic (Kitchener, 2002). In cities including New York, Philadelphia, and St. Louis, management consultants helped health care executives merge combinations of community providers, practice plans (comprising flows of physicians' fees, among other things), medical schools, and teaching hospitals (Commonwealth Fund, 2000). Elsewhere, in the face of opposition from civic groups and professionals, variants on the merger theme were labeled "alliances" and even "partnerships" in the case of two Harvard-affiliated teaching hospitals that combined contract negotiations but stopped short of shared asset ownership (Blumenthal and Edwards, 2000).

Four Barriers to Mergers in Professional Health Care Provider Organizations

While most analyses of mergers among health care providers present accounts of a "rational" managerial response to worsening market conditions, many also provide illustrations of four widely known characteristics of professional organizations that were not addressed adequately during planning and then frustrated implementation (Burns et al., 2000). This section briefly introduces the four issues and illustrates their consistent and well-documented implications for health care mergers.

Resilient Professional Logic and Power

Studies of health care mergers report consistently that the continuing strength of the professional logic requires that executives proceed through Byzantine webs of influence to negotiate with physicians and other professionals throughout the process. Nevertheless, it is tricky to develop the required influential cadre of "change champions" among professionals, who generally confirm their distaste for mergers. The failure of the merger between the academic health centers of the University of California at San Francisco (UCSF) and Stanford University demonstrates (1) what happens when the expectation of early professional involvement is violated, and (2) that management by fiat is not yet a taken-for-granted arrangement in all areas of the U.S. health market (Kitchener, 2002).

Loose Coupling

A remnant of professional logic in many health care organizations prescribes that autonomous work groups are accommodated within "loosely coupled" structures (Weick, 1976). This term refers to the situation whereby different occupational groups (e.g., nurses, physicians) are somehow attached (e.g., on strategic organization charts) yet retain their operational identity and separateness. A central doctrine of the professional logic holds that loose coupling contributes to organizational success by accommodating the pursuit of complex and varied missions, and by protecting the autonomy demanded by professionals. The continued strength of this doctrine helps to explain why accounts of health care mergers report executives' inability to quickly consolidate services or improve service coordination using managerial innovations such as "service lines." While the key idea of this managerial strategy—organizing service delivery around functionality rather than professional structures—seems rational to consultants, it violates professionals' preference for loosely coupled structures (Kitchener, 2002).

External Meddling

Perhaps to a greater extent than in any other field, health care executives must "sell" their plans for mergers to a variety of external stakeholders, including antitrust regulators, professional associations, the press, government, accreditation agencies, as well as the civic groups and local politicians who tend to protest their perceived loss of "local" control (Burns et al., 2000). This process typically slows decision making and reveals strategic plans to competitors. The UCSF–Stanford case illustrates how this need for transparency frustrates executives, especially those from private institutions who are less used to (what they see as) external meddling within their managerial prerogatives. While such external involvement involves important aspects of accountability, oversight, and due diligence, it also tends to induce a warfare mentality. As commitment escalates on both sides, executives hire consultants to justify mergers but not to critically assess research evidence, costs, or implementation barriers (Kitchener, 2002).

Absence of Enabling Factors

Research shows that merger implementation can be aided by "enabling factors"—namely, "slack" money to encourage (buy) support and effective monitoring systems. Given that health care mergers are designed primarily to achieve cost savings and/or increase market power, there is often little financial slack—so the first agenda item is quick budget cuts. Likewise, health care organizations often lack the information systems necessary to control and oversee mergers effectively (Burns et al., 2000). This helps explain the finding from a study of health care mergers in Boston, New York, and Northern California, which concluded, "despite what consultants say, saving money by merger is rare, and domination of managed care remains an unproven accomplishment supported only by anecdotal data" (Kastor, 2001).

WHY DO THEY DO IT?

Much of the evidence summarized above is readily available to health care executives and their consultants because it appears (albeit in fragments) in the orthodox management and health care literatures. While this begs the question that titles this section, previous analyses have tended to ignore the interests of those involved and suggest that merger represents a rational strategy to cope with worsening market conditions (created under the logic of managerialism). This section offers an alternative perspective by considering the beneficiaries and losers from the health care merger mania.

Beneficiaries

Orthodox analyses of health care mergers state (or imply) that provider organizations can benefit from mergers and that the mania is driven by executives' knowledge of, and desire to, replicate success stories. Certainly, not all health care mergers have harmed those involved in either financial or organizational terms. Some widely publicized success stories have achieved desired outcomes in terms of improved market share or power relative to purchasers (e.g., rural providers), survival (e.g., in cases of over-bedded hospitals), and cost savings. Some mergers may also have involved critical assessment of evidence concerning costs and barriers (Kassirer, 1995).

That said, to explain how, despite a weak evidence base, the merger myth attained such a taken-for-granted status that non-adoption came to threaten organizational legitimacy, it is instructive to examine how a loose alliance of advocates of managerial logic has spread and benefited from merger mania.

First, and despite their frequent and loud assertions of rational and altruistic behavior, the biggest beneficiaries from health care mergers (in the short run at least) are the corporate executives of the expanded for-profit HMOs and hospital systems, who command handsome salaries and bonuses (Kassirer, 1995). Other provider executives have also clearly benefited from merger implementation by securing enhanced compensation or even larger salaries with HMOs (Staw and Epstein, 2000). In the case of the failed UCSF–Stanford merger, two board members with investment banking backgrounds were also influential proponents of the merger (Kitchener, 2002). It could be seen that the decision to merge represented a "win" for their managerial logic over the professional logic they are (presumably) drafted onto health care boards to challenge.

Second, the management consultancy industry has added advice on mergers to the limited list of services that it offers to embattled health care executives. It has been estimated that merger consultants and advisers receive as much as 2% to 3% of their clients' annual revenues, and their total fees are growing by 20% to 25% per year (*The Economist,* 1995). The end of the UCSF–Stanford merger in 2001 did not prevent the total costs of the aborted effort from rising to an estimated $176 million. Indeed, one firm of consultants received fees of $3.5 million through 1999 alone (Kitchener, 2002).

Third, the gray literature—the business press (e.g., *Fortune* and *Forbes*), health care management journals, and standard business texts—have used anecdotal evidence to consistently and uncritically promote managerial myths such as mergers to health care executives (Arndt and Bigelow, 2000). Faced with this powerful normative barrage, it is not difficult to imagine how nonconforming executives could begin to feel (and be perceived as) negligent and/or illegitimate.

Losers

Physicians and other health care professionals typically protest that they lose out from mergers in terms of their jobs and/or autonomy lost to empowered managers (Kassirer, 1995). Of course, both CEOs in the UCSF–Stanford merger lost their jobs, half of the CEOs in another study of mergers suffered the same fate (Kastor, 2001), and lower down the hierarchy many managerial careers are disrupted by role changes and displacement. While these losers are worthy of note, their voices rarely go unheard.

By contrast, implications for patients and the wider U.S. health system receive less attention. Patients may face reduced choice if services are discontinued or facilities are closed during mergers. Indeed, the specific case of mergers between secular and religious (e.g., Catholic) organizations commands particular concern because of the loss of women's health and contraceptive services (American Public Health Association, 2002). People may also face higher premiums when mergers do deliver increased market power for providers. At the level of the health care system, while the total costs of merger mania remain unknown, it is interesting to wonder just how much has been paid to merger consultants and what else that money might have been spent on, had it not been diverted from service delivery.

CONCLUSION

The notion of evidence-based medicine is being invoked increasingly by health care executives and others to address the systematic nature of poor-quality care and medical errors. This analysis argues that the merger myth is, in part, caused by executives who systematically fail to perform the technical aspects of their work, such as critically evaluating strategies. It is to be hoped that executives pursue evidence-based management policies (Kovner et al., 2000) with vigor to encourage the systematic evaluation of managerial myths. This article has shown the truths behind one such myth: (1) Mergers typically cost more than originally estimated by those who profit handsomely from them; (2) 75% of all commercial mergers do not achieve the stated goals of cost savings, improved market share, and enhanced service coordination; and (3) health care mergers produce similarly disappointing results as they flounder against the powerful remnants of professional logic.

REFERENCES

American Public Health Association. (2000, January). Preserving consumer choice in an era of religious/secular health industry mergers. Retrieved November 14, 2002, from www.apha.org.

Andreopoulos, S. (1997). The folly of teaching hospital mergers. *New England Journal of Medicine* 336(1), 61–64.

Arndt, M., and Bigelow, B. (2000). Presenting structural innovation in an institutional environment: Hospitals' use of impression management. *Administrative Science Quarterly* 45(1), 494–522.

Blumenthal, D., and Edwards, N. (2000, May/June). A tale of two systems: The changing academic health center. *Health Affairs,* 86–102.

Bogue, R., et al. (1995). Hospital reorganization after merger. *Medical Care* 33(7), 676–686.

Burns, L. R., et al. (2000). The fall of the house of AHERF: The Allegheny bankruptcy. *Health Affairs* 19(1), 7–42.

Commonwealth Fund Task Force on Academic Health Centers. (2000). *Managing academic health centers: Meeting the challenges of the new health care world.* New York: Commonwealth Fund.

Davis, G. F., et al. (1994). The deinstitutionalization of conglomerate firms in the 1980s. *American Sociological Review* 59(4), 547–570.

Dranove, D., and Shanley, M. (1995). Cost reductions or reputational enhancement as motives for mergers: The logic of multihospital systems. *Strategic Management Journal* 16(1), 55–74.

Fuchs, V. R. (1997). Commentary: Managed care and merger mania. *Journal of the American Medical Association* 277(11), 920–921.

Garside, P. (1999). Evidence based mergers? *British Medical Journal* 318, 345–346.

Hayes, J. (1998, January 12). Health care services (annual report on American industry). *Forbes,* 180–181.

The health care industry's morning after. (1995, July 15). *The Economist.* pp. 45–46.

Kassirer, J. P. (1995). Managed care and the mortality of the marketplace. *New England Journal of Medicine* 333(1), 50–52.

Kastor, J. A. (2001). *Mergers of teaching hospitals in Boston, New York, and Northern California.* Ann Arbor: University of Michigan Press.

Kitchener, M. (2002). Mobilizing the logic of managerialism in professional fields: The case of academic health center mergers. *Organization Studies* 23(3), 391–420.

Kovner, A. R., et al. (2000). Evidence-based management. *Frontiers of Health Services Management* 16(4), 3–46.

Marks, M. L., and Mirvis, P. H. (2001). Making mergers and acquisitions work: Strategic and psychological preparation. *Academy of Management Journal* 15(2), 80–94.

Meyer, J., and Rowan, B. (1991). Institutionalized organizations: Formal structures as myth and ceremony. In: W. Powell and P. D. Maggio (Eds.), *The new institutionalism in organizational analysis.* Chicago: University of Chicago Press.

Scott, W. R., et al. (2000). *Institutional change and health care organizations: From professional dominance to managed care.* Chicago: University of Chicago Press.

Sirower, M. S. (1997). *The synergy trap: How companies lose the acquisition game.* New York: Free Press.

Snail, T. S., and Robinson, J. C. (2001). Organizational diversification in the American hospital industry. *Annual Review of Public Health* 19, 417–453.

Staw, B., and Epstein, L. (2000). What bandwagons bring: Effects of popular management techniques on corporate performance, reputation, and CEO pay. *Administrative Science Quarterly* 45(3), 523–556.

Weick, K. E. (1976). Educational organizations as loosely coupled systems. *Administrative Science Quarterly* 21(1), 1–19.

Weil, T. (2000). Horizontal mergers in the United States health field: Some practical realities. *Health Services Management Research* 13, 137–151.

The Transition from Excess Capacity to Strained Capacity in U.S. Hospitals

Gloria J. Bazzoli, Linda R. Brewster, Jessica H. May, and Sylvia Kuo

During the 1980s and 1990s, researchers and policymakers generally agreed that hospitals had substantial excess inpatient capacity (Ennis, Schoenbaum, and Keeler 2000; Gaynor and Anderson 1995; Green 2002; Keeler and Ying 1996; Madden 1999). Between 1980 and 1995, hospital inpatient admissions declined by approximately 15 percent, and occupancy rates nationwide fell from about 76 to 63 percent (American Hospital Association 2005). Certainly, no one expects a hospital to be completely full all the time, as it must maintain a reserve or standby capacity to deal with unanticipated health needs (Friedman 1999; Gaynor and Anderson 1995; Joskow 1980). Furthermore, some excess hospital capacity is desirable because it provides leverage to third-party payers in their rate negotiations with hospitals (Zwanziger, Melnick, and Bamezai 1994). In the late 1990s, however, the general perception was that the U.S. health system had several thousand unneeded hospital beds that, if closed, could reduce the nation's health expenditures on hospital care (Madden 1999).

In the last few years, however, reports of strained hospital capacity have been increasing, including reports of patients being held in one hospital unit because there were no beds available in a unit more appropriate to their needs and of hospitals temporarily closing their emergency departments because they were unable to accept more patients. One particular concern has been the growing number of emergency department diversions, in which ambulances are instructed to bypass particular hospitals, especially because this could have a domino effect in the community (California HealthCare Foundation 2002; Shute and Marcus 2001). Evidence of the rising rates of emergency department diversion was found in round 3 of the Community Tracking Study (CTS), which was conducted by the Center for Studying Health System Change in 2000 and 2001. A study of emergency room overcrowding by the General Accounting Office (2003) yielded similar findings, suggesting that strained capacity in various hospital units led to backups in emergency departments.

This article examines why the capacity of some hospitals in the U.S. health system appears to be constrained and how they have responded to it. In addition, given that hospital occupancy rates nationwide are still relatively low, averaging about 66 percent in 2003 (American Hospital Association 2005), it is important to understand why perceptions of strained capacity exist at all.

We examine data collected through the CTS for certain study markets. The CTS is an ideal platform for examining the preceding questions because it tracked key events and

Adapted from: Gloria J. Bazzoli, Linda R. Brewster, Jessica H. May, and Sylvia Kuo. (2006). The transition from excess capacity to strained capacity in US hospitals. *Milbank Quarterly, 84*(2), 272–304.

data longitudinally over the period in which perceptions about hospital capacity changed. The CTS began its intensive study of twelve markets in 1995/96, at which time most hospital executives and community leaders believed that hospitals had much unneeded capacity. As concerns about strained capacity began to materialize in round 3 of the CTS in 2000/01, interviews with community stakeholders included questions about capacity problems. Similar issues were included in round 4 of the study, in 2002/03.

A number of CTS publications have explored the issue of hospital capacity. Two CTS issue briefs examined emergency department diversions and how their occurrence and severity had changed over time (Brewster and Felland 2004; Brewster, Rudell, and Lesser 2001). Bazzoli and her colleagues (2003) looked at the degree to which specific hospital services were viewed as constrained and what contributed to these problems. They found that those service areas perceived as highly strained were the emergency department, medical/surgical ICU beds, and general medical/surgical beds. The main contributing factors reported by the CTS respondents were nursing and other personnel shortages and an insufficient supply of beds. The primary contribution of this article is an exploration of the specific ways in which these contributing factors arose, namely, what events led to these conditions. In addition, we looked at the relationships among various contributing factors, with our longitudinal approach revealing insights not identified in prior work. One of our main findings was that hospitals adjusted their capacity slowly in response to recent increases in service demand because they were having problems staffing existing beds, let alone new ones. Also, they may have been prevented by physical space or regulation from adding new beds.

STUDY FINDINGS

Each site had a number of multihospital systems in operation that together made up 50 to nearly 90 percent of the hospitals operating in each market. Three of the sites had a dominant health system in terms of the market share of discharges: Partners HealthCare in Boston (20.1 percent), Cleveland Clinic Health System in Cleveland (40.1 percent), and Banner Health Arizona in Phoenix (31.7 percent). Miami had four large systems with similar market shares. Many of the health systems have major teaching hospitals, such as Massachusetts General Hospital and Brigham and Women's Hospital in Partners HealthCare, Boston; the Cleveland Clinic Foundation Hospital in the Cleveland Clinic Health System; Jackson Memorial Hospital in the Jackson Health System, Miami; and Good Samaritan Regional Medical Center in Banner Health, Arizona. However, some systems are composed strictly of community hospitals, such as Caritas Christi Health Care in Boston and Lake Hospital System in Cleveland.

CROSS-CUTTING LESSONS AND IMPLICATIONS

Joskow (1980) noted a set of factors affecting the demand for a hospital's services and thus its perceptions and decisions about service capacity: (1) the size and demographic characteristics of the population, (2) the prices charged for services, (3) the extent of the population's insurance coverage, (4) the number of physicians, and (5) the hospital's quality and scope of services. We expanded on these by emphasizing the importance of the changing health insurance market, local physician practice patterns, and shifts in demand in a market over time.

Our examination of hospitals in the four selected CTS markets suggests that many of these factors influenced hospitals' perceptions of the adequacy of their capacity. Miami and Phoenix were particularly affected by increasing population growth leading to greater demand for hospital services. In addition, changes in the insurance environment in Boston, Miami, and Phoenix, notably the managed care backlash of the 1990s, likely led to increases in demand. Boston's teaching hospitals also appeared to have reduced their service capacity too much given initial expectations of HMO effects in their market that were subsequently proven wrong. Although Cleveland's hospitals were not influenced by these factors per se, some of them had an increase in demand after two local hospitals closed. Thus, the experiences of the hospitals in these four markets indicate that population growth, insurance market changes, and demand shifts shaped their thinking about the adequacy of their capacity.

Two other factors were components of the conceptual framework: physician supply and/or practice patterns and the quality or scope of a hospital's services. Our evidence for the first of these was more limited than that for the other factors.

We also examined theories of supply adjustment to better understand what might affect the pace at which firms change their supply of services. These theories emphasize that because change is expensive, it is likely to be slow. This certainly was true for the communities we examined. In all four communities, occupancy rates initially were low and there was a perception of excess capacity, but it took time for the pressure to mount before hospitals began to reduce their bed capacity. As demand began to rise, however, these actions had to be reversed.

Although preliminary, our research offers some important insights for policy and management. In regard to policy, CON's planning efforts are prominent when one considers the state's role in affecting hospitals' supply of services. Existing empirical evidence and market observations suggest that CON has not had a substantial effect on hospitals' expansion or cost of care (Conover and Sloan 1998; Mayo and MacFarland 1989; Solomon 1998). Our findings also provide mixed evidence for the value of CON in rationalizing changes in capacity in health markets. On the positive side, the hurdles of obtaining CON approval may force hospitals to think of approaches other than bed expansion to deal with their capacity problems. These include making better use of existing capacity throughout the hospital system, as observed in Boston, or by improving hospital throughput. But if CON simply slows the inevitable, namely, the expansion of beds, its long-term effect on hospitals will be minimal.

States can also help increase the supply of nursing and other hospital personnel, which was clear in both Miami and Phoenix. The efforts by the state of Florida, along with those of its hospitals, appear to have quickly boosted the supply of nurses. The state's actions included providing nursing scholarships and loan-forgiveness programs and easing licensure requirements for nurses moving to Florida from other states.

Certainly, both short-term and long-term strategies are needed to address immediate nurse shortages and to educate new nurses to replace an aging workforce.

From a management perspective, the events in Cleveland are perhaps most telling and should serve as a warning to hospitals that simply building new capacity in response to greater demand may not be the answer. The Cleveland market presented few obstacles to hospitals in expanding capacity, but capacity built does not necessarily mean capacity utilized, especially if underlying demand expectations prove to be wrong. An unanticipated decline in use can leave hospitals or their parent systems with costly new capacity that cannot be supported financially.

Given this uncertainty, hospitals may be better served by coupling better capacity management with limited expansion in particular service lines and geographic areas of a market. The strategies of strained Boston hospitals are particularly interesting in this regard, namely, their considering how they could shift volume around a system's hospitals to better use their existing capacity and more tightly manage care. Another advantage of better capacity management, both within hospitals and across hospitals in a system, is that it enables a more rapid adjustment of supply to meet the fluctuations of demand.

REFERENCES

American Hospital Association. 2005. *Hospital Statistics*. Chicago: HealthForum.

Bazzoli, G.J., L.R. Brewster, G. Liu, and S. Kuo. 2003. Does U.S. Hospital Capacity Need to Be Expanded? *Health Affairs* 22 (November/December):40–54.

Brewster, L.R., and L.E. Felland. 2004. Emergency Department Diversions: Hospital and Community Strategies Alleviate the Crisis. *Issue Brief* no. 78 (March):1–4. Washington, D.C.: Center for Studying Health System Change.

Brewster, L.R., L.S. Rudell, and C.S. Lesser. 2001. Emergency Room Diversions: A Symptom of Hospitals under Stress. *Issue Brief* no. 38 (May):1–4. Washington, D.C.: Center for Studying Health System Change.

California HealthCare Foundation. 2002. California's Emergency Departments: System Capacity and Demand. *Issue Brief* (April):1–7. Oakland: California HealthCare Foundation.

Conover, C.J., and F.A. Sloan. 1998. Does Removing Certificate-of-Need Regulations Lead to a Surge in Health Care Spending? *Journal of Health Politics, Policy, and Law* 23 (June):455–81.

Ennis, S., M. Schoenbaum, and T. Keeler. 2000. Optimal Prices and Costs for Hospitals with Excess Bed Capacity. *Applied Economics* 32(9):1201–12.

Friedman, B. 1999. Commentary: Excess Capacity, a Commentary on Markets, Regulation, and Values. *Health Services Research* 33 (February): 1669–82.

Gaynor, M., and G.F. Anderson. 1995. Uncertain Demand, the Structure of Hospital Costs, and the Cost of Empty Hospital Beds. *Journal of Health Economics* 14(3):291–317.

General Accounting Office. 2003. *Hospital Emergency Departments: Crowded Conditions Vary among Hospitals and Communities.* Report to the Ranking Minority Member, U.S. Senate Committee on Finance, GAO-03-460.

Green, L.V. 2002. How Many Hospital Beds? *Inquiry* 39(4):400–412.

Joskow, P.L. 1980. The Effects of Competition and Regulation on Hospital Bed Supply and the Reservation Quality of the Hospital. *Bell Journal of Economics* 11 (autumn):421–47.

Keeler, T.E., and J.S. Ying. 1996. Hospital Costs and Excess Bed Capacity. *Review of Economics and Statistics* 78(3):470–81.

Madden, C.W. 1999. Excess Capacity: Markets, Regulation, and Values. *Health Services Research* 33 (February):1651–68.

Mayo, J.W., and D.A. MacFarland. 1989. Regulation, Market Structure, and Hospital Costs. *Southern Economic Journal* 55:559–69.

Mulligan, J. 1985. The Stochastic Determinants of Hospital-Bed Supply. *Journal of Health Economics* 4(2): 177–85.

Shute, N., and M.B. Marcus. 2001. Code Blue Crisis in the ER. *U.S. News and World Report* (September 10). Available at http://www.usnews.com/usnews/health/articles/010910/archive_003670.htm (accessed February 20, 2006).

Solomon, L.S. 1998. Rules of the Game: How Public Policy Affects Local Health Care Markets. *Health Affairs* 17 (July/August):140–48.

Zwanziger, J., G.A. Melnick, and A. Bamezai. 1994. Costs and Price Competition in California Hospitals, 1980–1990. *Health Affairs* 13 (fall):118–26.

Health Industry Practices
That Create Conflicts of Interest:
A Policy Proposal for Academic Medical Centers

Troyen A. Brennan, MD, MPH, David J. Rothman, PhD,
Linda Blank, David Blumenthal, MD, MPP, Susan C. Chimonas, PhD,
Jordan J. Cohen, MD, Janlori Goldman, JD, Jerome P. Kassirer, MD,
Harry Kimball, MD, James Naughton, MD, and Neil Smelser, PhD

The current influence of market incentives in the United States is posing extraordinary challenges to the principles of medical professionalism. Physicians' commitment to altruism, putting the interests of the patients first, scientific integrity, and an absence of bias in medical decision making now regularly come up against financial conflicts of interest. Arguably, the most challenging and extensive of these conflicts emanate from relationships between physicians and pharmaceutical companies and medical device manufacturers.[1]

As part of the health care industry, pharmaceutical and medical device manufacturers promote the welfare of patients through their commitment to research and product development. Their investments in discovering, developing, and distributing new pharmaceutical agents and medical devices have benefited countless patients. Most companies also support continuing medical education (CME). However, their ultimate fiduciary responsibility is to their shareholders who expect reasonable returns on their investments. Indeed, manufacturers are acutely aware of the conflict between patient vulnerability and profit incentives.

Recent congressional investigations, federal prosecutions, and class action lawsuits have brought to light documents demonstrating how company practices frequently cross the line between patient welfare and profit-seeking behavior.[2-4] Concerned physicians, journalists, and federal prosecutors are exposing still other aspects of an unhealthy relationship between manufacturers and the medical profession.[5-7]

These transgressions have prompted pharmaceutical firms to regulate themselves more stringently. That effort is commendable, but physicians' behavior is a large part of the problem and industry efforts to date have not resolved the crisis. The standing of the profession, as much as the integrity of the pharmaceutical and medical device industries, is jeopardized by allowing obvious conflicts to continue.

Adapted from: Troyen A. Brennan, David J. Rothman, Linda Blank, David Blumenthal, Susan C. Chimonas, Jordan J. Cohen, Janlori Goldman, Jerome P. Kassirer, Harry Kimball, James Naughton, and Neil Smelser. (2006). Health industry practices that create conflicts of interest. *Journal of the American Medical Association*, 295(4), 429–433.

The serious threat that this state of affairs poses for professionalism, and for the trust that patients have in physicians, makes the need for effective guidelines on industry-physician relationships both apparent and urgent. Marketing and market values should not be allowed to undermine physicians' commitment to their patient's best interest or to scientific integrity.

To remedy the situation and prevent future compromises to professional integrity, academic medical centers (AMCs) must more strongly regulate, and in some cases prohibit, many common practices that constitute conflicts of interest with drug and medical device companies. The guidelines we suggest are designed to promote broader professional self-regulation.

WHY AMCS?

Academic medical centers, which include medical schools and their affiliated hospitals, should provide leadership for medicine in the United States. Just as pharmaceutical manufacturers look to AMCs for influential advice and support, so does the medical profession. Academic medical centers also have a major responsibility for training medical students and house staff. Research reveals that the habits learned or acquired during training persist into practice.[8] Objectivity and scientific integrity should be central tenets of physician training.

Academic medical centers are also in a position to take immediate action. They are sufficiently well organized to gain commitments to a set of new principles in relatively short time. Moreover, independent research into the impact of medications and devices on population health is concentrated in AMCs; therefore, unwarranted influence by manufacturers must be avoided. For these reasons, academic medicine should take the leadership in reforms, and other physicians and medical institutions should adopt their standards.

DEFINING CONFLICTS OF INTEREST WITH INDUSTRY

Conflicts of interest occur when physicians have motives or are in situations for which reasonable observers could conclude that the moral requirements of the physician's roles are or will be compromised. In terms of industry influences, financial conflicts of interest occur when physicians are tempted to deviate or do deviate from their professional obligations for economic or other personal gain.[9] The bias thus introduced violates both the best interests of patients and the standards of scientific integrity. Policing such conflicts clearly lies within the scope of professional responsibilities set forth in the *Physician Charter on Medical Professionalism.*[10,11]

Traditionally, marketing by pharmaceutical and device companies has centered on company representatives or "detail persons" who visit individual physicians and provide information on new products. This practice has increased in scale and many other marketing strategies are also used. Approximately 90% of the $21 billion marketing budget of the pharmaceutical industry continues to be directed at physicians, despite a dramatic increase in direct-to-consumer advertising.[12]

The following list, while not exhaustive, indicates the interactions with industry that must be addressed[13]: gifts, even of relatively small items, including meals; payment for attendance at lectures and conferences, including online activities; CME for which physicians pay no fee; payment for time while attending meetings; payment for travel to meetings or scholarships to attend meetings; payment for participation in speakers bureaus; the provision of ghostwriting services; provision of pharmaceutical samples; grants for research projects; and payment for consulting relationships.

MYTHS OF THE SMALL GIFTS AND FULL DISCLOSURES

Most of the recommendations from medical and industry groups share 2 key assumptions. The first is that small gifts do not significantly influence physician behavior. The second is that disclosure of financial conflicts is sufficient to satisfy the need to protect patients' interests. Although these 2 assumptions are widely accepted among physicians, compelling research findings using a variety of methods have called their validity into question.

Psychologists, sociologists, and economists have explored human behavior in a conflicted situation using innovative experimental techniques.[14] Their research has established that behavior is not entirely rational, individuals are not always conscious of their motives, and many popular beliefs about how individuals act in light of specific information are simply wrong.[15]

Social science research demonstrates that the impulse to reciprocate for even small gifts is a powerful influence on people's behavior. Individuals receiving gifts are often unable to remain objective; they reweigh information and choices in light of the gift.[16]

Researchers have specifically studied industry gifts to physicians. Receiving gifts is associated with positive physician attitudes toward pharmaceutical representatives.[17] Physicians who request additions to hospital drug formularies are far more likely to have accepted free meals or travel funds from drug manufacturers.[18] The rate of drug prescriptions by physicians increases substantially after they see sales representatives,[19] attend company-supported symposia,[20] or accept samples.[21] The systematic review of the medical literature on gifting by Wazana[22] found that an overwhelming majority of interactions had negative results on clinical care.

The assumption that disclosure to patients is sufficient to resolve problems created by physicians' conflicts of interest is also unfounded.

MORE STRINGENT REGULATION

Because gifts of even minimal value carry influence and because disclosure is an inadequate safeguard, the guidance presently provided by the medical profession, the pharmaceutical industry, and the federal government fails to protect the best interests of patients and the integrity of physician decision making. For these reasons, many current practices should be prohibited and others should be more strictly regulated to eliminate potential sources of unwarranted influence.

Gifting
All gifts (zero dollar limit), free meals, payment for time for travel to or time at meetings, and payment for participation in online CME from drug and medical device companies to physicians should be prohibited.

Pharmaecutical Samples

The direct provision of pharmaceutical samples to physicians should be prohibited and replaced by a system of vouchers for low-income patients or other arrangements that distance the company and its products from the physician.

Drug Formularies

Hospital and medical group formulary committees and committees overseeing purchases of medical devices should exclude physicians (and all health care professionals) with financial relationships with drug manufacturers, including those who receive any gift, inducement, grant, or contract. These policies would help ensure that decision making for formulary drugs and medical devices is based solely on the best available scientific evidence.

Continuing Medical Education

The widespread influence of drug manufacturers on current CME activities make more stringent regulation necessary.[23] Manufacturers should not be permitted to provide support directly or indirectly through a subsidiary agency to any ACCME-accredited program.

Funds for Physician Travel

Pharmaceutical and device manufacturers interested in having faculty or fellows attend meetings should provide grants to a central office at the AMC. That office could then disburse funds to faculty and training program directors. Trainees would no longer be directly dependent on industry largesse for educational opportunities.

Speakers Bureaus and Ghostwriting

Faculty at AMCs should not serve as members of speakers bureaus for pharmaceutical or device manufacturers. Speakers bureaus are an extension of manufacturers' marketing apparatus. Faculty should be prohibited from publishing articles and editorials that are ghostwritten by industry employees.

Consulting and Research Contracts

Because the process of discovery and development of new drugs and devices often depends on input from academic medicine, consulting with or accepting research support from industry should not be prohibited.

To promote scientific progress, AMCs should be able to accept grants for general support of research (no specific deliverable products) from pharmaceutical and device companies, provided that the grants are not designated for use by specific individuals.

To better ensure independence, scientific integrity, and full transparency, consulting agreements and unconditional grants should be posted on a publicly available Internet site, ideally at the academic institution.

Going Forward

What then might the world of medicine look like if these proposals are widely adopted? First, decisions by physicians on which prescription to write and which device to use might become more evidence-based; medical societies' practice guidelines might become less subject to bias. A greater reliance on objective sources for accurate and up-to-date information would also promote better patient outcomes. Second, total expenditures on prescription drugs might decline. An increased use of generic products, increased use of comparable but less expensive patent-protected products, and, in some cases, a decreased reliance on pharmaceutical agents might be observed. Third, although AMCs and professional societies would have to find alternative sources for funding programs, the absence of industry representatives at AMC meetings and lunches and in corridors would increase the sensitivity among medical students and house staff to the values of medical professionalism and scientific integrity. Rules would be standardized, not, as now, with some departments prohibiting drug company lunches, others allowing them; some hospitals permitting the sales representatives to see their physicians, others not. Medical society meetings would also assume a more professional tone and the substance of the programs would become more scientific.

Ultimately, the implementation of these proposals will substantially reduce the need for external regulation to safeguard against market-driven conflicts of interest, and the medical profession will reaffirm very publicly its commitment to put the interests of patients first.

REFERENCES

1. Schafer A. Biomedical conflict of interest: a defense of the sequestration thesis-learning from the cases of Nancy Oliveri and David Healy. *J Med Ethics.* 2004;30:8–24.

2. Studdert DM, Mello MM, Brennan TA. Financial conflict of interest in physician relationships with the pharmaceutical industry: self-regulation in the shadow of federal prosecution. *N Eng J Med.* 2004;351:1891–1900.

3. Matthews AW, Martinez B. Emails suggest Merck knew Vioxx's dangers at early stage. *Wall Street Journal.* November 1, 2004:A1.

4. Kassirer JP. Why should we swallow what these studies say? *Washington Post.* August 1, 2004: Outlook:B3.

5. Kassirer J. *On the Take: How Medicine's Complicity with Big Business Can Endanger Your Health.* New York, NY: Oxford University Press; 2004.

6. Angell M. *The Truth About Drug Companies.* New York, NY: Random House; 2004.

7. Avom J. *Powerful Medicine: The Benefits, Risks and Costs of Prescription Drugs.* New York, NY: Knopf; 2004.

8. McCormick BB, Tomlinson G, Brill-Edwards P, Detsky AS. Effect of restricting contact between pharmaceutical company representatives and internal medicine residents on post-training attitudes and behavior. *JAMA.* 2001;286:1994–1999.

9. Erde EL. Conflicts of interest in medicine: a philosophical and ethical morphology. In: Speece RG, Shimm DS, Buchanan AE, eds. *Conflicts of Interest in Clinical Practice and Research.* New York, NY: Oxford University Press; 1996:12–41.

10. American Board of Internal Medicine Foundation; American College of Physicians-American Society of Internal Medicine Foundation; European Federation of Internal Medicine. Medical professionalism in the new millennium: a physician charter. *Ann Intern Med.* 2002;136:243–246.

11. Blank L, Kimball H, McDonald W, Menino J. Medical professionalism in the new millennium: a physician charter 15 months later. *Ann Intern Med.* 2003;138:839–841.

12. Kerber R. Drug makers target consumers with their ads. *Boston Globe.* March 10, 2004:C1.

13. Blumenthal D. Doctors and drug companies. *N Engl J Med.* 2004;351:1885–1890.

14. Cain DM, Loewenstein G, Moore DA. The dirt on coming clean: possible effects of disclosing conflicts of interest. *J Legal Stud.* 2005;34:1–24.

15. Cialdini RB. *Influence: Science and Practice.* New York, NY: Harper Collins College Publishers; 1993:21.

16. Dana J, Loewenstein G. A social science perspective on gifts to physicians from undustry. *JAMA.* 2003;290:252–255.

17. Sandberg WS, Carlos R, Sandberg EH, Roizen MF. The effect of educational gifts from pharmaceutical firms on medical students' recall of company names of products. *Acam Med.* 1997;72:916–918.

18. Chren MM, Landefeld CS. Physicians' behavior and their interactions with drug companies: a controlled study of physicians who requested additions to a hospital drug formulary. *JAMA.* 1994;271:684–689.

19. Lurie N, Rich EC, Simpson DE, et al. Pharmaceutical representatives in academic medical centers. *J Gen Intern Med.* 1990;5:240–243.

20. Orlowski JP, Wateska L. The effects of pharmaceutical firm enticements on physician prescribing patterns: there's no such thing as a free lunch. *Chest.* 1992;102:270–273.

21. Cleary JD. Impact of pharmaceutical sales representatives on physician antibiotic prescribing. *J Pharm Technol.* 1992;8:27–29.

22. Wazana A. Physicians and the pharmaceutical industry: is a gift ever just a gift? *JAMA.* 2000;283: 373–380.

23. Bowman MA, Pearle DL. Changes in drug prescribing patterns related to commercial company funding of continuing medical education. *J Contin Educ Health Prof.* 1988;8:13–20.

The U.S. Long-Term Care Field: A Dialectic Analysis of Institution Dynamics

Martin Kitchener and Charlene Harrington

Sociological knowledge of the interplay between sets of beliefs and values (interpretive schemes) and patterns of social change has advanced significantly from analyses of health care fields comprising "sets of organizations that, in the aggregate, constitute an area of institutional life" (DiMaggio and Powell 1983:148–49). Research conducted at this level of analysis has recently begun to examine how the purposive action (agency) of participants is constrained and enabled by interpretive schemes and the templates of structure and action they prescribe (Kitchener 1998, 2002; D'Aunno, Succi, and Alexander 2000). This article, continues that line of inquiry through an analysis of organization dynamics in the U.S. field of long-term care.

The first goal of this article is to provide an account of the current institutional arrangements in long-term care—a recognized organizational field concerned with the delivery of health and social care, over a sustained period, to persons who lack some degree of functional capacity because of old age or disability (Kane and Kane 1987). While this field has received limited attention from institutional analysts, it has attracted growing interest from the public and from policy makers. In the context of a rapidly aging nation, long-term care is the source of persistent concerns about poor quality and escalating cost, not least because government is the largest payer (57 percent) of the estimated $123 billion in annual long-term care expenditures (Heffler, Levit, and Smith 2001; Institute of Medicine 2001).

The second aim of this study is to frame a historical analysis of the long-term care field that concentrates on the contest between interests aligned with two templates of organization (archetypes) that are underpinned by countervailing interpretive schemes: (1) the "traditional" nursing home archetype, which legitimates the provision of care in residential facilities under the control of medical professionals, and (2) the "insurgent" home and community-based services archetype, which emphasizes maintaining consumers' social integration through services such as home health and personal care. Consequently, this analysis employs a dialectic perspective to frame all institutional arrangements in the long-term care field as temporary resolutions in a battle between opposing social forces associated with the two archetypes (Benson 1977; Friedland and Alford 1991).

Adapted from: Martin Kitchener and Charlene Harrington. (2004). The U.S. long-term care field: A dialectical analysis of institutional dynamics. *Journal of Health and Social Behavior,* 45(extra issue), 87–101.

RESEARCH DESIGN AND CONCEPTUAL FRAMEWORK

Data Sources and Study Design

Given the early stage of institutional research in the long-term care field, the present analysis provides a historical analysis of documentary data from two main sources (Yin 1999). The first source involves the results from a systematic search for salient published material using on-line catalogues in health services (e.g., PubMed) and the social sciences (e.g., ABI Inform) that employed search terms including: key words (e.g., "long-term care," "institutional theory"), leading authors (e.g., "Scott"), and journals (e.g., "*Health Services Research*," "*Administrative Science Quarterly*"). The second source was the research archive compiled during the second author's program of long-term care policy studies conducted over the last 20 years. This rich source of historical information includes published and unpublished reports, working papers, and press cuttings.

INSTITUTIONAL DYNAMICS IN THE LONG-TERM CARE FIELD

Table 5.4.1 describes key features and tracks of change concerning the nursing home and home and community-based service archetypes.

The Nursing Home Archetype in the Era of Professional Dominance

Throughout the era of professional dominance in U.S. health care (Scott et al. 2000), many of its defining structural and normative features were reproduced in (and reinforced through) the nursing home archetype that characterized the long-term care field. For example, around the turn of the twentieth century, the social shifts (e.g., population growth and urbanization) that encouraged the growth of the hospital field also spurred the expansion of residential providers of long-term care. While the first constituents of this field included a variety of organizational types, including independent for-profit board and care homes, the most common form was the independent proprietary nursing home located in large (40 plus beds) houses that typically cared for local clients (Vladeck 1980).

In contrast to the hospital field, the influence (and concern) of physicians in nursing homes was (and still is) constrained by less frequent visits. However, while treatment regimes in nursing homes have typically fallen under the control of the nursing profession (Stevens 1989) physicians derive considerable power from a virtual monopoly over admissions and discharges. From the outset of the long-term care field, physician leaders worked hard to justify claims for extended influence through strategies such as labeling individuals' homes as inappropriate sites for modern care (Boas 1930).

Until the Great Depression, resource support for the long-term care field (i.e., nursing home archetype) was restricted because government financing remained limited largely to poorhouses administered by the fragmented welfare functions of county and state administrations (Hudson 1996). In 1935, the field received boosts of legitimacy, and resources when the Social Security Act provided pension funds to individuals who could use them to purchase private long-term care (U.S. Social Security Administration 2001). The Act also included an Old Age Assistance title that had two significant implications for the development of the long-term care field. First, federal and state governments were placed at the heart of the field, as administrators of grants for services including old age assistance for the poor. Second, because the Social Security Act prohibited payment of benefits to "inmates" of public institutions (until 1950) the state sponsored the growth of for-profit nursing homes (Vladeck 1980). By the end of World War II, the nursing home industry had grown to include approximately 8,000 facilities (Mechanic and Rochefort 1992).

By the mid-1950s, state financing and the power of the medical profession had combined to institutionalize within the long-term care field the prevailing set of normative and structural arrangements summarized as the nursing home archetype in Table 5.4.1. This configuration was underpinned by a dominant interpretive scheme that prescribed the need for sick patients (Parsons 1954) to receive institutional care under conditions of medical

TABLE 5.4.1   Summary Comparative Dimensions of Two Long-Term Care Archetypes

Dimension	*"Traditional" Nursing Home*	*"Insurgent" Home and Community-Based Services*
Interpretive Scheme		
Organizational Purpose	To institutionalize the aged & disabled & allow professional control over clients & their families	Maintain independence & quality of life of client through integration with family & community
Organizing Principles	Control by professions, confinement, & treatment of sick patients, 24-hour care in isolated facilities	Networks of inter-disciplinary agencies, independent contractors, & part-time providers. Increased management role for clients, nurses, & social workers, lesser role for physicians
Evaluation Criteria	Quality of treatment as determined by professionals, limited oversight of cost, & quality of care by others	Ideally, consumer-assessed but increasingly cost & quality of care as determined & assured through regulation & inspection
Structures	Originally locally-based cottage industry, increasingly for profit & chains	Originally not-for profit home health & personal care agencies, visiting nurse associations, & hospice. Increasing role of state programs & for-profit providers
Systems Aligned Interests	Medicaid, Medicare, private pay Government, professionals, & facility operators, industry associations, conservative politicians, organized labor	Medicaid, Medicare, private pay Home & community-based service providers, liberal politicians, consumers/advocates & some professionals

control, restricted autonomy, and limited external oversight by government (Estes and Binney 1989). State sponsorship of this interpretive scheme presented medical professionals and independent facility operators with an early monopoly over the economic and social rewards to be gained from long-term care (Estes and Binney 1993). As in the hospital field, corporate capital began to invade the field in search of profit using standard rationalizing techniques to produce larger bureaucratic facilities (Mendelson 1974).

LONG-TERM CARE IN THE ERA OF FEDERAL INVOLVEMENT

Through the 1965 enactment of Medicaid and Medicare, government became a third-party payer for long-term care and high public demand was secured. Political activity during the drafting of the programs ensured that interests aligned with the nursing homes archetype benefited heavily while home and community-based services received limited additional resource support (Estes, Harrington, and Pellow 2002). Medicare was designed primarily to pay for short-term, post-acute nursing home care and home health care. No capacity was included to pay for home and community-based service alternatives for the chronically ill such as personal care. Even within the construction of Medicare home health, homemaker services were excluded and medical professionals' continued power was displayed as physicians were allotted the gatekeeping role of determining program eligibility (Estes and Binney 1989).

In 1965, the Medicaid program introduced a joint federal-state system of funding health care for the poor that became the single largest payer of long-term care. In a similar way to the Medicare program, the majority of new resources were directed toward institutional providers leaving limited support for home and community-based services. Again, political activity by the institutional provider lobby secured program characteristics that benefited the nursing home industry. These features included: limited state regulation of nursing homes, cost-plus-profit payments for mandated nursing home care, the disqualification of competing old age homes, and a limited mandate for home health (Harrington 1996).

LONG-TERM CARE UNDER MARKET MANAGERIALISM

From the early 1980s, the two competing long-term care archetypes entered the current institutional era which is defined by an ideology of reduced welfare expenditure, weak regulation, increased personal responsibility, privatization, and decentralization (Quadagno 1999; Scott et al. 2000). In the long-term care field, a defining feature of the new era has been the use of legislation to encourage forms of privatization based on government subsidies for for-profit enterprises and the promotion of self-reliance and informal care (Estes and Alford 1990). In one example of the first trend, the Omnibus Reconciliation Acts of 1980 and 1981 encouraged the growth of for-profit home and community-based services that were traditionally provided by non-profit or public providers (Estes, Harrington, and Pellow 2002). By 1985, the number of for-profit home health agencies receiving Medicare reimbursement had increased six-fold. These home health enterprises benefited from both a new flow of government funding and the increased service demand that resulted from quicker hospital discharges after the introduction of the Medicare hospital prospective payment system (Benjamin 1993).

Throughout the 1980s and 1990s, the continued political strength of the nursing home archetype was demonstrated through a successful assault on non-profit home care providers. At the same time, nursing homes were subjected to a variety of cost containment methods including restrictions on bed supply and cuts in payments (Feder, Lambrew, and Huckaby 1997). Despite this, between 1985 and 1996 the number of facilities jumped from 14,500 to 17,200.

Re-theorizing Home and Community-based Services

As government searched for new ways of restricting long-term care spending, advocates re-framed their theorization (political justification) of home and community-based services away from the notions of social justice toward the idea that they offered a cheaper (or cost effective) alternative to nursing home care (Alecxih et al. 1996). In retaliation, the nursing home industry warned policy-makers of a posited woodwork effect whereby home and community-based services users and family members would demand more services if they were offered (Lynch and Estes 2001). Despite this, the re-theorization of home and community-based services against the prevailing concern for cost containment heralded a number of legislative and policy changes that gave increased resources to home care services. In one significant example, the Omnibus Reconciliation Act of 1981 allowed states to use Medicaid funds to pay for non-medical home and community-based services programs to avoid institutionalization. These "waiver" programs—so called because they involve waiving certain Medicaid regulations—allow states to provide (directly or through contract) a range of home and community-based services including personal care, case management, and home modifications.

By 1997, 49 states had developed 221 waivers for some or all of their long-term care target groups and national expenditures had risen to $8.1 billion to provide home and community-based services to 561,000 persons (Kitchener, Benon, and Harrington 2002). Additionally, by the mid-1990s many states had used federal funding to form task forces and demonstration projects to address what was now framed as a nursing home bias and limited home and community-based services options (Fox-Grage 1997).

The Formalization of the Home and Community-based Service Archetype

As home and community-based services received greater government funding, a larger market was constructed for corporate exploitation. Driven by the Reagan administration's ideology of extending for-profit service provision, and enabled by legislation in the early 1980s, corporations (often nursing home providers) colonized home health agencies and board-and-care facilities to cream-skim the most profitable clients and services (Hawes and Phillips 1986). In each case, any growth in home and community-based services provision was driven as much by corporate expansion into a new market as it was by consumer demand (Estes, Harrington, and Pellow 2002).

The Growth of Large Diversified Nursing Home Corporations

Between the 1970s and 1990s, Medicaid funding and state capital reimbursement policies fueled four tracks of change in the nursing home industry. First, there was a 25 percent increase in the number of facilities and a 37 percent increase in beds between 1978 and 1996 (Harrington and Carrillo 2000). Second, for-profit ownership increased from 39 percent in 1990 to 65 percent in 1999 (Harrington and Carrillo 2000). Third, a new class of huge corporate nursing home chains emerged from a series of more than 5,000 mergers and acquisitions (Banaszak-Holl et al. 2001). Many of these corporations integrated vertically and internationally to operate in fields including real estate, home health, and pharmacy.

During the 1990s, the proportion of large chains (51 plus homes) increased by 2.6 percent as the total number of chains fell from 725 to 624 (Banaszak-Holl et al. 2001). Because the government contributed 60 percent of the $90 billion that nursing homes earned in revenue in 1999 (Heffler, Levit, and Smith 2001), the largest chains were hugely profitable with, for example, Sun reporting a four-year average return on capital of 18.9 percent in 1998, compared with an industry median of 10.5 percent (Estes, Harrington, and Pellow 2002).

CONCLUSION

This article presented an account of institutional dynamics in the long-term care field that concentrated on the slow and contested institutionalization of the home and community-based services archetype and the continued dominance of the nursing home archetype. It has shown that within the traditional institutional arrangement the state legitimized and sponsored the nursing home archetype that presented medical professionals and independent facility operators with a virtual monopoly over the social and economic rewards to be gained from long-term care.

This pattern of change and inertia in the field of long-term care is vastly different from the descriptions of relatively quick transformations of institutional arrangements that emerge from studies of other health care fields (e.g., Kitchener 1998, D'Aunno, Succi, and Alexander 2000). Moreover, this portrayal of the long-term care field as comprising two archetypes does not stress the replacement of the nursing home archetype with home and community-based services. Rather, it acknowledges the uneasy accommodation of two contradictory interpretive schemes and interests, and an ongoing competition for legitimacy and resources. The dialectic approach of this study emphasized how a loosely-linked collection of institutional reform advocates mobilized against the powerful interests associated with the prevailing nursing home archetype. Despite their efforts being sidetracked, aborted, and resisted by nursing home interests, reformers mobilized around the home and community-based services interpretive scheme to challenge prevailing institutional arrangements.

The cumulative effect of a century of reform advocacy altered societal norms concerning patient choice and social integration to the extent that home and community-based services are now codified as the rights of citizens within policies (e.g., waivers) and law (e.g., the Olmstead case). This dialectic analysis also underscored the way that those aligned with the traditional archetype worked to frustrate home and community-based services advocates through, for example, their support for state policies and politicians who limit resource support for home and community-based services.

REFERENCES

Alecxih, Lisa, Steven Lutzky, and John Corea. 1996. *Estimated Savings from the Use of Home and Community-based Alternatives to Nursing Facility Care in Three States*. Washington, DC: American Association of Retired Persons.

Banaszak-Holl, Jane, Whitney B. Berta, Dilys Bowman, Joel A. C. Baum, and Will Mitchell. 2001. "Cauess and Consequences of Chain Acquisitions; Health Performance and Operating Strategy of U.S. Nursing Homes, 1991–1997." *Managerial and Decision Economics* 23:261–82.

Benjamin, A. E. 1993. "An Historical Perspective on Home Care Policy." *Milbank Quarterly* 71 (1):129–65.

Benson, Kenneth. 1977. "Organizations: A Dialectic View." *Administrative Science Quarterly* 22:1–21.

Boas, E. 1930. "The Care of the Aged Sick." Pp. 39–46 in *The Care of the Aged*, edited by J. M. Rubinow. Chicago, IL: University of Chicago Press.

D'Aunno, Thomas, Melissa Succi, and Jeff Alexander. 2000. "The Role of Institutional and Market Forces in Divergent Organizational Change." *Administrative Science Quarterly* 45:679–703.

DiMaggio, Paul J., and W. Walter Powell. 1983. "The Iron Cage Revisited: Institutional Isomorphism and Collective Rationality in Organizational Fields." *American Sociological Review* 48:147–60.

Estes, Carroll L., and Robert R. Alford. 1990. "Systematic Crisis and the Nonprofit Field: Toward a Political Economy of the Nonprofit Health and Social Services Field." *Theory and Society* 19 (2):173–98.

Estes, Carroll L., and Elizabeth A. Binney. 1989. "The Biomedicalization of Aging: Dangers and Dilemmas." *The Gerontologist* 29 (5):587–96.

———. 1993. "Restructuring the Nonprofit Field." Pp. 22–40 in *Long-term Care Crisis: Elders Trapped in the No-care Zone*, edited by Carroll L. Estes, James Swan and Associates. Newbury Park, CA: Sage.

Estes, Carroll, Charlene Harrington, and David Pellow. 2002. "Medical Industrial Complex." Pp. 1818–32 in *The Encyclopedia of Sociology*, edited by Edgar F. Borgatta and Rhonda J. Montgomery. New York: Macmillan.

Feder, Judith, Jeanne Lambrew, and Michelle Huckaby. 1997. "Medicaid and Long-term Care for the Elderly: Implications of Restructuring." *Milbank Quarterly* 75 (4):425–59.

Fox-Grage, Wendy. 1997. *The Task Force Report: Long-term Care Reform in the States*. Washington, DC: National Conference of State Legislators.

Friedland, Roger, and Robert R. Alford. 1991. "Bringing Society Back In: Symbols, Practices, and Institutional Contradictions." Pp. 232–63 in *The New Institutionalism in Organizational Analysis* edited by Walter W. Powell and Paul J. DiMaggio. Chicago, IL: University of Chicago Press.

Harrington, Charlene. 1996. "The Nursing Home Industry: Public Policy in the 1990s." Pp. 515–34 in *Perspectives in Medical Sociology*, edited by Phil Brown. Prospect Heights, IL: Waveland.

———. 2000. *Long Term Care Program and Market Characteristics State Survey Data Base*. San Francisco, CA: University of California, San Francisco.

Harrington, Charlene, Helen Carrillo, Valerie Wellin, Nancy Miller, and Alan LeBlanc. 2000. "Predicting State Medicaid Home and Community Based Waiver Participants and Expenditures." *The Gerontologist* 40 (6):673–86.

Hawes, Catherine, and Charles Phillips. 1986. "The Changing Structure of the Nursing Home Industry and the Impact of Ownership on Quality, Cost and Access." Pp. 492–541 in *For Profit Enterprise in Health Care*, edited by Bradford H. Gray. Washington, DC: National Academy Press.

Heffler, Stephen, Katherine Kevit, and Sheila Smith. 2001. "Health Spending Growth Up in 1999: Faster Growth Expected in the Future." *Health Affairs* 20 (2):193–203.

Hudson, Robert B. 1996. "Home and Community-based Care; Recent Accomplishments and New Challenges." Pp 53–69 in *From Nursing Homes to Home Care*, edited by Marie E. Cowart and Jill Quadagno. New York: Howarth.

Institute of Medicine. 2001. *Improving the Quality of Long-term Care*. Washington, DC: National Academy Press.

Kane, Rosalie A., and Robert L. Kane. 1987. *Long-term Care: Principles, Programs, and Policies*. New York: Springer.

Kitchener, Martin. 1998. "Quasi-market Transformation: An Institutionalist Approach to Change in UK Hospitals." *Public Administration* 76 (1):73–97.

———. 2002. "Mobilizing the Logic of Managerialism in Professional Organizations: The Case of Academic Health Center Mergers." *Organization Studies* 23 (3):391–421.

Kitchener, Martin, Malcolm Beynon, and Charlene Harrington. 2002. "QCA and Public Services Research: Lessons from an Early Application." *Public Management Review* 4 (4):485–504.

Lynch, Marty, and Carroll L. Estes. 2001. "The Underdevelopment of Community-Based Services in the U.S. Long-term Care System: A Structural Analysis." Pp 201–15 in *Social Policy and Aging: A Critical Perspective*, edited by Carroll L. Estes and Associates. Thousand Oaks, CA: Sage.

Mechanic, David, and David A. Rochefort. 1992. "A Policy of Inclusion for the Mentally Ill." *Health Affairs* 11 (1):128–50.

Mendelson, Mary A. 1974. *Tender Loving Greed*. New York: Alfred A. Knopf.

Parsons, Talcott. 1954. "The Professions and Social Structure." Pp. 185–99 in *Essays in Sociological Theory*. Glencoe, IL: Free Press.

Quadagno, Jill. 1999. "Creating a Capital Investment Welfare State: The New American Exceptionalism." *American Sociological Review* 64 (1):1–11.

Scott, W. Richard, Martin Ruef, Peter J. Mendel, and Carol A. Caronna. 2000. *Institutional Change and Healthcare Organizations: From Professional Dominance to Managed Care*. Chicago, IL: University of Chicago Press.

Stevens, Rosemary. 1989. *In Sickness and in Wealth: American Hospitals in the Twentieth Century*. New York: Basic Books.

U.S. Social Security Administration. 2001. *Social Security Bulletin, Annual Statistical Supplement, 2001*. Washington, DC: Social Security Administration.

Vladeck, Bruce C. 1980. *Unloving Care: The Nursing Home Tragedy*. New York: Basic Books.

Yin, Robert K. 1999. "Enhancing the Quality of Case Studies in Health Services Research." *Health Services Research* 34 (5 Part II):1209–25.

Primary Care, Race, and Mortality in U.S. States

Leiyu Shi, James Macinko, Barbara Starfield,
Robert Politzer, and Jiahong Xu

BACKGROUND

In the past decade, substantial literature suggested a significant association between income inequality and mortality both in the U.S. and abroad (Blakely, Lochner, & Kawachi, 2002; Wilkinson, 1996; Kennedy, Kawachi, & Prothrow-Stith, 1996; Lochner, Pamuk, Makuc, Kennedy, & Kawachi, 2001; Lynch et al., 1998; McLaughlin & Stokes, 2002; Subranumian, Blakely, & Kawachi, 2003). The greater the gap in income distribution between the rich and poor in a given area, the higher the mortality rate for the population of that area. However, several recent studies have failed to find a similar relationship between income inequality and various manifestations of health (Mellor & Milyo, 2001; Wagstaff & van Doorslaer, 2000; Lynch et al., 2004).

We assess the impact of primary care by examining if there is an independent relationship between primary care and mortality and by determining whether primary care attenuates the impact of socioeconomic characteristics on mortality. The logic of the connection between primary care and reduced mortality is reflected in the goal of primary care (Starfield, 1994, 1992) and mounting evidence that links primary care with better health status (Starfield, 1998; Shi, 1994, 1997; Macinko, Starfield, & Shi, 2003).

Primary care addresses the most common problems in the community to maximize health and well-being. It integrates care where there is more than one health problem, and deals with the context in which illness exists and influences the responses of people to their health problems. It is care that organizes and rationalizes the deployment of all resources, basic as well as specialized, directed at promoting, maintaining, and improving health. Findings of an independent effect of primary care on reduced mortality would be particularly relevant as it would represent a specific mechanism for addressing at least some of the health impact of growing social inequalities in the Unites States.

This study is unique in that it seeks to examine the independent relationship between income inequality and population mortality, shed light on the still contentious issue of the impact of racial composition on the observed relationship between income inequality and health, and assess the extent to which primary care might mediate this association. By using 11 years of data, we are able to examine the relationship among the variables of interest in more than one period, thus improving the robustness of our findings to changes over time. By performing race-stratified analysis, we are able to examine the differential

Adapted from: Leiyu Shi, James Macinko, Barbara Starfield, Robert Politzer, and Jiahong Xu. (2005). Primary care, race, and mortality in US states. *Social Science & Medicine,* 61, 65–75.

effects of income inequality and primary care on white and black mortality. As noted above, previous research has indicated that the effect of income inequality on health may be confounded by the inclusion of the fraction of African-Americans in the population (Deaton & Lubotsky, 2003).

RESULTS

During 1985–1995, there was a decline in all-cause mortality. The mean state age-adjusted mortality rate dropped from 821 to 762 per 100,000 population. In the same period, there was a steady increase in primary care physicians, from 5.02 to 6.04 per 10,000 population. Income inequality within states fluctuated during the period with an overall worsening trend: the mean of the Gini coefficient among states increased from 0.41 to 0.43 during the period.

Both primary care (inversely) and income inequality (positively) were significantly associated with total mortality. Among sociodemographic indicators, blacks and unemployment are significantly and inversely related to mortality. Metro is not significantly related to mortality. In addition, primary care is positively and significantly related to metro and education. Income inequality is significantly and positively related to black but inversely related to education.

A significant effect of income inequality on mortality was noted. Inclusion of sociodemographics, particularly *Percent of Black* reduces the regression coefficient of income inequality to insignificance. The inclusion of primary care reduces the magnitude of all sociodemographic regression coefficients, although only metro loses statistical significance. An increase of one primary care doctor per 10,000 population is associated with a reduction of 14.4 deaths per 100,000 population, or 1.44 deaths per 10,000 population, after taking into account the effects of income inequality and the sociodemographic correlates of mortality.

The magnitude of the association between primary care and mortality remains stable over time, suggesting a lagged effect of primary care on mortality. The association between income inequality and mortality remains insignificant in time-lagged analysis after controlling for sociodemographic characteristics.

Income inequality was significantly associated with mortality, where neither sociodemographic characteristics nor primary care were included in the model. The magnitude of the income inequality coefficient was significantly higher for black mortality than for white mortality. However, for both races, inclusion of sociodemographics rendered income inequality statistically insignificant.

Primary care exhibited a similar relationship between black and white mortality, although the magnitude of the association was higher for black mortality. Primary care is significantly and inversely associated with mortality, after controlling for income inequality and sociodemographic correlates of mortality. In the white population, an increase of one primary care doctor per 10,000 population is associated with a reduction of 1.58 deaths per 10,000 population. In the black population, primary care was associated with a reduction of 3.97 deaths per 10,000 population. For both populations, the inclusion of primary care reduces the magnitude of other sociodemographic variables. These results were replicated in time-lagged models. The effect of primary care on white and black mortality remains relatively stable over time. The effect of income inequality on mortality remains insignificant in time-lagged analysis after controlling for sociodemographic characteristics.

DISCUSSION

This study confirmed earlier findings that primary care was associated with lower mortality and partially mediated the association between socioeconomic variables and mortality (Shi et al., 1999, 2002; Shi & Starfield, 2000, 2001). These findings are significant because they provide more robust evidence of a relationship between primary care physicians and lower state mortality than was possible by previous cross-sectional analyses. That primary care remained significant after including income inequality and sociodemographic covariates of mortality indicates primary care is likely to be independently associated with lower population mortality. An increase of one primary care doctor is independently associated, on average, with a reduction of 14.4 deaths, per 100,000 population—about a 2 percent decline over current levels.

Race-specific stratified analyses demonstrated that the relationship between primary care and mortality was not confounded by race. Primary care is significantly and inversely associated with white and black mortality, after controlling for sociodemographics and income inequality. However, primary care exerted a greater impact on black mortality than white mortality (2.5 times or 3.97/1.58). These findings are consistent with previous studies demonstrating that an increase in primary care resources in areas of high social inequality would result in greater health improvements (lower mortality) than would the same increase of primary care resources in areas of lower social inequalities (Shi et al., 2002).

Results of time-lagged models demonstrate that in addition to a contemporaneous association, primary care also has a latent relationship on mortality. These findings are consistent with prior postulated benefits specific to primary care adequacy at the population level (Starfield, 1992, 1994, 1998; Shi, 1994, 1997; Macinko et al., 2003). According to the results of this study, primary care is associated with improvements in health—reductions in mortality over time—while other risk factors (e.g., unemployment, education) are positively associated with eroding health status over time. This result points to a longer-term contextual impact of primary care resources at the state-level and increasing primary care resources might represent one strategy to at least partially offset the effects of "accumulated disadvantage" on population health. There is evidence that (at least in Europe) differential access to primary care and other preventive services over the period of several decades may be partially responsible for current inequalities in health (Mackenbach, Stronks, & Kunst, 1989; Paterson & Judge, 2002).

These findings are also consistent with other research that attributes a significant percentage of the increase in life expectancy in the developed world over the past 50 years to advances in health care (Bunker, 2001). In all, clinical services, composed of preventive services as well as therapeutic intervention, were credited with approximately five of the 30 years of increase in life expectancy since 1950 (Bunker, Frazier, & Mosteller, 1995). One postulated mechanism for the impact of primary care is that access to a regular source of primary care may improve prevention and early detection of chronic diseases (Shea, Misra, Ehrlich, Field, & Francis, 1992). Primary care makes its contribution to health by providing comprehensive, coordinated, and longitudinal care upon first contact with the health system (Starfield, 1998). There is evidence that high-quality primary care can also lead to more efficient secondary and tertiary care (Casanova, Colomer, & Starfield, 1996; Casanova & Starfield, 1995). We hypothesize that the unique features of primary care such as continuous, longitudinal, and person-focused care, may also work to reverse some of the negative health effects of social inequalities by "short-circuiting" the ability of long-term stressors to produce chronic ailments.

From a policy perspective, the promotion of primary care may serve as a more feasible and less expensive strategy for combating mortality and for reducing socioeconomic disparities in health, compared with either social policy that addresses sociodemographic determinants of health or behavioral modifications. Such a hypothesis at least deserves consideration in the face of declining health levels of the US relative to comparably industrialized nations (Starfield & Shi, 2002).

Numerous ecological studies, mostly cross-sectional, have provided support for the hypothesis that unequal distributions of income are associated with high mortality in populations (Blakely et al., 2002; Wilkinson, 1996; Kennedy et al., 1996; Lochner et al., 2001; Lynch et al., 1998; McLaughlin & Stokes, 2002; Subramanian et al., 2003). Other studies, however, have challenged this finding (Mellor & Milyo, 2001; Wagstaff & van Doorslaer, 2000; Lynch et al., 2004). Our analysis indicates that income inequality is significantly associated with mortality only in analyses where it is the only variable. This effect becomes insignificant after taking into account population sociodemographic characteristics. This finding supports recent studies that claim income inequality has an apparent effect only because it is associated with other variables related to mortality. It reaffirms the significant association between population sociodemographic characteristics and mortality and implies that studies of the impact of income inequality on health need to include other determinants of health. From a policy perspective, improvement in population health is likely to require a multi-pronged approach that addresses sociodemographic determinants of health as well as strengthening primary care.

REFERENCES

Blakely, T. A., Lochner, K., & Kawachi, I. (2002). Metropolitan area income inequality and self-rated health—a multi-level study. *Social Science & Medicine, 54*, 65–77.

Bunker, J. (2001). *Medicine matters after all: measuring the benefits of medical care: a healthy lifestyle and a just social environment.* London, UK: Nuffield Trust.

Bunker, J. P., Frazier, H. S., & Mosteller, F. (1995). The role of medical care in determining health: creating an inventory of benefits. In B. C. Amick III, S. Levine, A. R. Tarlov, & D. C. Walsh (Eds.), *Society and health.* New York, NY: Oxford University Press.

Casanova, C., Colomer, C., & Starfield, B. (1996). Pediatric hospitalization due to ambulatory care-sensitive conditions in Valencia (Spain). *International Journal for Quality in Health Care, 8*, 51–59.

Casanova, C., & Starfield, B. (1995). Hospitalizations of children and access to primary care: a cross-national comparison. *International Journal of Health Services, 25*, 283–294.

Deaton, A., Lubotsky, D. (2003). Mortality, inequality and race in American cities and states. *Social Science & Medicine, 56*, 1139–1153.

Kennedy, B. P., Kawachi, I., & Prothrow-Stith, D. (1996). Income distribution and mortality: cross sectional ecological study of the Robin Hood index in the United States. *British Medical Journal, 312*, 1004–1007 (Erratum: *British Medical Journal 312*(7040), 1996, p. 1194).

Lochner, K., Pamuk, E., Makuc, D., Kennedy, B. P., & Kawachi, I. (2001). State-level income inequality and individual mortality risk: a prospective, multilevel study. *American Journal of Public Health, 91*, 385–391.

Lynch, J. W., Kaplan, G. A., Pamuk, E. R., Cohen, R. D., Heck, K. E., Balfour, J. L., & Yen, I. H. (1998). Income inequality and mortality in metropolitan areas of the United States. *American Journal of Public Health, 88*, 1070–1080.

Lynch, J., Smith, G. D., Harper, S., Hillemeier, M., Ross, N., Kaplan, G. A., & Wolfson, M. (2004). Is income inequality a determinant of population health? Part 1. A systematic review. *Milbank Quarterly, 82*, 5–99.

Macinko, J., Starfield, B., & Shi, L. (2003). The contribution of primary care systems to health outcomes within Organization for Economic Cooperation and Development (OECD) countries, 1970–1998. *Health Services Research, 38*, 831–865.

Mackenbach, J. P., Stronks, K., & Kunst, A. E. (1989). The contribution of medical care to inequalities in health: differences between socio-economic groups in decline of mortality from conditions amenable to medical intervention. *Social Science & Medicine, 29*, 369–376.

McLaughlin, D. K., & Stokes, C. S. (2002). Income inequality and mortality in US counties: does minority racial concentration matter? *American Journal of Public Health, 92*, 99–104.

Mellor, J. M., & Milyo, J. (2001). Reexamining the evidence of an ecological association between income inequality and health. *Journal of Health Politics, Policy and Law, 26*, 487–522.

Paterson, I., & Judge, K. (2002). Equality of access to healthcare. In J. P. Mackenbach & M. Bakker (Eds.), *Reducing inequalities in health* (pp. 169–187). London: Routledge.

Shea, S., Misra, D., Ehrlich, M. H., Field, L., & Francis, C. K. (1992). Predisposing factors for severe, uncontrolled hypertension in an inner-city minority population. *New England Journal of Medicine, 327*, 776–781.

Shi, L. (1994). Primary care, specialty care, and life chances. *International Journal of Health Services, 24*, 431–458.

Shi, L. (1997). Health care spending, delivery, and outcome in developed countries: a cross-national comparison. *American Journal of Medical Quality, 12*, 83–93.

Shi, L., & Starfield, B. (2000). Primary care, income inequality, and self-rated health in the United States: a mixed-level analysis. *International Journal of Health Services, 30*, 541–555.

Shi, L., & Starfield, B. (2001). The effect of primary care physician supply and income inequality on mortality among blacks and whites in US metropolitan areas. *American Journal of Public Health, 91*, 1246–1250.

Shi, L., Starfield, B., Kennedy, B. P., & Kawachi, I. (1999). Income inequality, primary care, and health indicators. *Journal of Family Practice, 48*, 275–284.

Shi, L., Starfield, B., Politzer, R., & Regan, J. (2002). Primary care, self-rated health, and reductions in social disparities in health. *Health Services Research, 37*, 529–550.

Starfield, B. (1992). *Primary care: concept, evaluation, and policy.* New York, NY: Oxford University Press.

Starfield, B. (1994). Is primary care essential? *Lancet, 344*, 1129–1133.

Starfield, B. (1998). *Primary care: balancing health needs, services, and technology.* New York: Oxford University Press.

Starfield, B., & Shi, L. (2002). Policy relevant determinants of health: an international perspective. *Health Policy, 60*, 201–218.

Subramanian, S. V., Blakely, T., & Kawachi, I. (2003). Income inequality as a public health concern: where do we stand? Commentary on "Is exposure to income inequality a public health concern?" *Health Services Research, 38*, 153–167.

Wagstaff, A., & van Doorslaer, E. (2000). Income inequality and health: what does the literature tell us? *Annual Review of Public Health, 21*, 543–567.

Wilkinson, R. G. (1996). *Unhealthy societies: the afflictions of inequality.* London: Routledge.

CHAPTER 6

Labor Issues

Doctor and nurse in hospital corridor

From the Doctor's Workshop to the Iron Cage? Evolving Modes of Physician Control in U.S. Health Systems

Martin Kitchener, Carol A. Caronna, and Stephen M. Shortell

INTRODUCTION

As national health systems pursue the common goals of containing expenditure growth and improving quality, many have sought to replace traditional modes (systems) of controlling physicians' resource use and practice that rely on initial professional training and subsequent peer review (Freidson, 2001; Kitchener, 2000; Pollitt & Bouckaert, 2000). Although variations in national systems and politics have spawned a variety of approaches, a common theme involves extending the use of bureaucratic controls such as hierarchical coordination, salaried positions, and performance management techniques (Hoggett, 1996; Power, 1997).

In the United States (US) market system, bureaucratic control of physicians has developed in a different way. Traditionally, the US medical profession avoided the forms of control experienced by their NHS counterparts as members worked individually, or in groups, under a fee-for-service remuneration system. From the early 1980s, purchasers of US healthcare (e.g., government and employers) increasingly blamed poor quality and rising costs on the limited capacity of the market to regulate physicians' resource-use and practice variation. In this decentralized context, reform efforts have concentrated on exposing physicians to bureaucratic control from inside the hospital organizations they once treated as "workshops" from which to accumulate fees and prestige (Pauly & Redisch, 1973).

For more than 20 years, researchers have examined alterations in relations between physicians, established bureaucratic forms (e.g., the NHS), and newer entities such as US hospital systems (Shortell, Gillies, Anderson, Erickson, & Mitchell, 2000). Prominent among the early US analyses, Scott (1982) specified three ideal-typical systems of structures and practices (modes) concerning physician control: autonomous, conjoint, and heteronomous. Despite two decades' of studies into aspects of change in the US healthcare industry, none has explicitly re-considered Scott's framework in the light of conceptual and practical developments.

A TYPOLOGY OF THREE BUREAUCRATIC MODES OF PHYSICIAN CONTROL

Studies of professional work in bureaucratic contexts such as US and British hospitals, UK social work, and Canadian hospitals demonstrate the value of Mintzberg's (1979) notion of

Adapted from: Martin Kitchener, Carol A. Caronna, and Stephen M. Shortell. (2005). From the doctor's workshop to the iron cage? Evolving modes of physician control in U.S. health systems. *Social Science and Medicine*, 60, 1311–1322.

the "professional bureaucracy" as a basis for understanding differences between modes of control over expert and other forms of labor (Ackroyd & Bolton, 1999; Denis, Lamothe, Langley, & Valette, 1999; Kitchener, 2000, 2002). Crucially, the "professional bureaucracy" reflects that expert labor is typically conducted in decentralized and "loosely coupled" organizations in which senior professionals perform the role most similar to that of the industrial supervisor (Weick, 1976).

Custodial Control

Ackroyd and colleagues (1989) identify a "custodial" mode of control in which the primary concern of professional line managers is to "preserve and perpetuate customary [professionally determined] kinds and standards of service provision" including the definition and measurement of quality. Senior professionals are typically represented on executive boards although their preference for loosely coupled structures ensures that some separation is maintained between professional and administrative jurisdictions.

The importance placed on high trust and collegial relations between practitioners requires that senior professionals demonstrate to junior staff their independence from management and disinclination to intrude in daily routines. Thus, within professional domains, work supervision involves senior professionals "coaching" or mentoring junior colleagues through peer review, rather than through more direct coercion (Scott, 1965). This mode is typified by traditional staff group arrangements in US hospitals (Friedson, 1970).

Conjoint Control

Scott's (1982) specification of the conjoint mode of control rests on a demarcation of responsibility whereby senior professionals maintain control over micro concerns (e.g., patient care) while managers take the lead in strategic organizational issues (Shortell, Morrisey, & Conrad, 1985). Conjoint control does, however, provide "overlapping roles and structures that allow administrators to co-opt professionals into decision bodies stressing macro-care goals, and professionals to co-opt administrators in decision areas stressing micro-care goals" (Scott, 1982; p. 236). The conjoint mode recognizes (more than the other modes) that conflict will occur when issues span professional and administrative domains and it places great emphasis on boundary spanning activities to bridge the gap. This exchange across domains may equalize the influence of physicians and managers both within organizations as a whole, and inside the traditionally separate managerial and professional jurisdictions.

Heteronomous Control

This mode of control emerges from Scott's (1965) study of US social work agencies in which practitioners traditionally have been more "managed" than have physicians. Under these arrangements, general managers and other bureaucratic controls are employed to regulate professional action against agency goals. Stopping well short of the control systems experienced by physicians in the former Soviet Union (Rafferty & McKinlay, 1993), the heteronomous mode is similar, in some ways, to that which is typical in fields of corporate professional firms. In that context, experts such as lawyers are typically constrained as corporate executives and stockholders set commercial goals (e.g. increased revenue, market share).

Fig. 6.1.1 presents a continuum of three ideal typical modes of bureaucratic physician control. Recognizing that none is ever likely to emerge in a pure form in the US or elsewhere, the present study used this conceptual framework to help analyze evolving bureaucratic modes of physician control in US health systems.

RESEARCH DESIGN AND METHODS

Casing Criteria and Method

Data for this analysis of bureaucratic modes of US physician control were collected between the summer of 1999 and the spring of 2000 from a sub-sample of the not-for-profit,

	Custodial	Conjoint	Heteronomous
Physician autonomy over terms of work	High	Moderate	Low
Physician autonomy over content of work	High	Moderate	Low
Physician remuneration	Fee for services (FFS)	Salary with some FFS	Salary
Quality assurance (QA)	Peer review of practice & coaching from senior colleagues	Negotiated combination of professional & managerial methods	Managerial systems e.g., benchmarking & TQM
Physician-organization integration	Low	Moderate	High
Explanations of mode			
Orthodox	Response to complex & uncertain work i.e. couple capability with discretion.	Physicians control "micro" care issues, managers control "macro" strategic issues.	Response to medical specializaiton & "need" for cost containment.
Alternative	Professional dominance	Eroded professional dominance	Managerial dominance

FIGURE 6.1.1   Comparative Dimensions of Bureaucratic Modes of Physician Control

hospital-based health systems involved in a 10-year program of research examining issues of physician integration and governance (Shortell et al., 2000).

Findings: Multiple and Flexible Modes of Bureaucratic Physician Control

We report considerable variation among modes of physician control. Our analysis classifies one system as being most similar to the custodial mode of physician control, four systems fit best with the conjoint control, and three systems are best understood in terms of the heteronomous mode. Within each broad category, some systems fit the ideal typical characteristics of the modes better than others. This feature underscores the diversity of modes of professional control within the emerging professional bureaucracies in US healthcare.

DISCUSSION AND CONCLUSIONS

This article has provided a conceptual and empirical analysis of the movement away from the autonomous mode of US physician control that relied on initial professional training and subsequent peer review, toward three emergent bureaucratic modes. In common with Light (1995), we suggest that this process arose from a combination of internal pressures (such as physicians' pursuit of income and prestige through specialization), and a rare combination of countervailing forces capable of challenging the autonomous mode (e.g., the buyers' revolt and waning professional legitimacy). Thus, somewhat ironically, the bureaucratization of the US medical profession is, in a part, an inevitable outcome of the entrepreneurial activity of physicians under the autonomous mode. It also represents a socially driven response to mounting evidence that neither the market system nor the autonomous mode of physician control could be relied upon to deliver social goals such as cost containment and quality improvement. In US healthcare, as new bureaucratic systems have evolved, there is little indication of a monolithic iron cage of physician subjugation. The bureaucratic modes of control encountered by physicians within the case systems bear little resemblance to those experienced by 19th Century English craft guildsmen and contemporary Detroit autoworkers. Rather, as in most other fields of professional bureaucracies, three modes of control have emerged in which expert labor maintains high levels of autonomy over the content of work. This finding adds further weight to arguments that bureaucratic forms can, and do, extend their structures and processes to accommodate the work, if not the self-interest, of professionals (DuGay, 2000).

If the core of bureaucratic organization is as Weber (1930, 1978) suggested, the exercise of control based on knowledge, a key issue for all national health systems will be to decide who is allowed to secure control over the acquisition and manipulation of medical practice and knowledge (Reed, 2000; Jacques, 1996). The US once allowed the medical -profession exclusive and autonomous control over this intellectual capital. As part of an international policy agenda to constrain public spending, address quality concerns, and render professionals "on tap rather than on top" (Pollitt, 2000), some control has been transferred to the administrative elite of physicians (Montgomery, 2001), US health systems and networks, and centralized governments in other countries. The effectiveness of these transfers in addressing the challenges involved is an important area for further research.

Although this study concentrated on the case of not-for-profit US health systems, the typology is likely to be useful in other national contexts because the modes of control were derived from studies of professional work in the US and elsewhere. It was noted earlier that in countries such as the UK, there have been extensions to the bureaucratic controls used to regulate professional practice against social goals including equity in the treatment of cases (DuGay, 2000). Recent studies of such developments provide some evidence of movement toward more heteronomous modes of control including: the introduction of formalized practice guidelines and performance management for British general practitioners (Exworthy et al., 2003) and New Zealand hospital doctors (Doolin, 2002), and the increasing use of general managers in British social work (Kitchener et al., 2000). Analyses of such developments may present opportunities to conceptually and empirically elaborate the typology presented here. They may also provide signals for the development of physician control in US hospital systems.

REFERENCES

Ackroyd, S., & Bolton, S. (1999). It is not Taylorism: mechanisms of work intensification in the provision of gynaecological services in an NHS hospital. *Work Employment and Society, 13*(2), 369–387.

Ackroyd, S., Hughes, J., & Soothill, K. (1989). Public sector services and their management. *Journal of Management Studies, 26*(6), 603–619.

Denis, J.-L., Lamothe, L., Langley, A., & Valette, A. (1999). The struggle to redefine boundaries in health care systems. In D. Brock, C. R. Hinings, & M. Powell (Eds.), *Restructuring the professional organization: accounting, health care and law* (pp. 105–130). London: Routledge.

Doolin, B. (2002). Enterprise, discourse, professional identity and the organizational control of hospital clinicians. *Organization Studies, 23*(2), 369–390.

DuGay, P. (2000). *In praise of bureaucracy.* London: Sage.

Exworthy, M., Wilkinson, E., McColl, A., Moore, M., Roderick, P., Smith, H., & Gabbay, J. (2003). The role of performance indicators in changing the autonomy of the general practice profession in the UK. *Social Science & Medicine, 56*(7), 1493–1504.

Freidson, E. (1970). *Professional dominance: the social structure of medical care.* New York: Atherton Press.

Freidson, E. (2001). *Professionalism: the third logic.* Chicago: University of Chicago Press.

Hoggett, P. (1996). New modes of control in the public service. *Public Administration, 74,* 9–32.

Jacques, R. (1996). *Manufacturing the Employee: Management knowledges from the 19th to 21st centuries.* London: Sage.

Kitchener, M. (2000). The bureaucratisation of professional roles: the case of clinical directors in UK hospitals. *Organization, 7*(1), 129–154.

Kitchener, M. (2002). Mobilizing the logic of managerialism in professional fields: the case of academic health center mergers. *Organization Studies, 23*(3), 391–420.

Kitchener, M., Kirkpatrick, I., & Whipp, R. (2000). Supervising professional work under new public management: evidence from an invisible trade. *British Journal of Management, 11*(3), 213–226.

Light, D. W. (1995). Countervailing powers: a framework for professions in transition. In T. Johnson, G. Larkin, & M. Saks (Eds.), *Health professions and the state in Europe* (pp. 25–41). London: Routledge.

Mintzberg, H. (1979). *The structuring of organizations: a synthesis of the research.* Englewood Cliffs, NJ: Prentice Hall.

Montgomery, K. (2001). Physician executives: the evolution and impact of a hybrid profession. *Advances in Health Care Management, 2,* 215–241. Greenwich: JAI Press.

Pauly, M., & Redisch, M. (1973). The not-for-profit hospital as a physicians' cooperative. *American Economic Review, 63*(1), 87–100.

Pollitt, C., & Bouckaert, G. (2000). *Public management reform: a comparative analysis.* Oxford: Oxford University Press.

Power, M. (1997). *The audit society.* Oxford: Oxford University Press.

Reed, M. (2000). From the "cage" to the "gaze"? The dynamics of organizational control in late modernity. In G. Morgan & L. Engwall (Eds.), *Regulation and organization: international perspectives* (pp. 17–49). London: Routledge.

Scott, W. R. (1965). Reaction to supervision in a heteronomous professional organization. *Administrative Science Quarterly, 10,* 65–81.

Scott, W. R. (1982). Managing professional work: three models of control for health organizations. *Health Services Research, 17*(3), 213–240.

Shortell, S., Gillies, R., Anderson, D., Erickson, K., & Mitchell, J. (2000) *Remaking health care in America: the Evolution of organized delivery systems.* San Francisco: Jossey-Bass.

Shortell, S., Morrisey, M., & Conrad, D. (1985). Economic regulation and hospital behavior: the effects on medical staff organization and hospital-physician relationships. *Health Services Research, 20*(5), 597–628.

Weber, M. (1930). *The protestant ethic and the spirit of capitalism.* Oxford: Basil Blackwell.

Weber, M. (1978). Economy & society: an outline of interpretive sociology. In: G. Roth & C. Wittich (Eds), Los Angeles: University of California Press.

Weick, K. (1976). Educational organizations as loosely coupled systems. *Administrative Science Quarterly, 21*(1), 1–19.

Projections and Trends in RN Supply: What Do They Tell Us About the Nursing Shortage?

Lynn Y. Unruh, PhD, RN, LHRM, and Myron D. Fottler, PhD

The current nursing shortage has been the subject of innumerable articles, research programs, and policy actions since the beginning of this century. Yet despite the attention that has been paid to the shortage, many questions remain regarding causes and solutions.

The shortage is typically viewed as RN supply that is insufficient to meet increasing demand. A recent U.S. Department of Health and Human Services (DHHS, 2002) projection of future RN shortages shows a timeline graph with demand for the number of full-time equivalent (FTE) RNs in nursing jobs increasing significantly by 2020, supply growing slowly until 2010, then numbers beginning a slow decline. From 2000 to 2020, demand is projected to grow 40% and supply is projected to increase only 6%. The gap, by then, will be 29%.

This projection is worrisome. Yet because it is based on raw numbers of RN FTEs, rather than the number of RNs per population, it may not accurately estimate the separate demand and supply contributions to the shortage. It is important to know whether demand will equal or outpace population growth and whether supply will keep up with or fall behind population growth. To compensate for our current RN shortage as well as our aging population, the optimum situation would be for the supply of RNs to grow at a commensurately greater rate than population.

The future supply of RNs could be threatened by inadequate growth in the number of RN licensees and of those, too few who work or want to work in nursing jobs and of those, too few who work or want to work at the bedside. If this is the case, policies need to focus not only on increasing the RN supply but also equally or even more so on increasing the active RN participants in nursing, especially at the bedside. At this time, however, we do not have much information about trends in these subsets of RN supply or about forces that are influencing the trends.

Because the extent of the supply problem and trends in subsets of RN supply are not well known, policy makers today may not be focusing on the most critical issues and solutions. To effectively deal with the current shortage, and to avoid future ones, research into these issues is needed.

In this article, we use data from the Census Bureau, the DHHS, and the National Sample Survey of Registered Nurses (NSSRN) to delve deeper into trends in RN supply. Although

---

Adapted from: Lynn Y. Unruh and Myron D. Fottler. (2005). Projections and trends in RN supply: What do they tell us about the nursing shortage? *Policy, Politics, and Nursing Practice, 6*(3), 171–182.

demand-side trends are of equal importance to the analysis, in this article we are concerned with assessing the extent of the RN supply problem and the RN supply trends that are giving rise to it. Based on our findings, we examine the possible role of education and employment conditions and present policy solutions.

RESULTS

Projected Supply of RN FTEs per U.S. Resident

Once the projected numbers of RNs demanded and supplied are weighted by the population projected for that period, we find that demand per U.S. resident grows 18% from 2000 to 2020 and supply falls 11%, leaving a shortage of 29% by 2020. This means that demand outstrips population growth by 18% and supply falls behind population growth by 11% in this 20-year time period. Although demand per U.S. resident rises steadily from 2000 to 2020, supply barely increases from 2000 to 2006, and declines sharply thereafter. This projection is shown in Figure 6.2.1.

Compared to the unweighted DHHS (2002) projections, the final gap between supply and demand is the same, but demand grows less and supply falls much more and several years sooner. This indicates that demand is somewhat less of a problem and supply is much more of a problem than initially thought, whereas the gap between supply and demand is still alarming.

Sources of the Projected Decline in RN FTEs Supplied per U.S. Resident

There are three major sources for the current slow growth and imminent downward trend in RN FTEs supplied per U.S. resident. First, between 1996 and 2000, RNs were entering the

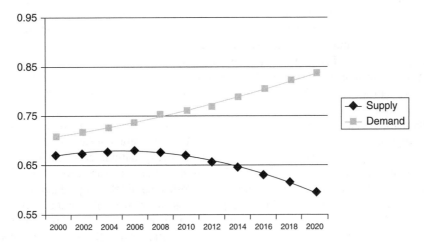

FIGURE 6.2.1   Projected Supply and Demand of RN Full-Time Equivalents per U.S. Resident, 2000 to 2020

Source: U.S. Census Bureau (2004); U.S. Department of Health and Human Services (2002).

license pool at a slower rate and leaving the license pool at a higher rate than before. Second, fewer RNs in the license pool were employed in nursing. Third, of those not employed in nursing, fewer have been looking for work in nursing.

Reasons for RNs Not Working in Nursing

The top five reasons RNs gave for not working in nursing in 1992 and 2000, as stated in the NSSRN (in terms of decreasing relative importance) are better hours, more rewarding work, better salaries, skills out of date, and safer working conditions. Four of these reasons, all but skills out of date, increased in importance during the 8-year period. The bottom line is that not only do there appear to be multiple interrelated factors that make employment in nursing unattractive but also that the significance of those factors is, for the most part, increasing.

It should be pointed out that the surveys did not provide an option for choosing workload or other staffing-related reasons for working outside of nursing. This is a significant omission, because other research indicates high workload/inadequate staffing is a significant determinant of RN dissatisfaction and turnover (Aiken, Clarke, Sloan, Sochalski, & Silber, 2002; Unruh & Fottler, 2002). Also, the 2000 survey listed additional reasons for not working in nursing: 6.8% of RNs in the 2000 survey cited "taking care of the home," 2.1% cited "retirement," 1.8% cited "disability or illness," and 0.7% cited "stress or burnout." Other nurses not working in nursing did not cite a reason.

Decline in Direct Patient Care RNs

Just because an RN is counted as an FTE in a "nursing job" does not necessarily mean that the RN was employed in a patient care area. Many non-patient care opportunities have opened up for RNs during the past several decades (Pindus et al., 2002). As a result, the "working in nursing" RN population must be distributed across a wider set of job types and a growing proportion of nonpatient care areas. The proportion of RNs employed in direct patient care peaked at 72% in 1992 and fell 14% between 1992 and 2000 to stand at only 62% of the RN workforce in 2000.

This distribution of RNs in nursing jobs would not be an issue if the demand for RNs in each type of job matched supply. However, that does not appear to be the case. The areas reporting RN shortages tend to be ones involving patient care, such as hospitals, nursing homes, home care, physician's offices, and ambulatory care centers (GAO, 2001b; Kovner et al., 2002; Pindus et al., 2002). On the other hand, shortages have not been reported in non-patient care areas in nursing such as insurance, sales, regulatory agencies, and others. The only non-patient care area reporting RN shortages is among faculty in nursing education (American Nurses Credentialing Center, 2004). So even if an RN stays in "nursing," the individual may not be working in a patient care area where shortages are occurring. The fact that patient care jobs are available in which RNs apparently choose not to be employed points to a supply shift away from the patient care areas.

DISCUSSION AND POLICY IMPLICATIONS

Our analysis of the data on RN supply indicates that if current trends continue, RN supply will be sooner and more severely threatened than was projected by DHHS (2002). As indicators of future supply problems, we find that between 1992 and 2000, there was a reversal of long-term trends. Specifically, we find decreases in the numbers entering nursing, together with an increase in the percentage of RNs leaving nursing; a decline in the percentage of RNs employed in nursing; a decrease in the percentage of RNs not working in nursing who are looking for work in nursing; an increase in the percentage of RNs citing specific reasons for not working in nursing; and a decline in the percentage of RNs working in patient care. Whether the 1992 to 2000 trend has reversed, continued, or accelerated between 2000 and 2004 will be determined when the 2004 data are released and analyzed.

Supply-Side Reasons for the Nursing Shortage: Educational Bottlenecks and Negative Employment Conditions

Why did fewer individuals between 1992 and 2000 become RNs, fewer stay RNs, fewer look for work as RNs, and fewer work in bedside roles? Two major possibilities are educational bottlenecks to producing more nurses and the unattractiveness of nursing due to negative employment factors. Regarding the first factor, an NLN (2004) survey of nursing programs reveals that although nursing schools are experiencing a strong increase in applications since 2003, they are turning away thousands of qualified applicants. A 2004 survey by the AACN (2005) reports that 76.1% of responding schools cited an insufficient number of faculty as a reason for not accepting all qualified applicants. The NLN identified the problem as a "critical shortage of faculty" and stated that unless this is addressed, the gap between supply and demand will continue to grow. A shortage of available clinical sites is an additional constraint exacerbating the faculty shortage and impeding expansion of nursing educational programs (AACN, 2005).

As important as it is to remove any bottlenecks to accepting all willing and qualified applicants into the nursing profession, the second shortage issue—attracting willing and qualified applicants and keeping them in the profession—is equally important. In fact, because RN educators generally come from the pool of RNs actively working in nursing, when those numbers decline, as occurred between 1992 and 2000, the supply of RN educators will likely be affected.

In this study and others, employment conditions are emerging as major causes of recruitment and retention difficulties. In this study, four of the five top reasons RNs cited for why they were not working in nursing were employment related: better hours, more rewarding work, better salaries, and safer working conditions in nonnursing jobs.

Maintaining adequate working conditions in patient care areas is vital to the stability of the workplace environment. If working conditions are poor, the physical and mental health of the nurse suffers, dissatisfaction grows, and nurse turnover and dropout rates increase (Burke, 2003; Burke & Greenglass, 2001; Hoogendoorn et al., 2002; Nolan, Lundh, & Brown, 1999; Taylor, White, & Muncer, 1999; Thompson & Brown, 2002; Tovey & Adams, 1999; Unruh & Byers, 2002). Furthermore, without adequate working conditions, the RN workplace is not seen in a positive light, thereby discouraging new and inactive RNs from entering/reentering the nursing profession and bedside nursing (Armstrong-Stassen & Cameron, 2003; Fottler & Widra, 1995). Given the expanding career opportunities inside and outside of nursing, many individuals consider other occupations and professions to be a better choice (Staiger, Auerbach, & Buerhaus, 2000).

An employment-related reason for the nursing shortage cited in some studies is low wages. RN wage rates grew approximately 3% per year in the 1980s but were essentially flat in the 1990s (Peterson, 2001). In fact, RN earnings growth for 1994 through 1997 and in 1999 fell short of the average rate of inflation in those years (GAO, 2001a).

Although several studies show that wages have a positive influence on nursing supply (Buerhaus, 1991; Chiha & Link, 2003; Phillips, 1995; Schumacher, 1997), surveys of nurses suggest that wage improvements may not be of the highest priority. Although 42% of nurses indicate that they would be induced to stay at their current jobs for better pay, only 1 in 4 thinks that raising wages is an effective way to manage the nursing crisis in the long run. About 18% want higher salaries compared to 56% who are concerned about the stress and physical demands of the job (Federation of Nurses & Health Professionals & American Federation of Teachers, 2001). In other words, although higher wages would be desirable, most nurses are more concerned about workplace factors such as stress and physical demands. A more recent survey, however, reports that wages are the top reason for nurses to leave their jobs (McIntosh et al. 2003), suggesting that wages may indeed be an important factor in retention and recruitment.

Supply-Oriented Solutions:
Educational Opportunities and Improved Employment Conditions

Based on our assessment above, two strategies to increase RN supply emerge: (a) providing increased educational opportunities and (b) improving employment conditions to make the profession more attractive, retain existing nurses, attract new entrants, and bring lapsed participants back into nursing.

Educational bottlenecks and negative employment conditions identified by nurses and researchers as significant negative factors in recruitment, enrollment, licensing, and retention of nurses must be addressed. The key policy question is, How can policy measures assist and motivate educational institutions and health care facilities to make the necessary changes? There are two fundamental policy approaches: legislative/regulatory and incentive.

Legislative and Regulatory Approaches

Legislative approaches are key to improving educational opportunities. Schools of nursing need added funding to hire additional faculty, to pay them the higher salary needed to attract them into academia, and to expand classrooms, labs, and other resources. Prospective students need funding to assist their education at both the graduate and undergraduate levels. Clinical sites, such as hospitals, need space and preceptors. The Nurse Reinvestment Act of 2002 has several provisions that provide educational scholarships, faculty educational loan cancellations, and career ladder grants (AACN, 2002). These provisions need to be expanded. However, this support of individuals in their pursuit of education does not adequately meet nursing schools' and clinical sites' financial needs for increasing nursing faculty and expanding classroom and clinical site space. Direct federal and state funding of nursing schools and health care facilities is necessary to adequately expand RN educational opportunities (AACN, 2003).

Several existing or proposed federal laws aim to improve nurse recruitment and retention through the improvement of working conditions (Pindus et al., 2002). The Nurse Reinvestment Act of 2002 provides programs to improve nurse retention, the nursing workplace, and quality of care (AACN, 2002). There are also current attempts to limit overtime, either through a prohibition on forced overtime or by tying limits on forced overtime to a hospital's status as Medicare provider (e.g., the Safe Nursing and Patient Care Act, H.R. 791, 2005; S. 351, 2005).

Regulation of employment is gaining support as it becomes apparent that there has been insufficient improvement in working conditions at the bedside despite the continuing evidence of problems. As a result, some are advocating a "policy shield" (such as mandated nurse-patient ratios) to alleviate these problems (Redman & Jacox, 2003). California has already instituted minimum licensed nurse-patient staffing ratios and enacted legislation that places limits on the activities of the unlicensed assistive personnel (American Nurses Association, 2001; Coffman, Seago, & Spetz, 2002).

Although mandatory staffing ratios have the potential for addressing extreme working conditions, they are blunt policy instruments with potentially negative effects, such as rigid ratios applied to dissimilar circumstances (Buerhaus, 1997; Coffman et al., 2002; Spetz, 2001). This is especially a problem if the ratios do not account for patient severity or throughput. It would be better to mandate a uniform, evidence-based staffing system that considers individual facility and unit factors contributing to workload variation, such as patient, staff, and unit characteristics. Regardless of the system of mandated ratios used, hospitals may find it difficult to achieve a mandated staffing level given the existing nursing shortage and continuing tight budgets.

Other public regulations could play a role in keeping nurses at the bedside. The U.S. Department of Labor, in conjunction with state departments of labor, could consider appropriate changes in legislation and regulation to address such issues as wages, mandatory overtime, worker safety, patient safety, and whistle blower protections (Pindus et al., 2002).

An example of private regulation is the Joint Commission on Accreditation of Healthcare Organizations' (2002) recent implementation of staffing standards. These new standards require health care organizations to assess their staffing effectiveness by continually screening for potential issues that can arise from inadequate or inefficient staffing.

Incentive Approaches

A major incentive to improve the work environment that is regaining popularity after two decades is magnet hospital status. Facilities awarded this honor by the American Nurses Credentialing Center have succeeded in attracting and retaining professional nursing staff based on the positive work environment that includes adequate staffing, support for professional development and autonomy, and attractive employment benefits such as salaries and scheduling (Aiken, Smith, & Lake, 1994; Havens, 2001). As of 2004, there were more than 100 hospitals nationwide that had attained the new magnet status (American Nurses

Credentialing Center, 2004). As an added incentive, the Nurse Retention and Quality of Care Act of 2001 provides US$40 million in grants to magnet hospitals to improve workplace settings by developing model practices (Havens, 2001).

To help many of its facilities with the task of recruitment and retention, the American Hospital Association is currently evaluating workplace issues through its Commission on the Workforce. Assigned to identify strategies that can be used for retention and recruitment of professional and support staff, this commission works through staff surveys to identify work environment issues, plan a response, and evaluate the program's success (Smith, 2001).

A final policy, proposed by the Joint Commission on Accreditation of Healthcare Organizations (2002), involves a financial incentive. This approach links public and private reimbursement to evidence of adequate working conditions, particularly staffing; the quality of nursing services; and patient outcomes. This could be an improvement on merely increasing public and private reimbursement to health care facilities in the hopes that they put the added reimbursement to good use by improving working conditions. However, it could have the disadvantage of reinforcing negative employment conditions in some facilities by keeping them outside the increased revenue loop. A remedy for this disadvantage could be to also provide "start up" money for improvements.

CONCLUSION

In conclusion, this study describes several negative trends in RN supply from 1992 to 2000 that may have significant impacts on future supply. Attracting, educating, graduating, retaining, and returning RNs to nursing and the bedside are and will continue to be among the most significant challenges for the health care system in the years ahead. Because educational roadblocks and negative employment conditions appear to be among the strongest set of reasons for these downward RN supply shifts, some combination of regulatory, legislative, and incentive systems focusing on the educational institutions and health care workplaces will be necessary to meet this challenge.

REFERENCES

Aiken, L. H., Clarke, S. P., Sloane, D. M., Sochalski, J., & Silber, J. H. (2002). Hospital nurse staffing and patient mortality, nurse burnout, and job dissatisfaction. *American Medical Association, 288*(16), 1987–1993.

Aiken, L. H., Smith, H., & Lake, E. (1994). Lower Medicare mortality among a set of hospitals known for good nursing care. *Medical Care, 32,* 771–787.

American Association of Colleges of Nursing. (2002). *Nurse Reinvestment Act at a glance.* Retrieved October 2004 to March 2005 from http://www.aacn.nche.edu/Media/NRAataglance.htm#1

American Association of Colleges of Nursing. (2003). *Faculty shortages in baccalaureate and graduate nursing programs: Scope of the problem and strategies for expanding the supply.* Retrieved October 2004 to March 2005 from http://www.aacn.nche.edu/Publications/WhitePapers/FacultyShortages.htm

American Association of Colleges of Nursing. (2005). *New data confirms shortage of nursing school faculty hinders efforts to address the nation's nursing shortage.* Retrieved October 2004 to March 2005 from http://www.aacn.nche.edu/Media/NewsReleases/2005/Enrollments05.htm

American Nurses Association. (2001). *Analysis of American Nurses Association staffing survey.* Warwick, RI: Cornerstone Communications Group. Retrieved October 2004 to March 2005 from http://nursingworld.org/staffing/ana_pdf.pdf

American Nurses Credentialing Center. (2004). *Frequently asked questions.* Retrieved October 2004 to March 2005 from http://www.nursecredentialing.org/magnet/faqs.html

Armstrong-Stassen, M., & Cameron, S. (2003). Nurses' job satisfaction and turnover intentions over a six-year period of hospital downsizing and amalgamation. *International Journal of Public Administration, 26*(14), 1607–1620.

Buerhaus, P. I. (1991). Economic determinants of annual hours worked by registered nurses. *Medical Care, 29*(12), 1181–1194.

Buerhaus, P. I. (1997). What is the harm in imposing mandatory hospital nurse staffing regulations? *Nursing Economics, 15*(2), 66–72.

Burke, R. (2003). Length of shift, work outcomes, and psychological well-being of nursing staff. *International Journal of Public Administration, 26*(14), 1637–1646.

Burke, R. J., & Greenglass, E. R. (2001). Hospital restructuring stressors, work-family concerns and psychological well-being among nursing staff. *Community, Work, and Family, 4*(1), 49–62.

Chiha, Y. A., & Link, C. R. (2003). The shortage of registered nurses and some new estimates of the effects of wages on registered nurses labor supply: A look at the past and a preview of the 21st century. *Health Policy, 64,* 349–375.

Coffman, J. M., Seago, J. A., & Spetz, J. (2002). Minimum nurse-to-patient ratios in acute care hospitals in California. *Health Affairs, 21*(5), 53–64.

Federation of Nurses & Health Professionals & American Federation of Teachers. (2001). *The nurse shortage: Perspectives from current direct care nurses and former direct care nurses.* Washington, DC: Peter D. Hart Associates. Retrieved October 2004 to March 2005 from http://www.aft.org/healthcare/downloadfiels/hart-report.pdf/

Fottler, M. D., & Widra, L. S. (1995). Intention of inactive registered nurses to return to nursing. *Medical Care Reserach and Review, 52*(4), 492–516.

Havens, D. S. (2001). Comparison of nursing infrastructure and outcomes: ANCC magnet and nonmagnet CNEs report. *Nursing Economics, 19*(6), 3–11.

Hoogendoorn, W. E., Bongers, P. M., De Vet, H. C., Ariëns, G. A., Van Mechelen, W., & Bouter, L. M. (2002). High physical work load and low job satisfaction increase the risk of sickness absence due to low back pain: Results of a prospective cohort study. *Occupational and Environmental Medicine, 59*(5), 323–328.

Joint Commission on Accreditation of Healthcare Organizations. (2002). *Health care at the crossroads: Strategies for addressing the evolving nursing crisis.* Retrieved October 2004 to March 2005 from http://www.jcaho.org/about+us/public+policy+initiatives/health+care+at+the+crossroads.pdf

Kovner, C., Mezey, M., & Harrington, C. (2002). Who cares for older adults? Workforce implications of an aging society. *Health Affairs, 21*(5), 78–89.

McIntosh, B., Rambur, B., Palumbo, M. V., & Mongeon, J. (2003). The older nurse: Clues for retention. *Nursing and Health Policy Review, 2*(2), 61–77.

National League for Nursing. (2004). *Startling data from the NLN's comprehensive survey of all nursing programs evokes wake-up call.* Retrieved October 2004 to March 2005 from http://www.nln.org/newsreleases/datarelease05.pdf

Nolan, M., Lundh, U., & Brown, J. (1999). Changing aspects of nurses' work environment: A comparison of perceptions in two hospitals in Sweden and the UK and implications for recruitment and retention of staff. *Work Environment, 4*(3) 221–234.

Peterson, C. A. (2001). Nursing shortage: Not a simple problem—No easy answers. *Online Journal of Issues in Nursing, 6*(1). Retrieved October 2004 to March 2005 from http://www.nursingworld.org/ojin/topic14/tpc14_1.htm

Phillips, V. L. (1995). Nurses' labor supply: Participation, hours of work, and discontinuities in the supply function. *Journal of Health Economics, 14*(5), 567–582.

Pindus, N., Tilly, J., & Weinstein, S. (2002). *Skill shortages and mismatches in nursing related health care employment* (Report to the U.S. Department of Labor, Employment and Training Administration). Washington, DC: Urban Institute.

Redman, B. K., & Jacox, A. K. (2003). On the necessity of policy shields. *Nursing and Health Policy Review, 2*(2), 59–60.

Safe Nursing and Patient Care Act of 2005, S. 351, 109th Cong. (2005). Retrieved October 2004 to March 2005 from http://thomas.loc.gov/cgi-bin/query/D?c109:2:./temp/~c109IRDIPT::

Schumacher, E. J. (1997). Relative wages and exit behavior among registered nurses. *Journal of Labor Research, 18*(4), 581–592.

Smith, G. (2001). *Smith introduces a bill to alleviate nurse shortage.* Retrieved October 2004 to March 2005 from http://www.senate.gov/~gsmith/press/011030a.htm

Spetz, J. (2001). What should we expect from California's minimum nurse staffing legislation? *Journal of Nursing Administration, 31*(3), 132–140.

Staiger, D., Auerbach, D., & Buerhaus, P. (2000). Expanding career opportunities for women and the declining interest in nursing as a career. *Nursing Economics, 18*(5), 230–236.

Taylor, S., White, B., & Muncer, S. (1999). Nurses' cognitive structural models of work-based stress. *Journal of Advanced Nursing, 29*(4), 974–983.

Thompson, T., & Brown, H. (2002). Turnover of licensed nurses in skilled nursing facilities. *Nursing Economics, 20*(2), 66–82.

Tovey, E. J., & Adams, A. E. (1999). The changing nature of nurse's job satisfaction: An exploration of sources of satisfaction in the 1990s. *Journal of Advanced Nursing, 30*(1), 150–158.

Unruh, L., & Byers, J. F. (2002). Hospital downsizing: International experiences and perspectives. *Nursing and Health Policy Review, 1*(2), 117–149.

Unruh, L., & Fottler, M. D. (2002). Nurse staffing and nurse performance: A review and synthesis of the relevant literature. In G. T. Savage, J. D. Blair, & M. D. Fottler (Eds.), *Advances in health care management* (Vol. 3, pp. 11–44). Amsterdam: JAI–Elsevier Science.

U.S. Department of Health and Human Services. (2002, July) *Projected supply, demand, and shortages of registered nurses: 2000–2020.* Retrieved October 2004 to March 2005 from http://bhpr.hrsa.gov/healthworkforce/reports/rnproject/default.htm

U.S. General Accounting Office. (2001a). *Nursing workforce: Emerging nurse shortages due to multiple factors.* Retrieved October 2004 to March 2005 from http://frwebgate.access.gpo.gov/cgi-bin/useftp.cgi?IPaddress=162.140.64.21&filename=d01944.pdf&directory=/ diskb/wais/data/gao

U.S. General Accounting Office. (2001b). *Nursing workforce: Recruitment and retention of nurses and nurse aides is a growing concern.* Retrieved October 2004 to March 2005 from http://www.gao.gov/new.items/d01750t.pdf

Costs of Occupational Injury and Illness Within the Health Services Sector

Geetha Waehrer, J. Paul Leigh, and Ted R. Miller

Costs of medical care in the United States have now reached 14.9 percent of the gross domestic product and are forecast to rise even more.[1] A significant but somewhat overlooked contributor to rising medical costs has been the rapidly rising costs for workers' compensation. For example, workers' compensation costs rose 21 percent in just three years from 1998 to 2001 for all industries combined.[2] A related concern is the long-term increasing cost associated with administration in the health services sector.[3] And nowhere is that concern greater than for the administrative costs of workers' compensation, which appear to be highest in the health services sector.[4] An Institute of Medicine report suggests that medical errors affecting patients are unacceptably high, killing 44,000 to 98,000 patients each year, and may be related to unacceptably high rates of occupational injuries to health care workers.[5] A research initiative is addressing correlations between workers' and patients' safety.[6] In part because of these concerns about costs and workers' compensation and medical errors, job-related injuries and illnesses among health care workers have received increased attention.[7,8] Incidence and prevalence of injury and illness, as well as costs, among health care workers appear to be exceptionally high. In a study of more than 20 occupations with high female employment, nursing aides were at the top of the list for costs of occupational injuries.[9] The hospital industry, a subcategory of the broad health services sector, has ranked in the top four of more than 300 industries generating occupational injuries and illnesses throughout the 1980s and 1990s.[10,11] In part, this is a result of the great number of employees in the health services industry—nearly 10 million people in 1998.

Only a handful of studies have addressed the costs of these injuries and illnesses,[12-14] but even among these, cost was the primary research interest in only two studies. In the first study,[13] hospital orderlies ranked sixth out of 223 occupations for workers' compensation costs. In the second,[14] the hospital industry ranked third of 313 industries for total costs. This lack of attention to cost is unfortunate, since cost has become increasingly important in our era of managed care. In fact, recent re-engineering and cost-reduction strategies in managed care organizations may be resulting in increasing numbers of injuries to nurses and orderlies in hospitals in the United States and Canada.[15,16] Finally, cost is a useful measure because it combines incidence, severity, injury, and illness.

In this study we estimated the costs of nonfatal occupational injuries and illnesses in the health services sector. We excluded deaths, because fatality data were not available in

Adapted from: Geetha Waehrer, J. Paul Leigh, and Ted R. Miller. (2005). Cost of occupational injury and illness within the health services sector. *International Journal of Health Services*, 35(2), 343–359.

207

the same rich categories as nonfatal data. However, 97 percent of the overall costs of injuries are due to nonfatal events, and fatal illnesses comprise less than 10 percent of the costs of all occupational injuries and illnesses combined for all industries.[17]

DATA AND METHODS

The Bureau of Labor Statistics (BLS) Annual Survey, which collects information on nonfatal cases, was the data source that served as a template onto which we merged cost information from other sources described below.[18,19] Medical cost information came from summaries of workers' compensation records in the Detailed Claims Information data set and the National Health Interview Survey.[20,21] We transformed work loss information from the Annual Survey into dollar values using wage data from the 1993 monthly Current Population Survey files.[22] We used a survey of jury verdicts related to occupational injuries and illnesses to predict pain and suffering costs for nonfatal cases in the Annual Survey.[23-25]

RESULTS

We estimated that job-related nonfatal injuries and illnesses resulting in work loss for all occupations and industries in the private sector cost $61 billion in 1993. The five health services industries combined (hospitals, nursing facilities, home care, physician offices, and laboratories) contributed $4.974 billion. This represented 8.1 percent of the total in the private sector. The three occupations combined (nursing aides, registered nurses, and licensed practical nurses) generated roughly $3.4 billion in costs, or 5.6 percent of the $61 billion. In a companion study[14] we ranked 313 U.S. industries for total cost including fatalities. Hospitals placed third. The number for the nursing and personal care facilities, 204 percent, means that the rate for nursing facilities was more than double the one for all industries combined (Table 6.3.1).

Nursing aides, attendants, and orderlies generated the most costs—$2.18 billion (or $2,180 million)—which comprised 64 percent of the combined $3.4 billion for all three. The corresponding dollar amounts and percentages were $841 million and 25 percent for RNs and $406 million and 11 percent for LPNs. The highest cost per case occurred among RNs and the lowest among aides. In part, this reflected the higher wage (indirect cost) paid to RNs than orderlies.

There were gender differences. Women generated the highest costs among LPNs (95 percent) and the lowest among RNs (89 percent). These differences were similar to employment differences. Females comprised 96 percent of LPNs, 93 percent of RNs, and 89 percent of aides in 1993.[26] There were racial and ethnic differences across occupations. However, race was not recorded in 20 to 30 percent of the cases, depending upon the classification. Such a large omission raised a concern about the validity of our race/ethnicity results. Non-Hispanic whites comprised roughly 85 percent of the labor force in 1993, and non-Hispanic blacks roughly 11 percent.[27] The remaining 4 percent consisted of Hispanics, Native Americans, Asians, and Pacific Islanders. The highest percentage of cases among blacks was for nursing aides (24 percent); the lowest was for RNs (5 percent).

TABLE 6.3.1   Employment, Injury, and Illness Statistics within the Bureau of Labor Statistics Annual Survey, 1993

Industry	Employment (millions)	Injury and Illness Rates[a]	Percentage of All Private Industry[b]
All health services	8.871	9.6	113%
Nursing and personal care facilities	1.615	17.3	204
Hospitals	3.816	11.8	139
Home health care services	0.474	9.6	113
Medical and dental laboratories	0.193	5.8	68
Physicians' offices	1.545	2.8	33
All private industry (combined)	91.932	8.5	100
Hazardous Industry Comparison			
Agriculture[c]	–	11.5	135
Coal mining	0.105	10.3	121
Construction	4.574	12.2	143

[a]Per full-time employed worker, per year.

[b]Ratio of the rate for a specific industry to the rate for all industries combined (for example, 113% = 9.6/8.5).

[c]BLS does not publish employment statistics that match injury and illness statistics for agriculture. Rate within agriculture is a BLS estimate with wide confidence intervals.

Source: Bureau of Labor and Statistics.

Across industries, the costs and percentage contribution per industry were: hospitals, $2,567 billion, 52 percent; nursing and personal care facilities, $1.879 billion, 38 percent; home health care services, $0.306 billion, 6 percent; and physicians' offices, $0.183 billion, 4 percent.

In all four industries, females contributed more than males to injury and illness costs. The highest percentage contribution occurred in physicians' offices (91.3 percent) and the lowest in hospitals (78.8 percent).

Regarding occupations, the ranking of greatest to least costs in hospitals was: RNs; aides, attendants, and orderlies; administrative support; LPNs; maids and janitors; and technologists. For nursing and personal care facilities the ranking was: aides, attendants, and orderlies; LPNs; RNs; maids and janitors; administrative support; and technologists.

Table 6.3.2 provides information on costs by occupation and four broad classifications of the injury or illness: nature of injury, part of body, event or exposure, and nature of disease or infection.

DISCUSSION

One finding was that the health services sector generated high costs for occupational injuries and illnesses. As Table 6.3.1 suggests, this finding in part reflects the sheer number

TABLE 6.3.2   Type of Injury or Illness within Occupations

	Nursing Aides, Attendants, Orderlies	*Registered Nurses*	*Licensed Practical Nurses*
Nature of Injury	1. Back sprains and strains ($900 million)	1. Back sprains and strains ($318 million)	1. Back sprains and strains ($142 million)
	2. Other sprains and strains ($643 million)	2. Other sprains and strains ($185 million)	2. Other sprains and strains ($122 million)
	3. Fractures, dislocations, excluding back, head, neck ($166 million)	3. Fractures, dislocations, excluding back, head, neck ($85 million)	3. Fractures, dislocations, excluding back, head, neck ($24 million)
	4. Surface wounds, bruises ($125 million)	4. Surface wounds, bruises ($42 million)	4. Surface wounds, bruises ($19 million)
	5. Other traumatic injuries, disorders ($61 million)	5. Multiple traumatic injuries, disorders ($22 million)	5. Other traumatic injuries, disorders ($15 million)
Part of Body Affected	1. Back ($992 million)	1. Back ($353 million)	1. Back ($157 million)
	2. Shoulder ($234 million)	2. Knee ($46 million)	2. Shoulder ($29 million)
	3. Knee ($132 million)	3. Shoulder ($45 million)	3. Knee ($28 million)
	4. Wrist ($95 million)	4. Neck, throat ($33 million)	4. Wrist ($17 million)
	5. Neck, throat ($44 million)	5. Wrist $27 million)	5. Neck, throat ($10 million)
Event or Exposure	1. Bodily reaction and exertion, unspecified ($1,463 million)	1. Bodily reaction and exertion, unspecified ($507 million)	1. Bodily reaction and exertion, unspecified ($248 million)
	2. Falls ($292 million)	2. Falls ($125 million)	2. Falls ($59 million)
	3. Assaults, violent acts ($161 million)	3. Exposure to harmful substances or environments ($76 million)	3. Exposure to harmful substances or environments ($30 million)
	4. Contact with objects, equipment ($136 million)	4. Contact with objects or equipment ($50 million)	4. Assaults or violent acts ($29 million)
	5. Exposure to harmful substances or environments ($63 million)	5. Assaults or violent acts ($37 million)	5. Contact with objects or equipment ($25 million)

	Nursing Aides, Attendants, Orderlies	*Registered Nurses*	*Licensed Practical Nurses*
Nature of Systematic Disease and Infections	1. Musculoskeletal disorder ($31 million)	1. Musculoskeletal disorder ($33 million)	1. Musuloskeletal disorder ($9 million)
	2. Carpal tunnel syndrome ($26 million)	2. Viral diseases ($20 million)	2. Disorders of the skin ($9 million)
	3. Disorders of the skin ($16 million)	3. Disorders of the skin ($17 million)	3. Respiratory disease ($7 million)
	4. Digestive system disease ($12 million)	4. Carpal tunnel syndrome ($10 million)	4. Carpal tunnel syndrome ($7 million)
	5. Viral disease ($7 million)	5. Respiratory disease ($8 million)	5. Viral disease ($3 million)

of employees. But the injury and illness rate was also high. The rate is a measure of risk. These high rates suggest that nursing and personal care facilities, hospitals, and home health care services are especially hazardous industries. A second finding was that injuries, especially back strains as well as "all other" sprains and strains, were far more prevalent than diseases. In this regard, the health services sector is similar to other large industrial sectors such as manufacturing, agriculture, and mining for which injuries, especially sprains and strains, far exceed diseases.[28]

Implications

The finding on the hazardous nature of nursing facilities, hospitals, and home care was somewhat surprising. Workers in this sector are thought to be the most knowledgeable about health and safety of all persons in society. One would think that employers in this sector would want their workplaces to be shining examples of health and safety.[5] The first implication of our results, therefore, pertains to workers' knowledge of hazards and employers' responses to hazards. One occupation (aides, attendants, and orderlies) and one industry (nursing facilities) stand out in this regard. Aides, attendants, and orderlies were at the top of the list in Table 6.3.2, and nursing facilities were at the top of Table 6.3.1. Aides and orderlies as well as most workers in the nursing facilities industries hold dangerous jobs.

There are second, related implications. Any reduction in occupational injury and illness costs has the potential to reduce costs in health services in general. Moreover, efforts to improve job safety are likely to have a positive spill-over effect to improve patient safety.

A third implication pertains to regulatory directions. The Occupational Safety and Health Administration (OSHA) has limited resources to police industries. To have the greatest impact, OSHA might consider targeting for intervention those industries and occupations with high costs. These include hospitals, nursing facilities, aides, orderlies, RNs, and LPNs.

REFERENCES

1. Levit, K., et al. Health spending rebound continues in 2002. *Health Aff.* 23(1): 147–159, 2004.
2. Williams, C. T., Reno, V. P., and Burton, J. F. *Workers' Compensation: Benefits, Coverage, and Costs, 2001.* National Academy of Social Insurance, Washington, D.C., July 2003.
3. Woolhandler, S., Campbell, T., and Himmelstein, D. Health care in the United States and Canada: Micro-management, macro costs. *Int. J. Health Serv.* 34(1): 65–78, 2004.
4. Leigh, J. P., and Bernstein, J. Public and private workers' compensation insurance. *J. Occup. Environ. Med.* 39(2): 119–121, 1997.
5. Kohn, L. T., Dorrigan, J. M., and Donaldson, M. S. (eds.). *To Err Is Human: Building a Safer Health System.* National Academy Press, Washington, D.C., 2000.
6. Agency for Healthcare Research and Quality. *The Effect of Health Care Working Conditions on Quality of Care.* RFA-01-005. Washington, D.C., March 26, 2001.
7. Engkvist, I. L., et al. Risk indicators for reported over-exertion back injuries among female nursing personnel. *Epidemiology* 11(5): 519–522, 2000.
8. Trinkoff, A. M., et al. Musculoskeletal problems of the neck, shoulder, and back and functional consequences in nurses. *Am. J. Ind. Med.* 41(3): 170–178, 2002.
9. Guo, H. R., et al. Back pain among workers in the United States: National estimates and workers at high-risk. *Am. J. Ind. Med.* 28(5): 591–602, 1995.
10. Engle, C. Health services industry: Still a job machine? *Monthly Labor Rev.* 122(3): 3–14, 1999.
11. U.S. Bureau of Labor Statistics. *Occupational Injuries and Illnesses: Counts, Rates, and Characteristics.* Bulletin 2538. U.S. Department of Labor, Washington, D.C., July 2001.
12. Goldman, R. H., et al. Prioritizing back injury risk in hospital employees: Application and comparison of different injury rates. *J. Occup. Environ. Med.* 42(6): 645–652, 2000.
13. Leigh, J. P., and Miller, T. R. Ranking occupations based upon the costs of job-related injuries and diseases. *J. Occup. Environ. Med.* 39(12): 1170–1182, 1997.
14. Leigh, J. P., et al. Costs of occupational injury and illness across industries. *Scand. J. Work Environ. Health* 30(3): 199–205, 2004.
15. Woodward, C. A., et al. The impact of re-engineering and other cost reduction strategies on the staff of a large teaching hospital: A longitudinal study. *Med. Care* 37(6): 556–569, 1999.
16. Heitlinger, A. The paradoxical impact of health care restructuring in Canada on nursing as a profession. *Int. J. Health Serv.* 33(1): 37–54, 2003.
17. Leigh, J. P., et al. Occupational injury and illness: Estimates of costs, mortality and morbidity. *Arch. Intern. Med.* 157(14): 1557–1568, 1997.
18. Toscano, G., and Windau, J. The changing character of fatal work injuries. *Monthly Labor Rev.* 117(10): 17–28, 1994.
19. U.S. Bureau of Labor Statistics. *Occupational Injuries and Illnesses in the U.S. by Industry, 1991.* Bulletin 2328. U.S. Department of Labor, Government Printing Office, Washington, D.C., 1992.
20. Miller, T. R., and Galbraith, M. Costs of occupational injury in the U.S. *Accident Anal. Prev.* 27(6): 741–747, 1995.
21. Miller, T. R., Pindus, N. M., and Douglass, J. B. Medically related motor-vehicle injury costs by body region and severity. *J. Trauma* 34(2): 270–275, 1993.
22. Weinberg, D. H., et al. Fifty years of data from the Current Population Survey: Alternatives, trends and quality. *Am. Econ. Rev.* 89(2): 18–22, 1999.
23. Rodgers, G. B. Estimating jury compensation for pain and suffering in product liability cases involving nonfatal personal injury. *J. Forensic Econ.* 6(3): 251–262, 1993.
24. Miller, T. R., Cohen, M. A., and Wiersema, B. *Victim Costs and Consequences: A New Look.* National Institute of Justice Research Report NCJ 155281 & U.S. GPO: 1996-495-037-20041. Government Printing Office, Washington, D.C., 1996.

25. Miller, T. R., et al. *The Consumer Product Safety Commission's Revised Injury Cost Model.* Final Report. Consumer Product Safety Commission, Washington, D.C., 1998.

26. U.S. Census Bureau. *Statistical Abstract of the United States: 1994.* Ed. 114. Washington, D.C., 1994.

27. U.S. Census Bureau. *Statistical Abstract of the United States: 1999.* Ed. 119. Washington, D.C., 1999.

28. Leigh, J. P., et al. *Costs of Occupational Injuries and Illnesses.* University of Michigan Press, Ann Arbor, 2000.

CHAPTER 7

Quality of Care

Business group at conference

The National Healthcare Quality and Disparities Reports: An Overview

Ed Kelley, PhD, Ernest Moy, MD, Daniel Stryer, MD,
Helen Burstin, MD, MPH, and Carolyn Clancy, MD

In its reauthorization legislation,[1] Congress directed the Agency for Healthcare Research and Quality (AHRQ) to lead an effort for the US Department of Health and Human Services (DHHS) to develop 2 annual reports: a National Healthcare Quality Report (NHQR) and a National Healthcare Disparities Report (NHDR). The legislation required that AHRQ report on the state of healthcare quality for the nation in the NHQR and track "prevailing disparities in health care delivery as they relate to racial factors and socioeconomic factors in priority populations"[2] in the NHDR. The NHQR and NHDR were designed and produced by AHRQ with support from DHHS and private sector partners. The first set of these annual reports was released in December 2003 and together they represent the broadest national examination of healthcare quality and disparities ever completed in the United States.

One objective of these reports is clearly to respond to the legislative mandate given AHRQ by Congress, namely to provide a baseline for the nation's healthcare system in quality of care and disparities in care delivery. A vital step in the effort to improve healthcare quality for all populations is the systematic collection and analysis of healthcare data. This will help policymakers and researchers discern the areas of greatest need, monitor trends over time, and identify successful programs for addressing those needs. Moreover, the NHQR and NHDR are resources that can help encourage consensus building on what is important to address in quality and disparities and how to measure it.

This *Medical Care* supplement presents major findings from the NHQR and NHDR across a spectrum of conditions and priority populations. This article presents the concepts and frameworks used for the first reports, lays out some common methodologic issues, and discusses the reports' key findings.

CONCEPTS AND DEFINITIONS IN QUALITY AND DISPARITIES

"Quality health care means doing the right thing at the right time in the right way for the right person and having the best results possible."[3] Quality health care means striking the right balance in the provision of health services by avoiding overuse (e.g., getting unnecessary tests), underuse (e.g., not being screened for high blood pressure), or misuse (e.g., being prescribed drugs that have dangerous interactions).[4]

Adapted from: Ed Kelley, Ernest Moy, Daniel Stryer, Helen Burstin, and Carolyn Clancy. (2005). The National Healthcare Quality and Disparities Reports: An overview. *Medical Care*, 43(3), 13–18.

"Disparity" can be defined as "the condition or fact of being unequal, as in age, rank, or degree." Synonyms for disparity include *inequality, unlikeness, disproportion,* and *difference.* There are many potential reasons for disparities. For example, a patient may receive fewer medications because of differences in underlying disease processes, individual choice, systemic barriers to obtaining needed medications, or some combination of these reasons.

Access to health care is a central aspect of healthcare quality.[5] Defined as "the timely use of personal health services to achieve the best health outcomes,"[6] access to care is an essential prerequisite to obtaining quality care, increasing the quality and years of healthy life, and eliminating health disparities. A recent Institute of Medicine (IOM) report asserts that "access-related factors may be the most significant barriers to equitable care, and must be addressed as an important first step toward eliminating healthcare disparities."[7]

The congressional mandate to produce the NHQR and NHDR did not specify the dimensions of quality and which conditions should be included in the report. AHRQ contracted with the IOM to create conceptual frameworks for the 2 reports. The NHQR conceptual framework (Fig. 7.1.1) is a matrix including components of health care quality (e.g., effectiveness, safety, timeliness, patient centeredness, equity) and patient needs (e.g., staying healthy, getting better, living with illness or disability, coping with the end of life). The NHDR conceptual framework expands on the NHQR conceptual framework by adding 1) a dimension representing the racial, ethnic, and socioeconomic disparities that are the focus of the NHDR, 2) measures of access to care, and 3) the construct of health status and healthcare need that are essential for understanding disparities in health care.

KEY FINDINGS FROM THE REPORTS

The NHQR and NHDR cover a huge range of dimensions of quality and disparities as well as priority conditions and have, between them, documentation on approximately 250 mea-

National Healthcare Quality Report Framework

Components of Healthcare Quality

Health care needs	Effectiveness	Safety	Timeliness	Patient centeredness
Staying healthy				
Getting better				
Living with illness or disability				
End of life care				

• Equity is a component of healthcare quality that applies to all cost in the market
* Resource consumption is another component discussed in the National Healthcare Quality Report
• The first NHQR is due to Congress in 2003.

FIGURE 7.1.1   NHQR Framework

Source: © 2005 Lippincott, Williams & Wilkins.

sures. Over 30 databases are used to generate the 350+ data tables associated with the 2 reports. It is difficult to synthesize findings across such a broad set of measures and data sources. However, Table 7.1.1 summarizes some broad findings that are based on the data presented in the report.

TABLE 7.1.1   Key Findings from the First NHQR and NHDR

High-quality health care is not a given in the US healthcare system.

Thirty-seven of 57 areas with trend data presented in the NHQR have either shown no improvement or have deteriorated.

Only 23% of those with hypertension have it under control. Control of hypertension is essential to continued successes in reducing mortality from heart disease, stroke, and complications of diabetes.

Half of the people with depression stop using their medicines within the first month, far shorter than is recommended by experts and scientific evidence.

In terms of patient safely, approximately 1 in 5 elderly Americans was prescribed medications that may be inappropriate for them and potentially harmful.

Gaps in healthcare quality are particularly acute for certain racial, ethnic, and socioeconomic groups.

Blacks and Hispanics experience worse quality of care for approximately half of the quality measures reported in the NHQR and NHDR.

Hispanics and Asians experience worse access to care for approximately two thirds of access measures.

Poor people experience worse care for approximately two thirds of the quality and access measures.

Quality of care and disparities in quality of care are particularly pronounced for preventive services.

Smoking is the single most preventable cause of mortality, but rates of smoking cessation counseling both in the hospital and during office visits are only 40% and 60%, respectively.

Screening for high cholesterol can prevent the development of heart disease, but only 67% of adults have had their cholesterol checked within the past 2 years and can state whether it is normal or high.

Black, Hispanic, and poor adults are significantly less likely to receive colorectal and breast cancer screening and influenza immunization.

Black, Hispanic, and American Indian women are less likely to receive prenatal care; black, Hispanic, and poor children are less likely to receive dental care; black, Hispanic, and poor elderly are less likely to receive pneumococcal vaccination.

Improvement in quality and disparities is possible.

Chosen as a national priority for improvement by the Medicare QIO program, the use of beta-blockers for patients sustaining heart attacks rose from 21% of eligible patients in the early 1990s[10] to 69% (This measure is the percentage of patients sustaining acute

TABLE 7.1.1   (continued)

myocardial infarction who are prescribed beta blockers at discharge.). In addition, improvement on this measure has been relatively universal. Fully 45 states are at or above 70% on this measure.

A majority of women over the age of 40 (70.3%) are being screened by mammography for breast cancer, exceeding the Healthy People 2010 objective.

Black women have higher screening rates for cervical cancer, perhaps related to significant investments in community-based cancer screening and outreach programs for cervical cancer. This may help explain why death rates among black women, although still over twice those of white women, have been falling at approximately twice the rate.[11]

Quality improvement efforts have resulted in demonstrable reductions in black-white differences in hemodialysis. A targeted intervention within a quality improvement culture may offer important lessons in disparity reduction.

Note: NHQR indicates National Healthcare Quality Report; NHDR, National Healthcare Disparities Report.

CONCLUSION: WHAT HAPPENS NEXT?

Although these reports represent a major step forward in terms of documenting quality and disparities gaps and progress in the American healthcare system, they are of course not the first or only attempt at such assessment. Reviews of the literature, data chartbooks, and international comparisons of health care quality and disparities from public and private organizations in recent years have contributed to the ongoing discussion on quality and disparities measurement.[8,9] These particular reports are scientific, data-driven reports and their contribution is not only in the narrative, but also in the data that they present. They offer the first ever national baseline for tracking the nation's progress on quality and disparities going forward. The debate that these reports should engender is not if the glass is half-full or half-empty now, but, in years to come, how do we get better? AHRQ encourages its partner organizations to examine the condition- and population-specific chapters and the many detailed data tables for greater depth on particular topics and findings. AHRQ is working now on tools that will enable users to access this rich data source more easily and quickly, including greater flexibility in its web site for the reports (www.qualitytools.ahrq.gov). In addition, AHRQ staff stand ready to help users get the most out of report data.

It is clear that this report is already making an impact at the state and national levels. Outreach conducted by AHRQ to state partners and to private sector organizations has resulted in policy activities at the state and local levels to align state healthcare quality reports with the NHQR framework and measure set. Such efforts can help to reduce the burden of quality measurement for providers and healthcare organizations and enable broader comparisons across our healthcare system. We expect these activities to continue as consensus activities continue for this report and for future reports. For DHHS, the NHQR and NHDR are expected to become a unifying tool for measurement and improvement activities in healthcare quality nationally as it is updated and improved in the future. Finally, for the American healthcare system, the NHQR and NHDR will be baselines to judge the future performance of the entire healthcare system.

The impact of these reports will depend on how the information is used. Currently, the picture of healthcare quality in America is fragmented and incomplete. With this first NHQR and NHDR, we are beginning the process of completing that picture.

REFERENCES

1. Section 913(b)(2) of the Public Health Service Act as added by Public Law 106–129.

2. Institute of Medicine. Committee on the National Quality Report on Health Care Delivery. In: Hurtado MP, Swift EK, Corrigon JM, eds. *Envisioning the National Healthcare Quality Report*. Washington, DC: National Academics Press; 2001.

3. Agency for Healthcare Research and Quality. *Your Guide to Choosing Quality Healthcare*.

4. Chassin M. The urgent need to improve health care quality. Institute of Medicine national roundtable on health care quality. *JAMA*. 1998:280.

5. Institute of Medicine. Committee on Guidance for Designing a National Healthcare Disparities Report. In: Swift EK, ed. *Guidance for the National Healthcare Disparities Report*. Washington, DC: National Academics Press; 2002:20.

6. Institute of Medicine. Committee on Monitoring Access to Personal Health Care Services. In: Millman M, ed. *Access to Health Care in America*. Washington, DC: National Academy Press; 1993.

7. Institute of Medicine. Committee on Understanding and Eliminating Racial and Ethnic Disparities in Health Care. In: Smedley BD, Nelson AR, eds. *Unequal Treatment: Confronting Racial and Ethnic Disparities in Health Care*. Washington, DC: National Academics Press; 2003:33.

8. McGlynn EA, Asch SM, Adams J, et al. The quality of health care delivered to adults in the United States. *N Engl J Med*. 2003;348:2635–2645.

9. *Doing What Counts for Patient Safety: Federal Actions to Reduce Medical Errors and Their Impact*. Washington, DC: Quality Interagency Coordination Task Force; 2000.

10. Soumerai et al. *JAMA*. 1997.

11. Ries LAG, Eisner MP, Kosary CL, et al., eds. *SEER Cancer Statistics Review. 1975–2000*. Bethesda, MD: National Cancer Institute; 2003. Available at: http:/seer.cancer.gov/csr/1975_2000/.

Quality of Care in For-Profit and Not-for-Profit Health Plans Enrolling Medicare Beneficiaries

Eric C. Schneider, MD, MSc, Alan M. Zaslavsky, PhD, and Arnold M. Epstein, MD, MA

Federal policy continues to encourage enrollment of Medicare beneficiaries in private health plans.[1] Proponents contend that managed care can improve quality of care and control cost growth.[2] During the 1990s, large numbers of Medicare beneficiaries enrolled in health plans. By 1998 for-profit plans enrolled the majority of approximately 4.5 million Medicare health plan enrollees.[3] Despite a reduction in the number of health plans after 2000, recent federal legislation included payment provisions designed to increase enrollment of Medicare beneficiaries in managed care. Some prior research suggests that the quality of care provided by for-profit health plans may be worse than that in not-for-profit health plans.[4,5] However, these studies, based on regional plans, surveys, or data voluntarily reported by health plans, may have been affected by biased selection, and none of them fully accounted for known geographic variations in the delivery of care.[6-8]

Since 1994, many health plans have voluntarily reported data to the National Committee for Quality Assurance (NCQA) using the Health Plan Employer Data and Information Set (HEDIS). HEDIS has become the most widely used method for assessing health plan quality.[9] The Balanced Budget Act of 1997 required all health plans that enroll Medicare beneficiaries to report Medicare HEDIS data annually.[10] The standardization of HEDIS quality measure specifications, the mandatory nature of the Medicare reporting in this program, and the special audit of the national 1998 data create an ideal opportunity to compare the quality of care provided in for-profit and not-for-profit health plans serving Medicare beneficiaries nationwide.

METHODS AND DATA

Beginning in 1997, all health plans that care for Medicare beneficiaries participating in the Medicare + Choice program (recently renamed "Medicare Advantage") have been required to report HEDIS data to the Centers for Medicare and Medicaid Services (CMS) through NCQA using a format that permits anonymous linkage to individual sociodemographic characteristics. In 1998, the Medicare HEDIS data set summarizing performance in calendar

Adapted from: Eric C. Schneider, Alan M. Zaslavsky, and Arnold M. Epstein. (2005). Quality of care in for-profit and not-for-profit health plans enrolling Medicare beneficiaries. *American Journal of Medicine,* 118, 1392–1400.

year 1997 included 4 measures of the quality of clinical care (NCQA's "clinical effectiveness" measures). Every health plan submitted an electronic file indicating which enrolled beneficiaries were eligible and selected for each HEDIS measure denominator and whether each selected individual received the measured clinical service. We included all 4 available clinical effectiveness measures in our analyses.

From CMS, we obtained the 1998 HEDIS file that included usable data with individual sociodemographic indicators from 294 health plans on 303,718 beneficiaries who had been included in at least 1 of the 4 HEDIS clinical effectiveness measures: breast cancer screening, use of beta blocker after myocardial infarction, diabetic eye examinations, and follow-up after hospitalization for mental illness.

ANALYSIS

The goal of the analysis was to compare the HEDIS performance in for-profit and not-for-profit health plans while adjusting for sociodemographic mix and other characteristics of each health plan, including geographic location.

STUDY RESULTS

Sixty-four percent of the study health plans were for-profit. Compared with not-for-profit health plans, for-profit health plans had lower total enrollment, were less likely to enroll Medicaid beneficiaries, were more likely to be Independent Practice Association (IPA) or network model types, had been in operation for a shorter period of time, and were less prevalent in the New England and Pacific regions. The sociodemographic characteristics of enrollees in for-profit and not-for-profit health plans differed in many ways. Compared with not-for-profit health plans, for-profit health plans enrolled, on average, smaller proportions of beneficiaries aged 65 to 69 years, women, whites, and rural residents. For-profit health plans also enrolled larger percentages of African Americans and beneficiaries with lower educational attainment.

On average, rates of plan performance (and 95% confidence intervals) were 70.4% (68.3%–72.4%) for breast cancer screening, 48.7% (46.1%–51.4%) for diabetic eye examination, 67.7% (63.9%–71.5%) for beta-blocker medication after myocardial infarction, and 48.2% (43.3%–53.2%) for follow-up after hospitalization for mental illness. For-profit health plans had significantly lower HEDIS scores than not-for-profit health plans (Table 7.2.1). Compared with not-for-profit health plans, the performance of for-profit health plans ranged from 7.3 percentage points lower for the breast cancer screening measure to 18.3 percentage points lower for the measure of follow-up after hospitalization for mental illness. All of these differences were statistically significant.

The adjusted results were similar to the unadjusted findings. Controlling for the sociodemographic case-mix of health plans had a small effect on the differences in performance of for-profit and not-for-profit health plans. Additional adjustment for the other characteristics of health plans further reduced the differences, but did not eliminate them. Across the 4 regression models, no single health plan characteristic was consistently an important mediator of tax status–related differences in performance, although health plan total enrollment, plan age, model type, and region seemed to mediate a portion of the tax status difference. Whether the plan was part of a national managed care firm had little impact on the primary results (data not shown).

TABLE 7.2.1   HEDIS Performance among For-Profit and Not-for-Profit Health Plans

	For-Profit	Not-for-Profit	For-Profit and Not-for-Profit Difference	95% CI (mean of plan means)
		%		
Breast cancer screening (n = 194)	67.5	74.8	−7.3†	−11.4, −3.2
Diabetic eye examination (n = 214)	43.7	57.7	−14.1†	−19.2, −8.9
Beta blockers after myocardial infarction (n = 162)	63.1	75.2	−12.1†	−19.8, −4.5
Follow-up after hospitalization for mental illness (n = 122)	42.1	60.4	−18.3†	−28.2, −8.4

CI = confidence interval; Health Plan Employer Data and Information Set (HEDIS).

†$P < .05$.

CONTROLLING FOR DIFFERENCES IN THE GEOGRAPHIC LOCATION OF FOR-PROFIT AND NOT-FOR-PROFIT HEALTH PLANS

Health plans included in this study sample operated in 1311 counties. Approximately 37% (479) of these counties had enrollees in both for-profit and not-for-profit plans; however, these latter counties included 92% (261,537) of the study's health plan enrollees. After matching enrollees by county and weighting for the distribution of enrollment among counties, the "within county" HEDIS scores (except for beta-blocker medication after myocardial infarction) were statistically significantly lower among enrollees in for-profit health plans than among enrollees in not-for-profit plans. Adjustment for individual sociodemographic characteristics had little impact on these differences. Adjustment for health plan characteristics reduced the differences further, but HEDIS scores remained lower among enrollees in for-profit health plans than enrollees in not-for-profit health plans. These differences remained statistically significant.

DISCUSSION AND POLICY IMPLICATIONS

Our results show that on all 4 available standardized HEDIS measures reflecting care delivered during 1997, the quality of care was significantly lower among the Medicare program's for-profit health plans than among its not-for-profit health plans. These results are particularly important for 2 reasons. First, since the late 1990s, the majority of health plans that have enrolled Medicare beneficiaries have been for profit. Second, the measures we studied are based on widely accepted standards of care for the clinical services they assess. There is a high degree of consensus that these clinical services can reduce morbidity and mortality if beneficiaries receive them.

The few prior studies that have compared the quality of care provided in for-profit and not-for-profit health plans have come to varying conclusions about the relationship between tax status and quality. Two studies suggested that for-profit health plans provide lower quality of care based on technical measures of quality performance and receive less favorable subjective ratings from enrollees with self-reported fair or poor health.[11] National survey data suggest that for-profit status is associated with lower ratings and reports about care and slightly higher rates of disenrollment.[4] However, other analyses suggested that the quality gap between for-profit and not-for-profit health plans is not significant or is explained primarily by other market level factors such as competition among health plans.[6] Our findings support the proposition that the quality of care is lower among for-profit health plans and that this result is not related to competing explanations.

Some might cite our results and conclude that for-profit health plans should be barred from participation in Medicare. We believe this would be problematic. First, the quality of care in for-profit plans, though not as high as that in not-for-profit plans, may nevertheless be higher than the quality of care under fee-for-service insurance.[12] Second, such an action would disrupt benefits available to potentially millions of beneficiaries who lack an alternative not-for-profit plan in their area. Third, a blanket prohibition on for-profit plans would remove some high-performing plans.

In conclusion, we found that the quality of care delivered to Medicare beneficiaries is substantially lower in for-profit health plans compared with not-for-profit health plans. The results seem important because of the prominent role of for-profit health plans in Medicare and the payment changes that are designed to accelerate enrollment in health plans. Our findings are not only consistent with prior research but also reinforce the concern that the financial incentives of for-profit plans lead to less aggressive efforts to manage the quality of care. The variability of performance within the 2 groups of plans and the limited number of measures we studied suggest that a blanket prohibition of for-profit health plans may be premature. However, monitoring health plan quality is clearly a worthwhile endeavor. Quality monitoring by itself may lead to institutional efforts that may improve the quality of care for Medicare beneficiaries.[13] At a minimum, quality monitoring should be a cornerstone of federal government efforts to optimize the quality of health care for Medicare beneficiaries.

REFERENCES

1. Centers for Medicare and Medicaid Services. *More Choices. Better Benefits: The Medicare + Choice Program.* Washington, DC: CMS; 2003.

2. Enthoven A, Kronick R. A consumer-choice health plan for the 1990s. Universal health insurance in a system designed to promote quality and economy (1,2) *N Engl J Med.* 1989;320:29–37, 94–101.

3. InterStudy Publications. *The Competitive Edge Database.* St. Paul, Minn: InterStudy Publications; 1998.

4. Landon BE, Epstein AM. MARKETWATCH: for-profit and not-for-profit health plans participating in Medicaid. *Health Aff.* 2001;20(3):162–171.

5. Tu HT, Reschovsky JD. Assessments of medical care by enrollees in for-profit and nonprofit health maintenance organizations. *N Engl J Med.* 2002;346:1288–1293.

6. Born PH, Simon CJ. Patients and profits: the relationship between HMO financial performance and quality of care. *Health Aff.* 2001;20:167–174.

7. Fisher ES, Wennberg DE, Stukel TA, et al. The implications of regional variation in Medicare spending. Part 1: the content, quality and accessibility of care. *Ann Intern Med.* 2003;138:273–287.

8. Fisher ES, Wennberg DE, Stukel TA, et al. The implications of regional variation in Medicare spending. Part 2: health outcomes and satisfaction with care. *Ann Intern Med.* 2003;138:288–298.

9. Iglehart JK. The National Committee for Quality Assurance. *N Engl J Med.* 1996;335:995–999.

10. Lied TR, Sheingold S. HEDIS performance trends in Medicare managed care. *Health Care Financ Rev.* 2001;23:149–160.

11. Tu HT, Kemper P, Wong HJ. Do HMOs make a difference? Use of health services. *Inquiry.* 1999;36(4):400–410.

12. Landon BE, Zaslavsky AM, Bernard SL, Cioffi MJ, Cleary PD. Comparison of performance of traditional Medicare vs Medicare managed care. *JAMA.* 2004;291(14):1744–1752.

13. Jencks SF, Huff ED, Cuerdon T. Change in the quality of care delivered to Medicare beneficiaries, 1998–1999 to 2000–2001. *JAMA.* 2003;289:305–312.

Improving Nurse-to-Patient Staffing Ratios as a Cost-Effective Safety Intervention

Michael B. Rothberg, MD, MPR, Ivo Abraham, PhD, RN,
Peter K. Lindenauer, MD, MSc, and David N. Rose, MD

In response to the current crisis in healthcare spending, hospitals have employed a variety of means to reduce costs, including limiting length of stay, restricting formularies, and gradually increasing patient-to-nurse (PTN) ratios, potentially undermining patient safety. In 2001, 75% of American nurses surveyed warned that increasing patient loads during the previous 2 years adversely affected quality of care,[1] and in Massachusetts, 29% of nurses surveyed knew of a patient death linked directly to understaffing.[2] A growing body of research confirms the link between nurse staffing and patient outcomes.[3-7] According to the Joint Commission on Accreditation of Healthcare Organizations (JCAHO), 24% of 1609 sentinel events (unanticipated events that result in injury, death, or permanent loss of function) were related to nurse staffing levels.[8]

In California, public concern led to legislation mandating minimum staffing levels to begin in 2004,[9] and a similar move is under way in Massachusetts.[10] At least 12 other states have introduced legislation to limit PTN ratios and have met with opposition from the hospital industry, which already is squeezed by soaring costs and shrinking reimbursement. In California, nursing unions have advocated PTN ratios as low as 3 to 1 for medical-surgical wards, whereas the California Healthcare Association (the state affiliate of the American Hospital Association) lobbied for a ratio of 10 to 1.[11] The state Department of Health Services settled on a ratio of 5 to 1 to be phased in over the course of 12 to 18 months.

Some advocates propose that lower PTN ratios might actually save money by decreasing nurse turnover, hospital complications, and length of stay.[11,12] If this were shown to be true, hospitals might limit PTN ratios without legislation. To date, research on nurse staffing has not considered the cost-effectiveness of different PTN ratios. We hypothesize that the improved outcomes associated with lower PTN ratios are not cost-saving, but cost less than many other commonly accepted patient safety interventions.

METHODS

We calculated the cost-effectiveness in dollars per life saved of various PTN ratios using national cost estimates combined with patient mortality data from one large study[3] and

Adapted from: Michael B. Rothberg, Ivo Abraham, Peter K. Lindenauer, and David N. Rose. (2005). Improving nurse-to-patient staffing ratios as a cost-effective safety intervention. *Medical Care, 43*(8), 785–791.

length of stay data from another.[4] The incremental cost-effectiveness of each PTN ratio relative to the next higher PTN ratio was calculated by dividing the difference in total cost by the difference in 30-day mortality.

RESULTS

We examined the results from 3 viewpoints: (1) labor costs alone, (2) labor costs plus savings from decreased length of stay, and (3) total costs assuming increased wage pressure from mandated 4:1 ratios. In each scenario, 8 patients per nurse is the PTN ratio with the lowest costs, but it is associated with the highest patient mortality. For each decrement in the ratio, nurse labor cost per patient increases and overall mortality declines. However, the rate of incremental cost increase accelerates, while the rate of mortality decrease decelerates, resulting in progressively higher incremental cost-effectiveness ratios for each one-patient decrement in the PTN ratio. Considering labor costs only and excluding savings from decreased length of stay, the cost associated with saving one life by changing from 8 to 7 patients per nurse is $46,000. By comparison, the cost of saving additional lives by changing from 5 to 4 patients per nurse is $142,000 per life saved. Including the savings from shortened length of stay improves the cost-effectiveness of increased staffing, but the savings offset only one-half of the increase in labor costs. In addition, if mandatory PTN ratios translate into higher wages for nurses, the incremental cost per life saved would be $71,000 at 5 patients per nurse and $136,000 at 4 patients per nurse.

Results of Probabilistic Sensitivity Analysis

In 99.8% of 10,000 analyses in which the values of key parameters were randomly chosen from a distribution of their ranges, lower PTN ratios resulted in fewer deaths than higher ratios (Figure 7.3.1). Lower PTN ratios always increased costs. Compared with a PTN ratio of 5:1, a ratio of 4:1 had an incremental cost-effectiveness of less than $316,000 per death averted 95% of the time. The 25th, 50th, and 75th percentiles were $101,000, $133,000, and $179,000 per death averted.

DISCUSSION

The United States has a severe shortage of nurses, with an estimated 126,000 nursing jobs unfilled.[12] With an aging population of 78 million baby boomers and an aging population of nurses, the shortage is projected to expand to 400,000 by 2020.[8] At the same time, career dissatisfaction associated with high PTN ratios leads to burnout and may exacerbate the situation. As inpatient care has become more clinically challenging, there is a growing consensus that high PTN ratios are dangerous. At the same time, stagnant or diminished reimbursement combined with continued advances in technology and pharmaceuticals have created a financial crisis for US hospitals. According to the American Hospital Association, one in 3 hospitals lost money in 2000, 58% reported negative margins on

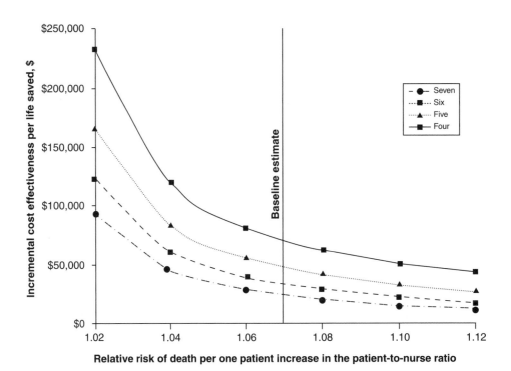

FIGURE 7.3.1   Incremental Cost per Life Saved of 4 Different Patient-to-Nurse Ratios as a Function of the Relative Increase in Mortality Associated with Each Additional Patient per Nurse

Medicare patients, and 73% lost money treating patients with Medicaid.[13] In advocating for minimum PTN ratios as high as 10:1,[12] hospitals have correctly assessed that increasing nurses' patient loads decreases labor costs, but until now no formal economic analysis of the consequences of these savings has been undertaken.

On the basis of national nursing wage data, we found that increasing the PTN ratio results in moderate labor cost savings. For example, increasing the PTN ratio from 6:1 to 7:1 would save hospitals $92 in labor costs per case on average, representing 1% of total hospitalization costs.[14] This savings is halved when additional costs related to increased length of stay are included. Moreover, as nurses are assigned additional patients, the associated savings in labor cost per patient declines, while the probability of a fatal error occurring increases, making higher ratios increasingly unattractive. Moving from a ratio of 6:1 to 7:1 costs 1.4 additional lives per 1000 admissions. Put more simply, we can prevent additional hospital deaths at a labor cost of $64,000 per life saved by decreasing the average PTN ratio from 7:1 to 6:1. Including all hospital costs, even if implementing lower ratios requires an increase in nursing wages, decreasing the PTN ratio from 5 to 4 would save additional lives at a cost of $136,000 per life saved.

Testing the US blood supply for HIV costs $22,000 per life saved.[15] Thrombolytic therapy in acute myocardial infarction costs $182,000 per life saved[16] and routine cervical cancer screening with Pap tests costs $432,000 per life saved.[17] Compared with these commonly accepted interventions, a PTN ratio of 4:1 seems reasonably priced.

Considering that there are approximately 38 million hospital admissions in the United States each year,[14] small changes in hospital mortality could result in a substantial number of lives saved. A recently introduced bill, the Nurse Staffing Standards for Patient Safety and Quality Care Act of 2004 (H.R. 4316), calls for mandatory federal staffing ratios, with a maximum PTN ratio of 4:1 on general medical and surgical wards. There are no available data on national PTN ratios, but if the national ratios resemble those in Pennsylvania, then mandating a ratio of 4:1 could potentially save 72,000 lives annually at a projected cost of $4.2 billion to $7.3 billion. If national ratios are higher than those in Pennsylvania, then both the number of lives saved and the costs will be greater.

Advocating for more staffing could exacerbate the current nurse shortage, and may require higher wages to attract new nurses. We tried to adjust for this by assuming higher wages for lower PTN ratios. Such adjustments are tricky because nonmonetary benefits, such as improved working conditions, may also attract more people to hospital nursing. One survey found that 65% of nurses working outside of hospitals would consider returning to hospital care if Safe Staffing legislation was enacted.[18] In short, lessons from nursing shortages caused by adverse working conditions may not apply to a shortage caused by mandated improvement in working conditions. Alternatively, by relying on average wages, we may have underestimated the cost of compliance in those areas where high wages have driven hospitals to adopt high PTN ratios. Our analysis suggests that even for areas in the 90th percentile of wages, a ratio of 4:1 is reasonably cost-effective ($211,000 per life saved).

What is the optimal level of staffing? It depends on what we as a society are willing to pay to decrease hospital patient mortality. The California Nurses Association called for PTN ratios of 3:1, while the State Hospital Association requested a level of 10:1.[12] Beginning in 2004, California medical and surgical nursing staff ratios will be set at 6:1, and decrease to 5:1 in 2005. Other states are considering similar initiatives. Some private health care providers, such as Kaiser Permanente in California, recognize nurse staffing as a quality issue, and have voluntarily chosen a staffing level of 4:1. Based on our analysis, Kaiser's choice seems a cost-effective one. However, state-mandated ratios may not produce the intended outcomes.[11] More research is needed to define how best to implement improved staffing in individual units.

Can the same benefits be achieved though the use of licensed practical nurses and nursing extenders? Both Aiken[3] and Needleman[4] found that decreases in adverse outcomes were related to registered nurse staffing alone. Increases in licensed practical nurse hours or the use of nurses' aides had no effect on any patient outcome. In another study, Aiken found that nurses' education level was also inversely correlated with patient mortality.[19] Results of other studies have been mixed.[20]

Conspicuously absent from this debate are physicians' voices, despite the fact that more than 50% of physicians identified understaffing of nurses in hospitals to be a very important cause of medical errors.[21] With the exception of a few articles published in medical journals, research of this type has appeared primarily in nursing journals, newspapers, and editorial pages. Physicians and hospital administrators have tended to view nurse staffing levels as part of the hospital infrastructure, as opposed to an intervention aimed at decreasing hospital-associated morbidity and mortality. Considering our results, hospital directors have correctly judged that increasing PTN ratios noticeably reduces labor costs. The resultant rise in mortality, complications and length of stay, however, are more difficult to measure at the level of a single institution. To truly estimate the impact of PTN ratios on patient outcomes, a large randomized trial with an accompanying economic analysis is in order.

Considered as a patient safety intervention, improved nurse staffing has a cost-effectiveness that falls comfortably within the range of other widely accepted interventions. If a hospital decided, for economic reasons, not to provide thrombolytic therapy in acute myocardial infarction, physicians would likely refuse to admit to that hospital, and patients would fear to go there. Physicians, hospital administrators, and the public must now begin to see safe nurse staffing levels in the same light as other patient safety measures.

REFERENCES

1. *Analysis of American Nurses Association Staffing Survey.* Warwick, RI: Cornerstone Communications Group; 2001.

2. Stewart R. Nurses see danger in short staffs. *Boston Globe.* Boston, MA, 2003:1.

3. Aiken LH, Clarke SP, Sloane DM, et al. Hospital nurse staffing and patient mortality, nurse burnout, and job dissatisfaction. *JAMA.* 2002;288:1987–1993.

4. Needleman J, Buerhaus P, Mattke S, et al. Nurse-staffing levels and the quality of care in hospitals. *N Engl J Med.* 2002;346:1715–1722.

5. Cho SH, Ketefian S, Barkauskas VH, et al. The effects of nurse staffing on adverse events, morbidity, mortality, and medical costs. *Nurs Res.* 2003;52:71–79.

6. Sasichay-Akkadechanunt T, Scalzi CC, Jawad AF. The relationship between nurse staffing and patient outcomes. *J Nurs Adm.* 2003;33:478–485.

7. Unruh L. Licensed nurse staffing and adverse events in hospitals. *Med Care.* 2003;41:142–152.

8. Joint Commission on Accreditation of Healthcare Organizations (JCAHO). *Health Care at the Crossroads: Strategies for Addressing the Evolving Nursing Crisis.* Oak Brook Terrace, IL: JCAHO; 2005:43.

9. Hymon S. New rules will tighten nurse-patient ratios. *Los Angeles Times.* 2003:7.

10. Powell JH. Effort intensify on setting nursing levels. *Boston Herald.* 2003.

11. Coffman JM, Seago JA, Spetz J. Minimum nurse-to-patient ratios in acute care hospitals in California. *Health Aff (Millwood).* 2002;21:53–64.

12. Steinbrook R. Nursing in the crossfire. *N Engl J Med.* 2002;346:1757–1766.

13. American Hospital Association. The State of Hospitals' Financial Health. 2002. Available at: http://www.hospitalconnect.com/aha/advocacy-grassroots/advocacy/advocacy/content/Wp2002Hosp Finances.doc. Accessed May 23, 2005.

14. Agency for Healthcare Research and Quality. HCUPnet, Healthcare Cost and Utilization Project. 2002. Available at: http://www.ahrq.gov/hcupnet/. Accessed May 23, 2005.

15. Blumberg N, Heal JM. Mortality risks, costs, and decision making in transfusion medicine. *Am J Clin Pathol.* 2000;114:934–937.

16. Castillo PA, Palmer CS, Halpern MT, Hatziandreu EJ, Gersh BJ. Cost-effectiveness of thrombolytic therapy for acute myocardial infarction. *Ann Pharmacother.* 1997;31:596–603.

17. Charny MC, Farrow SC, Roberts CJ. The cost of saving a life through cervical cytology screening: implications for health policy. *Health Policy.* 1987;7:345–359.

18. Opinion Dynamics Corporation. Survey of Registered Nurses in Massachusetts. Massachusetts Nursing Association. 2003. Available at: http://www.massnurses.org/. Accessed May 23, 2005.

19. Aiken LH, Clarke SP, Cheung RB, et al. Educational levels of hospital nurses and surgical patient mortality. *JAMA.* 2003;290:1617–1623.

20. Seago JA. *Nurse Staffing. Models of Care Delivery, and Interventions in Making Health Care Safer: A Critical Analysis of Patient Safety Practices. Evidence Report/Technology Assessment: Number 43.* Rockville, MD: Agency for Healthcare Research and Quality; 2001:423–46.

21. Blendon RJ, DesRoches CM, Brodie M, et al. Views of practicing physicians and the public on medical errors. *N Engl J Med.* 2002;347:1933–1940.

State Nursing Home Enforcement Systems

Charlene Harrington, Joseph T. Mullan, and Helen Carrillo

Poor nursing facility quality of care has been a national concern since the U.S. Senate Special Committee on Aging first began hearings in 1963 (this study follows hearing reports from 1963 to 1974; also see U.S. GAO 1987). Reports about poor quality continued into the 1980s and led to an Institute of Medicine (IOM) (1986) report on widespread quality problems and recommendations for stronger federal regulations. The IOM report, as well as the active efforts of many consumer advocacy and professional organizations, resulted in Congress passing a major reform of nursing facility regulation in the Omnibus Budget Reconciliation Act of 1987 (Public Law 100-203) (OBRA 1987). OBRA 1987 strengthened the quality standards, the survey process, and the enforcement mechanisms for nursing facility regulation. OBRA and its subsequent regulations mandated uniform comprehensive assessments for all nursing facility residents and required the survey process to focus on resident outcomes. The overall goal of the survey and enforcement process under OBRA 1987 was to achieve facility compliance with federal quality requirements.

Since 1965, when the Medicare and Medicaid programs were established, nursing facility regulation has been a joint federal and state responsibility. State survey agencies are responsible for licensing nursing facilities if they meet state legal requirements and for certifying facilities that meet the conditions for participation in the Medicare and Medicaid programs. State survey agencies have contracts with and are funded by CMS to undertake certification and enforcement activities. Even though the regulatory system is shared between CMS and states, the implementation of the regulations has been largely devolved to the states.

Although it was expected that the OBRA 1987 changes would improve the survey and enforcement system and ultimately improve quality, there are still many nursing facilities with quality of care problems. The U.S. General Accounting Office (GAO) (1998, 1999a) found that one-third to one-fourth of nursing facilities nationwide continue to be cited for deficiencies that either caused actual harm or the potential for harm and serious injury. A number of studies and reports have related the poor quality of some nursing facility care to serious ongoing problems with the survey and enforcement system (Edelman 1997, 1998; U.S. OIG 1999; Abt and U.S. DHHS 1998; U.S. GAO 1999b, 1999c, 1999d).

This article examines state agency survey and enforcement activities for nursing facilities five years after the 1995 federal enforcement procedures were adopted. The study had four aims: (1) to examine the variations in the survey process and enforcement actions across states, (2) to identify the barriers to effective enforcement from the perspective of state licensing and certification (L&C) officials, (3) to classify states on the basis of their enforcement stringency, and (4) to identify some factors that predict state regulatory enforcement activity.

The study presents interview and statistical data from a telephone and fax survey of state L&C agency officials (or their designees) and statistical data from CMS's Online Survey Certification and Reporting (OSCAR) system.

FINDINGS

In 1999, 15,724 facilities were surveyed in the United States by state agencies and 82 percent of these facilities received a total of almost 85,000 deficiencies for failure to meet federal regulations (not shown). Thirty-one percent of facilities (4,880) were given citations for violations that could or did cause harm or jeopardy to residents, and 811 facilities were classified by survey agencies as providing substandard care based on the number and type of deficiencies the facilities received. Overall, these nursing facilities had about 80,489 complaints lodged against them during 1999. These findings indicate that quality problems are substantial.

Civil Monetary Penalties

A total of 3,316 state and federal CMPs were issued in 1999. Of the total CMPs, 61 percent were issued by sixteen states under their own state CMP regulations, 3 percent of CMPs were issued by states for Medicaid-only facilities, and 36 percent were issued by CMS for Medicare and/or Medicaid certified facilities. Eight states did not issue any CMPs (Alaska, Connecticut, District of Columbia, Hawaii, Louisiana, Rhode Island, South Dakota, and Wyoming) and four states (Delaware, Montana, Nebraska, and North Dakota) only issued one to two CMPs in 1999.

Surprisingly only eight states (16 percent) considered CMS CMPs effective in bringing facilities into compliance, and nineteen states (37 percent) reported that CMS CMPs were not effective. The remaining states either did not use CMPs or used their own state systems for issuing CMPs. Almost every one of the sixteen states that had state CMP systems considered their state system to be more effective than the federal CMPs because it was easier and faster to use.

Denial of Payment for New Admissions

Thirty-two states used denials of payment for new admissions in 1,454 facilities in 1999. Of the total states using these sanctions, 57 percent of facilities were sanctioned under state regulations and 43 percent of facilities were sanctioned under the federal regulations (not shown). All states (except Utah) rated the denial of payments as an effective intermediate sanction, primarily because it protects the residents while it is imposed and facilities respond quickly to make corrections.

Temporary Management and Receivership

Only thirteen states used either the federal or the state temporary management or receivership regulations to sanction a total of forty-seven facilities in 1999. Of these sanctions, only six facilities were sanctioned under the federal temporary manager provisions in 1999, and the remainder was under state provisions. Twenty-eight states (55 percent) never had used this federal sanction, while most other states had tried to use it one or two times but were unsuccessful (four states did not report). Seventeen states (33 percent) had used their own state receivership or management program in the past, but only seven states reported using it in 1999.

Decertification or Revocation

Decertification (termination from the Medicare and Medicaid program), as the ultimate sanction against a facility, was seldom used. In 1999, seventeen states reported issuing forty-six decertification or termination notices for the Medicare and/or Medicaid program. Of these, thirty-nine facilities were later certified to return to the program (not shown). Fourteen states had never used decertification or had not used it for many years.

STATE ENFORCEMENT

State Enforcement Indicators

The average number of deficiencies issued per facility in a state in 1999 was 5.7. A closely related measure is the percentage of facilities that received a deficiency (82.5 percent) compared to those facilities that received no deficiencies in 1999 (17.5 percent). A third measure showed that 31 percent of facilities received a deficiency at the G level or above, indicating that the facilities were judged to have caused residents either harm or serious jeopardy (ranging from an isolated event, a pattern, or a widespread problem). The percentage of facilities that were cited for substandard care overall was 5.1 in 1999. Finally, the average number of CMPs issued to facilities under state or federal regulations was .21 per facility surveyed in 1999.

The summary ranking of all states across the five indicators was created by standardizing each of the five dependent variables and then adding them together. Using the five indicators, Washington, Arkansas, California, Oregon, and Idaho were ranked as the top five enforcement states. The five states ranked as the lowest were Colorado, the District of Columbia, Rhode Island, Virginia, and Vermont.

Predictors of Enforcement Stringency

During 1999, the average number of complaints per 1,000 nursing home beds was 43.87, with a range from .42 complaints in Pennsylvania to 181.9 in Nevada. The number of complaints represents perceived quality by the public or residents and was used as a control variable in the regression model.

Controlling for the number of nursing home complaints per 1,000 nursing home beds as a proxy for quality, states with higher percentages of the population age eighty-five and over gave more facilities at least some deficiencies. States with Democratic governors had higher summary scores on enforcement stringency.

In terms of facility characteristics, states with higher percentages of facilities with chains and higher percentages of hospital-based facilities gave higher percentages of facilities deficiencies. Higher percentages of hospital-based facilities led to lower average numbers of civil monetary penalties. States with more chain facilities also had higher percentages of facilities that received deficiencies for causing harm or jeopardy. States with lower facility occupancy rates gave citations to a higher number of facilities for substandard care and had higher summary scores on enforcement.

In terms of competition for beds, states with fewer nursing facility beds per 1,000 aged population gave more deficiencies per facility on average, but they did not have high summary scores on enforcement. States that had more generous Medicaid reimbursement rates had a higher percentage of facilities cited for causing harm or jeopardy to residents but did not have higher overall summary scores.

The model predicted 37.7 percent of the variance for the average number of deficiencies, 28.8 percent for the percentage of facilities that received deficiencies, 18.5 percent cited for substandard care, and 28.9 percent for the average number of CMPs per facility surveyed. But the model did not predict significant differences for the percentage of facilities causing harm or jeopardy. The model predicted 32.9 percent of the variance for the overall summary score across all measures.

Figure 7.4.1 shows a map of the overall rank of all the states on enforcement indicators for 1999. The states in the west and southwest are in the highest quartile on overall rank on enforcement stringency. States in the lowest two quartiles tend to be in the Rocky Mountain area, the central plains (except for Kansas), and the northeastern region of the country. Federal CMS oversight of the states is administered by ten regional offices.

DISCUSSION

This study showed a substantial number of quality problems as indicated by the total number of deficiencies issued, the almost one-third of facilities with violations that could or did cause harm or jeopardy to residents, the number of facilities (811) classified as providing substandard care, and the large number of complaints made about quality (over 80,000). These findings by state survey agencies suggest serious quality of care violations across the country.

In spite of the many facilities identified as having serious deficiencies, few facilities had follow-up enforcement actions or sanctions taken against them, even when all state and federal sanctions are combined. Less than 4 percent of violations were issued civil monetary penalties, 9 percent of facilities had a denial of payments issued for new admissions, and less than one-half of 1 percent of facilities had serious action taken against them (i.e., the imposition of a temporary manager/receiver [forty-seven facilities], the issuance of a decertification notice [forty-six facilities], or the revocation of the facility license [forty-two facilities]). The findings here are consistent with a number of earlier reports that documented the poor enforcement system and the ineffective use of both intermediate and permanent sanctions (U.S. GAO 1998, 1999a, 1999b, 1999c, 1999d; IOM 2001).

Without meaningful sanctions that serve as a deterrence to future violations, Brown's (1992) general critique of popular decentralized (state) behavioral regulations appears to be

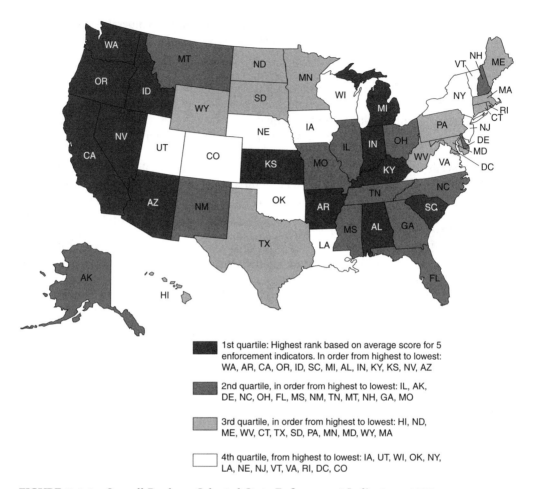

1st quartile: Highest rank based on average score for 5 enforcement indicators. In order from highest to lowest: WA, AR, CA, OR, ID, SC, MI, AL, IN, KY, KS, NV, AZ

2nd quartile, in order from highest to lowest: IL, AK, DE, NC, OH, FL, MS, NM, TN, MT, NH, GA, MO

3rd quartile, in order from highest to lowest: HI, ND, ME, WV, CT, TX, SD, PA, MN, MD, WY, MA

4th quartile, from highest to lowest: IA, UT, WI, OK, NY, LA, NE, NJ, VT, VA, RI, DC, CO

FIGURE 7.4.1   Overall Rank on Selected State Enforcement Indicators, 1999

relevant. In this situation, the federal-state nursing survey process gives the appearance that government is doing something about the quality of care problems, but in reality, the enforcement system does little to change or improve the system and generally does not remove the most serious violators from the system.

With widespread quality problems identified by state agencies, the variation in enforcement actions taken by states was considered problematic in terms of compliance with federal requirements. Because these variations are not entirely due to quality differences, nursing facility residents do not appear to have equal access to a high quality of care and equal protection from poor quality and abuse.

State officials reported problems in their ability to carry out the federal enforcement activities that are related to limited federal and state resources for regulatory activities. These resources were found to be less than one-half of 1 percent of the total expenditures on nursing facilities in the United States in 1999 (Walshe and Harrington 2002). The federal and state resources vary widely, in part based on historical expenditures for regulation, and some state agencies reported operating under serious financial and personnel constraints. Some states invest greater state resources than others in the regulatory process to make up for limited federal funds (ibid.).

In summary, CMS needs to develop approaches that bring greater standardization in the survey and enforcement process across states and to identify ways to encourage poor performing state agencies and regions to improve (U.S. GAO 2000). These issues are complex in a system that has been largely devolved to the states, with very different political and philosophical positions on regulation. Moreover, other factors such as reimbursement rates and occupancy rates suggest policy approaches that can be further studied as a means of improving regulation. Finally, ensuring adequate funding for state regulatory programs may also be a way to improve the state enforcement system.

REFERENCES

Brown, L. D. 1992. Political Evolution of Federal Health Care Regulation. *Health Affairs* 11:17–37.

Edelman, T. 1997. An Unpromising Picture: Implementation of Reform Law's Enforcement Provisions Troubles Advocates. *Quality Care Advocate,* March.

———. 1998. What Happened to Enforcement? *Nursing Home Law Letter* 1–2:1–46.

Institute of Medicine (IOM). Committee on Nursing Home Regulation. 1986. *Improving the Quality of Care in Nursing Homes.* Washington, DC: National Academy Press.

———. Committee on Improving Quality in Long-Term Care. 2001. *Improving the Quality of Long-Term Care,* ed. G. S. Wunderlich and P. O. Kohler. Washington, DC: National Academy Press.

U.S. General Accounting Office (GAO). 1987. Report to the Chairman, Subcommittee on Health and Long-Term Care, Select Committee on Aging, House of Representatives. *Medicare and Medicaid: Stronger Enforcement of Nursing Home Requirements Needed.* Washington, DC: U.S. GAO.

———. 1998. *California Nursing Homes: Care Problems Persist Despite Federal and State Oversight.* Report to the Special Committee on Aging, U.S. Senate. GAO/HEHS-98–202. Washington, DC: U.S. GAO.

———. 1999a. *Nursing Homes: Additional Steps Needed to Strengthen Enforcement of Federal Quality Standards.* Report to the Special Committee on Aging, U.S. Senate. GAO/HEHS-99–46. Washington, DC: U.S. GAO.

———. 1999b. *Nursing Homes: Complaint Investigation Processes Often Inadequate to Protect Residents.* Report to the Special Committee on Aging, U.S. Senate. GAO/HEHS-99–80. Washington, DC: U.S. GAO.

———. 1999c. *Nursing Home Care: Enhanced HCFA Oversight of State Programs Would Better Ensure Quality.* Report to the Special Committee on Aging, U.S. Senate. GAO/HEHS-00–6. Washington, DC: U.S. GAO.

———. 1999d. *Nursing Homes: Proposal to Enhance Oversight of Poorly Performing Homes Has Merit.* Report to the Special Committee on Aging, U.S. Senate. GAO/HEHS-99–157. Washington, DC: U.S. GAO.

———. 2000. *Nursing Homes: Sustained Efforts Are Essential to Realize Potential of the Quality Initiatives.* Report to the Special Committee on Aging, U.S. Senate. GAO/HEHS-00–197. Washington, DC: U.S. GAO.

U.S. Office of the Inspector General (U.S. OIG). Department of Health and Human Services. 1999. *Nursing Home Survey and Certification: Deficiency Trends.* OEI-02-98–00331. Washington, DC: Inspector General.

Walshe, K., and C. Harrington. 2002. The Regulation of Nursing Facilities in the U.S.: An Analysis of the Resources and Performance of State Survey Agencies. *Gerontologist* 42:475–486.

Relationship of Nursing Home Staffing to Quality of Care

John F. Schnelle, Sandra F. Simmons, Charlene Harrington,
Mary Cadogan, Emily Garcia, and Barbara M. Bates-Jensen

Nursing home (NH) staffing resources necessary to provide care consistent with regulatory guidelines are the subject of national debate due to emerging evidence that existing staffing resources may not be adequate (U.S. Department of Health and Human Services 2000b). One recent study for the Centers for Medicare and Medicaid Services (CMS) reported that 4.1 mean total (nursing aides [NAs] plus licensed nurses) direct care hours per resident per day (hprd) and 1.3 licensed nurse hprd (.75 for registered nurses [RNs] and .55 for licensed vocational nurses [LVNs]) were the minimum staffing levels associated with a lower probability of poor resident outcomes, such as weight loss and pressure ulcers (Kramer and Fish 2001). This study is supported by other correlational data documenting a relationship between staffing (particularly RNs) and a variety of outcomes, including: lower death rates, higher rates of discharges to home, improved functional outcomes, fewer pressure ulcers, fewer urinary tract infections, lower urinary catheter use, and less antibiotic use (Aaronson, Zinn, and Rosko 1994; Bliesmer et al. 1998; Harrington et al. 2000; U.S. Department of Health and Human Services 2000b). Few studies have specifically examined the relationship between staffing and the implementation of daily care processes, but inadequate staffing has been associated with inadequate feeding assistance during meals, poor skin care, lower activity participation, and less toileting assistance (Spector and Takada 1991; Kayser-Jones 1997; Kayser-Jones and Schell 1997). The results of these correlational studies led two Institute of Medicine committees to recommend higher nurse staffing in nursing facilities, including 24-hour registered nursing care.

A second study conducted for CMS focused on this care process implementation issue (Schnelle, Simmons, and Cretin 2001). This study used staff time estimates in computerized simulations to predict the nursing assistant (NA) staffing ratios necessary to provide care recommended in regulatory guidelines. Care processes related to incontinence care, feeding assistance, exercise, and activities of daily living (ADL) independence enhancement (e.g., dressing), all of which are typically implemented by NAs, were included in the simulation. The results of this study showed that 2.8 to 3.2 NA hprd, depending on the acuity level of the NH population, were necessary to consistently provide all of these daily care processes. Unfortunately, 92 percent of the nation's NHs report staffing levels below the

Adapted from: John F. Schnelle, Sandra F. Simmons, Charlene Harrington, Mary Cadogan, Emily Garcia, and Barbara M. Bates-Jensen. (2004). Relationship of nursing home staffing to quality of care. *Health Services Research*, 39(2), 225–250.

staffing minimums identified by the expert panel as well as the two recent CMS studies, and more than 50 percent of NHs would have to double current staffing levels to meet these minimums (U.S. Department of Health and Human Services 2000a).

The purpose of this study was to address this issue by describing the relationship between staffing levels in 21 NHs and directly measured processes of care that are both labor intense and recommended in NH regulatory guidelines. A total of 21 homes in southern California were studied: nine in the lowest quartile on staffing, 6 in the 75th to 90th percentile, and 6 in the upper decile on staffing in 1999 and 2000.

RESULTS

Characteristics of Participants in Key Comparison Groups

There were significant differences between participants in all three groups. In particular, participants in the upper-decile homes were significantly more likely to be female, older, private pay, and Caucasian when compared to participants in all the other homes; while participants in the lower quartile homes were significantly more likely to be minority and MediCal. In terms of participant acuity, participants in the lower quartile homes tended to be more independent for transfer and feeding assistance and had better cognitive functioning (MDS recall scores) when compared to participants in both the 75th to 90th percentile and upper-decile homes. There was no difference on five MDS based acuity measures (recall, transfer and eating dependency, incontinence, pressure ulcer RAP triggered) when comparisons were made between residents in the highest-staffed homes (upper decile) and those in the two lower-staffed homes.

Sample Characteristics: Staffing Data

There were large differences between high-decile homes and all remaining homes on all staffing variables except RN hours according to 2000 state staffing data. These differences are most dramatic for total staffing hours and aide staffing hours. In regard to total hours, high decile homes reported an average of 4.88 hours compared to lower quartile and 75th to 90th percentile homes that reported 2.7 and 3.4 hours per resident day, respectively. There were also significant but less dramatic differences between homes in the lower quartile and the 75th to 90th percentile on most staffing variables.

The primary comparisons on all care process measures were conducted between homes in the upper decile and the remaining sample.

NA Care Process Measures: Do Homes That Report the Highest NA Staffing Provide Different Care Than the Remainder of the Homes?

Table 7.5.1 illustrates that upper-decile homes were significantly different in the same direction on 13 of 16 different care process measures; and, in eight cases significance levels

TABLE 7.5.1   Observation and Interview Measurement Domains

Measurement Domains	(1) Low Homes < 25th Percentile	(2) High Homes 75–90th Percentile	(3) Highest Homes 91st+ Percentile	Significant Comparisons
Out of Bed/Engagement	N = 227	N = 205	N = 125	
1. Percent observations of residents in bed 7:00 A.M. to 7:00 P.M.	41	50	26	1 and 2 vs. 3**
2. Percent observations of residents engaged with nursing home staff, other residents, another person, or an organized group activity, or with an object (e.g., television, reading, sewing)	47	44	52	1 and 2 vs. 3*
Nutrition: Feeding Assistance	N = 407 meals	N = 350 meals	N = 252 meals	
3. Percent of resident meals in dining room	25	39	80	1 and 2 vs. 3**
4. Average duration of feeding assistance to residents in minutes	2.5 (5.9)	4.11 (8.6)	7.0 (11.7)	1 and 2 vs. 3**
5. Average resident tray access time in minutes'	26.9 (3.9)	32.5 (5.3)	38.2 (14.8)	1 and 2 vs. 3*
Providing assistance to residents with low intake:				
6. Percent of residents who eat < 50% and are provided > 1 minute of assistance	19 (n = 106)	31 (n = 96)	46 (n = 95)	1 and 2 vs. 3**
Providing assistance to physically dependent residents:				
7. Percent of residents feeding dependent, MDS 1, and who receive > 5 minutes assistance	66 (n = 83)	48 (n = 134)	80 (n = 72)	1 and 2 vs. 3**
Accuracy of food intake documentation:				
8. Percent of residents who ate less than 50%; NA recorded < 60%	24 (n = 106)	50 (n = 96)	52 (n = 95)	1 and 2 vs. 3*
9. Percent of mealtime observations with social interaction and verbal prompting	18 (n = 103)	28 (n = 137)	25 (n = 199)	—
10. Percent residents responding yes to "Do you have food choice during meals?"	84 (n = 99)	86 (n = 104)	98 (n = 55)	1 and 2 vs. 3*

Measurement Domains	(1) Low Homes < 25th Percentile	(2) High Homes 75–90th Percentile	(3) Highest Homes 91st+ Percentile	Significant Comparisons
Incontinence				
11. Number of toileting assists received; MDS Recall Score > 2	1.76 (1.18) (*n = 48*)	1.8 (1.25) (*n = 64*)	2.8 (1.12) (*n = 31*)	1 and 2 vs. 3**
12. Percent residents responding yes to "Do you have to wait too long for assistance?" All Recall Scores	49 (*n = 90*)	39 (*n = 89*)	31 (*n = 58*)	1 and 2 vs. 3*
Exercise Activities	*N = 42*	*N = 46.*	*N = 30*	
13. Number of exercise activities per hour (Day)–Thigh monitor (can't reposition or walk independently)	.20 (.15)	.18 (.13)	.27 (.20)	1 and 2 vs. 3*
14. Number of repositioning movements per hour (Night)–Thigh monitor (can't reposition independently)	.25 (.17)	.17 (.14)	.23 (.14)	1 and 2 vs. 3*
15. Number of repositioning movements per hour (Day)–Thigh monitor (can't reposition independently)	.26 (.40)	.20 (.14)	.36 (.28)	1 and 2 vs. 3**
16. Number of walking assists received MDS Recall Score > 2 and can bear weight	.51 (.72)	.76 (.68)	.69 (1.1)	

*P < .05;

**P < .001.

exceeded $p < .001$. The probability that 13 out of 16 comparisons would be significant at the .05 level by chance is less than .00001. The pattern of significant differences was consistent across all care areas, but the care process differences were most compelling for feeding assistance and least compelling for exercise and repositioning. In general, participants in the upper-decile homes spent more time out of bed during the day; were engaged more frequently; received better feeding and toileting assistance; were repositioned more frequently; and showed more physical movement patterns during the day that could reflect exercise. However, even participants in these highest-staffed facilities did not receive repositioning at the rate of once every two hours during the day or night and only received potential exercise activities at the rate of approximately one episode every four hours. In addition, there were no differences between the groups of homes in repositioning frequency at night; walking assistance frequency during the day as reported by the participants; or the amount of social interaction observed between residents and staff during meals.

Social interaction during meals could only be measured in the dining room, and participants in the upper-decile homes were observed significantly more often in the dining room than those in the remaining homes. If one assumes that there are very low or zero levels of social interaction between residents and staff if residents eat in their rooms, which is a reasonable assumption, then there would be significant overall differences in the amount of social interaction that participants in upper-decile homes received during meals as compared to participants in all remaining homes.

There were no differences on five MDS-based acuity measures that could explain why more residents ate in their rooms more often in the lower-staffed homes. The significant higher age of residents in the highest-staffed home would seem predictive of these residents spending more time in bed as opposed to less time as was observed. However, none of the demographic characteristics including age were correlated with in-bed or feeding assistance measures across all homes. A multiple regression analysis using staffing as a categorical variable (upper decile versus all others) and MDS acuity scores that were correlated with in-bed time (transfer and feeding assistance, recall scores, and prevalence of UI and pressure ulcer RAP triggered) revealed that staffing remained the only significant predictor of in-bed time.

DISCUSSION

Nursing home self-reported staffing statistics do reflect differences in quality between homes that report the highest staffing level (upper decile) and all remaining homes. There were few differences between homes that report staffing levels below the 90th percentile and the staffing levels in these homes were unstable across the different staffing measures. There appears to be a two-tiered staffing system with only the homes reporting the highest level of staffing showing both stability and significantly better care on most measures.

The most dramatic differences between the homes were reported for NA hours and the most dramatic quality improvement occurred for homes that reported a total staffing hrpd average from 4.8 (state data) to 4.5 (onsite interview data). There was also a significant improvement in these upper-decile homes for multiple care processes delivered by NAs even though residents in the upper-decile homes needed as much care according to multiple functional measures as residents in the lower-staffed homes.

There were smaller differences between homes in reported licensed nurse hours and particularly RN hours and there were also fewer differences between homes on licensed nurse performance measures. The differences that did exist favored the lower-staffed homes for two pressure ulcer assessment indicators derived from medical record data. In contrast, observation and resident interview measures related to pressure ulcer care actually received by residents (e.g., toileting assistance, repositioning care) favored the upper-decile homes. This finding highlights an important discrepancy between quality conclusions about NH care process implementation derived from different data sources (medical record versus observation and resident interview).

Despite this discrepancy, it is still surprising that the medical record documentation provided by licensed nurses in higher-staffed facilities was not better since other studies have reported a relationship between licensed nurses' hours and some quality measures (Kramer and Fish 2001). There are two potential explanations for this finding. First, it is possible that none of the homes in this study had adequate licensed nurses, particularly RNs, to improve care quality. Furthermore, RN hours failed to reach the minimum level recommended by a recent CMS study (.75 hours) in all homes, and RN hours were much less in all homes than that recommended by an expert panel (1.5 hours) (Harrington, Kovner et al. 2000). Second, licensed nurses in all facilities simply may be unaware of some care processes that define good quality (e.g., no homes documented a trial of toileting assistance for incontinent residents and all homes did poorly on all pain-related measures). This possibility reinforces arguments that licensed nurses who practice in NHs should receive more specialized training focused on the NH population.

It is also important to note that some care processes were poorly implemented in even the highest-staffed facilities, despite the fact that these facilities had sufficient numbers of NAs to potentially provide 100 percent of care to all residents. One plausible explanation for this finding is that all homes lacked management mechanisms necessary to assure that care was provided on a daily basis, in particular, for care processes that are difficult to measure and manage. For example, the fewest differences occurred between homes on care processes related to repositioning and walking exercise, both of which are difficult to measure when compared to more visible types of care (e.g., resident out of bed). In addition, even though the highest-staffed facilities provided better feeding assistance than other homes, there were still problems that could be traced to measurement issues. For example, even staff in the highest-staffed facilities did not accurately record that 48 percent of the residents were eating less than 50 percent of the food offered and that 54 percent of these low-intake residents were provided less than one minute of feeding assistance during meals. Both of these problems in higher-staffed homes could reflect the absence of a quality assessment technology to accurately measure and monitor these care processes.

We should also note that the differences in the care for the highest-staffing homes (Group 3, upper decile) and all lower-staffed homes were significantly greater than the differences in quality measured for homes that differed on MDS clinical quality indicators. This finding, as reported in other studies, suggests that staffing data may be the best information to give consumers (Bates-Jensen et al. 2003; Simmons et al. 2003; Schnelle, Cadogan et al. 2003; Cadogan et al. 2003; Schnelle et al. 2004).

Despite the limitations of this study, an excellent case can be made that the highest-staffed homes provided better care. Furthermore, NA staffing levels reported by only the highest-staffed homes exceeded those levels that were identified in two recent CMS reports as associated with higher care quality. This finding provides some verification that NA staffing above 2.8 hours per resident per day is associated with better quality.

REFERENCES

Aaronson, W. E., J. S. Zinn, and M. D. Rosko. 1994. "Do For-Profit and Not-For-Profit Nursing Facilities Behave Differently?" *Gerontologist* 34 (6): 775–86.

Bates-Jensen, B. M., M. Cadogan, D. Osterweil, L. Levy-Storms, J. Jorge, N. R. Al-Samarrai, V. Grbic, and J. R. Schnelle. 2003. "The Minimum Data Set Pressure Ulcer Indicator: Does It Reflect Differences in Care Processes Related to Pressure Ulcer Prevention and Treatment in Nursing Homes?" *Journal of the American Geriatric Society* 51 (9): 1203–12.

Bliesmei, M. M., M. Smayling, R. Kane, and I. Shannon. 1998. "The Relationship between Nursing Staffing Levels and Nursing Home Outcomes." *Journal of Aging and Health* 10 (3): 351–71.

Cadogan, M. P., J. F. Schnelle, N. Yamamoto-Mitani, G. Cabrera, and S. F. Simmons. "A Minimum Data Set Prevalence of Pain Quality Indicator: Is It Accurate and Does It Reflect Differences in Care Processes?" *Journal of Gerontology: Medical Science* (Accepted).

Harrington, C., C. Kovner, M. Mezey, J. Kayser-Jones, S. Burger, M. Mohler, R. Burke, and D. Zimmerman. 2000. "Experts Recommend Minimum Nurse Staffing Standards for Nursing Facilities in the United States." *Gerontologist* 40 (1): 5–16.

Harrington, C., D. Zimmerman, S. L. Karon, J. Robinson, and P. Beutel. 2000. "Nursing Home Staffing and Its Relationship to Deficiencies." *Journal of Gerontology: Social Sciences* 55B (5): S278–87.

———. 1997. "Inadequate Staffing at Mealtime: Implications for Nursing and Health Policy." *Journal of Gerontological Nursing* 23 (8): 14–21.

Kayser-Jones, J., and E. Schell. 1997. "The Effect of Staffing on the Quality of Care at Mealtime." *Nursing Outlook* 45 (2): 64–71.

Kramer, A. M., and R. Fish. 2001. "The Relationship between Nurse Staffing Levels and the Quality of Nursing Home Care." In *Appropriateness of Minimum Nurse Staffing Ratios in Nursing Homes.* Report to Congress, Phase 2 final, chap. 2, pp. 1–26. Washington, DC: U.S. Department of Health and Human Services, Health Care Financing Administration.

Schnelle, J. F., B. M. Bates-Jensen, L. Levy-Storms, V. Grbic, J. Yoshii, M. P. Cadogan, and S. F. Simmons. 2004. "The Minimum Data Set Prevalence of Restraint Quality Indicator: Does It Reflect Differences in Care?" *Gerontologist* 44 (2).

Schnelle, J. F., M. P. Cadogan, J. Yoshii, N. R. Al-Samarrai, D. Osterweil, B. M. Bates-Jensen, and S. F. Simmons. 2003. "The Minimum Data Set Urinary Incontinence Quality Indicators: Do They Reflect Differences in Care Processes Related to Incontinence?" *Medical Care* 41 (8): 909–22.

Schnelle, J. F., S. F. Simmons, and S. Cretin. 2001. "Minimum Nurse Aide Staffing Required to Implement Best Practice Care in Nursing Facilities." In *Appropriateness of Minimum Nurse Staffing Ratios in Nursing Homes.* Report to Congress, Phase 2 final, chap. 3, pp. 1–40. Washington, DC: U.S. Department of Health and Human Services, Health Care Financing Administration.

Simmons, S. F., E. T. Garcia, M. P. Cadogan, N. R. Al-Samarrai, L. F. Levy-Storm, D. Osterweil, and J. F. Schnelle. 2003. "The Minimum Data Set Weight Loss Quality Indicator: Does It Reflect Differences in Care Processes Related to Weight Loss." *Journal of the American Geriatric Society* 51 (10): 1410–18.

U.S. Department of Health and Human Services, Health Care Financing Administration (USHCFA). 2000a. *Executive Summary. Report to Congress: Appropriateness of Minimum Nurse Staffing Ratios in Nursing Homes.* Washington, DC: Health Care Financing Administration.

U.S. Department of Health and Human Services, Health Care Financing Administration (USHCFA). 2000b. *Appropriateness of Minimum Nurse Staffing Ratios in Nursing Facilities.* Vols. 1, 2, and 3. Report to Congress. Washington, DC: Health Care Financing Administration.

Wunderlich, G. S., and P. O. Kohler, eds. 2001. *Improving the Quality of Long-Term Care.* Report by the Committee on Improving the Quality in Long-Term Care, Division of Health Care Services, Institute of Medicine. Washington, DC: National Academy of Sciences, National Academy Press.

Initial Home Health Outcomes Under Prospective Payment

Robert E. Schlenker, Martha C. Powell, and Glenn K. Goodrich

The Prospective Payment System (PPS) for Medicare home health services was implemented in October 2000. The PPS replaced the Interim Payment System (IPS), which was implemented in 1997 as part of the Balanced Budget Act of 1997 (BBA). The IPS placed stringent limits on the Medicare cost-based reimbursement system then in effect. Both IPS and PPS were intended to constrain Medicare home health expenditures, which had increased rapidly in the preceding decade (from $2 billion to over $17 billion between 1988 and 1997 [MedPAC 1998]). IPS was associated with dramatic expenditure and visit reductions between 1997 and 1999. Medicare expenditures declined 53 percent to $7.9 billion (CMS 2003), still comprising about 5 percent of total Medicare expenditures. Two recent articles estimate that home health visits per user declined by about 40 percent (Komisar 2002; McCall et al. 2003).

Whether the reduction in visits per user under IPS affected patient outcomes is uncertain. McCall et al. (2002) found mixed results based on selected utilization measures derived from Medicare claims data as proxy outcome indicators. Based on multivariate analyses for fiscal years 1997 and 1999, in the 120 day period after home health admission, hospital admissions decreased while skilled nursing facility admissions, emergency room use, and mortality increased. Although the study authors urge caution in attributing the changes to IPS, it is possible that the stringency of IPS resulted in a decline in patient outcomes.

The PPS encouraged further visit reductions. Under PPS, a prospectively determined per-episode payment rate is case-mix adjusted using 80 mutually exclusive Home Health Resource Groups (HHRGs). Each Medicare episode is classified into an HHRG using a subset of items from the Outcome and Assessment Information Set (OASIS), which has been collected by all Medicare-certified home health agencies since mid-1999 (HCFA 1999a). The PPS creates strong financial incentives to minimize service provision because per-episode payments do not vary according to the quantity or mix of services provided. A study by the U.S. General Accounting Office (USGAO 2002) found that average visits per episode declined by 24 percent (29–22 visits) from just prior to PPS to the first half of 2001. The reduction in visits per episode under PPS compounded the already substantial decline under IPS and raises the possibility of poorer outcomes under PPS. Alternatively, if PPS outcome changes are minimal, then the visit reductions may represent a gain in the

---

Adapted from: Robert E. Schlenker, Martha C. Powell, and Glenn K. Goodrich. (2005). Initial home health outcomes under prospective payment. *Health Services Research*, 40(1), 177–193.

overall efficiency and cost-effectiveness of home health care. The OASIS data provide uniform, standardized outcome measures to test these possibilities. (The late-IPS period must be used as the baseline, since national OASIS data were not collected earlier.)

METHODS AND DATA

The objective of this analysis was to determine the changes in outcomes between the pre-FrS (1999–2000) and initial PPS (2001) periods, focusing on home health-care episodes of Medicare beneficiaries aged 65 years and over (the main Medicare group to which per-episode PPS payments apply or would apply in the case of pre-PPS episodes). Changes in visits per episode also were analyzed, both to check the above-mentioned GAO finding of fewer visits under PPS and to obtain a preliminary indication of possible changes in the system-level efficiency of Medicare home health care provision under PPS by examining visit and outcome changes for the same samples. The analyses compared random samples of Medicare home health care episodes for the two periods. In order to assess the impact of PPS based on measurement yardsticks that are in current use, we employed the outcome measures and risk factors adopted by CMS for reports to agencies and public reporting.

RESULTS

HHRG and Visit Changes

The pre-PPS and PPS changes in the HHRG distribution and visits per episode indicate a shift toward the higher levels of each dimension in the PPS period (i.e., toward more clinically complex and functionally dependent patients, with greater needs for therapy services). Such changes may indicate that providers responded to PPS by increasing the proportion of Medicare patients in the higher payment HHRGs. Such shifts also could result from more accurate reporting by agencies or from deliberate manipulation (i.e., "gaming") of the data to obtain higher per-episode payments. This finding heightens the importance of including risk factors beyond those used for HHRGs in the outcome models.

With adjustment for the shift in the HHRG distribution, total visits per episode were 16.6 percent lower in the PPS compared with the pre-PPS period (based on outcome, not payment, episodes). However, visit changes varied by discipline. The largest reduction (44.9 percent) occurred for aide visits, while therapy visits actually increased (8.4 percent), consistent with PPS financial incentives resulting from higher payment for patients in the high-therapy categories.

Outcome Changes

In the PPS period, unadjusted improvement rates range from 34.59 percent for ambulation/locomotion to 87.46 percent for urinary tract infection. All but two of the 26 improvement rates are below 70 percent, suggesting potential opportunities for outcome enhancement.

All stabilization rates (indicating nonworsening) are greater than 80 percent; however, the relatively small proportions of patients who do worsen are definitely important from a care perspective. (In some instances, of course, a decline in health status is inevitable.)

Overall, most outcome rate changes between the two periods are relatively small (based on either the unadjusted or adjusted PPS rates), although even a small change in percentage rates translates into a large number of patient episodes nationwide.

All (adjusted) ADL changes are statistically significant except for improvement in bathing, which is close to significance ($p = .0502$), and all but two ADL improvement and stabilization rates are higher in the PPS period.

Under PPS, hospitalization and emergent care rates decreased while the community discharge rate increased. These findings suggest positive changes under PPS and are counter to the hypothesis that fewer visits are likely to lead to more hospitalizations and emergent care.

DISCUSSION

The generally small changes in outcomes associated with visit reductions suggest a possible gain in system-level cost effectiveness during the first year under PPS (i.e., similar outcomes, lower cost). However, underlying this overall result are varied results across outcomes. The changes for functional measures, particularly improvement in ADLs, are positive. Additional positive findings are the utilization outcome changes, particularly the lower hospitalization rates. However, as mentioned above, subsequent hospitalization and other service use after the home health episode should be examined.

In contrast to the positive changes, the reductions in improvement rates for urinary incontinence and all four cognitive and emotional/behavioral outcomes suggest the possibility that patients with these typically chronic care problems may be more negatively affected by PPS than other patients. Analyses of changes for specific diagnoses could shed light on whether outcome effects under PPS differ by condition, with possibly more negative consequences for chronic care patients. The association between higher improvement rates for ADLs under PPS and more therapy visits should also be further explored.

The outcomes analyzed in this study are those used in the current national outcome reporting system. Additional outcome measures should be developed and analyzed, including aggregate outcomes combining the individual measures currently in outcome reports, variants based on the degree of change (rather than the current dichotomies), and measures using additional information from the OASIS items. Future outcome analyses should also explore the inclusion of risk factors beyond those in the current CMS models.

This analysis pertains to the first few years of OASIS data collection and the first calendar year under PPS. Since data inaccuracies are likely to be more prevalent in new than in mature systems, later time periods should also be studied. In addition, recently introduced quality improvement initiatives such as the OBQI approach are intended to encourage outcome enhancement efforts by home health agencies. The provision of outcome reports to home health agencies by CMS began in 2002 and represents the initial step in the OBQI process. Nationwide training efforts organized and funded by CMS have concentrated on how agencies can use outcome reports to improve care and patient outcomes.

Also, public reporting of 11 outcomes began for eight states in May 2003, and was implemented nationally in late 2003 (http://www.medicare.gov/HHCompare). The publicly reported outcomes are a subset of those included in agency outcome reports, and are likely to receive particular attention from agencies as they implement OBQI. Future analyses should assess these and other developments as both PPS and OBQI evolve.

REFERENCES

Centers for Medicare & Medicaid Services (CMS), U.S. Department of Health and Human Services. 2003. *Health Care Financing Review: Medicare and Medicaid Statistical Supplement, 2001.*

Health Care Financing Administration (HCFA), U.S. Department of Health and Human Services. 1999. "Medicare and Medicaid Programs; Mandatory Use, Collection, Encoding, and Transmission of Outcome and Assessment Set (OASIS) for Home Health Agencies and Privacy Act of 1974; Report of New System; Notices." *Federal Register* 64 (117): 32983–91.

Komisar, H. 2002. "Rolling Back Medicare Home Health." *Health Care Financing Review* 24 (2): 33–55.

McCall, N., J. Korb, A. Petersons, and S. Moore. 2002. "Constraining Medicare Home Health Reimbursement: What Are the Outcomes?" *Health Care Financing Review* 24 (2): 57–76.

McCall, N., A. Petersons, S. Moore, and J. Korb. 2003. "Utilization of Home Health Services before and after the Balanced Budget Act of 1997: What Were the Initial Effects?" *Health Services Research* 38 (1): 85–106.

Medicare Payment Advisory Commission (MedPAC). 1998. Report to the Congress: Context for a Changing Medicare Program. Washington, DC.

United States General Accounting Office (USGAO). 2002. "Medicare Home Health Care: Payments to Home Health Agencies Are Considerably Higher Than Costs." GAO Publication No. 02-663. Washington, DC.

PART IV

THE ECONOMICS OF HEALTH CARE

Health care costs have escalated at rates much higher than the general rate of inflation (consumer price index) since the early 1990s. In the United States, the $2 trillion spent on health care in 2005 is projected to increase dramatically, reaching $4 trillion by 2015. These spending patterns have continued largely unabated despite numerous policy interventions made in recent years. Not surprisingly, policy makers in the United States continue to see cost containment as the number one health policy problem facing the nation, as has been the case for the past 25 years.

These high growth rates in health care expenditures are a function of the privatized and unregulated health insurance industry and health care delivery system in the United States. Members of the private insurance industry can raise their premium rates as much as they like to pass through increases in hospital and physician charges to patients. When payment rates made by government payers (e.g., Medicare and Medicaid) are constrained, providers can shift costs to private payers. Thus the growth in private premiums and expenditures, in turn, increases the costs to government.

The Centers for Medicare and Medicaid Services (CMS; formally called the Health Care Financing Administration) publishes data on these increasing costs. The growth is primarily related to provider price increases over and above the general inflation rates (e.g., for food and salaries). The CMS has identified price inflation in the medical sector as a major factor in the overall expenditure growth, which might be called the "greed factor." One logical approach to cost containment is, therefore, to regulate the prices for all payers, including insurance premiums. Regulatory approaches could quickly bring the growth rate under control, but such approaches are adamantly opposed by insurers, providers, and the special-interest groups that influence public policy makers.

The health sector (or medical industrial complex) has benefited from the high inflation rates in health care. Every year *Forbes* and *Provider* magazines publish lists of the top companies in the health industry. Although profits are cyclical, the health industry has consistently enjoyed better returns on investment than many other areas. The return on equity for drug companies, for example, has been higher than that for other industries over the past 10 years. Growth in sales and profit margins in the health sector are all higher than that for other industries in the United States. The dangers of making profit the mission of the health care system, in terms of higher overall health care costs and poor quality, are clear.

Almost all policy issues involve economic issues. Max's article describes how economic analysis is playing an increasing role in health care. Health professionals need to know the different techniques of cost-of-illness studies, cost-effectiveness analysis, cost-utility analysis, and cost-benefit analysis to be conversant with the policy literature. Increasingly, today's health professionals must also be able to make their own cost estimates for new projects and for proposed legislation. Without being able to argue that new legislation will be somewhat cost-effective and in the overwhelming interest of the public, there is little chance of such laws' passage.

The fundamental reason that the United States has such high rates of spending on health care compared with other countries is that its prices for services are so much higher. Bodenheimer shows that costs are high in the United States compared to other countries owing to the unit price of care by physicians, hospitals, and pharmaceuticals. The higher prices cut across the board for all types of services in the United States, but are particularly notable in terms of their effects on pharmaceutical spending and total spending. The United States will have a difficult time sustaining these high prices without having a negative impact on its economy as a whole. Nevertheless, the increases in these prices will no doubt continue unless more effective regulatory controls are adopted.

Some policy makers have supported shifting greater costs onto consumers, particularly in the Medicare and Medicaid programs. Researchers, however, have shown that increasing co-payments has negative effects on consumers, discouraging them from seeking care for both minor and major illnesses. They conclude that cost sharing can have a serious negative impact on individuals with low incomes and patients with chronic illnesses.

PUBLIC FINANCING

The passage of the 1996 Welfare Reform Act eliminated welfare and Medicaid benefits for many women and children. In addition, this act changed Aid to Families with Dependent Children (AFDC) to Temporary Assistance for Needy Families (TANF) in the Omnibus Budget Reconciliation Act of 1996. Following this change, large enrollment declines occurred due to the reduction in Medicaid coverage for children. The negative effects on child health have proved serious. States were able to counter some of these coverage losses with the new State Children's Health Insurance Program (SCHIP), but many children who are eligible do not enroll because of the premium costs and other factors. SCHIP should be expanded through a variety of new public policies, and creative approaches are needed to ensure access to health care in the Medicaid and SCHIP programs.

Although the majority of Medicaid recipients are women and children, most of the expenditures are for the aged, blind, and disabled for long-term care services. Because of the high costs of nursing facility care, many older people and individuals with disabilities quickly use up their limited Medicare benefits (100 days of skilled nursing) and their own assets, making them eligible for the Medicaid program. Medicaid home and community-based service programs have grown dramatically across states and now include personal care services, home health, and special long-term care programs with waivers. Unfortunately, access to services varies widely across states, and many states have waiting lists for programs that sometimes result in unnecessary institutionalization of some individuals. Threatened cutbacks in federal and state Medicaid funding will potentially have the greatest impact on the Medicaid nursing facility program and the poor elderly and disabled who depend on the Medicaid program for their long-term care.

Medicare, which was originally designed to provide health care to the aged and disabled, has traditionally offered limited coverage for outpatient drugs, and it still covers only a small proportion of long-term care services. The Kaiser Family Foundation provides an overview of Medicare Parts A (hospital insurance), B (supplementary medical insurance), C (a managed care option), and D (prescription drugs). Most Medicare beneficiaries purchase supplemental insurance to make up for gaps in coverage and to reimburse the co-payments and deductibles.

Because of its rapidly growing costs, Medicare is a regular target for cutbacks by Congress and presidential administrations. As federal Medicare dollars become more tightly constrained, more costs are shifted to the aged, who are already paying for a large percentage of their care through premiums for private insurance or direct out-of-pocket payments. Given that most aged persons have low—and often fixed—incomes, the rapidly increasing care premiums for Medigap private insurance and prescription drugs are beyond many individuals' reach. The burden of the proposed cutbacks in the Medicare program would fall heavily on the most elderly, women, and those who have the lowest incomes, while those with higher incomes will be able to pay for their care privately.

One of the most problematic areas is the high costs of prescription drugs. Medicare did not cover outpatient prescription drugs until 2003, when Congress passed the Medicare Prescription Drug, Improvement and Modernization Act. The debates over this legislation were bitter, as members of Congress supported widely differing approaches to solving the problems. Unlimited price increases, increasing numbers of prescriptions, patent protection on drugs, and the high costs of direct-to-consumer marketing have all created a major crisis that will not be easily solved with the new drug benefit because Congress has been unwilling to regulate drug industry prices. Moon argues that the new legislation is less than ideal and has created new problems that threaten those with low incomes and the poor. The high premium costs and the break in coverage for those who have spending levels between $3,000 and $5,000 (called the doughnut hole) leave those with the most chronic illnesses and medication needs at risk. Revisions of the legislation have been widely suggested by health experts, but the political will for change has not been strong.

The proposals for privatizing the Medicare program have been popular with some policy makers who want to cut program costs. Geyman reviews the dangers of privatization. For example, the use of vouchers, which would pay a defined amount, would force Medicare beneficiaries to choose among the least costly managed care plans and pay more out of pocket for their insurance. Medicare operates with relatively low administrative costs and has been able to control its spending growth better than private health plans. Medicaid also has low administrative costs compared with private plans.

Health professionals have an obligation to educate their patients and the public about the benefits of public programs. The antigovernment movement in the United States continues to be unabated and is often used as a rationale for dismantling government programs and shifting dollars into the private health care sector.

PRIVATE HEALTH INSURANCE AND MANAGED CARE

Private health insurance companies and health plans have developed many ways to avoid covering individuals who need health care insurance. Unfortunately, little has changed over the past two decades regarding the methods used to exclude individuals who could have high health care costs. Health insurance reform passed by Congress and signed by President Clinton in 1996 was designed to help certain groups retain their insurance when they lose or change jobs and to prevent insurance companies from excluding individuals with preexisting conditions. There is no evidence that the legislation was successful, because prices of insurance were not regulated.

Almost all insured Americans (97%) receive their health care from managed care plans, either health maintenance organizations (HMOs; 21%), preferred provider organizations (PPOs; 61%), or point of service plans (15%). Millions of Americans have been forced into managed care by their employers, because many companies offer only one managed care plan option. Others require employees to pay for premiums beyond the lowest-cost plan's rates, forcing employees to choose managed care as the lesser of evils. Moreover, a number of large businesses are choosing to be self-insured. Self-insured businesses are exempt from state insurance regulation because of the rules under the Employee Retirement Income Security Act (ERISA) of 1974. Because of the inability of states to regulate ERISA plans, many advocates have urged the repeal of ERISA. Some businesses are dropping their health plan coverage altogether (only 60% in 2005 offered insurance, compared with 69% in 2000).

In the past, managed care was viewed by some as the best approach in general to constraining market costs in the United States without engaging in government regulation of insurers and health care providers. The latest data show that high health insurance premiums exist for all types of health plans, demonstrating a flaw in this viewpoint. Administrative costs, premiums, and profits are just as high for managed care corporations as in the fee-for-service system. Managed care companies increase their profits by controlling payment rates to providers and expenditures on patients, raising questions concerning access and quality.

There are some good reasons to be concerned about access to needed services and quality in managed care, which has a clear incentive to prevent individuals from using costly services. Researchers have reported lower use of hospital and other expensive resources and have comparable quality in HMOs compared to non-HMOs. At the same time, many HMO enrollees report problems with access to health care and lower levels of satisfaction with their plans. HMO care appears to be especially problematic for patients with chronic conditions and diseases, resulting in poor quality of care for those types of HMO enrollees.

These findings are troubling in view of the growing trend for states to mandate that Medicaid members enroll in managed care programs. Garrett and Zuckerman examine mandatory Medicaid managed care programs. Their findings reveal that mandatory enrollment in HMO programs lowered the probability of Medicaid adults using emergency rooms but had weaker effects on children's care. These programs, however, did not show a strong and consistent improvement in access to services and use of services. These findings suggest that states use Medicaid managed care to save costs but that the effects of these programs on access and quality are questionable.

Mechanic describes the rise and fall of managed care brought about by the public backlash to explicit rationing of services. This backlash resulted in a reduction in utilization management under HMOs and increased the popularity of PPOs. A number of states have now passed legislation prohibiting health plans from requiring hospital discharge of new mothers and infants in the first 24 hours after birth and mandating financial disclosure, external appeal processes, and other regulatory controls on plans. President Clinton's Patient's Bill of Rights was introduced in Congress in 1998, but the legislation, after many different versions and authors, continues to be contested between Republicans and Democrats. The managed care industry opposed most of the new regulatory provisions, and consensus was not achieved in Congress. The most controversial provision was the right to sue HMOs in federal court.

Some economists have argued that there is a need for greater competition among health plans, which might force health plans to lower prices and improve quality. Scanlon and colleagues have shown that greater competition among health plans in one area was associated with poorer health plan performance on three of six quality dimensions. They argue there is not a reason to believe that competition among HMOs will improve quality. If this is the case, then arguments about improving regulatory oversight of health plans can be made.

CHAPTER 8

Financing Health Care

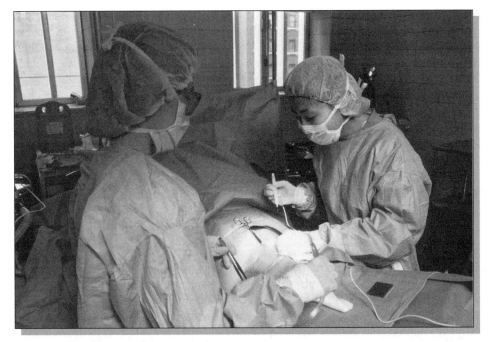

Surgeons operating on patient

Economic Analysis in Health Care

Wendy Max, PhD

INTRODUCTION

Economic analysis is playing an increasingly important role in the evaluation of health care. Where once the focus of health care decisions was only on the effectiveness of treatments and interventions, now the bottom line plays a critical role. Insurers are taking a careful look at what services they will cover and how extensive that coverage should be. Treatment decisions are being made by those paying for care, instead of by clinicians and patients. Policy makers are attempting to control public expenditures, often by limiting the health care coverage in terms of groups covered, services covered, setting and circumstances under which care will be reimbursed, and maximum allowable payment. Hence, attention is being given to providing care that satisfies economic as well as clinical criteria.

TYPES OF ANALYSES

A number of analytical techniques exist for evaluating the economics of health care programs and policies (Haddix, Teutsch, Shaffer, and Dunet, 1996; Eisenberg, 1989; Warner and Luce, 1982). These techniques include cost-of-illness studies, cost-effectiveness analysis, cost-utility analysis, and cost-benefit analysis. Cost-of-illness studies estimate the total cost of a disease and provide a measure of the order of magnitude of the illness. By contrast, cost-effectiveness, cost-benefit, and cost-utility analyses focus on both costs and outcomes, and analyze the incremental or additional costs or benefits of an intervention or treatment program. The purpose of these incremental analyses is to permit decision makers to select among alternative interventions by comparing those options in economic terms. The methodologies differ in whether the outcome or benefit is measured in "health units" (cost-effectiveness analysis), quality-adjusted life-years (cost-utility analysis), or dollars (cost-benefit analysis).

Cost-of-Illness Studies

A cost-of-illness study is used to estimate the total economic burden of a given illness or condition. Included are all the resources that are used to diagnose, treat, and otherwise

Wendy Max. (1997). Economic analysis in health care. Dr. Max is professor at the Institute for Health and Aging, University of California, San Francisco. This article was prepared specifically for the second edition of this book.

cope with the illness under consideration. There exists a substantial literature that esti-mates the cost of a number of illnesses, dating back to the early methodologic work of Rice (1966). Some studies use a "top-down" approach, in which total health expenditures are disaggregated by disease. For example, Rice and her colleagues estimated the economic burden of all illness in the United States to be $455 billion in 1980 (Rice, Hodgson, and Kopstein, 1985). Other studies build estimates of specific diseases from the "bottom up." For example, a study of the 18 most clinically significant birth defects estimated the cost per case in California of cerebral palsy at $445,000; truncus arteriosus at $437,000; and Down syndrome at $410,000 in 1988 (Waitzman, Romano, and Scheffler, 1994).

Cost-Effectiveness Analysis

Cost-effectiveness analysis combines the estimate of the incremental cost of a treatment or intervention for illness with a measurement of the incremental benefit or outcome of inter-est. Whereas the cost is measured in dollars, the benefits are measured in "health units" such as cases avoided or life-years gained. Alternative ways of achieving a given outcome can then be compared.

One alternative might be the current standard of care. For example, a study that ana-lyzed the cost-effectiveness of vaccinating healthy children in the United States for vari-cella used as a comparison program one in which children are not vaccinated (Lieu et al., 1994). The outcomes of interest were cases prevented, major sequelae prevented, long-term disability prevented, deaths prevented, and life-years saved. Compared to not vaccinating children, the cost of the vaccination program was estimated to be an additional $4.20 per case of chickenpox prevented, $1650 per major sequelae prevented, $837,000 per long-term disability prevented, $2,940,000 per death prevented, and $16,000 per life-year saved.

Another study compared the cost-effectiveness of alternative treatments to reduce serum cholesterol levels. Using cholestyramine, the cost was $59,000 per year of life saved compared to a cost of $17,800 per year of life saved using oat bran (Kinosian and Eisen-berg, 1988).

Cost-effectiveness analysis determines whether one treatment is cost-effective com-pared to another. That is, it answers the question, What is the cheapest means of achieving a given objective? It does not determine whether any treatment should be undertaken in the first place.

Cost-Benefit Analysis

When both costs and outcomes can be valued in dollar terms, cost-benefit analysis is the appropriate tool to use. The costs are then subtracted from the benefits to determine the net economic benefit. Interventions and programs can be ranked by net economic benefit, with all those with positive net economic benefits considered worthy of being undertaken. Results are sometimes presented as a benefit-cost ratio—that is, the ratio of net benefits to net costs. Cost-benefit analysis permits the comparison of alternatives with different objec-tives because all costs and benefits are converted to a common metric—dollars.

The varicella vaccine study described previously (Lieu et al., 1994) calculated the benefit-cost ratio to be 0.9 when only medical care costs were included, and 5.4 when the value of lost workdays was included.

Cost-Utility Analysis

Cost-utility analysis is somewhat of a hybrid between cost-effective analysis and cost-benefit analysis. In cost-utility analysis, the cost of an alternative is compared to the health outcome where that outcome is measured in quality-adjusted life-years (QALYs) gained (Drummond, Stoddart, and Torrance, 1987; Torrance, 1987; Loomes and McKenzie, 1989). The results can then be expressed in terms of costs per QALY gained. As analyses are performed on more interventions and programs, more measures of cost per QALY are becoming available and can be compared across programs.

Cost-utility analysis is appropriate when the outcome of interest can be expressed in terms of changes in the quality of life, such as reduced pain or disability. The QALY measure adjusts years of life using a weight that reflects the quality of health experienced by a person during those years. That is, a year of perfect health may be deemed equivalent to two years during which some level of pain is experienced. The weights can be derived using a variety of methods for interviewing patients or clinicians and reflect their assessment of the utility of various health states (Hargreaves and Shumway, 1996).

Revicki and colleagues (1996) estimated weights for QALYs in a study of major depression. They asked patients to rate 11 possible health states using the standard gamble approach. In this approach, the probability of living in each state for one month and a gamble between perfect health and untreated depression for one month is varied until the respondent is indifferent between them. The resulting utilities for a year in a given state were 0.036 for untreated depression, 0.797 to 0.875 for treated depression with various medications, and 0.895 for remission with no further treatment. In other words, the utility of a year of untreated depression would be 0.306 compared to 1.0 for a year of perfect health. Similarly, the utility of a year of treated depression would range from 0.797 to 0.875 depending on the medication used; the utility of a year of untreated remission would be 0.895 as compared to 1.0 for perfect health.

METHODOLOGY

Common to all of the economic methods discussed in the preceding section are a number of issues that must be addressed.

Defining the Problem

The first step in conducting an economic analysis is to define the problem. This step may not be as simple as it appears, but it is critical to the formulation of the analysis. For example, suppose the issue under consideration relates to birth outcomes for teenage mothers.

One might want to estimate the total economic burden associated with teen births. Alternatively, the problem might be defined as determining the best means of assuring successful birth outcomes for teenagers who are already pregnant. A third problem might be how to lower the cost to society of caring for low-birth-weight babies born to teenage mothers. A fourth statement of the problem might be how to improve the quality of life for teenage girls who are at risk of pregnancy. Each statement of the problem implies a different analytical approach.

Identifying Alternatives

The alternatives that should be considered follow from the statement of the problem and the outcomes to be measured. If the problem is defined as determining the best means of assuring successful birth outcomes for teenage mothers, then the alternatives will consist of various treatments for teenagers who are already pregnant. If the problem is to lower the cost to society of caring for low-birth-weight babies born to teenage mothers, then the alternatives might include smoking cessation and drug treatment programs. If the problem is defined as how to improve the quality of life for teenage girls at risk of pregnancy, then the alternatives might include job training and housing subsidies. Note that some of the alternative programs for achieving health-related outcomes, including tobacco taxes and housing subsidies, are not health related per se.

Determining the Relationship Between Inputs and Outcomes

What resources or inputs are used to produce the outcomes of interest? The inputs to produce health-related outcomes are likely to include the services of medical professionals such as nurses, physicians, and therapists. An appropriate unit of measure is necessary, which could take the form of hours or number of visits. Other inputs include the use of the facility (i.e., capital), medical supplies such as medications and bandages, and procedures such as laboratory tests. Inputs that are being used for other purposes must be accurately attributed to the treatment and process under consideration. For example, a clinic may be the site of a drug trial and many other programs. Therefore, only a portion of the cost of running the clinic is relevant for the evaluation of the drug trial. A distinction must also be made between the efficacy of an intervention—that is, the degree to which it works under ideal conditions such as those found in a controlled clinical trial—and effectiveness—that is, the impact of the intervention under real-world conditions (Haddix et al., 1996).

Estimating the Costs

Once the resources used for the illness or intervention under study have been identified, the next step is to estimate their cost. Costs are typically divided into three components: direct costs, which result in dollar expenditures; indirect costs, which represent lost opportunities but do not result in expenditures; and intangible costs, which pose a burden but are very difficult to measure in practice.

Direct Costs

Direct costs include the actual dollar expenditures related to the illness and treatment, including dollars spent on hospital care, physician and other professional services, home and community-based care, prescription and other medications, nursing home care, ambulance and helicopter transport, attendant care, and medical equipment. Direct costs may also be nonmedical in nature, such as health insurance overhead, vocational rehabilitation, and home modifications. Direct costs consist of resources that could be devoted to other purposes in the absence of illness.

To measure direct costs, we add up the dollar cost of each component. If these data are unavailable, a reasonable approach is to obtain data on the units of each resource used, such as hours of nursing care, physician visits, hospital days, and so forth, and to determine the cost per unit.

Indirect Costs

Indirect costs include morbidity and mortality costs. Morbidity costs are the value of lost output due to the reduced productivity of people who are ill or disabled—that is, people who are not able to perform their usual activities or may perform them at less than full capacity. Mortality costs are the value of lives lost due to premature death. Two methods are commonly used to value indirect costs: the human capital approach and the willingness-to-pay approach.

According to the human capital approach, lost productivity is valued using forgone market earnings and an imputed value for forgone household production. This estimation technique incorporates life expectancy for different age and gender groups, changing patterns of earnings over the life cycle, varying labor force participation rates, and discounting to estimate future productivity losses in terms of current dollars. Because the approach uses market earnings, the estimates for children, the retired elderly, and anyone who is undervalued in the labor market will be low using such an analysis.

The willingness-to-pay approach values life according to what someone would be willing to pay for a change that reduces the probability of illness or death (Schelling, 1968). The value of life based on willingness-to-pay has been estimated using three methodologies (Haddix et al., 1996). The required compensation approach studies wage differentials between occupations that differ in terms of fatality risk. The extra compensation required for someone to take a riskier job is used to infer the value placed on life. Another willingness-to-pay method looks at consumer markets for goods that reduce the risk of death, such as automobile air bags, and uses the price paid to infer a value for life. The most commonly used method is a contingent valuation study, in which a survey is conducted that asks what people would be willing to pay for something that reduces the probability of illness or death by a given amount.

Another indirect cost that may be relevant is the value of unpaid caregiving provided by the family or friends of a patient. Although no payment is made for the services performed, if the caregiver were not available, services would have to be either purchased in an institution or provided in the home.

The value of caregiving services can be imputed using one of several approaches. The replacement-cost approach values time according to what it would cost to hire someone to provide the same services. Rice and her colleagues (Rice et al., 1993; Max, Webber, and Fox, 1995) used this approach to estimate the economic cost of caregiving for Alzheimer's disease patients. They collected data on the hours of services provided and the care actually provided (e.g., cooking, cleaning, helping with grooming, managing finances); they then valued the time using the wage of the person most likely to be hired to provide that service (e.g., a nurse's aide, housekeeper, bookkeeper).

An alternative approach, the opportunity-cost approach, values the hours spent providing care using the value of that time in the caregiver's next best opportunity. Some studies have attempted to ask caregivers what income or other opportunities they have given up to provide services. In practice, however, it is difficult to solicit this information, particularly from caregivers who are retired or not in the labor market (Max, Webber, and Fox, 1995).

Intangible Costs
Many other aspects of illness are difficult to value, including pain and suffering, fear, and loss of social interactions. Many studies have identified these dimensions without attempting to assign dollar values to them. Others have sought to impute dollar values to these intangibles. Miller and his colleagues (1993) have estimated the cost of "quality of life lost to psychological injury" based on mental health care costs from average jury awards. They estimate this cost to be $30,000 per rape, $9,000 per robbery, and $5,000 per assault.

Measuring Benefits and Outcomes

Outcomes should be measurable and relevant to the treatment or program being evaluated. Some outcomes are easier to measure than others. For example, hospital days or dollars spent on health care can be summed, but it is more difficult to measure reductions in pain and suffering. Outcomes must be reasonable for the intervention under evaluation. If alternative drug therapies for patients with Alzheimer's disease are being compared, a benefit is more likely to be an improved quality of life for patients and their caregivers than a reduction in hospital stays.

The outcome selected may determine the final decision made. An analysis looking at mortality rates, for example, would almost certainly favor programs that treat heart disease over programs that treat arthritis.

Selecting a Perspective

The perspective taken in the analysis will determine which costs and outcomes should be considered (Hodgson, 1994). At least four perspectives may be relevant.

The Societal Perspective
The broadest perspective is that of society as a whole. From this viewpoint, all direct and indirect costs and benefits are relevant, regardless of to whom they accrue.

The Patient's Perspective

The patient and his or her family are interested only in costs and benefits that they experience. Therefore, they will consider the out-of-pocket co-payments for health care, but not the total costs. They will consider caregiving costs but may not be concerned about payments made on their behalf by public programs. They will also consider income loss, psychological cost, and pain and suffering.

The Payer's Perspective

The payer's perspective will incorporate the actual payments made for services covered, which may not necessarily reflect the cost of providing that service. Costs from this perspective are likely to be a subset of the direct costs, but probably will not include such components as unpaid caregiving services by family members.

The Provider's Perspective

The provider, such as a hospital, will be concerned with its actual cost of providing a service. This amount is likely to include the cost of labor, materials, and equipment. It may be quite different from both the amount charged to the payer and the payment ultimately received for that service.

The importance of defining the perspective is illustrated by the varicella vaccination program discussed earlier (Lieu et al., 1994). The cost-benefit ratio from the payer's perspective, including only medical care costs, was 0.9. Hence, the payer saved 90 cents for every dollar spent on the program. From the societal perspective, however, when the indirect costs associated with days lost from work by caregivers were included, the resultant cost-benefit ratio was 5.4, meaning that society saved $5.40 for every dollar spent on the program. From the payer's perspective, the program should not be undertaken; from the societal perspective, it is clearly beneficial.

Methodological Issues

Costs Versus Charges

Costs differ from charges (Finkler, 1982). The true economic cost of a resource should reflect the opportunities given up in using that resource. However, the charge for that resource is influenced by a number of other factors, including the bargaining clout of the buyer (e.g., a large health maintenance organization that is able to negotiate discounts), and cost shifting that may occur among payers, patients, and types of resources. Although it is preferable to obtain cost data for economic analyses, this information is usually not readily available. Therefore, charges are often used as a proxy, with an adjustment made to reflect the level of costs. Many hospitals are required to report their Medicare cost-to-charge ratio to the Healthcare Financing Administration. This ratio can then be used to adjust charges to obtain costs (Shwartz, Young, and Siegrist, 1995). If, for example, the hospital charges are $1,200 per inpatient day and the Medicare cost-to-charge ratio is 1.5, then per diem costs would be $800. Alternatively, payment or expenditure data may be used if the question addressed relates to the payer's perspective.

Comorbidity

Patients often have multiple health conditions. These comorbid conditions may make it difficult to isolate the cost associated with treating a given illness. For example, if a patient with Alzheimer's disease and a heart condition is hospitalized, part of the cost of the hospitalization should be attributed to Alzheimer's disease and part to the heart condition.

A number of approaches have been developed in practice to address this issue. Some studies have included only individuals who were free of confounding comorbid conditions. For example, Rice and colleagues, in their study of the cost of Alzheimer's disease, excluded patients with other conditions that might cause dementia (Rice et al., 1993). Alternatively, one could compare the cost of patients with a given condition to the cost of individuals who are free of the condition. This approach has been employed in looking at the medical costs of people with disabilities compared to those with no disabilities (Rice and LaPlante, 1988; Trupin, Rice, and Max, 1996). A multivariate model can be used to statistically control for other conditions in estimating the cost of the condition of interest. For example, a model of the cost of the health effects of smoking developed a regression model in which the presence of cardiovascular, neoplastic, and respiratory diseases are controlled for (Bartlett, Miller, Rice, and Max, 1994).

Discounting

Costs and benefits often occur at different points in time. For many programs, most of the costs are incurred early on, whereas the benefits may not be realized until several years have elapsed. The timing of the costs and benefits must be taken into account when they are compared. A dollar received today is more valuable than a dollar received in the future, because that dollar could be invested and earn interest. If the interest rate were 5%, a dollar today would be equivalent to $1.05 one year from now. Thus all dollars must be converted into common terms. This is done by using an appropriate discount rate, reflecting the rate at which one discounts the future. The higher the discount rate, the more one discounts the future, and the less future dollars are worth in today's terms. Although there is much debate over the appropriate discount rate (Olsen, 1993), most studies use discount rates ranging from 3% to 5% (Revicki and Luce, 1995).

Risk and Uncertainty

The outcomes of an intervention are not always known. *Risk* refers to the situation in which the probability of a given outcome occurring is known. For example, as a result of a clinical trial, it may be possible to determine the probability that certain side effects will occur when a drug is used. *Uncertainty* refers to the situation in which the probability is unknown, and the best one can do is to make an educated guess. This might be the case for a new medical technology that has never been used. If enough information exists to permit the assigning of statistical probabilities to the outcomes, then a decision tree can be constructed and outcomes can be weighted by the probability that they will occur.

Sensitivity Analysis

An analysis can be performed that tests the sensitivity of the findings of the study to the assumptions made. For example, a study might be performed using discount rates of 2%, 4%, and 6%. A sensitivity analysis might compare findings using alternative assumptions about the effectiveness of a treatment. If the findings differ when the value of a key variable changes, this discrepancy is noted and decision makers must be very careful about the assumptions adopted. A common approach is to analyze the worst-case scenario (Haddix et al., 1996). If the findings are favorable even in this case, the decision maker may feel more confident in the analysis.

Equity

A program may prove to be cost-effective compared to another, or it may have high positive, net positive, economic benefits, but the benefits may occur to one group disproportionately. For example, a program that screens for breast cancer may have a lower net economic benefit than a program that screens for prostate cancer. However, the benefits of the former program apply to women, whereas the latter program benefits only men. The ultimate decision of where to spend limited health care dollars must include value judgments about which group is to benefit.

CONCLUSION

Economic analysis can make an important contribution to the analysis of health care interventions and policies. However, several caveats must be kept in mind.

First, economic analysis includes many elements that are better classified as art than as science. That is, many judgments must be made in designing an analysis such as those described in this chapter. Which costs should be included? What is the best way to measure these costs? What is the relationship between inputs and outcomes? Do comorbid conditions need to be accounted for? What is the best way to measure the effect of an intervention? Can the outcome be valued and, if so, how? Which discount rate best reflects the tradeoff between the present, the past, and the future? How should risk and uncertainty be treated? The competent analyst needs to consider all of these issues and make decisions that will have an impact on the final analysis.

Second, it must be remembered that economic analysis is only one tool in the analytic toolbox. Other considerations must also be taken into account. Often, political factors are key to the passage of laws relating to health policy. Other times, resource constraints may be paramount, or timing may be crucial, as when a program is implemented in response to a legislative mandate.

Given the proper perspective, economic analysis has much to offer to the clinician or policy maker who is trying to make informed decisions about the use of scarce health resources and the allocations of the ever-smaller health care cost pie.

REFERENCES

Bartlett, J. C., Miller, L. S., Rice, D. P., and Max, W. B. (1994). Medical-care expenditures attributable to cigarette smoking–United States, 1993. *Morbidity and Mortality Weekly Report,* 43(26), 469–472.

Drummond, M. F., Stoddart, G. L., and Torrance, G. W. (1987). *Cost-utility analysis: Methods for the economic evaluation of health care programmes* (pp. 112–148). Oxford, UK: Oxford University Press.

Eisenberg, J. M. (1989). Clinical economics: A guide to the economic analysis of clinical practices. *Journal of the American Medical Association, 262*(20), 2879–2886.

Finkler, S. A. (1982). The distinction between cost and charges. *Annals of Internal Medicine,* 96, 102–109.

Haddix, A. C., Teutsch, S. M., Shaffer, P. A., and Dunet, D. O. (Eds.). (1996). *Prevention effectiveness: A guide to decision analysis and economic evaluation.* New York: Oxford University Press.

Hargreaves, W. A., and Shumway, M. (1996). Pharmacoeconomics of antipsychotic drug therapy. *Journal of Clinical Psychiatry,* 57, Suppl 9: 66–76.

Hodgson, T. A. (1994). Costs of illness in cost-effectiveness analysis: A review of the methodology. *PharmacoEconomics,* 6(6), 536–552.

Kinosian, B. P., and Eisenberg, J. M. (1988). Cutting into cholesterol: Cost-effective alternatives for treating hypercholesterolemia. *Journal of the American Medical Association,* 259, 2247–2254.

Lieu, T. A., Cochi, S. L., Black, S. B., Halloran, M. E., Shinefield, H. R., Holmes, S. J., Wharton, M., and Washington, A. E. (1994). Cost-effectiveness of a routine varicella vaccination program for US children. *Journal of the American Medical Association,* 271(5), 375–381.

Loomes, G., and McKenzie, L. (1989). The use of QALYs in health care decision making. *Social Science and Medicine,* 28(4), 299–308.

Max, W., Webber, P. A., and Fox, P. J. (1995). Alzheimer's disease: The unpaid burden of caring. *Journal of Aging and Health,* 7(2), 179–199.

Miller, T. R., Cohen, M. A., and Rossman, S. B. (1993). Victim costs of violent crime and resulting injuries. *Health Affairs,* 12(4), 168–197.

Olsen, J. A. (1993). On what basis should health be discounted? *Journal of Health Economics,* 12, 39–53.

Revicki, D. A., Brown, R. E., Palmer, W., Bakish, D., Rosser, W. W., Anton, S. F., and Feeny, D. (1996). Cost effectiveness of antidepressant treatment in primary care: Clinical decision analysis of nefazodone, imipramine, or fluoxetine for major depression. *PharmacoEconomics.* 8(6), 524–40.

Revicki, D. A., and Luce, B. R. (1995). Methods of pharmacoeconomic evaluation of new medical treatment in psychiatry. *Psychopharmacology Bulletin,* 31, 45–53.

Rice, D. P. (1966). *Estimating the cost of illness.* DHEW, PHS: Health Economics Series, no. 6.

Rice, D. P., Fox, P. J., Max, W., Webber, P. A., Lindeman, D. A., Hauck, W. W., and Segura, E. (1993). The economic burden of Alzheimer's disease care. *Health Affairs,* 12(2), 164–176.

Rice, D. P., Hodgson, T. A., and Kopstein, A. N. (1985). The economic costs of illness: A replication and update. *Health Care Financing Review,* 7(1), 61–80.

Rice, D. P., and LaPlante, M. F. (1988). Medical expenditures for disability and disabling comorbidity. *American Journal of Public Health,* 82(5), 739–741.

Schelling, T. C. (1968). The life you save may be your own. In: S. B. Chase (Ed.), *Problems in public expenditure analysis.* Washington, DC: Brookings Institute.

Shwartz, M., Young, D. W., and Siegrist, R. (1995). The ratio of costs to charges: How good a basis for estimating costs? *Inquiry,* 32, 476–481.

Torrance, G. W. (1987). Utility approach to measuring health-related quality of life. *Journal of Chronic Disease,* 40(6), 593–600.

Trupin, L., Rice, D. P., and Max, W. (1996). *Medical expenditures for people with disabilities in the United States, 1987.* Washington, DC: U.S. Department of Education, National Institute on Disability and Rehabilitation Research.

Waitzman, N. J., Romano, P. S., and Scheffler, R. M. (1994). Estimates of the economic costs of birth defects. *Inquiry,* 31, 188–205.

Warner, K. E., and Luce, B. R. (1982). *Cost-benefit and cost-effectiveness analysis in health care.* Ann Arbor, MI: Health Administration Press.

High and Rising Health Care Costs.
Part 1: Seeking an Explanation

Thomas Bodenheimer, MD

"Rising-health-care-costs" has become a household word—and worry—for the general public, governments, and employers who purchase health care for their employees. In 2002, the United States spent $5267 per person for health care. Switzerland, the second most expensive health system, posted a per capita figure of $3445, two thirds of the U.S. amount. The third, fourth, and fifth most costly health systems, those of Norway, Canada, and Germany, reported 2002 health expenditures per capita less than 60% that of the United States. The United Kingdom, a frugal system, spent $2160 per person in 2002, 41% of the U.S. amount.[1]

Not only does the United States outspend other nations in health care, but U.S. health care costs are growing rapidly. From 1988 to 1993, U.S. health expenditures rose by 9.7% per year. Following a slowdown from 1993 to 2000, costs jumped by 8.5% in 2001, 9.3% in 2002, and 7.7% in 2003.[2,3] The health care sectors with the most rapid growth in cost are prescription drugs and administrative costs of private health insurance (each increasing at 11% to 16% over the past 3 years). Hospital and physician expenditures have been growing at annual rates closer to 7% to 8% over the past 3 years.[3]

The federal government projected an average annual growth rate of 7.2% through 2013, with health expenditures rising from $1.6 trillion in 2002 (14.9% of gross domestic product, the value of all goods and services produced in a nation) to $3.6 trillion by 2013 (18.4% of gross domestic product).[4] It is undisputed that U.S. health expenditures are high and rising, but the mechanisms behind these phenomena are a topic of debate.

A QUICK SYNOPSIS OF THE HEALTH CARE SYSTEM

Four major actors occupy the health care stage: purchasers, insurers, providers, and suppliers.[5] Purchasers, including employers, governments, and individuals (some of whom are patients), supply the funds. Insurers receive money from purchasers and reimburse providers. The government can be viewed as an insurer or a purchaser in the Medicare and Medicaid programs. The term "payer" refers to both purchasers and insurers.

Providers include physicians and other health professionals, hospitals, nursing homes, home care agencies, and pharmacies. Suppliers—the pharmaceutical, medical supply, and computer industries—manufacture equipment, supplies, and medications used by providers.

Adapted from: Thomas Bodenheimer. (2005). High and rising health care costs. Part 1: Seeking an explanation. *Annals of International Medicine*, 142, 847–854.

Each dollar spent on health services represents an expense to payers and revenue to providers and suppliers. Payers generally wish to reduce the dollars flowing into health care, while providers and suppliers want to increase those dollars. Payers want to contain costs; providers and suppliers resist cost containment. That conflict is the fundamental battle in the health care economy.

Secondary skirmishes complicate this battle. Although insurance companies are payers and try to reduce reimbursements to providers and suppliers, they want more money from purchasers. Providers and suppliers may engage in ferocious conflicts; for example, hospitals purchasing pharmaceuticals negotiate for a low price while pharmaceutical manufacturers demand a high price. Providers may face off against one another. If a physician group receives a capitation payment from an insurer, primary care physicians and specialists may fight over how much of the capitation check goes to each group.

Health care costs represent a battleground among competing interests (Figures 8.2.1 and 8.2.2).

VARYING PERSPECTIVES ON HEALTH CARE COSTS

The literature—scientific, commercial, and popular—on health care costs contains a variety of perspectives on why costs are high and how to control their growth.

Perspective 1: Costs Are Not a Serious Problem

Some articles have argued that high and rising health expenditures present some difficulties but are not a serious problem. Organizations and individuals touched by the reality of costly health care do not share this opinion. Most employers, for whom the purchase of employee

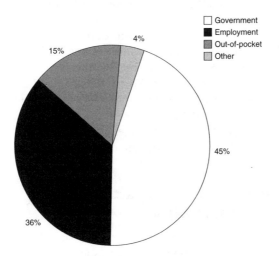

FIGURE 8.2.1   Where the Health Care Dollar Comes from, 2002

Adapted from Levit et al. (2) Copyright 2004. Project HOPE–The People-to-People Health Foundation, Inc.

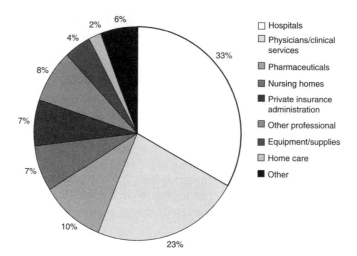

FIGURE 8.2.2　Where the Health Care Dollar Goes, 2002

Adapted from Levit et al. (2) Copyright 2004. Project HOPE–The People-to-People Health Foundation, Inc.

health insurance is an expense rather than a revenue, are anxious to reduce insurance premiums.[6] If premiums were lower, employers could augment employee wages, reduce consumer prices, or increase profits.[7] Expanding government health expenditures create budget deficits and crowd out spending for education, police, fire, and other services.[7] Rising costs increase the number of uninsured people through 3 mechanisms: Employers stop offering insurance to their employees,[6,8,9] employees decline employer-offered health insurance because they cannot afford the employee share of the premium,[10] and people are dropped from Medicaid as state governments respond to increased costs with eligibility reductions.[11] For the large proportion of the population that is uninsured or underinsured, higher costs make physician visits, preventive services, and prescription drugs less affordable, particularly for poor persons, elderly patients, and those in ill health.[12-14] When costs rise and governments reduce reimbursements, institutions serving as the safety net for the uninsured may close their doors.[15] These effects of rising costs demonstrate that increased cost often means decreased access.

In summary, while rising costs may not create major problems for the economy as a whole, they do negatively affect employers, employees, governments, and patients.

Perspective 2: High Costs Are Due to Factors External to the Health Care System

High health care costs might derive from factors outside the health sector rather than from characteristics of the health care system itself. One such external cause is the state of the overall economy. International comparisons of health spending consistently show that the level of health expenditures per capita is closely associated with total GDP per capita. In other words, richer nations spend more per capita on health care than poorer nations.[16]

Although no one disputes this association, one key fact stands out: The United States is a striking outlier. For example, the U.S. GDP per capita is 150% that of Sweden, but U.S. health spending per capita is 240% that of Sweden.[16] The same relationship is found between the United States and almost all other developed nations.[17] The U.S. outlier status suggests that high and rising costs in the United States cannot be explained simply by invoking GDP per capita.

Another possible external cause for rising health case costs is the aging of the populations of developed nations. Given that people older than 75 years of age incur per capita health expenditures 5 times higher than those of people age 25 to 34 years, it is logical to assume that nations with a higher proportion of elderly people would have higher per capita health expenditures than nations with younger age distributions.

Research, however, consistently shows that this demographic trend explains only 6% to 7% of health expenditure growth.[18-19] A cross-national regression analysis of the effects of aging on health spending found no significant relationship between the percentage of elderly persons in a nation's population and national health spending.[16,18]

Perspective 3: The Absence of a Free Market Creates High and Rising Costs

Some policy experts argue that costs could be reduced by introducing an unfettered free market in health care.[20,21]

At the level of patients seeking physician and hospital services, a free market means that patients, responsible for some or all of their costs, have sufficient information on the costs of different providers and seek low-priced physicians and hospitals. Physicians and hospitals would lower their fees to attract patients. In reality, patients do not purchase physician and hospital services in a free market, as shown by the following:

1. Patients cannot compare the cost of medical services because different health conditions lead to widely differing costs. A patient with a headache does not know whether the cost of care will be a $50 physician visit plus a bottle of aspirin or $60,000 neurosurgery for a brain neoplasm.
2. Because most health care is a necessity rather than a luxury, private and government insurance has evolved to shield patients from the financial disaster of serious illness, obviating the need for patients to shop for lower-cost services.
3. A free market might lead to patients becoming more cost conscious, but low-income and sick people who are responsible for all or part of their health care costs may incur unaffordable expenditures and be priced out of receiving needed services.

At the level of health insurance plans choosing which hospitals their enrollees could use, a free market requires that a sufficient number of hospitals, competing on the basis of price, exists in each geographic region.

In reality, these transactions do not take place in competitive free markets. Hospitals and insurance plans have consolidated in most geographic regions,[22] and entry of new hospitals or health plans into a market is difficult, thereby undermining the price competition that is a necessary component of a free market.

Cost-containment strategies based on the free market perspective include increased patient cost sharing and competition among health care providers and insurers.

Patient Cost Sharing

An influential school of thought advocates that consumers should be responsible for a greater share of their health care costs. Employers are requiring employees to pay more for health insurance premiums, deductibles, and copayments.[8] A deductible is the sum of money patients must pay to physicians or hospitals each year before the insurance company begins to pay for those services. A copayment is a small fee (often $5 or $10) that patients must pay for each health service received. Co-insurance is similar to a copayment but is the percentage (rather than a specific amount) of the cost of a service that the patient is responsible to pay. Taking the place of health maintenance organization (HMO) plans with no deductible and minimal copayments are products with $2500 deductibles and 25% co-insurance. Medical savings account plans may have deductibles reaching $10,000.[23]

Advocates of the patient cost-sharing strategy cite as evidence the 1970s RAND Health Insurance Experiment, which compared health expenditures of patients receiving free care with those of similar patients paying for 25%, 50%, or 95% of their care out-of-pocket. Cost-sharing patients had an upper limit on their costs. The study found that patients receiving free care utilized more services and had higher expenditures than cost-sharing patients.[24]

The effectiveness of patient cost sharing as a cost control mechanism has been challenged by other analysts[22] and by the RAND investigators themselves.[24,25] From 1950 to 1984, the spread of health insurance coverage (that is, the reduction in patient responsibility for health care costs) explains only 5% to 10% of spending growth.[19,24] Moreover, the United States has one of the highest levels of patient cost sharing among developed nations yet has the highest expenditures per capita.

Another fact buttresses the argument that patient cost sharing is marginally effective in containing costs: Seventy percent of health care expenditures are incurred by 10% of the population.[26] It is likely that patients in the high-cost 10% (that is, those who suffer an acute catastrophe or prolonged chronic illness) are far too sick to impose limits on their care because they must pay for part of that care. Thus, 70% of health expenditures may be unaffected by shifting costs to patients.

Competition

Controlling costs through free-market competition is an idea gaining currency in the United States. The barriers to a free market (discussed earlier in this section) make competition almost impossible at the level of patients paying out-of-pocket for medical services. However, competition is a realistic option for health insurance plans contracting with hospitals and purchasers choosing health plans.

Health Plans Contracting with Providers

Before the 1980s, hospitals competed for patients by competing for admitting physicians. To attract physicians, many hospitals constructed state-of-the-art radiology and surgical facilities. As a result of this "medical arms race," an oversupply of facilities existed in many metropolitan areas. This form of competition caused costs to rise rather than fall.[27] This situation reversed as health insurance plans—which formerly paid any hospital that cared for its enrollees—began to contract selectively with hospitals agreeing to lower prices. Hospitals became less concerned with competing for physicians and more concerned with competing for patients by contracting with insurance plans.

In response to insurers' success in cutting payments to hospitals that were competing for insurance contracts, the hospital industry consolidated, reducing the number of hospital entities and thereby reducing the amount of competition. From 1995 to 2000, the proportion of private hospitals in multihospital systems increased markedly; in some areas, 60% to 80% of acute private admissions went to hospitals in multihospital systems.[28] Insurers could no longer force hospitals to accept low reimbursement rates because insurers needed contracts with the 2 or 3 hospital systems in each geographic market to guarantee accessible medical services to their enrollees.[29]

Market power is the ability of a seller to raise prices without losing customers.[30] Hospitals have market power if they can raise rates without losing insurance contracts. As hospitals consolidated and competition waned, hospitals gained market power and prices of hospital care shot back up.[31-32] In 1 study, the merger of 2 competing hospitals led to price increases of 20% to 40%.[33]

To summarize, there is a fundamental difference between the pre- and postselective contracting eras. In the former era, hospital competition led to higher costs; in the latter, competition has been associated with lower costs and lower hospital revenues, leading hospitals to respond in an anticompetitive manner through consolidation.

Purchasers Choosing Health Plans

Competition can also take place in the market of purchasers—employers or government—buying health insurance. An example is provided by the experience of Medicare HMOs, which are insurance plans that accept a fixed payment from Medicare for enrolled Medicare beneficiaries. Medicare hoped that a system in which HMOs competed to enroll Medicare beneficiaries would reduce costs. The result was the opposite: Costs went up for the Medicare program. To reduce their own costs, Medicare HMOs attracted healthier beneficiaries; HMOs had only half of fee-for-service Medicare's proportion of people in poor health.[34] Medicare was paying several thousand dollars a year per patient for the 58% of HMO patients in good health,[34] patients who would cost few dollars under traditional Medicare. As a result, Medicare paid HMOs between 13% and 21% more per beneficiary than traditional Medicare.[35] This particular form of competition was not successful as a cost reduction measure.

Another variety of competition in the insurer market is "managed competition." Employers would provide employees a set amount of money for health insurance, perhaps $400 per month for a family. If the employee elected a health plan costing $600 per month, the employee would pay the extra $200 per month.

Managed competition was never implemented because the consolidation of health insurance plans and hospitals undermined the potential for competition. In all but 14 states, 3 insurers control over 65% of the market; their market clout enables them to negotiate high premiums from employers with scant risk for losing customers.[22] Higher concentrations of market share among a few HMOs are associated with higher HMO profits.[36] Because managed competition has never been implemented, it is not known whether it can control costs.[37]

In summary, competition can reduce health care costs under favorable conditions. These conditions existed for a brief period in the 1990s. With many competing health insurance plans, employers were able to reduce insurance premium growth; as long as there was a multiplicity of competing hospitals, health plans could control payments to hospitals. The consolidation of health plans and hospitals may have put an end to that brief competitive era.

CONCLUSION

In seeking an explanation for high and rising health expenditures, the economics and health policy literature offers several perspectives. The aging of the population is not an adequate explanation, nor is the post-1950s' spread of health insurance, which reduced patients' responsibility for the costs of care. The lack of well-developed competitive markets in health care may be partially responsible for high health expenditures.

REFERENCES

1. Organization for Economic Cooperation and Development (OECD). Health Data 2004. Accessed at www.oecd.org on 15 November 2004.

2. Levit K, Smith C, Cowan C, Sensenig A, Catlin A. Health spending rebound continues in 2002. *Health Aff* (Millwood). 2004;23:147–59.

3. Smith C, Cowan C, Sensenig A, Catlin A. Health spending growth slows in 2003. *Health Aff* (Millwood). 2005;24:185–94. [PMID: 15644387].

4. Heffler S, Smith S, Keehan S, Clemens MK, Zezza M, Truffer C. Health spending projections through 2013. *Health Aff* (Milwood). Web Exclusive. 11 February 2004. 10.1377/hlthaff.w4.79 Accessed at http://content.healthaffairs.org/cgi/content/full/hlthaff.w4.79vl/DC1 on 25 March 2005.

5. Bodenheimer T, Grumbach K. Conflict and change in US health care. In: *Understanding Health Policy: A Clinical Approach*. New York: McGraw-Hill; 2005:167–75.

6. Gabel J, Levitt L, Holve E, Pickreign J, Whitmore H, Dhont K, et al. Job-based health benefits in 2002: some important trends. *Health Aff* (Millwood). 2002;21:143–51.

7. Davis K, Anderson GF, Rowland D, Steinberg EP. *Health Care Cost Containment*. Baltimore: Johns Hopkins Univ Pr; 1990.

8. Gabel J, Claxton G, Holve E, Pickreign J, Whitmore H, Dhont K, et al. Health benefits in 2003: premiums reach thirteen-year high as employers adopt new forms of cost sharing. *Health Aff* (Millwood). 2003;22:117–26. [PMID: 14515887].

9. Gabel J, Claxton G, Gil I, Pickreign J, Whitmore H, Holve E, et al. Health benefits in 2004: four years of double-digit premium increases take their toll on coverage: five million fewer jobs provided health insurance in 2004 than in 2001, this new analysis finds. *Health Aff* (Millwood). 2004;23:200–9. [PMID: 15371386].

10. Gabel JR. Job-based health insurance, 1977–1998: the accidental system under scrutiny. *Health Aff* (Millwood). 1999;18:62–74. [PMID: 10650689].

11. Kaiser Commission on Medicaid and the Uninsured. *Medicaid Enrollment in 50 States*. Menlo Park, CA: Kaiser Family Foundation; December 2002. Accessed at www.kff.org on 6 December 2004.

12. Ayanjan JZ, Weissman JS, Schneider EC, Ginsburg JA, Zaslavsky AM. Unmet health needs of uninsured adults in the United States. *JAMA*. 2000;284:2061–9. [PMID: 11042754].

13. Blustein J. Drug coverage and drug purchases by Medicare beneficiaries with hypertension. *Health Aff* (Millwood). 2000;19:219–30. [PMID: 10718036].

14. Federman AD, Adams AS, Ross-Degnan D, Soumerai SB, Ayanian JZ. Supplemental insurance and use of effective cardiovascular drugs among elderly Medicare beneficiaries with coronary heart disease. *JAMA*. 2001;286:1732–9. [PMID: 15002637].

15. Instirune of Medicine. *America's Health Care Safety Net: Intact but Endangered*. Washington, DC: National Academies Pr; 2000.

16. Organization for Economic Cooperation and Development (OECD). *A Disease-based Comparison of Health Systems: What Is Best and at What Cost?* Paris: OECD; 2003. Accessed at www.oecd.org on 6 December 2004.

17. Reinhardt UE, Hussey PS, Anderson GF. Cross-national comparisons of health systems using OECD data. 1999. *Health Aff* (Millwood). 2002;21:169–81. [PMID: 12025981].

18. Reinhardt UE. Does the aging of the population really drive the demand for health care? *Health Aff* (Millwood). 2003;22:27–39. [PMID: 14649430].

19. Newhouse JP. An iconoclastic view of health cost containment. *Health Aff* (Millwood). 1993;12 Suppl:152–71. [PMID: 8477929].

20. Enthoven AC. Employment-based health insurance is failing: now what? *Health Aff* (Millwood). Web Exclusive. 28 May 2003. 10.1377/hlthaff.w3.237. Accessed at http://content.healthaffairs.org/cgi/content/full/hlthaff.w3.237vl1/CD1 on 25 March 2005.

21. Liebowitz S. *Why Health Care Costs Too Much*. Cato Policy Analysis No. 211. Washington, DC: Cato Institute; 23 June 1994. Accessed at www.cato.org/pub_display.php?pub_id=1070 on 15 January 2004.

22. Robinson JC. Consolidation and the transformation of competition in health insurance. *Health Aff* (Millwood). 2004;23:11–24. [PMID: 1584099].

23. Robinson JC. Renewed emphasis on consumer cost sharing in health insurance benefit design. *Health Aff* (Millwood). Web Exclusive. 20 March 2002. 10.1377/hlthaff.w2.139. Accessed at http://content.healthaffairs.org/cgi/content/ fullhlthaff.w2.139v1/DC1 on 25 March 2005.

24. Manning WG, Newhouse JP, Duan N, Keller EB, Leibowitz A, Marquis MS. Health insurance and the demand for medical care: evidence from a randomized experiment. *Am Econ Rev*. 1989;77:251–77. [PMID: 10284091].

25. Rice T. Who gets what and how much? In: Ginzberg E, ed. *Critical Issues in U.S. Health Reform*. Boulder, CO: Westview Pr; 1994:57–72.

26. Berk MI, Monheit AC. The concentraion of health care expenditures, revisited. *Health Aff* (Millwood). 2001;20:9–18. [PMID: 11260963].

27. Devers KJ, Brewster LR, Casalino LP. Changes in hospital competitive strategy: a new medical arms race? *Health Serv Res*. 2003;38:447–69. [PMID: 12650375].

28. Cuellar AE, Gertler PJ. Trends in hospital consolidation: the formation of loal systems. *Health Aff* (Millwood). 2003;22:77–87. [PMID: 1469434].

29. Devers KJ, Casalino LP, Rudell LS, Stoddard JJ, Brewster LR, Lake TK. Hospitals' negotiating leverage with health plans: how and why has it changed? *Health Serv Res*. 2003;38:419–46. [PMID: 12650374].

30. Ginsburg PB. Can hospitals and physicians shift the effects of cuts in Medicare reimbursement to private payers? *Health Aff* (Millwood). Web Exclusive. 8 October 2003. 10.1377/hylthaff.w3.472. Accessed at http://content.healthaffairs.org/cgi content/full/hlthaff.w3.472v1/DC1 on 25 March 2005.

31. Town R, Vistnes G. Hospital competition in HMO networks. *J Health Econ*. 2001;20:733–53. [PMID: 11558646].

32. Krishnan R. Market restructuring and pricing in the hospital industry. *J Health Econ*. 2001;20:213–37. [PMID: 11252371].

33. Goetghebeur MM, Forrest S, Hay JW. Understanding the underlying drivers of inpatient cost growth: a literature review. *Am J Manag Care*. 2003;9 Spec No 1:SP3–12. [PMID: 12817611].

34. *Current Medicare Current Beneficiary Survey, 2000*. Washington, DC: Center for Medicare & Medicaid Services; 2001. Accessed at www.cms.hhs.gov/MCBS/PubCNP00.asp on 7 December 2004.

35. Berenson RA. Mediare + Choice; doubling or disappearing? *Health Aff* (Millwood). Web Exclusive. 28 November 2001. 10.1377/hlthaff.w1.65. Accessed at http://content.healthaffairs.org/cgi/content/full/hlthaff.w1.65v1/DC1 on 25 March 2005.

36. Pauly MV, Hillman AL, Kim MS, Brown DR. Competitive behavior in the HMO marketplace. *Health Aff* (Millwood). 2002;21:194–202. [PMID: 11900077].

37. Luft HS, Grumbach K. Global budgets and the competitive market. In: Ginzberg E, ed. *Critical Issues in U.S. Health Reform*. Boulder, CO: Westview Pr; 1994:303–22.

High and Rising Health Care Costs.
Part 3: The Role of Health Care Providers

Thomas Bodenheimer, MD

PROVIDER MARKET POWER EXPLAINS HIGH AND RISING COSTS

Market power is the degree of influence that an organization has over another organization.[1] In economic terms, it is the ability of a seller to raise prices without losing business.[2] Take the common example of health insurance plans buying hospital services: If the hospital (the seller) can negotiate a contract with the insurer that gives the hospital the reimbursement (price) it wants, the hospital has market power. If the insurer can prevent the hospital from raising its price by refusing to sign a contract with the hospital (causing the hospital to lose the patients enrolled in that insurance plan), the insurer has market power.

Some observers believe that provider market power explains much of the outlier status of U.S. health expenditures compared with those of other nations.[3-5] According to this view, when payers have market power, costs rise more slowly; when providers or suppliers wield market clout, costs increase more rapidly. When health insurance developed in Canada, the market power of the sole payers of health services—provincial governments—enabled those payers to restrict prices paid to hospitals and physicians. In contrast, the U.S. health insurance industry was initially dominated by Blue Cross and Blue Shield, institutions that were controlled by hospitals and physicians. This uncontested provider market power allowed lucrative reimbursement formulas for hospitals and physicians. These formulas were replicated in Medicare as a result of the influence of Blue Cross, Blue Shield, the American Hospital Association, and the American Medical Association over the writing of Medicare regulations.[3-5] In addition, the pharmaceutical industry has deterred most governmental regulation of drug prices by using its influence over legislators.[6] The result of the historical domination of providers and suppliers over payers has been a price structure far different from that of health care in most developed nations.

Provider market power can be curbed in 2 ways: by the countervailing power of purchasers and payers (governmental and private) and by governmental regulation. Regulation of hospital and physician prices began to appear in the 1980s; the countervailing power of purchasers and payers grew in the late 1980s and early to mid-1990s, but then

Adapted from: Thomas Bodenheimer. (2005). High and rising health care costs. Part 3: The role of health care providers. *Annals of International Medicine, 142,* 996–1002.

waned. However, the prices of health services preceding those developments were already high relative to prices in other nations, and this historical gap has persisted.

Prices of Services

One important difference between costs of care in the United States and those in other developed nations is the price per unit of care—physician fees, payments per hospital day, and pharmaceutical prices.[7,8] Even though the United States does not provide a greater quantity of physician visits per capita than other nations, physician income is 3 times higher in the United States than in the average nation that belongs to the Organisation for Economic Co-operation and Development.

Each acute inpatient hospital day in the United States costs more than double that in Canada and almost 3 times the median of that in nations in the Organisation for Economic Co-operation and Development.[8] Inpatients in the United States also receive more intensive treatment (quantity) per bed-day than do inpatients in other nations. What appears to be a price differential is in fact a mix of price and quantity differences.

Many pharmaceutical products improve quality and prevent costly complications of chronic illness. However, the costs of these products has been increasing at a rapid pace—more than 15% each year from 1998 to 2002.[9] Comparing a similar "market basket" of medications, Canadian and French prices are about 60% and German and United Kingdom prices are about 85% of those in the United States. Differences are wider for brand-name than for generic produces. Nations whose governments control pharmaceutical prices have reduced prices compared with the United States.[10]

Price Controls

Controlling prices has been an effective mechanism of cost containment, particularly in nations other than the United States. Two experiments with governmental price controls have taken place in the United States. In the 1970s, President Nixon responded to inflation in the economy by instituting general price controls. Hospitals were not allowed to raise prices, and hospital costs slowed markedly. When the program ended, hospital costs shot back up. In the 1970s, 4 states (Maryland, Massachusetts, New Jersey, and New York) legislated mandatory hospital rate setting, thereby limiting growth in hospital charges. The programs applied to all payers, so that hospitals could not shift costs from 1 payer to another. These states created savings of 10% to 15%, with hospital cost growth 3% less than that in states without such programs.[3,11] Over time, as political forces weakened the legislation, the power of the regulators gradually eroded and hospital prices again increased.

In the 1990s, price controls on physician fees and hospital payments were administered by private insurers and by the government through Medicare. These controls were a major factor in slowing health expenditure growth. When the market power of insurance plans eroded because of hospital consolidation, hospital prices increased again.[12,13] Physicians, particularly in primary care, have not achieved economic clout because they have seldom consolidated into strong organizations; they therefore continue to feel the impact of reduced prices for their services.

For physician services, the effect of price reductions are partially offset by increases in the quantity of services provided.[14] For every 1% reduction in Medicare physician fees, the volume of physician services increases by 0.56%.[15] If Medicare cuts the fee for coronary artery bypass surgery, thoracic surgeons recoup about 70% of their revenue loss by increasing the volume of surgeries for both Medicare and private patients.[14]

Quantity of Services

Nations that have more physicians and hospital beds or deliver higher quantities of physician visits and hospital days per capita might be expected to have higher health expenditures. The United States has fewer physicians, hospital beds, and acute care hospital bed days per capita than the median country in the Organisation for Economic Co-operation and Development.[8] But the United States has a higher ratio of specialist to primary care physicians,[16] and it is specialists who perform high-cost innovative procedures.[17]

Why does the United States have a lower supply of providers but higher costs? There are at least 3 reasons. First, nations in which a greater proportion of physicians practice primary care medicine tend to have lower per capita health expenditures than does the United States, in which a greater proportion of physicians practice specialty care.[16] Second, the price of hospital care is far higher in the United States than in other nations. Finally, even though the United States has fewer physician visits and hospital beds than do other nations, it has a greater supply of expensive new technologies and uses them more intensively.[18]

Another influence on the quantity of services is the method of physician payment, which is predominantly fee-for-service in the United States. Economists debate whether fee-for-service physicians generate more visits, diagnostic procedures, or surgeries to increase their incomes, known as supplier-induced demand.[19] Regardless of whether one calls it supplier-induced demand or physician beliefs about how intensively to treat patients,[20] the groundbreaking research of Wennberg and Cooper[21] and Fisher and colleagues[22] uncovered large variations in the quantity of care delivered to Medicare patients between 1 geographic area and another.

Reimbursment
Presentin

Quantity Controls

Strategies to reduce the quantity of care include utilization management, limitation of the supply of resources, and shifting of financial risk to providers so that providers will benefit by delivering fewer rather than more services.

Utilization Management

In contrast to strategies to increase patient responsibility for costs, which try to reduce the quantity of services by influencing patient behavior, utilization management seeks to influence physician behavior. In the 1980s and 1990s, insurance plans denied payment for what they considered to be inappropriate services. These utilization management programs showed some cost savings[23] but angered physicians. Studies found that reviewers for the same case differed in their care decisions.[24,25]

Supply Limits

Supply limits are controls on the number of physicians or the quantity of health facilities, such as hospital beds or MRI scanners. The research showing that the quantity of services is associated with the supply of resources suggests that supply limits could be effective in reducing quantities of health care. In the 1970s, Certificate of Need programs required hospitals to ask permission to invest in more beds and expensive equipment.[3] The program failed, perhaps because the boards making the decisions were not at risk for increased costs and had strong hospital representation. In contrast, Canadian governments are at risk for increased spending, and they have controlled medical facility spread.[11] Supply limits are an alternative to utilization management as a quantity-limiting strategy. Metaphorically speaking, utilization management puts reins on physicians, whereas supply limits are akin to building a fence around the entire medical commons.[26] If an excess of MRI scanners exist, utilization management would reduce the quantity of MRI scans by requiring preauthorization of scans. A constrained supply of MRI scanners keeps the quantity of scans in check through a limited number of MRI appointments.

Shifting of Risk to Providers

Under the fee-for-service system, the predominant method of provider payment in the United States, payers are at financial risk (that is, they pay out more money when more services are provided), and providers earn more money by providing more services. Changing the method of provider payment can shift the risk from payers to providers. Capitation payment shifts the risk from payers to providers: Payers spend a fixed amount of money regardless of how many services are delivered, whereas providers do not receive additional money, but spend additional time, when they deliver more services. Capitation payment is a quantity control. Diagnosis-related-group payment to hospitals also shifts risk to providers and discourages them from providing a greater quantity of services. Shifting risk to providers, therefore, is a strategy used by payers to recruit providers to their cost-control agenda. Because money flowing into the health sector through fee-for-service reimbursement produces more medical care and higher provider incomes, providers paid by fee-for-service are generally opposed to cost control. Payment that places the provider at risk for increased costs may turn cost-increasing providers into cost-controlling providers.

SUMMARY

The strong historical influence of provider interests on the structure of public and private health insurance in the United States created lucrative reimbursement formulas for hospitals and physicians. As a result, hospitals and physicians in the United States were able to obtain considerably higher prices for their services than did providers of similar services in other nations.[7,8] Moreover, even though the quantities of physician visits and hospital days per capita have been lower in the United States than the average developed nation,[8] the use of expensive technologies—which is also influenced by provider market power—is higher in the United States.[7,8] Thus, according to this perspective on health care costs, the gap between health expenditures in the United States and those in other nations is explained by the higher prices of all services and the greater quantities of high-technology services in the United States. Measures to control both the prices and quantities of services have been only partially and temporarily effective.

What Strategies Are Available to Control the Growth of Health Expenditures?

Making patients responsible for the costs of their care can reduce expenditures for patients with low levels of expenditures; however, there is no convincing evidence that patient cost-sharing reduces expenditures for the 10% of the population that incurs 70% of health care costs. During the early 1990s, competition showed some promise of reducing costs for purchasers seeking health insurance and for health insurers contracting with hospitals. However, consolidation of health plans and hospitals thwarted efforts to develop markets in which competition could occur. The absence of a competitive free market for health care services reflects the market power of providers.

Because technologic innovation in the environment of strong provider market power is associated with increasing expenditures, cost-containment efforts directed at these 2 factors may hold promise for slowing health expenditure growth. An example would be technology assessment programs that set standards of appropriate care, which are in turn linked to a system of provider payment that reimburses diagnostic testing and medical procedures only if they have been used appropriately.

Global budgeting and strict expenditures caps—a strategy to limit the total amount of money that flows into the health care economy—are potentially the strongest cost-control measures. Whether such a strategy can (or should) withstand the imperative for technologic innovation is doubtful. Although most medical advances diffuse more rapidly in the United States than in nations with expenditure limits, per capita use of new technologies in other nations is catching up to U.S. rates.

REFERENCES

1. Scott WR. *Organizations, Rational, Natural, and Open Systems.* Englewood Cliffs, NJ: Prentice-Hall; 1987.

2. Ginsburg PB. Can hospitals and physicians shift the effects of cuts in Medicare reimbursement to private payers? *Health Affairs.* Web Exclusive. 8 October 2003. Accessed at http://content.healthaffairs.org/cgi/content/full/hlthaff.w3.472v1/DC1 on 2 Demcember 2004.

3. Davis K, Anderson GF, Rowland D, Steinberg EP. *Health Care Cost Containment.* Baltimore: Johns Hopkins Univ Pr; 1990.

4. Aaron HJ. *Serious and Unstable Condition.* Washington DC: The Brookings Institution; 1991.

5. Starr P. *The Social Transformation of American Medicine*. New York: Basic Books; 1982.

6. Angell M. *The Truth About the Drug Companies: How They Deceive Us and What to Do About It*. New York: Random House; 2004:196–205.

7. Organisation for Economic Co-operation and Development. *A Disease-based Comparison of Health Systems*. Paris: OECD; 2003. Accessed at www.oecd.org on 7 December 2004.

8. Reinhardt UE, Hussey PS, Anderson GF. Cross-national comparisons of health systems using OECD data, 1999. *Health Aff* (Millwood). 2002;21:169–81. [PMID: 12025981].

9. Levit K, Smith C, Cowan C, Sensenig A, Catlin A; Health Accounts Team. Health spending rebound continues in 2002. *Health Aff* (Millwood). 2004;23:147–59. [PMID: 15002637].

10. Danzon PM, Furukawa MF. Prices and availability of pharmaceuticals: evidence from nine countries. *Health Affairs*. Web Exclusive. 29 October 2003. Accessed at http://content.healthaffairs.org/cgi/content/full/hlthaff.w3.521v1/DC1 on 2 December 2004.

11. Rice TH. Containing health care costs. In: Andersen RM, Rice TH, Kominski GF, eds. *Changing the U.S. Health Care System*. San Franciso: Jossey-Bass; 1996:81–100.

12. Devers KJ, Casalino LP, Rudell LS, Stoddard JJ, Brewster LR, Lake TK. Hospitals' negotiating leverage with health plans: how and why has it changed? *Health Serv Res*. 2003;38:419–46. [PMID: 12650374].

13. Melnick G, Keller E, Zwanziger J. Market power and hospital pricing: are nonprofits different? *Health Aff* (Millwood). 1999;18:167–73. [PMID: 10388213].

14. Yip WC. Physician response to Medicare fee reductions: changes in the volume of coronary artery bypass graft (CABG) surgeries in the Medicare and private sectors. *J Health Econ*. 1998;17:675–99. [PMID: 10339248].

15. Christensen S. Volume repsonses to esogenous changes in Medicare's payment policies. *Health Serv Res*. 1992;27:67–79. [PMID: 1563954].

16. Starfield B. *Primary Care*. New York: Oxford Univ Pr; 1998.

17. Gelijns A, Rosenberg N. The dynamics of technological change in medicine. *Health Aff* (Millwood). 1994;13:28–46. [PMID: 7927160].

18. Bodenheimer T. High and rising health care costs. Part 2: technologic innovation. *Ann Intern Med*. 2005;142:932–7.

19. Phelps CE. *Health Economics*. Boston: Addison Wesley; 2003.

20. Skinner J, Wennberg JE. Perspective: exceptionalism or extravagance? What's different about health care in South Florida? *Health Affairs*. Web Exclusive. 13 August 2003. Accessed at http://content.healthaffairs.org/cgi/content/full/hlthaff.w3.372v1/DC1 on 2 December 2004.

21. Wennberg JE, Cooper MM. *The Dartmouth Atlas on Health Care*. Chicago: American Hosp Publishing; 1999.

22. Fisher ES, Wennberg DE, Stukel TA, Gottlieb DJ, Lucas FL, Pinder EL. The implications of regional variations in Medicare spending. Part 1: the content quality, and accessibility of care. *Ann Intern Med*. 2003;138:273–87. [PMID: 12585825].

23. Wickizer TM. The effect of utilization review on hospital use and expenditures: a review of the literature and an update on recent findings. *Med Care Rev*. 1990;47:327–63. [PMID: 10113408].

24. Dippe SE, Bell MM, Wells MA, Lyons W, Clester S. A peer review of a peer review organization. *West J Med*. 1989;151:93–6. [PMID: 2669350].

25. Light DW. Life, death, and the insurance companies [Editorial]. *N Engl J Med*. 1994;330:498–500. [PMID: 8289857].

26. Grumbach K, Bodenheimer T. Reins or fences: a physician's view of cost containment. *Health Aff* (Millwood). 1990;9:120–6. [PMID: 2289748].

Employer Health Benefits: 2006 Summary of Findings

The Kaiser Family Foundation

Between spring of 2005 and spring of 2006, premiums for employer-sponsored health insurance rose by 7.7%, a slower rare than the 9.2% increase in 2005 and 11.2% increase in 2004 (Figure 8.4.1).[1] Despite this slowdown, premiums continued to increase much faster than overall inflation (3.5%) and wage gains (3.8%). Premiums for family coverage have increased by 87% since the year 2000.

Although the average premium increase for 2006 is 7.7%, many covered workers are in firms that experienced premium changes that were substantially above or below the average: 42% of covered workers work for firms where premiums increased by 5% or less, while 13% of covered workers work for firms where premiums increased by more than 15%. Premiums in fully insured plans grew more quickly than premium equivalents in self-funded plans (8.7% versus 6.8%). Average annual premiums for employer-sponsored coverage are $4,242 for single coverage and $11,480 for family coverage.

Preferred provider organizations (PPOs) continue to cover a majority of workers (60%), with health maintenance organizations (HMOs) covering 20%, point of service (POS) plans covering 13%, high deductible health plans associated with a savings option (HDHP/SOs) covering 4%, and conventional plans covering 3%. PPO market share remains high despite the fact that premiums for PPOs are higher on average than premiums for HMOs, POS plans, and HDHP/SOs for both single and family coverage. Premiums for HDHP/SOs are lower than all other plan types for both single and family coverage.

Over 75% of covered workers with single coverage and over 90% of covered workers with family coverage make a contribution toward the total premium for their coverage. Workers on average contribute $627 annually toward the cost of single coverage and $2,973 annually toward the cost of family coverage. Since 2000, annual worker contributions have increased by $293 for single coverage and by $1,354 for family coverage. Covered workers in small firms (3–199 workers) on average make a significantly higher annual contribution toward single and family coverage than covered workers in larger firms (single: $515 vs. $689, family: $3,550 vs. $2,658). The average percentage of premiums paid by workers is statistically unchanged over the last several years, at 16% for single coverage and 27% for family coverage.

Adapted from: The Kaiser Family Foundation. (2006). *Employer health benefits: 2006 summary of findings*. Menlo Park, CA: The Kaiser Family Foundation.

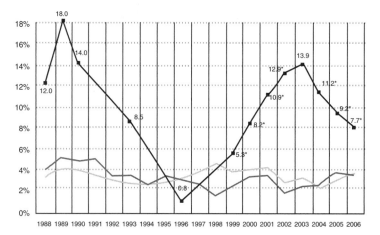

**Percentage Increase in Health Insurance Premiums
Compared to Other Indicators, 1988–2006**

1988	1989	1990	1993	1996	1999	2000	2001	2002	2003	2004	2005	2006	
12.0	18.0	14.0	8.5	0.8	5.3*	8.2*	10.9*	12.9*	13.9	11.2*	9.2*	7.7*	HEALTH INSURANCE PREMIUMS
3.9	5.1	4.7	3.2	2.9	2.3	3.1	3.3	1.6	2.2	2.3	3.5	3.5	OVERALL INFLATION
3.1	4.2	3.9	2.5	3.3	3.6	3.9	4.0	2.6	3.0	2.1	2.7	3.8	WORKERS' EARNINGS‡

*Estimate is statistically different from the estimate for the previous year shown at p < .05. No statistical tests are conducted for years prior to 1999.

‡Data on premium increase in workers' earnings are seasonally adjusted data from the Current Employment Statistics survey (April to April). For additional information about this data, see the Survey Design and Methods section in the full report.

Note: Data on premium increases reflect the cost of health insurance premiums for a family of four.

Source: Kaiser/HRET Survey of Employer-Sponsored Health Benefits, 1999–2006; KPMG Survey of Employer-Sponsored Health Benefits, 1993, 1996; The Health Insurance Association of America (HIAA), 1988, 1989, 1990; Bureau of Labor Statistics, Consumer Price Index, U.S. City Average Inflation (April to April), 1988–2006; Seasonally Adjusted Data from the Current Employment Statistics Survey (April to April), 1988–2006.

FIGURE 8.4.1   A Problem-Centered Public Policy-Making Process Model

Source: Kaiser/HRET Survey of Employer-Sponsored Health Benefits, 1999–2006; KPMG Survey of Employer-Sponsored Health Benefits, 1993, 1996; The Health Insurance Association of America (HIAA), 1998, 1989, 1990; Bureau of Labor Statistics, Consumer Price Index, U.S. City Average Inflation (April to April), 1988–2006; Bureau of Labor Statistics, Seasonally Adjusted Data from the Current Employment Statistics Survey (April to April), 1988–2006.

EMPLOYEE COST SHARING

In addition to their premium contributions, most covered workers make additional payments when they use health care services. Sixty-nine percent of covered workers with single coverage in PPOs are in a plan with a general plan deductible that must be met before many plan benefits are provided; this compares to 32% of covered workers in POS plans and only 12% of covered workers in HMOs.[2] Even workers in plans without a general plan deductible, however, may face a specific deductible, copayment, or other charge when they use hospital services or have an outpatient procedure.

For workers in plans with a general plan deductible, the average annual deductibles for single coverage are $352 for workers enrolled in HMOs, $473 for workers enrolled in PPOs, $553 for workers enrolled in POS plans, and $1,715 for workers enrolled in HDHP/SOs. Average deductibles for covered workers with single coverage in small firms (3–199 workers) are substantially higher than average deductibles in large firms (200 or more workers) for covered workers in PPOs, POS plans, and HDHP/SOs.[3]

About half of covered workers face cost sharing that is in addition to any general annual plan deductible when they are admitted to a hospital or have outpatient surgery. For hospitalizations, 25% of covered workers face a separate deductible or copayment for each hospital admission, with an average payment of $231, and 22% face separate coinsurance when they are hospitalized, with an average coinsurance rate of 17%.

The vast majority of covered workers face copayments when they go to the doctor. Among these covered workers, 60% are in plans with a copayment of $15 or $20, and an additional 15% are in a plan with a copayment of $25.

As with physician office visits, most covered workers face cost-sharing for prescription drugs. The majority of covered workers are in plans that have multi-tier cost-sharing for drugs.

AVAILABILITY OF EMPLOYER-SPONSORED COVERAGE

Sixty-one percent of firms offer health benefits to at least some of their employees, a similar percentage to last year (Figure 8.4.2). Since 2000, the percentage of firms offering health benefits has fallen from 69%. As we have seen in prior years, health benefit offer rates vary considerably by firm size, with only 48% of the smallest companies (3–9 workers) offering health benefits, compared to 73% of firms with 10 to 24 workers, 87% of firms with 25 to 49 workers, and over 90% of firms with 50 or more workers.

Even when a firm offers health insurance, not all workers get covered. Some workers are not eligible to enroll as a result of waiting periods or minimum work-hour rules, and others choose not to enroll perhaps because they must pay a share of the premium or can get coverage through a spouse. Within offering firms, 78% of workers are eligible for coverage, and 82% of eligible workers take-up coverage from that employer.

DENTAL AND VISION BENEFITS

Among firms offering health benefits, 50% offer or contribute to a dental benefit and 21% offer or contribute to a vision benefit that is separate from any dental or vision coverage provided by the firm's health plan. Large firms (200 or more workers) are more likely than small firms to offer or contribute toward separate dental and vision benefits.

	2000	2003	2006
3–9 Workers	57%	55%	48%
10–24 Workers	80	76	73
25–49 Workers	91	84	87
50–199 Workers	97	95	92
All Small Firms (3–199 Workers)	68%	65%	60%
All Large Firms (200 or More Wokers)	99%	98%	98%
ALL FIRMS	69%	66%	61%

*Estimate is statistically different from the estimate for the previous year shown at p<.05.

Note: As noted in the Survey Design and Methods section of the full report, estimates presented in this exhibit are based on the sample of 3,159 firms, which includes both firms that completed the entire survey and those who answered just one question about whether they offer health benefits.

Source: Kaiser/HRET Survey of Employer-Sponsored Heath Benefits, 1999–2006.

FIGURE 8.4.2　Percentage of Firms Offering Health Benefits, by Firm Size, 2000–2006

HIGH DEDUCTIBLE HEALTH PLANS WITH SAVINGS OPTION

This year the survey includes high deductible health plans with a savings option, or HDHP/SOs, as a plan type. HDHP/SOs include (1) health plans with a deductible of at least $1,000 for single coverage and $2,000 for family coverage offered with an health reimbursement arrangement (HRA), and (2) high deductible health plans that meet the federal legal requirements to permit an enrollee to establish and contribute to an health savings account (HSA). In most instances information about HDHP/SOs is presented in the same manner as information about PPOs, HMOs, and POS plans.

Seven percent of firms offering health benefits offer an HDHP/SO in 2006. This is statistically unchanged from the 4% we reported in 2005.

RETIREE COVERAGE

The implementation of the new Medicare Part D drug benefit, combined with cutbacks in retiree coverage by several large national firms, has put a spotlight on retiree health benefits. In 2006, 35% of large firms (200 or more workers) offer retiree health coverage, virtually the same percentage as last year, but down from 66% in 1988. Among large firms offering retiree benefits, the vast majority (94%) offer benefits to early retirees, while 77% offer benefits to Medicare-age retirees.

DISEASE MANAGEMENT AND WELLNESS

Twenty-six percent of employers offering health benefits include one or more disease management programs in their largest health plan, with large firms (200 or more workers) being more likely than smaller firms to do so (55% vs. 25%).

Twenty-seven percent of employers offering health benefits offer one or more wellness programs to their employees, with 19% offering an injury prevention program, 10% offering a fitness program, 9% offering a smoking cessation program, and 6% offering a weight loss program. Large firms (200 or more workers) are more likely than small firms (3–199 workers) to offer one or more wellness programs (62% vs. 26%).

OUTLOOK FOR THE FUTURE

Although growth in health insurance premiums has moderated in each of the last three years, it continues to outpace inflation and average wage growth. Since the year 2000, health insurance premiums have grown by 87%; compared with cumulative inflation of 18% and cumulative wage growth of 20%. During this period, the percentage of employers offering health benefits has fallen from 69% to 61%, and the percentage of workers covered by their own employer also has fallen.

Despite these cost pressures, relatively few employers offering health benefits report that they are very likely or somewhat likely to drop coverage (6%) or limit eligibility (6%) in the next year, although larger percentages report that they are very or somewhat likely to increase what employees pay for coverage (49%), increase plan deductibles (39%), increase copayments or coinsurance for office visits (39%), or increase worker payments for prescription drugs (39%). There is some interest among employers in new consumer-directed plan designs. Among firms offering benefits but not currently offering an HSA qualified HDHP, 4% say that they are very likely and an additional 19% say that they are somewhat likely to offer one in the next year. Employer interest in HDHP/HRAs is comparable.

While discussions about price transparency, consumerism, and consumer-directed plan designs are common topics in health policy circles, they are mostly theoretical: the number of employers offering and the number of employees actually enrolling in consumer directed plans is quite modest. It may take several years, assuming that enrollment in these plans continues to grow, before we can assess their potential impact on the marketplace.

REFERENCES

1. Data on premium increases reflect the cost of health insurance premiums for a family of four.
2. By the way that we define the plan type, all workers in HDHP/SOs are in plans with a general plan deductible.
3. For HMO coverage, there is insufficient data to report the result.

Squeezed: Why Rising Exposure to Health Care Costs Threatens the Health and Financial Well-Being of American Families

Sara R. Collins, Jennifer L. Kriss, Karen Davis,
Michelle M. Doty, and Alyssa L. Holmgren, The Commonwealth Fund

Employer-sponsored health insurance is the main source of coverage for working adults. Recently, there has been an erosion in both the proportion of workers covered under employer plans and the adequacy of such coverage, as rising health care costs have made it increasingly difficult for employers to continue offering comprehensive coverage.

Most workers who lose access to employer health insurance have few coverage options. Many turn to the individual insurance market, where coverage is often unaffordable—and sometimes unavailable—to older adults or people with health problems. For those families who continue to have employer coverage, ever-rising deductibles and other cost-sharing are consuming larger and larger shares of family income, particularly among families with low or moderate incomes.

The consequences are serious. According to this analysis of the Commonwealth Fund Biennial Health Insurance Survey, most adults who seek to purchase insurance coverage through the individual market never end up buying a plan, finding it either very difficult or impossible to find one that met their needs or is affordable (Table 8.5.1). Compared with adults with employer coverage, adults with individual market insurance give their health plans much lower ratings, pay more out-of-pocket for their premiums, face much higher deductibles, and spend a greater percentage of their income on health insurance premiums and health care expenses. Eight percent of adults ages 19 to 64 who are privately insured all year, or 8.5 million people, are covered through the individual insurance market. Only a third (34%), however, rate their coverage as excellent or very good, compared with over half (54%) of those enrolled in employer plans.

Other key survey findings on the individual insurance market include:

- Insurance in the individual market is often impossible to obtain or unaffordable. Nearly nine of 10 people who explored obtaining coverage through the individual market never bought a plan, citing difficulties finding affordable coverage or being turned down.

Adapted from: Sara R. Collins, Jennifer L. Kriss, Karen Davis, Michelle M. Doty, and Alyssa L. Holmgren, The Commonwealth Fund. (2006). *Squeezed: Why rising exposure to health care costs threatens the health and financial well-being of American families.* New York: The Commonwealth Fund.

TABLE 8.5.1   Individual Market Is Not an Affordable Option for Many People

Adults ages 19–64 with individual coverage or who thought about or tried to buy it in past three years who:	*Total*	*Health problem*	*No health problem*	*<200% poverty*	*200%+ poverty*
Found it very difficult or impossible to find coverage they needed	34%	48%	24%	43%	29%
Found it very difficult or impossible to find affordable coverage	58	71	48	72	50
Were turned down or charged a higher price because of a pre-existing condition	21	33	12	26	18
Never bought a plan	89	92	86	93	86

Source: The Commonwealth Fund Biennial Health Insurance Survey (2005).

- More than half of adults with coverage through the individual market have annual premium costs of $3,000 or more, compared with one of five covered by employer plans.
- Two of five adults (43%) covered through the individual market spent more than 10 percent of their incomes on premiums and family out-of-pocket medical expenses, compared with one of four (24%) of those insured through employer plans.

Rising health care costs can negatively affect all privately insured Americans, not only those covered in the individual insurance market. Adults with high deductibles—including both those with individual and employer-based coverage—have higher out-of-pocket medical expenses than adults with lower deductibles, have greater problems obtaining needed care, are paying off medical debt over time, and are less satisfied overall with their health care. Families with high-deductible plans said they take on credit card debt and dip into their savings to pay bills.

Key survey findings on high-deductible health care plans include:

- Thirty-seven percent of those insured through the individual market have per-person deductibles of $1,000 or more, as do 8 percent of those insured through employer plans, for a total of 11 million people (8 million covered by employer plans and 3 million covered by individual plans).
- Individuals covered by high-deductible plans—either through the individual insurance market or an employer—have financial burdens. Of those adults with per-person deductibles of $1,000 or more, two of five (43%) spent 10 percent or more of their incomes on premiums and family out-of-pocket medical expenses, compared with one of five (22%) of those enrolled in plans with deductibles of $500 or less.
- Privately insured adults enrolled in high-deductible plans are less satisfied with coverage and care than those with lower deductibles. Forty-one percent of those with

deductibles of $1,000 or more rated their coverage as fair or poor, compared with 15 percent of those enrolled in plans with deductibles of $500 or less. In addition, those with high deductibles were less satisfied with the quality of their health care. Only 29 percent of adults with deductibles of $1,000 or more said they were very satisfied with the quality of care they had received in the past 12 months, compared with more than half (54%) of adults with deductibles under $500.

- People with higher deductibles also are more likely to have problems getting needed care than those with lower deductibles. Forty-four percent of adults with deductibles of $1,000 or more reported one of four access problems: did not fill a prescription; did not see a specialist when needed; skipped a recommended test, treatment, or follow-up; or had a medical problem but did not see a doctor. Twenty-five percent of adults with deductibles under $500 cited similar access problems.
- Medical bill problems or accumulated medical debt were reported more frequently by those with higher deductibles compared with those with lower deductibles. Two of five (41%) of those with deductibles of $1,000 or more reported a medical bill problem or outstanding debt compared with one of four (23%) of those with deductibles of less than $500.

The erosion of comprehensive employer-based coverage disproportionately affects those who are most at risk: low- and middle-income families, and those with major illnesses or injuries. A substantial percentage of adults in families with incomes under $60,000 spend considerable shares of their annual income on medical expenses. For insurance to function as intended, risk must be pooled. Employer coverage is a natural pooling mechanism—those who obtain coverage do so because they become employed, not because they become sick. The individual insurance market, however, is often a last resort for those with no other alternative. Some states have required individual market insurance plans to accept all applicants. However, in most states, individuals with preexisting conditions are denied coverage, have conditions excluded, or face much higher and often unaffordable premiums. And while individual market regulations in some states have improved access for older and less healthy people, they also have made coverage more expensive for younger and healthier people.

Some states, such as Maine,[1] Massachusetts,[2] and Vermont,[3] have created new pooling mechanisms and have provided subsidies for lower-wage individuals to make coverage more affordable for those not insured under employer plans. Massachusetts and Vermont have taken the additional step of requiring some financial contribution from employers who do not provide coverage to their workers. By drawing upon the experience of these innovative states and others, policymakers at the national level may be able to devise effective ways to address this increasingly urgent problem.

REFERENCES

1. S. Silow-Carroll and T. Alteras, *States in Action; A Quarterly Look at Innovations in Health Policy*, vol. 1 (New York: The Commonwealth Fund, May 2005).
2. S. Silow-Carroll and F. Pervez, *States in Action: A Quarterly Look at Innovations in Health Policy*, vol. 5 (New York: The Commonwealth Fund, July 2006).
3. Ibid.

CHAPTER 9

Public Financing

Doctors in meeting

Medicaid at Forty

Diane Rowland, ScD

The Social Security Amendments of 1965 established both Medicare and Medicaid to provide health insurance coverage and assistance to the Nation's elderly and low-income population. Originally designed as a Federal-State program to pay for medical expenses as an extension of public assistance for the aged, blind, and dependent children, Medicaid has grown over the last four decades into the Nation's largest health care program and a source of assistance to over 52 million Americans.

In 2003, Medicaid provided health insurance coverage to 39 million children and adults in low-income families, health and LTC assistance to 8 million low-income people with disabilities, and supplementary coverage and LTC assistance to 7 million elderly and disabled Medicare beneficiaries (U.S. Congressional Budget Office, 2004; Holahan and Ghosh, 2005). Medicaid now covers one in four American children, 18 percent of Medicare beneficiaries, and 60 percent of nursing home residents (Kaiser Commission on Medicaid and the Uninsured, 2005a; Kaiser Commission on Medicaid and the Uninsured and Urban Institute, 2005; Harrington, Carrillo, and Crawford, 2004) (Figure 9.1.1).

To finance these multiple roles, the Federal and State governments combined spent $275 billion in 2003, accounting for 17 percent of overall personal health spending (Urban Institute, 2004; Centers for Medicare & Medicaid Services, 2005b). Of the total, $252 billion financed direct services, with the bulk of spending (69 percent) going to health and LTC services for the aged and disabled (Figure 9.1.2). The Federal share of Medicaid spending ranges from 50 to 77 percent, with a higher Federal share in poorer States.

As Medicaid marks its 40th year, it is timely to review the evolution, current role, and impact of Medicaid for its three major beneficiary groups—low-income families, people with disabilities, and elderly and disabled Medicare beneficiaries.

TODAY'S ROLE

Medicaid's most widely acknowledged role is as the source of insurance coverage for 39 million low-income children and parents (U.S. Congressional Budget Office, 2004). By providing fundamental health insurance protection, Medicaid keeps millions of poor children and their parents from adding to our growing uninsured population. Although more needs to be done to broaden outreach and facilitate enrollment to achieve full participation by all eligible uninsured children, coverage through Medicaid and SCHIP has helped to offset

Adapted from: Diane Rowland. (2005–06). Medicaid at forty. *Health Care Financing Review, 27*(2), 63–77.

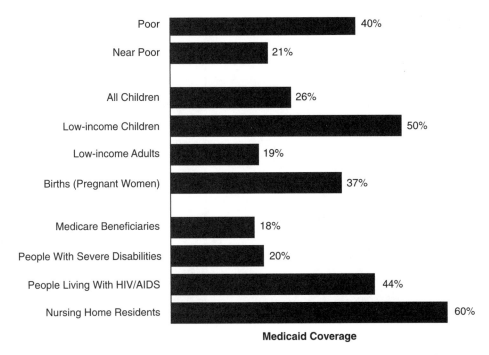

NOTE: "Poor" is defined as living below the Federal poverty level, which was $14,680 for a family of three in 2003.

FIGURE 9.1.1   Medicaid's Role for Selected Populations

Sources: Kaiser Commission on Medicaid and the Uninsured, Kaiser Family Foundation, and Urban Institute estimates: birth data: National Governors Association, 2003.

the decline in employer coverage and reduce the increase in the uninsured population (Holahan and Ghosh, 2004).

As a result of the legislative expansions and availability of Federal matching funds, Medicaid coverage remains mostly targeted at children and poor pregnant women. This translates into Medicaid coverage for 61 percent of children from poor families, but only 37 percent of poor parents and 28 percent of poor adults without children (Hoffman, Carbaugh, and Cooke, 2004). Medicaid is the dominant payer of prenatal care and delivery services for low-income women. Nationally, Medicaid covers more than one-third of all births, and in some States, over one-half of all births (National Governors Association Center for Best Practices, 2003).

For those eligible for Medicaid, the scope of coverage is geared toward meeting the health needs of a low-income population. The EPSDT program added in 1989 expanded coverage for preventive health services for children under age 21, including immunizations; vision, dental, and hearing services; and other treatment needed to correct health problems. Medicaid's benefit package is comprehensive, prohibits cost sharing on services for children, and allows only nominal cost-sharing amounts for adults. The goal is to promote access to care—especially preventive and primary care—without undue financial

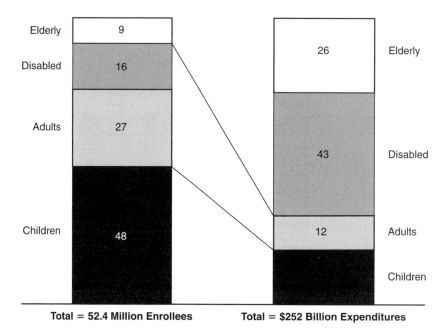

NOTE: Total expenditures on benefits excludes disproportionate share hospital payments

FIGURE 9.1.2   Medicaid Enrollees and Expenditures, by Enrollment Group: 2003

Sources: Kaiser Commission on Medicaid and the Uninsured estimates based on U.S. Congressional Budget Office and Office of Management and Budget data, 2004.

burden in recognition of the very low incomes and limited resources of the covered families. Reducing financial barriers to accessing necessary health services has been integral to Medicaid's role as the source of health coverage for the low-income population.

While Medicaid's role has expanded for America's low-income children, the program has been far more limited in its reach to low-income adults. Parents of covered or eligible children are most often not eligible themselves for coverage because the parent eligibility levels in most States remain far below the income levels now embraced for children. Only 17 States (including Washington, DC) offer coverage to parents at or above 100 percent of the FPL, in contrast to 39 States (including Washington, DC) covering children at or above 200 percent of FPL (Cohen Ross and Cox, 2004).

The lack of coverage for low-income adults without dependent children remains a major impediment to Medicaid's ability to provide coverage and reduce the uninsured rate within the low-income population.

IMPACT

Medicaid financing has helped move many low-income families from dependence on charity and free care to financial access to both public and private providers. In doing so, it has offered assistance to millions of low-income children and adults and provided a healthier start in life to many of the Nation's children. The coverage provided by Medicaid has helped to narrow the gaps in access to care faced by those without insurance and promoted broader use of preventive and primary care services. Medicaid's impact on low-income families can be seen both in the numbers of people served and the access to care provided.

Medicaid's greatest achievement for low-income families has been its sustained growth in covering a higher proportion of the low-income population, especially our Nation's youngest and poorest children. Without this program, millions of children would potentially be uninsured. As employment-based coverage continues to erode, Medicaid has been able to offset employment based losses for children—thus holding down overall growth in the uninsured. Between 2000 and 2003, while the percent of non-aged uninsured adults rose, the percent of children who were uninsured declined (Holahan and Ghosh, 2004).

Medicaid also has demonstrated success in improving access to care for the low-income population, most notably reflected in the comparability of Medicaid to private insurance for many access indicators where uninsured people fall far behind. Among low-income children, Medicaid, like private insurance, enables them to have a usual source of care—the key entry point into the health care system (Dubay and Kenney, 2001). For adults, those with Medicaid are less likely to report not receiving needed care and more likely to use preventive services than those who are uninsured (The Henry J. Kaiser Family Foundation and The Commonwealth Fund, 1997; Salganicoff, Ranji, and Wyn, 2005).

This achievement is particularly striking given that Medicaid serves both a sicker and poorer population than private insurance. Within the low-income population, those with Medicaid are predominately from families with income below the FPL (69 percent), nearly one-half (48 percent) report their health as fair or poor, and 61 percent have health conditions that limit work; compared to 27 percent poor, 16 percent in fair or poor health, and 15 percent with conditions that limit work with private coverage (Coughlin et al., 2004).

Medicaid also provides that coverage at a lower cost. In 2001, Medicaid's per enrollee cost is $749 for children's coverage and $1,752 for non-disabled adults compared to $1,098 and $2,253, respectively, for the low-income privately insured (Hadley and Holahan, 2003/2004).

Provider participation remains one area where improvement is needed to secure access to care for beneficiaries. Medicaid provider payments have historically been substantially below those of private insurance and Medicare. Medicaid's low payment rates coupled with administrative burdens for providers have resulted in limited access for some services, especially specialty care. As States have grappled with their budgets over the last few years, provider payments have been frequently targeted to curtail Medicaid spending.

State efforts over the last 20 years have broadened the use of managed care arrangements, both as a cost control mechanism and as a way to secure better provider networks for Medicaid beneficiaries. From 1994 to 2004, the percent of enrollees in managed care has grown from 23 to 61 percent of Medicaid—largely composed of low-income children and their parents (Centers for Medicare & Medicaid Services, 2005a). The use of managed care and its structure varies widely with some populations enrolled in primary care case management arrangements and others in capitated health maintenance organization (HMO)-

type plans. Nearly all States utilize managed care arrangements for family coverage and more than 30 States have moved into managed care arrangements for some of the special needs children and disability populations (Kaye, 2001). While managed care has the potential to improve the delivery and coordination of services, the inherent financial incentives to provide fewer services under capitated arrangements needs to be balanced against the higher utilization needed to address the health of those with disabilities and chronic conditions.

LOW-INCOME PEOPLE WITH DISABILITIES

Medicaid is now the largest single source of health and LTC coverage and public financial support for people with disabilities, covering 8 million children and adults with severe disabilities in 2003 (U.S. Congressional Budget Office, 2004). Medicaid's disabled population includes people with physical impairments and limitations, such as cerebral palsy, epilepsy, HIV/AIDS, and multiple sclerosis; mental or emotional conditions, such as depression, bipolar disorder, schizophrenia, and mental retardation; and other functional limitations.

Coverage for People with Disabilities

Under the 1965 legislation, States were only required to cover populations receiving cash assistance, including individuals age 18 or over receiving aid for the permanently and totally disabled under Title XIV of the Social Security Act, and the elderly qualifying for Old Age Assistance. Some States also offered coverage to the medically needy—those who met the categorical requirement for cash assistance and had high medical expenses that reduced their income to below the income cutoff for eligibility.

The most significant change in eligibility and coverage of people with disabilities and the elderly came in 1972 with the enactment of a Federal income-assistance program for people with disabilities—the Supplemental Security Income (SSI) program—which replaced the State-based welfare system with a Federal cash assistance program with national income and asset standards as well as a uniform national definition of disability. States were required to provide Medicaid coverage either to all their federally qualified SSI recipients or to all the elderly and individuals with disabilities using their State's eligibility standard in effect in 1972.

In addition to the eligibility-related changes, other major changes to Medicaid for people with disabilities involved making assistance in the community and at home an alternative to institutional nursing home care, promoting improvements in the quality of care in nursing homes, and assisting people with disabilities to return to work while retaining Medicaid coverage.

In 1986, Congress required States to continue Medicaid coverage for working disabled individuals with severe impairments who lose their eligibility for SSI due to earnings. Recognizing both the limits of private health insurance coverage and the disincentive to employers to bring a disabled individual into their health insurance pool, legislation in 1997 and 1999 allows States to help people with disabilities enter the workforce and retain Medicaid coverage with incomes that can exceed 250 percent of FPL.

Today's Role

All of these changes have combined to make Medicaid the primary source of coverage for people with disabilities and the low-income elderly, especially those needing LTC. Individuals with disabilities make up 16 percent of Medicaid beneficiaries, but account for 43 percent of total Medicaid spending due to their intensive use of services and the high cost of their LTC services. Medicaid spends, on average, seven times more on a disabled beneficiary than on a non-disabled child. In 2003, per capita expenditures were $12,300 per disabled beneficiary compared to $1,700 per child (Kaiser Commission on Medicaid and the Uninsured, 2005a).

Of the 25 million non-elderly Americans considered to have a specific, chronic disability—defined as a disabling condition or impairment that has lasted 1 year or is expected to last for 1 year—who live in the community, 20 percent are covered by Medicaid (Crowley and Elias, 2003). Medicaid covers 43 percent of poor non-elderly adults with disabilities and provides benefits to over 2 million disabled individuals who are also Medicare beneficiaries (Meyer and Zeller, 1999; Holahan and Ghosh, 2005). In addition, Medicaid is also the largest single payer of direct medical services for people with HIV/AIDS, covering over one-half (55 percent) of people with AIDS, and up to 90 percent of children with AIDS (Centers for Medicare & Medicaid Services, 2004).

Impact

Medicaid coverage helps to provide health insurance to the low-income disabled who are either not in the workforce or otherwise without access to private insurance. Private health insurance, including both employer-based and individually purchased coverage, is often unavailable or unaffordable for people with disabilities, as they are less likely to be working and more likely to have lower incomes (Hanson et al., 2003; Meyer and Zeller, 1999). Medicaid actually helps make the private insurance market work by removing many of the high-risk and -cost individuals with special health needs from insurance pools (Burwell, Crown, and Drabek, 1997; Hadley and Holahan, 2003/2004; Hanson et al., 2003).

Medicaid has a substantial role in financing care for those with severe mental health problems and developmental disabilities. In 1971, Congress authorized Federal Medicaid funding for care provided in residential intermediate care facilities for the mentally retarded (ICF/MR). Medicaid's role for people with mental health needs grew significantly in the 1970s, when SSI was established and tied to Medicaid, and further expanded in the mid-1980s due to changes in the SSA's disability eligibility criteria. The shift away from institutional care toward LTC provided in the home and community allowed States to close institutions and shift some of the costs of what was previously fully State financed to the Federal government. The shift was meant to improve care, but was not smooth or without consequences and in some cases contributed to an increase in the homeless population as institutions closed.

Although Medicaid is still the dominant source of financing for care in nursing facilities and ICF/MRs, covering 46 percent of spending, Medicaid has helped to shift more care to home and community-based settings, facilitating access to these services, as well as people's ability to maintain function and independence (Centers for Medicare & Medicaid Services, 2005b). Enacted in 1981, the home and community-based waiver program (1915(c) waivers), provides Federal matching payments.

In 2002, there were over 250 waivers in place across the country, allowing nearly 1 million individuals with mental retardation/developmental disabilities, physical disabilities, and the elderly to receive home and community-based care as an alternative to institutional care (Kitchener et al., 2005).

ROLE FOR MEDICARE'S BENEFICIARIES

Medicaid subsidizes care for some of the poorest of Medicare beneficiaries by providing coverage to fill in Medicare's gaps. Medicare's lack of LTC or prescription drug coverage and substantial financial requirements for premiums and cost sharing pose a financial burden that Medicaid eases for Medicare's lowest income beneficiaries, the population known as dually eligible beneficiaries. For the disabled who qualify for SSI, Medicaid provides full coverage during the 29-month waiting period for Medicare and wraps around Medicare coverage thereafter.

Medicaid helps relieve the financial burdens facing low-income Medicare beneficiaries in two ways. First, it pays their monthly Medicare Part B premium, which now amounts to over $900 a year, and pays the cost-sharing charges for many Medicare services. Second, Medicaid covers a range of important benefits excluded from Medicare: prescription drugs (until January 2006), LTC, dental and vision care, and other key services.

Quite simply, Medicaid wraps around Medicare coverage and assists with Medicare's financial obligations to make health coverage affordable and comprehensive for Medicare's poorest beneficiaries. Almost 7.5 million Medicaid beneficiaries (about 5 million elderly and 2.5 million non-elderly disabled) are dually eligible beneficiaries with joint enrollment in both programs (Holahan and Ghosh, 2005). Dually eligible beneficiaries account for 14 percent of Medicaid enrollees and 18 percent of Medicare beneficiaries (Holahan and Ghosh, 2005; Cubanski et al., 2005). Virtually all of the elderly and over one-third of the non-elderly with disabilities covered by Medicaid are dually eligible beneficiaries. These dually eligible beneficiaries are poorer, sicker, and more in need of LTC than other Medicare beneficiaries: 73 percent have annual incomes below $10,000 compared to 12 percent of all other Medicare beneficiaries. Over one-half are in fair or poor health, twice the rate of others in Medicare; and 19 percent live in LTC facilities compared to 3 percent of other Medicare beneficiaries (Cubanski et al., 2005).

One of Medicaid's key roles has been to provide LTC assistance for dually eligible beneficiaries. With the cost of nursing home care reaching $70,000 a year, many Medicare beneficiaries who need LTC quickly exhaust their resources and become eligible for Medicaid (Metlife Mature Market Institute, 2004). Per capita spending for beneficiaries in nursing homes averages $44,600, or about four times greater than spending for those living in the community ($10,900) or for other Medicare beneficiaries ($8,400). Because Medicare does not cover LTC, the high costs for the institutionalized fall heavily on the Medicaid Program and account for nearly 4 out of 5 dollars that Medicaid spends on dually eligible beneficiaries (Kasper, Elias, and Lyons, 2004). Many of these beneficiaries spend down to qualify for Medicaid LTC, but access to initial nursing home care can be difficult with long waiting lists and limited supply due to Medicaid payment rates.

LOOKING AHEAD

Over the last 40 years, Medicaid has been an essential and effective health safety net for millions of our poorest and sickest Americans. It has performed remarkably well in filling many of the cracks in our health system for the poor and the vulnerable. Its role in providing health and LTC services to our Nation's most vulnerable people and its widening safety net responsibilities have brought notable improvements in coverage of low-income families and assistance to the elderly and individuals with disabilities. As the primary source of financing and coverage for the low-income population, Medicaid has been a critical force in moderating the growth in America's uninsured population over the last four decades. Without Medicaid, millions of our Nation's poorest children could be added to our growing uninsured population.

Yet, one of the most daunting challenges facing Medicaid is how to meet the Nation's growing need for health and LTC coverage within the constraints of Federal and State financing. There are no easy answers to reducing the cost of providing care to over 50 million Americans who now depend on Medicaid. The high cost of caring for this population is reflective of their serious health problems, not excessive spending by the program. Program costs grow in response to downturns in the economy, the needs of an aging population, and emerging public health crises and emergencies. Medicaid costs rise because it is the Nation's health safety net.

The fiscal situation in the States, coupled with the growing Federal deficit, makes assuring adequate financing and meaningful coverage for low-income families, the elderly, and people with disabilities a growing challenge. In meeting this challenge, we need to not only recognize the role Medicaid has played in filling the gaps in our Nation's health system over the last four decades, but also begin filling those gaps.

Underlying the debate over Medicaid's future is thus a more fundamental debate about how we, as a Nation, fill the gaps in our health care system to provide and finance care for the poorest and sickest among us. The solution to making Medicaid more sustainable is to make it less necessary. If we had universal health coverage and assistance with the high cost of LTC, the need for Medicaid's safety-net role in the future would undoubtedly be dramatically reduced. But in the absence of broader solutions, policymakers need to find ways to maintain the Medicaid safety net, because without it, millions more would be uninsured, and many of our poorest and sickest citizens would be unable to obtain or afford the care they need. Until we solve the many gaps in our health system, we need to strengthen and improve Medicaid's ability to meet the many challenges we ask the program to address in its multiple roles.

REFERENCES

Burwell, B., Crown, W., and Drabek, J.: *Children with Severe Chronic Conditions on Medicaid.* U.S. Department of Health and Human Services. November 1997. Internet address: http://aspe. hhs.gov/daltcp/reports/children .htm (Accessed 2005.)

Centers for Medicare & Medicaid Services: *Medicaid and Acquired Immunodeficiency Syndrome (AIDS) and Human Immunodeficiency Virus (HIV) Infection.* January 2004. Internet address: http://www.cms.hhs.gov/hiv/hivfs.asp (Accessed 2005.)

Centers for Medicare & Medicaid Services: *Medicaid Managed Care Penetration Rates by State as of December 31, 2004.* 2005a. Internet address: http://www.cms.hhs.gov/medicaid/managedcare/mmcpr04.pdf (Accessed 2005.)

Centers for Medicare & Medicaid Services. Office of the Actuary, National Health Statistics Group: *National Health Accounts.* January 2005b. Internet address: http://www.cms.hhs.gov/statistics/nhe/historical/ (Accessed 2005.)

Cohen Ross, D., and Cox, L.: *Beneath the Surface: Barriers Threaten to Slow Progress on Expanding Health Coverage of Children and Families.* Kaiser Commission on Medicaid and the Uninsured. October 2004. Internet address: http://www.kff. org/medicaid/loader.cfm?url=/commonspot/security/getfile.cfm&PageID=47039 (Accessed 2005.)

Coughlin, T.: Unpublished Analysis of the 2002 National Survey of America's Families. Prepared by the Urban Institute for the Kaiser Commission on Medicaid and the Uninsured. 2004.

Crowley, J.S., and Elias, R.: *Medicaid's Role for People with Disabilities.* Kaiser Commission on Medicaid and the Uninsured. August 2003. Internet address: http://www.kff.org/medicaid/upload/Medicaids-Role-for-People-with-Disabilities.pdf (Accessed 2005.)

Cubanski, J., Voris, M., Kitchman, M., et al.: *Medicare Chartbook.* The Henry J. Kaiser Family Foundation. July 2005. Internet address: http://www.kff.org/medicare/7284.cfm (Accessed 2005.)

Dubay, L., and Kenney, G.M.: Health Care Access and Use Among Low-Income Children: Who Fares Best? *Health Affairs* 20(1):112–121. January/February 2001.

Hadley, J., and Holahan, J.: Is Health Care Spending Higher Under Medicaid or Private Insurance? *Inquiry* 40(4):323–342. Winter 2003/2004.

Hanson, K.W., Neuman, P., Dutwin. D., et al.: Uncovering the Health Challenges Facing People with Disabilities: The Role of Health Insurance. Web Exclusive. *Health Affairs* W3:552–565. November 19, 2003. Internet address: http://content.healthaffairs.org/webexclusives/index.dtl?year=2003 (Accessed 2005.)

Harrington, C., Carrillo, H., and Crawford, C.S.: *Nursing, Facilities, Staffing, Residents, and Facility Deficiencies, 1997–2003.* University of California San Francisco Department of Social and Behavioral Sciences. August 2004. Internet address: http://www.nccnhr.org/uploads/CHStateData04.pdf (Accessed 2005.)

Hoffman, C., Carbaugh, A., and Cooke, A.: *Health Insurance Coverage in America 2003 Data Update.* November 2004. Internet address: http://www.kff.org/uninsured/upload/Health-Insurance-Coverage-in-America-2003-Data-Update-Report.pdt (Accessed 2005.)

Holahan, J., and Ghosh, A.: *The Economic Downturn and Changes in Health Insurance Coverage, 2000–2003.* Kaiser Commission on Medicaid and the Uninsured. September 2004. Internet address: http://www.kff.org/uninsured/upload/The-Economic-Downturn-and-Changes-in-Health-Insurance-Coverage-2000-2003-Report.pdf (Accessed 2005.)

Holahan, J., and Ghosh, A.: *Dual Eligibles: Medicaid Enrollment and Spending for Medicare Beneficiaries in 2003.* Kaiser Commission on Medicaid and the Uninsured. July 2005. Internet address: http://www.kff.org/medicaid/upload/7346%20Dual%20Eligibles_Enrollment%20and%20Spending_Beneficiaries_Final_revised%207_28.pdf (Accessed 2005.)

Kaiser Commission on Medicaid and the Uninsured: *Medicaid: A Primer.* July 2005a. Internet address: http://www.kff.org/medicaid/upload/7334%20Medicaid%20Primer_Final%20for%20posting-3.pdf (Accessed 2005.)

Kaiser Commission on Medicaid and the Uninsured and Urban Institute: Unpublished Analysis of Data from the Medicaid Statistical Information System (MSIS) and CMS Medicare Enrollment Data. Internet address: http://cms.hhs.gov/statistics/enrollment/st02all.asp (Accessed 2005.)

Kasper, J., Elias, R., and Lyons, B.: *Dual Eligibles: Medicaid's Role in Filling Medicare's Gaps.* Kaiser Commission on Medicaid and the Uninsured. March 2004. Internet address: http://www.kff.org/medicaid/upload/Dual-Eligibles-Medicaid-s-Role-in-Filling-Medicare-s-Gaps.pdf (Accessed 2005.)

Kaye, N.: *Medicaid Managed Care: A Guide for States.* National Academy for State Health Policy. May 2001. Internet address: http://www.nashp.org/Files/MMC_62.pdf (Accessed 2005.)

Kitchener, M., Ng, T., Harrington, C., et al.: *Medicaid 1915(c) Home and Community-Based Service Programs: Data Update.* Kaiser Commission on Medicaid and the Uninsured. July 2005. Internet address: http://www.kff.org/medicaid/upload/7345%20rev081105.pdf (Accessed 2005.)

MetLife Mature Market Institute: *The MetLife Market Survey of Nursing Home & Home Care Costs.* September 2004. Internet address: http://www.metlife.com/WPSAssets/51768985701096047148V1F2004%20NH%20and%20HC%20 Market%20Survey.pdf (Accessed 2005.)

Meyer, J.A., and Zeller, P.J.: *Profiles of Disability: Employment and Health Coverage.* Kaiser Commission on Medicaid and the Uninsured. September 1999. Internet address: http://www.kff.org/medicaid/loader.cfm?url=/commonspot/security/getfile.cfm&PageID=13325 (Accessed 2005.)

National Governors Association Center for Best Practices: *MCH Update 2002: State Health Coverage for Low-Income Pregnant Women, Children, and Parents.* June 2003. Internet address: http://preview.nga.org/Files/pdf/MCHUPDATE02.pdf (Accessed 2005.)

Salganicoff, A., Ranji, U.R., and Wyn, R.: *Women and Health Care: A National Profile.* The Henry J. Kaiser Family Foundation. July 2005. Internet address: http://www.kff.org/womenshealth/upload/Women-and-Health-Care-A-National-Profile-Key-Findings-from-the-Kaiser-Women-s-Health-Survey.pdf (Accessed 2005.)

The Henry J. Kaiser Family Foundation and The Commonwealth Fund: *1997 National Survey of Health Insurance.* 1997. Internet address: http://www.cmwf.org/surveys/surveys_show.htm?doc_id=239489 (Accessed 2005.)

Urban Institute: Unpublished Analysis Based on Data from HCFA Financial Management Reports (HCFA-64/CMS-64). 2004.

U.S. Congressional Budget Office: *Fact Sheet for CBO's March 2004 Baseline: Medicaid and the State Children's Health Insurance Program.* March 2004. Internet address: http://www.cbo.gov/factsheets/2004b/Medicaid.pdf (Accessed 2005.)

How Well Does Medicaid Work in Improving Access to Care?

Sharon K. Long, Teresa Coughlin, and Jennifer King

Medicaid is the nation's largest health insurance program. More than 51 million people—about one in seven Americans—were enrolled in Medicaid at some time during 2002 (Holahan and Bruen 2003). Medicaid also plays a vital role in funding the health care safety net, including hospitals, community health centers, and school health programs. Consistent with this important role, federal and state Medicaid expenditures were more than $256 billion in 2002, about equal to what was spent on Medicare (Holahan and Bruen 2003).

Because of its cost, Medicaid is often at the center of budget discussions, both in Washington and state capitals. Currently, states, which are experiencing especially tough fiscal times, are proposing or implementing large cutbacks to Medicaid (Smith et al. 2003). And, at the national level, the Bush administration has reiterated its support for legislation proposed last year that would make sweeping changes to the program (U.S. Department of Health and Human Services 2003).

In an effort to inform this debate, we assess how well Medicaid works. Specifically, we look at how Medicaid beneficiaries' access to health care and use of medical services compares with that of both the privately insured and the uninsured. Do Medicaid beneficiaries do as well as their privately insured counterparts? Do they do better than the uninsured? We compare the experiences of Medicaid beneficiaries with the experiences of the uninsured because, in all likelihood, if Medicaid were cut, most of its beneficiaries would become uninsured.

Several previous studies have examined the relationship between access to care and insurance status. Several recent health services research studies have attempted to deal with selection bias in estimating the impacts of Medicaid on access to and use of care for children (Currie and Gruber 1996; Glied et al. 1998; Kaestner 1999), homeless adults (Glied et al. 1998/1999), and elderly Medicare beneficiaries (Pezzin and Kasper 2002). In general, these studies find that controlling for selection into insurance status has significant implications for estimates of the impacts of insurance coverage, although the direction of the bias in unadjusted estimates varies across populations and outcomes. Our work builds on this literature by estimating the relationship between insurance status and a number of access and use measures, while controlling for insurance choice.

Adapted from: Sharon K. Long, Teresa Coughlin, and Jennifer King. (2005). How well does Medicaid work in improving access to care? *Health Services Research*, 40(1), 39–58.

DATA

The data for this study are from the 1997 and 1999 National Survey of America's Families (NSAF), which provides detailed economic, health, and social characteristics for a nationally representative sample of almost 45,000 families. Of particular relevance, NSAF oversamples low-income families—defined as having incomes below 200 percent of the federal poverty level (Kenney et al. 1999). To ensure that we focus on a relatively homogenous population facing similar insurance choices, we limit our study sample to low-income women with children.

RESULTS

The probability of choosing private insurance versus Medicaid is higher for low-income mothers who are in a family with at least one member employed by a firm with more than 50 workers and lower for mothers who view welfare as helping people get back on their feet after family difficulties and for mothers in communities with higher levels of participation in public assistance programs. For the choice between uninsurance and Medicaid, mothers who live in states with more generous state Medicaid eligibility, in areas with higher levels of public assistance receipt, and who view welfare as helping people get back on their feet are also less likely to be uninsured than be on Medicaid. We also find that low-income women who are in a household with at least one member working for a large firm are less likely to be uninsured than on Medicaid.

Low-income mothers have better access to care under private coverage than Medicaid. The results also show that low-income mothers who are uninsured have significantly worse access to care relative to those with Medicaid coverage. For example, the simple differences show that mothers with private coverage are significantly less likely to lack a usual source of care (5 percentage points) and significantly more likely to have a dental visit (13 percentage points) and a clinical breast exam (7 percentage points) than mothers on Medicaid.

In contrast, uninsured mothers are significantly more likely to lack a usual source of care and to have unmet need and less likely to have a doctor visit, dental visit, pap smear, or clinical breast exam than Medicaid mothers. Medicaid mothers are significantly more likely to have hospital stays and emergency room visits than either mothers with private coverage or mothers who are uninsured.

OLS Model

The ordinary least squares (OLS) model, which controls for a range of individual and area characteristics, shows that many of the access and use disparities between private coverage and Medicaid observed in the simple difference model described reflect underlying differences in the characteristics of the populations. Many of the simple differences between mothers with private coverage and mothers with Medicaid are no longer significant in the OLS model. The OLS results do, however, suggest that mothers with private coverage are more likely to have a dental visit and less likely to have unmet need for medical care or surgery than are mothers on Medicaid. For uninsured mothers, the OLS results, like the simple differences, continue to indicate substantially worse access to and use of care relative to Medicaid mothers.

IV Estimation Model

The instrumental variable (IV) models include everything in the OLS models plus controls for unobserved factors that affect both selection into insurance status and access and use. With the IV models, we find that the access and use differences between low-income mothers with private insurance and those with Medicaid observed in the OLS estimates are no longer significant. Rather, the low-income Medicaid mothers and those with private coverage have comparable levels of access to and use of care across all of the measures considered. Comparing across the three models suggests that failing to account for unobserved factors (as in the simple differences and OLS models) overstates the benefits that private insurance confers relative to the benefits of Medicaid coverage.

In the IV model, the differences in hospital stays, emergency room visits, and unmet need that were found in the OLS model disappear. However, differences between uninsured mothers and mothers on Medicaid on all other access and use measures remain significant. Relative to mothers on Medicaid, uninsured mothers are significantly more likely to lack a usual source of care and significantly less likely to have a doctor visit, a dental visit, a pap smear, or clinical breast exam. Not only do differences between the uninsured and those on Medicaid persist, but the differences are bigger in the IV model than the OLS model. As with the previous comparison between private insurance and Medicaid mothers, the fact that the estimates changed across the three models suggests that failing to account for unobserved factors (as in the OLS and the simple differences models) produces biased estimates of the impact of Medicaid relative to uninsurance. In this case, not controlling for selection into insurance status leads one to understate the gains in access and use that Medicaid provides relative to being uninsured.

DISCUSSION

Over the past 20 years, a substantial body of research investigating the relationship between insurance status and access to health care has developed. An important shortcoming in much of this literature is a failure to account for an individual's selection of their insurance status. In this analysis, we examined the impact of the Medicaid program on health care access and use for low-income women with children, using an analytical approach that controlled for insurance choice. We found that, across a gamut of measures, Medicaid beneficiaries' access to care was significantly better than that obtained by the uninsured. Indeed, by controlling for insurance selection, the analysis showed that the benefits of having Medicaid coverage versus being uninsured are substantially larger than estimates that do not account for selection into insurance status suggest. This finding indicates that the importance of Medicaid coverage relative to being uninsured is greater than what has previously been reported. After controlling for selection into insurance status, low-income mothers on Medicaid are significantly more likely than uninsured mothers to have a usual source of care, doctor visits, and preventive care.

Our results also indicate that access to care for low-income mothers on Medicaid is comparable to that of low-income privately insured mothers. Once insurance selection was controlled, access to care for the two populations did not differ significantly. This dynamic was consistent across all the access measures examined. Importantly, without controls for insurance selection, the impact of Medicaid coverage relative to private coverage is underestimated: If selection is not controlled for, access for Medicaid beneficiaries is found—erroneously—to be significantly worse than for the low-income privately insured.

While we find that low-income mothers on Medicaid fare as well as low-income privately insured mothers, we cannot determine whether the low-income privately insured mothers have good access to care. For example, cost sharing generally associated with private insurance may limit or delay service use, especially for the low-income population (Newhouse 1993). If low-income privately insured women have limited benefit packages, this too could curtail service use. Similarly, if the low-income privately insured have benefit packages that emphasize selected services—for example, inpatient care—this could shift use patterns across services.

One puzzling finding is the lack of any differences in hospital and emergency room use between Medicaid and uninsured mothers after controlling for selection into insurance status. This suggests that the higher levels of use of other types of care that we see under Medicaid relative to the uninsured (e.g., doctor visits and preventive care) do not translate into a reduction in either emergency room use or hospitalizations for the Medicaid population. We also found no difference in emergency room use and hospital stays for the Medicaid population relative to those with private coverage. Together, these findings suggest broad inadequacies in care delivery for the low-income population and are also consistent with a recent study that finds increased emergency room use for both insured and uninsured populations over time in response to more difficulties obtaining primary care (Cunningham and May 2003). In future research, it will be important to examine ambulatory care, sensitive emergency room use, and avoidable hospitalizations to better understand what might be driving these findings.

Our results clearly show that the Medicaid program improved access to care for low-income mothers relative to being uninsured. Presumably, extending Medicaid to somewhat higher income uninsured parents would lead to a significant improvements in their access to care, including a greater likelihood of having a usual source of care and increased use of preventive care. However, with the current fiscal crisis facing the states and the mounting federal deficits, expansions in eligibility seem unlikely in the near term. On the contrary, states are seeking ways to contain Medicaid costs. For example, a recent survey by the Kaiser Commission on Medicaid and the Uninsured (Smith et al. 2003) found that 18 states plan to reduce Medicaid eligibility, 20 states plan to scale back benefits, and 21 states plan to increase copayments in 2004. An implication of our findings is that cutting Medicaid eligibility will lead to a substantial reduction in access to care for those who become uninsured. It is also likely that benefit reductions and increased copays would change the relationship between Medicaid and private coverage. If states significantly revamp Medicaid benefits and cost-sharing arrangements, it will be important to examine how well a scaled-back Medicaid program works.

REFERENCES

Cunningham, P., and J. May. 2003. "Insured Americans Drive Surge in Emergency Department Visits." Issue Brief No. 70. Washington, DC: Center for Studying Health System Change.

Currie, J., and J. Gruber. 1996. "Health Insurance Eligibility Utilization of Medicaid and Child Health." *Quarterly Journal of Economics* 3 (2): 432–66.

Glied, S., A. B. Garrett, C. Hoven, M. Rubio-Stipec, D. Regier, R. E. Moore, S. Goodman, P. Wu, and H. Bird. 1998. "Child Outpatient Mental Health Service Use: Why Doesn't Insurance Matter?" *Journal of Mental Health Policy and Economics* 1: 173–87.

Glied, S., S. Hoven, R. E. Moore, and A. B. Garrett. 1998/1999. "Medicaid and Service Use among Homeless Adults." *Inquiry* 35 (Winter): 380–7.

Holahan, J., and B. Bruen. 2003. "Medicaid Spending: What Factors Contributed to the Growth between 2000 and 2002?" Washington, DC: Kaiser Commission on Medicaid and the Uninsured.

Kaestner, R. 1999. "Health Insurance, the Quantity and Quality of Prenatal Care, and Infant Health." *Inquiry* 36 (Summer): 162–75.

Kenney, G., F. Scheuren, and K. Wang. 1999. "National Survey of America's Families: Survey Methods and Data Reliability." NSAF Methodology Series, No.1. Washington, DC: The Urban Institute.

Newhouse, J. P. 1993. *Free for All? Lessons from the RAND Health Insurance Experiment.* Cambridge, MA: Harvard University Press.

Pezzin, L. E., and J. D. Kasper. "Medicaid Enrollment among Elderly Medicare Beneficiaries: Individual Determinants, Effects of State Policy, and Impact on Service Use." *Health Services Research* 37 (4): 827–47.

Smith, V., R. Ramesh, K. Gifford, et al. 2003. "States Respond to Fiscal Pressure: State Medicaid Spending Growth and Cost Containment in Fiscal Years 2003 and 2004, Results from a 50-State Survey," Washington, DC: Kaiser Commission on Medicaid and the Uninsured.

U.S. Department of Health and Human Services. 2003. *FY 2004 Budget in Brief.* Washington, DC: U.S. Government Printing Office.

Medicare at a Glance

The Kaiser Family Foundation

OVERVIEW OF MEDICARE

Medicare is the federal health insurance program created in 1965 for all people age 65 and older regardless of their income or medical history. The program was expanded in 1972 to include people under age 65 with permanent disabilities. Medicare now covers nearly 43 million Americans. Most people age 65 and older are entitled to Medicare Part A if they or their spouse are eligible for Social Security payments and have made payroll tax contributions for 10 or more years. People under age 65 who receive Social Security Disability Insurance (SSDI) generally become eligible for Medicare after a two-year waiting period, while those with End Stage Renal Disease and Lou Gehrig's disease become eligible for Medicare when they begin receiving SSDI payments.

Medicare plays a vital role in ensuring the health of beneficiaries by covering many important health care services, including a new prescription drug benefit. However, there are also gaps in coverage, notably dental, vision, and long-term care. Medicare benefits are expected to total $374 billion in 2006, accounting for 14% of the federal budget (CBO, 2006).

CHARACTERISTICS OF PEOPLE ON MEDICARE

Medicare covers a diverse population: 35% have three or more chronic conditions, 17% are African American or Hispanic, 14% have limitations in three to six activities of daily living, and 12% are age 85 and older (Figure 9.3.1). Many people on Medicare have modest incomes and resources: 39% have incomes below 150% of poverty ($19,600/single and $26,400/couple in 2006). Fifteen percent—nearly 7 million in 2006—are under age 65 and permanently disabled.

MEDICARE'S STRUCTURE

Medicare is organized into four parts (Figure 9.3.2).

Part A pays for inpatient hospital, skilled nursing facility, home health, and hospice care. Accounting for 41% of benefit spending in 2006, Part A is funded mainly by a dedicated tax of 2.9% of earnings paid by employers and workers (1.45% each).

Part B pays for physician, outpatient, and home health visits and preventive services. Part B is funded by taxpayers through general revenues and beneficiary premiums and

---

Adapted from: The Kaiser Family Foundation. (2006). *Medicare at a glance*. Menlo Park, CA: The Kaiser Family Foundation.

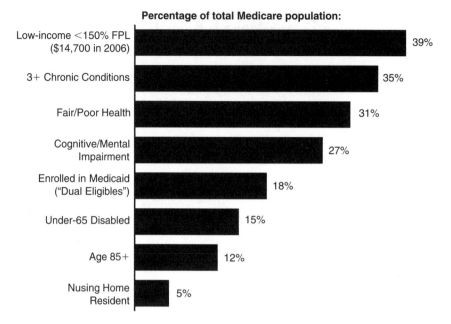

Percentage of total Medicare population:

Low-income <150% FPL ($14,700 in 2006) 39%

3+ Chronic Conditions 35%

Fair/Poor Health 31%

Cognitive/Mental Impairment 27%

Enrolled in Medicaid ("Dual Eligibles") 18%

Under-65 Disabled 15%

Age 85+ 12%

Nusing Home Resident 5%

FIGURE 9.3.1   Selected Characteristics of the Medicare Population

Source: Low-income, chronic conditions, and cognitive/mental impairment data from Medicare Current Beneficiary Survey 2002; all other data from Medicare Current Beneficiary Survey 2003.

accounts for 35% of benefit spending in 2006. Medicare beneficiaries pay a monthly Part B premium of $88.50 in 2006 (estimated to increase to $98.40 in 2007). Starting in 2007, those with annual income over $80,000 ($160,000 per couple) will pay a higher, income-related monthly Part B premium.

Part C refers to the Medicare Advantage program, through which beneficiaries can enroll in a private managed care plan, such as an HMO, PPO, or private fee-for-service (PFFS) plan. These plans offer combined coverage of Part A, Part B, and in most cases, Part D (prescription drug) benefits. Part C accounts for 14% of benefit spending in 2006.

Part D is the new outpatient prescription drug benefit, delivered through private plans that contract with Medicare. The benefit includes additional assistance with plan premiums and cost-sharing amounts for low-income beneficiaries. Part D, which is funded by general revenues, beneficiary premiums, and state payments, accounts for 8% of benefit spending in 2006. Enrollees in Medicare drug plans pay a monthly premium that averages $25 across plans in 2006.

BENEFICIARY COST SHARING AND OUT-OF-POCKET SPENDING

Medicare has relatively high cost-sharing requirements and covers less than half (45%) of beneficiaries' total costs. Medicare premiums and cost-sharing requirements are indexed to rise annually; the monthly Part B premium has nearly doubled between 2000 and 2006. In

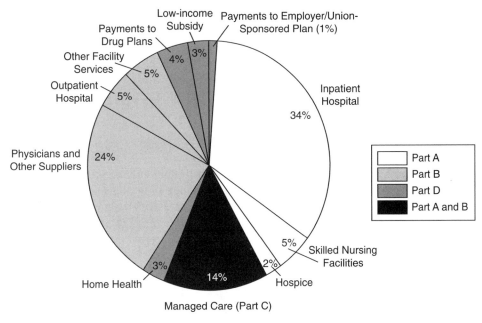

Total Benefit Payments = $374 billion

NOTE: Does not include administrative expenses such as spending for implementation of the Medicare drug benefit and the Medicare Advantage Program.

FIGURE 9.3.2   Medicare Benefit Payments by Type of Service, 2006

Source: Congressional Budget Office, Medicare Baseline, March 2006.

2006, the Parts A, B, and D (standard) deductibles are $952, $124, and $250, respectively. Unlike most employer-sponsored plans, Medicare has no cap on out-of-pocket spending.

A significant share of beneficiary out-of-pocket spending in 2002 was for long-term care (36%) and prescription drugs (22%). Even with the new drug benefit, beneficiaries are likely to face significant out-of-pocket costs in the future to meet their long-term care needs.

THE ROLE OF PRIVATE PLANS IN MEDICARE

Private plans are playing a larger role in Medicare through a revitalization of the Medicare managed care program, now known as Medicare Advantage, as well as through the new Part D drug benefit.

Medicare Advantage

Medicare HMOs have been an option under Medicare since the 1970s, although the majority of beneficiaries have remained in the traditional fee-for-service program. The Medicare

Modernization Act of 2003 (MMA) included several provisions to encourage private plan participation and beneficiary enrollment. In 2006, virtually all beneficiaries have a choice of one or more Medicare Advantage plans, with enrollment now at 16% of the total Medicare population. Medicare pays HMOs and other plans to provide all Medicare-covered benefits. The average Medicare payment to Medicare Advantage plans for Part A and B services is 111% of the cost of similar benefits in the fee-for-service program (MedPAC, 2006).

Medicare Prescription Drug Plans

Beneficiaries can obtain the new Medicare drug benefit through private stand-alone prescription drug plans (PDPs) and Medicare Advantage prescription drug plans (MA-PDs). Medicare pays plans to provide the standard drug benefit, or one that is actuarially equivalent.

As of June 2006, 22.5 million beneficiaries were enrolled in Medicare Part D plans, including 16.5 million in PDPs and another 6 million in MA-PDs (HHS, 2006) (Figure 9.3.3).

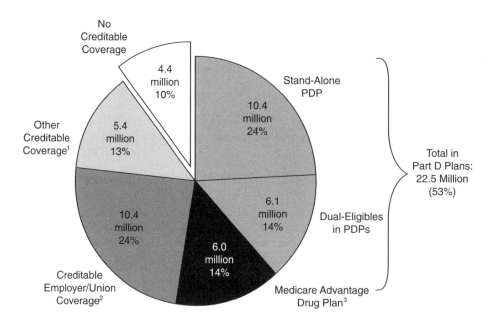

Total Number of Beneficiaries = 43 Million

NOTE: Numbers do not sum to 100% due to rounding. [1]Includes coverage from Veterans Administration, Indian Health Service, employer plans without retirees subsidiaries, and employer plans for active workers. [2]Includes employer/union SEHB, and TRICARE coverage. [3]Approximately 0.5 million are eligibles and enrolled in Medicare Advantage drug plan and are reported in this category.

FIGURE 9.3.3   HHS Estimates of Prescription Drug Coverage Among Medicare Beneficiaries, 2006

Source: HHS; June 14, 2006, Data as of June 11, 2006.

ADDITIONAL SOURCES OF COVERAGE

In addition to Medicare, most beneficiaries have some form of supplemental coverage.

Employer-Sponsored Plans

Employers are a key source of supplemental coverage, assisting about 11 million retirees on Medicare. However, retiree health benefits are on the decline; only 33% of large firms offered retiree benefits in 2005, down from 66% in 1988 (KFF/HRET, 2005). An additional 2.6 million Medicare beneficiaries are active workers (or spouses) for whom employer plans are the primary source of coverage.

Medicaid

More than 7 million low-income beneficiaries are dually eligible for Medicare and Medicaid. Most qualify for full Medicaid benefits, including long-term care and dental, and get help with Medicare's premiums and cost-sharing requirements. Some do not qualify for full Medicaid benefits, but get help with Medicare premiums and some cost-sharing requirements under the Medicare Savings Programs, administered under Medicaid.

Medigap and Other Coverage

Many beneficiaries purchase private supplemental policies, known as Medigap (nearly 9 million in 2002). Another 3 million beneficiaries receive supplemental assistance through the Veterans Administration or some other government program, according to HHS.

MEDICARE SPENDING AND OUTLOOK

With the aging of the population and the new drug benefit, net federal spending on Medicare is estimated by CBO to grow from $331 billion in 2006 to $524 billion in 2011. Annual growth in Medicare spending is influenced by factors that affect health spending generally, including increasing volume and utilization of services and higher prices for health care services. Although Medicare spending increases each year, the average per capita spending growth rate between 1970 and 2004 was lower for Medicare (8.9%) than for private health insurance (9.9%) for common benefits (excluding prescription drugs) (CMS Office of the Actuary, 2006). Looking to the future, Medicare faces many challenges, but none greater than financing care for an aging population with a declining ratio of workers to beneficiaries. Medicare spending as a share of GDP is expected to increase from 2.7% in 2005 to 4.7% in 2020. The Part A Trust Fund reserves are projected to be exhausted in 2018, and a "Medicare funding warning" is expected to be triggered next year by the Medicare Trustees, as required by law. Maintaining benefits for future beneficiaries will require more resources over time. In addition to these fiscal challenges, others include: ensuring the successful implementation of the drug benefit; setting fair payments to providers and plans; improving care for those with multiple chronic conditions; and providing adequate financial protections for those with low incomes and health security for an aging U.S. population.

Are Women Better Off Because of the New Medicare Drug Legislation?

Marilyn Moon, PhD

Any legislation that affects Medicare beneficiaries, by definition, is crucial for women because they make up a disproportionate share of enrollees in the program. Women's longer lives mean that they represent more than 6 of every 10 Medicare recipients (Health Care Financing Review: Medicare and Medicaid Statistical Supplement, 2001). But prescription drug legislation for Medicare is of even greater significance as a woman's issue because women are more likely to use prescription drugs than are men (Moon & Herd, 2002).

Because women are disproportionately more likely to suffer from chronic conditions, good drug therapies are particularly important to them (Collins et al., 1999). Yet these new drugs are expensive, adding substantially to the out-of-pocket costs that Medicare beneficiaries experience. Further, older women have lower incomes on average than men, so that even equal amounts of out-of-pocket costs impose a higher toll on women (American Institutes for Research Calculation from the Current Population Survey, 2003). In many cases, they have faced the difficult decisions of doing without the drugs they need or cutting back on other expenses. Further, women are less likely to have employer-sponsored retiree coverage, which often comes with a drug benefit (Moon & Herd, 2002). They are more likely to purchase private supplemental coverage (which is often more expensive and less comprehensive) or do without. Mitigating the problem somewhat, women are more likely to be on the Medicaid program, which supplements Medicare coverage and provides drug benefits for those with very low incomes. Overall, however, adding good prescription drug coverage to the Medicare program is an issue of greater concern to women than to men. Consequently, the details of the Medicare legislation create a number of special issues for women.

In the 1990s, prescription drugs became an essential part of the health care delivery system. Increasingly, medications for chronic conditions taken on a daily basis can improve the quality of life and extend life expectancy. But recognition of the importance of drug coverage, especially for older Americans, did not guarantee passage of a new Medicare drug benefit: lack of such coverage under Medicare meant an increasingly large gap in the comprehensiveness of the benefit but filling that gap would be very expensive given the 41 million people on the program. As a consequence, until late in 2003, the U.S. Congress stalemated over the issue of providing a new prescription drug benefit to persons

Adapted from: Marilyn Moon. (2005). Are women better off because of the new Medicare drug legislation? *Women's Health Issues,* 15,1–4. Copyright (2005), with permission from The Jacob's Institute of Women's Health.

on Medicare. Despite strong public support and a proven need for such coverage, its high costs and the controversy over expanding a government program in a time of suspicion of government and an aversion to any increase in taxes made it difficult to craft a bill. Somewhat to the surprise of many pundits, the Medicare Prescription Drug and Improvement Act of 2003 (MMA) became law.

But almost immediately this legislation proved controversial (Harwood, 2004). Many beneficiaries were hoping for a simpler, more stable source of drug coverage than what was contained in the legislation. This can be seen by the dissatisfaction expressed by beneficiaries, again catching many by surprise (Douglas, 2004). What about prospects for improving the legislation? Changes in the drug benefit and other parts of the legislation may be difficult to achieve, and any effort in this direction needs to recognize three elements, key to gaining Republican support, which are likely to create major barriers to be overcome: limits on the comprehensiveness of coverage to hold down the costs; reliance on the private insurance market for any drug benefit; and lack of any effort to establish a sound financing mechanism.

THE SHARE OF DRUG COSTS COVERED

Altogether, beneficiaries are expected to spend about $1.6 trillion on drugs during the first 8 years of the drug benefit. Thus, although the expected federal costs will be over $400 billion, this will still represent only a little more than a fourth of drug spending (Congressional Budget Office, 2003). The difference arises because of a less than comprehensive benefit structure and a substantial number of beneficiaries declining to participate. (Figure 9.4.1.)

Although this new benefit may not be viewed as adequate, it still will provide help to a substantial number of beneficiaries who now cannot find or afford such coverage. In particular, persons with low incomes not now receiving Medicaid coverage will receive the most substantial reductions in out-of-pocket spending because of substantial subsidies to this group in excess of the standard benefit. Further, women—particularly widows and other unmarried women—are more likely than men to have incomes low enough to qualify for the additional subsidies. Women just above the income qualification limits (under 150% of the federal poverty lines) will receive only the standard coverage, which is likely to prove highly inadequate over time.

Many Medicare beneficiaries with substantial drug costs will get lower coverage as a share of their spending than those with only modest needs. Yet it will be difficult to propose filling in the coverage gaps because of the high costs that would result. Changing the benefit in a cost-neutral way to better target those in need would make this voluntary benefit less attractive to healthier persons, potentially leading to escalating costs over time if the healthy opt out of the benefit. Raising the income limits for the improved subsidies would also prove to be very expensive.

THE ROLE OF PRIVATE INSURANCE

Less noticed as yet but likely to be as important for Medicare's future is the emphasis in the new legislation on the private insurance market, not only for drug coverage but also as

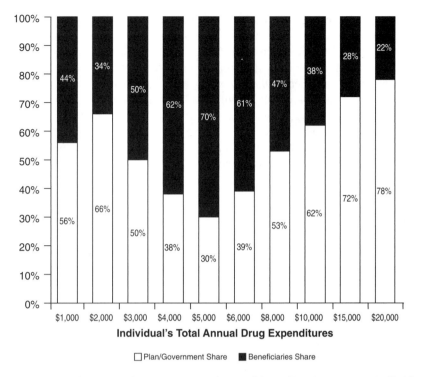

FIGURE 9.4.1   Beneficiary and Government Share of Spending in 2006, at Individual Expenditures Levels, under the New Medicare Drug Benefit

a potential full replacement for the traditional program (in which the government is the insurer of a fee-for-service program).

Anyone desiring to stay in traditional Medicare must get his or her drug coverage from a private stand-alone plan (Medicare Prescription Drug, Improvement, and Modernization Act, 2003). Thus, many are likely to end up with three sources of coverage: Medicare, private supplemental insurance, and the drug plan. On administrative grounds alone, this is likely to result in inefficiency and higher costs than necessary. Beneficiaries will bear considerable burdens in making decisions about their coverage. Moreover, wives and daughters are often the ones caught up in such efforts, as they are often the caregivers and the health care decision makers in families, both before and after age 65 (Barrett & Lynch, 1999).

Stand-alone drug plans are risky for insurers and have been soundly criticized by the industry. Nearly 90% of all beneficiaries are currently in traditional Medicare, so these stand-alone drug plans will be crucial to the success of the drug benefit.

A second way in which private plans are promoted in the new legislation arises from higher payments to the comprehensive plans (now called Medicare Advantage plans) for each Medicare enrollee, both from changes in the payment formula and from $14 billion in bonuses that the Secretary of Health and Human Services will be allowed to bestow on plans. Because evidence indicates that private plans are already overpaid on average because of adverse selection, private plans will be able to offer more generous benefits than traditional Medicare (General Accounting Office, 2000). The resulting inequities will likely hurt the very sick, who disproportionately choose to remain in the traditional option (Moon & Storeygard, 2001), and have varying effects across the country depending on payment level variations and availability of private plan options.

Although there would certainly be ways to offer options to Medicare beneficiaries that are both simpler and do not overpay plans, the political feelings on this issue run very high. Despite evidence to the contrary, supporters of a greater private insurance role cling to this approach with nearly religious fervor.

FINANCING ISSUES

By claiming that the private options under Medicare will restrain cost growth, supporters of the legislation have ignored the fact that they were generating over $400 billion in new government expenditures at a time when the deficit is soaring. Even without the $400 billion in new expenditures, Medicare will need to either substantially hold down the costs of care or increase the revenues needed to fund it. And when the higher estimates that the executive branch had made were released in early 2004, some members of Congress who had supported the legislation expressed doubts about continuing support for it (Welch, 2004).

Because costs will likely continue to be shifted onto beneficiaries, the oldest (overwhelmingly women) will face the prospect of ever higher costs each year as their incomes remain constant or even decline.

Medicare is a program in which the number of beneficiaries will double in the next 25 years and the costs of benefits will likely rise faster than general inflation (Board of Trustees, Federal Hospital Insurance and Federal Supplementary Medical Insurance Trust Funds, 2004). It is difficult to imagine how any cost containment effort can be expected to avoid the need for greater revenues over time. Ironically, this is a benefit that taxpayers have expressed a willingness to support. If baby boomers are to be asked to help with the future costs of Medicare, tax increases should occur while this important cohort is at the peak of its earning power. It would be a breath of fresh air for some politician to step up to the plate and suggest that new revenues should be raised for this important source of security for older and disabled persons.

Most difficult will be ensuring Medicare's future by recognizing that if it is a valuable benefit, we must be willing to pay for it. Cutting spending on Medicare will not solve the problem of insurance coverage of seniors; rather, it will simply shift the costs onto beneficiaries and their families. Here the only solution is for taxpayers to stop pretending that we can get something for nothing and signal a willingness to pay for those programs we value. Older women deserve assurance of a stable and viable Medicare program over time.

REFERENCES

American Institutes for Research Calculation from the Current Population Survey, 2003 Annual Social and Economic Supplement.

Barrett, A. E., & Lynch, S. M. (1999). Caregiving networks of elderly persons: variations by marital status. *Gerontologist,* 39, 695–704.

Board of Trustees Federal Hospital Insurance and Federal Supplementary Medical Insurance Trust Funds. (2004). *2004 Annual Report of the Boards of Trustees of the Federal Hospital Insurance and Federal Supplementary Medical Insurance Trust Funds.* Washington, D.C.: U.S. Government Printing Office.

Collins, K. S., Schoen, C., Joseph, S., Duchon, L., Simantov, E., & Yellowitz, M., et al. (1999, May). Health concerns across a woman's lifespan: The Commonwealth Fund 1998 survey of women's health. Report no. 332, Commonwealth Fund. New York: Commonwealth Fund. Available: http://cmwf.org/programs/ksc_whsurvey99_332.asp. Accessed November 9, 2004.

Congressional Budget Office. (2003). Letter from the Congressional Budget Office to Congressman Bill Thomas, Chairman Ways and Means Committee, November 20.

Douglas, W. (2004). Medicare a problem issue for Bush camp. Knight Ridder Newspapers. Available: http://www.thestat.com. Accessed October 20, 2004.

General Accounting Office. (2000). Medicare + Choice: payments exceed cost of fee-for-service benefits, adding billions to spending. GAO/HEHS-00-161. Washington, D.C.: U.S. Government Printing Office.

Harwood, J. (2004). Capital journal: despite Rx benefit, White House faces a Medicare problem. *Wall Street Journal.* Available: http://www.wsj.com. Accessed October 20, 2004.

Health Care Financing Review: Medicare and Medicaid Statistical Supplement. (2001). Maryland: U.S. Department of Health and Human Services.

Medicare Prescription Drug, Improvement, and Modernization Act. (2003). Pub. L. No 108–173, 117 Stat. 2066.

Moon, M., & Herd, P. (2002). *A place at the table: women's needs and Medicare reform.* New York: The Century Foundation.

Moon, M., & Storeygard, M. (2001). One-third at risk: the special circumstances of Medicare beneficiaries with health problems. Report no. 474, Commonwealth Fund. New York: Commonwealth Fund.

Welch, M. (2004). More seniors now against drug-benefit law, poll says. Political attacks, news that benefit's true cost withheld seen as factors. *USA Today.* Available: http://www.usatoday.com. Accessed October 20, 2004.

Medicare and Medicaid: Trends and Issues Affecting Access to Care for Low-Income Elders and People with Disabilities

Ellen O'Brien

The projected cost increases in both Medicare and Medicaid reflect the steady rise in healthcare costs that affect both private insurance and public programs. However, efforts to cut both of these programs are premised on the belief that they will grow faster than the general economy and are thus "unsustainable" over the long-term. Medicaid is the primary target for federal budget savings this year—with Medicare expenditures expected to grow significantly with the addition of a drug benefit in 2006, and large increases in payments to private health insurance plans in Medicare. However, cost trends in both programs have spurred efforts by both federal and state governments to rein in spending, and those reforms are likely to seriously erode the protections that both programs are designed to provide in the form of crucial healthcare coverage to millions of older and disabled individuals. This paper describes five key issues and trends that threaten to undermine access to care for low-income beneficiaries in both programs, including high and rising Medicare cost sharing, limited participation of low-income Medicare beneficiaries in Medicare savings programs, overpayments to Medicare managed-care plans, and federal and state efforts to reduce Medicaid spending.

MEDICARE'S HIGH AND RISING COST SHARING

Medicare's cost sharing has risen rapidly, eroding the protection Medicare was designed to provide. Both the Part A deductible and the Part B premium have risen rapidly in real terms, growing far faster than consumer prices or beneficiaries' incomes over the past four decades. Only the Part B deductible is lower in real terms today than it was in 1966 (Davis, 2001). These cost-sharing requirements impose significant burdens on Medicare beneficiaries, especially those with low incomes. In 2000, elders paid about 22 percent of income out-of-pocket on Medicare premiums and cost sharing; disabled beneficiaries in Medicare (ages 45 to 64) had even higher out-of-pocket burdens, spending 29 percent of income on

Adapted from: Ellen O'Brien. (2005). Medicare and Medicaid: Trends and issues affecting access to care for low-income elders and people with disabilities. *Generations, 29*(1), 65–69.

healthcare. The poor and the sick in Medicare have even higher burdens; healthcare costs absorb more than half the income of older, low-income women in poor health (Maxwell, Moon, and Segal, 2001).

Without policy changes, out-of-pocket burdens are expected to rise significantly in the future. However, recent reforms signal that options for enhancing tax revenues that could reduce beneficiary burden are "off the table." For example, the Medicare drug law enacted in 2003 requires the Medicare trustees to estimate in their annual report the year in which general revenues will finance at least 45 percent of Medicare costs. (If current cost trends continue, it is estimated that the threshold will be met by 2012.) Once the trustees estimate in two successive years that this 45 percent level will be reached within the next six years, the president is required to include a proposal in his next budget—and to submit legislation within fifteen days of the budget's release—to alter Medicare so the 45 percent threshold will not be reached. With enhanced general-revenue financing off the table, the 45 percent trigger will necessitate deep cuts in Medicare and cost shifting to beneficiaries, rather than real solutions to help address beneficiaries' already high out-of-pocket burdens (Greenstein, Kogan, and Park, 2005).

HIGHER PAYMENTS TO MANAGED CARE

Substantially higher payments to Medicare managed-care plans may do little to expand access for low-income beneficiaries. Many modest-income Medicare beneficiaries (often those with incomes just above the eligibility levels for the Medicare Savings Programs) have elected to enroll in Medicare managed-care plans as a way of lowering their Medicare cost-sharing burdens and receiving expanded benefits, including prescription drugs. Medicare's managed-care program disproportionately enrolls low-income Medicare beneficiaries: 35 percent of Medicare HMO enrollees have income between $10,000 and $20,000, compared to 25 percent of beneficiaries in traditional, fee-for-service Medicare. In contrast, lower-income beneficiaries (with annual incomes below $10,000) and higher-income beneficiaries (with incomes above $40,000) remain disproportionately in fee-for-service Medicare (Murgolo, 2002).

Since the late 1990s, however, the managed care program in Medicare has been marked by steadily increasing premiums, declining benefits, and rising out-of-pocket costs for beneficiaries. Dozens of plans quit the program, leaving hundreds of thousands of beneficiaries to find new options (Thorpe and Atherly, 2002). The average Medicare managed-care enrollee spent about $1,964 out-of-pocket in 2003, an increase of 10 percent from the previous year, and a doubling from 1999. Medicare beneficiaries in poor health spent more than three times that amount ($5,305 on average in 2003) and experienced an even greater increase in out-of-pocket costs (out-of-pocket costs for enrollees in poor health increased by 322 percent between 1999 and 2003, compared to a 52 percent increase for those in good health) (Gold and Achman, 2003). Recent analysis also suggests that at least some Medicare managed plans have charged significantly higher cost-sharing than is allowed in fee-for-service Medicare, undermining the very goal of prepaid health plans—which is to provide the same or better coverage while reducing Medicare beneficiaries' financial burdens. According to the Medicare Payment Advisory Commission (2003), some plans have imposed substantial cost sharing for nondiscretionary services like chemotherapy and dialysis, resulting in high out-of-pocket costs for the sickest enrollees, without imposing out-of-pocket caps to limit enrollees' overall liability.

In 2003, Congress sought to stabilize the market by increasing payments to private plans, raising average plan payments from 103 percent to 107 percent of estimated costs for similar beneficiaries in traditional fee-for-service Medicare. Payment changes have helped to stem the erosion in benefits. Plans reduced premiums and physician office copayments, and, to a more limited extent, have improved prescription drug and other supplemental coverage (Achman and Gold, 2004). However, many close observers of the Medicare managed-care program have expressed doubt that Medicare Advantage plans will achieve penetration rates seen in the late 1990s. High payments to plans thus won't guarantee access to a lower cost, managed care option for Medicare's low-income beneficiaries, and, at the same time, those payments threaten to undermine traditional Medicare. Managed care has not saved money for Medicare in the past. The dramatically higher payments to plans guarantee that they won't produce savings any time soon (Biles, Dallek, and Nicholas, 2004).

PROPOSED REDUCTIONS IN FEDERAL MEDICAID

Proposed reductions in federal Medicaid spending don't address underlying cost trends. In Medicaid, federal and state reforms designed to extract savings will shift costs to poor and near-poor beneficiaries and erode their access to care. Though Medicaid spending grows at roughly the same rate as other public and private insurance costs, Medicaid reform at the federal level has been framed as a response to federal deficit pressures, and the discussion has largely been about how much Medicaid will be cut, rather about whether it should be cut at all.

In April of 2005, House and Senate conferees reached agreement on a congressional budget resolution that calls for significant cuts in domestic programs—most notably Medicaid—over the next five years. The budget resolution cuts $30.5 billion from the growth of entitlement programs through 2010, more than a third of which comes from Medicaid (Horney, 2005). Though half the amount of the Medicaid cuts originally proposed by the House, the cuts are nonetheless substantial. The budget resolution directs the Secretary of Health and Human Services to establish a Medicaid Commission to identify federal policy changes to achieve savings, with recommendations to be delivered by September 2005, before Congress enacts legislation to codify the budget savings (Weisman, 2005).

If states are not able to make up for the lost federal payments with state and local funds, it is likely that some Medicaid beneficiaries will lose eligibility, and others will lose coverage for services and items they currently receive or be forced to pay a higher share of the costs. Since the majority of Medicaid spending (70 percent) pays for services for the elderly and people with disabilities, they are a likely target of reform.

THREATS TO ACCESS FROM MEDICAID WAIVERS

States have also taken action to reduce Medicaid spending, often by applying for waivers of federal Medicaid rules. Under section 1115 of the Social Security Act, the federal government may permit states to establish comprehensive demonstration projects that waive federal Medicaid requirements related to who is eligible for Medicaid, the benefits they receive, and the cost sharing they pay for covered services. In 2001, the Centers for Medicare and Medicaid Services developed the Health Insurance Flexibility and Accountability (HIFA) waiver program in Medicaid, which encourages states to scale back benefits significantly and increase cost sharing.

Greater state flexibility is available with regard to "optional" Medicaid populations: individuals whom federal law allows but does not require states to cover and whom states have elected to cover. Under HIFA waivers, states are allowed to limit Medicaid benefits for optional groups and to impose substantially greater cost sharing on these beneficiaries. There is no limit on the level of cost sharing a state can impose; though, under current law, only nominal cost sharing is permitted.

In 2002, Utah became the first state to receive federal approval to operate a waiver program that adopted many of the principles of the HIFA initiative. The Utah waiver reduces benefits and increases cost sharing for low-income parents previously covered by Medicaid in order to expand coverage to other low-income adults who were previously uninsured and ineligible for Medicaid.

Although the Utah waiver reduced benefits and increased cost sharing for low-income parents, more than half (56 percent) of the five million elders in Medicaid, including many of the elderly people who live in nursing homes and who receive home- and community-based care, are "optional" Medicaid beneficiaries. In addition, more than 3.5 million adults and children with catastrophic medical expenses who do not meet the program's low-income eligibility levels but who "spend down" to these very low income eligibility levels due to their high medical costs are also optional (Weinstock, 2005). These groups are also at risk of losing valuable benefits as states implement waivers to fundamentally redesign Medicaid.

SUMMARY

Efforts to slow the growth of entitlement spending threaten access to care for the most vulnerable elderly and disabled beneficiaries in Medicare and Medicaid. Addressing rising federal costs for Medicare by shifting costs to beneficiaries fails to address the underlying cost problem in health care and will erode access for the most vulnerable beneficiaries with significant health care needs. Reliance on private plans has not saved money for Medicare in the past, and large increases in payments to private plans assure that they won't deliver Medicare cost savings in the future. In Medicaid, reduced federal contributions will lead many states to restrict eligibility or benefits for the elderly and disabled who account for the majority of program expenditures. States seeking "flexibility" through waivers to restrict benefits and raise cost sharing for optional populations may hit very low-income elderly and beneficiaries hard. Cost burdens are already high in Medicare and Medicaid beneficiaries are unlikely to be able to pay more for their own health care. Thus, recent reforms threaten to erode access to care and health for millions of the poorest beneficiaries in Medicare and Medicaid.

REFERENCES

Achman, L., and Gold, M. 2004. "Are the 2004 Payment Increases Helping to Stem Medicare Advantage's Benefit Erosion?" New York: Commonwealth Fund.

Biles, B., Dallek, G., and Nicholas, L. H. 2004. "Medicare Advantage: Deja-Vu All Over Again." *Health Affairs* Web Exclusives: W4-586-97.

Davis, L. 2001. "Medicare's Cost-Sharing: Implications.for Beneficiaries." *Hearing on Strengthening Medicare: Modernizing Beneficiary Cost Sharing.* New York: Commonwealth Fund.

Gold, M., and Achman, L. 2003. "Average Out-of-Pocket Costs for Medicare + Choice Enrollees Increase 10 Percent in 2003." New York: Commonwealth Fund.

Greenstein, R., Kogan, R., and Park, E. 2005. "Element of Medicare Trustees' Report Could Spell Trouble for Beneficiaries in Future Years." Washington, D.C.: Center on Budget and Policy Priorities.

Horney, J. 2005. "Assessing the Conference Agreement on the Budget Resolution." Washington, D.C.: Center on Budget and Policy Priorities.

Maxwell, S., Moon, M., and Segal, M. 2001. "Growth in Medicare and Out-of-Pocket Spending: Impact on Vulnerable Beneficiaries." New York: Commonwealth Fund.

Medicare Payment Advisory Commission. 2003. "Report to the Congress: Benefit Design and Cost Sharing in Medicare Advantage Plans." Washington, D.C.: Medicare Payment Advisory Commission.

Thorpe, K. E., and Atherly, A. 2002. Medicare + Choice: Current Role and Near-Term Prospects." *Health Affairs* Web Exclusives: W242–W52.

Weinstock, B. 2005. "Cut Medicaid—Increase Health Disparities: How Cuts to 'Optional' Beneficiaries Will Affect Minority Health." Washington, D.C.: Families USA.

Weisman, J. 2005. "Budget Deal Sets the Stage for Arctic Drilling and Tax Cuts?" *Washington Post.* P. AOI. Washington, D.C.

Privatization of Medicare:
Toward Disentitlement
and Betrayal of a Social Contract

John P. Geyman

The intense political battle waged in recent years over adding a prescription drug benefit to Medicare has again brought out in the open polarized ideologic views that go way beyond the drug benefit itself. Finally passed by a slim majority in the U.S. Congress in November 2003, the Medicare Prescription Drug, Improvement and Modernization Act of 2003 ended up providing a confusing and meager drug benefit to Medicare beneficiaries while creating lucrative new markets for the pharmaceutical and insurance industries. The underlying issue—the uncontrolled escalation of drug prices and their unaffordability for millions of Americans—was completely avoided, even to the point of prohibiting the federal government from negotiating deep discounts of drug prices through its bargaining clout, as it already does for the Veterans Administration. Conservative interests pushed for privatizing Medicare further, under the guise of increasing choice and the claimed efficiency of markets, but with the more basic goal of limiting the government's responsibility for Medicare as an entitlement program. The final bill displeased many conservatives in not going far enough in this direction, but still contains provisions to promote preferred provider organizations (PPOs) with a goal that 35 percent of Medicare beneficiaries will be so enrolled by 2007.[1,2]

THE SOCIAL CONTRACT OF ORIGINAL MEDICARE

After three failed attempts in the United States to establish a program for universal coverage through national health insurance (1912–1917, 1932–1938, and 1945–1950), Medicare was enacted in 1965 as the country's first program of publicly financed social health insurance. The issue of health insurance for the elderly had been a major issue during the presidential election campaigns of 1960 and 1964. The Medicare program was modeled after Blue Cross and Aetna insurance plans, with benefits protecting beneficiaries against the increasing costs of hospitalization and physician services. Although never intended to cover all health care costs of the elderly, Medicare did provide them with a government promise to help finance that care. A social contract was established through strong bipartisan support in Congress, covering 10 percent of the population at the time of its passage in 1965.[3]

Adapted from: John P. Geyman. (2004). Privatization of Medicare: Toward disentitlement and betrayal of a social contract. *International Journal of Health Services*, 34(4), 573–594.

Passage of Medicare was preceded by a hard-fought political battle among the major interests, with many similarities to earlier and later battles over health policy. Organized medicine vehemently opposed Medicare, as it had when national health insurance was raised on earlier occasions.[4] The American Hospital Association and Blue Cross joined forces in support of the program, especially after they were assured that Blue Cross would process claims for hospital services and that the rules on costs were both vague and generous.[5] Many employers saw Medicare as a way of decreasing their responsibility for their retirees' health care and reducing public pressure for larger government interventions in health care.[6] As soon as the bill was expected to pass, all the parties scrambled to best serve their own interests. Indeed, the 1970s and 1980s were halcyon years for physicians and hospitals, with most of their services well reimbursed through a large industry of intermediaries. Initial federal budget estimates projected a $10 billion outlay for Medicare in 1990, but the actual budget had grown over 25 years to $100 billion in 1990.[7] Later observers of the health care debate in this country have called attention to the "corporate compromise" among employers, insurers, physicians, and hospitals, as illustrated by Medicare and later health care legislation.[8]

A study panel of the National Academy of Social Insurance explored the social values underlying Medicare. It its 1999 report *Medicare and the American Social Contract,* these key findings were noted[9]:

- Medicare was created as a response to a serious problem: The private market did not and could not work for a large proportion of the nation's elderly and disabled population.
- Medicare was originally designed as a social insurance program, rather than a social welfare program.
- Decisions about Medicare's future, including its ability to deal with health care utilization and costs, will not (and cannot) be made on purely economic or medical criteria.

Seven criteria were recommended to be considered and weighed against each other as values and public policy concerns in the ongoing debate over Medicare's future: (*a*) financial security, (*b*) equity, (*c*) efficiency, (*d*) affordability over time, (*e*) political accountability, (*f*) political sustainability, and (*g*) maximizing individual liberty.[9]

A LONG DRIVE TO PRIVATIZE MEDICARE

Attempts to privatize Medicare have a long history, beginning during the early 1960s as its opponents promoted an alternative plan whereby the federal government, instead of operating its own single-payer program, would subsidize beneficiaries to purchase private health insurance.[10] During the Nixon administration in 1972, Social Security amendments were enacted authorizing Medicare to contract with HMOs on a "risk" capitation basis, with requirements that participating plans were subject to retrospective cost adjustments and constraints upon their profits.[11] Not surprisingly, only one plan had signed up by 1979.[12]

There has been growing concern among policymakers since the 1970s about the rising costs of Medicare, and cost containment has been a continuing goal since then. Medicare managed care gained impetus with the passage of the Tax Equity and Fiscal Responsibility Act of 1982, which authorized Medicare to contract with HMOs and pay them 95 percent of traditional Medicare's adjusted average per capita cost in each county of the United States. That formula was established with the expectation that HMOs would actually save Medicare money.

A vigorous new push to privatize Medicare was ushered in with the 1994 elections, in which Republicans gained control of both houses of Congress. It was argued that the long-term financial viability of Medicare is bleak, especially with the anticipated enrollment of the baby boomer generation after 2010, and that markets are more efficient. The ultimate goal was to transform and privatize Medicare as much as possible while reducing the role of government and the Medicare budget.[13] A 1995 Balanced Budget Amendment called for complete privatization of the Medicare program. While it did not pass in Congress, BBA 1997 created the Medicare + Choice program, with the hope that Medicare HMOs and other private Medicare plans would cover 34 percent of all Medicare enrollment by 2005.[14]

Conservative policymakers embrace the goal of replacing Medicare as an entitlement program with a system wherein all beneficiaries would take more personal responsibility for their own care and pay their own way in a private market system, including the use of medical savings accounts, vouchers, and tax credits for the poor.[15] A three-year $30 million media campaign launched in 1995 by the conservative Heritage Foundation helped to promote market-based solutions to the "Medicare problem," including advocacy for modeling Medicare after the Federal Employees Health Benefits Program (FEHBP).

Since 1999, the number of participating Medicare + Choice HMOs has fallen steadily, and many others have reduced their service areas. Almost 2.4 million people have lost their coverage since 1997 as Medicare + Choice HMOs have left the market.[16] The federal government attempted to reverse the abrupt decline in numbers of participating Medicare HMOs by passage of the Balanced Budget Refinement Act of 1999 and the Medicare, Medicaid, and SCHIP Benefits Improvement and Protection Act of 2000. Both bills provided for increases in private reimbursement and decreased regulatory burdens sought by industry. Medicare HMOs still claimed their reimbursement was inadequate, and continued to exit the market.

With Republicans controlling Congress as well as the executive branch, the continued battle to privatize Medicare resulted in the Medicare Prescription Drug, Improvement and Modernization Act of 2003, a bonanza for the insurance and pharmaceutical industries. This more than 600-page bill is full of provisions that increase cost sharing, limit some benefits, and subsidize the private sector. Here are some of these provisions:

- The Congressional Budget Office (CBO) estimates that the new drug benefit will cover only 22 percent of the costs Medicare beneficiaries are expected to spend on prescription drugs over the period 2004–2013.[17]
- Starting in 2006, seniors will pay $670 in premiums and deductibles as well as 25 percent of their drug costs up to $2,250 that year; a "doughnut hole" gap then kicks in, with no coverage until total drug costs reach $5,100, when 95 percent coverage is provided.[18]

- Premiums and deductibles will increase by 78 percent between 2006 and 2013, much higher than seniors' income growth; while the threshold for catastrophic drug coverage rises to $9,066, so that drug benefits will become less affordable each year.[19]
- Beneficiaries with annual incomes above $80,000 will have to pay higher premiums for outpatient care and drug coverage.[1]
- The CBO estimates that 3.8 million retirees will see reductions or elimination of their more generous private coverage.[1]
- According to the Center on Budget and Policy Priorities, more than 6 million elderly people will lose their drug coverage under Medicaid, many of whom will be worse off with the new Medicare drug benefit.[1]
- In order to attract or retain participating Medicare HMOs, a federal bonus subsidy of $1.3 billion will be paid during 2004 and 2005, even before drug coverage starts in 2006.[20]
- Overpayments and subsidies for participating private health plans, originally expected by the CBO to cost $14 billion, are projected by White House actuaries to require $46 billion, more than three times as much.[21]
- Although employers will receive federal subsidies if they continue to provide drug coverage, they can reduce these below 40 to 50 percent of total drug costs and pocket the subsidies as profit.[22]
- The legislation mandates a six-year privatization experiment to begin in 2010 in six, as yet undecided, metropolitan areas.[1]
- The bill restricts importation of less expensive drugs from Canada and other countries.[1]

TRACK RECORD FOR PRIVATIZATION: CLAIMS VERSUS REALITY

Here we examine the track record of private Medicare plans from eight different perspectives.

Choice

While the Medicare + Choice (M + C) program was intended to expand choices for Medicare beneficiaries, its experience is quite the opposite. A thorough study of this issue was reported by Marsha Gold in 2001, with this major conclusion: "Existing plans have withdrawn from M + C, few new plans have entered the program from among the newly authorized plan types, greater choice has not developed in areas that lacked choice."[23]

The BBA 1997 also included a lock-in requirement that limits Medicare beneficiaries' freedom of choice of health plans. If dissatisfied with a private plan, they may find themselves unable to make a change back to Original Medicare for up to a year, and also unable to afford alternative Medigap coverage.[24] They may at the same time lose continuity of care with trusted physicians and have a restricted choice of providers.

Physical health, cognitive, or literacy factors present additional barriers to free choice of plans by Medicare beneficiaries. Nearly one-quarter of all Medicare beneficiaries have cognitive problems that limit their ability to make good choices.[25]

Reliability

Private Medicare plans are much less reliable than Original Medicare, as 2.4 million people found when their Medicare HMOs left the market between 1999 and 2003.[16] In addition, enrollees in Medicare HMOs frequently lose continuity of care by their physicians, either by change of health plans or by their physician not being included in their plan.

Even as private Medicare plans lobby for overpayment from the federal government, many attempt to increase their profits by enrolling healthier people and avoiding or disenrolling sicker people.[26] It is well documented that favorable risk selection has frequently been pursued by these plans.[27,28]

Cost Containment

From their inception, private sector Medicare plans have claimed their ability to contain costs and be more efficient than Original Medicare. Their track record over two decades belies that claim. They do not contain costs as well as does fee-for-service Medicare,[29] and actually cost the government more money than it would otherwise have spent within traditional Medicare.[30] Medicare's capability in cost control is based largely on its ability to aggressively set prices for the services it covers.[29] Medicare is administered with an overhead of about 3 percent, compared with overhead costs five to nine times higher for private plans.[31]

Benefits

Many Medicare + Choice HMOs have reduced benefits as they raise premiums, particularly among the two-thirds of HMOs that are for-profit. Current Medicare policies are intended to attract more private Medicare plans back into the market through continued overpayments, and some plans are again promising, as they have in past years, that they will use these payments to expand benefits or reduce co-payments and deductibles.[32]

Quality of Care

The record of privatized Medicare plans concerning quality of care is still mixed and inconclusive. However, there remains a widespread suspicion that privatized plans may compromise quality of care in their search for profits for their shareholders.

Efficiency

Of all the claims made by the private sector in health care, the claim of greater efficiency than in public programs is the hardest to defend. Private health insurance is especially bloated with bureaucracy, higher administrative overhead, duplication, and inefficiency compared with the public sector. With regard to the Medicare population, several examples make the point:

- While covering 40 million people 65 years of age and older, Medicare spends about 98 cents of every funded dollar on patient care, compared with about 80 cents for private health plans,[33] and still contains costs better than private plans.[29]
- Medigap policies spend on average more than 20 cents of each premium dollar on agents' fees, marketing, advertising, administration, and profits,[34] compared with administrative costs of Medicare in the 2 to 3 percent range.[35]
- According to the Inspector General of Health and Human Services, HMOs that contract with Medicare spend about 15 percent of their revenue on administrative costs rather than on health care,[36] while some spend up to 32 percent on administration.[35]

Public Satisfaction

In addition to being more efficient and more effective in controlling costs than private Medicare plans, Original Medicare is rated much more highly than private employer coverage. A 2001 study by the Commonwealth Fund found that these differences are consistent across income and health status categories.[37]

Fraud

Fraud within the Medicare program has been a persistent problem since the program's inception. The government initially focused its anti-fraud activities on providers, but by the mid-1990s, it became clear that private fiscal intermediaries, mostly Blue Cross/Blue Shield (BCBS), were complicit or actively fraudulent themselves. These Medicare contractors pay and monitor claims, audit providers; and are responsible for most of the Health Care Financing Administration prescribed program integrity.[38]

IMPACTS OF PRIVATIZATION ON MEDICARE AND ITS BENEFICIARIES

Privatizing Medicare increases the costs of the program to the government and encourages healthier seniors to enroll in private insurance plans.[36] Not only do these plans have an incentive to avoid sicker enrollees, but less healthy elderly are hesitant to join private plans that limit their choice of providers.[39] As a result, the advantages of sharing risk on a broad basis are lost as risk pools are segmented, with the ultimate threat of a "death spiral" of the Original Medicare program through adverse selection.

For its beneficiaries, privatization of Medicare means increased cost sharing, which leads inevitably to decreased access to care, lower utilization of services (including essential drugs), and impaired clinical outcomes, especially for lower-income, fragile, or disabled elderly patients.[40] Out-of-pocket spending for Medicare beneficiaries in poor health grew almost 300 percent from 1999 to 2002, and in 2003 was estimated to be about 3.4 times higher than for those in good health.[41] In 2000, average elderly Medicare beneficiaries spent 21 percent of their annual income on their medical care, while disabled beneficiaries spent 27 percent of their income.

MEDICARE AS A POLITICAL FOOTBALL

As we have seen, an intense political battle is being waged over the future of Medicare. The basic issue is whether it will remain an entitlement program within a 40-year-old social contract with the elderly and disabled or be privatized and dismantled as an obligation of government.

The AARP, among the most powerful of Washington interest groups, representing 35 million seniors, played a pivotal role in the passage of the 2003 Medicare legislation by throwing its weight in support of the bill. It soon found itself in the middle of an intense political crossfire, including from its own members, reminiscent of the 1988 backlash described earlier. About 60,000 AARP members either cancelled or refused to renew their membership in protest of the AARP's support of a flawed bill.[42] Critics pointed out the inherent and long-standing conflict of interest of the AARP because of its commercial interests.[43] About 60 percent of its revenue is derived from insurance-related activities, including the sale of Medigap Policies and its membership list.[44] In its attempt to quell the backlash, AARP has launched a new advertising campaign to educate seniors about the new Medicare drug benefit, and is trying to regain its credibility as an advocacy organization by restating its commitment to make prescription drugs more affordable.[45]

The current Bush administration, with the backing of Republicans, some moderate Democrats, and powerful economic interests within a very large medical-industrial complex, still promotes market-based solutions to the "Medicare problem," despite a 20-year track record of their failure. This issue remained at the center of the political debate through the 2004 election campaigns and beyond. Whether, and how, this battle will be resolved is unclear. Meanwhile, one cannot escape concluding that privatization of Medicare is a bold strategy to disenfranchise the elderly and disabled, the most vulnerable in our society, to their detriment and the gain of private interests.

REFERENCES

1. Pear, R. Sweeping Medicare change wins approval in Congress; President claims a victory; Senate backs bill. *New York Times,* November 26, 2003.

2. Pear, R. Medicare law's costs and benefits are elusive. *New York Times,* December 9, 2003.

3. Somers, A. R., and Somers, H. M. *Health and Health Care: Policies in Perspective,* pp. 179–180. Aspen Systems, Germantown, Md., 1977.

4. Campion, F. D. *The AMA and U.S. Health Policy since 1940.* Chicago Review Press, Chicago, 1984.

5. Andrews, C. *Profit Fever: The Drive to Corporatize Health Care and How to Stop It,* pp. 3–8. Common Courage Press, Monroe, Me., 1995.

6. Gordon, C. *Dead on Arrival: The Politics of Health Care in Twentieth Century America,* p. 238. Princeton University Press, Princeton, N.J., 2003.

7.   Ginsberg, E. Ten encounters with the U.S. health sector, 1930-1999. *JAMA* 282: 1665, 1999.

8.   Himmelstein, D. U., and Woolhandler, S. The corporate compromise: A Marxist view of health policy. *Monthly Rev.* 14: 20–22, May 1990.

9.   National Academy of Social Insurance. *Medicare and the American Social Contract.* February 1999.

10. Feingold, E. *Medicare: Policy and Politics: A Case Study and Policy Analysis,* pp. 100–156. Chandler, San Francisco, 1996.

11. Social Security Amendments of 1972, Pub. L. 92-603, § 226, 86 Stat 1320, 1391 (1972) adding § 1876 to the Social Security Act.

12. Oberlander, J. B. Managed care and Medicare reform. *J. Health Polit. Policy Law* 595: 598, 1997.

13. Thomas, B. Medicare at a crossroads. *JAMA* 274: 276–278, 1995.

14. Christensen, S. Medicare + Choice provisions in the Balanced Budget Act of 1997. *Health Aff. (Millwood)* 17(4): 224–231, 1998.

15. Jost, T. S. *Disentitlement? The Threats Facing Our Public Health-Care Programs and a Rights-Based Response,* p. 17. Oxford University Press, New York, 2003.

16. Centers for Medicare and Medicaid Services. *Medicare Fact Sheet.* Washington, D.C., September 2002.

17. Shearer, G. *Medicare Prescription Drugs: Conference Committee Agreement Asks Beneficiaries to Pay Too High a Price for Modest Benefit.* Consumers Union, Washington, D.C., November 17, 2003.

18. Altman, D. E. The new Medicare prescription drug legislation. *N. Engl. J. Med.* 350: 9–10, 2004.

19. Sherman, M. Seniors to face increasing costs for drugs. *Seattle Post Intelligencer,* November 26, 2003.

20. Headstart for HMOs. *Medicare Watch* 6(25): 2, 2003.

21. Pear, R., and Andrews, E. L. White House says congressional estimate of new Medicare costs was too low. *New York Times.* February 2, 2004.

22. Medicare Rights Center. MRC Advocacy Update. MRCAdvocacyUpdate@medicarerights.org (January 9, 2004).

23. Gold, M. Medicare + Choice: An interim report card. *Health Aff. (Millwood)* 20(4): 120–138, 2001.

24. Medicare Rights Center. *Ensuring Choice of Doctors.* Medicare Facts and Faces. Washington, D.C., January 2002.

25. Moon, M. Will the care be there? Vulnerable beneficiaries and Medicare reform. *Health Aff. (Millwood)* 18(1): 107–117, 1999.

26. Morgan, R. O., et al. The Medicare-HMO revolving door—The healthy go in and the sick go out. *N. Engl. J. Med.* 337: 169–175, 1997.

27. Neuman, P., et al. Marketing HMOs to Medicare beneficiaries. *Health Aff. (Millwood)* 17(4): 132–139, 1998.

28. U.S. General Accounting Office. *Fewer and Lower Cost Beneficiaries with Less Chronic Conditions Enroll in HMOs.* Washington, D.C., 1997.

29. Boccuti, C., and Moon, M. Comparing Medicare and private insurers: Growth rates in spending over three decades. *Health Aff. (Millwood)* 22(2): 230, 2003.

30. Bodenheimer, T. *The Dismal Failure of Medicare Privatization,* p. 18. Senior Action Network, San Francisco, June 2003.

31. Physicians for a National Health Program. Slide set. Chicago, 2002. www.pnhp.org.

32. Pear, R. Insurers plan broader Medicare coverage. *New York Times,* February 4, 2003.

33. Kleinke, J. D. *Oxymorons: The Myths of the U.S. Health Care System,* p. 192. Jossey-Bass, San Francisco, 2001.

34. Scanlon, W., U.S. General Accounting Office. Testimony before the Subcommittee on Health, Committee on Ways and Means, U.S. House of Representatives, March 14, 2002.

35. Board of Trustees of the Federal Hospital Insurance and Federal Supplemental Medical Insurance Trust Funds. *2002 Annual Report.* Washington, D.C., 2002.

36. Inspector General, Department of Health and Human Services. *Adequacy of Medicare's Managed Care Payments after the Balanced Budget Act of 1997.* Washington, D.C., September 2000.

37. Davis, K. Medicare versus private insurance: Rhetoric and reality. *Health Aff.*, Web exclusive, W321, October 9, 2002.

38. Sparrow, M. K. *License to Steal: How Fraud Bleeds America's Health Care System,* pp. 74–75. Westview Press, Boulder, Colo., 2002.

39. Moon, M., and Storeygard, M. *One-third at Risk: The Special Circumstances of Medicare Beneficiaries with Health Problems.* Commonwealth Fund, New York, September 2001.

40. Neuman, P. Testimony to the Subcommittee on Health, Committee on Ways and Means, House of Representatives, Washington, D.C., May 1, 2003. http://waysandmeans.house.gov/hearings.asp?formmode=view&id+338.

41. Achman, L., and Gold, M. *Medicare + Choice Plans Continue to Shift More Costs to Enrollees.* Commonwealth Fund, New York, 2003.

42. Broder, D. S. AARP's tough selling job. *Washington Post National Weekly Edition.* March 22–28, 2004.

43. Freudenheim, M. Opponents of Medicare bill say AARP has conflicts. *New York Times,* November 21, 2003.

44. Drinkard, J. AARP accused of conflict of interest. *USA Today,* November 21, 2003.

45. Novelli, W. D. As we see it: Medicare—next steps. *AARP Bull.,* p. 30, April 2004.

CHAPTER 10

Private Insurance and Managed Care

Skyscrapers

National Estimates of the Effects of Mandatory Medicaid Managed Care Programs on Health Care Access and Use, 1997–1999

Bowen Garrett, PhD, and Stephen Zuckerman, PhD

The 1990s saw a rapid increase in the number of Medicaid beneficiaries enrolled in Medicaid managed care (MMC). State governments viewed Medicaid managed care as a means both to improve access to care for beneficiaries and to slow the growth in Medicaid expenditures.[1] By 2001, 57% of Medicaid beneficiaries were enrolled in some type of managed care program in 49 states, compared with 10% in 1991.[2,3]

The development of Medicaid managed care occurred in 2 distinct phases. The first phase took place in the 1980s. States were primarily focused on using managed care as a means of improving access.[4] Many states implemented Primary Care Case Management (PCCM) plans, in which primary care providers were paid a monthly fee for coordinating the care received by Medicaid enrollees, with services continuing to be paid on a fee-for-service (FFS) basis. The expectation was that access to primary care would improve, resulting in better quality care at a lower cost.

During the second phase of Medicaid managed care implementation, states most often were relying on contracts with health maintenance organizations (HMOs) that would be paid a capitated rate for providing a contractually specified set of services. The expectation was that holding Medicaid HMOs at risk for the costs of providing services would create an incentive to achieve cost savings by negotiating discounts with providers and by encouraging more cost-effective forms of care.[5] However, capitation could also provide incentives to underprovide needed care. For this reason, Medicaid programs often develop comprehensive contract requirements and impose external review of plan operations.

Most states overlooked the fact that Medicaid fee-for-service rates were already well less than those of private payers[6] and that the potential for Medicaid plans to generate savings through provider discounts was much more limited than in the private sector.[7] In the end, evidence suggests that Medicaid spending grew at about the same rate in Medicaid managed care states as elsewhere.[8,9] However, the question of how Medicaid managed care affects beneficiaries' access and use of services remained open.

We used data from the 1997 and 1999 National Survey of America's Families (NSAF) to explore the effects of the various types of mandatory Medicaid managed care approaches (i.e., PCCMs, HMOs, and combinations of PCCMs and HMOs) on beneficiary access and use. We

Adapted from: Bowen Garrett and Stephen Zuckerman. (2005). National estimates of the effects of mandatory Medicaid managed care programs on health care access and use, 1997–1999. *Medical Care,* 43(7), 649–657.

compared adults and children who receive Medicaid in counties with each mandatory type of Medicaid managed care to those in counties whose Medicaid programs remain FFS. Because unobserved county differences may bias estimates based on cross-sectional comparisons by county MMC type, we estimate difference-in-difference models that correct for such bias.

RESULTS

Turning first to adults, we see that Medicaid enrollees in counties with mandatory HMO programs are less likely to have a visit to an ER during the 12 months before the survey than adults in FFS counties. Mandatory HMO programs decrease the probability of an ER visit by 18% points relative to a base rate of 49% among Medicaid adults in FFS counties. However, this reduction in ER use is not accompanied by an increase in other ambulatory care. We estimate a 13% point decrease in the likelihood of having an ambulatory physician visit (from a FFS base of 80%) as well as a 30% decrease in the number of these visits (from a FFS base of 7.9 visits during the 12 months before the survey). For women, the probability of getting a Papanicolaou test or a breast examination also decreases by 13% points (from a FFS base of 72%) for women in mandatory HMO counties. Therefore, it appears that mandatory HMO programs are not offsetting a lower dependence on emergency rooms with greater access to ambulatory and preventive care.

In programs that require adult enrollees to choose between HMOs and a PCCM, we also found that the probability of an ER visit is reduced by a similar magnitude to the effect in mandatory HMO programs. In addition, we found that these mixed mandatory programs increased the probability of having a usual source of care that is not an ER by 9% points from a FFS base of 75%. These combined programs also reduced unmet health care needs among Medicaid adults by almost eliminating the probability of unmet medical, surgical, or prescription drug needs relative to FFS counties. The probability decreases by 12% points from 15% in FFS counties. However, for this type of MMC program, there are no significant effects on adults' probability of seeing a doctor, the number of doctor visits, or the probability of a woman receiving preventive care.

Mandatory PCCM programs had only one significant effect on adult Medicaid enrollees across the outcomes studied here. Medicaid enrollees who saw a doctor or other health professional in counties with mandatory PCCM requirements had 35% fewer visits relative to the 7.9 visits occurring in FFS counties. This reduction is similar to our finding with respect to mandatory HMOs.

The effects of MMC programs are far less evident among children enrolled in Medicaid. We find no significant effect on having a usual source of care, receiving well-child care, reporting unmet health care needs, or on the number of visits that children make to a doctor or health care professional. In fact, there is only one significant effect that we detected, but the effect is large. Mandatory PCCM programs increase the probability of an ER visit by 14% points relative to the FFS base for children of 36%.

CONCLUSIONS AND DISCUSSION

There are 3 broad conclusions that can be drawn from this study. First, the effects of Medicaid managed care vary with the type of program implemented. Policy makers should not expect programs that rely on the PCCM model to have the same effects as those that incorporate mandatory HMO enrollment. Second, none of the program models had strong and consistent effects across all of the access and use indicators that we considered. This suggests that although Medicaid managed care may have some beneficial effects, there are also some potentially adverse consequences. Third, the effect of MMC appears to be greater for adults than children.

Our strongest result is that HMOs lower the probability of ER use among Medicaid adults, when implemented alone or in combination with a choice of a PCCM program. The chance of having an ER visit is more than one-third lower in counties with HMOs than in FFS counties. A further effect of mixed mandatory programs is that they increase the chance of an adult having a usual source of care that is not an ER. To the extent that an aim of HMO programs is to make a structural change in the way that Medicaid beneficiaries interact with the health care system, the policy seems to be effective for adults, which is consistent with the evidence on adults presented in Garrett et al.[10] (for mixed mandatory programs) and Zuckerman et al.[11]

Although those earlier studies also showed similar benefits of HMOs for children, this analysis does not support that conclusion. Counties with only mandatory HMO programs seem to be lowering the number of provider visits for adults and lowering rates of use of preventive care for women relative to FFS Medicaid. In the case of visits, the reductions appear to be clinically meaningful. The probability of a visit is more than 15% lower and, among those adults with a visit, the number of visits is 30% lower than for beneficiaries in Medicaid FFS counties. These differences are large, given that our models control for self-reported health status and disability within the sample.

We would expect HMOs to put greater emphasis on primary care and therefore the lower rates of preventive use for women are somewhat surprising. However, mandatory HMOs are not supposed to maintain visits at some specific level. To the extent that Medicaid FFS programs embody some excess use, the mandatory HMO programs may reduce the numbers of visits as a move in the direction of greater efficiency, which is consistent with the Hurley et al. review, which also showed that HMOs tend to reduce the number of physician visits. However, given the incentives of health plans receiving capitated payments to potentially under-provide services, the federal requirements imposed on states to conduct independent quality reviews of Medicaid managed care plans seem warranted.[12] In counties in which Medicaid managed care is only defined by a PCCM program, we found only one significant effect on beneficiary access and use relative to counties that remain FFS. Given how similar PCCM programs are to FFS Medicaid, the lack of significant effects is not surprising. Of course, to the extent that some states (e.g., Massachusetts, Arkansas, and North Carolina) have developed enhanced PCCMs that go beyond earlier models and incorporate provider management techniques used in HMOs, the impact of these new forms of PCCMs may be greater than we detected during the study period. This is a question that remains for future studies. However, the results of this study and a look back at the existing literature suggest that MMC has been neither the panacea that some of its supporters had hoped for nor the barrier to access that created a backlash in the private sector.

REFERENCES

1. Holahan J., Zuckerman S., Evans A. et al. Medicaid managed care in thirteen states. *Health Affairs.* 1998;17:43–63.

2. Centers for Medicare and Medicaid Services. National Summary of Medicaid Managed Care Programs and Enrollment. July 30, 2002. 2002. Available at: http://cms.hhs.gov/medicaid/managedcare/trends01.pdf. Accessed April 15, 2005.

3. Centers for Medicare and Medicaid Services. National Summary of Medicaid Managed Care Programs and Enrollment. July 30, 1996. 1997. Available at: http://cms.hhs.gov/medicaid/managedcare/trends1.asp. Accessed April 15, 2005.

4. Freund D., Hurley R. Managed care in Medicaid: selected issues in program origins, design, and research. *Ann Rev Public Health*. 1987;8:137–163.

5. Hurley R., Freund D., Paul J. *Managed Care in Medicaid: Lessons for Policy and Program Design*. Ann Arbor, MI: Health Administration Press; 1993.

6. Norton S. Medicaid fees and the Medicare fee schedule: an update. *Health Care Financing Review*. 1995;17:167–181.

7. Hurley R., Zuckerman, S. *Medicaid Managed Care: State Flexibility in Action*. Urban Institute Discussion Paper 02-06. (March). Washington, DC: The Urban Institute; 2002.

8. Ormond B.A., Ku L., Bruen B. *Engine of Change or One Force among Many? Section 1115 Demonstration Projects and Trends in Medicaid Expenditures*. Report prepared for the Health Care Financing Administration. Washington, DC: The Urban Institute; 2001.

9. Brown R., Wooldridge J., Hoag S. et al. *Reforming Medicaid: The Experiences of Five Pioneering States with Mandatory Managed Care and Eligibility Expansions*. Report prepared for the Health Care Financing Administration. Princeton, NJ: Mathematica Policy Research, Inc.; 2001.

10. Garrett B., Davidoff A., Yemane A. Effects of Medicaid managed care programs on health services access and use. *Health Services Res*. 2003;38:575–594.

11. Zuckerman S., Brennan N., Yemane A. Has Medicaid managed care affected beneficiary access and use? *Inquiry*. 2002;39:221–242.

12. Centers for Medicare and Medicaid Services. *Protocols for External Quality Review of Medicaid Managed Care Organizations and Prepaid Inpatient Health Plans*. September 16, 2004. Available at: http://www.cms.hhs.gov/medicaid/managedcare/mceqrhmp.as. Accessed April 15, 2005.

Medicare Beneficiary Out-of-Pocket Costs: Are Medicare Advantage Plans a Better Deal?

Brian Biles, Lauren Hersch Nicholas, and Stuart Guterman,
The Commonwealth Fund

OVERVIEW

The Medicare Advantage (MA) program established by the Medicare Modernization Act of 2003 is intended to increase the role of private health plans in Medicare. The program's creators envisioned that beneficiaries would opt out of traditional fee-for-service Medicare to take advantage of the lower monthly premiums, lower cost-sharing, and additional benefits available in private plans.

Proponents of private plans have suggested that MA enrollment is financially a good deal for Medicare beneficiaries. In a June 2005 press release, the U.S. Department of Health and Human Services announced:

> Nearly all Medicare beneficiaries have access to Medicare coordinated care plans and other health plan options in 2005, and these plans are providing significant new out-of-pocket savings to Medicare beneficiaries, particularly those with chronic illnesses.[1]

A specific comparison with Medigap coverage—the private insurance plans that many beneficiaries purchase to supplement their Medicare coverage—claimed particularly large savings:

> Beneficiaries who buy Medigap coverage on their own or who cannot afford Medigap will save just over $100 a month, on average, based on plans approved in March [2005], compared to traditional Medicare with Medigap. Those average savings include $29 in extra benefits, $2 in Part B premium reduction, and $70 in reduced average out-of-pocket expenses for Medicare-covered services compared to the national actuarial value.[2]

Earlier research, however, indicates that broad generalizations about the financial advantages of Medicare private health plan enrollment may be misleading for some beneficiaries.[3] According to an analysis of MA plans in 10 cities across the nation, out-of-pocket costs for enrolled seniors vary widely. These variations correspond with the health status of individual beneficiaries and the benefit package provided by individual plans.

Adapted from: Brian Biles, Lauren H. Nicholas, and Stuart Guterman, The Commonwealth Fund. (2006, May). Medicare beneficiary out-of-pocket costs: Are Medicare Advantage plans a better deal? New York: The Commonwealth Fund.

Drawing on 2005 data, this issue brief examines out-of-pocket costs for beneficiaries in good, fair, and poor health throughout the country. The results show that the earlier finding of wide variation in MA plan benefits still holds. Annual out-of-pocket costs for MA plan members now range from under $100 a year for beneficiaries in good health in cities such as Las Vegas, Fort Lauderdale, and San Antonio, to over $6,000 a year for beneficiaries in poor health in Philadelphia, Providence, Portland, Ore., and suburban Westchester County, N.Y.

In a number of these plans, beneficiaries in poor health pay more out-of-pocket than they would have with a combination of traditional fee-for-service Medicare and Medigap— despite the well-documented shortcomings of Medigap coverage.[4]

For individuals in good health, annual out-of-pocket costs in 2005 were lower in all of the 88 MA plans examined than they would have been in the fee-for-service program. It was nearly the same case for beneficiaries in fair health, with lower out-of-pocket costs in 86 of the 88 plans. But the story was different for beneficiaries in poor health: annual out-of-pocket costs in 2005 would actually be higher than fee-for-service in 19 of the 88 MA plans we examined.[5]

Despite the high payments, relative to fee-for-service costs, that MA plans receive from Medicare to enrich enrollee benefits, these plans may not always be a good deal for beneficiaries who, because of their poor health, use more health care services.[6] If a more comprehensive benefit package were made available as part of traditional fee-for-service Medicare, it might well be able to compete with MA plans on an equal footing.[7]

HISTORY OF PRIVATE PLANS IN MEDICARE

From the beginning, private plans have been a part of the Medicare program. The Tax Equity and Fiscal Responsibility Act of 1982 set payments for health maintenance organizations (HMOs) participating in the Medicare risk program at 95 percent of the adjusted average per capita cost for fee-for-service beneficiaries residing in each county. When Medicare payments were projected to exceed a plan's projected cost for providing the standard Medicare benefit package to enrollees, the plan was required to return the surplus to enrollees in the form of extra benefits or reduced cost-sharing.[8]

HMOs were expected to manage their costs more successfully than fee-for-service Medicare. But they also tended to enroll beneficiaries who were healthier, and therefore less costly, on average.[9] As a result of the widening discrepancy between their payments and base costs, Medicare managed care plans were able to offer substantial extra benefits: in 1994, the value of extra benefits offered by the average plan was $43 per member per month; by 1996, that amount had risen to $83.[10] Because of the better benefits the plans were able to provide, their enrollment jumped from 2.3 million (6% of all Medicare beneficiaries) to 4.1 million (11%) over the two-year period.[11]

Medicare+Choice

The role of private plans was expanded when the Balanced Budget Act of 1997 established the Medicare+Choice program, which gave beneficiaries a broader range of private plan choices and changed the way plans were paid. That legislation severed the tie between a plan's adjusted average per capita cost and its payment rates, narrowing the gap in payment rates between the highest-cost areas and other areas, particularly rural communities.

Halting payment rate growth in the highest-cost areas, however, made it less attractive for plans to locate there. Moreover, despite the higher rates now available in rural areas, plans locating to these regions were unable to flourish—for many of the same reasons that had kept them out of those areas before, including difficulty in establishing provider networks and sparse population. As a result, many private plans left the Medicare+Choice program; those that stayed, meanwhile, could not maintain their previous level of benefits. Enrollment in the program peaked in 1999 at 16 percent of Medicare beneficiaries. By 2003, it had fallen to 12 percent.[12]

Medicare Advantage

In the Medicare Modernization Act, Congress attempted to reverse that trend by allowing for substantial additional payments to Medicare Advantage plans in many areas. This change has increased the number of plans willing to participate: the Centers for Medicare and Medicaid Services (CMS) recently announced its approval of 163 new MA plans. It also enabled MA plans to offer more benefits: 70 percent of Medicare beneficiaries have access to a plan that does not require them to pay a premium for their prescription drug coverage.[13] These changes appear to have been successful in attracting more beneficiaries: nearly 7 million beneficiaries were members of MA plans as of April 2006, with enrollment increasing by about 1 million since enrollment in the new prescription drug benefit began (on November 15, 2005).[14]

OUT-OF-POCKET COSTS IN MEDICARE ADVANTAGE

Three factors are responsible for the current variation in out-of-pocket costs for Medicare Advantage plan enrollees, especially those who are in poor health:

- The high use of health services by Medicare beneficiaries in poor health, as well as the high costs associated with this use.
- Medicare policies that do not: a) sufficiently adjust (raise or lower) MA plan payments based on the costs actually incurred by enrollees, or b) limit MA plans' flexibility in designing their benefit packages.
- The ability of plans to adjust their benefit packages in response to these incentives.

High-Cost Beneficiaries

The most fundamental factor underlying the pattern of out-of-pocket costs by Medicare Advantage enrollees is the great variation in the use of health care services, and the annual cost of services, by individual Medicare beneficiaries. Enrollees in poor health use far more services and have higher costs than enrollees in good health.

It could cost an MA health plan as much to pay for the services for one person in poor health in the most expensive 5 percent group of beneficiaries as it would cost the plan to pay for more than 100 beneficiaries in good health within the least expensive 50 percent.[15]

This pattern provides a substantial incentive for MA plans to avoid the new or continued enrollment of beneficiaries who are in poor health.

Medicare Policies

Currently, Medicare policies only partly counteract the strong incentive for MA plans to avoid enrolling beneficiaries who are in poor health. At the same time, the government allows plans to design their benefit packages in a manner that favors beneficiaries who are in good health.

Risk Adjustment

MA plan payments are adjusted to reflect the anticipated costliness of the enrollee, with plans paid more for high-cost enrollees in poor health and less for low-cost members in good health. This risk adjustment is intended to counteract the incentive for plans to avoid sicker beneficiaries while protecting plans that might attract a disproportionate number of these higher-cost individuals. However, the current MA payment system does not completely meet these objectives.

Through 1999, plans' payment rates were adjusted only for demographics and other broad characteristics; they did not reflect the enrollee's specific clinical condition or medical history. Beginning in 2000, CMS began to phase in use of a clinical risk adjuster (referred to as the PIP-DCG, or principal inpatient diagnostic cost groups, model), and since 2004 a new, more sophisticated risk adjuster (referred to as the CMS-HCC, or hierarchical condition categories, model) has been used to adjust payments to MA plans.[16] While a great improvement over the previous system, the current model, however, does not completely remove the incentive to avoid potentially expensive enrollees, because it explains only a small proportion of the variation in costs across individual beneficiaries.

Recent analysis by the Medicare Payment Advisory Commission (MedPAC) found that the CMS-HCC model, even when fully implemented, would systematically underpay plans for enrollees who have the highest costs and overpay for those who have the lowest costs.[17]

Flexibility in MA Plan Benefits

Given the incentives in the MA payment system, private plans can be expected to take steps that would encourage the enrollment of healthy beneficiaries and discourage new or continued enrollment of high-cost members. These steps may involve: the design of the benefit package; the targeting of marketing campaigns; the selection of physicians and other providers for the plan network; and utilization review practices.

Medicare policies generally allow MA plans great latitude in the design of one or more benefit packages. MA plans are prohibited from imposing out-of-pocket costs that, on average, would be expected to exceed the amount in traditional fee-for-service Medicare, which was estimated at $119 per month in 2005.[18] So while the expected average of out-of-pocket costs for all MA plan members is limited, costs for individual plan members, such as those in poor health, are not.[19]

Medicare policy also provides that plans should not discriminate on the basis of health status. Compliance with this broad policy is not carefully defined and enforced by CMS, and many MA plans across the nation have benefit packages with high out-of-pocket costs for hospital, chemotherapy, and other non-discretionary health services.

Medicare Advantage Benefit Packages

Medicare Advantage plans avail themselves of the great discretion they are allowed in the design of monthly premiums and benefits to offer a wide variety of benefit packages.

A number of MA plans have designed benefit packages with greater out-of-pocket costs for health services. Some plans, for example, have a copayment of $200 or $300 per hospital day. For individuals in poor health requiring three hospital stays a year, each an average of four days, the out-of-pocket costs can total up to $3,600.

In addition, some plans charge coinsurance of $25 per physician visit. For enrollees in poor health who have 24 physician visits a year, this can amount to over $600 annually. Some MA plans offer benefit packages with out-of-pocket costs of as much as $5,600 for cancer chemotherapy.[20]

The features of MA plan benefit packages can also vary by geographic region. In several areas, the largest MA plans have hospital copayments of $200 per day or more. In others, there are major plans with no copayments for hospital care.

In addition, MA plans may change their benefit packages from year to year. Under the previous program, Medicare+Choice, out-of-pocket costs for enrollees consistently increased between 1999 and 2003, as payments to private plans were constrained by the provisions of the Balanced Budget Act; out-of-pocket costs began to level off as the extra payments provided by the Medicare Modernization Act took effect in 2004 and 2005. Analysis by Marsha Gold and colleagues, moreover, finds that out-of-pocket costs for those in poor health were greater and increased much more rapidly than for those in good health in every year through 2004.

COMPARISON OF OUT-OF-POCKET COSTS

To compare out-of-pocket costs for MA plan enrollees with costs for fee-for-service beneficiaries, the authors focused on 44 areas across the nation for closer study. The selected areas all share the following characteristics: (1) a substantial enrollment in MA plans, with greater than 10 percent of total beneficiaries in plans; (2) at least two competitive MA plans, each with enrollment of more than 2 percent of total beneficiaries; (3) information on out-of-pocket costs of MA enrollees available from HealthMetrix; and (4) coverage under the AARP Medigap Plan F available at a community-rated premium. Estimates, of annual out-of-pocket costs for enrollees in MA plans and Medigap Plan F are based on utilization packages for three broad categories of health status: good, fair, and poor.

Overall, this analysis found that that total annual out-of-pocket costs for beneficiaries in:

- *good health* are lower for all 88 MA plans than they are in Medigap Plan F.
- *fair health* are lower for all but two of the 88 MA plans than they are in Medigap Plan F.
- *poor health* are higher for 19 of the 88 MA plans than they are in Medigap Plan F.

Therefore, in 22 percent of the plans analyzed, MA enrollees in poor health have higher costs than they would have had with the combination of traditional fee-for-service Medicare and Medigap Plan F. These MA plans are located in 15 cities across the nation and are in 11 of the 18 states with cities in the study. They had a total of 343,037 Medicare enrollees in 2005. Estimated out-of-pocket costs for enrollees in poor health varied substantially among MA plans, from less than $1,400 to more than $7,500 among the plans we examined. Out-of-pocket costs for the same people under traditional Medicare would have varied much less. As a result, while many MA plans offer much better protection to enrollees in poor health, that protection is not universally available, and the additional costs faced by the sickest beneficiaries in some plans can be substantial.

ACCOUNTING FOR EXTRA PAYMENTS TO MEDICARE ADVANTAGE PLANS

As mentioned earlier, MA plans may be able to provide more benefits than traditional fee-for-service Medicare because the Medicare Modernization Act included provisions that set MA payments greater than per capita fee-for-service costs in every county in the nation. These extra payments to MA plans averaged over 11 percent ($800 per enrollee) in 2005.[21]

Through 2005, MA plans were required to provide additional benefits if their Medicare payment rate exceeds anticipated costs of providing the standard Medicare benefit package. These excess payments could be used to reduce premiums, deductibles, or copayments or to add coverage of services not covered by traditional fee-for-service Medicare.[22] It follows, therefore, that if plans had not received the extra payments provided under the MMA, their benefit packages would likely have been leaner and their members' out-of-pocket costs greater, and the comparison described above would not have been as favorable to MA plans—not only for enrollees in poor health, but also for some of those in fair and even good health.

CONCLUSION

The Medicare capitated payment system used for MA plans provides a fixed payment per enrollee per month. This type of arrangement provides a strong incentive for plans to manage the costs of their enrollees so that they stay below the corresponding payment amount.

This may be done by promoting healthier lifestyles and offering more preventive care so that potentially expensive episodes of illness may be avoided, by organizing care so that waste is minimized and effectiveness is maximized, and by coordinating care for chronically ill enrollees so that their conditions can be kept in check and expensive hospitalizations limited. All of these strategies not only make health care more efficient and effective, they help beneficiaries avoid illness when they are healthy and keep conditions under control when they are sick.

However, capitation also provides incentives to stint on health care and to avoid enrollees who are in poor health and represent a greater risk of high costs. Although the application of risk adjustment to the payment rates received by MA plans is intended to eliminate the incentive to avoid enrollees who are in poor health, it is not completely effective in doing so.

The analysis reported here indicates that the benefit packages offered by MA plans often result in substantial out-of-pocket costs for beneficiaries in poor health: in more than 20 percent of the MA plans we examined, located all across the nation in 15 cities in 10 states, enrollees in poor health would have had greater out-of-pocket costs in 2005 than if they had been in traditional fee-for-service Medicare with Medigap Plan F. If not for the extra payments provided to MA plans across-the-board, this pattern could have been even more pronounced.

Even with the completion of the transition to fully risk-adjusted MA payment rates and planned improvements in the risk adjustment methodology, the incentives for plans to avoid enrollees in poor health are unlikely to disappear. Moreover, as increased pressure to control Medicare spending makes continuation of the current level of extra payments to MA plans more difficult to justify, the incentive to shift costs from healthy to sick enrollees will become stronger. To address this situation, several changes in MA policies might be considered.

Suspend the annual MA plan lock-in for beneficiaries. Given the current potential for confusion regarding MA plan benefit packages and the risk of substantial out-of-pocket costs for sicker enrollees, the policy that locks in Medicare beneficiaries to an MA plan for an entire calendar year—which began in January 2006—could be suspended until new limits on out-of-pocket costs and improved risk adjustment are implemented. Suspension of the new annual lock-in policy would simply reinstate the previous Medicare policy (which gives beneficiaries the right to switch plans or between MA and fee-for-service with 30 days' notice) that was in place for the Medicare+Choice and Medicare Advantage programs from 1997 through 2005.

Meanwhile, senior counselors, the media, and others who advise the elderly and disabled regarding MA plan enrollment should be especially cautious about the advice they provide, particularly to beneficiaries in poor health. Senior advisors and beneficiaries themselves should carefully review the benefit packages of all MA plans and identify MA plans with benefit package features—such as high copayments for hospital care and chemotherapy—that increase costs for seniors who because of health conditions must use large quantities of health services.

Increase standardization of MA benefit packages. A broader policy that would both protect beneficiaries in poor health and clarify the selection of plans for all Medicare beneficiaries would be for Medicare to require some standardization of benefit packages that MA plans could offer. This type of policy might range from requiring that the definition of terms used to describe benefit packages be consistent across plans, to enumerating the combinations of benefits that could be offered.

Faced with widespread confusion among beneficiaries over premiums and benefits of Medigap polices in 1989, Medicare worked with the state insurance commissioners to develop a set of 10 uniform policies Medigap insurers must offer. These uniform policies have now been in place for over a decade. A similar process could bring order to the Medicare Advantage market, which offers elderly beneficiaries in many areas across the country dozens of Parts A and B acute care and Part D prescription drug benefit packages.

Improve payment accuracy. Improving the ability to risk-adjust payments to MA plans appropriately should be a high priority for CMS over the next five years. In addition, more information is needed on the utilization experience of beneficiaries in MA plans, so that future risk adjustment mechanisms can be appropriately calibrated. Earlier proposals for Medicare private plans to be paid based on partial capitation could be revisited as well; this could diminish the incentive to avoid costly enrollees or shift more costs to them.

Limit the vulnerability of MA plan enrollees to excessive out-of-pocket costs. Current Medicare policy regarding MA plan benefit packages could be strengthened to prohibit out-of-pocket costs that impose a significant financial burden on enrollees in poor health. We found that among the MA plans we studied, the 6 percent of enrollees who were in poor health had annual out-of-pocket costs of $4,844 in 2005, while those in fair and good health had estimated costs of $2,647 and $1,556, respectively.[23] Enrollees in poor health could be helped by prohibiting excessive copayments or by requiring that plans cap out-of-pocket payments at some reasonable amount.

It should also be noted that the analysis described in this paper was conducted in an environment in which the only alternative to Medicare Advantage for most beneficiaries is an increasingly complicated patchwork of coverage requiring some combination of traditional Medicare, Medigap or some other supplemental coverage, and now a third source of prescription drug coverage through a private plan. If Medicare were to offer a true alternative to private coverage—such as a more comprehensive fee-for-service option—market forces could be expected to work more effectively, and beneficiaries could choose between comparable alternatives on an equal footing.[24]

NOTES

1. Centers for Medicare and Medicaid Services, "Medicare Beneficiaries to Have More Health Plan Choices and Greater Savings with Medicare Advantage Plans Than Ever Before" (Washington, D.C.: CMS, 2005). Available at http://www.cms.hhs.gov/media/press/release.asp?Counter=1497.

2. Ibid.

3. B. Biles, G. Dallek, and L. H. Nicholas, "Medicare Advantage: Deja Vu All Over Again?" *Health Affairs* Web Exclusive (Dec. 15, 2004): W4-586-W4-97; G. Dallek, A. Dennington, and B. Biles, *Geographic Inequity in Medicare+Choice Benefits: Findings from Seven Communities* (New York: The Commonwealth Fund, Sept. 2002).

4. See, for example, U.S. Government Accountability Office, *Medigap Insurance: Plans Are Widely Available But Have Limited Benefits and May Have High Costs* (Washington, D.C.: GAO, July 2001).

5. In this analysis, out-of-pocket costs for beneficiaries in good, fair, and poor health, respectively, are estimated using profiles developed by HealthMetrix Research; Medigap premiums and coverage are based on Medigap Plan F offered through AARP by United Healthcare in each of the 44 counties we examined. See the discussion in Appendix 1.

6. See B. Biles, L. H. Nicholas, and B. S. Cooper, *The Cost of Privatization: Extra Payments to Medicare Advantage Plans—2005 Update* (New York: The Commonwealth Fund, Dec. 2004).

7. See, for example, K. Davis, M. Moon, B. S. Cooper, and C. Schoen, "Medicare Extra: A Comprehensive Benefit Option for Medicare Beneficiaries," *Health Affairs* Web Exclusive (Oct. 4, 2005):W5-442-W5-454.

8. Plans also had the option of returning the excess payment amount to Medicare, but no plans to our knowledge chose that option. See Prospective Payment Assessment Commission, *Medicare and the American Health Care System: Report to the Congress* (Washington, D.C.: ProPAC, June 1997):44.

9. R. S. Brown, J. W. Bergeron, D. G. Clement, et al., *The Medicare Risk Program for HMOs: Final Summary Report on Findings from the Evaluation* (Princeton, N.J.: Mathematica Policy Research, Feb. 1993).

10. ProPAC, *Medicare & American Health Care System,* 1997.

11. Ibid.:36.

12. M. Gold, "Private Plans in Medicare: Another Look," *Health Affairs,* Sept./Oct. 2005 24(5):1302-10.

13. Centers for Medicare and Medicaid Services, "Medicare Advantage Plans Provide Lower Costs and Substantial Savings" (Washington, D.C.: CMS, Apr. 3, 2006). Available at http://www.cms.hhs.gov/apps/media/press/release.asp?Counter=1825.

14. Ibid.

15. Congressional Budget Office, "High Costs Medicare Beneficiaries" (Washington, D.C.: CBO, May 2005). Available at http://www.cbo.gov/showdoc.cfm?index= 6332&sequence=0. Accessed August 2, 2005. It should be noted that other studies have similar findings including A. C. Monheit, "Persistence in Health Expenditures in Short Run: Prevalence and Consequences," *Medical Care,* July 2003 41 (7 suppl.): III53-III64.

16. G. C. Pope, J. Kautter, R. P. Ellis, et al., "Risk Adjustment of Medicare Capitation Payments Using the CMS-HCC Model," *Health Care Financing Review,* Summer 2004 25(4):119-41.

17. Medicare Payment Advisory Commission, *Report to the Congress: Issues in a Modernized Medicare Program* (Washington, D.C.: MedPAC, June 2005).

18. Medicare Payment Advisory Commission, *Report to the Congress: Benefit Design and Cost Sharing in Medicare Advantage Plans* (Washington, D.C.: MedPAC, Dec. 2004).

19. MedPAC, *Benefit Design,* 2004.

20. MedPAC, *Benefit Design,* 2004.

21. Commonwealth Fund estimate (unpublished), May 2006.

22. MedPAC, *Report to the Congress,* 2005.

23. L. Achman and L. Harris, *Early Effects of the Medicare Modernization Act: Benefits, Cost Sharing, and Premiums of Medicare Advantage Plans, 2005* (Washington, D.C.: AARP Public Policy Institute, Apr. 2005).

24. Davis et al., "Medicare Extra," 2005.

The Rise and Fall of Managed Care

David Mechanic

In a recent paper in the *Journal of the American Medical Association,* James Robinson (2001) proclaimed the death of managed care, a verdict widely shared in the health policy community. At the very least, managed care has been transformed into what some analysts call "managed care lite." There are few health images in American life that elicit displeasure comparable to managed care. Managed care companies and cigarette companies share the lowest levels of public confidence in social surveys. A Harris poll in May 2000 found that respondents' reports of industries doing a good job ranged from a high of 80 percent to a low of 28 percent. Tobacco companies defined the floor at 28 percent with managed care companies next at 29 percent (Blendon and Benson 2001). Although tobacco companies had low ratings for each of the prior three years as well, managed care was on a falling trajectory in public confidence over the four years covered by the report from 51 percent in 1997 to 29 percent in 2000. Repeated surveys in recent years also report that a majority of the public have unfavorable views of Health Maintenance Organizations (HMOs) (kaisernetwork.org 2002). Managed care also has been a source of derision in movies, television dramas, and in late show comedy routines.

Although satisfaction in more recent years has been less than in traditional practice (Miller and Luft 1997, 2002), most enrollees in managed care health plans report reasonable levels of satisfaction. Nevertheless, managed care has been the object of thousands of legislative proposals in Congress and state legislatures and an object of criticism by many politicians who find it an easy target (Mechanic 1997). The negative managed care symbolism is suggested by President Bush's 2003 State of the Union address, where after asserting to applause that "Instead of bureaucrats and trial lawyers and HMOs, we must put doctors and nurses and patients back in charge of American medicine," he proposed financial incentives to push the elderly into HMOs.

Managed care encompasses many organizational forms, strategies, and approaches, but any overall evaluation of the performance of this hybrid industry would have to conclude that there has been little performance difference between managed care and traditional fee-for-service medicine in access or quality (Miller and Luft 1994, 1997, 2002). Evaluation is complicated by the fact that significant proportions of respondents to surveys are confused as to whether they are in managed care (Nelson et al. 2000). Most surveys of managed care enrollees find that while they have a variety of complaints, as do members of traditional plans, most are reasonably satisfied with their plans and the medical care they have received. Those in managed care have generally preferred the cost

Adapted from: David Mechanic. (2004). The rise and fall of managed care. *Journal of Health and Social Behavior,* 45(Extra Issue), 76–86.

advantages, while those in fee-for-service were more satisfied with choice and interpersonal amenities (Miller and Luft 2002). The restriction of choice clearly has a negative effect on satisfaction (Gawande et al. 1998; Ullman et al. 1997). Nevertheless, it is difficult to account for the large gap between reported personal experience with managed care and public perception and response.

Managed care is credited with containing health care costs over the period of its growth. Many of the cost reductions came by negotiating, some would say dictating, lower rates of reimbursement for hospitals, doctors, other professionals, and a variety of ancillary services. Some significant cost reductions have come from utilization review and utilization management, particularly substantial reductions in length of hospital stays and some more prudent use of expensive diagnostic modalities. However, in fact, managed care approaches, while varying from one company to another, have not to any large degree limited access to hospital admission or to general medical care (Remler et al. 1997). The impact of its strategies have been more to constrain reimbursement than access to services. This hasn't made many friends and supporters in the health provider community. One important strategy for hospitals and providers has been to consolidate to achieve more market dominance and strengthen bargaining position in negotiations with large managed care organizations (Burns and Pauly 2002). Whatever uncertainty there might be about objective experience, there is little disagreement that managed care practices now have been substantially eroded, that costs are rising significantly, and that health care premiums are increasing substantially (Strunk, Ginsburg, and Gabel 2001; Center for Studying Health System Change 2002; Draper et al. 2002; Kaiser Health Poll Report 2003). Other factors, of course, contribute to cost increases, such as new medical technologies and drugs, aggressive direct advertising of pharmaceuticals and new medical services, and growing public awareness of treatable conditions and the value of medical care (Cutler 2001).

The failure of managed care speaks as much to American culture, the nature of mass communications, and the character of the medical marketplace as it does to the intrinsic qualities and performance of managed care (Mechanic 2002a). While many errors are rightfully attributed to managed care practices, errors are common in all medical activities (Institute of Medicine 2001; Kohn, Corrigan, and Donaldson 2000). In the pre-managed care era, such errors were attributed to the individual failures of hospitals, physicians, and other health care personnel. With the centralization of medical care into a more limited number of large health insurance companies and managed care providers, errors are more readily generalized to the now more visible centralized target (Mechanic 1997). Thus, the organization of medicine itself, and its increasing centralization, contributed to the public relations problems experienced by managed care plans and providers.

Basic to the backlash against managed care is the underlying American cultural preference for independence, autonomy, choice, and activism, and the view shared by many Americans that there should be no barriers to their access and choices in seeking and receiving medical care. Interest groups understand that the idea of "rationing" is unacceptable in the American context, and there is a long history of attacks on health reform by professional medicine and other health interests through assertions that it would "ration health care." Unlike in the United Kingdom, for example, health policy makers in the United States understand that they cannot have serious discussions about rationing in a political context. The intense interest by academics in Oregon's rationing scheme for its Medicaid program is an exception that helps prove the rule. Oregon went through an elaborate process of evaluating the value of medical and surgical interventions so that reductions in the Medicaid program would be limited to less valuable services. A major motivation was to extend valuable coverage to more people. What really happened in Oregon, however, is often misunderstood (Jacobs, Marmor, and Oberlander 1999).

The rejection of managed care was not simply that it rationed. There is much implicit rationing in health care programs (Mechanic 1995). However, utilization management and other strategies used by managed care providers were clearly explicit, making both patients and their doctors aware at the time of service that their choices and autonomy were being restricted. In popular parlance, it was "in your face" rationing. It was the constraints on preferred choice and managed care's inclination to temper the activism characteristic of American physicians that contributed to its negative reputation. Physicians complained bitterly that managed care was restricting their decisions (Kassirer 1998). The American patient has been socialized to value having all health care options and opportunities. They may endorse the rationality of cost containment measures in a general sense but resist any limitations when they believe that their health or the health of their loved ones might be at stake.

The public's unhappiness with rationing was an important factor, but it was not the only factor that led to the collective outburst perhaps best illustrated by movie audiences around the country cheering when actress Helen Hunt denounced HMOs in the 1997 movie hit, "As Good As It Gets." The tensions can be traced back to the failure of the Clinton health plan and the broad opposition it aroused from conservatives, businesses, health plans, physicians, hospitals, and the broader health care community. As Skocpol (1997) has noted, Clinton's efforts to be a new fiscally responsible Democrat led him to propose National Health Insurance that was cheap, substituting tight new cost-constraining regulations for large new expenditure commitments. Threatened by the potential loss of profits and autonomy, interest groups unleashed their public relations campaigns in opposition, such as the "Harry and Louise" ads that became famous after Hillary Clinton attacked them.

Managed care ultimately attempted what Clinton was unable to achieve: constraints that threatened the reimbursement and autonomy of health institutions and providers. Health organizations mobilized their media resources against managed care, as did many advocacy groups who feared restrictions on services. Public trust in medical institutions and leaders had been falling for some time, as was the case with leaders in many other social sectors, but patients still retained high trust in their personal physicians. Physicians' hostile responses to managed care reinforced patients' worries that health plans would put profits ahead of their welfare.

CORE VALUES CHALLENGED BY MANAGED CARE

Surveys in the United States have long indicated that most Americans see medical care as different from other products and services and believe it should be available to those who need it regardless of socioeconomic status or geography (Blendon et al. 1994; Lewis et al. 1976). Moreover, academic experts have noted the numerous ways that medical care has deviated from a traditional market environment (Arrow 1963; Mechanic 1978; Rice 1998). Nevertheless; many economists have argued that health care is most efficiently produced and distributed through a market approach, a view that resonates with conservative policy makers philosophically wedded to competitive markets and the belief that markets are more efficient than planned programs. This value assumption is widely shared by the general public, who distrust government and government regulation (Nye, Zelikow, and King 1997; Skocpol 1997). This eases the path for those who advocate a minimum of government intervention and oppose centralized reforms such as national health insurance. The popular conception of the marketplace also reinforces other strongly held public values such as consumer autonomy, choice, activism, and technical progress.

Perhaps most surprising about the final decades of the 20th century was that the enhanced rhetoric about market competition and choice accompanied an extraordinary degree of market consolidation in what were substantially decentralized and local markets (Burns and Pauly 2002). Hospitals, nursing homes, and other facilities were brought into national chains, and even medical groups—the last bastion of proclaimed independence—were organized into larger collectivities and parts of larger networks. These developments limited patients' options, their choices among health plans, and even their choices of doctors. Although choice of care and community rating had previously been strong community values, these were now superceded by reduced choice and risk rating. Many employers, and most small ones, now offer employees only HMO options, and decreasing numbers offer a choice of both HMOs and indemnity plans (Rice et al. 2002). Many employees in low paid employment receive no health benefits at all, while others have coverage for themselves but not for their families.

The growth of managed care, and what were perceived publicly as its most onerous practices, followed the failures of government intervention. After the demise of the Clinton health plan in the early 1990s (Mechanic 1996), the business sector endorsed a managed care approach, private regulation of health care choice, and provisions that went well beyond anything government could or would have done. Managed care, and its implicit challenge to consumer choice and physician autonomy, was a product of big business, privatization, and a quest for larger profits. Profit has always played a significant part in health care, but in the 1990s the tide turned demonstrably from small entrepreneurs and localized cottage industries to equity capitalism and the large corporation.

The American experiment in managed care was substantially built on a set of strategies of managerial capitalism and not one motivated by philosophical commitments comparable to those of the early managed care innovators. As employee complaints increased and the public expressed dissatisfaction with restrictions on choice, both employers and health plans retreated by relaxing the utilization controls that gave managed care advantages in constraining costs. On the positive side, private plans and provider groups showed ingenuity in devising new types of practice arrangements that adapted to changing circumstances (Robinson 1999). By the new century, health providers were increasingly successful at consolidating and strengthening their bargaining position as well, making it more difficult for health plans to demand low reimbursement rates. This new equilibrium has again brought us into a cost spiral with little sense of what countervailing forces will restrain it (Heffler et al. 2002).

FUTURE UNCERTAINTIES

Managed care bas not been the disaster the media portrays, but neither has it fulfilled its promise. The optimistic claim that managed care would bring improved clinical practices, higher quality of care, and maintain the public's health, and all at reduced cost, has been an illusion. There have been significant innovations in some of the established prepaid group practices (Hurtado, Greenlick, and Saward 1969; Wagner, Austin, and von Korff 1996) that offer guidance for putting in place good disease management programs and quality assurance practices, but such group structures are a shrinking part of the health care sector. The forms of managed care that have prevailed have been virtual networks rather than group structures, for-profit in contrast to not-for-profit organizations, and systems that manage costs more than care. Non-profit plans have performed better than profit organizations (Tu and Reschovsky 2002), and they are more likely than for-profit ones to put in place service arrangements that more broadly enhance care (Mechanic and Rosenthal 1999).

As we proceed further into this century there is a renewed focus on quality, on reducing hospital and medical error, and on managing disability and chronic disease more effectively (Institute of Medicine 2001). Although much has been written on the clinical integration of services, there are many barriers, and clinical integration rarely has occurred (Burns and Pauly 2002; Shortell et al. 2000). Advances in information technology, however, make disease management approaches more possible in virtual systems, and many companies now offer high risk and high cost patient management services, as well as the ability to usefully process massive claims data to improve patient population management (Mechanic 2002). The barriers are more human and organizational than technical; developing appropriate incentives and redirecting physician and other professional behavior toward these new approaches and systems are difficult and slow (Mechanic 2002b).

There is growing realization that the high prevalence of error and injury and the failure to provide high quality care are structural challenges and not simply individual problems. Spurred on by two influential Institute of Medicine reports (Institute of Medicine 2001; Kohn et al. 2000) and a collaboration of major business groups in the Leapfrog Group (2001), efforts are being made to use purchasing power to correct some deficiencies of health care systems. There appears to be a significant, widespread realization that, despite our vast expenditures for health care, quality is often poor and simple errors abound. It remains to be seen whether remedial efforts are sustained and grow or whether this is another example of adaptation and co-optation to just one more passing challenge.

The fact remains that the American health care system is disorganized and irrational. The interest groups who have a stake in its size and operations are powerful, making significant changes challenging their interests exceedingly difficult. The spiral of cost and premium increases accompanying the dilution of managed care will exacerbate the problems of insurance coverage and maintenance of the safety net for those who lack coverage. As employers and government face increased costs and budget constraints they will transfer more cost to patients. Medicine has more to offer than in the past, and the gaps in coverage for prescription drugs, preventive services, long-term care, and even the most basic services will be felt more strongly. The course of health care in America remains uncertain, and prediction is always hazardous. However, one thing is certain: If managed care is truly dead, a proposition I believe is doubtful, a functional substitute will be required. More likely, we will see managed care take iterative forms that dispense with gatekeepers and limited choices, that force patients into more self-conscious frugality, and that reintroduce rationing more implicitly. This is what experience should lead us to anticipate (Klein et al. 1996; Mechanic 1995).

In the final analysis, the underlying fault is in the failure of the United States to introduce a rational system of universal health care. While 60 percent of all health expenditures are from government through health programs, tax subsidies, and coverage of health benefits for government employees (Woolhandler and Himmelstein 2002), we maintain the illusion of a private health care system and pay a high price for it. Experience suggests that converting from our present system to a more rational insurance program is not politically possible without payoffs to established interests. Whether the failure is an example of American exceptionalism or a product of other cultural expectations and values, the likely prognosis under the current arrangement is one of greater inequalities in access and treatment and growth in the uninsured and under-insured, among other problems. There certainly will be efforts to muddle through and patch the cracks, but fundamental changes are unlikely until a significant proportion of the population is threatened and personally dissatisfied. Unfortunately, things are likely to get much worse before getting much better.

REFERENCES

Arrow, Kenneth J. 1963. "Uncertainty and the Welfare Economics of Medical Care." *American Economic Review* 53:941–73.

Blendon, Robert J. and John M. Benson. 2001. "Americans' Views on Health Policy: A Fifty-Year Historical Perspective." *Health Affairs* 20:33–46.

Burns, Lawton R. and Mark V. Pauly. 2002. "Integrated Delivery Networks: A Detour on the Road to Integrated Health Care?" *Health Affairs* 21:128–43.

Center for Studying Health System Change. 2002. *Navigating a Changing Health System, 2001 Annual Report.* Washington, DC: Health System Change. Accessed December 8, 2004 (www.hschange.com/CONTENT/452).

Cutler, David M. 2001. "Declining Disability among the Elderly." *Health Affairs* 20:11–27.

Draper, Debra A., Robert E. Hurley, Cara S. Lesser, and Bradley C. Strunk. 2002. "The Changing Face of Managed Care." *Health Affairs* 21:11–23.

Gawande, Atul A., Robert J. Blendon, Mollyann Brodie, John M. Benson, Larry Levitt, and Larry Hugick. 1998. "Does Dissatisfaction with Health Plans Stem from Having No Choices?" *Health Affairs* 17:184–94.

Heffler, Stephen, Sheila Smith, Greg Won, M. Kent Clemens, Sean Keehan, and Mark Zezza. 2002. "Health Spending Projections for 2001–2011: The Latest Outlook." *Health Affairs* 21:207–18.

Hurtado, Arnold V., Merwyn R. Greenlick, and Ernest W. Saward. 1969. "The Organization and Utilization of Home-Care and Extended-Care-Facility Services in a Prepaid Comprehensive Group Practice Plan." *Medical Care* 7:30–40.

Institute of Medicine (ed). 2001. *Crossing the Quality Chasm: A New Health System for the 21st Century.* Washington, DC: National Academy Press.

Jacobs, Lawrence, Theodore Marmor, and Jonathan Oberlander. 1999. "The Oregon Health Plan and the Political Paradox of Rationing: What Advocates and Critics Have Claimed and What Oregon Did." *Journal of Health Politics, Policy and Law* 24:161–80.

Kaisernetwork.org. 2002. "Health Poll Search." Accessed December 8, 2004 (http://www.ropercenter.uconn.edu/cgi-bin/hsrun.exe/roperweb/HPOLL/HPOLL.htx;start=hpollsearchAM?sid=F6).

"Kaiser Health Poll Report." 2003. Accessed December 8, 2004 (www.kff.org/healthpollreport/currentedition/about.cfm).

Kassirer, Jerome P. 1998. "Doctor Discontent." *New England Journal of Medicine* 339:1543–45.

Klein, Rudolf, Patricia Day, and Sharon Redmayne. 1996. *Managing Scarcity: Priority Setting and Rationing in the National Health Service.* Philadelphia, PA: Open University Press.

Kohn, Linda T., Janet M. Corrigan, and Molla S. Donaldson (eds). 2000. *To Err Is Human: Building a Safer Health System.* Washington, DC: National Academy Press.

Leapfrog Group for Patient Safety. 2001. "Rewarding Higher Standards." Accessed December 8, 2004 (www.leapfroggroup.org).

Lewis, Charles E., Rashi Fein, and David Mechanic. 1976. *A Right to Health.* New York: Wiley-Interscience.

Mechanic, David. 1978. *Medical Sociology.* 2nd ed. New York: Free Press.

Mechanic, David. 1995. "Dilemmas in Rationing Health Care Services: The Case for Implicit Rationing." *British Medical Journal* 310:1655–59.

Mechanic, David. 1996. "Failure of Health Care Reform in the USA." *Journal of Health Services Research and Policy* 1:4–9.

Mechanic, David. 1997. "Managed Care as a Target of Distrust." *Journal of the American Medical Association* 277:1810–11.

Mechanic, David. 2002a. "Socio-cultural Implications of Changing Organizational Technologies in the Provision of Care." *Social Science and Medicine* 54:459–67.

Mechanic, David. 2002b. "Improving the Quality of Health Care in the United States of America: The Need for a Multi-Level Approach." *Journal of Health Services Research and Health Policy* 7(Supplement 1):S35–S39.

Mechanic, David and Marsha Rosenthal. 1999. "Responses of HMO Medical Directors to Trust Building in Managed Care." *Milbank Quarterly* 77:283–303.

Mechanic, Robert E. 2002. "Disease Management: A Promising Approach for Health Care Purchasers." *Executive Brief.* Washington, DC: National Health Care Purchasing Institute.

Miller, Robert H. and Harold S. Luft. 1994. "Managed Care Plan Performance Since 1980: A Literature Analysis." *Journal of the American Medical Association* 271:1512–19.

Miller, Robert H. and Harold S. Luft. 1997. "Does Managed Care Lead to Better or Worse Quality of Care?" *Health Affairs* 16:7–25.

Miller, Robert H. and Harold S. Luft. 2002. "HMO Plan Performance Update: An Analysis of the Literature, 1997–2001." *Health Affairs* 21:63–86.

Nelson, David E., Betsy L. Thompson, Nancy J. Davenport, and Linda J. Penaloza. 2000. "What People Really Know about Their Health Insurance: A Comparison of Information Obtained from Individuals and Their Insurers." *American Journal of Public Health* 90:924–28.

Nye, Joseph S., Jr., Philip D. Zelikow, and David C. King. 1997. *Why People Don't Trust Government.* Cambridge, MA: Harvard University Press.

Remler, Dahlia K., Karen Donelan, Robert J. Blendon, George D. Lundberg, Lucian L. Leape, David R. Calkins, Katherine Binns, and Joseph P. Newhouse. 1997. "What Do Managed Care Plans Do to Affect Care? Results from a Survey of Physicians." *Inquiry* 34:196–204.

Rice, Thomas. 1998. *The Economics of Health Reconsidered.* Chicago, IL: Health Administration Press.

Rice, Thomas, Jon Gabel, Larry Levitt, and Samantha Hawkins. 2002. "Workers and Their Health Plans: Free to Choose?" *Health Affairs* 21:182–87.

Robinson, James C. 1999. *The Corporate Practice of Medicine: Competition and Innovation in Health Care.* Berkeley: University of California Press.

Robinson, James C. 2001. "The End of Managed Care." *Journal of the American Medical Association* 285:2622–28.

Shortell, Stephen M., Robin R. Gillies, David A. Anderson, Karen Morgan Erickson, and John B. Mitchell. 2000. *Remaking Health Care in America: the Evolution of Organized Delivery Systems.* 2nd ed. San Francisco, CA: Jossey-Bass.

Skocpol, Theda. 1997. *Boomerang: Health Care Reform and the Turn against Government.* New York: W.W. Norton.

Strunk, Bradley C., Paul B. Ginsburg, and Jon Gabel. 2001. "Tracking Health Care Costs." Health Affairs Web Exclusive, posted September. Accessed December 9, 2004 (www.healthaffairs.org).

Tu, Ha T. and James D. Reschovsky. 2002. "Assessments of Medical Care by Enrollees in For-Profit and Nonprofit Health Maintenance Organizations." *New England Journal of Medicine* 346:1288–93.

Ullman, Ralph, Jerrold W. Hill, Eileen C. Scheye, and Randall K. Spoeri. 1997. "Satisfaction and Choice: A View from the Plans." *Health Affairs* 16:209–17.

Wagner, Edward H., Brian T. Austin, and Michael von Korff. 1996. "Organizing Care for Patients with Chronic Illness." *Milbank Quarterly* 74:511–44.

Woolhandler, Steffie and David U. Himmelstein. 2002. "Paying for National Health Insurance—And Not Getting It." *Health Affairs* 21:88–98.

Competition and Health Plan Performance
Evidence from Health Maintenance
Organization Insurance Markets

Dennis P. Scanlon, PhD, Shailender Swaminathan, PhD,
Michael Chernew, PhD, James E. Bost, PhD, and John Shevock, MSM

For more than 3 decades, Health Maintenance Organizations (HMOs) have been promoted as effective vehicles for introducing competition within the healthcare sector.[1] Proponents of managed competition hoped that competing plans would produce more efficient market outcomes either by reducing costs and/or improving quality. However, others have noted that competition between plans may be counterproductive if the result is nonvalued product differentiation.[2] Recent evidence regarding quality deficiencies and medical errors has renewed interest in HMO competition as a potential catalyst for improving quality.[3,4]

The degree to which HMOs compete on attributes such as clinical quality and member service, relative to price, is still an unanswered empirical question because standardized measures of health plan quality have been lacking historically. The recent availability and use of measurement systems, such as the Health Plan Employer Data and Information Set (HEDIS©) and the Consumer Assessment of Health Plans Survey (CAHPS©), now make it possible to investigate the relationship between HMO competition and these measures of plan quality. HEDIS is a set of clinical process and outcome measures derived from scientific evidence and measured for relevant health plan populations, whereas CAHPS is a survey of health plan members regarding their opinions about the quality of care and service provided by their plan and its contracted physicians. Because these are the most widely used measures of HMO performance, understanding their relationship to market factors is important.

We present estimates from models that examine the relationship between HMO quality and competition, controlling for important characteristics of market demand and supply. We used data for 341 plans operating across various markets in the United States. Although the cross-sectional and nonexperimental nature of our data means that we cannot draw causal inferences about the impact of competition, our estimates report whether competition was correlated with HMO performance in 1999.

Adapted from: Dennis Scanlon, Shailender Swaminathan, Michael Chernew, James E. Bost, and John Shevock. (2005). Competition and health plan performance: Evidence from health maintenance organization insurance markets. *Medical Care*, 43(4), 338–346.

RESULTS

Plans in more competitive markets (a lower HHI) have worse performance in all 6 domains, holding HMO penetration constant. This relationship is statistically significant for the 2 CAHPS domains and the women's care domain.

Our estimates suggest, all else constant, the health plan in the more concentrated market would have 0.37 and 0.58 of a standard deviation better performance on the plan service and plan satisfaction domains, respectively.

Greater HMO penetration is significantly associated with better performance for all 4 of the HEDIS domains. Plans that allow NCQA to publicly report their results perform significantly better on all domains.

There is generally no statistically significant difference between for-profit and not-for-profit plans or across plan model types. Commercial plan enrollment also is not associated with plan performance. Plan age is estimated to be positively and significantly related to performance in 3 of the 6 domains, while plans affiliated with a national firm perform between one-half to three-quarters of a standard deviation worse on the 2 CAHPS domains.

Taken together, the market demographic variables suggest that population, economic, and sociodemographic characteristics are significantly related to plan performance for many domains, which suggests these variables may collectively reflect broader regional differences in the practice of medicine.

DISCUSSION

Theory is equivocal about the relationship between competition and plan performance. There are several potential explanations for our finding that less competition, as measured by the HHI, is associated with better performance for 3 of the 6 domains. First, competition among plans may result in providers finding it more difficult to respond to HMOs' competing quality initiatives with the incentive to respond to any one plan reduced if the market is fragmented. Second, competition may have driven down premiums, resulting in lower quality, though the relationship between quality and costs (or premiums) is not well established.[5] Third, although lower premiums and reduced quality may be optimal if consumers and purchasers are well informed, this outcome could result from information imperfections rather than voluntary decisions. Fourth, plans that provide poor quality may have exited the market, leaving fewer better performing plans. Our study design does not allow us to resolve these issues, but the results point to hypotheses that should be explored in future studies.

Our finding that plans in markets with greater HMO penetration perform better on the HEDIS performance dimensions may mean that providers in these markets are under greater pressure from plans to improve performance on the HEDIS indicators. The lack of a relationship between HMO penetration and the CAHPS domains might reflect a situation where incremental HMO enrollment in high penetration markets includes individuals less receptive to HMO care.

The positive and significant relationship between public reporting and quality suggests the importance of plan disclosure. Although the number of nonpublic reporters has dropped in recent years, this finding suggests that voluntary reporting dilutes the market signal, perhaps stifling competition, because consumers and purchasers are shielded from knowing the true degree of quality variation. As long as reporting remains voluntary, it is important for health plan report cards to denote plans that refuse to report their data.

In summary, our results offer little support for the notion that HMO competition is related to better performance in 1999. Although not definitive regarding causality, our analysis suggests the need to reassess the belief that competition inherently will improve performance. As concerns about the cost and quality of health care continue to mount, policymakers, regulators, and purchasers need to understand the effects of procompetitive policies on outcomes in the complicated, multilayered health care environment.[2]

REFERENCES

1. Enthoven AC The history and principles of managed competition. *Health Aff (Millwood)*. 1997;16: 125–136.

2. Nichols LM, Ginsburg PB, Berenson RA, et al. Are market forces strong enough to deliver efficient health care systems? Confidence is waning. *Health Affairs*. 2004;23:8–21.

3. Institute of Medicine. *Crossing the Quality Chasm*. Washington, DC: National Academy Press; 2001.

4. Scanlon DP, Rolph E, Darby C, et al. Are managed care plans organizing for quality? *Med Care Res Rev*. 2000;57(Suppl 2):9–32.

5. McLaughlin CG, Ginsburg PB. Competition, quality of care, and the role of the consumer. *Milbank Q*. 1998;76:737–743.

The Effects of Recent Employment Changes and Premium Increases on Adults' Insurance Coverage

Jack Hadley

The percentage of nonelderly adults (ages 18 to 64) without insurance coverage declined from 19.6 percent in 1997 to 17.8 percent in 2000 (calculated from DeNavas-Walt, Proctor, and Mills 2004). By 2003, following the recession that began in 2001 and several years of double-digit increases in the cost of private insurance (Kaiser Family Foundation and Hospital Research and Education Trust 2005), the number of nonelderly adults without insurance coverage jumped by 5.4 million people to 36.3 million people, representing 20.2 percent of nonelderly adults (DeNavas-Walt, Proctor, and Mills 2004). Since Medicaid coverage of nonelderly adults expanded somewhat during this period from 6.5 percent in 2000 to 7.2 percent in 2003, the increase in uninsurance reflects a substantial decrease in the proportion of nonelderly adults with private insurance coverage.

The trend of declining insurance coverage coupled with the simultaneous increases in unemployment and the cost of private insurance raises several questions. Was falling employment or private insurance price inflation the more important factor underlying the increase in uninsurance? How do changes in employment and the cost of private insurance affect public insurance coverage? If employment loss was the dominant reason for the drop in insurance coverage, then economic recovery should lead to improved insurance coverage. However, if insurance price inflation is the primary reason for the drop in coverage, policy should focus on the factors behind the rising cost of insurance.

NEW CONTRIBUTION

This article addresses these questions by estimating empirical models of the relationships between employment, the cost of insurance, and the distribution of insurance coverage using data from surveys fielded in 1997, 1999, and 2002, years that encompassed major changes in unemployment and the cost of private insurance, and modest expansions of nonelderly adults' eligibility for public insurance. This work extends and complements two previous strands of research, one focusing on the effects of unemployment and the other on the effects of insurance costs on insurance coverage. First, the article analyzes the

---

Adapted from: Jack Hadley. (2006). The effects of recent employment changes and premium increases on adults' insurance coverage. *Medical Care Research and Review,* 64(4), 447–476.

distribution of choices among private coverage, public coverage, or no coverage among all nonelderly adults without regard to employment status or access to employer-sponsored insurance (ESI). Second, the empirical models explicitly consider the linkages between employment status and insurance coverage and incorporate the costs of private insurance, public insurance, and being uninsured into the insurance choice models. Third, the models use novel measures of the costs of alternative insurance states. In contrast, most of the prior research analyzed a single type of coverage (private, public, or uninsured) for a narrowly defined population (e.g., workers with or without access to employer-sponsored insurance, people potentially eligible for public coverage), usually as a function of only the price of that type of coverage.

CONCEPTUAL FRAMEWORK

The underlying conceptual framework (Phelps 1973, 1976) posits that families evaluate alternative insurance options, including being uninsured, and choose the option that offers the greatest expected utility. In particular, the probability of selecting a particular option depends on the costs associated with each of the choices as well as on factors (e.g., family income, wealth, education, health, and demographic characteristics) that affect the underlying demand for medical care and the need for insuring against large medical expenses.

In general, an increase in the price of any one insurance option should reduce the probability of choosing that option and increase the probabilities of choosing the other options, while increases in the costs of the alternative insurance options should have nonnegative effects.

EMPIRICAL APPROACH

Data Sources

The National Survey of America's Families (NSAF), fielded in 1997, 1999, and 2002, is the primary data source for this analysis (Kenney, Scheuren, and Wang 1999). The NSAF is a nationally representative household survey conducted primarily by telephone. Each survey collected information on type of insurance coverage, access to ESI, employment status, income, and family and sociodemographic characteristics for more than 100,000 people. The analysis sample pools data from all three NSAF surveys and is limited to nonelderly adults (ages 19 through 64) who do not have any Medicare coverage.

RESULTS

The cost of private insurance is negative and statistically significant in the private-insurance equations and positive and statistically significant in the models for public insurance and uninsurance both for low- and high-income people. The measure of the cost of being uninsured is negative and statistically significant in the uninsurance equations and positive and statistically significant in both private-insurance models. Contrary to expectation, this variable has a negative sign in the public-coverage models, but its coefficients are very small and statistically insignificant.

The indicator for categorical eligibility is statistically significant in all three equations for low-income people and has the hypothesized positive sign in the public-insurance equation and negative coefficients in the models for private coverage and uninsurance. For people who are categorically eligible, the cost of public coverage (income that would have to be forgone to meet income eligibility standards) is negative and significant in the public-insurance equation and positive and significant in the private-insurance and uninsurance models. Public insurance coverage is inversely related to the extent of Medicaid managed care and positively related to the presence of a medically needy program, which increases the probability of public coverage for people in poor health or with a work-limiting disability.

Controlling for the prices of the alternative insurance states, family income among low-income adults has a strong positive effect on private coverage and corresponding negative effect on being uninsured. However, as expected, its effect on public coverage flattens after 150 percent of the FPL, that is, once a family's income is too high for public coverage, the probability of public coverage does not decrease with further increases in family income relative to poverty. Increasing income among high-income adults increases private coverage, but its quantitative impact is relatively small. Private coverage also goes up with increasing wealth for both low- and high-income adults.

DISCUSSION

The main policy implication suggested by these results is that the rapid increase in cost of private insurance during the past few years is the primary factor behind the decrease in private insurance among nonelderly adults and the corresponding increase in uninsurance. Since employees' out-of-pocket share of premium costs has remained steady in recent years (Kaiser Family Foundation and Hospital Research and Education Trust 2005), private insurance premium inflation has been fueled mainly by the increase in the underlying cost of insurance reinforced by a drop in the proportion of small firms offering employer-sponsored coverage (Kaiser Family Foundation and Hospital Research and Education Trust 2005), which also is related to the rapidly escalating cost of insurance, and an increase in the proportion of workers in small firms (Holahan and Ghosh 2004). In spite of the fact that the elasticity (marginal probability) of private coverage with respect to cost of private insurance is very low, the cumulative increase in the cost of private insurance during the years studied was sufficiently large to have a substantial effect on coverage. The decrease in employment was associated with only a small rise in aggregate uninsurance. The increase in the cost of private insurance was also the largest factor contributing to the increase in public coverage, accounting for two-thirds of the simulated increase of 0.6 percentage points. Moreover, as indicated by the actual coverage changes, the increase in simulated public coverage absorbs less than 20 percent of the decrease in private coverage.

Increases in the cost of private insurance potentially affect the entire population. In contrast, the loss of employment has a substantial effect primarily on the relatively small proportion of people who lose employment. Even though the 2001 recession had a considerable effect on employment, only 2.6 percent of the adult population was affected directly. Without minimizing the effect of job loss on job losers and their dependents, changes in their insurance coverage are not sufficiently large to explain the aggregate loss of private coverage and increase in uninsurance.

These implications suggest that even if employment returns to its peak value of just less than 65 percent, continuing inflation in the cost of private insurance will continue to undermine private insurance coverage. Furthermore, growing federal and state budget pressures make it extremely unlikely that public insurance coverage, primarily Medicaid, can be expanded sufficiently to keep uninsurance from increasing. This certainly was the case during the 2000–2003 period before the effect of rising government deficits was transmitted fully to Medicaid eligibility, coverage, and payment policies.

Ironically, even though the increase in the cost of private insurance is the primary culprit behind the recent increase in uninsurance, the very low price elasticity of demand implies that subsidies to encourage people to buy private insurance will have to be very large to have much effect. Although low-income adults are more price sensitive than high-income adults, the rate of private insurance-coverage is so low among low-income people that modest subsidies, such as through tax credits that reduce premium cost by 25 to 30 percent, will increase private insurance coverage by only a few percentage points, which would still leave around 20 percent of low-income people uninsured. Moreover, some of the increase in private coverage would be likely to come from public coverage. While this would be beneficial to some government programs, it does not serve the primary goal of reducing uninsurance.

Conversely, the even lower price sensitivity found for high-income people coupled with their very high rate of private insurance coverage suggests that eliminating existing tax subsidies for private insurance coverage for high-income people would have very little effect on their insurance coverage. The total size of the tax subsidy is substantial, more than $180 billion in 2004, and most of it goes to high-income people (Sheils and Haught 2004). This would be more than enough to pay for the estimated $48 billion of additional medical care the uninsured would use if they had insurance coverage (Hadley and Holahan 2004). Although eliminating the tax subsidy would in effect reduce income for high-income people, the analysis suggests that private coverage for these people would fall by only 1 to 2 percentage points and remain higher than 90 percent.

This research does not have any implications for the best strategies for reducing both insurance and medical-care cost inflation. However, it does suggest very strongly that successful cost-control policies may be critical for improving insurance coverage. Limiting medical- and insurance-cost inflation will make private insurance more affordable and also will make the cost of government programs and subsidies for both public and private insurance more manageable.

REFERENCES

DeNavas-Walt, C., B. Proctor, and R. Mills. 2004. *Income, poverty, and health insurance coverage in the United States: 2003*. Washington, DC: U.S. Government Printing Office.

Hadley, J., and J. Holahan. 2004. The cost of care for the uninsured: What do we spend, who pays, and what would full coverage add to medical spending? Report prepared for the Kaiser Commission on Medicaid and the Uninsured. Washington, DC: Kaiser Family Foundation.

Holahan, J., and A. Ghosh. 2004. The economic downturn and changes in health insurance coverage, 2000–2003. Washington, DC: Kaiser Commission on Medicaid and the Uninsured.

Kaiser Family Foundation and Hospital Research and Education Trust. 2005. *Employer Health Benefits 2005 Summary of Findings.* Washington, DC: Kaiser Family Foundation. Last accessed April 7, 2006, from http://www.kff.org/insurance/7315/summary/index.cfm.

Kenney, G., F. Scheuren, and K. Wang. 1999. *National survey of America's families: Survey methods and data reliability.* NSAF Methodology Series No. 1. Washington, DC: The Urban Institute.

Phelps, C. 1973. The demand for health insurance: A theoretical and empirical investigation. RAND research paper series no. R-105-OEO. Santa Monica, CA.

———. 1976. The demand for reimbursement insurance. In *The Role of Health Insurance in the Health Services Sector,* edited by R. Rosett. New York: National Bureau of Economic Research.

Sheils, J., and R. Haught. 2004. The cost of tax-exempt health benefits in 2004. *Health Affairs Web Exclusive,* February 25: W4-106-12. Available from http://www.healthaffairs.org/Web Exclusives.php.

Health Savings Accounts and High-Deductible Health Plans: Why They Won't Cure What Ails U.S. Health Care

Sara R. Collins, PhD, The Commonwealth Fund

Some maintain that health savings accounts (HSAs), coupled with high-deductible health plans (HDHPs), are an important part of the solution to our health system's cost, quality, and insurance problems. Asking families to pay more out-of-pocket, the reasoning goes, will create more prudent consumers of health care, driving down cost growth and improving the quality of care as providers compete for patients. And the tax incentives associated with HSAs will lure previously uninsured people into the individual market, reducing the numbers of families without health insurance.

But while it is comforting to believe that such a simple idea could help solve our health care problems, nearly all evidence gathered to date about HSAs and HDHPs points to the contrary. Indeed, there is evidence that encouraging people to join such health plans will exacerbate some of the very maladies that undermine our health care system's ability to perform at its highest level.

MANY AMERICANS ARE ALREADY BURDENED BY HIGH HEALTH CARE COSTS

- Americans already pay far more out-of-pocket for their health care than residents of other industrialized countries, and real per capita out-of-pocket spending has been steadily rising since the late 1990s.
- The Commonwealth Fund Biennial Health Insurance Survey found that in 2005, 60 percent of working-age adults with private insurance with annual household incomes of under $40,000 spent 5 percent or more of their income on out-of-pocket expenses and premiums, and 40 percent spent 10 percent or more.
- There is considerable evidence that high out-of-pocket costs lead patients to decide against getting the health care they need. The Commonwealth Fund Biennial Survey found that 44 percent of privately insured adults with deductibles of $1,000 or more avoided getting necessary health care or prescriptions because of the cost, compared with 25 percent of adults with deductibles under $500.

Adapted from: Sara Collins, The Commonwealth Fund. (2006, September). Health savings accounts and high-deductible health plans: Why they won't cure what ails U.S. health care. New York: The Commonwealth Fund.

- There is also evidence that rising cost exposure leads people to accumulate medical debt, take on credit card debt, and reduce their savings. The Commonwealth Fund survey found that 40 percent of privately insured adults with deductibles of $1,000 or more had problems paying medical bills or had accumulated medical debt, compared with 23 percent of adults with deductibles under $500.

EARLY EXPERIENCE WITH HSA-ELIGIBLE HDHPs REVEALS LOW SATISFACTION, HIGH OUT-OF-POCKET COSTS, AND COST-RELATED ACCESS PROBLEMS

- The EBRI/Commonwealth Fund Consumerism in Health Care Survey found in 2005 that people enrolled in HSA-eligible HDHPs were much less satisfied with many aspects of their health care than adults in more comprehensive plans.
- People in these plans allocate substantial amounts of income to their health care, especially those who have poorer health or lower incomes.
- Adults in HDHPs are far more likely to delay or avoid getting needed care, or to skip medications, because of the cost. Problems are particularly pronounced among those with poorer health or lower incomes.
- Few Americans in any health plan have the information they need to make decisions. Just 12 to 16 percent of insured adults have information from their health plan about the quality or cost of care provided by their doctors and hospitals.

PATIENTS' USE OF INFORMATION ALONE IS NOT LIKELY TO DRAMATICALLY REDUCE HEALTH CARE COSTS OR IMPROVE QUALITY

- It is unrealistic to expect that patient financial incentives, even if better information is available, will lead to dramatic improvements in quality and efficiency.
- Most health care costs are incurred by people who are very ill, often in emergencies. Ten percent of the sickest patients account for about 70 percent of all health care spending.
- Payers, federal and state governments, accrediting organizations, and professional societies are much better positioned to insist on high quality and efficiency.

HSAs WILL NOT SOLVE OUR UNINSURED PROBLEM

Economists Sherry Glied and Dahlia Remler estimate that under current law, fewer than 1 million currently uninsured Americans are expected to gain coverage as a result of HSAs. This is primarily because 71 percent of the uninsured are in a 10-percent-or-lower income tax bracket—and thus would benefit little from the tax savings associated with HSAs.

THE INDIVIDUAL INSURANCE MARKET IS NOT AN EFFICIENT OR EQUITABLE SOLUTION TO THE UNINSURED PROBLEM

- The Commonwealth Fund Biennial Health Insurance Survey found that nearly 90 percent of adults who sought coverage in the individual insurance market in the last three years never ended up buying a plan.
- One-third (34%) of those who sought individual market insurance said they found it very difficult or impossible to find a plan with the coverage they needed.
- Nearly three of five (58%) adults who sought individual market insurance found it very difficult or impossible to find a plan they could afford. The problem was particularly acute among people with health problems or low incomes.
- About one-fifth (21%) of adults who had ever sought coverage in the individual market were turned down by an insurance carrier, charged a higher price, or had a specific health problem excluded from their coverage.
- The individual market is also inefficient: the administrative costs of individual coverage consume an estimated 25 to 40 percent of each premium dollar, compared with 10 percent for group coverage.

WHAT NEEDS TO BE DONE

We as a nation should focus on more promising strategies for expanding coverage, improving affordability, and improving quality and efficiency. These strategies include:

- Expanding group insurance coverage, with costs shared among individuals, employers, and government. This could be done by expanding employer-based coverage, eliminating Medicare's two-year waiting period for coverage of the disabled, letting older adults "buy in" to Medicare, and building on Medicaid and the State Children's Health Insurance Program (SCHIP) to cover greater numbers of low-income families, young adults, and single adults.
- Ensuring affordable coverage for families by placing limits on family premium and out-of-pocket costs as a percentage of income (e.g., 5% of income for low-income families).
- Greater transparency with regard to provider quality and the total costs of care.
- Pay-for-performance incentives to reward health care providers that deliver high quality and high efficiency.
- Development of "value networks" of high performing providers under Medicare, Medicaid, and private insurance.
- Better management of high-cost care and chronic health conditions.
- Improved access to primary care and preventive services.
- Investment in health information technology to facilitate the transfer of information among patients, providers, and payers.

PART V

Reforming the U.S. Health Care System

INTERNATIONAL HEALTH SYSTEMS

Americans have long been convinced that the United States has the finest system of health care in the world, and that the health care systems in other countries have nothing to offer. This perspective has been promoted by the media and by the American Medical Association, both of which have consistently opposed national health insurance. Anderson and colleagues compared the high level of U.S. spending for health care with the expenditures of other industrialized countries that provide national health insurance for their entire population. In spite of high health care expenditures, U.S. life expectancies are lower than those in many other countries and infant mortality rates are higher than those in all but five other countries. Thus U.S. health indicators are poor compared with other countries. In part, this relatively poor showing is related to the lack of national health insurance. Only the United States considers health services to be a commodity that is for sale to only those who can afford it.

The United Kingdom has provided universal health care with comprehensive coverage, including long-term care, for everyone in the country since just after World War II. This system has been financed by the government through taxes and has been owned and operated by the government's National Health Service. The quality of care and satisfaction with the National Health Service care have been strongly supported by the public in the United Kingdom. In the 1980s, however, the conservative government began to underfund the system after launching a series of attacks on its inefficiency. In 1991, the U.K. government introduced what it considered to be market reforms to create internal competition within its system. Pollock critiques the privatization of the British system and highlights the serious negative impact that this policy direction has had on access to free care at the point of service. Current U.K. policies use public funds from taxes to subsidize the private system and have dismantled a widely acclaimed system of public hospitals and a comprehensive primary care system.

The Canadian health care system has long been considered by many to be a good model for the United States. This approach has a single payer (the government) for all health care services, with health care providers remaining largely private. Once a year, the government negotiates with private providers to set reimbursement rates for the year. This approach has the advantage of controlling Canada's costs while ensuring access to services for all its citizens and reducing the administrative overhead associated with costly billing mechanisms. U.S. health care administrative costs are dramatically higher than those in Canada, owing to the complex and costly billing systems, marketing, competition, duplication of equipment and personnel, and other factors in the United States. Although the benefits of the Canadian model over the U.S. system are clear, recent fiscal pressures in Canada have reduced funding for the program, which in turn has reduced access and eroded satisfaction with care in that country.

Lasser, Himmelstein, and Woolhandler show that Americans are less likely to have a regular doctor, more likely to have unmet needs for health care, and more likely to not receive needed medications than Canadians. The universal health care in Canada reduces health disparities in access to care and could serve as a model for reform of the U.S. system.

Numerous studies have found that the United States has the lowest levels of satisfaction with health care compared to other industrialized countries. Recent studies confirm that Americans are less satisfied than the public in five other nations with how the system works as a whole. They believe the country is spending too much on health care, and they have problems paying medical bills, accessing care, and receiving high-quality care. These studies reconfirm that the United States is paying more for care, getting less for its expenditures, and excluding one fifth of its population from any care. White describes the health and income security arrangements employed in other countries. His work shows that long-term care and social security systems are better supported in other industrialized countries.

Jasso-Aguilar, Witzkin, and Landwehr describe the international expansion of multinational health care corporations, especially in Latin America. They show that this growth has been influenced by the United States, which has influenced organizations such as the World Bank, International Monetary Fund, and World Trade Organization to encourage reduction in public services and a growth in the privatization of health care and public health. The growth of multinational companies has resulted in less access to needed services and increased the strain on the remaining public service organizations. The processes of globalization of health care and privatization of health services, as promoted by U.S. corporations, have had serious negative impacts on access to health care in Mexico, Brazil, and other Latin American countries.

Navarro argues that the important problems in the world are poverty and hunger. These problems are made worse by the policies of industrialized countries such as the United States, which has supported U.S. corporate and financial interests that have prevented redistributional policies.

HEALTH REFORM FOR THE FUTURE

The key to the future is developing a shared vision of what type of health reform is needed. Americans need to embrace key values and goals that would foster a justice-based health care system, in which they support the idea of contributing to equality of opportunity and minimizing inequities in access and quality of care. The ideal system would ensure access to health care for all, promoting health and minimizing disease. It would support active, responsible, and informed community members and allow for local control and decision making.

Light has outlined how private health insurers and voluntary insurance fail to provide adequate coverage. These health plans use techniques of charging higher prices, denying coverage or excluding coverage to high-risk individuals, implementing indirect techniques of risk rating such as co-payments and deductibles, and avoiding payment of claims and other schemes. Light argues that a fair health care system should meet seven benchmarks: good public health programs, democratic accountability and empowerment, universal access, equitable financing based on ability to pay, comprehensive and uniform benefits, universal access, and clinical efficacy.

A single-payer national health insurance system could provide real coverage for everyone. Indeed, coalitions of physicians, nurses, and community leaders have developed a viable vision for national health insurance that represents a modification of the Canadian health plan and would provide universal health care. This proposal is similar to the Canadian plan in that it would be financed and paid for directly by government. It would be similar to a Medicare program for the entire population. The health care organizations and providers would continue to be private, but their incentives for profit making would be reduced. This system has many advantages—for example, budgets could be made globally without detailed fee-for-service billing and the rates would be negotiated annually with greater controls on overall system costs. Such a system would allow for stability among providers and access to services regardless of ability to pay.

Another approach is to continue to work for health care coverage at the state level. The original Canadian plan was initiated by provinces before it became a national plan, and these provinces continue to administer the program with some variations among them. Thus state models could lead to a national health movement. Several states, such as Hawaii, Tennessee, and Oregon, are currently experimenting with wider health insurance coverage for the population. Others, such as California, have been the subject of initiatives and state legislative efforts to adopt universal coverage for the population in the state.

The link between a national health insurance system and overall cost containment must be made. Instead of increasing costs, a national health system could help gain control over all payer costs. Although the health industry argues that the United States cannot afford health reform because Americans would have to pay more taxes, members of the health industry are really opposed to what may be economic limits on their current inflationary practices. Universal health insurance systems are able to involve cost controls more effectively, while ensuring access to care for a greater proportion of the population. The excess funds now spent on administrative costs and profits to the health industry could be brought under control and used to pay for those individuals who currently lack health insurance.

Health and equity need to be considered in an era of globalization, according to Navarro. He questions the activities and discourse used by international agencies and shows that some of these organizations have contributed to growing inequalities in wealth within countries and a growing polarization of various factions of the population. These policies have diminished the public health care programs in many countries and have led to the privatization of health care and reductions in services in less developed countries. As a consequence, globalization has become a major political and policy concern in the health arena.

CHAPTER 11

International Health Systems

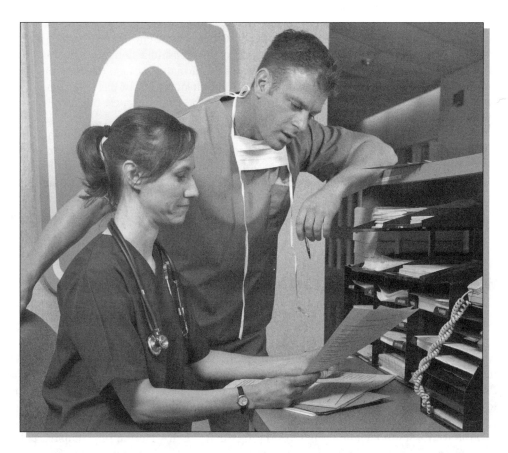

Nurse and doctor look at chart

The World Health Situation

Vincente Navarro

Analyses of the most important public health issues in today's world show that the greatest problem facing the world population is famine. According to a recent report on children's health, 10 million children die each year, most of them because of starvation and malnutrition.[1,2] This number of deaths is equivalent to 25 Hiroshima bombs exploding every year—and they explode without producing a sound. As a matter of fact, these deaths are so much a part of everyday reality that they do not appear on the front page: or even on the last page, of any prominent newspaper in Europe or the United States. Meanwhile, every two seconds, a child dies of hunger.

The paradox of this reality is that the world has enough food to feed the human population many times over. Let's not forget that the governments of the European Union and the United States are paying farmers not to produce food. Even countries where the majority of people are hungry have enough productive land to feed their populations many times over. According to a recent study, for example, Bangladesh, a country where hunger is endemic, has enough productive land to feed five times its population.[3,4] And this is true for most countries where hunger is endemic.

WHY DO WE HAVE THIS SITUATION?

The reason for this state of affairs is the huge concentration of economic, political, social, and cultural power in the world today. The world order—or, better, world disorder—is characterized by a massive concentration of economic, political, and cultural power. As is widely known, a very few countries in the North control or have a major influence over the world's economic, political, and cultural resources. This does not mean, however, that the primary division in today's world is between the North and the South. It is important to stress that the problem of the South is not a lack of resources. The South has enough resources to feed a population many times its size.

The North-South dichotomy ignores the fact that the distribution of economic, political, and social resources is highly concentrated both in the North and in the South. The North has dominant classes and groups and races, as well as a dominant gender, and dominated classes, groups, races, and gender. The same is true in the South: there are dominant and dominated classes, groups, races, and gender in the South as well. Twenty percent of

---

Adapted from: Vincente Navarro. (2004). The world health situation. *International Journal of Health Services,* 34(1), 1–10.

the richest persons in the world live in the South. For example, that while most populations in the Arab nations are extremely poor, the sheikhs live in opulence.

HOW IS THIS SITUATION REPRODUCED?

Within this context, what is the pattern of influences on the world today, including on the health sector? I believe the evidence is very strong: the economic, political, and health establishments of the North, and most especially of the United States (including its federal agencies, foundations, and leading academic institutions), have an enormous influence in shaping the culture, discourse, practices, and policies of the western world, including its international agencies such as the International Monetary Fund (IMF), the World Bank, the World Trade Organization (WTO), the World Health Organization (WHO), and the Pan American Health Organization (PAHO). Dominant ideologies in establishment circles in developed countries (and, again, very much in particular in the United States) appear, for example, in WHO documents shortly after they appear in U.S. mainstream medical and economics journals. The latest example of this situation is the document evaluating countries' health systems (*Health Systems: Improving Performance*),[5] prepared by the WHO two years ago (see [6] for a critique of that report). This is a heavily ideological document, reproducing the dominant ideology that has existed in the United States, and to a lesser degree in the United Kingdom, since the 1980s.

While managed competition, privatization, and for-profit medicine are fashionable doctrine with the U.S. establishment, they are not popular at the street level in the United States. The majority of people profoundly dislike insurance companies. Poll after poll confirms this. You may have seen the movie *John Q* (which in the United States means "average citizen"). When the main character in the movie—a blue-collar worker—curses the for-profit health insurance companies, the audiences in many U.S. movie theaters applauded. They clearly hold the private, for-profit health insurance-dominated system responsible for the situation of working people in the United States, where 44 million people lack any form of health insurance and 52 million have insufficient insurance.

THE ROOTS OF THE PROBLEM

It would be erroneous, however, to put all the blame on the establishments of the countries of the North. The establishments of the developing countries share a large part of the blame. Usually forgotten is that underdevelopment is rooted not only in international power relations but also in the power relations existing within the developing counties—that is, the class and other power relations in those countries. The roots of the problem are to be found in the developing countries themselves—in the patterns of class control over governments, assisted by governments of the North that are heavily influenced by their own dominant classes and dominant economic groups.

The solution, therefore, cannot be the replacement of consultants, academics, or international civil servants of the Northern establishments by their counterparts from the South. We have seen professionals from developing countries directing many international agencies that, while using a more radical discourse, have not behaved very differently in practice. Sometimes they have done even worse.

THE NEED FOR CHANGE

Contrary to what is usually assumed, the solutions to the problems we encounter in the world are not difficult solutions from the scientific point of view. Analyzing the situations in the world, we could easily find the solutions: to empower the dominated populations—the popular classes (in both the North and the South)—to make their governments responsive to their needs. We have enough experience to know how this can be done. And within that new order, the WHO should be a technical agency that supports such empowerment. Part of that support would be the criticism and denunciation of those dominant groups and classes (in both North and South) that, through the governments they so strongly influence, reproduce their interests. We have seen many occasions in which the WHO has failed to stand up to powerful governments and interests whose practices have interfered with the health of populations.

Some solutions: a health option that enables the empowerment of populations, facilitating their active participation in the shaping of their societies; a health system in which resources are allocated according to need and funds are obtained according to the ability of people to contribute; a health system linked to redistributive policies within each country and between countries—complemented by full-employment policies that ensure adults have the right to satisfactory work in an environment-friendly system of production and distribution, guided by public interventions and regulations. The enormous distance between these solutions (all of them easily doable) and the possibility of achieving them tells us much about the extreme political difficulties we still face.

Finally, the WHO should require each country, as a condition for membership, to provide health information as well as demonstrate a respect for human and health rights, and should denounce those countries, including the United States, that do not abide by the WHO Constitution. It rarely does that, but it should.

REFERENCES

1. Black, R. E., Morris, S. S., and Bryce, T. Where and why are 10 million children dying every year? *Lancet* 361: 2226–2233, 2003.

2. Dreze, J., Sen, A., and Hussain, A. *The Political Economy of Hunger.* Oxford University Press, Oxford, 1995.

3. *The Malnutrition Problem in Bangladesh.* The Social Policy Program, Paper No. 34. Johns Hopkins University, Baltimore, 2003.

4. Yong Kim, T., et al. *Dying for Growth: Global Inequality and the Health of the Poor.* Common Courage Press, Monroe, Maine, 2000.

5. World Health Organization. *World Health Report 2000: Health System-Improving Performance.* Geneva, 2000.

6. Navarro, V. Assessment of the World Health Report 2000. *Lancet* 356; 1598–1601, 2000.

Health, Poverty, and MDG

World Health Organization

2005

One billion people globally live in extreme poverty on an income of just $1 a day, of whom 700 million live in Asia and the Pacific. Many of the poor lack access to basic health services.

The Millennium Development Goals (MDG) aim to cut poverty by half by the year 2015. As health is central to poverty reduction, three goals focus directly on health, covering maternal mortality, infant mortality, HIV/AIDS, malaria and tuberculosis. Other MDG concern issues related to health, such as nutrition, water and sanitation, and the environment.

Asia-Pacific nations will need to invest considerable action and resources to meet these goals. Governments also need to look beyond individual diseases. Major investments will need to be made in strengthening health systems, promoting equity, securing and managing resources and promoting partnerships with non-health sectors.

CHILD HEALTH

More than 4 million children die before their fifth birthday in Asia and the Pacific every year, mostly from causes that can easily be prevented or treated, such as diarrhoeal diseases and pneumonia. In south Asia alone, 9 of 100 children die before five years.

The number of child deaths globally every year is huge—twice as many children died in 2002 than all deaths among adults from AIDS, tuberculosis and malaria.

Girls denied an education are more vulnerable to poverty, violence, abuse, death during childbirth and at the risk of disease, including HIV/AIDS.

REPRODUCTIVE HEALTH

Reproductive problems are the biggest cause of ill-health for women. Pregnancy and child birth are the major causes of death for women of reproductive age, killing more than one half million every year.

India accounts for more than one quarter of all maternal deaths worldwide.

In most countries, women have limited access to reproductive health services. Nearly 40% of all births worldwide are not attended by a skilled health worker.

Adapted from: World Health Organization. (2006). *Health, poverty and millennium development goals*. Geneva, Switzerland: World Health Organization.

TUBERCULOSIS

Every minute, roughly four people die of TB and 15 others newly develop the disease worldwide. One third of these people live in Asia.

TB is preventable and, in 90% of cases, can be completely cured for as little as $15 per course. Yet it accounts for 1 in 4 adult preventable deaths.

HIV/AIDS

About 40 million people are living with HIV/AIDS globally.

AIDS is the leading cause of death of adults aged 15–49 worldwide, killing 3 million in 2003.

Asia-Pacific countries have relatively low HIV prevalence rates, but large numbers of infected people. India has a prevalence one twentieth that of South Africa yet the same number of people infected. Similarly, Viet Nam and Swaziland have the same number of infected people yet have prevalence rates of 0.4% and 40%.

ENVIRONMENTAL HEALTH

Two-thirds of people in Asia and the Pacific lack access to safe water, including 300 million in China alone.

About 900 million people worldwide are estimated to live in slum-like conditions, which usually lack access to water and sanitation. In many south Asian cities, slum dwellers account for more than 70% of the urban population.

HEALTH SYSTEMS

Shortages of health workers in some countries are an acute problem, and in some Pacific nations are at a crisis level. Expansion of antiretroviral treatment for AIDS is currently being hampered by a lack of trained staff.

Up to 15% of professional health workers have migrated from most Pacific islands in recent years. In Samoa, 5%–10% of doctors are leaving each year and in Tonga, half the doctors now work outside the country. The main reasons include: low salaries, poor working conditions and environment, and shortages of supplies.

Better health information systems are urgently needed in Asia and the Pacific. Information needs to be disaggregated by sex, geographic area and ethnicity to enable analysis on health equity. Few countries have efficient information systems.

HEALTH FINANCING

An estimated $30–$40 per capita is needed annually to finance a *minimum* health service package, but many countries invest far less. Bangladesh, Cambodia, Mongolia, Pakistan and Viet Nam all spend less than $10 per capita per annum.

Some 100 million people are driven into poverty due to "out-of-pocket" health expenditures every year.

Some of the highest "out-of-pocket" payments, as a proportion of total health expenditure, are in this region. Such payments account for 80% of all health spending in Cambodia and India and about 50% or more in Bangladesh, Indonesia and the Philippines.

In poor countries worldwide, roughly one third of the disease burden in 1990 could have been averted at a total cost per person of only $12.

INEQUITIES IN HEALTH

Less than one third of the rural population in Cambodia, the Lao People's Democratic Republic, Mongolia and Papua New Guinea had improved drinking water in 2000. In these countries, the percentage of households with an improved drinking water source was twice as high in urban areas compared to rural areas.

In the Philippines, over 90% of women from the poorest quintile of the population gave birth at home while a mere 20% of the richest quintile had home births.

Less than 20% of mothers from the poorest quintile of the population in Cambodia and the Philippines were assisted during delivery by trained health professionals, while more than 80% of mothers from the richest quintile in Cambodia and 90% in the Philippines received assistance.

Most of the poor live in rural areas, yet these areas are often neglected. In Cambodia, only 13% of health professionals work in rural areas, where 85% of the population reside. In Nepal, only 20% of rural physician posts are filled compared with 96% in urban areas.

The likelihood of a woman dying in pregnancy and childbirth is more than 50 times higher in India and Nepal than in Japan. The probability of a child dying before its 5th birthday is more than 100 times higher in Cambodia and Myanmar than in Japan.

ACTION IN NON-HEALTH SECTORS

Mothers with more education are more likely to adopt appropriate health-promoting behaviors, such as having young children immunized.

A study of several countries found that child mortality declines by 3%–4% if access to drinking water is improved by 10%. Child mortality also declines by 3% if the years of schooling among mothers are increased by 10%.

Gender inequalities in schooling and urban jobs accelerate the spread of HIV.

Developed countries have been urged to give 0.7% of national income to help uplift the world's poor. So far, only five countries have met that target.

Rising Health Costs Put Pressure on Public Finances, Finds OECD

Organisation for Economic Co-operation and Development

Health spending continues to rise in OECD countries and, if current trends continue, governments will need to raise taxes, cut spending in other areas or make people pay more out of their own pockets in order to maintain their existing healthcare systems, new OECD data indicate.

According to OECD Health Data 2006, health spending has grown faster than GDP in every OECD country except Finland between 1990 and 2004 (Figure 11.3.1). It accounted for 7% of GDP on average across OECD countries in 1990 but reached 8.9% in 2004, up from 8.8% in 2003. OECD Health Data 2006 provides a comprehensive database of comparable health statistics in major developed countries, with more than 1200 indicators including some time series going back to 1960.

In most OECD countries, the bulk of healthcare costs is financed through taxes, with 73% of health spending on average publicly funded in 2004 (Figure 11.3.2). Ensuring sustainable financing of health systems is critical for governments, as health spending as a share of GDP is projected to increase further due to costly new medical technologies and population ageing.

Although the public share of health spending has fallen in countries such as Poland, Hungary and the Czech Republic which had a relatively high public share of health spending in 1990, it has risen in countries where it was low, such as Korea, Mexico, Switzerland and the United States. In Korea, for example, the public share of health spending rose from 38% in 1990 to just over 50% in 2004. In the United States, it increased from 40% to 45% between 1990 and 2004. Although the private sector in the United States continues to play the dominant role in financing, public spending on health per capita is still greater than that in most other OECD countries, because overall spending on health is much higher than in other countries.

PRIVATE SPENDING IS AN IMPORTANT SOURCE OF FINANCING

Private payments for health include those financed by private insurance and those paid directly out of the pocket of private households. Direct, out-of-pocket spending is an important source of financing in some OECD countries, particularly where private health insurance is low. In 2004, the share of direct, out-of-pocket spending was highest in Mexico (51%), followed by Greece (45%), and Korea (37%) (Figure 11.3.3).

Adapted from: Organisation for Economic Co-operation and Development. (2006). *Rising health costs put pressure on public finances.* Paris, France: Organisation for Economic Co-operation and Development.

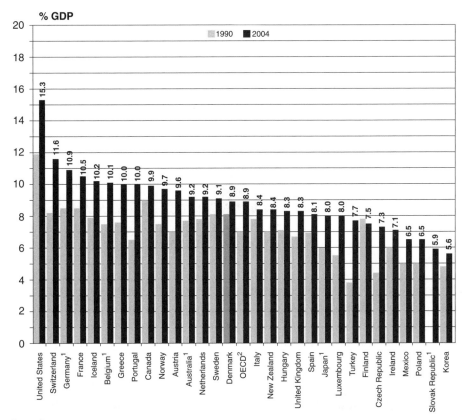

[1]2003. [2]OECD average for 1990 excludes Slovak Republic as expenditure data is not available.

FIGURE 11.3.1   Change in Health Expenditures as a Share of GDP, OECD Countries, 1990 and 2004
Source: OECD Health Data 2006, June 2006.

Private health insurance, that is, the money paid out by insurance companies on health services, represents only around 6% of total health spending on average across OECD countries, but it plays a large role for certain population groups in Germany and the Netherlands, and for most of the non-elderly population in the United States, where private health insurance accounted for 37% of health spending in 2004. In France and Canada, private health insurance covers 10 to 15% of overall spending, providing optional, enhanced coverage in a public system with universal coverage.

Private sources tend to play a much greater role in paying for pharmaceuticals than for hospital or ambulatory care, because drugs are less well-covered under many publicly-financed insurance schemes. But there are large variations across countries. In 2004, public coverage of spending on drugs was lowest in Mexico (12%), the United States (24%), Poland (37%) and Canada (38%). By comparison, more than two-thirds of spending on drugs was paid by public sources in a number of countries, including Austria, France, Germany, Spain and Sweden.

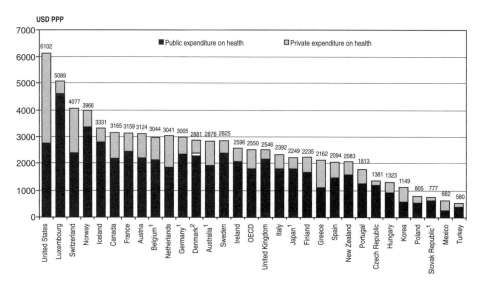

¹2003. ²For Denmark, current public and current private expenditures are shown as well as total investment, which cannot be separated into public and private.

FIGURE 11.3.2   Health Expenditure per Capita, Public and Private Expenditure, OECD Countries, 2004

Source: OECD Health Data 2006, June 2006.

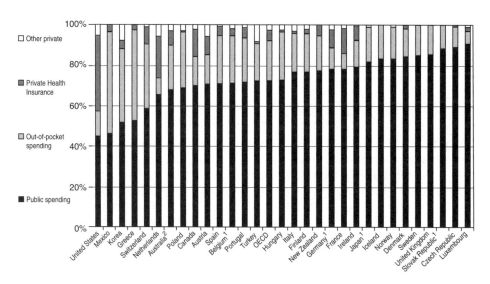

¹2003. ²2002.

FIGURE 11.3.3   Percentage of Health Expenditures by Source of Financing, OECD Countries, 2004

Source: OECD Health Data 2006, June 2006.

Access to Care, Health Status, and Health Disparities in the United States and Canada: Results of a Cross-National Population-Based Survey

Karen E. Lasser, MD, MPH, David U. Himmelstein, MD, and Steffie Woolhandler, MD, MPH

Canada, with a system of universal health insurance, spends about half as much on health care per capita as does the United States, yet Canadians live 2 to 3 years longer.[1] Few population-based data are available on health habits and processes of care in the 2 countries that might explain this paradox. Blendon et al.[2] found that both US residents and Canadians were dissatisfied with their health care systems, that low-income US residents reported more problems obtaining care than their peers in 4 other English-speaking countries (Australia, Canada, New Zealand, and the United Kingdom), and that quality-of-care ratings were similar in the 5 countries.[3] Among other studies, some,[1] but not all,[4] have found better health care quality in Canada. Socioeconomic inequalities in health, commonly perceived as pervasive in the United States, seem less stark in Canada.[2,5,7]

We analyzed population-based data from the recently released Joint Canada/US Survey of Health (JCUSH) to compare health status, access to care, and health care utilization in the 2 countries. We also sought to explore whether universal health insurance can mitigate disparities in health[7,8]—a question complicated by differences in race, poverty, and immigrant status in the 2 nations.

METHODS

The JCUSH assessed health status, disease prevalence, behavioral risk factors, health care utilization, and access to care in the 2 countries.[10] Conducted jointly by Statistics Canada and the US National Center for Health Statistics, the survey was administered between November 2002 and March 2003.

Adapted from: Karen E. Lasser, David U. Himmelstein, and Steffie Woolhandler. (2006). Access to care, health status, and health disparities in the United States and Canada: Results of cross-national population-based survey. *American Journal of Public Health*, 96(7), 1300–1303. Reprinted with the permission of the American Public Health Association.

RESULTS

Demographic Characteristics, Behavioral Risk Factors, and Health Status

The study population was representative of 206 million US adults and 24 million Canadian adults residing in households during 2002. United States residents were more likely to be non-White and native-born than were Canadians. United States residents had, on average, higher incomes and greater relative poverty rates (the proportion of respondents with income less than 60% of the median income) than did Canadians. With the important exception of having lower rates of cigarette smoking, US respondents were less healthy than Canadians, with higher rates of obesity, physical inactivity, diabetes, hypertension, arthritis, and chronic obstructive pulmonary disease.

Access to Care, Receipt of Health Services, and Perceived Quality and Satisfaction

In unadjusted analyses, fewer US residents than Canadians had a regular medical doctor. United States residents were more likely to have forgone needed medicines in the past year. Compared with Canadian women, US women had higher Pap test rates (at both 3- and 5-year intervals). US women reported higher rates of mammography screening "within less than 2 years" but not within the past 5 years. US respondents were slightly more likely than Canadians to give a rating of excellent to their hospital care (but not to their physician or community-based care). United States respondents also were more satisfied than Canadians with their hospital and community-based care, but not with their physician care. Although more US respondents had unmet health care needs than did Canadians (13.2% and 10.7%, respectively), their reasons for having such needs differed. Seven percent of US respondents (and less than 1% of Canadians) had unmet needs because of financial barriers, whereas 3.5% of Canadians had unmet needs because of waiting times (vs less than 1% of US residents).

Across virtually all measures, uninsured US residents had much worse access to care, received fewer medical services, and rated the quality of their care lower than did insured US residents. The uninsured were also less satisfied with the care they received. The US uninsured fared much worse than Canadians on most of these measures, whereas the US insured fared slightly better than Canadians (results of statistical testing not shown). Non-Whites were more obese than were Whites in the United States, but the opposite was true in Canada. In both countries, non-Whites were more sedentary. Racial differences in access to care were less marked in Canada than in the United States. Yet among the approximately 8% of respondents who reported depression in the past year, non-Whites in both countries (and the US uninsured) were less likely to receive treatment than were Whites or the US insured. Unlike non-White US residents, non-White Canadians were less likely to have received a Pap test within the past 3 years. Non-Whites in both countries had lower perceived quality of care and satisfaction than did Whites.

Unadjusted analyses of health status, access to care, and receipt of health services according to country, immigrant status, and income are available from the authors by request. These analyses revealed that the US foreign-born residents have worse access to care than do the US native-born residents, and that US respondents with incomes in the lowest quintile were less likely to have a regular medical doctor or to have contacted any medical doctor in the past 12 months than were US respondents in the highest quintile. Such differences in access were not present in Canada.

Multivariate Results

US residents (compared with Canadians) were less likely to have a regular doctor, more likely to have unmet health needs, and more likely to forgo needed medicines. US respondents were also more likely to say that they were very satisfied with the way health care services were provided. At the same time, US respondents were more likely to report that they were somewhat or very dissatisfied with health care services (odds ratio = 1.27, 95% confidence interval = 1.04, 1.54). In both the United States and Canada, respondents in the highest income quintile (compared with those in the lowest income quintile) had better access to care by most measures. The foreign-born respondents in both countries were less likely to perceive their quality of care as excellent than were the native born, although only in the United States were foreign-born respondents less likely to have a regular medical doctor, to have contacted a medical doctor in the past year, or to be very satisfied with their care. Non-Whites in both countries were less likely to be very satisfied with their health care than were Whites, although only in the United States were the former more likely to report unmet health care needs or to forgo needed medicines and less likely to have had a dental visit or to rate their quality of care as excellent.

DISCUSSION

Compared with Canadians, US residents are one third less likely to have a regular medical doctor, one fourth more likely to have unmet health care needs, and more than twice as likely to forgo needed medicines. Problems accessing medical care are particularly dire for the US uninsured. When they do receive medical care, US residents are more likely than Canadians to rate their satisfaction at the extremes (high and low) of the satisfaction scale. Health disparities on the basis of race, income, and immigrant status are present in both countries, but appear to be more pronounced in the United States.

Our finding that US residents have slightly higher rates of unmet health care needs confirms previous findings.[10] As in previous studies,[10] we found that barriers to care differed in the 2 countries: in the United States cost was the principal barrier, whereas in Canada waiting times were an issue. Canada's waiting times have received substantial press attention in the United States.[11] Nonetheless we found that long waiting times led to an unmet health need for only a small percentage (3.5%) of Canadians.

Racial disparities in health, present in both countries,[12,13] were more extreme in the United States. In multivariate analyses, non-Whites in the United States, but not in Canada, were more likely to have unmet health needs, to forgo needed medicines, and to have lower perceived quality of care than were Whites. Yet non-White Canadians had lower Pap test rates and lower rates of treatment for depression than did White Canadians.

It is possible that equalization of financial access may not ensure receipt of culturally conditioned services such as pelvic exams and psychiatric care. Comparing racial disparities in the 2 nations is complicated by the fact that each has a very different non-White population. The reasons for disparities involving Aboriginal Canadians and Asian Canadians may be different from those involving African Americans in the United States. Furthermore, the JCUSH did not provide language data on respondents; it is possible that the observed differences in both countries may in part reflect language barriers.

Income disparities may explain much, but not all, of racial disparities in health.[14] For Canadians, we, like others,[15] found income disparities in access to care. Like Katz et al.[16] we also observed that low-income Canadians have better access to medical care than do low-income US residents. Our study adds to others[2] in finding marked income disparities in perceived quality of care. Health disparities on the basis of immigrant status are also more pronounced in the United States than in Canada. Yet this comparison is problematic because the immigrant populations of the 2 countries differ. In Canada, many recent immigrants are Asian,[17] whereas in the United States, Latinos are the largest immigrant group, followed by Asians. Unfortunately, the JCUSH contains no data on the country of origin or the date of immigration, precluding more refined comparisons of immigrant health.

Comparisons of access to dental care in the 2 countries are of interest, given that neither country has universal dental coverage. Unlike physician services in Canada, which are fully insured in every province, dental coverage varies from province to province. In Canada, income disparities were much more pronounced for dental care than for medical care and were of a similar magnitude to the US disparities.

Universal coverage attenuates inequities in health care and should be implemented in the United States. However, adequate funding to avoid waits for care is essential; otherwise, satisfaction with care may diminish. Moreover, universal coverage is not sufficient to eliminate all health disparities. We also must address inferior systems of care in institutions serving the poor and nonfinancial access barriers such as cultural and language barriers. Simultaneously, policies to address unfavorable social conditions that impact health are sorely needed. Such policies could include reduction of income inequality through tax reform, improved housing, and expanded educational and employment opportunities for the poor.

REFERENCES

1. *OECD Health Data 2004: A Comparative Analysis of 30 Countries.* Paris: Organisation for Economic Co-operation and Development; 2004.

2. Blendon RJ, Schoen C, DesRoches CM, Osborn R, Scoles KI, Zapert K. Inequities in health care: a five-country survey. *Health Aff (Millwood).* 2002;21:182–191.

3. Hussey PS, Anderson GF, Osborn R, et al. How does the quality of care compare in five countires? *Health Aff (Millwood).* 2004;23:89–99.

4. Katz SJ, Hofer TP. Socioeconomic disparities in preventive care persist despite universal coverage. Breast and cervical cancer screening in Ontario and the United States. *JAMA.* 1994;272:530–534.

5. Hwang SW. Mortality among men using homeless shelters in Toronto, Ontario. *JAMA.* 2000;283:2152–2157.

6. Alter DA, Iron K, Austin PC, Naylor CD, and the SESAMI Study Group. Socioeconomic status, service patterns, and perceptions of care among survivors of acute myocardial infarction in Canada. *JAMA.* 2004;291:1100–1107.

7. Pincus T, Esther R, DeWalt DA, Callahan LF. Social conditions and self-management are more powerful determinants of health than access to care. *Ann Intern Med.* 1998;129:406–411.

8. Andrulis DP. Access to care is the centerpiece in the elimination of socioeconomic disparities in health. *Ann Intern Med.* 1998;129:412–416.

9. National Center for Health Statistics Web site. Joint Canada/United States Survey of Health, 2002-03. Available at: http://www.cdc.gov/nchs/data/nhis/jcush_analyticalreport.pdf. Accessed December 6, 2004.

10. Donelan K, Blendon RJ, Schoen C, Davis K, Binns K. The cost of health system change: public discontent in five nations. *Health Aff (Millwood).* 1999;18:206–216.

11. Krauss C. Canada looks for ways to fix its health care system. *New York Times.* September 12, 2004: A3.

12. Ng E. Disability among Canada's aboriginal peoples in 1991. *Health Rep.* 1996;8:25–32 [English]; 25–33 [French].

13. Chen J, Wilkins R, Ng E. Health expectancy by immigrant status, 1986 and 1991. *Health Rep.* 1996;8:29–38 [English]; 31–41 [French].

14. Isaacs SL, Schroeder SA. Class—the ignored determinant of the nation's health. *N Eng J Med.* 2004;351:1137–1142.

15. Chen J, Hou F. Unmet needs for health care. *Health Rep.* 2002;13:23–34.

16. Katz SJ, Hofer TP, Manning WG. Physician use in Ontario and the United States: the impact of socioeconomic status and health status. *Am J Public Health.* 1996;86:520–524.

17. Chen J, Ng E, Wilkins R. The health of Canada's immigrants in 1994-95. *Health Rep.* 1996;7:33–45 [English]; 37–50 [French].

Privatising the NHS: An Overview

Allyson M. Pollock, with Colin Leys, David Price,
David Rowland, and Shamini Gnani

Although elements of the privatisation process pre-date the Thatcher government, 1980 was when privatisation began to be official policy. By then the NHS had suffered thirty years of serious underfunding and a good deal of administrative reshuffling. Its hospitals were often dilapidated and some still dated from the Victorian era. Staff shortages were common and there were long waiting times for non-urgent hospital treatment. Pay for nurses and support staff had been kept low and morale was wearing thin. But a more equitable geographical distribution of resources had gradually been achieved, and the NHS's founding principles of comprehensive, universal care, equally available to all on the basis of need, not ability to pay, continued to prevail. What is more, the country's overall health statistics compared well with those of other industrialised countries, not to mention those of the USA, which spent twice as much per head on health care (see Tables 11.5.1–11.5.3). And in spite of its weaknesses the NHS remained extremely popular.

But in 1980 the Thatcher government began radically reshaping the NHS, fragmenting its structures, significantly reducing its coverage, and undermining evenness of provision from one district to another, while financial targets increasingly displaced health care needs as the focus of concern. Twenty-three years later the NHS had abandoned to the private sector almost all long-stay inpatient care, all routine optical care and most dental care, and multinational corporations from across the world were being invited to take over the running of 'failing' NHS hospitals and to provide routine NHS surgery in private Treatment Centres. The government had also just finished pushing through legislation under which most if not all NHS services, including hospitals, will eventually become more or less independent corporations, run on business lines.

2000–2003: NEW LABOUR'S DRIVE TOWARD A "MIXED ECONOMY OF HEALTH CARE"

By the autumn of 1999 Gordon Brown's two-year lock on new public spending had produced a situation in the NHS that resembled the Thatcher-induced crisis of 1987. Public discontent was acute and the government was in danger of forfeiting one of its greatest

Adapted from: Allyson M. Pollock with Colin Leys, David Price, David Rowland, and Shamini Gnani. (2004). Privatising the NHS. In: *NHS pc: The privatization of our health care*. London: Verso, Chapter 3: 34–80.

TABLE 11.5.1 Health Expenditure per Capita (£) and as Percent of GDP (in brackets)

	1970	*1980*	*1990*	*2000*
OECD average	74 (6.0)	346 (7.3)	839 (8.7)	1,500 (10.0)
EU 15 average	53 (5.4)	333 (7.3)	837 (7.8)	1,193 (8.7)
USA	145 (6.9)	506 (8.7)	1,553 (11.9)	3,057 (13.0)
UK	41 (4.5)	234 (5.6)	555 (5.7)	1,126 (7.1)

Source: OHE, *Compendium of Health Statistics 2002*

TABLE 11.5.2 Life Expectancy at Birth (years)

	1960–65	*1970–75*	*1980–85*	*1990–95*
OECD	66.4	67.8	70.0	72.2
EU 15	67.6	68.7	70.8	72.9
USA	66.7	67.5	70.9	72.2
UK	67.9	69.0	71.0	73.7

Source: OHE, *Compendium of Health Statistics 2002*

TABLE 11.5.3 Infant Mortality Rates per 1000 Live Births

	1970	*1980*	*1990*	*1998*
OECD	28.3	17.5	10.7	7.0
EU 15	31.1	19.4	11.1	7.4
USA	20.0	12.6	9.2	7.2
UK	18.5	12.1	7.9	5.7

Source: OHE, *Compendium of Health Statistics 2002*

electoral assets: Labour's identification with the NHS. On the other hand Brown's spending restrictions, coupled with the US-led boom of the late 1990s, had by now produced major fiscal surpluses. So early in January 2000, smarting from universal criticism over the latest 'winter beds crisis', the government pledged to raise spending on the NHS by 6.1 percent a year in real terms over the next four years—a roughly 30 percent increase in all, raising NHS spending to 8.2 percent of GDP (which, combined with private spending on health care, would be close to the current EU average). In return for the increases in pay and staffing and equipment that the new spending would permit, the government wanted pledges from everyone in the NHS to push through 'reforms' in every sector of the service, including the breaking down of professional barriers and the introduction of 'flexible' labour markets. In March 2000 133 senior NHS staff and informed outsiders were hurriedly organised into a set of 'modernisation action teams' which duly endorsed a plan of action that appeared in July. This was the *NHS Plan.*[1]

The NHS Plan

The *NHS Plan*'s goals, though expressed in sometimes overheated prose, were extremely positive, extensive and detailed. By 2010 there would be over 100 new hospitals (including those already under construction), 7,000 more hospital and intermediate-care beds, 500 new 'one-stop' primary care centres comprising dentists, opticians, pharmacies and social workers as well as GPs, and new information technology linking primary care and hospitals. There would be 7,500 more consultants, 2,000 more GPs, 20,000 more nurses and over 6,500 more therapists. By 2005 waiting times for hospital treatment would be reduced from an average of seven months to a *maximum* of six months, and eventually to a maximum of three months. A new system of resource allocation would end the unevenness in primary care provision that meant there were still 50 percent more GPs per capita in Richmond than in Bamsley, and NHS dentistry would become available 'to all who want it by September 2001'. (This last commitment seemed unrealistic, and so it proved. In August 2003, after a well-publicised incident in Wales when 600 people queued for 300 new 'places' in an NHS dental practice, the government announced that in future dentists would follow GPs and have contracts with their local PCTs, not the Secretary of State for Health.)

Further Privatisation

The *NHS Plan's* targets were ambitious and made great headlines. What was not so quickly absorbed by the general public was how far the *NHS Plan* would be accompanied by a much more radical marketisation of the NHS, both by opening it up to private providers of health care and by making even the publicly owned institutions of the NHS more and more like commercial companies. It is hard to tell whether the Department of Health's policy team had this radical marketisation of the NHS in mind in July 2000 when the *NHS Plan* was published. They were, as always, under heavy pressure from market enthusiasts in the Treasury, and it seems likely that they already envisaged some mixture of the continental European and the US models, both of which had been advocated in various forms by right-wing think-tanks and many of the department's external advisers. Pressure from both local and global market forces presumably also played a role in what eventually happened. The one body of opinion that was *not* consulted was the British public's. The far-reaching policy changes in the *Plan,* pointing the NHS ever farther down the road to privatisation, had not been put out for public discussion in a Green Paper. And the *Plan* itself, while eventually described officially as a White Paper, was from the first treated as official policy, endorsed by the NHS luminaries in the government-appointed 'modernisation action teams', not as a set of proposals for debate.

An important factor was the situation of the UK private health provider industry which had not benefited from any of the internal market reforms. The rising cost of health care meant that private medical insurance was now beyond the means of most people; rising insurance, premiums also meant that the numbers of people with company-paid medical insurance had stopped growing, and had continued to stagnate even when the economy expanded in the late 1990s (see Table 11.5.4). From the point of view of the private health care industry, the only solution was to get NHS tax revenues diverted to it, and it lobbied hard accordingly.

TABLE 11.5.4   Number of People Covered by Private Medical Insurance (millions), UK

1955	1960	1965	1970	1975	1980	1985	1990	1995	2000
0.58	1.0	1.45	2.0	2.3	3.6	5.1	6.7	6.7	6.9

Source: OHE. *Compendium of Health Statistics 2002.* Table 2.22

Most EU countries, with their mixture of state, independent nonprofit and private provision, looked capable of being penetrated in time. The NHS, however, with its universal publicly funded and publicly provided service, free at the point of delivery, still offered fewest openings to the private sector. It became fashionable among market-oriented health journalists and Conservative MPs to refer to its 'Soviet-style' centralised organisation, and to call for it to be broken up into something offering more 'choice', and for people to be able to 'put more of their own money' into the system and let private enterprise 'close the gap between demand and supply'. Behind these calls lay the commercial interests of not only insurance companies and private hospital and nursing home owners, but also nursing agencies, pharmaceutical companies, property development companies, facilities management companies and many more, which were all lobbying hard to erode the boundaries between the NHS and the private sector and get access to the NHS's tax revenues.

One of the boundaries targeted concerned hospital pharmacies. 'PFI is delivering improvements of up to 15 per cent in value for money', declared Tim Stone, now the 'PFI chair' at KPMG; 'if you got even 10% off the drugs budget at acute hospitals you would be talking about humungous amounts of money'. How humungous savings could be made by privatising hospital pharmacies the press report did not say. The prospect of humungous profits was easier to see. New Labour said it remained committed to the NHS and its founding principles, but it accepted the idea that private enterprise was more efficient than public enterprise and responded to all these pressures with ever greater concessions.

The Concordat with the Private Sector

The *NHS Plan* explicitly renounced what it called the 'standoff' that had existed between the NHS and private health care providers up till then. 'This has to end,' it said. 'Ideological boundaries or institutional barriers should not stand in the way of better health care for patients. . . . The private and voluntary sectors have a role to play in ensuring that NHS patients get the full benefit from this extra investment.' The NHS would therefore make a new 'Concordat' with the private sector about providing both critical and elective surgery, and intermediate care for NHS patients, paid for by the NHS. In addition the government would explore with the private sector the potential for investment in services such as pathology and imaging and dialysis. The *NHS Plan* also envisaged involving the pharmaceutical industry in 'the development and implementation of national service frameworks' or protocols for drug therapies for particular conditions, i.e. direct involvement in 'disease management'—a long-held goal of the pharmaceutical industry—rather than relying for their sales on doctors' prescriptions.

In fact the negotiations were already far advanced which led to the signing in October 2000 of a 'Concordat' between the government and the Independent Healthcare Association (IHA). In it the government made 'a commitment towards planning the use of private and voluntary care providers, not only at times of pressure but also on a more proactive longer term basis' which could be 'reflected in Long Term Service Agreements'.[2]

But just as few private nursing homes had the facilities to provide NHS standards of care, however 'intermediate', without substantial investment, much the same was true of most private hospitals, which provided a limited but profitable range of elective treatments, using NHS surgeons (and always with the option of moving patients to the nearest NHS hospital if complications arose). So the point was not just to agree to cooperate in general, but to 'signal a commitment' (in the words of the Concordat) on the part of the government to underwrite the necessary investment to upgrade private facilities by entering into long-term "contracts with the private sector to pay for clinical services—in effect, shifting more work by NHS consultants from NHS to private facilities, since virtually all private clinical work is done by NHS consultants, outside NHS hours.

By the end of 2003, however, it was becoming clear that the Concordat was largely a dead letter. The prices demanded by the UK private sector had proved so much higher than the cost of equivalent services provided by the NHS that the government could not defend accepting them. Eventually the government declared that it would continue to pursue the privatisation of clinical services, but by opening up the competition to international providers.[3]

Foundation Trusts

Foundation trusts were first foreshadowed in a speech by Alan Milburn in February 2002. No mention of them had been made in the Labour Party's election manifesto of the previous year, nor was any White Paper issued about them, though the legislation providing for them, and the detailed guidance later issued by the Department of Health for trusts applying for foundation status, showed that they had been a long time in preparation. According to Milburn, the idea emanated from NHS chief executives. It was presented as merely formalising the greater freedom which the *NHS Plan* promised for the highest-rated NHS trusts. Yet in reality it represented a drastic further step towards a fully marketised system.

Legislation followed swiftly and was completed in the autumn of 2003.[4] Under it all NHS hospitals, and all PCTs, will eventually be eligible for 'foundation' status. Foundation status will be awarded by an independent regulator. Provided they stay within the terms of the regulator's authorisation, foundation trusts will cease to be subject to control by the Department of Health and its regional arms, the strategic health authorities. They will become 'public benefit corporations', to be run as non-profit but nonetheless commercial concerns. Their assets will cease to belong to the state. They will be free to set their own pay scales, borrow on the private market, enter into contracts with private providers, and determine their own priorities.

They will be subject to some legislative constraints, which the government presented as ensuring that the NHS's founding principles would remain intact. They may not charge fees to NHS patients, and fees from private patients may never constitute a larger share of their revenue than at the time they become foundation trusts. There are no shareholders and so no profits. There are limits on how they may dispose of the assets they have inherited. And there will be boards of governors, a majority elected by members of the public in the local area. Indeed the government represented foundation trusts as a democratic advance.[5]

But the legislative constraints are weak, if not deliberately deceptive, above all because foundation trusts' freedom to enter into contracts with private sector companies means that all the things they are themselves prohibited from doing may be done by these joint ventures. A joint venture can for example charge fees, to constitute whatever proportion of its revenues it wants, and it may—indeed must, if it is a joint venture with a private company—make profits and distribute them to its shareholders. It will also be free to finance private loans out of its NHS revenues. In addition, it seems likely that the proceeds from any assets a foundation trust is allowed to sell will not go to the NHS as a whole, for use where needs are greatest, but will boost the balance sheets of the foundation trust alone.

There is also in reality no provision for local control. How many 'members' there are, and how they are selected from the local population, is provided for in each foundation trust's constitution, approved without any public consultation—by the regulator. There is no requirement for the 'members' to be representative of the local population or accountable to them, and in the first ten foundation trusts the total number of 'members', including patients and hospital staff, was less than three percent of the local population.[6]

Critics were quick to point out these and many other aspects of this complex change. MPs were particularly concerned that the first hospitals to become foundation trusts, being free to set their own pay scales and to borrow money, would drain other hospitals of their best staff, creating huge new inequalities, both between hospital staffs and between the facilities available to patients in adjacent areas. But the inequalities that worried the MPs are not a transitional problem; rather they are inherent in the whole idea. Foundation trusts will become like commercial companies. Their sole responsibility is to provide NHS health services 'effectively, efficiently and economically', i.e. to focus on their balance sheets, not on meeting patient needs. Even the regulator is not explicitly charged with meeting patient needs, as the Secretary of State for Health is under the NHS's founding Act, but only to act 'in a manner consistent with' the general duties of the Secretary of State. Foundation trusts will 'not be required to comply with management and operational guidance from the Department of Health', the Department told parliament, and so will be under no obligation to cooperate in service planning covering regions or even the country.[7] They will have the same ability to block area-wide improvements that impinge on their privileges that teaching hospitals have always tended to have.

When hospitals have foundation status, these kinds of problem seem bound to become worse, if not insuperable. The services available to patients will become a by-product of corporate planning focused on financial viability and growth. Not only will they be uneven between areas, they will be uneven between needs. Unglamorous, complex, costly kinds of care will inevitably lose out. What foundation trust will choose to specialise in mental health, geriatrics, patients with chronic diseases, or refugees' health? Who will provide them with an incentive to do so? The strategic health authorities will have no authority over them, PCTs will lack the necessary power, and it is not the job of the regulator. Who will even know what the health needs of their area are?

Regulating Standards

By 2001, even the core of the NHS—its hospital and family medicine services—was being transformed into a network of local corporations—the hospital and primary care trusts, and the private companies entering the new NHS 'mixed economy'—operating in a managed market, increasingly like the privatised public services such as water, telephone, electricity and gas. Foundation hospitals would carry this process further still, operating alongside for-profit providers. In effect, a quasi-monopolistic market was emerging which needed regulating.

The government seems to have only gradually come to see the need for regulation in this way. The initial motive seems to have been a desire to identify poorly performing hospitals and bring their performance up to the level of the rest. Another motive was the wish to strip hospital consultants of their remaining policy-making power and give cost-oriented managers exclusive authority. The fiercely defended principle that doctors' clinical judgement must be respected made it difficult even for hospital chief executives to change the balance of service provision or to curb spending that was wanted by some powerful senior consultants. But a series of medical scandals centred around individual doctors, helped turn public opinion against the authority of doctors generally, and made it possible to try to introduce more binding guidelines on clinical practice.

'National Service Frameworks', which outlined protocols and service arrangements for improving the treatment of a series of specified conditions including diabetes, coronary heart disease, and mental health, were one means of control. Another was the creation in 2000 of a well-funded Commission for Health Improvement (CHI), to undertake 'clinical governance' reviews in hospitals across the NHS. By early 2002 it had more than 300 full-time staff plus a pool of 500 part-time staff from which teams were drawn to carry out the reviews. A National Institute for Clinical Excellence (NICE), with an initial budget of £9 million, was set up for England and Wales, with a counterpart in Scotland, to assess the effectiveness of drugs and other medical technologies.

None of the elements in this rather haphazard structure proved initially very effective. NICE appeared to be quickly 'captured' by the pharmaceutical industry, which was in any case represented on NICE's governing body. NICE's first attempt to discourage the use of a drug, Relenza, which its expert assessors found to have too little therapeutic benefit, was reversed, and NICE also shied away from evaluating the cost-effectiveness of drugs it did approve.[8] CHI also proved ineffectual.

In May 2002 the government moved to improve this state of affairs by creating a single new body, to be called the Commission for Health Audit and Inspection (CHAI), which would combine the work of CHI with the work already done on the NHS by the Audit Commission. CHAI would also take over the work of the National Care Standards Commission which had recently been established to regulate private health care (since, under the Concordat, private nursing homes and hospitals would increasingly be treating NHS patients), and there would be a parallel new Commission for Social Care Inspection. CHAI was intended to become more like Ofsted, 'a single rigorous inspectorate armed with the ability to expose poor practice and highlight good practice'.

THE EMERGING NHS LANDSCAPE

The transformation of something as big and complex as the NHS can only be summarised, in the way this chapter has tried to do, at the cost of many simplifications and omissions. Even so it can be hard to see the overall picture, especially since so many of the changes are still in process while others, like foundation trusts, are just beginning. It is especially hard to distinguish between changes that are welcome in themselves, and those that are not. For example everyone benefits from medical advances, such as less intrusive 'keyhole surgery', that allow people to be discharged much sooner, or even to have 'day surgery' and go home afterwards. On the other hand they do not benefit if the reason for early discharge is financial, not clinical, and leads to suffering, and costly re-admissions. Likewise, with much more money going into the system from 2000 onwards, real improvements are being made; but if this money is diverted to pay for more expensive privately provided plant, like PFI hospitals, or more expensive private services, like those to be provided by for-profit DTCs or ITCs, it is highly undesirable. It is not easy to disentangle changes that are science-driven and rational from those that are ideology-driven and irrational.

One way to see the new shape of things is to relate changes to the NHS's founding principles of comprehensiveness, universality and equity. Comprehensiveness has clearly been abandoned, whether explicitly, as with most long-term residential care and routine optical care, or implicitly, as with dentistry, which has become available on NHS terms only to children and adults fortunate enough to live near a dentist still willing to work at NHS rates. Universality has gone in as much as the services provided both by GPs and by hospitals vary increasingly from place to place. The push to rectify the unequal geographical distribution of resources, such as GPs and hospital beds, has been largely abandoned too. The emphasis is now on 'decentralisation' and 'choice', but there are no mechanisms for providing democratic local control. If you need a heart bypass operation, your chances of getting one in good time still vary widely according to where you live, and the emerging foundation trust system offers no mechanism for remedying this.

As for equal access in the sense of access based on need, not income, this has been steadily eroded both through the abandonment of comprehensiveness—so that many quite poor people now have to pay as much as the affluent for long-term care, optical care, domiciliary services, etc.—and through charges ('co-payments', in the language of the World Bank) for prescriptions, dentistry, and non-clinical hospital services (such as phones and television). It has also become routine for patients needing elective surgery, such as cataracts or hip replacements, to be told at the hospital what the waiting time is, and then asked if they would like to have the surgery done much sooner, privately. Access to primary care is improving, and should improve still further as more funds reach general practices and specialist clinics of various kinds, more GPs are appointed, and nights and weekends are better covered—improvements that should make hospital accident and emergency facilities less burdened. If this happens the private primary care services that the private health care industry is promoting ('walk-in' clinics and insurance policies for primary care) should not be needed. Otherwise inequity will start to become familiar in primary care too. More problematic is the break-up of continuity in primary care that is implied in the sharing out of primary care services among a range of new providers, including private providers.

Harder to see are the effects of the marketisation of NHS hospitals, and the penetration of NHS hospital services by private industry. The now-required focus on the bottom line already means that profitable services get priority, while costly services such as mental health are as far as possible cut back. Some of the signs are all too clear, even if the root cause is usually officially denied—new PFI hospital buildings with too few beds and too few staff to cope with demand; outsourced meals too unappetising to eat; substandard cleaning or sterilisation of equipment by underpaid outsourced workers, contributing to the rise in dangerous infections; medical accidents due to faulty work by private pathology labs.

At a deeper level still are the implications of the so-called mixed economy of health care. Quite apart from some £4 billion a year of tax revenues going to the private long-term care industry, more and more of the NHS budget itself now ends up in the accounts of private companies providing everything from weekend GP cover and GP premises to surgery in private hospitals. Not only do these services tend to cost more, as the case of the DTCs brought to everyone's attention, but they also tend to destabilise the finances and organisation of NHS hospitals and other services, and so raise their costs too.

With each new insertion of private provision into the NHS the political clout of the private providers increases, and the dominant culture shifts still further in a private enterprise direction, while the structures of national control are being progressively dismantled. Once most if not all NHS hospitals have foundation status, and share the 'market' for hospital care with a wide range of private hospitals in a 'mixed economy of health care', the only remaining mechanism of coordination will be the independent regulator, whose mandate says nothing about comprehensiveness, universality or equity.

By the time most hospital trusts have foundation status and are free to function increasingly like private corporations, unsupervised by the strategic health authorities, this shift in the power balance seems bound to become even more significant. The most expensive part of the NHS—the hospital sector—will then be in the hands of chief executives dealing constantly with a growing system of private providers within and around the hospitals they are operating. It does not follow that they will absorb the ambient corporate culture and start awarding themselves higher salaries, and restructuring hospital services on more and more market-oriented lines. But it takes a lot of optimism not to believe that this is a rather likely outcome, especially in the foreseeable context of the eventual return of a Conservative government pledged to push the privatisation of health services further still.

REFERENCES

1. *The NHS Plan: a plan for investment and reform*, cm. 4818-I, The Stationery Office, 2000.
2. Department of Health/Independent Healthcare Association, *For the Benefit of Patients: a concordat with the private and voluntary health care provider sector*, Department of Health, 2000.
3. John Carvel, 'Reid to drop deal with private hospitals', *Guardian*, 6 April 2004.
4. Health and Social Care Act, 2003.
5. Ian McCartney, 'Keep your nerve; this is the rebirth of popular socialism', *Guardian*, 2 December 2002.
6. ONS, *National Accounts Sector Classifications of NS Foundation Trusts and NHS Trusts: PSSC decision case 2002/22*, 2 July 2003.
7. Department of Health Response to the Health Select Committee Report on Foundation Trusts, July 2003.
8. Richard Cookson, David McDaid and Alan Maynard, 'Wrong SIGN, NICE Mess', *British Medical Journal*, Vol. 323, 2001, pp. 743–5.

Multinational Corporations and Health Care in the United States and Latin America: Strategies, Actions, and Effects

Rebeca Jasso-Aguilar, Howard Waitzkin, and Angela Landwehr

The process of globalization raises several problems regarding health care and public health. Influenced by public policy makers in the United States, such organizations as the World Bank, International Monetary Fund (IMF), and World Trade Organization (WTO) have advocated policies that encourage reduction and privatization of health care and public health services previously provided in the public sector (Stocker et al. 1999; Iriart et al. 2001; Rao 1999; Turshen 1999; World Health Report 2000). These policies in turn have affected policies of the World Health Organization. (WHO), the Pan American Health Organization, and the U.S. National Institutes of Health (NIH). The latter organizations have accepted funding from the World Bank and have initiated programs influenced by the Bank's policies (NIH Fogarty International Center 2002; McMichael and Beaglehole 2000).

In addition to these non-commercial organizations, multinational corporations based in the United States have expanded worldwide. Managed care organizations, health care consulting firms, and pharmaceutical and medical equipment companies have entered foreign markets. U.S. industrial corporations also have operated in foreign countries; the participation of workers and the promotion of products in those countries have raised concerns about the impacts on local economies, environmental health, and occupational health (Kim et al. 2000). The "flight" of multinational corporations to foreign sites with less costly labor and environmental regulations has led to unemployment and loss of health insurance for U.S. workers (Stocker et al. 1999; Kim et al. 2000). As MCOs have faced declining rates of profit in U.S. markets, they have entered foreign markets, usually seeking access to public social security funds designated for health care and retirement benefits (Iriart et al. 2001). When MCOs shift their focus to foreign public trust funds as a source of new capital, they tend to withdraw from U.S. Medicare and Medicaid markets, with consequent disruption of services for patients.

OBJECTIVES

In this paper, we aim to achieve the following objectives:

1. To identify the strategies that multinational corporations, based in the United States, have developed to penetrate the Latin American health care market (although we

Adapted from: Rebeca Jasso-Aguilar, Howard Waitzkin, and Angela Landwehr. (2004). Multinational corporations and health care in the United States and Latin America: Strategies, actions, and effects. *Journal of Health and Social Behavior*, 45(extra issue), 136–157.

focus on Latin America, the same corporations also expanded into Africa and Asia);

2. To examine the actions of multinational corporations that affect health care delivery and public health policies in Latin America; and
3. To evaluate the effects of multinational corporations on health care delivery and public health policies in Latin America.

METHODS

Data Collection

Bibliographic Research
We reviewed the research and archival literature, published and unpublished, with the purpose of tracing the actions and strategies of multinational corporations in the United States and in the Latin American health care market.

Interviews
We conducted interviews with respondents in Mexico City and Guadalajara, Mexico, and in Brasilia, Brazil. The purpose of the interviews was to investigate specific practices in the corporations' health care delivery, such as health programs they offered and how these programs compared to those offered by the public sector.

FINDINGS

The Changing Characteristics of the Health Care Market in the United States

The Chronic Crisis of U.S. Health Care
Navarro (1994) points out some key issues in the U.S. health care industry and in health reforms enacted between 1980 and 1994. The massive involvement of for-profit hospital chains in the delivery of health services during the 1980s created a considerable growth of the for-profit sector (see also Caronna 2004). This involvement was facilitated by federal policies and programs such as Medicare, which provided about one-third of the revenue for these chains. The government paid for but did not control the delivery of health services and provided subsidies representing a large proportion of overall health expenditures. These conditions contributed to the crisis of health services in the 1980s. The medical-industrial complex acquired influence by financing members of Congress sitting in powerful committees that draft health legislation. From 1981 to the first half of 1991, for example, insurance political action committees (PACs) contributed about $60 million to congressional campaigns. The medical professional, pharmaceutical, and hospital PACs contributed, respectively, $28 million, $9 million, and $6 million.

The Rise and Fall of Managed Care Organization Profitability
Despite the penetration of managed care in the United States MCOs in the United States have faced a declining rate of profit. The MCOs reaped major earnings initially by paying hospitals a fixed capitation for each patient at a low negotiated rate (Freudenheim and

Krauss 1999). However, the rate of profit fell as the market became increasingly saturated (Stocker et al. 1999). By 1996 private health insurance premiums were rising at a much lower rate than MCO costs. Reasons for higher costs included rapidly increasing prices of medications, greater bargaining power for doctors and hospitals as they have consolidated, and a sicker population available for recruitment by MCOs after healthier populations initially were recruited (Winslow 1997).

MCOs' Exit from U.S. Markets

In light of declining revenues in the U.S. market, MCOs began to pull away from U.S. markets. As previously mentioned, MCOs also expanded domestically, although this expansion did not necessarily improve their financial conditions.

In summary, during the 1990s managed care in the United States evolved with an initial cycle of tremendous expansion and then a notable contraction. After attaining substantial rates of profit in the early stages, MCOs have reduced benefits and have raised premiums due to increasing costs. Managed care organizations have abandoned markets in the United States, specially those that involve partients with Medicare and Medicaid.

Corporations and International Health Care Markets

As the domestic market became more contentious and less attractive, a transition from national to multinational managed care emerged. U.S. and European multinational corporations, including pharmaceutical companies, long-term care corporations, and MCOs, turned to the international service sector as an alternative source of profits (Price et al. 1999). Other factors drove this transition as well. One of them was the triumph of marketplace ideology. From Eastern Europe to Latin America this ideological change led to governments setting aside welfare state ideologies and initiating privatization policies (Vranjes 1998). Some governments' moves to control costs and to privatize what were perceived as wasteful health care delivery systems increased the demand for U.S. managed care organizations around the world (Kertesz 1997).

In Latin America, the health care market presented very lucrative opportunities during the second half of the 1990s (Swafford 1996; Cisneros 1997; Financial Times 1997). The health care sector, still untouched by the privatization wave that had swept the region in the previous years, underwent reforms that opened the door to private capital (Swafford 1996). After implementation of reforms, favorable economic conditions created advantages for investors. By 1999, Latin America had become ripe for U.S. companies' investments and operations (Freudenheim and Krauss 1999).

The Role of International Financial Institutions in Health Reform

International financial institutions intervene in social policy making by requiring major health care and social security reform (Armada et al. 2001). Loan conditions and renegotiation of external debt payments have comprised the major tools of political leverage used by international financial institutions. "Letters of intent" that debtor countries have submitted to the IMF provide evidence of how health and pension reforms become embedded in major economic policies.

Effects of Multinational Corporations' Penetration in Latin America

Corporate managed care has exerted several important effects on health care and public health programs in Latin American countries. These effects include restricted access for vulnerable groups of patients and reduced spending for clinical services as a result of higher spending on administration and return to investors. Because copayments required under managed care plans have created barriers to access, they have led to increasing use of and strain on public hospitals and clinics (Iriart et al. 2001; Stocker et al. 1999; Waitzkin and Iriart 2001).

CONCLUSION: THE BEGINNINGS OF A THEORY AND PRAXIS

Economic Motivations for Globalization Policies

Since Adam Smith, economists have recognized that, over the long term, firms face a falling rate of profit as the market for a good or service becomes increasingly saturated. Our own research group and others have observed that one motivation for exporting managed care involves the falling rate of profit in U.S. markets. Some for-profit managed care organizations abandoned specific Medicare and/or Medicaid markets in the United States, as they entered new markets in Latin America and other regions. In health care, the falling rate of profit resembles that experienced in most other goods and services over time (Moseley 1991; Marx 1998).

When the rate of profit falls, corporations may develop several strategies, which include: increasing the productivity of labor, diversification into new product lines, and searching for new markets abroad. The managed care industry, for instance, has used all these strategies but has emphasized the search for foreign markets. Thus, in a largely correct prediction during 1996, the president of the Academy for International Health Studies noted the relationship between market saturation and exportation for managed care organizations: "By the year 2000, it is estimated [that] 80% of the total U.S. population will be insured by some sort of MCO. Since 70% of all American MCOs are for-profit enterprises, new markets are needed to sustain growth and return on investment" (Lewis 1996). The dynamics of globalization facilitate the movement of insurance companies and managed care organizations from U.S. to foreign markets, and globalization also affects services within the United States.

Globalization, "Silent Reform," and "Common Sense"

In our research, we have found that crucial decisions about privatization and the entry of multinational corporations into the public sector generally occur in the executive branch of government. In the United States, the pertinent agencies of the executive branch include the Office of the U.S. Trade Representatives and the Department of Health and Human Services. For instance, in late 2001, the U.S. Congress approved "fast-track" authority for the executive branch to enact international agreements in trade for health care and other services, with only a yes or no vote permitted by Congress, rather than legislative consideration of a trade agreement's details. In Latin America, the pertinent agencies of the executive branch usually comprise the Ministry of Health and/or the Ministry of the Economy.

After consultation with international financial institutions such as the World Bank or International Monetary Fund, policy decisions reach implementation usually through executive decrees or changes in regulations, rather than through new laws debated in the legislative branch. These policy changes receive little attention among lawmakers, the public media, or professional associations and consumer groups. The political process that accompanies such reforms therefore is usually a silent one, restricted to the executive branch of government.

Why do citizens in many cases consent to privatization schemes? The concept of "common sense" refers to the acceptance of new ideological discourses that challenge the role of the welfare state and transform the expectations of citizens in the face of growing crises. "Experts" in health care construct this common sense, according to several "fundamentals": the causes of the health care crisis are financial; administrative rationality is indispensable to solving the crisis; financing and delivery must be separated to increase efficiency; demand rather than supply should be subsidized; private administration is more efficient and less corrupt than public administration; the market is the best regulator of quality and costs; and deregulation of social security allows the user freedom of choice (Iriart et al. 2001:1250).

The legitimacy of such policy changes often contributes to the dismantling of the public sector. In Mexico, for example, "a gestation period of almost a decade," during which public institutions were slowly undermined and discredited, was necessary to legitimize the reform (Laurell 2001:299). Yet the worsening of the crisis in the public system—such as shortages of medications—could be traced to political decisions and appointments made by the same actors who became advocates of privatization. These examples show how governments can create artificial crises and then use them to build their cases for privatization (Schuld 2003:43–44).

Praxis

Action informed by theory, or praxis, has focused on the detrimental effects of economic globalization on health and health care, as well as alternative projects that aim toward improvements in health conditions (cf. Waitzkin 2000, 2001). Opposition to policies which generate adverse effects on health and health services has increased worldwide. Specific examples of organized resistance have shown that such policies can be blocked or reversed. For instance, a campaign to eliminate users' fees in public-sector health services and education led to a major change in the World Bank's policies of enhancing privatization and corporate trade in services. Through a series of protests, a coalition of health professionals, non-professional health workers, and patients who use public hospitals in El Salvador have blocked, at least temporarily, the privatization of those institutions.

Alternative projects favoring international collaboration have countered some effects of globalization on health and health services. For instance, the Brazilian Workers Party, which won the presidency in late 2002, has emphasized the expansion of public hospitals and clinics at the municipal level. Adopting the principle of community participation in municipal budgets, the new government has encouraged the strengthening of municipal public services and has tried to limit the participation of multinational corporations in health (Merhy et al., 2003). Such efforts have occurred in the context of a global network of advocacy organizations, political parties, labor unions, and organizations of professional and non-professional workers. This network aims to develop alternative models of service delivery that emphasize a strengthened public sector, and to counter the corporate dominance in health care that globalization encourages.

Linkages between economic globalization and health deserve more critical attention. A growing network of professionals and advocates has drawn attention to the new policies affecting health and health services that derive from the new conditions of global trade. Such profound changes arise as part of broader processes of economic globalization that lead to widespread unrest. Those concerned with health and security worldwide no longer can afford to ignore these changes.

REFERENCES

Armada, Franciso, Carlos Muntaner, and Vicente Navarro. 2001. "Health and Social Security Reforms in Latin America: The Convergence of the World Health Organization, the World Bank, and Transnational Corporations." *International Journal of Health Services* 31:729–68.

Caronna, Carol A. 2004. "Filling the Gaps in the Managed Care Story: The Organizational Field Approach." *Journal of Health and Social Behavior* 45 (Extra Issue):26–58.

Cisneros, Roberto. 1997. "International Benefits and Risk Management: Managed Care Makes Inroads in Latin America; Employers Driving Expansion of Benefit Plans." [Electronic version]. *Business Insurance*, October 6, p. 3.

Financial Times. 1997. "Healthcare Dream for Insurers: Will Social Security Changes Lead to Major Surgery on the Medical System?" [Electronic version]. *Financial Times*, October 23, p. 6.

Freudenheim, Milt and Clifford Krauss. 1999. "Dancing to a New Health Care Beat; Latin America Becomes Ripe for U.S. Companies' Picking." [Electronic version]. *The New York Times*, June 16, p. 1.

Iriart, Celia, Emerson E. Merhy, and Howard Waitzkin. 2001. "Managed Care in Latin America: The New Common Sense in Health Policy." *Social Science and Medicine* 52:1243–53.

Kertsez, Louise. 1997. "The New World of Managed Care." [Electronic version]. *Modern Healthcare*, November 3, p. 115.

Kim, Jim Yong, Joyce V. Millen, Alec Irwin, and John Gershman, eds. 2000. *Dying for Growth: Global Inequality and the Health of the Poor*. Monroe, ME: Common Courage Press.

Laurell, Asa Cristina. 2001. "Health Reform in Mexico: The Promotion of Inequality." *International Journal of Health Services* 31:291–321.

Lewis, John C. 1996. "Latin American Managed Care Partnering Opportunities." Presented at the Eighth Congress of the Association of Latin American Pre-paid Health Plans, Sao Paulo, Brazil. November 8.

Marx, Karl. 1998. *Capital: A Critique of Political Economy*. Vol. 3. London: The Electric Book Company.

McMichael, Anthony J. and David R. Beaglehole. 2000. "The Changing Global Context of Public Health." *Lancet* 356:495–99.

Merhy, Emerson E. and Gastão Campos. 2003. Unpublished research on municipal health programs. Campinas, Brazil: University of Campinas.

Moseley, Fred. 1991. *The Falling Rate of Profit in the Postwar United States Economy*. New York: St. Martin's Press.

National Institutes of Health, Fogarty International Center. 2002. *International Studies on Health and Economic Development.* Retrieved July 21, 2001 (http://www.fic.nih.gov/programs/econ.html).

Navarro, Vicente. 1994. *The Politics of Health Policy: The U.S. Reforms, 1980–1994.* Oxford, U.K.: Blackwell Publishers.

Pice, David, Allyson Pollock, and Jean Shaoul. 1999. "How the World Trade Organization is shaping domestic policies in health care." [Electronic version]. *Lancet* 354:1889–92.

Rao, Mohan, ed. 1999. *Disinvesting in Health: The World Bank's Prescriptions for Health.* Newbury Park, CA: Sage.

Schuld, Leslie. 2003. "El Salvador: Who Will Have the Hospitals?" *NACLA Report on the Americas* 36(3):42–45.

Stocker, Karen, Howard Waitzkin, and Celia Iriart. 1999. "The Exportation of Managed Care to Latin America." *New England Journal of Medicine* 340:1131–36.

Swafford, David. 1996. "A Healthy Trend." [Electronic version]. *Latin Finance*, December, p. 55.

Turshen, Meredeth. 1999. *Privatizing Health Services in Africa.* New Brunswick, NJ: Rutgers University Press.

Vranjes, Toni. 1998. "Devise Industry Impacted by Managed Care Going Global." [Electronic version]. *Medical Industry Today*, August 31.

Waitzkin, Howard. 2000. *The Second Sickness: Contradictions of Capitalist Health Care,* Rev. ed. Lanham, MD: Rowman and Littlefield.

Waitzkin, Howard. 2001. *At the Front Lines of Medicine: How the Health Care System Alienates Doctors and Mistreats Patients . . . And What We Can Do About It.* Lanham, MD: Rowman and Littlefield.

Waitzkin, Howard and Celia Iriart. 2000. "How the United States Exports Managed Care to Third World Countries." *Monthly Review* 52(1):21–35.

Winslow, Ron. 1997. "Oxford to Post First Quarterly Loss Ever—MCO's Stock Plunges 62 Percent; Forecasts for 4th Period, Year Also to Be Missed." [Electronic version]. *The Wall Street Journal*, October 28, p. A3.

World Health Organization. 2000. *World Health Report 2000.* Geneva, Switzerland: World Health Organization.

Compared to Other Countries, How Exceptional Are the Health and Income Security Arrangements of the United States?

Joseph White

The Bush administration seeks to make individuals much more dependent on personal savings (even if mandatory) for retirement income by reducing shared Social Security guarantees. The administration has also promoted reliance on individual insurance rather than social insurance for healthcare. This campaign to restructure the Social Security and Medicare programs in the United States uses some of the language and arguments of a conventional not-quite-wisdom that has spread across the globe over the past two decades, propagated especially by officials of the World Bank (1994). The view has two components: The first suggests that a rising ratio of retired elderly beneficiaries to workers necessarily makes decent defined-benefit pensions (and perhaps healthcare) unaffordable. The second suggests that requiring individuals to save for themselves for pensions (and perhaps even healthcare), through defined-contribution schemes, would solve the supposed problem.

With the muscle of the World Bank behind it, the push for defined-contribution rather than defined-benefit pensions has had extensive influence on policy makers in the "global south." The view has had a more modest effect on policies in the advanced industrial countries that most resemble the United States.

This group, the "rich democracies," as Wilensky (2002) refers to them, faces the same basic sociological and economic forces as the U.S., while having similar capacity to respond to the challenges. Concerns about defined-benefit pensions, like concerns about healthcare costs, have enough basis in reality that officials in rich democracies have contemplated a range of alterations of their systems.

Are the Bush administration's attempts to replace part of Social Security with personal accounts and Medicare with a voucher program then simply the logical U.S. component of a worldwide trend? Or are the attempts just part of seventy years of U.S. conservative objection to social insurance? Mostly it is the latter. Even where comparable countries are cutting benefits or creating some sort of hybrid arrangement such as the "notional defined-contribution" pension described below (Williamson, 2004), they tend to be starting from a better guarantee than that offered by Social Security and are maintaining substantial shared-risk arrangements.

Adapted from: Joseph White. (2005). Compared to other countries: How exceptional are the health and income security arrangements of the United States? *Generations,* 29(1), 7–12.

INCOME SECURITY

The economic or budgetary consequences of "dependency" reflect what workers guarantee to dependents. That guarantee can be very hard to measure because government and quasi-government programs take so many forms even in the same country. Even if there is one main scheme, as with Social Security, there may be a different provision for some—for example, a means-tested benefit like Supplemental Security Income for those who fall through the cracks. Redistribution can be done within a single pension system (as in the United States and Germany) or by having a flat-rate pension (which is redistributive because lower-earners pay much less for the benefit) plus an earnings-related pension (as in Canada or Finland). In some countries, such as the Netherlands and Sweden, pension arrangements negotiated between associations of workers and employers are so widespread, and so binding, that they should be treated as mandatory guarantees even though they did not originate in legislation. The mix of arrangements will also have different consequences according to a person's earnings history and family type (Whitehouse, 2003).

Hence it is difficult to compare what the U.S. guarantees (through Social Security and a bit of SSI) to the guarantees from other systems. Nevertheless, Whitehouse's (2003) analysis of nine countries as of 2000 is in line with other studies. He reports benefits as a proportion of the national average wage and concludes that the United States' guaranteed income is slightly more generous than Germany's and slightly less so than that of Japan. Whitehouse found guarantees in Finland, Italy, the Netherlands, and Sweden to be more generous than those in the U.S., particularly at higher income levels. Canada's pension system was more generous for very low incomes and then less for average or higher earnings, while the U.K.'s guarantee was shown to be less generous (or adequate) across the board. In short, the U.S. system was in the lower middle class for generosity (or adequacy) among these nine nations.

Social Security's finances tend to be in better shape than those of similar funds in continental Europe for a number of reasons (in varying combinations). First, U.S. demographics are more favorable. Second, other systems often have higher benefits. Third, Social Security's payroll tax is applied to a larger share of earnings than in the less generous European systems (e.g., Germany and France). And fourth, the normal retirement age is sometimes higher, and the penalty for earlier retirement greater, in the U.S. This latter fact means that Whitehouse's comparison of benefits payable at age 65 somewhat overstates the relative generosity of Social Security.

To summarize, Social Security is on the whole somewhat less generous (or adequate) and is in much better financial condition than systems in other countries, save for the other English-speaking nations.

MEDICAL COST SECURITY

Medical care is a different story. If spending were the measure, American healthcare-finance arrangements would be about 40 percent more generous than any other system in the world. Unfortunately, we also manage to have over 40 million people uninsured, and not particularly great health outcomes, so spending is not a good measure. We spend more because we pay more for services (Anderson et al., 2003). This difference has nothing to do with aging, for the U.S. population is younger than the populations of most other countries, and, in any event, aging is a relatively minor factor in the increase of healthcare costs (Gruber and Wise, 2002; White, 2004). Yet, because of the peculiar structure of our guarantees, aging *seems* to be a major factor in increased American healthcare costs.

In all other rich countries, older people and other citizens are in the same insurance pools, whether public or public law (for example, sickness funds in Germany), or private. When multiple pools exist in the same geographic area, as in Germany or Japan, there are arrangements to transfer revenues from the funds that have smaller proportions of older people to those with larger shares. But the costs of the elderly population per se do not appear as a separate expense on public budgets. When a person turns 65 in Canada or France or the Netherlands, the cost difference for the insurer is the difference between that person's costs at age 64 and 65.

In the United States, however, a person who turns 65 will normally go from some private budget to the government's Medicare budget. Suddenly the government is paying $6,000 or so per year that it was not paying before. Therefore, if you look at Medicare alone, the "aging society" seems to portend a huge relative increase in healthcare costs. In reality, however, much of this increase in Medicare costs is just a shift from private to public accounts. Moreover, the same assumptions used to project Medicare costs as increasing to 8 percent of GDP by the year 2075 predict that other healthcare would consume 30 percent of GDP in 2075 (Technical Review Panel, 2000). If these assumptions are correct, Medicare is not exactly the major burden, and privatizing is not the solution.

To summarize, the United States pays for medical care for its elderly population much the way other countries do. The benefits are somewhat less extensive yet much more expensive per person, because all healthcare is more expensive in the United States. The big difference, though, is not in how we pay for the elderly population, but in how we pay—or do not pay— for medical care for everyone else. As a result, a view that focuses on government budgets alone makes aging look like much more of a healthcare cost challenge than it really is.

LONG-TERM CARE

For both healthcare and pensions, social insurance is the norm among advanced industrial countries. Social insurance for long-term care, however, is not the norm (Glaser, 1991). For years there has been doubt about how "insurable" some aspects of long-term care really are. Need can be hard to define, and demand for services can be easily expanded. Moreover, when a person is not expected to get well and support a family, a case can be made for means-testing. Social insurance payment for older people in nursing homes would largely protect inheritances, which may not be the best goal for social guarantees. Each country has some history of community or religious or other charitable nursing homes or other care. At the level of national policy-making, however, long-term care needs are a relatively new focus compared to basic medical care.

The Dutch, in 1968, and the Germans and Japanese in the 1990s did create forms of social insurance for long-term care. Aside from where to find new money, perhaps the most basic question in long-term-care policy is the degree to which the care provided by families should be replaced (or compensated). Germany did but Japan did not adopt reforms that would compensate family care giving by allowing the beneficiary to receive cash rather than professional services in kind (so as to pay, for example, a daughter or daughter-in-law who was providing needed care if that is what the beneficiary preferred) and providing temporary relief for such caregivers (Campbell and Ikegami, 2000; Cuellar and Wiener, 2000). Most countries, like the U.S., have some mix of subnational programs with some national funding and often a means test (Merlis, 2000). Government supports a smaller proportion of identifiable long-term care in the United States than in Australia, Canada, France, Germany, Japan, and the United Kingdom, and American means and assets tests appear to be more severe than most (Anderson and Hussey, 2000).

WHAT LESSONS FOR THE UNITED STATES?

Separate from the clash between visions of social insurance and of a high-risk "ownership" society, a look at other countries can highlight some more modest issues that deserve consideration for reform.

One issue is the tax treatment of benefits. The effective replacement rate from pensions is higher virtually everywhere than the gross benefit would suggest, because pensions are taxed less than earnings (Whitehouse, 2003).

A second point is the variety of ways that can be used to vest people in pension systems. For example, it is possible to base full benefits not just on age but on a mix of age and years in the workforce, as is done in Italy. Such a mix could be the basis for a Social Security alteration that would recognize increasing longevity yet protect blue collar workers who begin and end work at younger ages than do white collar workers (White, 2003).

A third point is the decline of voluntary employer-based defined-benefit plans, which means that, if there is any merit to defined-benefit guarantees, they will need to be mandated by governments.

Review also shows that the United States is only truly exceptional in its lack of national health insurance. The U.S. adopted social-insurance principles for pensions in advance of the other English-speaking countries. Pension guarantees in Canada are less extensive than in the U.S. Australia has a fairly generous basic pension and a plausible mandatory defined-contribution plan on top of that, but the country never adopted a further defined benefit plan (Sass, 2004). The long-term trend of guarantees in the U.K. is shockingly negative. Because the British basic pension is not related to earnings and rises only with inflation, the pension will become less and less adequate relative to living standards in the future.

Other rich democracies are not abandoning the socialization of pension risk, are not embracing "competition" to insure healthcare, and if anything are expanding social insurance for long-term care. They most likely will shave pension promises, but in most cases their remaining guarantees will resemble the promises of our current Social Security system more than the shrunken defined benefit that President Bush seems to envision.

REFERENCES

Anderson, G. E., and Hussey, P. S. 2000. "Population Aging: A Comparison Among Industrialized Countries." *Health Affairs* 19(3): 191–203.

Anderson, G. E., Reinhardt, U. E., Hussey, P. S., and Petrosyan, V. 2003. "It's the Prices, Stupid! Why the United States Is So Different from Other Countries." *Health Affairs* 22(3): 89–105.

Campbell, J., and Ikegami, N. 2000. "Long-Term Care Insurance Comes to Japan?" *Health Affairs* 19(3): 26–39.

Cuellar, A., and Wiener, J. 2000. "Can Social Insurance for Long-Term Care Work? The Experience of Germany." *Health Affairs* 19(3): 8–25.

Glaser, W. A. 1991. *Health Insurance in Practice.* San Francisco: Jossey-Bass.

Gruber, J., and Wise, D. 2002. "An International Perspective on Policies for an Aging Society." In S. H. Airman and D. I. Shactman, eds., *Policies for an Aging Society.* Baltimore: The Johns Hopkins University Press.

Merlis, M. 2000. "Caring for the Frail Elderly: An International Review." *Health Affairs* 19(3): 141–49.

Sass, S. A. "Reforming the Australian Retirement System: Mandating Individual Accounts." Center for Retirement Research at Boston College Global Brief 2 (April).

Technical Review Panel on the Medicare Trustees Reports. 2000. Review of Assumptions and Methods of the Medicare Trustees' Financial Projections. Baltimore: Health Care Financing Administration, Dec. www.cms.gov/publications/technical/panelreport/report.pdf.

White, J. 2003. *False Alarm: Why the Greatest Threat to Social Security and Medicare Is the Campaign to "Save" Them.* Baltimore: The Johns Hopkins University Press.

White, J. 2004. "(How) Is Aging a Health Policy Problem?" *Yale Journal of Health Policy, Law and Ethics* 4(1): 47–68.

Whitehouse, E. 2003. 'The Value of Pension Entitlements: A Model of Nine OECD Countries." OECD Social, Employment and Migration Working Papers No. 9, DELSA/ELSA/WD/SEM(2003)9 (June 6).

Wilensky, H. L. 2002. *Rich Democracies: Political Economy, Public Policy, and Performance.* Berkeley, Calif.: University of California Press.

Williamson, J. B. 2004. "Assessing the Notional Defined Contribution Model?" Center for Retirement Research at Boston College Issue Brief 24 (October).

World Bank. 1994. *Averting the Old Age Crisis: Policies to Protect the Old and Promote Growth.* A World Bank Policy and Research Report. New York: Oxford University Press.

CHAPTER 12

Health Reform for the Future

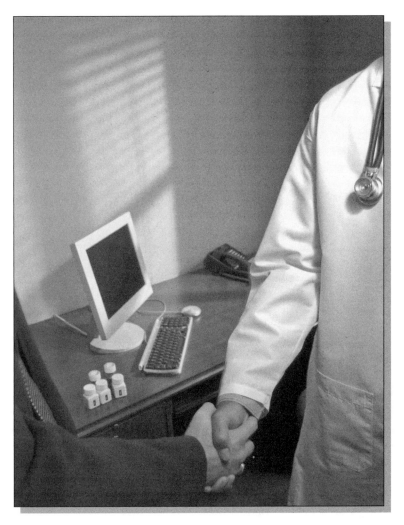

Doctor shaking hand of businessman

Myths as Barriers to Health Care Reform in the United States

John P. Geyman

As on many occasions over the last century in the United States, the issue of health care reform is again moving toward center stage on the nation's agenda. There is growing recognition that the present system is sick, and many feel that structural reform is required.

There have been five well-motivated and serious attempts to enact a system of universal coverage in the United States over the last 100 years. On each occasion, health care stakeholders have pulled no punches in using disinformation and obfuscation to confuse and mislead the public. Thus, the American Medical Association (AMA) has repeatedly fought national health insurance by labeling it "socialized medicine" (instead of socialized insurance), while the insurance industry distorted the debate in 1994 by raising fears of decreased choice of physicians and the role of government in health care. Since disinformation and intentional misrepresentation of the real issues will certainly occur again as new reforms are debated, this article briefly examines six myths concerning U.S. health care, which are recurrently used to cloud the debate, maintain the status quo, and defeat systemic efforts to reform our health care system.

MYTHS OF U.S. HEALTH CARE

These six well-worn myths have been perpetuated over the years by stakeholders in our present market-based system.

1. "Everyone gets care anyhow"

Purveyors of this myth assume that the uninsured and underinsured are able to access health care within an extensive safety net of community health centers; emergency rooms and outpatient clinics of public hospitals and not-for-profit community hospitals; local health departments; or other public sector clinics and hospitals, such as the Veterans Administration or National Health Service Corps. While this belief may absolve their guilt about serious access problems within the present system, it is a total misperception on many counts. Access to health care is more complex than it may appear, even for the insured. Eisenberg and Power (1) have drawn the analogy between access to health care and

Adapted from: John P. Geyman. (2003). Myths as barriers to health care reform in the United States. *International Journal of Health Services*, 33(2), 315–329.

electrical current passing through resistance—even for the insured, access suffers with each voltage drop, whether their needed services are actually covered, their choice is informed and available, or primary and specialty services are available.

While the plight of the uninsured is more obvious, there are many misperceptions here as well. For example, 80% of the uninsured live in working families, and still cannot qualify for or afford health insurance (2). Whether insured, underinsured, or uninsured, people suffer serious outcomes of lack of access to primary care. Three examples make the point. A 1997 study of low-income patients hospitalized for preventable or avoidable conditions found, for example, that 60% reported receiving no care before admission, while only 17% had been seen in an emergency room (3). A 2001 study by Baker and colleagues (4) of 7,500 adults aged 51 to 61 who lacked continuous health insurance found that almost three times as many persons experienced a decline in their health or functional status if continuously uninsured than if insured. In another recent study of 1,900 Medicare beneficiaries, only 4% without prescription drug coverage were receiving statins, compared with an estimated 60% who could benefit from their use (5).

2.   "We don't ration care in the United States"

This is a common notion, often used as a "put-down" for those countries with national health systems without full coverage for every conceivable health care service (e.g., chronic renal dialysis for elderly patients, cosmetic surgery). This myth flourishes while the prevailing public attitude (fueled by powerful stakeholders in the present system) is outright denial that rationing is common, necessary, or moral.

It is an often overlooked given that our market-based health care economy implicitly denies services to those who can't pay for them. Another type of rationing—denial of services to those who can pay for them—also is common (and highly contentious). Thus, there is a growing field of litigation challenging the prerogatives of HMOs to deny services. Some may be inappropriate denials, while others (e.g., coverage of autologous bone marrow transplants for women with metastatic breast cancer) may be well grounded in evidence-based clinical science (6). What is typically missing in public attitudes in the United States, however, is a societal (vs. individual) perspective on what services can be made available to those who can pay without compromising basic health services for those who cannot.

3.   "The free market can resolve our problems in health care"

This myth continues to underpin pro-market health care policies of both major political parties, with the belief that the marketplace can effectively resolve access, cost, and quality problems in delivery of health care services. Touted as the "American way," this view reflects the belief that a private, competitive market exists in health care. Yet, there is incontrovertible evidence that health care markets do not behave in a freely competitive way. Robert Evans, health care economist at the University of British Columbia, has pointed out how market mechanisms in health care yield distributional advantages for particular groups, including providers, suppliers, insurers, and more affluent and healthier people (7). He calls attention to the natural alliance between providers, suppliers, and higher-income citizens in support of private financing of health care, leaving the burden of financial care for the sick and uninsured to the public sector. As a result, the farther such privatization goes, the more difficult it is to finance basic health care services for sick and lower-income people through a smaller risk pool. It is well documented that the public interest is not well served by an unfettered private health care market.

4. "The U.S. health care system is basically healthy, so incremental change will address its problems"

Incrementalism has been the prevailing approach to health care reform for at least 30 years in the United States, and is still the most politically popular. Strongly supported by influential stakeholders in the present system, incremental changes are periodically put in place, which fail to address the more fundamental problems of the system. Examples include the attempt to contain rising hospital costs by the DRG (diagnosis related groups) prospective payment system (costs soared again 11 years later) (8) and the State Children's Health Insurance Program (SCHIP) enacted in 1997 (but by 2000 up to 21 million American children were still estimated to have significant access problems) (9).

Incrementalism best serves advocates of privatizing health care, reflecting values often diametrically opposed to the public interest. If incrementalism as the dominant health policy instrument over the last 30 years was effective, a 1998 RAND analysis of many studies would not give the following findings: 50% of people receive recommended preventive care; 60% receive recommended chronic care; 70% receive recommended acute care; 30% receive contraindicated acute care; and 20% contraindicated chronic care (10). Under the banner of incrementalism and increased consumer choice, there is now a vigorous effort by pro-market interests, supported by government, to shift more and more costs of health care to consumers, thereby discriminating against lower-income people and the sick.

The "invisible hand" deserves special comment, for much of the lobbying by the stakeholders in the pro-market system is almost transparent behind the scenes.

5. "The United States has the best health care system in the world"

That such a view is not only untenable but also arrogant toward countries with better-performing health care systems is demonstrated by these examples:

- The average ranking for the United States on 16 health indicators in a 1998 comparative study of 13 countries by Starfield was twelfth, second from the bottom. The top five, in decreasing order, were Japan, Sweden, Canada, France, and Australia (11).
- In another study by Starfield of 11 Western countries, the United States was ranked last with respect to its primary care base and its per capita health care expenditures (the highest), while ranking poorly on public satisfaction, health indicators, and use of medication (12).
- A 2000 study by the World Health Organization based on various indicators (including disability-adjusted life expectancy, child survival to five years of age, social disparities in care, experiences with the health care system, and out-of-pocket health care expenditures) found the average ranking of the United States to be fifteenth out of 25 countries (13).

6. "National health insurance is so unfeasible for political reasons that it should not be given serious consideration as a policy alternative"

Since national health insurance (NHI) would require fundamental restructuring of the health care system, it poses a threat to the stakeholders in the present system. For many reasons, when NHI is raised as a policy alternative, it therefore becomes a target of opportunity for interests vested in the status quo. Each time this occurs it obscures a national debate on the real issues, which should focus on which of the policy alternatives best serves the public interest.

NHI proposals in the United States have been attacked by their critics in past years on many counts, including alleged lack of affordability, overly intrusive roles of government, questions of quality, threat to the physician-patient relationship, and lack of political acceptance. The closer that NHI comes to serious consideration, the harder its opponents battle to denigrate such a proposal or distort the issues.

Despite the constant pressure by stakeholders in the pro-market status quo to keep single-payer NHI off the table of policy alternatives for health care reform, the myth of its alleged lack of feasibility can be well countered by the facts. In California, for example, where 22% of the population is uninsured, nine alternative reform proposals have been carefully studied under the California Health Care Options Project (HCOP). These include public program expansions, individual and employer tax credits, employer and individual mandates, single-payer models, and combination approaches. These options were analyzed and compared using a micro-simulation model developed by the Lewin Group. Most of the options are incremental proposals, all of which would increase health care costs without providing universal coverage. Only the single-payer proposals would provide comprehensive care for the state's entire population while reducing costs by $8 billion (14). In terms of affordability of NHI at the national level, the $1.4 trillion now being spent on health care (about $5,000 for every adult and child in the United States) could easily fund universal coverage of comprehensive care, if the wasteful for-profit insurance industry were replaced by a single, publicly administered insurance program.

DISCUSSION

The United States is alone among developed Western industrialized nations in still not having some form of national health insurance. Some have suggested that this is because the American public has not wanted it (15). Vicente Navarro makes a convincing case for another explanation—that the power and influence of the labor movement are the most important factors in establishing national health insurance in any country. With a low rate of unionization and without a strong and cohesive political party representing labor, the capitalist and management class in the United States has so far effectively thwarted any populist movement toward NHI (16). A recent position paper developed for the Wisconsin State AFL-CIO further contends that a class-based struggle has been fought by the right against labor since the 1930s, with the right persistently promoting its own economic interests and unlimited corporate power as an overall anti-worker agenda (17).

Although opponents of NHI have discounted the level of popular support for NHI on many occasions over the years, there is good evidence that a majority or plurality of

Americans have expressed support for it, as early as the 1940s and even at a cost of higher taxes (18). Growing evidence in recent years indicates that the public is increasingly dissatisfied with the health care system and more supportive of an expanded role of government in assuring access to care. There is now widespread support, even in the conservative South, for government regulation of HMOs (19). The most recent national poll by Harris Interactive (August 2002) found that one-half of respondents (physicians, employers, hospital managers, health plan managers, and public citizens) now favor radical reform, not incremental change. Only 19% of physicians and smaller percentages of the other four groups felt that "on the whole the health care system works pretty well and only minor changes are necessary" (20).

As editor of the *New England Journal of Medicine*, Relman (21) warned in 1980 of the corrosive effects of the medical-industrial complex in medicine and health care. The ensuing years have fully demonstrated these effects. In 1990, Coddington and colleagues (22), in their book *The Crisis in Health Care: Costs, Choices, and Strategies*, predicted these outcomes under our market-based system:

- More than 40 million uninsured
- Continued gaps in safety net coverage
- Double-digit health plan rate increases
- Smaller employers cutting coverage or even dropping health plans
- Increased copayments and deductibles for employees
- Large rate increases for private insurers in shrinking markets
- Numerous failures of HMOs and withdrawal from the market by larger insurance companies
- Continued cost shifting in an increasingly fragmented market
- Continued inflation of health care costs

Twelve years later, every one of these outcomes has taken place, precisely as predicted.

In the early 1990s, Mark Peterson (23), well-known policy analyst and scholar in government affairs, noted that the "iron triangle" of closely allied stakeholders in the pro-market health care system (business, the insurance industry, and the medical profession) was starting to break down into competition among themselves.

A battle is raging over the future of U.S. health care, much of it behind the scenes. In their defense against growing pressure by stake challengers for effective change, the corporate class will promulgate the myths described here in well-funded campaigns of disinformation. However, a fresh proposal for fundamental reform of the health care system could well succeed the next time around if these six myths are seen as such and a national debate can be sharply focused on the public interest. The middle class, not just the lower class, is affected by the increasing unaffordability of health care. The length and depth of the current recession will broaden the constituency adversely affected by the present system and increase the influence of grassroots activism for reform. The aftermath of the September 11 tragedy will stretch the nation's resources and call into question the value being returned on the country's already huge investment in health care.

Americans want, and deserve, a system assuring them of access to health care, free choice of physician, affordable care of high quality, trust, and respect. What many now get is a disorganized, failing, and nonsustainable system with increasingly serious problems of access, cost, quality, and equity. The most unfortunate aspect of previous reform efforts is how successful their opponents have been in purveying myths in order to change the subject, distort the debate, and promote hopes that tinkering around the edges of the current system will succeed. Neither of the two major political parties is yet prepared to address fundamental reform, still subscribing to an incrementalism that has been a complete failure for more than 25 years. The current experiment with consumerism conveys a cruel illusion of "progress," is unfair, and won't resolve system problems.

Medicine has the opportunity to take a leadership role in promoting a broad consensus supporting what should be unassailable principles of reform against which reform alternatives can be assessed. These principles could well include (a) guaranteed universal coverage; (b) free choice of physicians; (c) continuity of primary care; (d) a comprehensive, basic set of clinically effective benefits; (e) cost containment with affordability; and (f) commitment to continuous quality improvement. Hopefully, the time for much needed structural reform of the nation's ailing health care system will soon be at hand.

REFERENCES

1. Eisenberg, J. M., and Power, E. J. Transforming insurance coverage into quality health care: Voltage drops from potential to delivered quality. *JAMA* 284: 2100–2107, 2000.

2. Committee on the Consequences of Uninsurance, Board on Health Care Services, Institute of Medicine. *Coverage Matters: Insurance and Health Care*, pp. 2–3. National Academy Press, Washington, D.C., 2001.

3. Billings, J., Minanovich, T., and Blank, A. *Barriers to Care for Patients with Preventable Hospital Admissions*. United Hospital Fund, New York, 1997.

4. Baker, D. W., et al. Lack of health insurance and decline in overall health in late middle age. *N. Engl. J. Med.* 345: 1105, 2001.

5. Federman, A. D., et al. Supplemental insurance and use of effective cardiovascular drugs among elderly Medicare beneficiaries with coronary heart disease. *JAMA* 286: 1732–1739, 2001.

6. Eddy, D. M. *Clinical Decision Making: From Theory to Practice—A Collection of Essays from JAMA*. Jones and Bartlett, Boston, 1996.

7. Evans, R. G. Going for the gold: The redistributive agenda behind market-based health care reform. *J. Health Polit. Policy Law* 22: 427–465, 1997.

8. VHA. *1998 Environmental Assessment: Setting Foundations for the Millennium*. Irving, Tex., 1992.

9. Friedrich, M. J. Medically underserved children need more than insurance card. *JAMA* 283: 3056–3057, 2000.

10. Schuster, M., McGlynn, E. A., and Brook, R. H. How good is the quality of health care in the United States? *Milbank Q.* 76(4): 517–563, 1998.

11. Starfield, B. *Primary Care: Balancing Health Needs, Services, and Technology*. Oxford University Press, New York, 1998.

12. Starfield, B. *Primary Care: Concept, Evaluation, and Policy*. Oxford University Press, New York, 1992.

13. Gray, B. H., and Rowe, C. Safety-net health plans: A status report. *Health Aff.* (Millwood) 19(1): 185–193, 2000.

14. California Health Care Options Project. http://www.healthcareoptions.ca.gov/doclib.asp

15. Fuchs, V. R. *The Health Economy*, p. 269. Harvard University Press, Cambridge, 1986.

16. Navarro, V. Why countries have national health insurance, others have national health services, and the United States has neither. *Int. J. Health Serv.* 19(3): 383–404, 1989.

17. Ricca, J. Politics in America: The Right Wing Attack on the American Labor Movement, 2002. http://www.wisaflcio.org/political_action/rightwing.htm

18. Coughlin, R. *Ideology, Public Policy, and Welfare Policy: Attitudes toward Taxes and Spending in Industrialized Societies,* p. 77. Research Series No. 42. Institute of International Studies. University of California, Berkeley, 1980.

19. Duff, C. Americans tell government to stay out—Except in case of health care. *Wall Street Journal,* June 25, 1998.

20. Attitudes toward the United States health care system: Long-term trends—Views of the public, employers, physicians, health plan managers are closer now than at any time in the past. *Harris Interactive* 2(17), August 21, 2002.

21. Relman, A. S. The new medical-industrial complex. *N. Engl. J. Med.* 303: 963–970, 1980.

22. Coddington, D. C., et al. *The Crisis in Health Care: Costs, Choices, and Strategies.* Jossey-Bass, San Francisco, 1990.

23. Peterson, M. A. Political influence in the 1990s: From iron triangles to policy networks. *J. Health Polit. Policy Law* 18(2): 395–438, 1993.

Why Congress Did Not Enact Health Care Reform

Vincente Navarro, MD

Many explanations are given for the failure of the 103rd Congress to enact health care reform. The most frequent explanation in the mainstream media and academic press is that people were not ready and were confused. Congress, it is said, merely reflects the voice of the people because the U.S. political system represents the population. Thus the roots of health care reform's failure can be found in people's ambivalence: They wanted health care reform but were not quite ready; they were confused or misinformed.

I believe this view is wrong. The American public certainly has a voice in its political system, but it is not one of the most important voices that shape the federal government's decisions, including those about federal health policies. Most people agree with this perception. Seventy-four percent believe that the U.S. Congress does not represent their interests but rather the interests of what they call the "rich," the popular term for the corporate and upper middle classes.[1] And much evidence supports the accuracy of this perception. The gap between what people want from their government and what they get is substantial and growing, which may explain citizens' increasing anger with the political establishment. Since 1954, whenever polled on whether they favor a universal health care program, large pluralities or majorities have supported it.[2] Even during the 1980s and early 1990s, when concepts such as the "greed" of the privileged few and austerity for the many were supposed to be fashionable, most Americans supported a government-run national health care program (Shapiro and Young 1986). Yet Congress has failed time after time to enact such a program.

Another proposed explanation for Congress' failure to pass health care reform is that government experts have not yet got it right. In this scenario, professionals and experts are primarily responsible for establishing public policies and convincing key political actors of the merits of various proposals. But this scenario is clearly insufficient to foster an understanding of the failure of health care reform. It ignores the sociopolitical context in which these "experts" operate and the interests with which they are identified or represent. Hillary Rodham Clinton's Health Care Task Force, for example, was not merely a group of experts. Its key members were persons identified, for the most part, with some of the primary forces (including the insurance industry) responsible for the current predicament of the U.S. health

---

1. These are the electorate's views of the U.S. Congress, as determined by a Gallup poll in November 1992.

2. For an analysis of popular support for a universal health program since the 1950s, see Navarro (1994).

care system. I offer just one example: The chairman of the Governance Committee, a critical committee of the task force, was for many years a high-ranking official of the Health Insurance Association of America. The task force was a predominantly white, male, upper middle class group in which the interests of insurance companies (large and small) and other components of the medical industrial complex were well represented. Obviously, these persons were not on the task force as "representatives" of these groups, but their positions were, for the most part, the same as those of the industries in which they worked and with which they were identified. Others who had no professional association with these interest groups accepted the theoretical framework dictated to them by their spokespersons—the Jackson Hole Group. Indeed, the primary objective of the task force initially was to achieve a synthesis of the major interests at work in the health care sector, to develop a blueprint—managed competition—that could be approved by the major players in this sector.

Similarly, the members and staff of key committees of the House and Senate that craft health care-related legislation have long-standing relationships with these health sector interests. The list of recipients of donations from insurance and professional groups reads like a Who's Who of federal health policy circles (Kemper and Novak 1992). Of course, part of the official discourse is that such intercourse between politicians and lobbyists does not influence policy makers. None other than Congressman Thomas Foley, then Speaker of the House (and himself a recipient of health care industry funds), has denied the existence of such influence. Empirical evidence shows, however, that lobbyists and their financial contributions do influence the behavior of congressional recipients (New York Times 1994). Common Cause has also documented how most Washington lobbyists for the medical industrial complex previously worked within the U.S. Congress, with which they retain close ties (Kemper and Novak 1992).

This link between the medical industrial complex and the legislative and executive branches of government offers better grounds for understanding the failure of health care reform than does simply examining what the "experts" recommended. Who those experts represent is far more important. The relationship between the components of the medical industrial complex, the large and small insurance lobbies, the large and small employer associations, the representatives of professional associations, and other interest groups, on the one hand, and the U.S. government, both the executive and legislative branches, on the other, is critical to our understanding of that failure. Many authors writing in the "interest group" theoretical tradition have provided useful information on the key relationship between the medical industrial complex and political power (Marmor 1994). Yet this approach, however helpful, is insufficient to explain why health care reform failed. We cannot understand the behavior of U.S. political institutions by focusing only on the interplay of groups and actors while failing to analyze the social, political, and economic contexts in which these political institutions and interest groups operate. In other words, we cannot understand the nature of the tree—the existence or absence of health care reform—without understanding the forest—the structure of power in the United States and how these power relations are reproduced through the state.

In the United States, power is distributed according to race, sex, and, most importantly, class. Alain Enthoven, the principal theoretician of managed competition, the dominant framework in the health care debate, recognized as much when he wrote "The U.S. political system is incapable of forcing change in such power institutions as the insurance industry, the hospital industry, organized medicine, the medical devices industry and the pharmaceutical industry" (Marmor 1994). What these components of the corporate and upper middle classes have in common with the other components, the large and small employers, is not only their composition of race and sex but, most importantly, their class composition: corporate class for large employers, large and small insurers, and the medical industries, and upper middle class for small employers and professionals. Conventional wisdom now dictates that the single-payer proposal, the only proposal that clearly threatened that class dominance, was politically unfeasible because it was unacceptable to those classes.

The reality is that the United States lacks a national health care program because of its specific class relations. The focus on interest group behavior without understanding class behavior leads to wrong conclusions. For example, why did the major associations representing large employers oppose the single-payer proposal when they would most likely benefit from this proposal by paying considerably less in fringe benefits for their workers? According to their short-term interest group interests, they should have supported it, but the overwhelming majority of large employers and their trade associations did not. As employers, members of the corporate or capitalist class, they most value control over their own labor force, and employment-based health benefits coverage gives them enormous power over their employees. The United States is the only country where the welfare state is, for the most part, privatized. Consequently, when workers lose their jobs, health care benefits for themselves and their families are also lost. In no other country does this occur. This is why the corporate class and its instruments in the United States oppose establishing government-guaranteed universal entitlements: They strengthen the working class and weaken the capitalist class. The staggering power of the capitalist class and enormous weakness of the working class explains why health care reform failed again. The United States, the only major capitalist country without government-guaranteed universal health care coverage, is also the only nation without a social-democratic or labor party that serves as the political instrument of the working class and other popular classes. These two facts are related. In most advanced countries, the establishment of universal entitlement programs has been based on the political alliances of the working class with the middle classes, through the election of social-democratic governments or through their pressure on non-social-democratic governments (Navarro 1989).

The Democratic party has traditionally presented itself as the party of working people and of the disenfranchised. And during and after the New Deal, most of the working class supported the Democratic party, largely because of the identification of the party with the popular New Deal programs such as Social Security, the most popular insurance program in the United States. Such an identification, however, has been diluted considerably, and for many decades the Democratic party leadership has distanced itself from the New Deal. In fact, the anti–New Deal measures taken by Reagan and Bush were supported by most Democrats in Congress. This situation is responsible for discrediting the two parties, which are now seen as very similar, and has been greatly facilitated by money's growing influence in politics. Both the Republican and Democratic parties now depend heavily on moneyed interests. As William Greider, author of the best analysis of the Democratic party, concludes, "Anomalous as it may seem, Wall Street is a major source of financing for the party of working people" (1993: 259). Not only is the United States the only capitalist country without a national health program and without a social-democratic party but it is also the country where democracy is most limited by the overwhelming power of money, the milk of U.S. politics.

This situation explains the anti-establishment mood in the country and why all 1992 presidential candidates, Clinton, Perot, and Bush, had to run as anti-establishment candidates, a difficult position for Bush to sustain because he had been part of the Washington establishment for two decades. Clinton (unlike Carter, Mondale, and Dukakis) ran as a left-of-center, anti-establishment populist, with a New Deal platform (which the *New York Times* called "a Roosevelt platform") and with a class war campaign, the type of campaign Republicans most fear. As noted by conservative Republican strategist Kevin Phillips, "class war was the strategy most feared by Republicans since they were highly vulnerable (particularly after the pro-rich and pro-business policies of the Republican administrations) to be presented as the party of the rich" (1994), that is, the capitalist and upper middle classes. A clear class polarization occurred during the 1980s and early 1990s. For the upper 20% of the population, incomes increased by 125%; for the lower 60%, incomes declined by 6%.

Despite the class discourse Clinton used to mobilize alienated voters, he was a "new Democrat" who did not believe in class confrontation but rather in the development of consensus policies. Clinton's desire to please was not a personal character flaw, as is often reported. It was part of a political strategy to create consensus among forces with very uneven power, and some of these forces were pleased more consistently than others. The Health Care Reform Task Force was an example of this strategy. It was supposed to develop a blueprint that would be acceptable to the principal interest groups in the medical sector, and to large and small employers. These compromises defined the terms of the subsequent debate, moving it farther to the right. Predictably, the compromises did not satisfy the major players—large employers and large insurance companies, which developed their own proposals (Cooper and others)—nor did they satisfy the major grassroots constituencies of the Democratic party, such as labor, civil rights, and other social movements. These constituencies felt increasingly alienated from the Clinton administration, which was increasingly perceived, since the North American Free Trade Agreement debate, as aligned too closely to corporate America. As Mrs. Clinton indicated, the problem faced by the Clinton administration was the strong mobilization of those who opposed health care reform and the lack of support and mobilization by those who supported it. There is growing disenchantment of the working and middle classes, the New Deal coalition, with the Democratic party, which is responsible for its electoral defeat on November 8, 1994. Only 33% of Democrats voted, compared with 82% of Republicans.

Another alternative strategy, never considered, would have been the mobilization and development of alliances between the working class and the lower middle class, which represent most of the U.S. population. Clinton could have put forward a single-payer, left-wing position at the start of the debate, which would have been diluted in Congress, eventually reaching a center position as the final outcome. After wasting several months, however, Clinton began the debate from a center-right position that moved so far to the right that he could no longer mobilize popular support, the grass roots of the Democratic party. Clinton's plan was very complex and cumbersome because of his commitment to leave unchanged the current system's major partners of financing and organization. He was actually stimulating a process already occurring in the medical care sector: the corporatization of medicine in the United States. A key element of Clinton's plan was control by the large insurance companies over the medical care sector. As stated by Starr and Zelman (1993), two of Clinton's advisors, "the integration of health insurance companies and health care provision into the same organization, i.e., health plans" would be the key element of managed competition.

In the debate, the major media and academia (also heavily influenced by the hegemonic ideology of corporate America) systematically excluded alternatives that would have had a stronger effect on the core of the corporate and upper middle classes: the large employers, large insurance companies, and the medical industrial complex. Not only the *New York Times* (whose editorial board includes several CEOs of insurance companies) but also the *Washington Post* and the major television networks marginalized and ridiculed the single-payer position, presenting it as "fundamentalist," "extreme," "utopian," and the like (Brundin 1993). As Miliband (1969) has eloquently written, "Class dominant value generating systems contribute to the fostering of a climate of conformity, not by total suppression of dissent, but by the presentation of views which fall outside the consensus as curious heresies, or, even more effectively, by treating them as irrelevant eccentricities, which serious and reasonable people may dismiss as of no consequence." This is how class power is reproduced in the United States. Strengthening the exclusion of alternative proposals was the absence not only of a mobilizing discourse but of an instrument that could facilitate such a mobilization. The Democratic party was not such an instrument. The conditions for establishing a national health care program include active mobilization to democratize the political institutions, with the formation of political instruments that better represent the interests of most of the working population. Such mobilization cannot occur without a substantial confrontation with the pattern of not just race and sex but also primarily class-dominant relations in the United States.

REFERENCES

Brundin, J. 1993. How the U.S. Press Covers the Canadian Health Care System. *International Journal of Health Services* 23(2):275–77.

Greider, W. 1993. *Who Will Tell the People?* New York: Basic Books.

Kemper, V., and V. Novak. 1992. What Is Blocking Health Care Reform? *Common Cause Magazine* 18(1):8–13, 25.

Marmor, T. 1994. *Understanding Health Care Reform.* New Haven: Yale University Press.

Miliband, R. 1969. *The State in Capitalist Society: An Analysis of the Western System of Power.* London: Weidenfeld and Nicolson.

Navarro, V. 1994. *The Politics of Health Policy.* Oxford: Blackwell Publishers.

———. 1989. Why Some Countries Have National Health Insurance, Others Have National Health Services, and the U.S. Has Neither. *International Journal of Health Services* 19(3):383–404. *New York Times.* 1994, 4 October.

Phillips, K. 1994. *Arrogant Capital: Washington, Wall Street and the Frustration of American Politics.* Boston: Little, Brown.

Shapiro, R., and J. T. Young. 1986. The Polls: Medical Care in the U.S. *Public Opinion Quarterly* 50:423.

Starr, P., and W. Zelman. 1993. Bridge to Compromise: Competition under a Budget. *Health Affairs* 12 (Suppl):7–23.

Why the United States Has No National Health Insurance: Stakeholder Mobilization Against the Welfare State, 1945–1996

Jill Quadagno

The right to health care is recognized in international law and guaranteed in the constitutions of many nations (Jost 2003). With the sole exception of the United States, all industrialized countries—regardless of how they raise funds, organize care, or determine eligibility—guarantee comprehensive coverage of primary, secondary, and tertiary services. To the extent that care is rationed, it is done on the basis of clinical need, not ability to pay (Keen, Light, and May 2001; Dixon and Mossialos 2002). Universal health care has proven to be a major tool for restraining cost increases. Planning avoids widespread duplication that underlies the high percentage of empty beds in the United States; high rates of unnecessary procedures, tests, and drugs; and ineffective use of some technologies. Although many nations have flirted with competition, most are wary because the most competitive system, the United States has consistently been least successful in controlling costs (Anderson et al. 2003).

Most countries allow, and some encourage, private insurance as an upgrade or second tier to a higher class of service and a fuller array of services (Keen, Light, and May 2001; Ruggie 1996). However, the practices of these companies are heavily regulated to prevent them from engaging in the more pernicious forms of risk rating. That is not the case in the United States, where private insurance companies are allowed to use sophisticated forms of medical "underwriting" to set premiums and skim off the more desirable employee groups and individuals (Light 1992). The United States is the only nation that fails to guarantee coverage of medical services, rations extensively by ability to pay, and allows the private insurance industry to serve as a gatekeeper to the health care system (Jost 2003). This arrangement leaves approximately one-sixth of the population uninsured at any given time, and it leaves others at risk of losing insurance as a result of such life course events as divorce, aging, widowhood, or economic downturn (Harrington Meyer and Pavalko 1996). The uninsured are sicker, receive inferior care, and are more likely to die prematurely (Institute of Medicine 2004).

Adapted from: Jill S. Quadagno. (2004). Why the U.S. has no national health insurance: Stakeholder mobilization against the welfare state, 1945–1996. *Journal of Health and Social Behavior,* 45 (Extra Issue), 25–44.

The lack of national health insurance in the United States is the prime example of a larger historic issue captured by the phrase "American exceptionalism." The question to be answered is not just why every proposal for national health insurance has failed but also how commercial enterprise became the preferred alternative. Neither political sociologists nor medical sociologists have fully explained this puzzling pattern. Political theorists of the welfare state usually attribute the failure of national health insurance in the United States to broader forces of American political development but ignore the distinctive character of the health care financing arrangements that do exist. Medical sociologists emphasize the way that physicians parlayed their professional expertise into legal, institutional, and economic power but not the way this power was asserted in the political arena.

A THEORY OF STAKEHOLDER MOBILIZATION

The theory of stakeholder mobilization suggests that the health care financing system in the United States was constructed through contentious struggles between reformers and powerful stakeholder groups who mobilized politically against national health insurance or any government programs that might compete with private sector products or lead to government regulation of the market. Stakeholder mobilization involves the same processes that social movement theorists usually associate with the mobilization of politically powerless groups (Jenkins and Perrow 1977). To be effective in the political arena, stakeholders share with the politically powerless a need for leadership, an administrative structure, incentives, some mechanisms for garnering resources and marshalling support, and a setting (whether it be a workplace or a neighborhood) where grassroots activity can be organized (McAdam, McCarthy, and Zald 1996). Even though dominant groups may have privileged and systematic access to politics and to elected representatives, they require these same resources to exert political influence.

Stakeholder mobilization also involved the use of cultural "schemas" to shape public perceptions of the issues, strategically frame ideas, and establish shared meanings (Young 2002). Implicit in this emphasis on symbolic politics is a rejection of the notion that political decisions are made on the basis of objective information and a recognition instead that political enemies, threats, crises, and problems are social constructions that create solidarity between groups and individuals and ultimately determine whose framing of an issue is authoritative (Edelman 1988; Kane 1997; Pedriana and Stryker 1997). How issues are defined can activate new groups to take an interest in the policy, fragment the existing configuration of support and limit potential options for change. As West and Loomis (1999) assert, the ability to define the alternatives is the supreme instrument of power.

From the New Deal of the 1930s to the 1970s, the chief obstacle to national health insurance was organized medicine. However, physicians succeeded because their political objectives meshed with those of other powerful groups, notably employers, insurance companies, and trade unions. Physicians also had political allies in Congress among Republican opponents of the New Deal welfare state and among southern Democrats who controlled the key committees through which all social welfare legislation had to pass and who refused to support any program that might allow federal authorities to intervene in the South's racially segregated health care system (Quadagno 2004). Across two-thirds of a century, physicians and their allies lobbied legislators, cultivated sympathetic candidates through large campaign contributions, organized petition drives, created grassroots protests, and developed new "products" whenever government action seemed imminent (Gordon 2003).

Then the excesses of the profession produced a counter-reaction from the government, corporations, and insurance companies that were activated to challenge the protected provider markets (Light 1995). Ironically, the most effective challenge came from the private health insurance system that physicians had helped to construct as an alternative to government intervention and took the form of billion-dollar, for-profit managed care firms. Managed care helped to dismantle physicians' cultural authority by undermining their claims of specialized knowledge, putting them at financial risk for their medical decisions, and placing decision-making power in the hands of non-physicians (Luft 1999). The arousal of corporations and insurance companies also had consequences for national health insurance. Their political mobilization brought powerful stakeholders into debates about health care reform. While corporations were primarily concerned with containing costs, insurers had a vested interest in preventing the federal government from creating competing products and in structuring any new programs in ways that would preserve the private market.

NATIONAL HEALTH INSURANCE REVISITED

In 1991 national health insurance moved to the forefront of political debates when Senator John Heinz (D-Pa.) died in a plane crash and the governor of Pennsylvania appointed Harris Wofford, the sixty-five-year-old former president of Bryn Mawr College, to replace him. Wofford was only supposed to serve until a special election could be held, but he decided to run for the regular Senate seat. The little-known Wofford was trailing far behind his opponent, Richard Thornburgh, the twice elected, popular former governor and U.S. attorney general until Wofford raised the topic of health insurance. Wofford crushed Thornburgh in the election, and polls subsequently showed that voters identified health care as a key factor (Johnson and Broder 1996).

Other candidates seized the issue, and the Democratic party candidate, Bill Clinton, made it a feature of his campaign (Hacker 1997). After Clinton won the election, he promised to have a health reform bill for Congress within his first 100 days. Instead a crisis in Somalia and a battle over the North American Free Trade Agreement absorbed the president's attention. The NAFTA battle had a secondary consequence of depriving the Clinton administration of a key ally. Before the election, the president of the AFL-CIO had promised Clinton that the labor movement would be the "storm troopers" for national health insurance. However, labor leaders viewed NAFTA as an effort to shift production to low-wage countries with more lax environmental and labor standards, so instead of working for health care reform, the AFL-CIO became involved in fighting NAFTA (Skocpol 1996).

The president's Health Security plan was finally released in October of 1993. The most comprehensive domestic policy proposal since 1965, it would guarantee universal coverage through an employer mandate and contain inflation through purchasing alliances and a national health budget. The purchasing alliances would be similar to the corporate purchasing coalitions of the 1980s and dominated by the five largest health insurers: Aetna, Prudential, MetLife, Cigna, and Travelers. However, smaller specialty firms stood to lose 30 to 60 percent of their business, and insurance agents would be put out of business entirely. The plan also called for repeal of the health insurance industry's antitrust exemption under the McCarren-Ferguson Act and made insurers subject to federal anti-trust provisions and consumer protection mandates (Johnson and Broder 1996; Skocpol 1996).

The lengthy planning period provided stakeholder groups the opportunity to develop a strategy and plan an attack. The most vehement opponent of Health Security was the Health Insurance Association of America, which spent more than $15 million in a multi-faceted advertising campaign. In the summer of 1993, the HIAA created the Coalition for Health Insurance Choices, involving many of the same organizations that had fought the home care bill. Initially, the Coalition sponsored vague commercials about health care reform. One ad said the purchasing alliances might be "the first step to socialized medicine" (Skocpol 1996: 137). Another series of ads featured a white, middle-class couple confronting the worrisome possibility of government bureaucrats choosing their health plan. As Health Security won public support, the ads zeroed in on fears people had about how their current insurance coverage would be affected (Jacobs and Shapiro 1995). All the ads invoked an antistatist theme, that Health Security would create a vast, inefficient, and unresponsive government bureaucracy and thousands of new bureaucrats (Goldsteen et al. 2001; Jacobs and Shapiro 2000).

The Coalition for Health Insurance Choices set up an 800 number to enlist grassroots supporters. The Coalition also formed "swat teams" of supporters to write letters and lobby lawmakers (Center for Public Integrity 1995). Concerned employers received a thick manual spelling out ways to get employees, vendors, and other sympathizers involved in the battle against the Clinton plan. The effort produced more than 450,000 contacts with members of Congress, almost a thousand for each senator and congress person (Johnson and Broder 1996).

Insurance companies and insurance agents' organizations increased their campaign contributions substantially, with the largest sums going to members of the House Ways and Means Committee and the Senate Finance Committee, both of which had jurisdiction over health reform. Members of two House committees that debated health care bills received contributions averaging four times that of members not on these committees (Center for Public Integrity 1995). Insurance agents also organized their own grassroots effort (Johnson and Broder 1996). A political force in their own right, they were located in every congressional district, active in their communities, and involved in state and local politics (Quadagno 2005).

The HIAA had an ally among small business owners who opposed an employer mandate and any tax increase. The NFIB mobilized its own grassroots effort against Health Security, dispatching streams of faxes and action alerts from its Washington office to tens of thousands of small business owners. Every week the NFIB polled 600,000 members on their attitudes toward the Clinton plan and sent their responses to their congressional representatives. The NFIB also organized groups of activists who attended local meetings whenever their congressional representatives visited their home districts, and it also conducted seminars in states that had members on key congressional committees. The NFIB also worked through the press, using the influential radio talk shows to kindle public opposition (Johnson and Broder 1996). When the first poll was taken on the Clinton plan in September of 1993, 59 percent of the public favored it. By June of 1994 public support had declined to only 44 percent (West and Loomis 1999).

Interestingly, unlike the 1940s, when the AMA had been the most vocal political opponent of the Truman plan, in the 1990s physicians were nearly invisible in the fracas over Health Security. The AMA initially endorsed the concept of universal coverage but opposed any stringent cost controls or regulations that would give managed care an advantage. Some organizations of specialists endorsed the basic features of the Clinton plan; other physician organizations opposed the same features (Tuohy 1999). These disagreements made it impossible for physicians to convey a clear message about health care reform. Tellingly, the various accounts of Clinton's failed effort scarcely mention the AMA or the physicians it represented (Johnson and Broder 1996; Skocpol 1996; Hacker 1997).

After the demise of Health Security, health policy making moved toward shoring up the private health insurance system by tightening regulations to make private insurance less insecure. The Health Insurance Portability and Accountability Act of 1996 (HIPAA) narrowed the conditions under which companies could refuse coverage, allowed people who itemized deductions on their income taxes to deduct a portion of long-term care insurance premium: and made employer contributions toward the cost of group long-term care insurance a tax deductible business expense. After HIPPA long-term care insurance sales increased an average of 21 percent a year, with the biggest increase occurring in group insurance plans offered by employers (Quadagno 2005).

CONCLUSION

Medical sociologists have aptly described the shifting configuration of power within the health care system from providers to purchasers but have failed to specify the way that the rise of these "countervailing powers" transformed the political terrain. From the New Deal to the 1970s, the most vehement opponents of national health insurance were physicians. Fearful that government financing of health services would lead to government control of medical practice, they mobilized against this perceived threat to professional sovereignty. Physicians were able to realize their political objectives through the American Medical Association, which then had the organizational capacity to marshal resources, command a response from members, achieve deep penetration into local community politics, shape public opinion through antistatist campaigns, and subsequently influence electoral outcomes. The historical irony is that the private health insurance system that physicians helped to construct became a mechanism for undermining their sovereign rule, as the abuses of professional authority following the enactment of Medicare and Medicaid roused large firms and the insurance industry to seek redress in the form of managed care. The outcome demonstrates the fragility of physicians' power base.

As physicians' antipathy to national health insurance dwindled—tempered by the benefits of guaranteed payment, splits among various specialty groups, and the loss of allies among other health professionals and employer groups—health insurers moved to the forefront of public debates, determined to prevent passage of national health insurance and defeat any program that might compete with their products. In some cases, traditional lobbying tactics were sufficient to ward off government intervention; in other instances, they formed political coalitions with like-minded organizations—whether they be small business owners, pharmacists, or insurance agents—to create "grassroots" social movement activities and fund public information campaigns designed to convince politicians that the public opposed health care reform. The changing composition of the anti-reform coalition, dominated first by physicians, then by insurers, has obscured the persistence of stakeholder mobilization as the primary impediment to national health insurance.

The ironic outcome of each failed attempt to enact national health insurance was federal action that stimulated the growth of commercial insurance and entrenched a market-based alternative to a public program. In the 1940s the failure of national health insurance provided a stimulus to the private health insurance industry. The enactment of Medicare in 1965 removed a key constituency, the aged, from the political debate while preserving a profitable segment of the market for private insurers. The compromises involved in Medicare also led to health care inflation, creating a dilemma that would jinx all subsequent efforts to enact national health insurance. Health care reformers could never again define the problem solely in terms of improving access to health care for worthy and deserving groups. They now also had to promise to control costs and reform the system. A national health insurance plan proposed in the 1970s was redirected and led instead to federal support for private HMOs. The defeat of home care legislation in the 1980s provided a stimulus to the long-term care insurance market.

The centuries-long struggle for national health insurance illuminates fundamental features of American political development. First, it suggests that while anti-statism is not a causal force in and of itself it does provide a powerful weapon that can be deployed in political struggles over the welfare state. Second, it suggests that labor movements can use their "power resources" in ways that reinforce rather than transform the play of market forces, but also that the trade union movement has the capacity to transform the welfare state without forming a political party. Because the American trade unions viewed national health insurance as an unachievable political goal in the postwar era, they instead concentrated on winning benefits through collective bargaining. Once won, these private health benefits created a conundrum in the form of costly retiree health benefits that encouraged the AFL-CIO to lead a successful campaign for health insurance for the aged. The Medicare victory resulted from a confluence of historical conditions and favorable political opportunity structures that included an internally unified labor movement, Democratic party control of Congress and the Presidency, and a national climate that was sympathetic to initiatives to aid the less privileged. Third, it is apparent that the institutional structure of the state in the United States channels political activities in ways that blur the distinction between the tactics and strategies of less privileged groups and normal political processes. Just as challengers not only engage in grassroots activities but also attempt to gain privileged access to mainstream politics, so, too, do powerful stakeholders with privileged access also manufacture grassroots protests to convince political leaders that their interests represent the public will.

The similarities in tactics and strategies used by opponents and successful reformers suggest that the structure of the state organizes political activity in systematic ways. This insight provides a framework for identifying what might be required to transcend the network of powerful, vested interests to achieve universal coverage. Specifically, it suggests that prospects for reform are enhanced when a coalition is organized in ways that closely mirror the representative arrangements of the American state (Skocpol, Ganz, and Munson 2000). In keeping with this argument, any reform movement needs an organizational structure with a federal framework. At the top there must be a national leadership responsible for mapping out a grand plan to disseminate ideas, recruit members nationwide, and cultivate political insiders (influential congressional committee chairs and civil servants) who can introduce bills and devise ways to attach health care initiatives to less visible budget measures. At the middle level, a reform movement needs intermediate institutions, such as state labor federations whose leaders can coordinate activities, tap into indigenous social networks, and disseminate the organizations' models and ideas (Nathanson 2003). Finally, a reform movement needs local chapters to funnel money to the higher levels of the federation and provide grassroots activists who can engage in social action to influence politics at the local level. This structure ties leaders to one another, links local groups to larger issues, and affords opportunities for political leverage at the local, state, and national levels. Thus, social movement theorists' focus on informal, emergent social and political processes needs to be coupled with an analysis of the way the structure of the state systematically organizes political activity (McAdam and Su 2002).

REFERENCES

Anderson, G.F., U.W. Reinhardt, P.S. Hussey, and V. Petrosyan. 2003. "It's the Prices, Stupid: Why the United States Is So Different from Other Countries." *Health Affairs* 22(3):89–105.

Center for Public Integrity. 1995. "Well-heeled: Inside Lobbying for Health Care Reform: Part II." *International Journal of Health Services* 25:593–632.

Dixon, Anna and Elias Mossialos. 2002. *Health Care Systems in Eight Countries.* London, England: European Observatory on Health Care Systems.

Edelman, Murray. 1988. *Constructing the Political Spectacle.* Chicago: University of Chicago Press.

Goldsteen, Raymond, Karen Goldsteen, James Swan, and Wendy Clemens. 2001. "Harry and Louise and Health Care Reform: Romancing Public Opinion." *Journal of Health Politics, Policy and Law* 26(6):1325–52.

Gordon, Colin. 2003. *Dead on Arrival.* Princeton, NJ: Princeton University Press.

Hacker, Jacob S. 1997. *The Road to Nowhere.* Princeton, NJ: Princeton University Press.

Harrington Meyer, Madonna and Eliza K. Pavalko. 1996. "Family, Work and Access to Health Insurance among Mature Women." *Journal of Health and Social Behavior* 37:311–25.

Institute of Medicine. 2004. *Insuring America's Health: Principles and Recommendations.* Washington, DC: Institute of Medicine.

Jacobs, Lawrence R. and Robert Shapiro. 1995. "Don't Blame the Public for Failed Health Care Reform." *Journal of Health Politics, Policy and Law* 20(5):411–23.

———. 2002. *Politicians Don't Pander.* Chicago: University of Chicago Press.

Jenkins, J. Craig and Charles Perrow. 1977. "Insurgency of the Powerless: Farm Worker Movements 1946–1972." *American Sociological Review* 42:249–68.

Johnson, Haynes and David Broder. 1996. *The System.* Boston, MA: Little, Brown.

Jost, Timothy. 2003. *Disentitlement? The Threats Facing Our Public Health Care Programs and a Rights-Based Response.* New York, NY: Oxford University Press.

Kane, Anne E. 1997. "Theorizing Meaning Construction in Social Movements: Symbolic Structures and Interpretation during the Irish Land War, 1879–1882." *Sociological Theory* 15:249–76.

Keen, Justin, Donald Light, and Nicholas May. 2001. *Public-Private Relations in Health Care.* London: Kings Fund.

Light, Donald. 1992. "The Practice and Ethics of Risk-related Health Insurance." *Journal of the American Medical Association* 267(18): 2503–2508.

———. 1995. "Countervailing Powers: A Framework for Professions in Transition." Pp. 24–41 in *Health Professions and the State in Europe,* edited by Terry Johnson, Gerry Larkin, and Mike Saks. London, England: Routledge.

Luft, Hal. 1999. "Why Are Physicians So Upset about Managed Care?" *Journal of Health, Politics and Law* 24(5):957–66.

McAdam, Doug, John McCarthy, and Meyer Zald. 1996. "Introduction: Opportunities, Mobilizing Structures and Framing Processes—Toward a Synthetic, Comparative Perspectives on Social Movements." Pp. 1–20 in *Comparative Perspectives on Social Movements,* edited by Doug McAdam, John McCarthy, and Meyer Zald. Cambridge, England: Cambridge University Press.

McAdam, Doug and Yang Su. 2002. "The War at Home: Antiwar Protests and Congressional Voting, 1965–1973." *American Sociological Review* 67:696–721.

Nathanson, Constance. 2003. "The Skeptics Guide to a Movement for Universal Health Insurance." *Journal of Health, Politics and Law* 28(2–3):443–72.

Pedriana, Nicholas and Robin Stryker. 1997. "Political Culture Wars 1960s Style: Equal Employment Opportunity-Affirmative Action Law and the Philadelphia Plan." *American Journal of Sociology* 102:323–91.

Quadagno, Jill. 2004. "Physician Sovereignty and the Purchasers' Revolt." *Journal of Health Politics, Policy and Law* 29(4–5): 815–34.

———. 2005. *One Nation, Uninsured: Why the US Has No National Health Insurance.* New York: Oxford University Press. (Scheduled for publication in 2005).

Ruggie, Mary. 1996a. *Boomerang.* New York: W.W. Norton.

———. 1996.b *Realignments in the Welfare State.* New York: Columbia University Press.

Skocpol, Theda, Marshall Ganz, and Ziad Munson. 2000. "A Nation of Organizers: The Institutional Origins of Civic Volunteerism in the United States." *American Political Science Review* 94(3): 527–46.

Tuohy, Carolyn. 1999. *Accidental Logics.* New York: Oxford University Press.

West, Darrell and Burdette Loomis. 1999. *The Sound of Money.* New York: W.W. Norton.

Young, Michael. 2002. "Confessional Protest: The Religious Birth of U.S. National Social Movements." *American Sociological Review* 67:660–88.

Crowd-out and the Politics of Health Reform

Judith Feder

Critics of the gaps in our nation's health insurance decry the absence of a health insurance "system" and the resulting "patchwork" of private and public insurance that leaves so many Americans unprotected. There is no question that these gaps are unconscionable; but they are also no accident. They are the result of policy and political choices with substantial consequences for those who remain uncovered. In my view (based on experience as well as the excellent scholarship of others)[1] the fundamental political barrier to universal coverage is that our success in insuring most of the nation's population has "crowded out" our political capacity to insure the rest.

BARRIERS TO UNIVERSAL COVERAGE

Given the health insurance financing system currently in place in the U.S., the simplest way to explain the nation's political failure to enact universal coverage is that the "haves" have health insurance; it's the "have-nots"—or more precisely the "have-nots" deemed "undeserving"—who do not. Although it is true that any of us can fall out of employer-sponsored coverage—if, for example, we lose our job or get divorced—the vast majority of Americans can count on receiving health insurance through their jobs. The roughly 15 percent of Americans who are uninsured are overwhelmingly workers in low- and modest-wage jobs that do not offer health insurance and working-aged adults who do not qualify for Medicaid. The primary political and policy problem we face is that it is almost impossible to insure the "have-nots" without in some way disrupting the status quo of the "haves."

The most obvious form of "disruption" comes from the need to raise financial resources to subsidize health insurance for the economically disadvantaged uninsured. The full cost of employer-sponsored coverage of a typical family is now about $9000 per year. If comparable insurance were available to individuals outside employment, it would absorb more than 20 percent of income for the bulk of the uninsured. Virtually every health insurance expansion proposal, regardless of its form, recognizes that the cost of health insurance is too high to expect the uninsured to purchase it without subsidies. Unavoidably, subsidization entails redistribution—taxing those who have health insurance to subsidize health insurance for those who don't, or, in political terms, taxing those who vote, for the benefit of those who don't. Historically, that has posed an obvious and substantial political barrier to reform.

But less obvious and equally problematic is the policy—and therefore political—difficulty of getting health insurance to the uninsured without in some way disrupting not just

Adapted from: Judith Feder. 2004. Crowd-out and the politics of health reform. *Journal of Law, Medicine & Ethics.* 32(3), 461–464.

the pocketbooks, but the actual insurance of the already-insured. National health insurance via a single-payer or Medicare-for-all strategy actually intends disruption—or, more accurately, replacement—of employer-sponsored insurance with what its advocates believe is a simpler, more equitable, and more efficient system. Whether or not they are correct, reluctance to disrupt Americans who have insurance—specifically, to legislate both the redistribution of financing and the shift from private to public coverage a single-payer would entail—has inhibited most politicians from taking displacement head on.

On the contrary, the most recent initiative for achieving universal coverage (put forth by President Clinton in 1993) was built on a strategy explicitly aimed at avoiding redistribution and private-to-public coverage shifts. This result would have been achieved by securing and extending existing employer-sponsored coverage and by relying on financing arrangements that would not have required tax increases on the already-insured. In designing its health insurance strategy, the Clinton Administration kept its eye at least as much on those who had health insurance as on those who lacked it.

What did that strategy entail? First, the plan was built on an employer mandate. All employers would have been required to provide coverage for their workers, at benefit levels that matched benefits held by the well-insured. This mandate aimed to appeal to the currently covered in two ways: requiring employers to provide coverage locked in their health insurance, which otherwise could be at risk in a weak economy; and, because most of the uninsured were working, employers and employees would bear the immediate responsibility for paying for the expansion without having to impose new taxes on the already-insured.[2]

Second, the Clinton proposal contained an approach for financing subsidies for lower income families without the imposition of new taxes. Indeed, the proposal contained myriad subsidies. There were subsidies to lessen employers' premium obligations (especially small employers of low-wage workers, for whom new insurance costs might lead to job reductions). There were subsidies for households who were also required to contribute. Finally there were subsidies to finance coverage for the minority of uninsured persons who were outside the workforce. Public funds to finance these subsidies were generated through aggressive cost containment, which produced savings in federal health programs that could be reinvested. Specifically, it was estimated that slower health cost growth would reduce projected federal spending (most importantly, for Medicaid)[3] and also would reduce federal revenue losses or "tax expenditures" for employer-sponsored health insurance. Lower-than-projected public expenditures and higher-than-expected tax revenues made room in the federal budget to finance the new subsidies that were essential to the success of the Clinton plan.

Gaining sufficient room in the federal budget meant holding health care cost growth to levels of general inflation—a level never previously achieved. The Clinton Administration advocated "managed competition" for this purpose. Specifically, the proposal sought to guarantee everyone 80 percent of the average cost of a choice of health plans, all of which offered a guaranteed scope of benefits and uniform cost-sharing. These competing plans would be made available to consumers through newly structured and highly regulated insurance markets (labeled "alliances"). Consumers (either directly or, in very large firms, through their place of employment) would shop for—and financially benefit from—selecting a lower-cost plan. The theory was that insurers would compete for consumers by keeping their costs down. Prohibited from competing on benefit levels or by avoiding high-risk enrollees, plans would be forced to compete by securing the efficient delivery of quality care.

Were it not for the Congressional budget process, the proposal's cost containment might have stopped there. But under budget rules then in place, it was the Congressional Budget Office (CBO) that determined whether the Clinton proposal provided sufficient financing to cover its costs. CBO did not share the Clinton Administration's (and other proponents') high expectations for cost containment through managed competition. To avoid the need for new revenues, satisfying CBO required the proposal's designers to include what they described as a "back-up" mechanism: caps on the rate of growth in insurance premiums, enforced through reductions (as necessary) in provider payments.

In combination, then, mandatory contributions from employers and individuals, accompanied by aggressive cost containment that produced federal budget savings, enabled the Clinton Administration to claim that it guaranteed health insurance to all Americans at no new federal cost.[4] And with that claim, the Administration sought to overcome the obstacles posed by resistance to redistribution from and disruption of the already-insured.

Despite its creativity, the Clinton strategy was no more successful than previous national health insurance efforts at avoiding controversy about disruption and redistribution. Rather than being welcomed as simplifying and securing private coverage, the Clinton proposal's new insurance markets (the "alliances") were attacked as "big government" interference with employer-sponsored insurance. Rather than being applauded for reducing health care cost growth, the Clinton proposal's cost containment was criticized as "rationing care." Rather than making everyone a "winner," as its designers intended, the plan was characterized as making all those who already had insurance "losers" in terms of access to quality care, in no small part because their health benefits would be subject to aggregate, alliance-wide standards and the cost of their coverage, to aggregate controls. At the end of the Clinton health reform debate, polls indicated that only about one in five Americans believed reform would make them better off—in general and with respect to quality of care. A far larger proportion—more than one in three, believed they would be worse off from enactment of the proposed health reform.[5]

It was undoubtedly these concerns that led the public to resonate with advertisements run by the Health Insurance Association of America and featuring an all-American couple named Harry and Louise, who memorably lamented, "There's got to be a better way." But, holding the specifics of the Clinton plan aside, the truth is there simply is no way to design a policy for universal coverage that can cover the uninsured without affecting the already-insured; and no way to achieve political success if the already-insured perceive that they are worse off as a result.

This dilemma is not limited to expansions aimed at universal coverage. Incremental expansion proposals that focus on achieving small improvements for low-income populations not only make redistribution from the "haves" to the "have-nots" explicit (since only the latter receive new benefits)—they, too, affect the coverage of the already-insured. Except for a proposed expansion that would limit eligibility to individuals with incomes below the federal poverty level (a group in which hardly anyone has employer coverage), any coverage proposal is likely to make new publicly subsidized benefits available not only to the uninsured but also to significant numbers of people who already have insurance. With a new coverage option available, even individuals with employer coverage might replace that coverage with free or near-free benefits provided at public expense. And should those benefits be made available, employers—particularly employers whose employees earn relatively low wages—might decide to drop the coverage they currently offer, essentially forcing their employees to find coverage elsewhere.[6]

Why is this a political problem? First, by allowing or forcing the privately insured to move into public coverage, what was understood to be fully private health expenditures (despite the substantial tax expenditures that support them) becomes fully public. Shifting private expenditures to the public ledger is politically unpopular, even if it makes people better off (by providing broader benefits or reducing premium costs). In enacting the State Children's Health Insurance Program (SCHIP), for example, Congress limited eligibility for new benefits to children who lacked employer-sponsored coverage—a provision aimed at what is popularly labeled as the "crowd-out" of private coverage by public benefits. The result is a convoluted policy with questionable impacts. SCHIP imposes waiting periods on uninsured children who previously had private coverage. These waiting periods are intended to deter shifts from private to public coverage, but also are likely to leave some previously insured children with gaps in coverage, while simultaneously failing to deter others from moving on to the public rolls—sometimes at their employers' behest. With SCHIP, this threatened substitution occurred alongside an actual expansion of coverage to the uninsured.[7] But in other proposals (such as tax credits for people who lose the jobs that provide their insurance)[8] or even more broadly applicable tax credits,[9] the bulk of the impact would be substitution of public for private coverage. Tax-payer dollars, ostensibly mobilized to reduce uninsurance, would, in practice, have little effect, since most of the funds simply would be used to displace other sources of coverage.

But for people who lose insurance because it is no longer available, political concerns go beyond efficiency or effectiveness in expanding coverage. Making tax credits available for the purchase of health insurance outside employment would likely lead some employers to drop coverage, as well as lead some states to reduce their Medicaid benefits.[10] Although employers and state officials might welcome tax credits as an opportunity to reduce their insurance obligations, the "losers" would be the formerly well-covered individuals and families now left to shop for health insurance in a market with higher costs and fewer benefits.[11] The issue here becomes not only who will gain but who will lose insurance (putting people with the greatest need for health care at highest risk); and the political opponents become activists most committed to using public dollars to support expanded coverage.

Faced with the political dilemma posed by existing health insurance, coverage advocates continually try to target narrowly defined groups who may be politically attractive and whose coverage may not threaten the already-insured—like unemployed workers, early retirees, and low-income parents. But unless the target is poor, working-aged adults, who remain politically unattractive, coverage for any of these groups raises the potential that new public benefits will replace existing private benefits (wasting taxpayers' dollars) and the fear that the already-insured will end up with less protection than they already have.

ACHIEVING UNIVERSAL COVERAGE

Recent debates about coverage expansions have consistently drawn attention to the fiscal "crowd-out" effect—the degree to which the newly available, publicly financed coverage will replace privately financed coverage currently in effect. But a review of the nation's policies and politics indicates that from a political perspective, the problem is exactly the opposite. It is the attachment to existing private coverage that "crowds out" the political potential for proposals that would truly expand coverage to the uninsured.

The primary lesson of this experience is that coverage advocates must recognize, not avoid, the overlap of new and existing coverage—and generate political support for the fiscal resources necessary to secure, as well as extend, health insurance coverage. First and foremost that means going beyond incremental initiatives focused on narrowly defined groups. Having already covered the elderly, people with disabilities, and children, the truth is that all the "good" (that is, politically attractive) populations are taken. To make a real dent in the uninsured, it is time to end the systematic exclusion from coverage of poor and many near-poor/low-income, working-aged adults.

Preserving coverage for the insured during expansions clearly increases an initiative's costs. Previous strategies have relied on employer mandates to acquire these resources and, despite historical difficulties, that remains a legitimate and advocated plan. Alongside it, however, the 2004 Presidential campaign has generated another strategy—that is, to substantially subsidize, rather than require, existing employer-sponsored coverage, essentially using tax dollars to reduce premiums. Congressman Dick Gephardt initiated the proposal and devoted the most resources to it; Senator John Kerry continued it, on a smaller but still substantial scale (estimated to account for almost a third of the proposal's ten-year, roughly $900 billion cost). Mandating coverage has the political advantage of avoiding taxation. Subsidizing coverage has the equity advantage of replacing regressive payroll burdens with progressive tax revenues. The choices, though politically challenging, are conceptually simple: either require or pay for the continuation of existing coverage, while extending coverage to those without it.

Whether it is any easier to generate taxpayer than employer resources—or easier than the third alternative of mustering support for replacing all private coverage with a tax-financed, publicly run, single-payer system—remains to be seen. But it seems unlikely that the resource costs of an effective coverage strategy can be ignored or denied.

Securing those resources will require not only an offense but a defense. The offense is to persuade that effective insurance rests on community-wide coverage and that, as citizens and taxpayers, all Americans are part of that community. Bringing together the healthy and the sick enables us to pool risk—gathering resources from all of us (as taxpayers and premium-payers) to finance health care for those of us who need it. Including everyone, regardless of income or health status, in that pool requires that government—whom we elect to represent our community—make the rules and gather resources from the better off, as taxpayers, to support those whose incomes are too limited to fend for themselves. The defense is to prevent the unraveling of community—through tax cuts and tax-preferred "accounts" that tout individual self-reliance as the best insurance protection. Such strategies may work for the better-off and the lucky. But self-reliance is the opposite of community, and invariably such an approach segments the healthy from the sick, and the well-off from the less well-off. Indeed, it becomes the very opposite of insurance—shifting risks to individuals, rather than sharing risks across individuals.

Whether on offense or on defense, the challenge to improving or achieving universal coverage is to decide whether we are a society in which it is every man, woman, or child for him/herself or one in which we are all in it together. It is time we opted and fought for the latter.

REFERENCES

1. See, e.g., C. Howard, *The Hidden Welfare State* (Princeton, N.J.: Princeton University Press, 1997); J. Hacker, *The Divided Welfare State* (New York: Cambridge University Press, 2002).

2. The Congressional Budget Office ultimately judged this employer mandate to constitute a "tax," though whether the public perceived it as such is an open question.

3. Medicare savings were dedicated to the proposal's prescription drug and long-term care benefits.

4. Although the Congressional Budget Office did not find these and other projected savings entirely sufficient to finance the program, its estimates came close (and indeed were achievable with modest adjustments to some of the proposed benefits and subsidies).

5. R. T. Blendon, M. Brodie, and J. Benson, "What Happened to Americans' Support for the Clinton Health Plan," *Health Affairs* 14, no. 2 (1995): 7–23.

6. For a discussion of this issue, see J. Feder, L. Levitt, E. O'Brien, and D. Rowland, "Assessing the Combination of Public Programs and Tax Credits, Covering the Uninsured" (Washington, D.C.: Economic and Social Research Institute, 2001).

7. P. J. Cunningham, J. D. Reschovsky, and J. Hadley, *The Effects of SCHIP on Children's Health Insurance Coverage* (Washington, D.C.: Center for the Study of Health Systems Change, 2002).

8. J. R. Baumgardner, "Providing Health Insurance to the Short-Term Unemployed," *Inquiry* (1998): 266–279; J. A. Klerman, *Uninsured and Unemployed: Policy Issues Raised by Expanded Coverage for Those Losing Health Insurance as a Result of Job Loss* (Washington, D.C., RAND Mimeo, 1997).

9. J. Gruber and L. Levitt, "Tax Subsidies for Health Insurance: Costs and Benefits," *Health Affairs* 19, no. 1 (2000): 72–85.

10. Feder et al., *supra* note 6.

11. Feder et al., *supra* note 6.

Improving Medical Practice and the Economy Through Universal Health Insurance

Donald W. Light, PhD

Other industrialized countries provide universal access to medical services in a variety of ways, one of which is called by Americans "single payer." The term refers to structuring the financing so that premiums or taxes are collected by a single payer, usually the government. Other systems, including the oldest (Germany), limit the government's role to acting as the rules committee that sets fair rules for everyone and then lets insurers, providers, and others run the health care system. The government also acts as the referee, when one of the players (like the insurers or hospitals) begins to skew the system, and as the left-overs crew that takes care of bits and pieces left over (like providing coverage for medical students and residents). Still other systems are quite mixed: a national pool and single-payer arrangement for people with lower incomes or high medical bills, a mandatory but private market, and a voluntary do-what-you-like approach for the affluent. The Nether-lands (a model for the U.S.) has a quarter of its population covered by voluntary health in-surance, and yet it provides one of the most comprehensive, universal services for sick patients in the world, especially for the "uninsurable," the tragically ill and disabled.[1-3]

Two American myths among clinicians are that universal health care means becoming government employees and losing professional clout. Most medical services in universal health care systems are delivered by physicians in private practice or in arrangements that give them more autonomy and control than American physicians enjoy. In fact, the basic mistake that organized medicine made here was to oppose universal health care in the name of autonomy, choice, and freedom and to favor corporate task-masters who compro-mise all three much more than physicians experience in other affluent countries.[4] All uni-versal systems give the medical profession great powers to decide issues of payments, organization of services, and divisions of labor—they have to.

Medical professions everywhere complain and protest nevertheless; but if one looks closely at the nature and scope of the issues, one finds they are relatively minor compared to the systemic, basic problems that American physicians face. Many of the terms that American physicians are forced to accept are illegal everywhere else. With furious energy, state and national medical societies have opposed having "the government in your medical cabinet" and preferred having corporations concerned about their profits decide what is covered and how much will be paid. In such a system, for-profit corporations dictate

Adapted from: Donald Light. (2005). Improving medical practice and the economy through universal health insurance. *New Jersey Medicine,* 102(1–2), 39–44. Reprinted with permission of the Medical Society of New Jersey.

reforms, like the extended coverage in Medicare for prescription drugs. An analysis of the costs found that less than 4% of huge new costs (about $535 billion over the first ten years) is accounted for by the cost of new drugs.[5] The other 96% goes largely to additional profits for the pharmaceutical companies and to corporate middlemen who do not exist in any other universal health care system, because they are unnecessary. If this is the price of boondoggling, of relieving medical debts, and enabling physicians to prescribe what they think their patients need—$25 to corporations for every $1 to pay for medicine—there is no chance that physicians and nurses will practice in a stable health care system that honors their work and pays them for needed care.

"Single payer" plans should be called "more choice, less cost" plans, because patients and their doctors have more choice, and single payer systems have the least overhead as well as the best structure for controlling costs of any universal health care arrangement. They are also far more equitable. Funds collected from income taxes, for example, are more equitable and efficient than any alternative. America's single-payer plan is Medicare, and it is based on social fairness, but it operates in a world of private, competitive plans based on "actuarial fairness," the concept that it is unfair to make healthier people pay for sicker people.[6] This ethos works against clinicians, of course, because it avoids or denies the obvious: sick people need medical services, and those who provide them should be paid well and honored for doing so. The goal, instead, is to maximize profits by minimizing the proportion of a population's illnesses and disabilities one has to pay for. Table 12.5.1 summarizes most of the techniques used to do this. They all make both the lives of patients who need medical services and those who provide them miserable, especially manipulations of benefit design and techniques of claims harassment. They are distinctive features of American health care.

There are advantages of universal health care not often heard in the United States, yet of central importance to the medical profession and the nation. First, universal health care is *the* key tool for containing costs equitably, rather than reducing the proportion of medical bills covered and making sick people pay more out of their pockets. (*All* the U.S. and foreign evidence shows that co-payments save little, if any, money; but they do keep patients from getting the medical services they need.) None of the reforms to contain costs, past or present, in the United States, can or did work, because there is no national budget or universal framework.

The history of cost containment since the 1970s is a history of cost-shifting, "squeezing the balloon," as the metaphor goes, only with more and more being pumped in from uncontrollable sources.[4,7] A major reason is that competition works poorly in most health care. This was a widely accepted reality, even among economists, up to the late 1970s, when a new generation of economists declared it was not so and launched the revolution of managed competition and managed care. But they never proved their case, just declared it was so. When markets do not meet the requirements for beneficial competition, the result is *pernicious competition*.[8] Stronger or more clever competitors exploit their victims and then lobby to preserve what they call "free markets," that is, free to charge what they want or cover what they want. Physicians both exploit and are exploited. Since the early 1970s, when physicians incorporated their practices, many have become deeply invested in corporate medicine and provide far more services, at far higher charges, than do their counterparts in the best health care systems in the world.

TABLE 12.5.1 Benchmarks of Fairness for Health Care Systems

BENCHMARK 1: GOOD PUBLIC HEALTH AND BASICS

Funds, programs, and infrastructure to assure basic nutrition, housing, sanitary conditions, public safety, basic education, health literacy

Good monitoring systems for these

BENCHMARK 2: DEMOCRATIC ACCOUNTABILITY AND EMPOWERMENT

Open, public debates about system design and performance
Explicit, deliberative procedures for allocation decisions
Full public reports on use and performance by private and public organizations
Fair grievances procedures
Adequate privacy protection

BENCHMARK 3: UNIVERSAL ACCESS-COVERAGE AND PARTICIPATION

Mandatory coverage and participation
Prompt phase-in: coverage/participation not held hostage to cost control
Full portability and continuity of coverage

BENCHMARK 4: EQUITABLE FINANCING-BY ABILITY TO PAY

All direct and indirect payments and out-of-pocket expenses scaled to household budget and ability to pay
Non-discrimination by degree of illness or risk

BENCHMARK 5: COMPREHENSIVE AND UNIFORM BENEFITS

All effective and necessary services deemed affordable, by all effective and needed providers; no categorical exclusion of services
Reduced tiering and uniform quality
Benefits not dependent on savings

BENCHMARK 6: UNIVERSAL ACCESS–MINIMIZE NON-FINANCIAL BARRIERS

Minimize mal-distributions of personnel, equipment, facilities
Reforms of health professions education
Minimize language, cultural, and class barriers
Minimize educational/informational barriers

BENCHMARK 7: VALUE FOR MONEY–CLINICAL EFFICACY

Emphasis on effective public health, prevention, and primary care
Systematic assessment of outcomes
Minimize over-utilization and under-utilitization

BENCHMARK 8: FAIR AND EFFICIENT COSTS

Minimize administrative overhead
Tough contractual bargaining

(continues)

TABLE 12.5.1   continued

Minimize cost-shifting through fee schedules and risk-adjusted budgets
Minimize fraud and abuse

BENCHMARK 9: PATIENT AUTONOMY AND CHOICE

Fair choice ensured by the other benchmarks
Informed choice of primary-care provider, specialists, other health care providers, and
  procedures as much as is practicable

Source: Based on N. Daniels, D. Light, and R. Caplan. *Benchmarks of Fairness for Health Care Reform* (New York: Oxford University Press, 1996); and Daniels et al. *"Benchmarks of Fairness . . ." Bulletin, World Health Organization* 78 (2000): 740–750.

Second, reducing fragmentation and error cannot go far without universal health care. It is a key to good quality. This is the central flaw of the Institute of Medicine's solutions for the quality crisis in American health care. *Crossing the Quality Chasm* identifies the systemic sources of flawed medicine but poses solutions that require a common financial and institutional foundation.[9] The complexity and fragmentation of American health care is the source of huge revenues, and integration is less profitable. The huge inefficiency of the American system is a major source of profits, for subspecialties as well as for insurers, health plans, and billing services.[10] They have overturned a basic law of economics, and for that they should win a Nobel prize: Inefficiency and waste do not impede economic growth but are major sources of growth and profit. As cost-shifting continues, as parasitic corporations siphon more money away from paying for clinical care, and as pernicious competition destroys the ethos of professionalism, what are state medical societies going to do about it?

REFERENCES

1.   H. Maame. "Netherlands," in *Health Care Reforms in Industrialized Countries,* M. W. Raffel, ed. (University Park, Penn.: Pennsylvania State University Press, 1997): 135–162.

2.   S. Thomson and E. Mossialos. "Private Health Insurance and Access to Health Care in the European Union," *Euro Observer* 6, no. 1 (2004): 1–3.

3.   D. W. Light. "Two Forms of Public-Private Health Insurance Partnership (the Netherlands and Ireland)," in *Public-Private Relations in Health Care,* J. Keen, D. Light, and N. Mays, eds. (London: The King's Fund, 2001): 129–167.

4.   D. W. Light. "Ironies of Success: A New History of the American Health Care 'System'," *Journal of Health and Social Behavior,* forthcoming.

5.   A. Sager and D. Socolar. *Sixty-One Percent of Medicare's New Prescription Drug Subsidy Is Windfall Profit to Drug Makers* (Boston: Boston University School of Public Health, Health Reform Program, 2003).

6.   D. W. Light. "The Practice and Ethics of Risk-Rated Health Insurance," *JAMA* 267 (1992): 2503–2508.

7.   P. Starr. *The Social Transformation of American Medicine* (New York: Basic Books, 1982).

8.   D. W. Light. "Good Managed Care Needs Universal Health Insurance," *Ann Intern Med* 130 (1999): 686–689.

9.   Institute of Medicine. *Crossing the Quality Chasm: A New Health System for the Twenty-First Century* (Washington, D.C.: National Academy Press, 2001).

10. S. Woolhandler, T. Campbell, and D. U. Himmelstein. "Costs of Health Care Administration in the United States and Canada," *N Engl J Med* 349 (2003): 768–775.

CONCLUSIONS

Health policy is the art and science of making public policy decisions about financing organizations and delivery systems for health care services. As the United States embarks on major reform, policy makers have many options for the future. Dramatic change is bound to occur and needs to be addressed with creativity and courage.

If national health care reform adopts a play-or-pay approach (the use of private health plans to insure and manage the health care system rather than a public national health plan), the following scenario for the future can be envisioned. Health care would be financed through private health plans, and businesses would be mandated to pay for basic coverage for employees through either private or government insurance plans. The federal government would pay for individuals who are not otherwise covered. Under this approach, the private insurance industry might increase its efficiency, resulting in the elimination of small or disreputable companies and streamlining of billing procedures and other administrative practices. The private health insurance industry, however, is unlikely to accept any reductions in its profits and administrative costs, which currently absorb at least 14% of total premiums.

In contrast, a government-administered health plan, such as Medicare or Canada's single-payer system, would be significantly less expensive than private health plans. Moreover, a government plan would be more open and equitable in its policies, delivery, and management of services than private plans. The current health insurance industry strongly opposes any public plan that would prevent its members from maintaining and expanding their profits. Opposition to a government health plan is joined by the medical profession, which fears the power of a single-payer approach to reduce not only physician incomes, but also physician management and control over the health care system. The health insurance and provider lobbies continue to wield great political influence in Congress through campaign contributions and political action committees.

The advantage of a play-or-pay approach is that less direct tax money is necessary to finance the system. Politicians do not believe the public will understand or accept a shift of private health dollars into the tax system. Moreover, U.S. taxpayers, who want health insurance but are unwilling to pay higher taxes, are convinced that private-sector management is better than public-sector management. Thus a public–private partnership approach is born of the political expediency of policy makers. In contrast, a publicly administered health plan would be significantly less expensive and more efficient. Funds from current employer tax exemptions and other sources could be used to finance a national health plan.

A national plan based on employer mandates is unlikely to satisfy anyone except those who are currently uninsured. One concern is that employers who are required to offer such a plan might reduce their current health care coverage to a basic plan. Thus middle-class employees who currently enjoy good health benefits might lose their expanded coverage or have to pay for their health care costs beyond the basic coverage through supplemental insurance policies. If small businesses are required to pay for basic plans, they may reduce the number of their employees. Businesses might increase the proportion of part-time and temporary employees hired to avoid paying for their health benefits. In the long run, the population would have greater access to health care coverage but might be paying for more of these costs on an out-of-pocket basis. These problems could be avoided with a national health plan.

If national health insurance comes under consideration, the lobbying efforts by physicians, hospitals, pharmaceutical companies, and health insurers will intensify. All elements of the health industry will continue to fight for maximum funding with minimal government control over administration and service patterns. The groups with the greatest power within the health industry—pharmaceutical companies, physicians, and health insurers—might advocate for reductions in payments to other health providers so as to protect their own incomes and profits.

Incremental health policy changes could modify existing premiums, benefits, and other components of public or private insurance. Innovative alterations in eligibility or cost controls could be introduced. In contrast, fundamental changes could revise the entire health financing and delivery system. Perhaps in complex societies, there is no alternative to incremental change. Thus health reform efforts inevitably may need to move slowly through a transition from the current chaos to a public–private approach before a more rational government-financed national health plan can be developed. In any case, the process and the speed of health care reform will be determined by the legislative and policy efforts of the day. Such reform could build a transformed system and a healthier nation in the future.

GLOSSARY

AFDC (Aid to Families with Dependent Children): Also known as *welfare*. A joint federal–state assistance program that provides monthly cash payments to income-eligible families to support dependent children and the primary caretaker. This program was changed to the Temporary Assistance for Needy Families (TANF) in the Omnibus Budget Reconciliation Act of 1996.

Ambulatory care: Care that does not involve overnight hospitalization. It includes clinic visits in outpatient clinics or doctors' offices, and includes "ambulatory surgery," which may be performed in a hospital or free-standing surgery center.

Beneficiary: A person enrolled in the Medicare program. (See also *enrollee.*)

Capitated or prepaid coverage: A method of financing health care wherein a provider organization (a group of physicians, a hospital, or an integrated delivery system) agrees to accept a fixed dollar amount per member per month to deliver care to a given population. The monthly payment is given no matter how much or how little care is actually rendered. This scheme is distinguished from fee-for-service coverage in which reimbursement is given for each itemized service rendered.

Carrier: An organization, typically an insurance company, that has a contract with the Healthcare Financing Administration to administer claims processing and make Medicare payments to health care providers for most Medicare Part B benefits. (See also *fiscal intermediary* and *Medicare Part B.*)

Case management: Coordination of the health care and health-related social services for a person, generally for an individual with complex problems requiring the expertise of different types of care providers. A case manager may be a physician, nurse, social worker, or occupational or physical therapist.

Case mix: The mix of patients treated within a particular institutional setting, such as the hospital. Patient classification systems such as the DRG system can be used to measure hospital case mix. (See also *DRG.*)

CDC (Centers for Disease Control and Prevention): The major federal body responsible for the prevention and control of diseases and other preventable conditions and for responding to public health emergencies.

Charges: The posted prices of services provided by a facility. Medicare requires hospitals to apply the same schedule of charges to all patients, regardless of the expected sources or amount of payment.

Coinsurance: A portion (often 20%) of the total charges for medical services that an insured person is billed directly for each clinic visit after his or her insurance company pays a percentage (e.g., 80%).

Co-payment: A fixed dollar amount (e.g., $5, $10, or $15) that a person insured through an HMO or PPO must pay at the time of the clinic visit to receive care.

Deductible: A dollar amount that an insured person has to pay out-of-pocket in a given year before any reimbursement by his or her insurance company starts (e.g., $500, $1,000, or $2,000, depending on the policy).*

Disability insurance: Two types of federal disability insurance are available through the Social Security Administration. All employers, employees, and the self-employed pay into Old Age, Survivors, and Disability Insurance (OASDI), which is a national program of contributory social insurance. If a worker becomes disabled and has paid into the system for 7 out of at least 10 years in total, and for at least 5 of the last 10 years, then he or she is eligible for disability insurance under OASDI. The Supplemental Security Income (SSI) program is a disability program for aged, blind, or disabled persons who are not eligible for OASDI. SSI is financed through general governmental revenues.*

DRG (diagnosis-related group): A system developed for "prospective payment" (meaning that the payment level is predetermined according to the diagnosis, as opposed to according to how many services are used) for hospitalization of persons on Medicare. Now used by other third-party payers.

Employee Retirement Income Security Act (ERISA) of 1974: Businesses are allowed to self-insure for health care rather than offer health insurance through commercial companies. Self-insured businesses are exempt from state insurance regulation because of the federal ERISA rules.

Employment-based insurance: An employer pays all or part of an insurance premium for an employee.

Enrollee: A person who is covered by health insurance. (See also *beneficiary.*)

FDA (Food and Drug Administration): Part of the U.S. Department of Agriculture responsible for licensing pharmaceuticals and medical devices, and monitoring for impure and unsafe foods, drugs, and cosmetics in the United States.*

Fee-for-service payment: The care provider is paid separately for each service delivered (distinguished from capitated or prepaid coverage).

Fiscal intermediary: An entity, usually an insurance company, that has a contract with HCFA to determine and make Medicare payments for Part A and certain Part B benefits to hospitals and other providers of services and to perform related functions. (See also *Medicare Part A* and *Medicare Part B.*)

Fiscal year: A 12-month period for which an organization plans the use of its funds, such as the federal government's fiscal year (October 1 to September 30). Fiscal years are referred to by the calendar year in which they end; for example, the federal fiscal year

---

*Definition adapted from: Calkins, D., Fernandopulle, R. J., and Marino, B. S. (1995). *Health care policy.* Cambridge, MA: Blackwell Scientific.

1994 began October 1, 1993, and ended September 30, 1994. Individual providers can designate their own fiscal years, and this is reflected in differences in the time periods covered by the Medicare Cost Reports.

GA (General Assistance): Temporary monetary assistance provided by state governments to individuals with incomes below a certain level who do not qualify for assistance under AFDC, Medicaid, SSI, OASDI, or other programs.

Gatekeeping: A cost-control mechanism used in many health care financing arrangements in which a primary care physician must give a referral before his or her patient can seek a specialist or other services.*

Generalist: See *primary care provider.*

Global budget: A method of cost containment in which an overall limit is placed on health spending for a nation, region, state, or hospital or other health care facility.

Gross domestic product (GDP): The value of all goods and services produced within a country's (e.g., U.S.) boundaries during a given period.

Group practice: A clinic or medical practice site operated by physicians, some of whom may be part owners of the clinic and others of whom are purely staff. Overhead costs are shared. The practices are often multispecialty, with collaboration among the physicians in the group.

Group private insurance: A situation in which a group of individuals comes together to obtain a better rate from an insurance company; the insurance company offers a better premium to the group as a whole than an unaffiliated individual would receive because the risk of high medical expenses has been pooled across individuals in the group.

HCFA (Healthcare Financing Administration): The federal agency responsible for the management of Medicare, the federal portion of Medicaid, and related quality assurance activities.*

Health insurance premium: The amount of money paid to the insurer for a person's coverage. Premiums are mostly paid by employers in the United States, but the insured person may pay part of the premium and some people buy their own insurance (and hence pay their own premiums).

HEDIS (Health Plan Employer Data and Information Set): A set of standardized measures of health plan performance. HEDIS allows comparisons between plans on quality, access and patient satisfaction, membership and utilization, financial information, and health plan management. HEDIS was developed by employers, HMOs, and NCQA.

HMO (health maintenance organization): A staff-model HMO directly employs all providers, who are on salary and work at HMO-owned or leased facilities; the financing and delivery systems are through the HMO. A group-model HMO (e.g., Kaiser) involves a close arrangement between a group of salaried physicians and the payer organization, but the physician group and the payer organization are at least legally separate entities. The HMO provides the facilities. A network-model HMO involves a looser affiliation between

---

*Definition adapted from: Calkins, D., Fernandopulle, R. J., and Marino, B. S. (1995). *Health care policy.* Cambridge, MA: Blackwell Scientific.

the insurer and a network of physicians in private offices, who are generally not salaried, but receive capitated payment per patient enrolled in their practice. The HMO may also provide its own facilities.

Individual private insurance: Insurance premiums are paid directly to an insurance company by an individual rather than through a group. The insurance company then either reimburses the provider for care given, or the individual pays the provider and the insurance company reimburses the individual.

Inpatient care: Involves an overnight hospital/nursing facility stay, as opposed to outpatient care.

IPA (independent practice association):   Several independent physicians in different private practices form a group so that they can negotiate with third-party payers for rates and patients, generally under capitated coverage.

Long-term care: Ongoing health and social services provided for individuals who need assistance on a continuing basis because of physical or mental disabilities. Services can be provided in an institution, the home, or the community, and they may include informal services provided by family or friends as well as formal services provided by professionals or agencies.

Managed care: A term that is much overused and has lost a specific definition. Originally, it referred to health care delivered with a capitated financing mechanism. Then it included health care delivered through contracting networks. It now refers to almost any structure of health care delivery that is different from unregulated fee-for-service health care delivery.

Medicaid: Publicly financed health "insurance" for the poor. Cofinanced by the federal government and the states, it has different eligibility criteria in different states. Medicaid and Medicare legislation passed in 1965, with the idea that Medicaid would cover poor children and their families while Medicare would cover the elderly. In reality, the bulk of Medicaid expenditures goes to cover long-term care for the elderly and disabled, because Medicare doesn't cover long-term care.

Medi-Cal: California's version of Medicaid.

Medicare: A federal program that provides health "insurance" for all persons 65 years or older, regardless of income/assets; also covers blind/permanently disabled and persons with end-stage renal disease, regardless of their age. It pays for acute care (e.g., hospitals, doctors) but not for long-term care.

Medicare Part A: Medicare Hospital Insurance (HI) (Part A of Title XVIII of the Social Security Act), which covers beneficiaries for inpatient hospital, home health, hospice, and limited skilled nursing facility services. Beneficiaries are responsible for deductibles and co-payments. Part A services are financed by the Medicare HI Trust Fund, which consists of Medicare tax payments. (See also *fiscal intermediary* and *Medicare Part B*.)

Medicare Part B: Medicare Supplementary Medical Insurance (SMI) (Part B of Title XVIII of the Social Security Act), which covers Medicare beneficiaries for physician services, home health agency services, medical supplies, and other outpatient treatment. Beneficiaries are responsible for monthly premiums, co-payments, deductibles, and balance billing. Part B services are financed by a combination of enrollee premiums and general tax revenues. (See also *carrier* and *Medicare Part A*.)

Medigap policy: A privately purchased insurance policy that supplements Medicare coverage and meets specified requirements set by federal statutes and the National Association of Insurance Commissioners.

National health insurance: A government guarantee that everyone is insured for basic health care.

NHS (National Health Service): The British health care system, a highly regionalized and coordinated system with defined interfaces between primary, secondary, and tertiary care. Under the NHS, each person enrolls with a general practitioner (GP). The GP is paid a capitated amount per month for each enrollee, regardless of the number of visits that enrollee makes. Patients can freely change from one GP to another. For specialist care, the patient must receive a referral from his or her GP. Referral services (e.g., specialist care, laboratory test, hospitalization) are paid for through a separate funding mechanism.

Nursing facility: An institution that provides skilled nursing care and rehabilitation services to injured, functionally disabled, or sick persons. Formerly, distinctions were made between intermediate care facilities (ICFs) and skilled nursing facilities (SNFs). The Omnibus Budget Reconciliation Act of 1987 eliminated this distinction, effective October 1, 1990, by requiring ICFs to meet SNF certification requirements. (See also *skilled nursing facility*.)

Out-of-pocket expenses: Costs of health care that people pay out of their own pockets (i.e., cash, check), as opposed to costs covered by insurance.

Outpatient care: Most strictly defined as hospital-based care not involving an overnight stay, but often used synonymously with "ambulatory care," whether in hospital or nonhospital settings.

Population-based health services: Preventive health services provided to the entire population of a region, state, or nation, or to all members of a particular HMO.

PPO (preferred provider organization): A benefit plan that provides incentives for subscribers to use providers on a preferred list. Patients pay a lower or no co-payment if they go to preferred providers, but they have the freedom to go to whichever provider they choose.

Premium (insurance premium): See *health insurance premium*.

Prepaid coverage: See *capitated or prepaid coverage*.

Primary care: Ongoing care for the common health problems affecting the population. It includes preventive medicine and patient education. Care is delivered by a primary care provider and can be given in a hospital setting, although it usually takes place in a clinic or community setting.

Primary care provider: A family practitioner, general internist, general practitioner, pediatrician, or other caregiver, such as a nurse practitioner, who provides primary care. Primary care physicians are also responsible for making appropriate referrals to specialists when necessary, and coordinating the complexities of care for a given individual patient. Whether obstetrician/gynecologists are primary care physicians is an area of controversy.

Prospective payment: Predetermined payment to a health care provider or hospital for a hospitalization, an episode of illness, or a pregnancy/delivery. The amount is predetermined according to the diagnosis (sometimes with adjustment for age and presence of complications).

Prospective payment system (PPS):   Medicare's acute care hospital payment method for inpatient care. Prospective per-case payment rates are set at a level intended to cover operating costs in an efficient hospital for treating a typical inpatient in a given diagnosis-related group (DRG). Payments for each hospital are adjusted for differences in area wages, teaching activity, care to the poor, and other factors. Hospitals may receive additional payments to cover extra costs associated with atypical patients (outliers) in each DRG. Capital costs, which were originally excluded from PPS, are now being placed into the system. As of 2001, capital payments are being made on a fully prospective, per-case basis. (See also *DRG* and *prospective payment*.)

Public assistance: Monetary assistance or insurance provided to low-income people by the government. It includes AFDC, GA, SSI, and Medicaid, but is distinguished from social insurance.

Public health: Actions focused on maintaining the overall health of the entire population rather than on providing care only for particular individuals who seek health services.

Rate setting: A method of paying health care providers in which the federal or state government establishes payment rates for one or more payers for various categories of health services.

Regionalized care: Health service delivery designed so that a particular region is served by a center or coordinated network of services. The goal is to ensure coverage of an entire population and to avoid wasteful duplication of services and facilities.

Risk adjustment: Increases or reductions in the amount of payment made to a health plan on behalf of a group of enrollees to compensate for health care expenditures that are expected to be higher or lower than average. (See also *risk selection*.)

Risk contract: An arrangement between a managed health care plan and HCFA under section 1876 of the Social Security Act. Under this contract, the enrolled Medicare beneficiary must use the plan's network of providers. Payment to the plan is made on a capitated basis using the AAPCC (adjusted average per capita cost). (See also *capitated or prepaid coverage*.)

Risk selection: Enrollment choices made by health plans or enrollees on the basis of perceived risk relative to the premium to be paid. (See also *risk adjustment*.)

Secondary care: Care for problems requiring medical care that is more specialized than primary care but less specialized than tertiary care. Some people consider secondary care to mean any hospital overnight care, but most consider it to be care delivered by secondary providers.

Single payer: A universal coverage system in which health care is financed entirely by a single source, usually the government.

Skilled nursing facility (SNF):   An institution that has a transfer agreement with one or more hospitals, provides primary inpatient skilled nursing care and rehabilitation services, and meets other specific requirements for licensing and certification. (See also *nursing facility*.)

Social insurance: A government program in which everyone is entitled to benefits, regardless of income, but only if they have paid into a fund (e.g., one required through employment). Examples of social insurance include Social Security and Medicare.

Social Security: A national pension program for the aged and disabled who have paid Social Security payroll taxes through their employment for a certain time period.

Solo practice: A provider who operates his or her own practice alone, being responsible for all overhead, malpractice insurance, and billing. A solo practitioner may still belong to an HMO or PPO.

Specialist: A provider who specializes in a particular area (e.g., cardiology or radiology) and provides care only in that area. Specialists are distinguished from generalists or primary care providers.

Subspecialist: A physician with board certification or training in a particular area within a given specialty such as surgery or pediatric cardiology. Subspecialists generally practice in academic medical centers or other tertiary care settings.

Supplemental insurance: Any private health insurance plan held by a Medicare beneficiary, including Medigap policies and post-retirement health benefits. These plans generally pay the co-payments and deductibles that would otherwise be required of a Medicare beneficiary.

Supplemental Security Income (SSI): A program that subsidizes the income of individuals who meet the federal qualifications for being poor and being categorized as aged, blind, or disabled. The federal program pays a uniform benefit for individuals and couples across the country. States may supplement this income with state funds.

Tertiary care: Treatment of uncommon, highly specialized, or obscure conditions sometimes requiring sophisticated technology. This care is generally given in academic medical centers and other special hospitals.

Third-party payer: The first two parties are the patient and the care provider. The third party pays the bills to the provider on behalf of the patient. Types of third-party payers include private health insurance, Medicare, Medicaid, and self-insured employers, among others.

Underinsured: An individual with third-party coverage that does not adequately meet his or her health care needs.

Uninsured: An individual with no third-party coverage (private or public); sometimes called a self-payer if the individual can pay for his or her own care.

Welfare: Usually refers to AFDC, General Assistance, Supplemental Security Income, or other government-provided subsidies to the poor.

Workers' compensation: A federal–state program for employees who are injured on the job. Workers' compensation pays the medical bills incurred because of injury and provides short-term salary compensation to replace lost income until the employee can return to work.

INDEX